Dominican Republic

North Coast
p145

Central Highlands
p180

Península de Samaná
p124

HAITI
p223

Punta Cana & the Southeast
p91

The Southwest & Península de Pedernales
p203

Santo Domingo
p56

Ash 2018

Contents

PLAN YOUR TRIP

ON THE ROAD

MATT MUNRO/LONELY PLANET ©

SANTO DOMINGO P56

MATT MUNRO/LONELY PLANET ©

EAT & DRINK
LIKE A LOCAL P38

ANDREY PROKHOROV/500PX ©

Contents

CABARETE P161

Welcome to the Dominican Republic

The Dominican Republic is one of the Caribbean's most geographically diverse countries, with stunning mountain scenery, desert scrublands, evocative colonial architecture and beaches galore.

Coastal Country

Hundreds of kilometers of coastline define the Dominican Republic (DR) – some of it white-sand beaches shaded by rows of palm trees, other parts lined dramatically with rocky cliffs, wind-swept dunes or serene mangrove lagoons. Whether it's fishing villages where the shoreline is used for mooring boats or indulgent tourist playgrounds with aquamarine waters, the sea is the common denominator. Some of the bays and coves where pirates once roamed are the temporary home of thousands of migrating humpback whales, and part of an extensive network of parks and preserves safeguarding the country's natural patrimony.

Peaks & Valleys

Much of the DR is distinctly rural: driving through the vast fertile interior, you'll see cows and horses grazing alongside the roads and trucks and burros loaded down with fresh produce. Further inland you'll encounter vistas reminiscent of the European Alps, rivers carving their way through lush jungle and stunning waterfalls. Four of the five highest peaks in the Caribbean rise above the fertile lowlands surrounding Santiago and remote deserts stretch through the southwest, giving the DR a physical and cultural complexity not found on other islands.

Past & Present

The country's roller-coaster past is writ large in the physical design of its towns and cities. Santo Domingo's Zona Colonial exudes romance with its beautifully restored monasteries and cobblestone streets where conquistadors once roamed. The crumbling gingerbread homes of Puerto Plata and Santiago remain from more prosperous eras, and scars from decades of misrule are marked by monuments where today people gather to celebrate. New communities have arisen only a few kilometers from the ruins where Christopher Columbus strode and where the indigenous Taíno people left traces of their presence carved onto rock walls.

People & Culture

The social glue of the DR is the all-night merengue that blasts from *colmados* (combined corner stores and bars) and this is true everywhere from the capital Santo Domingo to crumbling San Pedro de Macoris to Puerto Plata, where waves crash over the Malecón. Dominicans greatly appreciate their down time and really know how to party, as can be seen at Carnival celebrations held throughout the country and each town's own distinctive fiesta. These events are windows into the culture, so take the chance to join the fun and elaborate feasts.

Why I Love the Dominican Republic

By Ashley Harrell, Writer

Although the idyllic beaches and all-included rum cocktails of Punta Cana have their place, for me, the DR is about other things – the wizened men puffing cigars and slapping down dominoes by the fire atop Pico Duarte, or dancing the merengue inside the crumbling ruins of the New World's first monastery. I've never felt so inspired as when I zipped through desert hills on a scooter, past grazing goats and drying laundry, headed for a faraway fishing village where some ambitious expat started a kitesurfing school.

For more about our writers, see p320

Above: Bike riding on a dirt road

Dominican Republic & Haiti

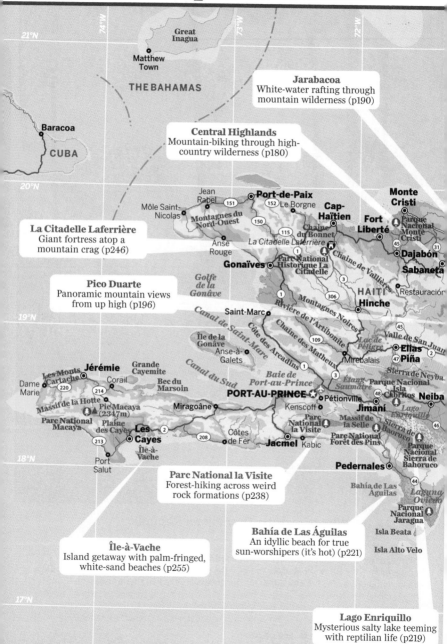

Jarabacoa
White-water rafting through
mountain wilderness (p190)

Central Highlands
Mountain-biking through high-
country wilderness (p180)

La Citadelle Laferrière
Giant fortress atop a
mountain crag (p246)

Pico Duarte
Panoramic mountain views
from up high (p196)

Parc National la Visite
Forest-hiking across weird
rock formations (p238)

Île-à-Vache
Island getaway with palm-fringed,
white-sand beaches (p255)

Bahía de Las Águilas
An idyllic beach for true
sun-worshipers (it's hot) (p221)

Lago Enriquillo
Mysterious salty lake teeming
with reptilian life (p219)

THE BAHAMAS

Great
Inagua

Matthew
Town

Baracoa

CUBA

Jean
Rabel

Môle Saint-
Nicolas

Montagnes du
Nord-Ouest

Port-de-Paix

Le Borgne

Cap-
Haïtien

Fort
Liberté

Monte
Cristi

Parque
Nacional
Monte
Cristi

Dajabón

Sabaneta

Anse
Rouge

La Citadelle Laferrière

Chaîne
du Bonnet

Parc National
Historique La
Citadelle

Chaîne de Vallières

Gonaïves

Golfe
de la
Gonâve

Montagnes Noires

HAITI

Hinche

Restauración

Saint-Marc

Rivière de l'Artibonite

Île de la
Gonâve

Anse-à-
Galets

Côte des Arcadins

Chaîne des Matheux

Canal de Saint-Marc

Lac de
Péligre

Valle de San Juan

Elías

Piña

Jérémie

Grande
Cayemite

Corail

Bec du
Marsoin

Canal du Sud

Baie de
Port-au-Prince

Mirebalais

Étang
Saumâtre

Sierra de Neyba

Parque Nacional
Isla
Cabritos

Neiba

Les Monts
Cartache

Dame
Marie

Massif de la Hotte

Pic Macaya
(2347m)

Parc National
Macaya

Plaine
des Cayes

Les
Cayes

Miragoâne

PORT-AU-PRINCE

Pétionville

Kenscoff

Parc
National
la Visite

Jimaní

Massif de
la Selle

Lago
Enriquillo

Sierra de
Bahoruco

Côtes
de Fer

Jacmel

Kabic

Parc National
Forêt des Pins

Parque
Nacional
Sierra de
Bahoruco

Port
Salut

Île-à-
Vache

Pedernales

Bahía de Las
Aguilas

Laguna
Oviedo

Parque
Nacional
Jaragua

Isla Beata

Isla Alto Velo

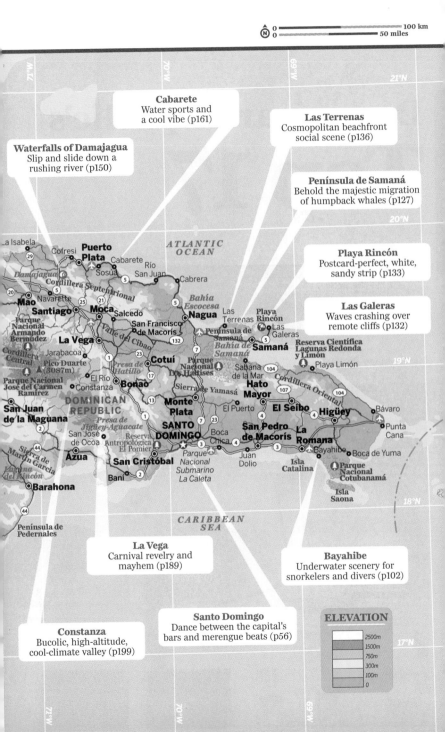

Cabarete
Water sports and
a cool vibe (p161)

Las Terrenas
Cosmopolitan beachfront
social scene (p136)

Waterfalls of Damajagua
Slip and slide down a
rushing river (p150)

Península de Samaná
Behold the majestic migration
of humpback whales (p127)

Playa Rincón
Postcard-perfect, white,
sandy strip (p133)

Las Galeras
Waves crashing over
remote cliffs (p132)

La Vega
Carnival revelry and
mayhem (p189)

Bayahibe
Underwater scenery for
snorkelers and divers (p102)

Constanza
Bucolic, high-altitude,
cool-climate valley (p199)

Santo Domingo
Dance between the capital's
bars and merengue beats (p56)

ELEVATION

2500m
1500m
750m
300m
100m
0

0 — 100 km
0 — 50 miles

ATLANTIC
OCEAN

La Isabela
Cofresí
Puerto Plata
Cabarete
Sosúa
Río San Juan
Cabrera
Damajagua
Navarrete
Mao
Cordillera Septentrional
Santiago
Moca
Salcedo
Nagua
Las Terrenas
Playa Rincón
Las Galeras
San Francisco de Macorís
Parque Nacional Armando Bermúdez
La Vega
Jarabacoa
Valle del Cibao
Península de Samaná
Bahía Escocesa
Bahía de Samaná
Samaná
Reserva Científica Lagunas Redonda y Limón
Playa Limón
Cordillera Central
Pico Duarte (3087m)
El Río
Presa de Hatillo
Cotuí
Parque Nacional Los Haitises
Sabana de la Mar
Cordillera Oriental
Parque Nacional José del Carmen Ramírez
Constanza
Bonao
Sierra de Yamasá
Hato Mayor
Bávaro
San Juan de la Maguana
DOMINICAN REPUBLIC
Presa de Jiguey-Aguacate
Monte Plata
El Puerto
El Seibo
Higüey
Punta Cana
San José de Ocoa
Reserva Antropológica El Pomier
SANTO DOMINGO
Boca Chica
San Pedro de Macorís
La Romana
Bayahibe
Boca de Yuma
Azua
San Cristóbal
Parque Nacional Submarino La Caleta
Juan Dolio
Isla Catalina
Parque Nacional Cotubanamá
Sierra de Martín García
Baní
Laguna del Rincón
Isla Saona
Barahona

CARIBBEAN
SEA

Península de Pedernales

Dominican Republic's
Top 17

1

Santo Domingo's Zona Colonial

1 Take a walk through history in the oldest city in the New World. With its cobblestone streets and beautifully restored mansions, churches and forts, many converted into evocative museums and restaurants, it's easy to imagine Santo Domingo's landmark quarter (p56) as the seat of Spain's 16th-century empire. But the past and present coexist rather gracefully here; follow in the footsteps of pirates and conquistadors one moment, the next pop into a 4D movie theater or shop selling CDs from the latest Dominican merengue star. Below left: Catedral Primada de América (p68)

Bahía de Las Águilas

2 The remoteness and loneliness of the country's most far-flung and beautiful beach adds savor and spice to the adventure of getting to Bahía de Las Águilas (p221), a stunning 10km-long stretch of postcard-perfect sand nearly hugging Haiti in an extreme corner of the Península de Pedernales. The fact that you take a boat that weaves in and out through craggy cliffs and sea-diving pelicans to get here – and you'll only share it with a few other tourists – only adds to its allure.

WALTER BIBIKOW/GETTY IMAGES ©

2

MATT MUNRO/LONELY PLANET ©

Hiking Pico Duarte

3 Hispaniola has some surprisingly rugged, pine-tree-covered terrain in the Central Cordillera, including Pico Duarte (p196), the Caribbean's highest mountain (3087m). You'll need a sturdy pair of shoes, warm clothing, good stamina and several days, but if you summit when the clouds have dispersed, the views out to both the Atlantic and the Caribbean are more than worth the blisters. Along with the memories of a night huddling around the fire out under the stars, you'll take home a well-earned feeling of accomplishment.

Sun, Sea & Sand at Playa Rincón

4 Consistently rated one of the top beaches (p133) in the Caribbean by those in the know – people who courageously brave heatstroke and sunburn in a quest for the ideal – Rincón's 3km of pitch-perfect sands is second only to Bahía de Las Águilas in the DR. It's large enough for every day-tripper to claim their own piece of real estate without nosy neighbors peeking over the seaweed and driftwood. A thick palm forest provides the backdrop and fresh seafood can be served upon request.

Whale Watching

5 North Americans and Europeans aren't the only ones who migrate south to the Caribbean in the winter. Every year, thousands of humpback whales congregate off the Península de Samaná (p124) to mate and give birth, watched (from a respectful distance) by boatloads of their human fans. For sheer awe-inspiring, 'the natural world is an amazing thing' impact, seeing whales up close is hard to beat, and Samaná is considered to be one of the world's top 10 whale-watching destinations. Get a front row seat to this spectacle from mid-January to mid-March.

Mountain Biking the Dominican Alps

6 Hardcore cyclists rave about the rough trails of the DR's central highlands (p51), where they feel like pioneers. Free styling their way on rocky descents, through alpine meadows and through coursing streams, is an adventurer's dream. Less strenuous rides abound, too: pedal along dirt roads through farming communities and sugarcane fields, and smiles and friendly invitations to stop and grab a Presidente or two will greet you along the way.

Winter Baseball

7 Dominicans don't just worship at Sunday Mass: baseball makes a solid claim for the country's other religion. Hometown fanatics cheer their team on with a passion and enthusiasm equal to bleacher creatures in Yankee Stadium or Fenway Park, but with better dancers and possibly a wider selection of stadium fare. The Dominican league's six teams go *cabeza a cabeza* several nights a week – Estadio Quisqueya (p84) in Santo Domingo is home field for two longtime rivals – culminating in a championship series at the end of January.

Leisurely Las Galeras

8 This sleepy fishing village at the far eastern end of the Península de Samaná is an escape from your getaway. Fewer tourists and therefore less development means that the area around Las Galeras (p132) includes some of the more scenic locales in all the DR. Swaying palm trees back beaches ready-made for a movie set, and waves crash over hard-to-get-to cliffs. Even more cinematic are the astounding views from a few elevated dining and sleeping options, which take in the surrounding expanses of jungle, mountain and sea.

Mountain Vistas in Constanza

9 The scenery found in the central highlands is a surprise to most. Cloud-covered peaks, with slopes of well-tended agricultural plots and galloping forest growth rising from the valley floor are vistas not often associated with Caribbean islands. A stay on the outskirts of Constanza (p199), truly a world away from the developing coastline, provides tableaus of often spectacular sunsets – it's also this time of day when the temperature begins to dip and the chilly air calls for sweaters and blankets.

BATECHENKOFF/SHUTTERSTOCK ©

White-Water Rafting

10 The Caribbean's only raftable river, the Río Yaque del Norte near Jarabacoa (p191) in the central highlands of the DR, is tailor-made for those looking to recharge their batteries after too much sun and sand. A short but intense series of rapids will get the adrenalin going, as will a spill in the cold roiling river; fortunately, however, there are stretches of flat water where you can loosen your grip on the paddle and gaze at the mountain scenery in the distance, or jump in for a refreshing swim.

MARIA GRAZIA CASELLA/ALAMY STOCK PHOTO ©

SAMI SARKIS/GETTY IMAGES ©

La Vega Carnival

11 Carnival is a huge blowout everywhere in the DR, but especially so in La Vega (p189); the entire city turns out for the parade and every corner and park is transformed into a combination impromptu concert and dance party. Look out for the whips when dancing with costumed devils. Garish, colorful, baroque and elaborately and painstakingly made outfits – capes, demonic masks with bulging eyes and pointed teeth – are worn by marauding groups of revelers.

Aquatic Bayahibe

12 Underwater visibility and consistent ocean conditions make this coastal village (p102), near La Romana in the southeast, the country's best scuba-diving destination bar none. You'll find boat services to the islands of Saona and Catalina, and the island's best wreck dive, the *St George*, is out here, too. Snorkelers will find themselves equally well catered to, and there's the unique opportunity to spend a few hours cruising the shoreline in a traditional fishing vessel.

Las Terrenas Cafe Culture

13 Mellow out in this cosmopolitan beachfront town (p136) where French and Italian accents are as common as Dominican. International camaraderie is contagious when every day begins and ends with espresso at open-air cafes and restaurants overlooking the ocean. The relaxed vibe of this former simple fishing village is a marriage between watersports adventurers swapping tips and tales and the more sedentary set, content to admire their exploits from afar, while relishing the town's European flare.

13

Santo Domingo Nightlife & Dancing

14

14 Get dressed to the nines, do some limbering up and get your dance moves on. Nightclubs in the seaside resort hotels host some of the best merengue and salsa bands this side of Havana. Downtown (p82) has trendy, sceney clubs for the fashionable set, the Zona Colonial is chockablock with drinking holes, from sweaty corner stores and boozy bohemian hangouts to upscale restaurants, hipster-y craft cocktail bars and hideaways with magnificent colonial-era courtyards.

Descending the 27 Waterfalls of Damajagua

15 A short drive from Puerto Plata, a hard-won slosh to the far side of the river and a trek through the lush forest lead to these falls (p150). Experiencing this spectacular series of cascades involves wading through clear pools, swimming inside narrow, smooth-walled canyons, hiking through dripping tropical forest, and climbing rocks, ropes and ladders through the roaring falls themselves. The adrenalin-pumping fun culminates when you can leap and slide down the falls, with some jumps from as high as 10m.

Kitesurfing in Cabarete & Beyond

16 Year-round strong offshore breezes make Cabarete (p163) on the DR's north coast one of the undisputed capitals for the burgeoning sport of kitesurfing, and the wind-whipped shallows of a newer spot called Buen Hombre, just west of Punta Rucia, are also gaining traction. Harnessing the wind's power to propel you over the choppy surface of the Atlantic isn't like another day at the beach. It takes training and muscles, not to mention faith, before you can attempt the moves of the pros from around the world.

Lago Enriquillo

17 Toward the border with Haiti you'll find Lago Enriquillo (p219), an enormous saltwater lake 40m below sea level and a remnant of the strait that once bisected the island from Barahona to Port-au-Prince. Several hundred crocodiles call the lake home, and everywhere you'll see rocks of fossilized coral. Waters have receded somewhat in recent years, unveiling an eerily picturesque sunken forest. Around the lake, colonies of seemingly menacing Ricord and rhinoceros iguanas roam freely and cacti thrive while swarms of butterflies color the landscape every June.

Right: Rhinoceros iguana

Need to Know

For more information, see Survival Guide (p293)

Currency
Dominican peso (RD$)

Language
Spanish

Visas
The majority of would-be foreign travelers in the Dominican Republic do not need to obtain visas prior to arrival.

Money
ATMs widely available. Credit and debit cards accepted in many hotels and restaurants.

Cell Phones
Local SIM cards can be used or phones can be set for roaming.

Time
Atlantic Standard Time (GMT/UTC minus four hours).

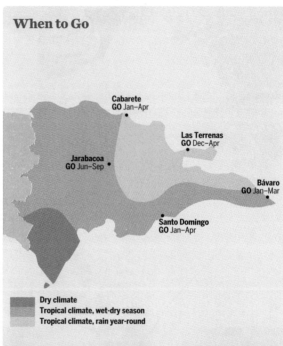

When to Go

Cabarete
GO Jan–Apr

Las Terrenas
GO Dec–Apr

Jarabacoa
GO Jun–Sep

Bávaro
GO Jan–Mar

Santo Domingo
GO Jan–Apr

Dry climate
Tropical climate, wet-dry season
Tropical climate, rain year-round

High Season
(mid-Dec–Feb)

➡ July to August and the week before Easter are also high season.

➡ Whale-watching runs from around mid-January to mid-March.

➡ Most water sports are prohibited the week before Easter.

Shoulder
(Mar–Jul)

➡ Short but strong rains in Santo Domingo (through October).

➡ March is dry in Samaná; April is ideal throughout the country (also breezy).

➡ May to June is partly cloudy or partly sunny; chance of afternoon showers.

Low Season
(Aug–early Dec)

➡ Hurricane season June to December (impacting the east), but still beautiful.

➡ Temperatures don't vary much (mountains an exception).

➡ Deeply discounted rooms and some properties in resort areas close in October.

Useful Websites

Debbie's Dominican Travel
(www.debbiesdominicantravel.
com) Reviews of sites and accommodations.

DR1 (www.dr1.com) Busy online
forum with engaged members
posting travel and DR-living
related news and opinions.

Go Dominican Republic (www.
godominicanrepublic.com)
Official tourism site.

Lonely Planet (lonelyplanet.
com/dominican-republic) Destination information, hotel bookings, traveler forum and more.

Important Numbers

For all calls within the DR (even
local ones), you must dial ☏1 +
809 or 829 or 849. There are no
regional codes.

Country code	☏1
Emergency	☏911
Fire	☏112

Exchange Rates

Australia	A$1	RD$36
Canada	C$1	RD$36
Europe	€1	RD$50
Haiti	HTG1	RD$0.71
Japan	¥100	RD$42
New Zealand	NZ$1	RD$33
UK	UK£1	RD$58
US	US$1	RD$47

For current exchange rates, see
www.xe.com.

Daily Costs
Budget:
Less than US$60

➡ Budget room: RD$1500
(US$35)

➡ Meal at local *comedor*:
RD$250–300 (US$5–6)

➡ Small bottled water: RD$10
(US$0.21)

➡ Six-pack of 12oz
Presidentes: RD$62 (US$1.30)

➡ Rides on *motoconchos*
(motorcycle taxis) and *guaguas*
(small buses) to get around:
RD$47 (US$1)

Midrange: US$60–200

➡ Internet deal on all-inclusive
accommodations: RD$2800
(US$65)

➡ First-class bus tickets
between major destinations:
RD$420 (US$10)

➡ Group tours for activities
like snorkeling, hiking, etc:
RD$1648 (US$35)

Top End:
More than US$200

➡ Beachfront resort:
RD$8500 (US$200)

➡ Meal at top restaurant
in urban or resort areas:
RD$1500 (US$35)

➡ Car rental for a week, at an
average daily rate (including
insurance): RD$1412 (US$30)

Opening Hours

Opening hours vary throughout
the year. We've provided high-
season opening hours; hours generally decrease in the shoulder
and low seasons.

Banks 9am to 4:30pm Monday
to Friday, to 1pm Saturday.

Bars 8pm to late, to 2am in Santo
Domingo.

Government Offices 7:30am to
4pm Monday to Friday (in reality
more like 9am to 2:30pm).

Restaurants 8am to 10pm Monday to Saturday (some closed
between lunch and dinner); to
11pm or later in large cities and
tourist areas.

Supermarkets 8am to 10pm
Monday to Saturday.

Shops 9am to 7:30pm Monday
to Saturday; some open half-day
Sunday.

Arriving in the DR

**Aeropuerto Internacional Las
Américas** (Santo Domingo,
p302) Taxi fares to the city are
US$40. *Motoconchos* take you to
the nearby highway *guagua* bus
stop for the slow, crowded ride
26km west to the center.

**Aeropuerto Internacional
Punta Cana** (Punta Cana, p302)
Resort minivans transport the
majority of tourists to nearby
resorts, but taxis (US$30 to
US$80) are plentiful.

**Aeropuerto Internacional
Gregorío Luperón** (Puerto Plata,
p302) Many resorts and hotels
in the area can arrange minivan
pick-up. Taxis cost US$35 to
US$55, depending on destina-
tion, for the 18km ride.

Getting Around

Although the DR is a fairly small
country, the inadequate road
network makes getting across the
country by car or public transportation more time consuming.

Air Useful if short on time, though
the most expensive option and
sometimes unreliable depending
on time of year.

Bus Two major companies,
Caribe Tours and Metro, provide
comfortable; frequent service
along a network of major cities
and towns.

Car Most convenient option if
seeking freedom of movement,
especially if interested in exploring rural and mountain regions.

Guaguas Small buses or
minivans, ubiquitous, least expensive and least comfortable, but
often the only available public
transport.

PLAN YOUR TRIP NEED TO KNOW

For much more on
getting around,
see p303

First Time Dominican Republic

For more information, see Survival Guide (p293)

Checklist

➡ Make sure your passport is valid for at least six months after your arrival date.

➡ Inform your debit-/credit-card company.

➡ Arrange for appropriate travel insurance.

➡ Decide on whether to get any recommended vaccinations.

➡ Brush up on your Spanish.

➡ Pack a $10 bill to pay for your tourist visa at the airport.

What to Pack

➡ High SPF sunscreen, hat, sunglasses, bug spray

➡ Warm-weather dressy outfits for Santo Domingo

➡ Sweater for cool evenings and buses; full-on cold-weather gear if hiking at high altitudes

➡ River shoes for water-based adventures

➡ Earplugs for a good night's sleep in the city

Top Tips for Your Trip

➡ Get out into the countryside to see how the majority of Dominicans live. If driving, grab a map and allow time to wander the back roads. Or hop in a *guagua* (local bus) to rub elbows with locals and see how most get around.

➡ Even if staying at an all-inclusive, experience the local dining scene, whether it's reservations at a nice restaurant or the *plato del día* at a *comedor* (eatery). Best case scenario, chow down late night on *sancocho* – basically a soupy stew and a Dominican specialty.

➡ Few experiences are more quintessentially Dominican than milking a couple of Presidente *grandes* at a plastic table on a beach or sidewalk patio of some no-name restaurant or *colmado* (combined corner store and bar).

What to Wear

Dominicans, especially in Santo Domingo, Santiago and other large towns, dress well (never shorts or tank tops) and take pride in their appearance, even in the warmest weather. High heels and starched shirts are the norm for nights out. Unless you want to stand out like a sore *turista* and unless you're on the beach or poolside, consider long pants and comfortable, semi-formal tops.

Sleeping

Online room rates are usually cheapest. Book early if you're visiting during high season, especially in tourist-heavy areas.

All-inclusive resorts What most people associate with the DR; quality ranges from top-flight luxury to neglected properties with low standards.

Apart-hotels & condos For longer stays, fully furnished units can be your best bet.

B&Bs A few rooms with owners living on the premises; breakfast included.

Hotels From boutique European-owned places with style and intimacy to business-class behemoths in the capital.

Hostels A few of these have popped up in recent years, complete with dorm beds and international camaraderie.

Sorting through the All-Inclusives

Consider the following questions if you're trying to choose an all-inclusive resort:

Location What part of the country is the resort in? What sights are nearby?

The fine print Other than the buffet, are all restaurants included? All alcoholic beverages? Motorized water sports?

Ocean front Is the resort on the beach, across the street, a bus ride away?

Children Is this a kid-friendly resort? Is there a kids' club? Babysitting service?

Entertainment Are there nightly performances or live-music venues? How about a disco?

Busy? Your mood and experience can be affected, depending on your tastes, if it's too crowded or too empty.

Tipping

A shock to many first-timers, most restaurants add a whopping 28% (ITBIS of 18% and an automatic 10% service charge) to every bill. Menus don't always indicate whether prices include the tax and tip.

Hotels A 10% service charge is often automatically included; however, a US$1 to US$2 per night gratuity left for cleaning staff is worth considering.

Taxis Typically, round up or give a little extra change.

Tours Tip tour guides, some of whom earn no other salary.

Restaurants Tipping generally not expected since 10% automatically added to total. If especially impressed, you can add something more.

Language

Some amount of English is widely spoken by Dominicans working in the tourism industry. Otherwise, especially in small towns and rural areas, little to none. Italian, French and German might come in handy in expat hideaways. Keep in mind that Dominican Spanish is spoken very fast with lots of slang and Dominicans tend to swallow the ends of words, especially those ending in 's' - *tres* sounds like 'tre' and *buenos días* like 'bueno dia.'

Bargaining

When shopping for jewelry, handicrafts, artwork or other souvenirs, bargaining is fairly common. Even when the price is marked on the item, it's worth a shot and usually turns out to be a casual, low-pressure affair.

Etiquette

Dominicans are generally very polite, but observe a couple of strict rules for dining and etiquette. Generally, it's a laid back, leisurely culture, so be patient if things are moving slower than you'd like.

Dining Lively background music in restaurants is the norm, so loud conversations aren't unusual.

Attention Rather than calling out, hissing is the preferred method for getting someone's attention.

Eating

Some visitors to the Dominican Republic never experience a meal outside of their all-inclusive resort, which can seem like a bargain. For travelers hoping to eat out on their own, food can be surprisingly expensive. Of course, prices tend to be much higher in heavily touristed areas, such as the Zona Colonial in Santo Domingo (comparable to US and European prices), and cheaper in small towns and isolated areas. However, outside of informal food stands and cafeteria-style eateries, a meal without drinks at most restaurants will cost a minimum of RD$325 or US$7 (after the 16% ITBIS tax and 10% service charge have been added on). Many restaurants have a range of options, from inexpensive pizza and pasta dishes to pricey lobster meals.

What's New

The Colonial Gate 4D Cinema

This super-cool Santo Domingo theater shows 4D short films (including *The Battle of Santo Domingo*) with effects like mist, fog, wind and heat. Admission includes three short films and headsets that translate them into nine languages. (p84)

Island Life Backpacker's Hostel

A derelict Santo Domingo colonial home was recently restored into this Zona Colonial hostel and erstwhile Unesco World Heritage site, which features courtyard hammocks, a great bar and a dipping pool. It's a true traveler's paradise. (p72)

La Alpargatería

It looks like a shoe shop, but step past the artisanal espadrilles (light canvas shoes people started making in the Pyrenees in the 14th century) and the place opens into a trendy cafe with comfy seating and delicious craft cocktails. (p82)

Kite School Buen Hombre

A new kitesurfing school, complete with eight beach bungalows and a simple but tasty restaurant, has been established in the faraway town of Buen Hombre, on the country's remote, northwestern shore. (p176)

Eze Bar & Restaurant

The Italian chef is known around town for opening ambitious restaurants, but this beachfront Cabarete hideaway is his first home-run. The tuna tartar might be the best in all the Caribbean. (p170)

Casa El Paraíso

The astonishing six rooms at this new B&B near Las Galeras offers some of the most jaw-dropping spots to hang your hat in ... well, anywhere. Entire walls are gone, revealing sea and mountain views most folks only see in their travel dreams. (p135)

El Monte Azul

Nobody dines in Las Galeras without dining at El Monte Azul, perched high in jungle surrounds a few kilometers outside town. The food (French/Thai), the cocktails, the service and the views are all stunning. (p135)

Dominican Tree House Village

These new rustic-luxe tree houses tucked away in jungly mountain scenery not far from Samaná are a perfect spot to live out your sky-high getaway fantasies. (p129)

Eco del Mar

Glamping in style near Bahía de Las Águilas is the calling of this new Italian-run beach lodging on the Península de Pedernales, but it's the idyllic beach bar that truly steals the show. (p221)

Macao Beach Hostel

This new and very rustic hostel on Playa Macao in Punta Cana is a great spot to immerse yourself in the rural Dominican Republic, with an excellent community-tourism angle to boot. (p114)

For more recommendations and reviews, see **lonelyplanet.com/ dominican-republic**

If You Like...

White-Sand Beaches

Full of breathtaking beaches, from oases of calm to party hotspots, the country's coastline can satisfy every taste. It is blessed with year-round warm temperatures and waters, so bring a boatload of lotion to avoid sunburn.

Playa Rincón Three kilometers of tropical paradise with a nearby freshwater stream to wash off the salt water. (p133)

Bahía de Las Águilas This far-flung, hard-to-get-to beach with cacti hugging the cliffs is definitely worth the trip. (p221)

Playa Macao Not far north of Bávaro, a palm-lined beauty, mostly undeveloped but for a surf camp and informal beach shacks. (p110)

Punta Cana Long strand of sand and the epicenter of the all-inclusive resorts. (p110)

Playa Grande Half-moon cove with turquoise water, good surf waves and readily available seafood lunch. (p171)

Playa Limón Three-kilometer-long strip lined with coconut trees, plus wetlands and mangroves nearby. (p119)

Playa Blanca Tens of kilometers of white sand on the northern coast of Isla Beata, part of Parque Nacional Jaragua. (p217)

Outdoor Adventures

Blessed with a varied geography, both inland and coastal, the DR is an extreme-sport mecca. Ditch the car and try one of these alternative methods of transportation.

Canyoning Involving rappelling, jumping, climbing and swimming down a river, basically emulating a Navy Seal on a recon mission. (p193)

White-water rafting The Río Yaque outside of Jarabacoa is the only river in the Caribbean for this adrenaline-pumping experience. (p191)

Kitesurfing Skim across the waves at high speeds powered by strong year-round winds in Cabarete and Buen Hombre. (p163)

Hiking Overnight it to Pico Duarte, the highest peak in the Caribbean, for potentially panoramic views. (p196)

Mountain biking Explore the network of little-used trails through striking landscapes and past little-visited villages of the central highlands. (p199)

Relaxing at a Resort

Many of the DR's best beaches are colonized by all-inclusive resorts, the quintessential Caribbean beach break. Certainly, they come in all shapes and sizes, though sprawling 'city-states' seem to be the norm.

Punta Cana The country's largest concentration of developments and widest range of accommodations, with more on the way. (p91)

Playa Dorada Good deals in the geographic center of the north coast, with easy access to other regional destinations. (p152)

Las Terrenas Of course there are beaches but also water sports and waterfall adventures in this charming town with a European feel. (p136)

Juan Dolio Convenient because of its close proximity to Santo Domingo, with shallow, calm water. (p94)

Playa Dominicus A small enclave of resorts on a crowded but pretty stretch near the town of Bayahibe. (p103)

Wildlife

A large national park system and an increasing number of scientific preserves ranging from semideserts to lush valleys protect the country's biological diversity and a surprising number of endemic species.

Whale-watching These massive mammals take their winter break in Bahía de Samaná. (p124)

Parque Nacional Los Haitises Birdwatching (plus manatees, boas and marine turtles) from a boat cruising through mangrove forest. (p121)

Lago Enriquillo & Isla Cabritos Crocodiles and iguanas (and flamingos and egrets December to April) in a remote saltwater lake and desert island. (p219)

Laguna Oviedo Flamingos, ibis, storks and spoonbills, not to mention egg-laying turtles and iguanas. (p216)

Estero Hondo Climb a watchtower or hop in a boat to spot a manatee in the mangroves around Punta Rucia. (p175)

Nightlife & Dancing

Whether it's an impromptu neighborhood block party gathering around the local *colmado* (corner store), swanky hotel nightclub or local fiesta, Dominicans love to drink, socialize and get down. Wherever you are in the country, the central square is a likely nighttime gathering place.

Santo Domingo *Capitaleños* know how to let loose and the city has more bars and nightclubs than anywhere else in the country. (p56)

Top: Merengue dancers, Santo Domingo (p56)
Bottom: Flamingos fly over Laguna Oviedo (p216)

Santiago Rub elbows and booties at one of the dozen-plus bars and clubs around *el Monumento* in the city's center. (p181)

Cabarete More than just an action-sports destination, the beach here is lined with restaurants and bars. (p161)

Sosúa Granted, there's a decidedly raunchy and illicit vibe to nightlife here, but it is lively and diverse. (p155)

Jarabacoa Post-adventure Presidentes are on tap in the raucous bars at this mountain town's center. (p190)

Romantic Getaways

Couples, both those on silver wedding anniversaries and those whose relationships are only a few hours old, will find plenty of places in the DR to make their hearts pound. From secluded hideaways to candle-lit restaurants, there is no shortage of options.

Casa Bonita Out-of-the-way hillside retreat to the south of Barahona. (p215)

Plaza España Come to Santo Domingo for an intimate dinner on the balcony of one of this plaza's many atmospheric restaurants. (p65)

Alto Cerro Balcony mountain views – either from the restaurant or your villa – will make your heart go pitter-patter; outside Constanza. (p200)

Aroma de la Montaña Good wine, food, twinkling lights from the valley floor and the DR's only rotating dining room at this restaurant near Jarabacoa. (p195)

Sunset Horseback Ride It may sound like a cliché but ocean waves lapping at your horse's feet and holding your partner's hand... (p119)

Casa El Paraíso In Las Galeras, rooms here are the most romantic the author has seen in his entire life, and he's seen a lot of rooms. (p135)

Diving & Snorkeling

With hundreds of miles of coastline it's no surprise that the DR's subaquatic adventures are the priority for many visitors. Warm waters and consistently good year-round conditions mean every region has something to offer.

Bayahibe Experienced divers consider this the best destination in the country. (p102)

Playa Frontón Boat out to the reefs here, some of the best on the Península de Samaná. (p132)

Sosúa The base for north-coast underwater adventures as far afield as Luperón and Monte Cristi. (p155)

Boca Chica Two small wrecks and shallow reefs a short drive from Santo Domingo. (p97)

Laguna Dudu A sinkhole with natural spring water leads to several underwater caverns near the town of Río San Juan. (p172)

Architecture

In addition to an enduring economic and social legacy, the Spanish colonizers left a physical one in the form of early-16th-century churches and buildings. Homes built

by beneficiaries of several industrial boom-bust cycles have also had a lasting impact on urban design.

Zona Colonial Santo Domingo's compact neighborhood of cobblestone streets steeped in history and colonial-era buildings. (p61)

Puerto Plata Elegant, pastel gingerbread Victorian homes around Parque Central. (p147)

Churches From colonial-era gothic to contemporary postindustrial, the cathedral is often a town's most striking building. (p181)

Ruins

Evidence of Hispaniola's rich and tumultuous history, where Carib and Taíno cultures once prospered and Columbus, Cortés, Ponce de León and Sir Francis Drake once strode, have been written onto the island's landscape.

La Vega Vieja Remains of a fort built on Columbus' orders and destroyed by a 1562 earthquake. (p189)

Parque Nacional La Isabela Trace the foundation of the second-oldest New World settlement on a picturesque ocean bluff. (p175)

Cueva de las Maravillas Easily accessible, massive cave with hundreds of pictographs and petroglyphs. (p99)

Cueva del Puente Cave of pictographs near the remains of a large Taíno city in the Parque Nacional Cotubanamá. (p103)

Reserva Antropológica Cuevas del Pomier Site of the most extensive prehistoric cave art in the Caribbean. (p209)

MICHAEL RUNKEL/GETTY IMAGES ©

Top: Horse-drawn carraige tour (p72), Santo Domingo

Bottom: Playa Rincón (p133)

Month by Month

TOP EVENTS

Whale-Watching, mid-January–mid-March

Carnival, February

Santo Domingo Merengue Festival, end of July

Festival of the Bulls, August

Winter Baseball, end of October–end of January

January

The North American winter coincides with the start of whale-watching season in the Bahía de Samaná, making this a popular time of year to visit. Winds on the north coast are generally strongest this time of year.

Day of Duarte

Public fiestas are held in all the major towns on January 26, and there are gun salutes in Santo Domingo, celebrating the birthday of the Father of the Country.

Día de Altagracia

One of the most important religious days of the year falls on January 21, when thousands of pilgrims flock to the basilica in Higüey to pray to the country's patron saint. (p108)

Whale-Watching

This seasonal display of thousands of humpback whales doing their best impersonation of gymnasts takes place in the Bahía de Samaná and Silver Bank area. January is the beginning, but things get into full swing in February.

February

This is a month of intense partying throughout the DR; hotel prices rise and popular tours can be booked solid. February to March are generally the driest months in Samaná.

Carnival

Celebrated with fervor throughout the DR every Sunday in February, culminating in blowouts on the last weekend of the month or the first weekend of March. The largest and most traditional Carnivals outside of Santo Domingo are in Santiago, La Vega, Cabral and Monte Cristi.

Master of the Ocean

Called a 'triathlon of the waves', this thrilling competition in the last week in February sees the world's best windsurfers, kitesurfers and surfers go board-to-board on Playa Encuentro outside Cabarete. (p166)

Independence Day

February 27, 1844, is the day that the DR regained its independence from Haiti; the holiday is marked by raucous street celebrations and military parades.

March

Semana Santa (Holy Week), the week before Easter, is when the DR takes a vacation; businesses close, Dominicans flock to beaches, and reservations are vital. Water sports are mostly prohibited. Spring Breakers arrive.

Sailing Regatta

On the Saturday of Semana Santa, the seaside village of Bayahibe turns out to watch a race of traditionally handcrafted fishing boats.

April

Dominicans travel domestically during the end of April around Good Friday. This is also a good time to visit Laguna Oviedo and the southwest; from March to June cactus flowers bloom in the desert.

🏃 Nighttime Turtle-Watching

Make your way to the out-of-the-way beaches of Parque Nacional Jaragua in the southwest where hawksbill and leatherback turtles lay and hatch their eggs. (p211)

May

⭐ Espiritu Santo

Santo Domingo's barrio Villa Mella comes alive to the sounds of drum rhythms on May 3rd when this community celebrates its African heritage honoring the (formerly) Kingdom of Kongo's paramount diety Kalunga.

June

From May to November Santo Domingo can experience strong daily rains, though usually only for short periods, while from June to September the north coast experiences generally sunny skies.

🏃 Lago Enriquillo Flora & Fauna

Blooming cactus flowers, butterflies, iguanas and crocodiles all converge in June on a desert island in the middle of Lago Enriquillo.

⭐ San Pedro Apóstal

A raucous festival on June 29 in San Pedro celebrating *cocolo* (non-hispanic African) culture. Roving bands of *guloyas* (dancers) perform this traditional dance routine on the streets.

July

The beginning of the holiday season for Dominicans and Europeans. Scorching temperatures are recorded in the southwest around Lago Enriquillo: don't forget to wear that sunscreen!

⭐ Santo Domingo Merengue Festival

Santo Domingo hosts the country's largest and most raucous merengue festival. For two weeks at the end of July and the beginning of August the world's top merengue bands play for the world's best merengue dancers all over the city. (p72)

August

The beginning of hurricane season, which can last all the way to December, means you should keep an eye out for developing storms. Sunny days prevail, though, and you can find good deals on accommodations.

⭐ Festival of the Bulls

Higüey's *fiesta patronal* (patronage festival dedicated to the town's saint) sees horseback-borne cowboys and herds of cattle mosey down the city's streets.

⭐ Restoration Day

August 16, the day the DR declared its independence from Spain, is marked by general partying and traditional folk dancing and street parades throughout the country, but it's especially festive in Santo Domingo and Santiago.

⭐ Puerto Plata Merengue Festival

During the first week in November the entire length of Puerto Plata's Malecón is closed to vehicular traffic, food stalls are set up and famous merengue singers perform on a stage erected for the event. Also includes a harvest festival and an arts-and-crafts fair. (p149)

October

Rain showers a few days a week are common throughout the country, especially inland around Santiago. Tropical storms are a threat, but expect mild temperatures, fewer visitors, some hotel closings and reduced accommodations costs.

November

🎎 DR Jazz Festival

Top Dominican and international musicians play on alternating days in Santiago, Puerto Plata and on the beach in Cabarete in late October and nearly November. (p166)

☆ Winter Baseball

The boys of winter get into full swing in November. Six teams in five cities (Santo Domingo has two) play a few games a week.

December

Hotel and flight prices rise as Americans and Canadians begin their yearly migration to the Caribbean, including the DR. Surfers head to the north coast where the waves are best from December through March.

🎎 Christmas

Decorations are ubiquitous and extended families gather to celebrate the holiday. Specialties like *puerco en puya* (pork roasted on a stick) are part of traditional family meals, and holiday songs are played nonstop.

Top: Painted hands at Carnival
Bottom: Humpback whale, Samaná (p127)

Itineraries

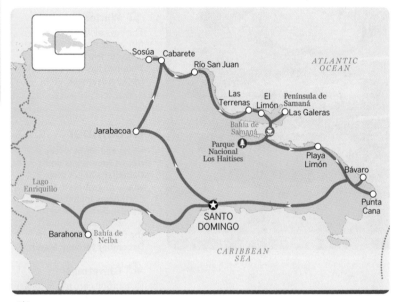

2 WEEKS Dominican Circuit

This 'greatest hits' itinerary visits every major attraction in the DR, from the New World's oldest city and the adrenaline-packed central highlands to the country's best beaches and natural environs.

Start with two days exploring **Santo Domingo**, the Zona Colonial and essential Dominican experiences of baseball and dancing to merengue. On day three head to **Jarabacoa**. Visit the waterfalls in the afternoon, with white-water rafting or canyoning the next day. Head north to **Cabarete**, which has world-class water sports and mountain biking. Spend several days diving and beach-bumming in nearby **Sosúa** and **Río San Juan**, then bolt for whale-watching from **Península de Samaná**. If it's the off-season take a boat trip to **Parque Nacional Los Haitises** to see mangroves, cave paintings or the waterfall near **El Limón**. Spend two days hiking and boating to the beaches around **Las Galeras**, or for more nightlife, base yourself in **Las Terrenas**. The southeast is perfect for some more relaxing beach time – go for either deserted **Playa Limón** or perennially popular **Bávaro and Punta Cana**. Return to Santo Domingo. To the southwest is a spectacular drive to **Barahona**, and crocodiles in **Lago Enriquillo**. Spend a night or two before returning to Santo Domingo.

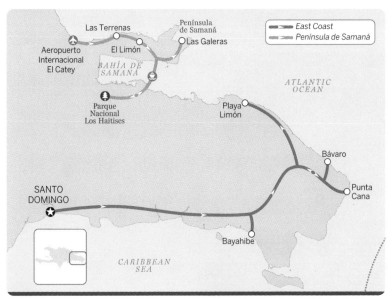

 **East Coast**

An east-coast sampler efficiently combines the colonial charm of the Americas' oldest city with total beach relaxation.

Fly into Santo Domingo or Punta Cana, and regardless of where you start, allow a full day to explore the old colonial center of **Santo Domingo**.

Base yourself in the southeast at the hub of Dominican tourism, **Bávaro and Punta Cana**, where the all-inclusive resorts are tailor-made for families; if all you want to do is splash about in the water, you could do worse than check in here. Many are particularly child-friendly, and activities include go-karts, bowling, sailing trips and parasailing. Resorts also offer tours to local sights; for more independence, rent a car and head out on your own. Singles, couples and those seeking nightlife can certainly find their own Shangri-la here as well.

Not far south of this area is **Bayahibe**, a tiny town on the edge of a national park, with the best scuba diving in the DR and a number of excursions, including catamaran tours to an island beach and snorkeling trips. For more privacy, head to deserted **Playa Limón** further up the coast.

 **Peninsula de Samaná**

From beaches to whale-watching to waterfall hikes, this itinerary is all about water.

If you can, fly directly into Aeropuerto Internacional El Catey, the closest airport to the peninsula. Otherwise, get in a puddle jumper from another DR airport or consider taking a bus or driving from Santo Domingo – the new highway makes it a painless transfer.

If possible, plan your trip for mid-January to mid-March, when humpback whales migrate to the **Bahía de Samaná** and whale-watching tours are in full steam.

Base yourself either in Las Terrenas or Las Galeras. **Las Terrenas** has a cosmopolitan mix and a relatively sophisticated European vibe. Kitesurfing and other water sports are deservedly popular here and you can choose from day-trips horseback riding to the waterfall near **El Limón** or a boat trip to **Parque Nacional Los Haitises** to see the mangroves and cave paintings.

Las Galeras is a small laid-back town at the far eastern tip of the peninsula. The beaches around here rival any in the DR and there are chances to really get to the proverbial end of the road.

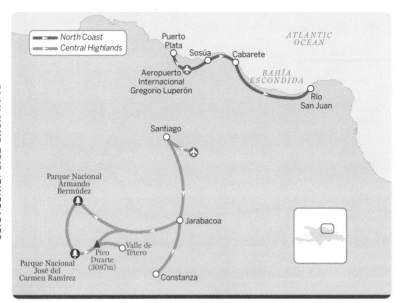

North Coast

For a less-traveled beach holiday that comes with a side of thrill-seeking and a splash of history and culture, head due north.

Fly into the Aeropuerto Internacional Gregorio Luperón. From here, choose your base for the week, but allow yourself at least an afternoon in **Puerto Plata**. Wander the city's downtown streets lined with restored Victorian homes, explore the city's museums and have a drink at a Malecón restaurant.

Active types will want to stay in or around the water-sports mecca of **Cabarete**, east of Puerto Plata; it also has a lively bar and restaurant scene. Carve out several hours or days learning the ropes of kitesurfing, windsurfing or just plain surfing from the best. Of course, the beaches are equally alluring for doing absolutely nothing but sipping cocktails and reading a good book. Scuba divers and those looking for a more raucous nightlife should look into staying in **Sosúa**.

Further east near the quiet town of **Río San Juan** are several terrific beaches, and there are snorkeling and even cave-diving opportunities nearby.

Central Highlands

The most extreme adventures in the Caribbean are concentrated here, along with a window into rural life in the DR.

Fly into the airport outside **Santiago** and spend a day exploring downtown and taking in Dominican painting at the Centro León. Take a tour of a tobacco factory and see a baseball game at the stadium if you're here during the winter season.

On the following day, head to **Jarabacoa**, gateway to **Parques Nacionales Armando Bermúdez and José del Carmen Ramírez**. The two parks cover much of the DR's central mountain range, including Pico Duarte. Visit the waterfalls in the afternoon, with white-water rafting, or canyoning or mountain biking for the next day or two. Or arrange your trip around climbing **Pico Duarte**. The standard trip is three days, but consider arranging a side trip to beautiful **Valle del Tétero**, which adds two days.

Unwind in the mountain town of **Constanza**, only a short drive from Jarabacoa, where you'll find cooler temperatures and stunning views. Rent a 4WD and off-road it through mountain passes to remote valleys and waterfalls.

Above: Cascada El Limón (p140)

Right: View of Plaza de España (p61), from the Alcázar de Colón

ENERGIEZER/GETTY IMAGES ©

Off the Beaten Track: Dominican Republic

BUEN HOMBRE
This far-flung fishing village is now home to a kitesurfing camp, complete with rustic beachfront bungalows and a shallow, windy cove. (p176)

RESERVO CIENTIFICA VALLE NUEVO
You'll need a 4WD to access this remote park with the coldest temps in the country. Situated on a high plain, fresh mountain air and beautiful vistas await. (p199)

CACHÓTE
Bathed in cloud forest – rare for a sun-drenched tropical island – these remote cabins are reached by 25km of impressively bad road that fords the same river a dozen times. (p215)

BAHÍA DE LAS ÁGUILAS
Reached via a near-deserted one-lane highway, a pot-holed secondary road and a spectacular boat ride, the DR's most beautiful beach is as much about the journey as the destination. (p221)

LOS PATOS
Stock up with gas and cash before you set out south of Barahona on the stunning drive to Paraíso. You'll probably find this *balneario* (swimming hole) and polished-stone beach free of other tourists. (p214)

Parque Nacional Monte Cristi

BUEN HOMBRE

Monte Cristi

Punta Rucia

Puerto Plata

Dajabón

Mao

Santiago

Sabaneta

Parque Nacional Armando Bermúdez

La Vega

Parque Nacional José del Carmen Ramirez

Elías Piña

RESERVO CIENTIFICA VALLE NUEVO

San Juan de la Maguana

PORT-AU-PRINCE **HAITI**

Parque Nacional Isla Cabritos

Jimaní

Neiba

Ázua

Parque Nacional Sierra de Baoruco

CACHÓTE Barahona

Pedernales

LOS PATOS

Parque Nacional Jaragua

BAHÍA DE LAS ÁGUILAS

Isla Beata

0 — 100 km
0 — 50 miles

DOMINICAN TREE HOUSE VILLAGE

Tucked away in El Valle, this sustainable ecotourism project offers 19 tree houses open on three sides to dramatic tropical forest views. (p129)

ATLANTIC OCEAN

⑤ ○ Cabrera

Moca
○

Nagua ○ **DOMINICAN TREE HOUSE VILLAGE**
○
⑤ **CASA EL PARAÍSO** ○
Bahía de Samaná ○ Samaná

Cotuí
○ ㉓

PLAYA LIMÓN

Bonao ○
⑰
🏕 Parque Nacional Los Haitises
①

Monte Plata ○

Hato Mayor ○

El Seibo ○

○ Bávaro

④ Higüey ○

San Cristóbal ○
㉓
④
San Pedro de Macorís ○
⑩①

La Romana ○

🏕 Parque Nacional del Este

✪ **SANTO DOMINGO**
③
②

Isla Saona

CASA EL PARAÍSO

An extraordinary six-room B&B in La Guázuma that practically tumbles out of the jungle into the whale-packed sea below. (p135)

PLAYA LIMÓN

North of Punta Cana, this far-flung beach is the antithesis of the resorts. Pass colorful *colonias* (settlements) and sugar plantations to discover these coconut tree-lined sands. (p119)

CARIBBEAN SEA

Tostones (fried plantain slices)

Plan Your Trip

Eat & Drink Like a Local

Though the DR isn't known as a culinary capital, eating and drinking are the social glue that binds its people together. A hybrid of Spanish, African and indigenous flavors and styles, DR cuisine is big on starches – rice, potatoes, bananas, yucca and cassava, served in large portions. Low-carb dieters beware.

STEFANO EMBER/SHUTTERSTOCK ©

Vegetarian DR

Vegetarianism is not widely practiced in the Dominican Republic, and there are certainly a large number of Dominicans who view it as downright strange. Still, there are enough nonmeat side dishes in Dominican cuisine – rice, salad, plantains, eggplant, yucca, okra and more – to ensure that vegetarians and even vegans shouldn't have too much problem finding something to eat. Beans are another easy-to-find staple, though they are often cooked with lard.

Pizza and pasta restaurants are ubiquitous in the DR and there is always at least one vegetarian option on the menu (and if not, it's easy enough to request).

For those vegetarians who make an exception for fish and seafood, there is no problem whatsoever. There are a couple of vegetarian restaurants in the DR – Ananda (p77) in Santo Domingo included – but virtually all the restaurants we've listed will have at least some nonmeat alternatives.

Food Experiences
Meals of a Lifetime

Passion by Martín Berasategui (p117) Michelin-starred owner from Basque country does a fabulous seven-course tasting menu.

Mares Restaurant & Pool Lounge (p151) Renowned chef combining Dominican flavors with European culinary inspiration.

Castle Club (p169) Elaborate, locally sourced meals in out-of-the-way mountain-top home.

Pat'e Palo (p79) Creatively conceived dishes in sparkling setting overlooking Santo Domingo's Plaza España.

El Monte Azul (p135) Fresh seafood in one of the most dramatically beautiful locations in the DR; go at sunset.

Mi Corazon (p143) Inventive tasting menu served in a romantic colonial-style courtyard.

La Terrasse (p142) Sophisticated French bistro on the Las Terrenas beachfront.

Casa Bonita (p215) Organic and locally sourced fare in a boutique hotel with postcard perfect views.

Aroma de la Montana (p195) The DR's only rotating dining room has panoramic views of the Jarabacoa countryside.

Local Specialties
To Eat

La Bandera The most typical Dominican meal consists of white rice, *habichuela* (red beans), stewed meat, salad and fried green plantains, and is usually accompanied by a fresh fruit juice. It's good, cheap, easy to prepare and nutritionally balanced. Red beans are sometimes swapped for small *moros* (black beans), *gandules* (small green beans) or *lentejas* (lentils).

Guineos (bananas) A staple of Dominican cuisine and served in a variety of ways, including boiled, stewed and candied, but most commonly boiled and mashed, like mashed potatoes. Prepared the same way, but with plantains, the dish is called *mangú*; with pork rinds mixed in it is called *mofongo*. Both are filling and can be served for breakfast, lunch or dinner, either as a side dish or as the main dish.

The Year in Food

The most widely consumed crops in the DR, beans and rice, are planted and harvested throughout the year.

➡ Spring (March–June) Some cacao is harvested during this time, along with lowland corn, yuca and potatoes.

➡ Summer (June–August) This is prime time for mango, pineapple and papaya, with June producing the ripest and most abundant fruit; cherry trees also bear fruit in June and July.

➡ Winter (Oct-March) Two coffee harvests take place during these months, with the exact timing dependent on elevation.

Seafood Most commonly a fish fillet, usually *mero* (grouper) or *chillo* (red snapper), served in one of four ways: *al ajillo* (with garlic), *al coco* (in coconut sauce), *al criolla* (with a mild tomato sauce) or *a la diabla* (with a spicy tomato sauce). Other seafood such as *cangrejo* (crab), *calamar* (squid), *camarones* (shrimp), *pulp* (octopus), *langosta* (lobster) and *lambí* (conch) are similarly prepared or *al vinagre* (in vinegar sauce), a variation on ceviche.

Chivo Goat meat is popular and presented in many ways. Two of the best are *pierna de chivo asada con ron y cilantro* (roast leg of goat with rum and cilantro) and *chivo guisado en salsa de tomate* (goat stewed in tomato sauce). It's a specialty of the northwest: the highway between Santiago and Monte Cristi is lined with restaurants serving *chivo*.

Locrio This Dominican version of paella comes in a number of different variations and is also known as *arroz con pollo* (chicken with rice). The dish features caramelized chicken and vegetables atop fluffy flavored rice sometimes colored with achiote.

To Drink

Ron (Rum) Known for its smoothness and hearty taste, as well as for being less sweet than its Jamaican counterparts, Dominican rum is of a quality that's tough to beat. Dozens of local brands are available, but the big three are Brugal, Barceló and Bermudez. Within these brands, there are many varieties, including *blanco* (clear), *dorado* (golden) and *añejo* (aged), which contains caramel and is aged in special wooden casks to mellow the taste. Bermudez, established in 1852, is the oldest of the distilleries.

Try a *santo libre* (rum and Sprite), which is just as popular among Dominicans as the more familiar *cuba libre* (rum and Coke). *Ron ponche* (rum punch) – a blend of rum and sweet tropical juices – is more often ordered by foreigners than by locals.

Beer Local brews include Quisqueya, Bohemia, Soberante and the ubiquitous Presidente. The most popular way to enjoy a beer is to share a *grande* (large) with a friend or two. A tall 1.1L beer is brought to your table in a sort of insulated sleeve, made from either wood or bamboo or from plastic and Styrofoam, along with a small glass for each of you.

Whiskey Popular in the DR and a number of familiar brands, plus a few Dominican variations, are available at most bars – purists will want a *trago de etiqueta roja* (Johnny Walker Red Label) or *trago de etiqueta blanca* (Dewar's White Label).

Mamajuana The DR's own homemade version of Viagra is a mixture of herbs, dried bark, rum, wine and honey, which is then steeped for around a month. If you can keep it down, locals believe it can cure various illnesses and, in general, is a substitute for vitamins.

Coffee Grown in six different regions by over 60,000 growers, coffee is a staple of any menu and most Dominicans' diets. It's typically served black in an espresso cup with sugar; a *café con leche* is a coffee with hot milk.

Batidas (smoothies) Made from crushed fruit, water, ice and several tablespoons of sugar. A *batida con leche* contains milk and is slightly more frothy. Popular varieties include *piña* (pineapple), *lechoza* (papaya), *guineo* (banana), *zapote* (sapote) and *morir soñando* (literally, 'to die dreaming'), made of the refreshing combination of orange juice, milk, sugar and crushed ice.

CASABE

From ancient Taíno cooking fires to elegant presidential banquets, there is at least one common thread: a starchy bread known as *casabe*. High in carbs and low in fat, *casabe* is made from ground cassava roots (also known as manioc and a close relation to yucca). Cassava was one of the Taíno's principal crops, as it was for numerous indigenous peoples throughout the Caribbean and South America. Easy to plant – just bury a piece of the root or stalk into the ground – it's also fast growing. Europeans brought the hardy plant from the Caribbean to their colonies in Africa and Asia, where it was quickly and widely adopted. *Casabe* is still popular today, especially at traditional meals with soups and stews, where it's great for soaking up every last drop. Rather tasteless on its own, *casabe* is best topped with butter, salt, tomato or avocado. A modern variation is the *catibía*, fried cassava flour fritters stuffed with meat.

Grilled lobster

Jugos (juices) Sometimes referred to as *refrescos* (this also means carbonated soda), *jugos* are typically made fresh in front of you. Popular flavors include *chinola* (passionfruit), *piña* (pineapple peel) and *tamarindo* (tamarind). Orange juice is commonly called *jugo de china*, although most will understand you if you ask for *jugo de naranja*.

Coco Coconut juice from a *cocotero* (a street vendor who hacks out an opening with a machete), is available everywhere.

Jugo de caña (sugarcane juice) Another drink sold from vendors, usually on tricycles with a grinder that mashes the cane to liquid; equally popular are the sticky pieces inside that people chew on.

Mabí Delicious drink made from the bark of the tropical liana vine.

Cheap Treats

Pastelito Usually beef or chicken, which has first been stewed with onions, olives, tomatoes and a variety of seasonings, and then chopped up and mixed with peas, nuts and raisins – all tucked into a patty of dough and fried in boiling oil.

Empanada Similar to *pastelitos* except typically containing ham or cheese.

Chimi Sandwich of seasoned ground meat, cooked cabbage, carrots, red onions and tomatoes; typically served in a plastic bag to catch the juices.

Quipe Lebanese-inspired afternoon snack of bulger stuffed with ground meat and fresh mint and fried.

Frituras de batata Sweet-potato fritters.

Fritos maduros Ripe plantain fritters.

Tostones Fried plantain slices.

Yaniqueques Johnny cakes.

Frío-frío Dominican version of snow cone; shaved ice and syrup.

Agua de coco Fruits like oranges, bananas and pineapples mixed with sliced coconuts and sugarcane juice.

Mangú (p39)

How to Eat & Drink

When to Eat

Dinner *(cena)* is the biggest meal (except on Sunday when the midday meal is generally the biggest meal), though neither breakfast *(desayuno)* nor lunch *(almuerzo)* are exactly light. All three meals usually consist of one main dish – eggs for breakfast, meat for lunch and dinner – served with one or more accompaniments, usually cold cuts, fresh fruit, rice, beans, salad and/or boiled vegetables. Dinner, at restaurants at least, isn't usually eaten until 8 or 9pm.

Menu Decoder

a la parrilla (a la pa-ree-ya) broiled

al carbon (al car-bone) grilled

al horno (al or-no) oven-baked

al vino (al vee-no) cooked in wine

frito (free-to) fried

guisada (gui-sa-da) any stew

parillada (pa-ri-yada) barbecue

sopa (so-pa) soup

Celebrations

There are a number of dishes usually reserved for special occasions, such as baptisms, birthdays and weddings: puerco asado (roast pork), asopao de mariscos (seafood) and the more modest locrio de pica-pica (spicy sardines and rice). Dishes such as sancocho de siete carnes (seven-meat soup), made with sausage, chicken, beef, goat and several pork parts, all combined with green plantains and avocado into a hearty stew, are sometimes on restaurant menus.

Christmas time in the Dominican Republic is associated with a few specialties: jengibre, a drink made of cinnamon, fresh ginger root, water and sugar; pastelitos (fried pastry treat stuffed with chicken or beef mixed with peas, nuts and raisins); moro de guandules (rice with pigeon, peas and coconut milk); and ensalada rusa (basically, potato salad).

Top: Tropical cocktail served in a pineapple

Bottom: Fried fish with *tostones*

Surfing (p45)

Surfing (p45)

Plan Your Trip

Outdoor Activities

No doubt, lounging by the pool or on the beach is what draws many visitors to the Dominican Republic. This is certainly an attractive option, but if you want to get the blood flowing, there's a wide range of sports and skill- and stamina-challenging adventures.

Best Outdoors

Best Mountain Biking

From Jamao near Moca to the isolated Magante Beach near Río San Juan; country roads in central highlands; Septentrional range around Cabarete.

Best Month to Go

February for migratory birds in the southwest, whale-watching in Samaná, and wind sports in Cabarete.

Best Adventures to Try for the First Time

Kitesurfing, canyoning, paragliding, whitewater rafting and wakeboarding.

Best Base for Active Adventures

Jarabacoa in central highlands, Cabarete on the north coast, Las Terrenas in Península de Samaná or Bayahibe in the southeast.

Best Places for More Leisurely Exploration

Parque Nacional Los Haitises, Parque Nacional Jaragua, San José de las Matas, Parque Nacional Cotubanamá or Parque Nacional Sierra de Bahoruco.

Water Sports

If it involves standing on a board, the Dominican Republic's got it in spades – you'll find world-class kitesurfing, windsurfing, surfing and wakeboarding. The undisputed water-sports capital of the DR is Cabarete on the north coast, and Las Terrenas on the Península de Samaná is the runner-up, but the adventurous can find a few other more-isolated spots as well.

Kitesurfing

Kitesurfing (also known as kiteboarding) involves strapping a board to your feet and a powerful kite to your torso, which propels you through the waves at sometimes breakneck speeds. The learning curve to get good enough to enjoy it – not to mention learning the lingo for tricks like 'kitelooping' and 'back-side handle passes' – is steep. On average, it takes a week's worth of lessons to go out solo, and months of practice to get competent. It's also expensive – to make this a regular hobby, you'll end up spending a few thousand dollars on lessons and gear. So it's no wonder that around 90% of wannabes who try it out don't generally advance to become regular kitesurfers.

That said, if you've got the time and the money, and you relish a challenge, the DR is one of the world's leading kitesurfing destinations – so much so that the International Kiteboarding Organization has its headquarters in Cabarete. Plenty of kitesurfing schools offer instruction in Cabarete or Las Terrenas in Samaná (where the wind is lighter and water shallower); Puerto Plata is another excellent spot to learn the sport, and Buen Hombre is a far-flung but up-and-coming kite destination. Most people need a minimum of four days of lessons at a cost of around US$350 to US$450. Schools and instructors vary considerably in personality, so spend some time finding one where you feel comfortable.

Surfing

According to many, the very first person to surf in the Dominican Republic was an American Army colonel, part of the US occupying force in Santo Domingo in 1965. Before leaving he sold his board to locals and the sport grew steadily from there. Until the late 1970s, specifically August 31, 1979, when hurricane David struck the southern coast, the waves around Playa Guibia on Santo Domingo's Malecón were some of the best in the country. The exact explanation of the storm's impact is unclear. What is known, is that Sosúa experienced its first tourism boom when surfers began flocking to nearby beach breaks soon after.

PLAN YOUR TRIP OUTDOOR ACTIVITIES

The north coast, especially Cabarete's Playa Encuentro, has grown into the capital of surfing in the DR. Of course, with nearly 800 miles of coastline, there's nary a region where adventurous surf gypsies can't find gnarly sets. In addition to the specific breaks listed here, the independent-minded can explore waves in Río San Juan, Playa Grande, Playa Preciosa, Cabrera and Nagua along the north coast; Playa Cosón and Playa Bonita near Las Terrenas on the Península de Samaná and Punta Cana and Macao in the east. The best season is December through March, when waves can get up to 4m high.

There are a number of surf shops in Cabarete, Playa Encuentro and Las Terrenas where you can rent boards or take surfing lessons. Rentals cost US$25 to US$30 for half a day; courses vary from three-hour introductory sessions (US$45 to US$50) to a full-blown five-day surf camp (US$200 to US$225 per person). Surfboards can be rented at a handful of other beaches including Playa Grande.

La Borja Near Santo Domingo's Las Americas airport and large shipping terminal at Boca Chica. A right reef break with long lines; not for beginners.

Pato West of Santo Domingo near the town of Nizao. A long left break near a river mouth good for beginners.

Tankline & La Puntillo Class A breaks, the former a right and the latter a left, both in front of Puerto Plata's fortress along the Malecón. Best time is November to March.

Playa Encuentro This, the epicenter of Dominican surf culture, is just 4km west of Cabarete with five separate breaks.

Windsurfing

Cabarete's bay seems almost custom-made for windsurfing, and it's here that the sport is most popular – although you'll also find a small windsurfing school in Las Terrenas. The best time to come is generally in winter, when the wind is strongest – in general, windsurfing requires stronger winds than kitesurfing does.

The beach at Cabarete has a few dedicated outfits renting windsurfing equipment and offering lessons for beginners. Renting a board and sail will cost about US$35/65/300 per hour/day/week. Lessons

Snorkelling

range from just one hour (US$50) to a complete four-session course (US$200).

In general, windsurfing is much easier to learn than kitesurfing, meaning you can be out on the water enjoying yourself within a few days' time. Lessons and equipment rentals are also significantly cheaper.

Diving & Snorkeling

Compared to other Caribbean islands, the DR is not known as a diving destination. That being said, it has some great places for underwater exploring – the offshore area around Bayahibe on the southeast coast is generally considered the best. The warm Caribbean waters around here have pretty fields of coral and myriad tropical fish that make for fun easy dives. Two national parks east of Santo Domingo – Parque Nacional Submarino La Caleta and Parque Nacional Cotubanamá – can be reached through dive shops in Boca Chica and Bayahibe, respectively.

La Caleta is an underwater preserve covering just 10 sq km but is one of the country's most popular dive destinations.

Kitesurfing (p45)

The main attraction is the *Hickory,* a 39m salvage ship with an interesting past that was intentionally sunk in 1994. Parque Nacional Cotubanamá has a number of interesting dives, too, including another wreck – a massive 89m cargo ship – and a site ominously called Shark Point.

The DR's north coast provides a very different diving experience. Facing the Atlantic, the water is cooler and somewhat transparent, but the underwater terrain is more varied, making for challenging dives and unique profiles.

Sosúa is the dive capital here and excursions can be organized to all points along the coast. Divers exploring the waters near the Península de Samaná can sometimes hear humpback whales singing; Las Terrenas and Las Galeras have a few small dive shops.

Other off-the-beaten-track options are two diveable freshwater caves – Dudu Cave, near Río San Juan, and Padre Nuestro, near Bayahibe. Dudu, with two openings, three different tunnels and a spacious stalactite-filled chamber, is one of the most memorable cave dives in the Caribbean (generally needed is an Advanced Diver certificate or at least 20 logged dives in order to come out here). Located within the Parque Nacional Cotubanamá, Padre Nuestro is a challenging 290m tunnel that should be attempted only by trained cave divers. With the exception of the cave dives, most of the sites also make for excellent snorkeling.

Dive prices vary from place to place, but average US$40 to US$60 for one tank, plus US$5 to US$10 for equipment rental. Most people buy multi-dive packages, which can bring the per-dive price down to around US$25. You must have an Open Water certificate; if you're new to the sport, dive shops offer the Discover Scuba and Open Water certification courses. Snorkeling trips cost around US$25 to US$40 per person.

White-Water Rafting

The Dominican Republic has the only navigable white-water river in the Caribbean, the Río Yaque del Norte. It's mostly a Class II and III river, with a couple of serious rapids, and the rest consists of

Freshly caught fish

Fishing

Like most places in the Caribbean, there is good sport fishing to be had for those so inclined. Blue marlin peaks in the summer months, there's white marlin in springtime, and mahi-mahi, wahoo and sailfish in wintertime.

The best places to go deep-sea fishing are the north-coast region and Punta Cana. Expect to pay around US$70 to US$100 per person (US$60 to US$70 for watchers) for a group half-day excursion. Most captains will also gladly charter their boats for private use; expect to pay upwards of US$700/900 for a half-/full day.

Land Sports
Cascading & Canyoning

Cascading – climbing up through a series of waterfalls, and then jumping and sliding down into the pools of water below – is hugely popular at the 27 waterfalls of Damajagua, on the north coast. For many travelers it's their favorite experience in the DR. You'll be issued a life jacket and safety helmet, and guides will lead you, sometimes pulling you through the force of the water. Some of the jumps down are as much as 10m high. You can visit the waterfalls by yourself – foreigners pay RD$500 per person, and while a guide is mandatory, there's no minimum group size. Alternatively, you can come with a tour group, but all the package 'jeep safari' tours go only to the 7th waterfall – disappointing. Only a very few tour agencies offer the trip to the very top.

Canyoning – often referred to as 'canyoneering' in the US – is cascading's technical, older brother and is even more of an adrenaline rush, involving jumping, rappelling and sliding down a slippery river gorge with a mountain river raging around you. You'll be issued a safety helmet and usually a shorts-length wetsuit. It's becoming more popular in the DR, but there are really only three reliable and experienced companies: Iguana Mama (p166) and Kayak River Adventures (p164) in Cabarete on the north coast and Rancho Baiguate (p193) in Jarabacoa in the mountains. It's wild and highly recommended.

fun little holes and rolls. The river winds through bucolic hilly countryside and makes for a fun half-day tour. Be aware that the water can be cold – you'll be issued a wetsuit along with your life vest and helmet. While you can make this a day trip from the north coast or Santo Domingo, it's a long journey in a bus – you'll enjoy yourself a great deal more if you spend a couple of nights in Jarabacoa. Trips cost around US$50 per person.

Kayaking

The DR holds great potential for both sea and river kayaking. A few scattered shops and hotels rent sea kayaks for a paddle along the beach, and gung-ho river kayakers looking for some crazy rapids (and who don't mind traveling with a kayak in their luggage) should head to Jarabacoa, where Class III, IV and V rapids surge past on the Río Yaque del Norte, which flows nearby. Or get in touch with Kayak River Adventures (p164) in Cabarete to customize a trip.

MATT MUNRO/LONELY PLANET ©

Top: Swimming at the base of the Twenty-Seven Waterfalls (p150)

Bottom: Horseback riding on Playa Rincón, (p133)

Hiking

Pico Duarte

The most famous hike in the DR is the ascent of Pico Duarte (3087m), the tallest peak in the Caribbean. First climbed in 1944 as part of the 100th anniversary celebration of the Dominican Republic's independence from Haiti, it's a tough multiday hike, but involves no technical climbing, and mules carry supplies and equipment up the mountain (best time to go is December to March, with the exception of February when the mountain is full of college students). There are two main routes to the summit and several side trips you can take along the way, including hikes through two beautiful alpine valleys and up the Caribbean's second-highest peak, La Pelona, just 100m lower than Pico Duarte.

While the destination – the peak itself and the views – is stunning, the well-traveled walker may be disappointed by the journey required to get there. You pass quickly through the ferns and moss-bound rainforest of the lower elevations, and once you hit 2200m all you see are burnt-out forests of Caribbean Pine, spaced at regular intervals, with no animals and only cawing crows for company. Still, if it's clear at the top when you get there – and you have time to linger at the summit – then the hard work to get there may be worth it.

Shorter Hikes

The DR is not a world-class hiking destination. Still, there are a number of waterfalls and quite a few challenging trails around Jarabacoa. The Península de Samaná has some beautiful hikes near Las Galeras, with picturesque deserted beaches as your reward at the end. In the southwest, there's some decent half-day and full-day hikes just outside Paraíso, although they are best visited as part of a tour.

Lesser-known trails are slowly being developed for organized hikes in the Cordillera Septentrional south of Sosúa. Contact Tubagua Plantation Eco-Village (p155) for customized itineraries. And rising out of flat plains near San Francisco de Macorís, Reserva Científica Loma Quita Espuela (p202) is surrounded by organic cocoa plantations and swimming holes.

Golf

Known as one of the premier golf destinations in the Caribbean, the DR has more than two dozen courses to choose from. Signature courses from high-profile designers like Tom Fazio, Robert Trent Jones Sr, Pete Dye, Jack Nicklaus, Nick Faldo and Arnold Palmer continue to be built at a steady pace. The majority are affiliated with (or located nearby) the top all-inclusive resorts (the most by far are located along the southeastern coast between La Romana and north of Punta Cana; none are west of an imaginary line that runs south to north from Santo Domingo to Jarabacoa, Santiago and Puerto Plata), but are open to guests and nonguests alike. Almost all take advantage of their Caribbean setting (of course this means many were built on former mangrove areas) and feature fairways and greens with spectacular ocean views. A few of the best in the country:

HANDY WEBSITES FOR OUTDOOR ACTIVITIES

www.drpure.com An overview of outdoor adventure activities; good place to start.

www.activecabarete.com Features listings, information and reviews about sporting activities in and around Cabarete.

www.windalert.com Up-to-the-minute wind reports and forecasts to help plan your wind-powered water activities.

www.godominicanrepublic.com Information on outdoor activities, golfing and beach activities.

www.ambiente.gob.do (in Spanish) The home page of the federal Department of the Environment has information on national parks.

Hispaniolan woodpecker

Teeth of the Dog One of four highly rated Pete Dye–designed courses in Casa de Campo (p98).

La Cana Golf Course Best in the area; design completed by Pete Dye's son Paul Burke (p111).

Punta Espada One of three Jack Nicklaus Signature courses at Cap Cana (p111).

Corales Tom Fazio–designed course opened in Punta Cana area in 2010; part of the Puntacana Resort & Club.

Playa Grande Amanera's course was designed by Robert Trent Jones Sr (p172).

Mountain Biking

The Jarabacoa and Constanza areas are the best and most popular areas for mountain-bike riding. The crisp air and cool climate make for ideal cycling, and dirt roads and single-track trails offer challenging climbs and thrilling descents through thick forests, with a number of waterfalls within easy reach.

Cabarete also has a number of good rides and is home to the DR's best cycling tour operator, Iguana Mama (p166), and one of its more passionate advocates/

guides, Maximo Martinez (p166). It offers mountain-bike tours ranging from half-day downhill rides to 12-day cross-country excursions. It can also customize a trip to fit your interests, available time and experience level.

Tour prices vary widely depending on the length of the ride, but begin at around US$50 per person for half-day trips.

Birdwatching

The DR is a popular destination for gung-ho birders looking for the island's endemic bird species – 32 in all (depending on who you ask and how you count). The very best place to go birding is the southwest, especially the north slope of the Sierra de Bahoruco, where you can spot nearly all the endemics, including the high-altitude threatened La Selle thrush, western chat-tanager, white-winged warbler, rufous-throated solitaire and Hispaniolan trogon. Lago Enriquillo and Laguna Oviedo are known for populations of wading birds.

WHALE WONDERS

Between mid-January and mid-March more than 80% of the reproductively active humpback whales in the North Atlantic – some 10,000 to 12,000 in all – migrate to the waters around the Península de Samaná to mate. The Bahía de Samaná is a favorite haunt of the whales, and one of the best places in the world to observe these massive, curious creatures. Most tours depart from the town of Samaná, and you are all but guaranteed to see numerous whales surfacing for air, lifting their fins or tail, jostling each other in competition, and even breaching – impressive jumps followed by an equally impressive splash. Whale-watching season coincides with Carnival (every weekend in February) and Independence Day (February 27) – major holidays here – so you should make reservations well in advance.

The Jardín Botánico Nacional (p70) in Santo Domingo is, surprisingly, also a good spot to look for birds, especially the palm chat, black-crowned palm tanagers, Hispaniolan woodpeckers, vervain hummingbirds and Antillean mangoes. In the Punta Cana area, head to the Ojos Indígenas Ecological Park (p110); and near Bayahibe, Parque Nacional Cotubanamá (p102), where 112 species have been recorded.

Parque Nacional Los Haitises (p121) is the only place you're likely to see the highly endangered Ridgway's hawk.

Around Tubagua Plantation Eco-Village (p155) in the central highlands you can spot both the narrow-billed and the broad-billed todies.

Tody Tours (p72) offers birdwatching trips in the DR.

Paragliding

Head out to Jarabacoa for the thrill of soaring on a thermal with a bird's-eye view of the spectacular mountains surrounding this valley town, with its unusual sights of pine trees and Swiss-type A-frame houses – right in the middle of the Caribbean. There's a great local group of pilots living here year-round.

Horseback Riding

Aspiring equestrians will find good riding on beaches and in the mountains. You may be somewhat disappointed in the horses, however – Dominicans themselves tend to use mules, and the few horses are principally for tourists and rich Dominicans. Don't expect to ride a thoroughbred; however a handful of well-run, independent operations, especially in the Sosúa and Cabarete region, can be recommended.

A number of stables offer their services through tour agencies and resorts. Expect to pay roughly US$50 to US$70 per person for a half-day ride. You can also ride a mule to the top of Pico Duarte.

The most popular trip is to the waterfalls around Limón on the Península de Samaná.

Regions at a Glance

Santo Domingo

History
Nightlife
Food

Colonial Charm

The heart of the Spanish empire's original seat in the New World is chockablock with museums, sights and courtly looking plazas surrounded by exquisitely restored 16th-century buildings. However, daily life continues apace amid a picturesque backdrop.

Bars & Beats

Whether it's at a modest *colmado* (corner store) or posh nightclubs that wouldn't be out of place in any major world capital, Santo Domingo, the largest city in the Caribbean, is the place to party. Merengue, *bachata* and salsa reverberate on the streets, gritty and posh alike.

Gastronomic Gem

This is truly a cosmopolitan dining scene and the country's culinary capital. There's little reason to settle for the *plato del día* when you can feast alfresco on the balcony of a colonial-era building on locally caught seafood with a haute cuisine twist.

p56

Punta Cana & the Southeast

Beaches
Resorts
Water Sports

Varied Shorelines

Planeloads of tourists make a beeline for the postcard-perfect stretches of white sand around Baváro and Punta Cana. But there are less-developed patches to the north for the more adventurous.

All-Inclusive Leisure

Much of the country's reputation as a sybaritic holiday land is based on this region. Regardless, there's something very intoxicating about having every indulgence, food, drinks, pools and beachfront, at hand.

Liquid Adrenaline

Bayahibe, a fishing village near La Romana, is the center of what's widely regarded as the country's best scuba diving. Snorkelers have offshore reefs to choose from too.

p91

Península de Samaná

Landscapes
Water Sports
Social Scene

Natural Paradise

Rolling mountains with hard-to-get-to waterfalls, a sea of hillocks pushing their way to a long coastline of protected beaches and picturesque coves, plus cliffs and hidden lagoons that were once refuges for pirates.

Water Playtime

Be it surfing, kitesurfing, snorkeling or scuba diving, active travelers will find it all here, as well as a community of experienced pros to show beginners how it's done.

Cafe Culture

A motley crew of mainly Europeans and North Americans have brought a cosmopolitan flavor to the peninsula: Las Terrenas is the center of cafe culture and nightlife, while Las Galeras' sophistication flies under the radar.

p124

North Coast

Beaches
Water Sports
Nightlife

Enticing shores

Rivaling the southeast in terms of the beauty of its shoreline, the long ocean corridor stretching from Monte Cristi to Río San Juan offers seclusion or development, whatever your fancy.

Riding Waves

Generally considered the mecca of water-based sports in the DR, the north coast offers virtually every means of propelling yourself across or through liquid. From kitesurfing to wakeboarding to canyoning, the conditions are close to ideal.

Party Scene

Indulge in *la dolce vita* sipping tropical cocktails on Cabarete's beachfront or a leisurely sundowner on Puerto Plata's Malecón. More rowdy Sosúa or resort discos round out your options.

p145

Central Highlands

Adventures
Scenery
Tranquility

Natural Playground

Blessed with a roaring river and four of the five highest peaks in the Caribbean, the Cordillera Central is an adventure-sport destination where you can get up high while paragliding or scramble on your hands and knees down a canyon.

Mountain Vistas

Pastoral panoramas of forested slopes are more evocative of the European Alps than a Caribbean island. A drive along one of the winding roads passes from cloud-shrouded jungle to sun-dappled plateaus.

Highland Calm

Because it can be relatively challenging to access, tourism is less developed and you're likely to slow down and rise and shine to the rhythms of the sun.

p180

The Southwest & Península de Pedernales

Landscapes
Nature
Escape

Geographic Gem

Millennia-old tectonic movements have given the peninsula its unique geographic features: unspoiled sanctuaries, characterized by the beautiful beach along the Bahía de las Águilas and cactus-covered deserts.

Wildlife Watching

This emerging ecotourism destination is the best place on the island for endemic birdwatching, as well as crocodiles, lizards, turtles and marine life.

Hidden Retreats

Get away from the coastal crowds, to where any stranger is sure to turn heads. Despite this thinly populated region's remoteness, there are still a few luxurious retreats.

p203

On the Road

North Coast
p145

Central Highlands
p180

Península de Samaná
p124

HAITI
p223

Punta Cana & the Southeast
p91

The Southwest & Península de Pedernales
p203

Santo Domingo
p56

Santo Domingo

☎ 809, 829, 849 / POP 2 MILLION

Best Places to Eat

➡ Pat'e Palo (p79)

➡ Adrian Tropical (p80)

➡ La Pesca de Oro (p81)

➡ Samurai (p82)

➡ Mesón D'Bari (p79)

Best Places to Sleep

➡ Island Life Backpacker's Hostel (p72)

➡ Hostal Nicolás de Ovando (p75)

➡ El Beaterío Guest House (p74)

➡ Hotel Villa Colonial (p74)

Why Go?

Santo Domingo, or 'La Capital' as it's typically called, is a collage of cultures and neighborhoods. It's where the sounds of life – domino pieces slapped on tables, backfiring mufflers and horns from chaotic traffic, merengue and *bachata* blasting from corner stores – are most intense. At the heart of the city is the Zona Colonial, where you'll find one of the oldest churches and the oldest surviving European fortress, among other New World firsts. Amid the cobblestone streets it would be easy to forget Santo Domingo is in the Caribbean. But this is an intensely urban city, home not only to colonial-era architecture, but also to hot clubs, vibrant cultural institutions and elegant restaurants. Santo Domingo somehow manages to embody the contradictions central to the Dominican experience: a living museum, a metropolis crossed with a seaside resort, and a business, political and media center with a laid-back, affable spirit.

When to Go

➡ Carnival, at the end of February and beginning of March, is a big deal in the capital. The city hosts an international book fair in April and a blowout merengue festival in July.

➡ Baseball is played almost five nights a week at Estadio Quisqueya from the end of October to the end of January.

➡ Hurricane season, from August through December, means strong rains and developing storms can be a threat, though sunshine usually prevails. On average September sees the most precipitation and February the least.

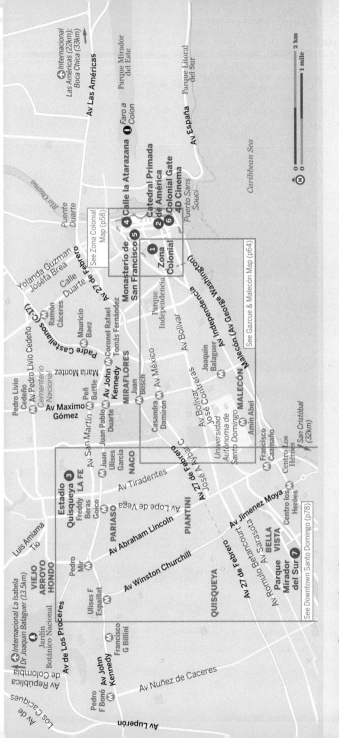

Santo Domingo Highlights

1 Zona Colonial (p61)
Wandering the 500-year-old cobblestone backstreets of the New World's first city.

2 Catedral Primada de América (p68) Entering the first church in the New World and imagining how 16th-century worshippers felt.

3 Estadio Quisqueya (p84) Rooting for the home team at one of the best places to watch a baseball game in the DR.

4 Calle la Atarazana (p77) Spending a relaxing night after dinner along romantic Plaza España.

5 Monasterio de San Francisco (p66) Dancing to merengue music with amid 16th-century ruins.

6 Colonial Gate 4D Cinema (p84) Beholding *The Battle of Santo Domingo* with at a 4D movie theater.

7 Parque Mirador del Sur (p71) Strolling in the trees, Zumba with locals or cocktails at dazzling restaurants.

Zona Colonial

SANTO DOMINGO

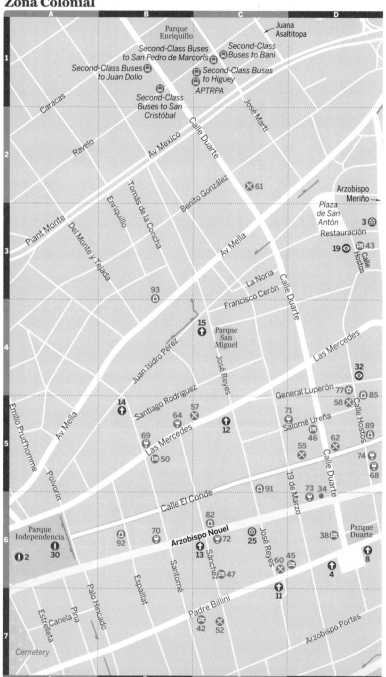

Parque Enriquillo

Juana Asaltitopa

Second-Class Buses to San Pedro de Marcorís

Second-Class Buses to Bani

Second-Class Buses to Juan Dolio

Second-Class Buses to Higuey

APTRPA

Second-Class Buses to San Cristóbal

Caracas

Ravelo

Av Mexico

Calle Duarte

José Marti

Tomás de la Concha

Enriquillo

Benito González

61

Arzobispo Meriño

Plaza de San Antón

Restauración

3

Piant Monte

Del Monte y Tejada

Av Mella

19

43

Calle Hostos

La Noria

Calle Duarte

Francisco Cerón

93

15

Parque San Miguel

Juan Isidro Pérez

José Reyes

Las Mercedes

32

Santiago Rodríguez

General Luperón

77

85

14

64

57

58

71

89

69

12

Salomé Ureña

46

62

74

Las Mercedes

50

55

Calle Duarte

68

Emilio Prudhomme

Av Mella

Polvorín

Calle El Conde

91

19 de Marzo

73 34

82

Parque Independencia

2

30

70

92

Arzobispo Nouel

72

25

José Reyes

38

Parque Duarte

13

Sánchez

60

45

8

Santomé

47

4

11

Espaillat

Estrelleta

Pina

Canela

Palo Hincado

Padre Billini

Arzobispo Portes

42

52

Cemetery

Calle Hostos

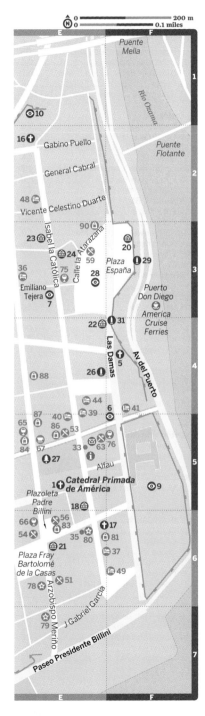

History

In a way, it can be said that the founding of Santo Domingo was an act of desperation. Columbus' first settlement, Villa La Navidad in present-day Haiti, was burned to the ground and all settlers killed within a year. His second settlement, La Isabela, west of present-day Puerto Plata, lasted only five years and was beset from the beginning by disease and disaster. Columbus' brother Bartolomé, left in charge of La Isabela and facing rebellion from its disgruntled residents, pulled up stakes and moved clear around to the other side of the island. He then founded Nueva Isabela on the east bank of the Río Ozama. The third time, evidently, was the charm for Columbus, and this city – though moved to the west bank and renamed Santo Domingo – has remained the capital to this day.

That's not to say the city hasn't had its fair share of troubles. In 1586 the English buccaneer Sir Francis Drake captured the city and collected a ransom for its return to Spanish control. And in 1655 an English fleet commanded by William Penn attempted to take Santo Domingo but retreated after encountering heavy resistance. A century and a half later a brazen ex-slave and Haitian leader by the name of François Dominique Toussaint Louverture marched into Santo Domingo. Toussaint and his troops took control of the city without any resistance at all; the city's inhabitants knew they were no match for the army of former slaves and wisely didn't try to resist. During the occupation many of the city's residents fled to Venezuela or neighboring islands. It was in Santo Domingo on February 27, 1844, that Juan Pablo Duarte – considered the father of the Dominican Republic – declared Dominican independence from Haiti, a day still celebrated today.

Sights

Most sights are conveniently concentrated within walking distance of one another in the Zona Colonial. Surprisingly, for a city with 15km of Caribbean waterfront, Santo Domingo is more inland-oriented, and the Malecón has been developed haphazardly or neglected. One small spot that has been reclaimed for the public is Playa Guibia (Avs George Washington and Maximo Gomez), which has a beach area (packed on weekends), a sandy volleyball court, a kids' playground, gym equipment and free wi-fi access.

Zona Colonial

⊙ Zona Colonial

For those fascinated by the origin of the so-called New World – a dramatic and complicated story of the first encounter between the native people of the Americas and Europeans – the Zona Colonial, listed as a Unesco World Heritage site, is a great place to explore. It is 11 square blocks, a mix of cobblestone and pavement on the west bank of the Río Ozama, where the deep river meets the Caribbean Sea. Calle El Conde, the main commercial artery, is lined with *casas de cambio* (money changers), cafes, restaurants, shoe, clothing and jewelry stores, and vendors hawking cheap souvenirs.

Museums

Museo Alcázar de Colón   MUSEUM
(Museum Citadel of Columbus; Map p58; ☑ 809-682-4750; Plaza España; adult/child RD$100/20; ⊙9am-5pm Tue-Sat, to 4pm Sun) Designed in the Gothic-Mudéjar transitional style, this was the early-16th-century residence of Columbus' son, Diego, and his wife, Doña María de Toledo. The magnificent edifice underwent three historically authentic restorations in 1957, 1971 and 1992, and the building itself, along with the household pieces on display (said to have belonged to the Columbus family), are worth a look.

Recalled to Spain in 1523, Diego and Doña Maria left the home to relatives who occupied the handsome building for the next hundred years. It was subsequently allowed to deteriorate, then was used as a prison and a warehouse, before it was finally abandoned. By 1775 it was a vandalized shell of its former self and served as the unofficial city dump. Less than a hundred years later, only two of its walls remained at right angles.

Tickets can be purchased in the stand-alone building in Plaza España a few steps from the museum's entrance.

Museo Memorial de la Resistencia Dominicana   MUSEUM
(Map p58; Arzobispo Nouel 210; adults/under 12yr RD $150/50; ⊙9:30am-6pm Tue-Sun) For those interested in the details on one of the darkest periods of Dominican history, this austere memorial honors Dominicans who fought against the brutal regime of dictator Rafael Trujillo. 'El Chivo' (the goat) ruled with an iron fist from 1930 until 1961, often touting his own greatness and wiping out some 50,000 political dissenters. The museum features torture-center replicas and 160,000 photographs, films and other objects belonging to resistance fighters. Admission includes an audioguide (English or Spanish).

Museo de las Casas Reales   MUSEUM
(Museum of the Royal Houses; Map p58; ☑ 809-682-4202; Las Damas; adult/under 7yr RD$100/ free; ⊙9am-5pm Tue-Sat, to 4pm Sun) Built in the Renaissance style during the 16th century, this building was the longtime seat of Spanish authority for the Caribbean region, housing the governor's office and the powerful Audiencia Real (Royal Court). It showcases colonial-period objects, including treasures recovered from sunken Spanish galleons. Rooms have been restored according to their original style, with Taíno artifacts and period furnishings displayed.

Several walls are covered with excellent maps of various voyages of European explorers and conquistadors. Also on exhibit is an impressive antique weaponry collection acquired by dictator-president Trujillo from a Mexican general (ironically, during a 1955 world peace event); you'll see samurai swords, medieval armor, ivory-inlaid crossbows and even a pistol/sword combo. Admission includes an audioguide available in a number of languages, including English.

Larimar Museum   MUSEUM
(Map p58; ☑ 809-689-6605; www.larimarmuseum.com; 2nd fl, Isabel la Católica 54; ⊙9am-6pm Mon-Sat) **FREE** Thorough exhibits on larimar – a rare, light-blue mineral found only in the remote southwestern mountains of the Dominican Republic – have signage in Spanish and English. Of course, the museum is meant to inspire you to make a purchase from the strategically located jewelry store on the 1st floor.

Amber World Museum   MUSEUM
(Map p58; ☑ 809-682-3309; www.amberworldmuseum.com; cnr Arzibispo Merino & Restauracion; RD$50; ⊙9am-6pm Mon-Sat, to 1pm Sun) This museum features an impressive collection of amber samples from around the world and excellent exhibits explaining (in Spanish and English) amber's prehistoric origins, its use throughout the ages, Dominican mining processes, and its present-day value to the science and art worlds. The 1st-floor shop sells jewelry made from amber, larimar and more ordinary stones.

MATT MUNRO/LONELY PLANET ©

MATT MUNRO/LONELY PLANET ©

1. Baseball
One of the best places to experience Dominican baseball is at Estadio Quisqueya (p84), the home field of two of the DR's six professional teams, Licey and Escogido.

2. Parque Colón (p66)
This historic park contains a large statue of Admiral Columbus, and is a fantastic spot for people-watching.

3. Zona Colonial (p61)
Listed as a Unesco World Heritage site, the Zona Colonial is 11 square blocks of cobblestone and pavement on the west bank of the Río Ozama.

4. Faro a Colón (p70)
This massive monument to Christopher Columbus contains a long series of exhibition halls displaying documents relating to his voyages and artefacts from indigenous communities.

3

HOLGER METTE/GETTY IMAGES ©

Gazcue & Malecón

500 m
0.25 miles

Caribbean Sea

Las Mercedes

Santomé

Espaillat

Parque Independencia

Palo Hincado

Piña

Canela

Estrelleta

16 De Agosto

Cemetery

Padre Billini

El Número

Av 30 de Marzo

Ozema Pellerano

Enrique Henríquez

Fco J Peynado

Fabio Fiallo

Av Independencia

Pte V Burgos

Osvaldo Baez

Pichardo

GAZCUE

Dr Delgado

Av Pasteur

Calle Danae

Calle Santiago

Calle

Calle Cervantes

Av Bolívar

Rosa Duarte

Calle José J Peréz

Calle Hermanos Deligne

Calle Rodríguez Objío

Socorro Sánchez

Casimiro de Moyá

Av Independencia

Malecón (Av George Washington)

Asociación Dominicana de Rehabilitación (470m); Fundación Dominicana de Ciegos (1.2km)

Leopoldo Navarro

Benito Moncíon

Expreso Bávaro Punta Cana

Joaquín Balaguer

Mahatma Gandhi

Av México

César Nicolas Penson

Plaza de la Cultura

Av Máxmo Gómez

Universidad Autónoma de Santo Domingo

José Contreras

Av Bolívar

MALECÓN

Calle Arístedes Fíalo Cabral

Benigno F Rojas

Dr Piñeyro

Casandra Damirón

LA ESPERILLA

Av Pedro Henríquez Ureña

Av Del Pedro México

Dr Nuñez de Caceres

Amín Abel

Av Alma Mater

AV 27 de Febrero

Luis Al Berti

Gazcue & Malecón

Museo del Ron y la Caña   MUSEUM

(Map p58; Isabel la Católica 261; ⊙9am-5pm Mon-Sat) FREE Housed in a restored 16th-century building, exhibits here celebrate rum and sugarcane, two of the country's most important exports. Displays and photographs explain the history of their production and importance to the DR's economy. At the bar you can sample the wares, which are distilled in-house and include passionfruit and cinnamon flavors, or buy some to go.

Museo del Duarte   MUSEUM

(Map p58; ☑809-687-1436; Isabel la Católica 308; ⊙8am-6pm Mon-Fri, 9am-3pm Sat & Sun) FREE The 1813 birthplace of Juan Pablo Duarte was converted into a modest museum and renovated in late 2016. Three rooms display documents, artifacts and photos from his life and from La Trinitaria, the underground independence organization he founded. Several new exhibits and an additional floor opened in January 2017.

Historical Sites

Fortaleza Ozama   HISTORIC SITE

(Map p58; ☑809-686-0222; Las Damas; RD$70; ⊙9am-5pm Tue-Sun) This is the New World's oldest colonial military edifice. The site, at the meeting of the Río Ozama and Caribbean, was selected by Fray Nicolás de Ovando and construction began in 1502. Over the centuries the fort served as a military garrison and prison, flying the flags of Spain, England, France, Haiti, Gran Columbia, the US and the DR. Public tours began in the 1970s. Multilingual guides at the entrance charge around US$3.50 per person for a 20-minute tour.

As soon as you walk into the site, you'll see the oldest of the buildings here: the impressive **Torre del Homenaje** (Tower of Homage). Its 2m-thick walls contain dozens of riflemen's embrasures and its rooftop lookout offers 360-degree views of the city. To its right, solid and windowless, stands **El Polvorín** (the Powder House), which was added in the mid-1700s; look for the statue of St Barbara (the patron saint of the artillery) over the door.

Running along the fort's riverside wall are two rows of cannons: the first dates from 1570, the second was added in the mid-1600s. Both served as the first line of defense for the city's port. The living quarters, now almost completely destroyed, were added along the city-side wall in the late 1700s. On the esplanade is a bronze statue of Gonzalo Fernández de Oviedo, perhaps the best-known military chronicler of the New World.

Plaza España   PLAZA

(Map p58) The large, open area in front of the Alcázar de Colón has been revamped many times, most recently during the 1990s in honor of the 500th anniversary of Christopher Columbus' New World 'discovery.' Running along its northwest side is **Calle la Atarazana**, fronted by a half dozen restaurants in buildings that served as warehouses through the 16th and 17th centuries.

This is a great place for a meal or drink at an outdoor table around sunset.

Parque Colón
PARK

(Map p58; cnr El Conde & Isabel la Católica) Beside the Catedral Primada de América, this historic park contains several trees and a large statue of Admiral Columbus himself. It's the meeting place for residents and is alive with tourists, townsfolk, hawkers, guides, shoeshine boys, tourist police and thousands of pigeons. The corner of Calle El Conde and Arzobispo Meriño is the premier people-watching corner in the Zona Colonial.

Las Damas
HISTORIC SITE

(Ladies' Street; Calle de las Damas) Heading north and south in front of Fortaleza Ozama is the first paved street in the Americas. Laid in 1502, the street acquired its name from the wife of Diego Columbus and her lady friends, who made a habit of strolling the road every afternoon, weather permitting.

Panteón Nacional
MONUMENT

(National Pantheon; Map p58; Las Damas; ⊙ 8am-7pm Tue-Sun, from 11am Mon) Built in 1747 as a Jesuit church, this was also a tobacco warehouse and a theater before dictator Trujillo restored it in 1958 for its current use as a mausoleum. Today many of the country's most illustrious persons are honored here, their remains sealed behind two marble walls. The building, including its neoclassical facade, was constructed with large limestone blocks.

As befits such a place, an armed soldier is ever present at the mausoleum's entrance – along with a powerful fan since it does get hot. Shorts and tank tops are discouraged.

Reloj del Sol
MONUMENT

(Map p58; Las Damas) Across from the Museo de las Casas Reales, this sundial was built by Governor Francisco Rubio y Peñaranda in 1753 and positioned so that officials in the Royal Houses could see the time with only a glance from their eastern windows. It was among the first time-telling devices constructed in North America, and remains accurate today.

Monasterio de San Francisco
HISTORIC SITE

(Map p58; Hostos) The first monastery in the New World belonged to the first order of Franciscan friars who arrived to evangelize the island. Dating from 1508, the monastery originally consisted of three connecting chapels. It was set ablaze by Drake in 1586, rebuilt, devastated by an earthquake in 1673, rebuilt, ruined by another earthquake in 1751 and rebuilt again. Later it served as a mental asylum until a hurricane shut it down; today the dramatic ruins host wild dance nights every Sunday (p72).

Hostal Nicolás de Ovando
NOTABLE BUILDING

(Map p58; Las Damas) A handsome building with a Gothic facade built in 1509, this was originally the residence of Governor Nicolás de Ovando, who is famous for ordering Santo Domingo rebuilt on the west bank of the Río Ozama following a hurricane that leveled most of the colony. Today it houses the posh Hostal Nicolás de Ovando (p75). To appreciate the building's massive size and solidity, take the steps leading down from the alleyway on El Conde towards Puerto Don Diego.

Ruinas del Hospital San Nicolás de Barí
HISTORIC SITE

(Map p58; Hostos) Standing next to the bright, white Iglesia de la Altagracia are the ruins of the New World's first hospital. They remain as a monument to Governor Nicolás de Ovando, who ordered the hospital built in 1503. So sturdy was the edifice that it survived Drake's invasion and centuries of earthquakes and hurricanes. It remained virtually intact until it was devastated by a hurricane in 1911, and public-works officials ordered much of it knocked down so that it wouldn't pose a threat to pedestrians.

Today visitors can still see several of its high walls and Moorish arches. Note that the hospital's floor plan follows the form of a Latin cross.

Puerta del Conde
MONUMENT

(Gate of the Count; Map p58; El Conde) This gate is named for the Count of Peñalba, Bernardo de Meneses y Bracamonte, who led the successful defense of Santo Domingo against 13,000 invading British troops in 1655. It's the supreme symbol of Dominican patriotism because beside it, in February 1844, brave Dominicans executed a bloodless coup against occupying Haitian forces; their actions created an independent Dominican Republic.

It also was atop this gate that the very first Dominican flag was raised. Just west of the gate inside Parque Independencia look for the Altar de la Patria (Map p58; Parque Independencia) FREE, a mausoleum that holds the remains of three national heroes: Juan Pablo Duarte, Francisco del Rosario Sánchez and Ramón Matías Mella. The park itself has a few benches but little shade.

SANTO DOMINGO IN TWO DAYS

Fuel up with a Dominican breakfast at **El Conde Restaurant** (p83) by Parque Colón, and plan your attack. Santo Domingo's Zona Colonial brims with New World firsts, and you'll need to hit them all, most importantly **Catedral Primada de América** (p68), **Fortaleza Ozama** (p65) and **Museo Alcázar de Colón** (p61), which can be linked as a walking tour (p73). Consider ducking into the **Colonial Gate 4D Cinema** (p84), where the award-winning short film *The Battle of Santo Domingo* transports all the senses back to 1586. Grab dinner at **Pat'e Palo** (p79) on the romantic **Plaza España** (p65) and a libation at **La Alpargatería** (p82) or **Mercado Colón** (p83).

For day two, hire a guide to whisk you over the Río Ozama to **Los Tres Ojos** (p70) for a beat-the-crowds-early cave tour. After admiring the underground lagoons and stalactite-filled passages, shoot over to **Faro a Colón** (p70), the massive cement monument that may or may not hold Columbus' remains but definitely contains a bunch of weird artifacts and exhibition halls. Back in town, hit up some shops for **larimar** (p61) and mamajuana souvenirs, then grab some octopus *mofongo* (a mashed plantain dish) at **D'Luis Parrillada** (p80) on the Malécon, or a touristy and traditional meal and dance performance at **El Conuco** (p81) in Gazcue.

SANTO DOMINGO SIGHTS

Fuerte de Santa Bárbara
HISTORIC SITE

(Map p58; cnr Juan Parra & Av Mella) Built during the 1570s, this fort served as one of the city's main points of defense. It proved no match for Drake, however, who, along with his fleet of 23 pirate-packed ships, captured the fort in 1586. Today the fort lies in ruins at the end of a lonely street. There isn't much to see here any more, mostly rooftops and occasionally a ship in the distance.

Puerta de San Diego
MONUMENT

(Map p58; Av del Puerto) For a time, this imposing gate, built in 1571 downhill from the Alcázar de Colón, was the main entrance into the city. Beside it you can still see some of the original wall, which was erected to protect the city from assaults launched from the river's edge.

Puerta de la Misericordia
MONUMENT

(Gate of Mercy; Map p64; Arzobispo Portes) This gate was erected during the 16th century and for many decades served as the main western entrance to the city. It obtained its name after a major earthquake in 1842, when a large tent was erected beside it to provide temporary shelter for the homeless.

Casa de Francia
NOTABLE BUILDING

(French House; Map p58; Las Damas 42) This was originally the residence of Hernán Cortés, conqueror of the Aztecs in present-day central Mexico. It was in this building that Cortés is believed to have organized his triumphant – and brutal – expedition. While visitors are not permitted past the lobby, this marvel of masonry is worth a walk by, if only to check out its facade.

Although the Casa de Francia served as a residence for nearly three centuries, it has had several incarnations since the beginning of the 19th century: a set of government offices, the Banco Nacional de Santo Domingo, a civil courthouse and the headquarters of the Dominican IRS. Today it houses the French embassy. It was built in the early 16th century and shares many elements with the Museo de las Casas Reales. Experts theorize that these buildings were designed by the same master; both have a flat facade and a double bay window in the upper and lower stories, repeating patterns of doors and windows on both floors, and top-notch stone rubblework masonry around the windows, doors and corner shorings.

Casa del Cordón
NOTABLE BUILDING

(House of the Cord; Map p58; cnr Isabel la Católica & Emiliano Tejera; ⊙8:15am-4pm) Said to be not only one of the first European residences in the Americas, but also one of the first residences in the Western hemisphere with two floors, this was briefly occupied by Diego Columbus and his wife before they moved into their stately home down the street. Today the structure is home to Banco Popular, so visiting the house beyond the main lobby is not permitted.

Named after its impressive stone facade, which is adorned with the chiseled sash-and-cord symbol of the Franciscan order, it is also believed to be the site where Santo

Domingo's women lined up to hand over their jewels to Drake during the month he and his men held the city hostage.

Churches

★**Catedral Primada de América** CHURCH
(Nuestra Senora de la Anunciacion; Map p58; ☑ 809-682-3848; Parque Colón; adult/child RD$60/free; ◷ 9am-4:30pm Mon-Sat) The first stone of this cathedral, the oldest standing in the Western hemisphere, was set in 1514 by Diego Columbus, son of the great explorer (the ashes of father and son supposedly once resided in the chapel's crypt). Construction, however, didn't begin until the arrival of the first bishop, Alejandro Geraldini, in 1521. From then until 1540, numerous architects worked on the church and adjoining buildings, which is why the vault is Gothic, the arches Romanesque and the ornamentation baroque.

It's anyone's guess what the planned bell tower would have looked like: a shortage of funds curtailed construction, and the steeple, which undoubtedly would have offered a commanding view of the city, was never built.

The cathedral's current interior is a far cry from the original – thanks to Drake and his crew of pirates, who used the basilica as their headquarters during their 1586 assault on the city. They stole everything of value that they could carry away and extensively vandalized the church before departing.

Among the cathedral's more impressive features are its awesome vaulted ceiling and its 14 interior chapels. Bare shoulders and legs are prohibited, but shawls are provided for those who need to cover up.

Although Santo Domingo residents like to say their cathedral was the first in the Western hemisphere, in fact one was built in Mexico City between 1524 and 1532; it stood for four decades, until it was knocked down in 1573 and replaced by the imposing Catedral Metropolitano.

Tickets, purchased at the entrance in the southeastern corner of the site, include an audioguide available in a variety of languages (RD$40 without audioguide). Daily mass is at 5pm Monday to Saturday and noon and 5pm Sundays.

**Capilla de Nuestra Señora
de los Remedios** CHURCH
(Chapel of Our Lady of Remedies; Map p58; cnr Las Damas & Las Mercedes; ◷ varies) The Gothic-style chapel was built during the 16th

century by alderman Francisco de Avila and was intended to be a private chapel and family mausoleum. Early residents of the city are said to have attended Mass here under its barrel-vaulted ceiling. It was restored in 1884.

**Convento de la Orden
de los Predicadores** CHURCH
(Convent of the Order of Preachers; Map p58; cnr Duarte & Padre Billini; ◷ varies) Built in 1510 by Charles V, this is the first convent of the Dominican order founded in the Americas. It also is where Father Bartolomé de las Casas – the famous chronicler of Spanish atrocities committed against indigenous peoples – did most of his writing. The vault of the chapel, remarkable for its stone zodiac wheel carved with mythological and astrological representations, is worth a look. On the walls are various paintings of religious figures, including Pope Saint Pius V.

Iglesia de San Lázaro CHURCH
(Map p58; cnr Santomé & Juan Isidro Pérez; ◷ varies) Completed in 1650, but altered several times since, this church was erected beside a hospital that treated people with infectious diseases. The church was constructed to give the patients hope – a commodity that no doubt was in short supply for patients with tuberculosis, leprosy and other common diseases of colonial times.

Iglesia de la Regina Angelorum CHURCH
(Map p58; cnr Padre Billini & José Reyes; ◷ varies) Paid for by a woman who donated her entire fortune to construct this monument for the cloistered Dominican Sisters, this church was built toward the end of the 16th century. In addition to its imposing facade, the church is known for its elaborate, 18th-century baroque altar, which is crowned with the king's coat of arms.

Iglesia de Santa Bárbara CHURCH
(Map p58; cnr Gabino Puello & Isabel la Católica; ◷ varies) This baroque church was built in 1574 to honor the patron saint of the military. After being done over by Drake, however, the church was rebuilt with three arches – two of these are windowless and the third frames a remarkably sturdy door.

Iglesia de Santa Clara CHURCH
(Map p58; cnr Padre Billini & Isabel la Católica; ◷ morning Sun) Home to the first nunnery

in the New World built in 1552. Years after being sacked by Drake and his men (who apparently hated all things Catholic), it was rebuilt with funds from the Spanish Crown. This simple, discreet church has a severe Renaissance-style portal with a gable containing a bust of St Claire.

Iglesia de San Miguel
CHURCH

(Church of Michael the Archangel; Map p58; cnr José Reyes & Juan Isidro Pérez; ⊘varies) In 1784 Spain ordered that the Iglesia de San Miguel be turned into a hospital for slaves. The decree, however, was never followed. Note the appealing juxtaposition of its rectangular stone doorway with the curved shape of the structure's exterior.

Iglesia de Nuestra Señora del Carmen
CHURCH

(Map p58; cnr Sánchez & Arzobispo Nouel; ⊘varies) Since 1596 this church has served as a hospital, a jail and an inn, but is now famous for its carved-mahogany figure of Jesus, which is worshipped every Holy Wednesday during Easter Week. The small church, originally made of stone, was set aflame by Drake in 1586 and was rebuilt using bricks. During colonial times its small square was used to stage comedies.

Iglesia de Nuestra Señora de las Mercedes
CHURCH

(Church of Our Lady of Mercy; Map p58; cnr Las Mercedes & José Reyes; ⊘varies) Constructed during the first half of the 16th century, the church was sacked by Drake and his men and reconstructed on numerous occasions following earthquakes and hurricanes. The church is remarkable for its pulpit, which is sustained by a support in the shape of a serpent demon. The intricate baroque altarpiece is carved from tropical hardwood. Of the group of buildings that pay homage to the Virgin Mary, only the cloister adjacent to the church is in original condition.

Capilla de la Tercera Orden Dominica
CHURCH

(Chapel of the Third Dominican Order; Map p58; cnr Duarte & Padre Billini) Built in 1729 and the only colonial structure in Santo Domingo that remains fully intact. These days the building is used by the office of the archbishop of Santo Domingo. It's not open to the general public, but the graceful baroque facade is worth a look.

◉ Gazcue

Palacio Nacional
NOTABLE BUILDING

(Map p64; ☑809-695-8000; Uruguay, btwn Av Pedro Henríquez Ureña & Moisés Garcia) The Dominican seat of government which occupies most of a city block was designed by Italian architect Guido D'Alessandro and inaugurated in 1947. Built of Samaná roseate marble in a neoclassical design, the palace is outfitted in grand style with mahogany furniture, paintings from prominent Dominican artists, magnificent mirrors inlaid with gold, and a proportionate amount of imported crystal.

Primarily used as an executive and administrative office building, it has never been used as the residence of a Dominican president, who is expected to live in a private home. Of special note is the **Room of the Caryatids,** in which 44 sculpted draped women rise like columns in a hall lined with French mirrors and Baccarat chandeliers.

Not regularly open to the public, nevertheless you may be able to wrangle a tour; free and by appointment only on Monday through Friday. No flip-flops, shorts or T-shirts.

Plaza de la Cultura
PLAZA

(Map p64; Av Maxímo Gómez) This large, centrally located park, mostly a sun-baked, fairly unkempt plaza, has three museums (two of which are worth visiting), the national theater (p84) and the national library. The land was once owned by the dictator Trujillo, and was 'donated' to the public after his assassination in 1961.

Museo de Arte Moderno
MUSEUM

(Map p64; Plaza de la Cultura; adult/child RD$50/20; ⊘9am-5pm Tue-Sun) The museum's permanent collection includes paintings and a few sculptures by the DR's best-known modern artists, including Luís Desangles, Adriana Billini, Celeste Woss y Gil, José Vela Zanetti, Dario Suro and Martín Santos. temporary exhibits tend to be fresher and more inventive – more installation and multimedia pieces. Note that the entrance is on the 2nd floor – don't miss the artwork on the bottom level.

Museo del Hombre Dominicano
MUSEUM

(Museum of the Dominican Man; Map p64; ☑809-687-3622; Plaza de la Cultura; RD$100; ⊘10am-5pm Tue-Sat, to 4pm Sun) Highlights here include an impressive collection of Taíno artifacts, including stone axes and intriguing urns and carvings and an interesting section on Carnival. Other exhibits focus on slavery and the colonial period, African influences in the DR (including a small section on Vodou) and contemporary rural Dominican life. Old-fashioned displays include captions in Spanish, but English-speaking guides are available.

Small tips are customary.

Museo Nacional de Historia Natural MUSEUM
(Map p64; ☎809-686-0106; www.mnhn.gov.do; Plaza de la Cultura; adult/child RD$50/25; ☺9am-5pm Tue-Sun) This museum explores the natural environs of the Dominican Republic, with the massive jaw of a sperm whale welcoming visitors at the door. Attractions include rock collections, butterfly exhibits, and a stuffed, endemic bird display. Children will be thrilled, and everybody will appreciate the planetarium, where a 35mm film on the planets is shown. A guide is included with the entrance fee.

Palacio de Bellas Artes NOTABLE BUILDING
(Palace of Fine Arts; Map p64; ☎809-687-0504; Av Máximo Gómez) This huge neoclassical building was used infrequently in the past for exhibitions and performances. Check the weekend edition of local papers for events.

◉ Outlying Neighborhoods

Faro a Colón MONUMENT
(Columbus Lighthouse; ☎ext 251 809-592-1492; Parque Mirador del Este; RD$100; ☺9am-5pm Tue-Sun) Resembling a cross between a Soviet-era apartment block and a Las Vegas–style ancient Mayan ruin, this massive monument is worth visiting for its controversial history. Located on the east side of the Río Ozama, the Faro's cement flanks stand 10 stories high, forming the shape of a cross. At the intersection of the cross' arms is a tomb, guarded by white-uniformed soldiers and purportedly containing Columbus' remains. Spain and Italy dispute that, however, both saying *they* have the Admiral's bones.

Inside the monument a long series of exhibition halls display documents (mostly reproductions) related to Columbus' voyages and the exploration and conquest of the

Americas. The most interesting (though deeply ironic) displays are those sent by numerous Latin American countries containing photos and artifacts from their respective indigenous communities.

High-power lights on the roof can project a blinding white cross in the sky, but are only turned on once a year because doing so can cause blackouts in surrounding neighborhoods.

Los Tres Ojos CAVE
(Three Eyes; Parque Mirador del Este; RD$100; ☺8am-5pm) Consisting of three humid caverns with dark blue lagoons connected by stalactite-filled passages, this site is lovely if you show up early to beat the crowds. Upon entrance, a long stairway takes visitors down a narrow tunnel in the rock, and a cement path at the bottom leads through the caves. At the third *ojo*, a small boat can be hired for RD$20 to visit a fourth *ojo*, which is actually a gorgeous lake beneath open sky, filled with fish.

On certain days, a man whom locals refer to as 'cave tarzan' accepts tips for climbing the cave wall and plunging 20ft into the water. Visitors, however, are not allowed to swim. On the way out, vendors aggressively hawk their services and wares – if you're not interested, say 'no gracias' and run.

Jardín Botánico Nacional GARDENS
(National Botanic Garden; ☎809-385-2611; Av República de Colombia; RD$200; ☺9am-5pm; ⊞) The lush grounds span 2 sq km and include vast areas devoted to aquatic plants, orchids, bromeliads, ferns, palm trees, a Japanese garden and much more. The grounds are spotless and the plants well tended, and it's easy to forget you're in the middle of a city with a metropolitan population of over 2 million people. The exhibits in the on-site Ecological Museum explain the country's ecosystems, including mangroves and cloud forests, plus a display on Parque Nacional Los Haitises.

An open-air trolley (operating every 30 minutes until 4:30pm) takes passengers on a pleasant half-hour turn about the park and is especially enjoyable for children. The garden hosts a variety of events, including an orchid exhibition and competition in March and a bonsai exhibition in April. A taxi from the Zona Colonial costs around RD$300.

Museo Bellapart MUSEUM
(Map p78; ☑ 809-541-7721; www.museobellapart. com; cnr Av JF Kennedy & Dr Peguero; ⊙ 9am-6pm Mon-Fri, to noon Sat) **FREE** Incongruously located on the 5th floor of the Honda building, which looks like a parking garage, is this significant private collection of Dominican painting and sculpture from the late 19th century to the 1960s. The museum contains around 2000 works, and was founded in 1999 by Catalan businessman Juan Jose Bellapart. Art aficionados will dig it.

Parque Mirador del Sur PARK
(Southern Lookout Park; Map p78; Av Mirador del Sur) A long tree-filled corridor atop an enormous limestone ridge, this park is riddled with caves, some as big as airplane hangars. One of the caves has been converted into a restaurant, and the park's seemingly endless paths are a popular jogging route for 30-something professionals, many of whom live in the middle- and upper-class neighborhoods north of the park.

Zumba has become quite popular at the eastern, sports-oriented end of the park, and on clear days hundreds of practitioners gather after work for the free dance classes.

Courses

Hispaniola Academy LANGUAGE
(Map p58; ☑ 809-689-8350; www.hispaniola.org; Arzobispo Nouel 103) Offering eight levels of Spanish-language instruction, this Zona Colonial school offers week-long courses consisting of 20 lessons per week (four 50-minute classes per day). Prices begin at US$150, and accommodations, from homestays to hotels, can be arranged. Medical Spanish, Haitian Creole, cooking and dance classes are also offered.

Instituto Intercultural del Caribe LANGUAGE
(Map p64; ☑ 809-571-3185; www.edase.com; Aristides Fiallo Cabral 456, Zona Universitaria) More than a dozen price combinations are offered here, depending on the length and intensity of instruction and whether or not accommodations are included. The school also offers private dance lessons (four hours per week or one hour a day) and maintains a language school in Sosúa.

EIFFEL TOWER OR WHITE ELEPHANT?

Though former president Joaquin Balaguer gets the lion's share of credit, the idea of commemorating Columbus' landing with a lighthouse wasn't Balaguer's: the **Faro a Colón** (p70) was suggested as early as the middle of the 18th century and later revived at the Fifth International American conference in Santiago, Chile, in 1923. The site of the memorial was always Santo Domingo. An international design competition was launched in 1929 and after sorting through hundreds of submissions from dozens of countries, the reward of US$10,000 eventually went to JL Gleave, a young British architect. Trujillo finally broke ground for the project in 1948, though one that incorporated his own design plans, but financial pledges from other Latin American governments never materialized and the project was scrapped.

Balaguer took up the issue again in 1986, appointing Nicolas Lopez Rodriguez, archbishop of Santo Domingo and a friend, as head of a commission for the celebration of the centenary of the 'discovery and evangelization of America' (he had also recently provided a blessing for the inaugural test run of the Santo Domingo metro). More than 50,000 shantytown dwellers were moved from their homes and tens of millions of dollars were spent on the project (some estimate the final cost to be around US$100 million) so that the beacon could project light visible 320km to the east in Puerto Rico – this in a city and country that at the time was often without power because of a poorly maintained electrical grid and high gas prices. The joke, not without some basis in fact, was that when the lighthouse was switched on the rest of the country went black.

Balaguer pulled the switch for the first time on October 12, 1992, with Pope John Paul II and King Juan Carlos and Queen Sofia of Spain in attendance – contemporary representatives of the dual powers that initiated the historic journey over 500 years ago. When responding to critics, supporters of the project – government officials at the time and some Dominicans – compared the lighthouse to the Eiffel Tower, explaining that both are in essence function-free white elephants.

⌒ Tours

Walking tours of the Zona Colonial are offered by a number of official guides – look for men dressed in khakis and light-blue dress shirts. Motorized scooters, sort of a cross between Segways and skateboards, are available for rent through **Trikke** (Map p58; ☑ 809-221-8097; www.trikke.do; Padre Billini 54; 1hr US$35; ☺ 9am-6pm Mon-Sat, from 10am Sun); audioguides included. A more leisurely option is a **horse-drawn carriage tour** (Map p58; cnr Las Damas and El Conde; with/without guide US$50/30). Or for a cross between the two, you can hop aboard the **Chu Chu Colonial** (Map p58; ☑ 809-686-2303; www.chuchucolonial.com; cnr El Conde & Isabel La Católica; adult/child US$12/7; ☺ 9am-5pm), a bunch of little 'train cars' hooked together that leaves every hour.

If you want to hook up with a bus tour that may include outlying sights in addition to the Zona Colonial, try one of the local agencies that provide city tours to guests of all-inclusive resorts. A few popular ones include **Ecodotours** (☑ 809-815-1074; www.ecodotours.com; half/full day tours per person approx US$75/100) and **Turinter** (Map p64; ☑ 809-686-4020; www.turinter.com; Leopaldo Navarro 2, Gazcue; ☺ 9am-6pm Mon-Fri, to 12:30pm Fri). This isn't a bad option if you're short on time.

If you're looking for birding tours, **Tody Tours** (☑ 809-686-0882; www.todytours.com; José Gabriel Garcia 105; per day US$250) is a Former Peace Corps volunteer who specializes in tropical birding tours all over the country.

⚜ Festivals & Events

Carnival   CARNIVAL

Carnaval (in Spanish) is celebrated throughout the country every Sunday in February, culminating in a blowout in Santo Domingo during the last weekend of February or first weekend of March. Av George Washington (the Malecón) becomes an enormous party scene day and night. Central to the celebration are the competitions of floats, and costumes and masks representing traditional Carnival characters.

Monastery Sundays   MUSIC

(Hostos; ☺ 5-10pm Sun) **FREE** Every Sunday night, the 16th-century ruins of the Monasterio de San Francisco (p66) come to life for a raging dance party. Beloved band Grupo Bonye plays a mix of salsa, *bachata*, merengue and Caribbean rhythms, and hundreds of locals and tourists gather to drink and

dance. The City Council has declared the event part of Santo Domingo's 'artistic patrimony.'

DR Environmental Film Festival   FILM

(www.dreff.org/dreff2016; ☺ Sep) Since 2011, this film festival has been held each September in Santo Domingo to raise awareness about environmental issues. The festival screens high-quality films on the environment and climate change, and also hosts panel discussions with environmental experts and filmmakers.

Merengue Festival   MUSIC

(☺ late Jul-early Aug) The largest in the country, this two-week celebration of merengue, *bachata*, salsa, Caribbean rhythms, reggaeton and reggae is held yearly. Most of the activity is on the Malecón, but there are related events across the city.

Chinatown street market   FERIA

(Av Duarte btwn Mella & Benito Gonzalez; ☺ 6am-1pm Sun) Every Sunday, shoppers descend on Avenida Duarte for a thriving Chinatown street market. Enormous fruits and vegetables, live chickens, dim sum and various sea creatures are all on offer, and haggling is compulsory. A note for those sensitive to animal cruelty: the scene can feel a bit brutal.

🛏 Sleeping

Zona Colonial

The Zona Colonial is the most distinctive part of the city and therefore where most travelers stcutuay. Sights and restaurants are within walking distance and there's an excellent choice of midrange and top-end hotels to choose from, including several European-owned boutique-style places in restored colonial-era buildings. A few new options for budget travelers have opened recently.

★**Island Life Backpacker's Hostel**   HOSTEL $

(Map p58; ☑ 809-333-9374; http://islandlifebackpackershostel.com; Isabel La Católica 356; dm incl breakfast from RD$695, d from RD$1620, tr from RD$1760; ❄ @ ☺ 🏊) The expat owner of this Zona Colonial oasis traveled the world for years observing what backpackers like. Then he found a derelict colonial abode from the 1600s and transformed it into the best hostel in Santo Domingo. From the comfy dorm beds and courtyard hammocks to the super chill bar and dipping pool, this is a true traveler's paradise.

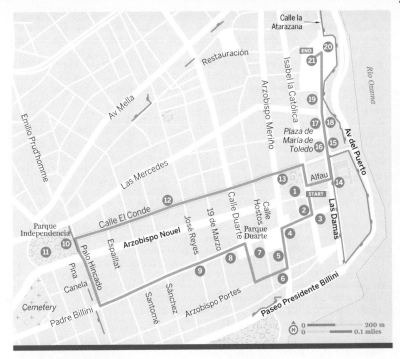

🏃 City Walk
Zona Colonial

START CATEDRAL PRIMADA DE AMÉRICA
END PLAZA ESPAÑA
LENGTH 2.4KM; FOUR HOURS

Start at ❶ **Catedral Primada de América** (p68), the New World's oldest working church. Turn south on Isabel la Católica: you'll see the ❷ **Larimar Museum** (p61) and the simple ❸ **Iglesia de Santa Clara** (p68). Turn west on Padre Billini and walk to the ❹ **Museo de la Familia Dominicana** (adult/under 12yr RD$100/free; ⊙ 9am-5pm Tue-Sun) with its famous Gothic window. Turn south onto Arzobispo Meriño and you'll pass ❺ **Casa de Teatro** (p84); ask about upcoming performances. Continue south to the ❻ **Centro Cultural Español** (p84) with a full calendar of events. Head west then turn right onto Calle Duarte, which opens onto a plaza with two churches: the spectacular ❼ **Convento de la Orden de los Predicadores** (p68) and the baroque ❽ **Capilla de la Tercera Orden Dominica** (p69).

Head west along Padre Billini to the ornate façade of the ❾ **Iglesia de la Regina Angelorum** (p68). Continue west before taking Palo Hincado north to the ❿ **Puerta del Conde** (p66), the supreme symbol of Dominican patriotism. Inside the gate is Parque Independencia and the ⓫ **Altar de la Patria** (p66), a mausoleum of three national heroes. Then take ⓬ **Calle El Conde**, the Zona Colonial's busy commercial walkway, to leafy ⓭ **Parque Colón** (p66).

From the park take Alfau, a small pedestrian street, to the entrance of ⓮ **Fortaleza Ozama** (p65), the New World's oldest military structure. Take Las Damas north, checking out the lovely facades of the ⓯ **Hostal Nicolás de Ovando** (p66) and the ⓰ **Casa de Francia** (p67). Further up Las Damas, you'll pass the ⓱ **Panteón Nacional** (p66) and the ⓲ **Capilla de Nuestra Señora de los Remedios** (p68). Next you'll come upon the interesting ⓳ **Museo de las Casas Reales** (p61) before reaching ⓴ **Museo Alcázar de Colón** (p61) in the ㉑ **Plaza España** (p65), a large plaza overlooking the Río Ozama.

The two-story building, which is also a Unesco World Heritage site, houses several dorms and private rooms, giving travelers options at different price points. Coffee and pancakes are provided each morning in a small kitchen in the leafy courtyard, and a full bar – along with a pool table and a dartboard – keeps the party going around the clock. The hostel also arranges all-inclusive day tours at bargain prices to attractions all over the country.

Portes 9 B&B $
(Map p58; ☑849-943-2039; info@portes9.com; Arzobispo Portes 9; r incl breakfast from US$55; ✹ 🛜) In a 400-year-old home, eight tastefully furnished rooms with wood floors and high ceilings make up this lovely, family-owned B&B fronting a quiet plaza in the neighborhood's southeast corner. It's an intimate spot where guests socialize over breakfast, and a rooftop deck features ocean views and a Jacuzzi. The location and atmosphere are superlative at this price point.

The owners also run some nice apartments near Plaza de España for longer stays, offering special deals for weekly and monthly stays.

Casa Naemie HOTEL $
(Map p58; ☑809-689-2215; www.casanaemie. com; Isabel la Católica 11; s/d incl breakfast RD$2000/3000; ✹ 🛜) This charming oasis only a few blocks from the oldest cathedral in the Americas feels like a European pension. Surrounding a narrow central courtyard are three floors of cozy, clean rooms with large modern bathrooms. An elegant lobby with a vaulted entranceway and brick flooring does double duty in the morning when the excellent breakfast is served.

Hostal Tierra Plana HOSTEL $
(Map p58; ☑809-686-0120; www.hostaltierraplana. com; Hostos 357; s/d incl breakfast RD$1500/1600; 🅿 🛜) The plain white exterior of this newer, two-story budget option in the Colonial Zone isn't much to look at, but the inside is cozy and clean, and staff members are kind and knowledgeable. Backpackers will enjoy taking breakfast and dinner on the rooftop terrace, with views of the neighboring Monasterio de San Francisco and its raucous Sunday-night dance parties.

Self-parking costs $4 per night.

Residencial La Fonte APARTMENT $
(Map p58; ☑809-686-3265; www.residenciallafonte. net; Las Mercedes 364; r with fan/aircon US$30/40; ✹ 🛜) Worth considering for the self-sufficient and long-term deal seekers (discounts for monthly stays) are the large apartment-style units (all have kitchens) in this three-story, purple-pastel building, a block off El Conde. There's no front desk per se and the furnishings are basic, but the top floor has a nice outdoor common area with chairs and hammocks.

Hostel Plaza Toledo GUESTHOUSE $
(Map p58; ☑809-688-7649; marshallbettye@ hotmail.com; Plaza de María de Toledo, Isabel la Católica 163; dm US$22, r US$50; ✹ 🛜) Look for the nondescript iron doorway opening onto Plaza de María de Toledo; don't be discouraged by the messy art-gallery space. There are several dorm rooms (one has a fan) with five to six beds, and while the spaces are hectic, they get good light and there's access to a common kitchen and bathroom.

For privacy but not quiet, a private room opens directly onto Isabel la Católica – the bathroom is extremely small. If no one answers the door, taxi drivers lounging around the plaza may be able to help.

★Hotel Villa Colonial HOTEL $$
(Map p58; ☑809-221-1049; www.villacolonial.net; Sánchez 157; s/d incl breakfast US$75/95; 🛜 🌊) The French owner has created an idyllic oasis, an exceptionally sophisticated combination of European elegance with a colonial-era facade and an art-deco design. The rooms lining the narrow garden and pool area all have high ceilings and four-poster beds, as well as flatscreen TVs and bathrooms with ceramic-tile floors.

Rocking chairs and a Balinese-style lounge bed provide plenty of character and comfort for those wishing to socialize. A few studios set in back, past the open-air breakfast area, are more basic but have stovetops and sinks and reduced weekly and monthly rates.

★El Beaterío Guest House GUESTHOUSE $$
(Map p58; ☑809-687-8657; http://elbeaterio.fr; Duarte 8; s/d incl breakfast US$80/100; ✹ 🛜) Get thee to this nunnery – if you're looking for austere elegance. Each of the 11 large rooms is sparsely furnished, but the wood-beamed ceilings and stone floors are truly special; the tile-floored bathrooms are modern and well maintained. It's easy to imagine the former function of this 16th-century building, with its heavy stone facade, and dark, vaulted front room.

These days it serves as a beautiful reading room and dining area with classical music playing softly, giving way to a lush and sunny inner courtyard inspiring peace and tranquility. Recently the owners created a mini-museum on the exterior walls, with placards explaining the history of convents in the DR.

Hostal Suite Colonial   HOTEL $$
(Map p58; ☎809-685-1082; www.suitecolonial. net; Padre Billini 362; s/d incl breakfast US$68/82; ❄️🛜) A solid, extremely friendly midrange choice with an exterior that blends in with the facades of the neighboring colonial-era buildings. However, once past an attractive high-ceilinged lounge area, some of the charm fades. Heavy couches and linoleum-floored hallways lead to rooms with relatively basic furnishings and some haphazard choices. Breakfast is served in a small backyard patio.

Hodelpa Caribe Colonial   HOTEL $$
(Map p58; ☎809-688-7799; www.hodelpa.com; Isabel la Católica 159; r incl breakfast from US$85; Ⓟ❄️🛜) Only a block from Parque Colón, the Hodelpa Caribe is a convenient choice for those seeking modern comforts without the colonial vibe. A full revamp in 2016 gave the lobby and 45 rooms a sleeker new look, the beds are comfortable and service is attentive. The onsite restaurant Azul serves local favorites like stewed goat, and a rooftop solarium has several lounge chairs and good views.

Hotel Doña Elvira   HOTEL $$
(Map p58; ☎809-221-7415; www.dona-elvira. com; Padre Billini 207a; s/d incl breakfast from US$64/89; Ⓟ❄️@🛜) Housed in a renovated colonial building, Doña Elvira is a friendly place geared toward travelers; you can hang out in the inner courtyard, take a dip in the pool (it's too small for swimming), lounge on the rooftop solarium or read in the lobby/dining area. For such a pretty building, it's unfortunate the 13 rooms are a somewhat haphazard amalgam of mostly plain styles and furnishings.

Hostal La Colonia   HOTEL $$
(Map p58; ☎809-221-0084; hostallacolonia@yahoo. com; Isabel la Católica 110a; s/d US$50/60; ❄️) Ideally located around the corner from Parque Colón, La Colonia is a good option if character is not an issue. In addition to shiny, polished floors and large rooms, each of the floors has its own spacious street-side sitting area and

balcony. Rooms are mostly shielded from the noise on this lively block.

Antiguo Hotel Europa   HOTEL $$
(Map p58; ☎809-285-0005; www.antiguoho-teleuropa.com; cnr Arzobispo Meriño & Emiliano Tejera; r incl breakfast US$80; Ⓟ❄️@) Considering the impressive-looking facade, spacious lobby and uniformed bellboys of this hotel only two blocks west of Plaza España, the 19 rooms are fairly unremarkable. Ask for one with a balcony to ensure your room receives light. Continental breakfast is served on a rooftop terrace.

Hotel Palacio   HOTEL $$$
(Map p58; ☎809-682-4730; www.hotel-palacio. com; Duarte 106; r incl breakfast from US$117; Ⓟ❄️🛜) Cross colonial with a touch of medieval and you have the Palacio, a maze-like hotel occupying a 17th-century mansion only a block north of El Conde. Service is exceptional and you'll need it to find your way past the charming nooks and crannies, which include reading areas, a gym, a small bar, a lush interior courtyard and stone-walled walkways.

First-floor rooms are German minimalist while the larger 2nd-floor rooms are more modern and generic. Though it lacks shade, the small rooftop pool is a big plus, as is the gym.

★Hostal Nicolás de Ovando   HISTORIC HOTEL $$$
(Map p58; ☎809-685-9955; Las Damas; r US$209-354, ste US$365; Ⓟ❄️🛜) Even heads of state must get a thrill when they learn they're sleeping in the former home of the first governor of the Americas. Oozing old-world charm, the Nicolás de Ovando was recently purchased by local hotel chain Hodelpa, but it remains one of the nicest stays in the city, featuring 97 rooms packed with 21st-century amenities.

There's a variety of room types: some have four-poster beds, exposed-timber ceilings and 500-year-old walls with views of the port and river. The split-level contemporary-style rooms are more basic. Cobblestone walkways run through lushly shaded courtyards and the fabulous pool has commanding views of the Río Ozama. An excellent buffet breakfast is included in the rate; La Residence, the hotel's superb and elegant French restaurant (mains US$17 to US$35), has a separate entrance down the street and opens for lunch and dinner.

Malecón

Less appealing than you might otherwise expect considering its waterfront Caribbean setting, Santo Domingo's Malecón, a long expanse of baking concrete, has several high-rise hotels. The upside is that many rooms have views and resort-style amenities like swimming pools and tennis courts; the downside is that you'll have to take a taxi almost everywhere – you'll sweat just walking from the street to the hotel entrance.

La Llave Del Mar   HOTEL $
(Map p64; ☑809-682-5961; Av George Washington 43; r incl breakfast US$58; [P][✲][🕸]) This cozy, affordable 10-room stay is ideally located on the edge of the Zona Colonial and near a bunch of good restaurants and cigar bars along the Malecón. Its restaurant is newly revamped and features an elegant dining room festooned in shark replicas, an old-timey piano and dinner tables propped on aquariums. The crab *criollo* (RD$400) is divine.

Catalonia Santo Domingo   HOTEL $$$
(Map p64; ☑809-685-0000; www.cataloniacaribbean.com; Av George Washington 500, Malecón; r from US$166; [P][✲][@][🕸][⛱]) Among the nicest of the luxury hotels on the Malecón, Catalonia Santo Domingo is part of a huge complex including a casino and movie theater. The highest of the high-rises, it's a long elevator ride from the atrium to the 21st floor at the top. Rooms have better views than nearby competitors, and a bar and restaurant feature stunning ocean views.

Sheraton Santo Domingo   RESORT $$$
(Map p64; ☑809-221-6666; www.sheratonsantodomingo.com; 365 Av George Washington, Malécon; r from US$150; [P][✲][@][🕸][⛱]) Changing hands for the third time in a decade, this aging, sky-high hotel is once again called Sheraton. A decent midrange option relatively close to the Zona Colonial, it boasts sweet views out to the Caribbean sea, cheerful staff members and a recent remodel that gave breakfast buffet room Café Casaba a glamorous new look.

Rooms are modern and tidy, and the hotel offers oodles of event and meeting space for business travelers, as well as a spa, a pool and a 24-hour gym. Annoyingly, wi-fi costs US$12 per day.

Renaissance Jaragua Hotel   RESORT $$$
(Map p64; ☑809-221-2222; www.marriott.com; Av George Washington 367; r from US$127; [P][✲][@][🕸][⛱]) Under the Marriott brand, the spacious rooms in the 10-story tower and low-slung annex have been upgraded, though furnishings are still dated. It's generally good value considering the resort-style facilities; there's a large casino on the premises.

Gazcue

Gazcue, a quiet residential area southwest of Parque Independencia, has several hotels in the midrange category, though there are far fewer eating options and you're likely to have to rely on taxis, especially at night.

Hostal Riazor   HOTEL $$
(Map p64; ☑809-685-5566; hostal_riazor@hotmail.com; Av Independencia 457; s/d incl breakfast US$65/75; [P][✲][🕸]) The Riazor boasts professional English-speaking front-desk staff and extremely well-kept rooms (some of the nicest in this price range) with fauxwood floors and flatscreen TVs. An elevator means you don't have to lug your bags to whatever floor you're on. Breakfast is served in Manolo, the recommended next-door restaurant.

Hotel San Marco   HOTEL $$
(Map p64; ☑809-686-2876; hotelsanmarco@claro.net.do; Santiago 752; s/d incl breakfast US$71/83; [P][✲][🕸][⛱]) Housed in an old colonial-style home, San Marco's *pièce de résistance* is the shady, inner courtyard pool area furnished with hammocks and lounge chairs. Rooms are simply but tastefully furnished.

The San Marco is located around the corner from a metro stop and the stop for Expreso Bávaro buses. It's also within walking distance of the Malecón, while the campus of the Universidad Autonoma de Santo Domingo is a few blocks west.

Hostal San Francisco de Asis   HOTEL $$
(Map p64; ☑809-685-0101; www.hostalsanfranciscodeasis.com; Av Luis Pasteur 102; s/d US$45/65; [P][✲][🕸]) Despite chintzy bed linens and little natural light, the sparkling-clean rooms with flatscreen TVs at this modern multistory hotel can be recommended. A miniature snack bar is attached to the lobby.

Hotel Barcelo Santo Domingo HOTEL **$$$**
(Map p64; ☑ 809-563-5000; www.barcelo.com; cnr Maximo Gomez & 27 de Febrero; r from US$231; P ❄ @ 🛜 ≊) Still known to locals as Barcelo Lina, this outpost of the Spanish chain is within walking distance of the Plaza de la Cultura and is steps away from the city's main east–west artery. The spacious rooms have all of the features of a business-class hotel, and a swanky VIP rooftop lounge includes a hot tub. Bathrooms are especially nice.

The inner courtyard pool and lounge area is equal to any of the Malecón hotels. A casino, bakery, cigar lounge, piano bar and two restaurants – one Japanese and the other a recommended buffet – mean some guests never leave the property. The downside is the $12-per-day wif-fi.

Downtown

West of Gazcue between Avs Tiradentes and Winston Churchill is a fairly high-end area with several shopping malls and two chic new chain hotels that will appeal particularly to business travelers.

JW Marriott Santo Domingo HOTEL **$$$**
(Map p78; ☑ 809-807-1717; www.marriott.com/hotels/travel/sdqjw-jw-marriott-hotel-santo-domingo; Blue Mall, Av Winston Churchill 93; r RD$320; P ❄ @ 🛜 ≊) Housed within the upper floors of downtown's chic Blue Mall, the new JW Marriott Santo Domingo is stylish and modern, with a snazzy cocktail bar, a relaxing infinity pool and a Peruvian restaurant with Asian flair. Rooms are pristine and state-of-the-art, with an option for an LED mirror TV in the bathroom. Amenities also include a 24-hour gym and cinema.

**InterContinental
Santo Domingo** BUSINESS HOTEL **$$$**
(Map p78; ☑ 809-683-6060; www.realhotelsandresorts.com/rep_do/real_sto_domingo/home; cnr Av Winston Churchill & Porfirio Herrera; r incl breakfast from $230; P ❄ @ 🛜 ≊) A new arrival to Santo Domingo's downtown scene, this chain establishment is a conventional but comfortable stay. Its plush rooms, three restaurants, wrap-around infinity pool and spa are housed in a sleek glass tower, and common areas feature sky-high ceilings and glitzy chandeliers. Nonguests can grab a cocktail at the pool bar Blu, which offers excellent city views.

✖ Eating

Unsurprisingly, Santo Domingo is the culinary capital of the country. It offers the full range of Dominican cuisine, from *pastelitos* (pastries with meat, vegetable or seafood fillings) sold from the back of street-vendors' carts to extravagantly prepared meals in picturesque colonial-era buildings. The Zona Colonial has some of the best restaurants and is most convenient for the majority of travelers.

✖ Zona Colonial

A handful of Chinese restaurants serve inexpensive Cantonese-style meals in the small Chinatown neighborhood just north of Av Mella and Calle Duarte; typical of the bunch is **Restaurante Asadero Chino** (Map p58; Duarte; mains RD$160; ⊙ 11am-11pm; ❄). For a meal full of ambience choose from the options on Plaza Espana's **Calle la Atarazana** – the best option is Pat'e Palo (p79). And of course, Calle El Conde has its fair share of cafes and eateries.

Supermercado Nacional (Map p58; cnr El Conde & Duarte; ⊙ 8am-9pm Mon-Sat 9am-8pm Sun) is the place to load up on cheap water, soda, alcohol and juice.

La Cafetera Colonial DINER **$**
(Map p58; ☑ 809-682-7114; www.lacafeteradominicana.com; El Conde 253; dishes RD$125; ⊙ 7:30am-10pm Mon-Sat, 8:30am-8pm Sun) Once a well-known hangout for artists, intellectuals and journalists, this long and narrow greasy spoon opened in 1932 and still caters to a regular clientele. Grab a stool at the counter for an egg sandwich, burger or a strong espresso (RD$50).

Bamban Sushi SUSHI **$**
(Map p58; ☑ 809-379-2009; Arzobispo Meriño 107; dishes RD$200; ⊙ 7pm-11:30pm Tue-Sun) Ensconced in the hip courtyard of a gorgeous 16th-century edifice, this sushi establishment triples as an erstwhile design store and cocktail lounge. The atmosphere is exceedingly hip, often luring a fabulous 20-something crowd for the live DJs and the sushi, which is expertly rolled with fresh ingredients. Don't miss the sangria.

Ananda VEGETARIAN **$**
(Map p64; ☑ 809-476-7341; Casimiro de Moya 7; mains RD$200; ⊙ 11:30am-6pm Mon-Fri, to 4pm Sat & Sun; ✔) Vegetarians will want to try out this pleasant cafeteria-style restaurant and yoga center (beginner hatha classes 6pm to 7pm Monday, Wednesday and Thursday) run by the 'International Society of Divine Realization.' Dominican dishes such as brown rice and roast beans outnumber the Indian offerings.

Downtown Santo Domingo

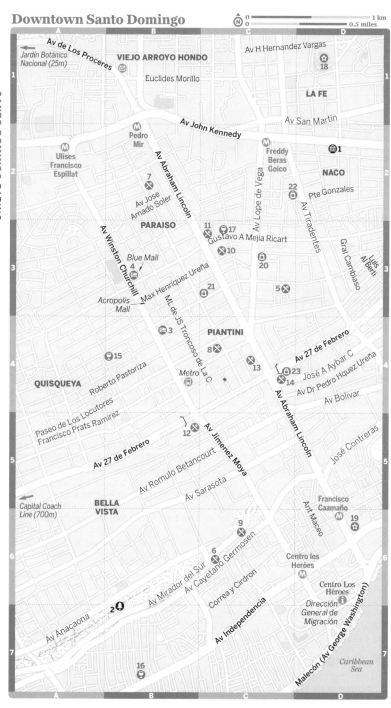

Downtown Santo Domingo

Mesón D'Bari
DOMINICAN **$$**

(Map p58; ☎809-687-4091; cnr Hostos & Salomé Ureña; mains RD$350; ⊙noon-midnight) A Zona Colonial institution popular with tourists and sophisticated *capitaleños* on weekends, Mesón D'Bari occupies a charmingly decaying colonial home covered with large, bright paintings by local artists. The menu has Dominican and international standards, and different versions of grilled meats and fish; the long attractive bar is equally appealing. Live music on some weekend nights.

El Rey del Falafel
MIDDLE EASTERN **$$**

(Map p58; cnr Sánchez & Padre Billini; mains RD$330; ⊙4:30pm-midnight Sun-Thu, to 1am Fri & Sat) This restaurant's stunning, open-air dining room is the courtyard of a ruined building lit by shimmering candles, which makes it at least as good a place for a drink as a meal. The kitchen has stepped up its game and now the food, fare like falafel and juicy shwarma platters, lives up to the ambience.

Pizza Colonial
ITALIAN **$$**

(Map p58; ☎809-689-4040, 809-689-3604; cnr Billini & José Reyes; mains RD$350; ⊙6pm-midnight, closed Sun & Tue) Sophisticated and stylish, with oversized framed poster reproductions of European Renaissance paintings decorating the triple-height ceilings, Pizza Colonial wouldn't be out of place in a fashionable district of Rome. The owner keeps a watchful eye on the kitchen and the exposed-brick pizza oven, which does excellent pies and a handful of pasta dishes.

Mamey Librería Café
CAFE **$$**

(Map p58; ☎809-688-9111; www.mameylibreria. com; Las Mercedes 315; mains US$15; ⊙10am-9pm, Wed-Sun) This new cafe, art gallery and bookstore is housed within the charming former abode of Emilio Rodríguez Demorizi, one of the Dominican Republic's first historians. Featuring elaborate courtyards, fountains and vertical gardens, the space is ideal for relaxing with a book or grabbing juice with a friend. The small menu includes a bacon steak sandwich and humus with grilled vegetables.

Zorro
MEXICAN **$$**

(Map p58; ☎809-685-9569; El Conde 54; mains RD$325; ⊙8am-1am Sun-Thu, to 3am Fri & Sat) Awash in bold primary colors like a Mondrian painting, this casual Mexican place with indoor and outdoor seating adds some spice to the alleyway just east of Parque Colón. It has quality tacos, enchiladas and quesadillas, plus churros with chocolate and flan for dessert: tequila and margarita round out the offerings.

★ Pat'e Palo
SPANISH, MEDITERRANEAN **$$$**

(Map p58; ☎809-519-9687; La Atarazana 25; mains RD$650-1200; ⊙noon-1am) The most happening and deservedly longest surviving of Plaza España's restaurant row, Pat'e Palo is for anyone tired of the same old bland pasta and chicken. Large, both physically and in terms of its selection, the menu includes creatively designed dishes such as foie gras with dark-beer jam and risotto in squid ink and shrimp *brunoise* with lobster tail and roasted arugula.

The lobster ravioli (RD$630), one of the least expensive items on the menu, is excellent. Stick around for dessert – crème brûlée is the specialty – and an extensive wine and cigar list are for those who want to spend an extra hour or two hanging out in the candlelight.

Because of its popularity (or maybe a reason for it), there's something of a pre-packaged vibe to the efficiently professional waitstaff's service; pirate-like headscarves are part of the uniform. English and French menus available.

Lulú Tasting Bar
TAPAS $$$

(Map p58; ☑ 809-687-8360; www.lulu.do; cnr Arzobispo Meriño & Padre Billini; all-you-can-eat tapas RD$800, Sun brunch RD$1920; ☺ 6pm-3am Mon-Sat, from 11am Sun) Class it up at Lulú, the most recent concept from the same team that brought Santo Domingo Pat'e Palo (the city's best restaurant) and Jalao (its most ostentatiously Dominican). This Zona Colonial tapas bar lures a fabulous after-work crowd looking to unwind over cigars and cocktails and nibble on small plates of *carpaccio de foie gras* and salmon satay.

The tapas are less rewarding than the steep price might imply, but the atmosphere at Lulú, with its towering arches, grand courtyards and charming koi pond, is unmatched in the city. Those looking to save a buck can purchase a bottle of wine at Cava Billini next door and pay a small corking fee. Sunday brunch includes bottomless mimosas.

La Bricola
ITALIAN $$$

(Map p58; ☑ 809-688-5055; Arzobispo Meriño 152; mains RD$850, brunch RD$400; ☺ 11am-1am) From the candlelit open-air patio to the soft melodic piano, La Bricola embodies romance – a meal here is the perfect place to pop the question. Set in a restored colonial-era palace, the ambience can't help but trump the food, which is international- and Italian-inspired mains, including fresh fish specials. Despite the almost regal, fairytale setting, service is more welcoming than stuffy.

Jalao
DOMINICAN $$$

(Map p58; ☑ 809-689-9509; www.jalao.do; El Conde 103; mains RD$750; ☺ 11am-2am) A towering restaurant brimming with Dominican style, newcomer Jalao is over-the-top touristy but attracts a local crowd, too. The walls and ceiling are decked out in traditional kites, decorative crosses and reclaimed wood from country homes, and live *bachata* and merengue bands play regularly. The food is pricey but adventurous; try the goat confit or the crab stew.

Gazcue & Malecón

Gazcue, only a short walk from the Malecón, has a number of good choices, and the grocery La Cadena (Map p64; ☑ 807-246-0004; cnr Cervantes & Casimiro de Moya; ☺ 7:30am-10pm Mon-Sat, 9am-8pm Sun) carries produce, meats and everything you should need.

Hermanos Villar
DOMINICAN $

(Map p64; ☑ 809-682-1433; cnr Avs Independencia & Pasteur; mains RD$175; ☺ 7am-11pm, to 10pm Sun) Occupying almost an entire city block, Hermanos Villar has two parts: the bustling Dominican-style diner serving cafeteria food and hot, grilled deli sandwiches, and a large outdoor garden restaurant that is slightly more upscale in terms of menu. Finding an empty table inside during the heavy lunchtime traffic is a challenge, so getting things to go is always an option.

Adrian Tropical
DOMINICAN $

(Map p64; ☑ 809-221-1764; Av George Washington; mains RD$200; ☺ 24hr; ⊞) This popular family-friendly chain occupies a spectacular location overlooking the Caribbean. Waiters scurry throughout the two floors and outdoor dining area doling out Dominican specialties like yucca or plantain *mofongo* as well as standard meat dishes. An inexpensive buffet (RD$200) is another option and the fruit drinks hit the spot. There are three other outposts in Santo Domingo.

D'Luis Parrillada
DOMINICAN $$

(Map p64; ☑ 809-686-2940; Paseo Presidente Billini; dishes RD$350; ☺ 8am-1am Sun-Thu, to 3am Fri & Sat) This casual, open-air restaurant perched over the ocean only a few blocks from the Zona Colonial is one of only a few restaurants to take advantage of the Malecón's setting. The large menu includes fajitas, grilled and barbecue meats, sandwiches, seafood and little-found *pulpofongo* (*mofongo* with Creole-style cuttlefish; RD$330). Wonderful place for a drink as well.

Il Cappuccino
ITALIAN $$

(Map p64; ☑ 809-682-8006; Av Máximo Gómez 60; mains RD$400; ☺ 7:30am-11:30pm; ⊞ ☎) You might leave this oasis of comfort and sophistication (on an otherwise gritty stretch) feeling envious of the regulars who are welcomed like family. It's the sort of place where the Italian owner bustles around, doling out pats and quips. Nearly three-dozen types of really top-notch pizza and pasta, plus fish and meat dishes round out the menu.

Great-looking pastries, cakes, gelato and wine are on display in the bright and welcoming cafe side. The larger dining room is a dreamy fantasyscape of papier-mâché trees and structures such as canopied beds.

Tres Cerditos
LATIN AMERICAN **$$**

(Map p64; ☑809-686-2940; Av George Washington 25; mains RD$350; ⊙11am-1am) On a raised platform at the eastern end of the Malecón, this *chicharronera* (fried pork eatery) is a new hot spot from the people behind D'Luis Parrillada across the street. The menu is small but heavy on fried pork, with *chicharrón* nachos (RD$200), pig legs (RD$350) and tacos, burritos and quesadillas stuffed with, you guessed it, pork.

Maniqui Restaurant & Lounge
INTERNATIONAL **$$**

(Map p64; ☑809-689-3030; Av Pedro Henríquez Ureña, Plaza de la Cultura; mains RD$650; ⊙11am-midnight Mon-Sat; P☀) Decked out like a burlesque club, this lavishly and curiously decorated space, seemingly inspired by modeling, is in the middle of the Plaza de la Cultura. Pizza and pasta dishes are identified as a 'model's nightmare' on the menu; other choices include beef carpaccio, crepes and croquettes. Live music Friday nights; karaoke and even stand-up comedy other nights.

Manolo
DOMINICAN **$$**

(Map p64; ☑809-685-5566; Av Independencia; mains RD$200-600; ⊙24hr) Owned by Hotel Riazor next door, Manolo has an indoor dining room and an elevated outdoor terrace that is great for a leisurely meal or drink. The menu runs the gamut from basic sandwiches to elaborately prepared lobster and steaks.

El Conuco
DOMINICAN **$$**

(Map p64; ☑809-686-0129; Casimiro de Moya 152; mains RD$300; ⊙11am-11pm) Unashamedly touristy, El Conuco is stereotypically Dominican in the same way the Hard Rock Cafe is authentically American. Nevertheless, Dominicans as well as tour groups come here to get traditionally prepared dishes while taking in merengue and *bachata* performances – the real highlight – in a palapa-topped dining room covered with traditional decorations.

Vesuvio Malecón
ITALIAN **$$$**

(Map p64; ☑809-221-1954; Av George Washington 521; mains RD$700; ⊙noon-midnight) A Malecón institution only a few blocks from Hotel Catalonia and one of the city's better restaurants since 1954, Vesuvio is elegant without being snooty. Expect refined Neapolitan-style seafood and meat dishes; lobster and shellfish are featured in beautifully plated antipasti.

✖ Downtown

The downtown area north and west of Gazcue, between Av Tiradentes and Av Winston Churchill, is a fine area for dining, with a large number of restaurants, many of which come and go rather quickly. For self-caterers, **Plaza Lama La Supertienda** (Map p78; cnr Avs Jímenez Moya & 27 de Febrero) and **Supermercado Nacional** (Map p78; ☑809-565-5541; cnr Avs Abraham Lincoln & 27 de Febrero; ⊙9am-10pm Mon-Sat, to 8pm Sun) live up to their names, the former (an enormous megastore occupying several city blocks) especially so.

La Pesca de Oro
SEAFOOD **$$**

(Map p78; ☑809-565-1723; www.facebook.com/lapescadeoro; Federico Geraldino 14; mains RD$450; ⊙11am-11:30pm Mon-Sat, to 11pm Sun) This new seafood place in hip Piantini gets its catch fresh from the seaside town Juan Dolio (also the location of a sister restaurant). The amiable chef explains what's good each day, often

---

SANTO DOMINGO FOR CHILDREN

Santo Domingo isn't particularly kid-friendly. Outside of the Zona Colonial, it doesn't cater to pedestrians, and there are few beaches or parks. **Parque Colón** (p66) and Parque Duarte in the Zona Colonial are basically flagstone plazas where you can sit on a bench and feed pigeons. **Playa Guibia** (Map p64; cnr Avs George Washington & Maximo Gomez) on the Malécon offers a kids' playground and is popular with families on weekends.

Adrian Tropical (p80) is a good place to eat with unruly youngsters. Hotels with pools, all those along the Malecón, are especially recommended and will allow you and the kids to take a break from the sightseeing for several relaxing hours.

suggesting ceviche, rock lobster, octopus and pompano, a delicious fish best grilled with garlic. A side of pasta (which comes in a crab shell) completes the meal.

Galette
CAFE $$

(Map p78; ☑809-565-2765; www.facebook.com/galette.rd; Plaza Mezzaluna, Federico Geraldino 83; mains RD$450; ☺7am-11pm Tue-Sun) Beloved for its sweets and juices, this adorable restaurant on the 2nd floor of downtown's Plaza Mezzaluna is an ideal stop for a churro waffle (RD$350) with *dulce de leche* (caramel) and whipped cream. Breakfast, salads, sandwiches and heartier meals are also on offer, and health-conscious yogis from the studio next door regularly drop in for the yummy ginger lemonade (RD$200).

Mecenas Café
INTERNATIONAL $$

(Map p78; ☑849-206-6651; Av Mirador Sur; mains RD$400; ☺7pm-midnight Wed & Sun, to 1am Thu, to 2am Fri & Sat) In tranquil Parque Mirador del Sur, this cafe and culture center beckons artsy Dominicans and travelers in the know. The menu is all over the globe, with dishes like plantain *mofongo* but also Hawaiian pulled-pork sliders or bruschetta camembert. Guests dine on an elegant terrace then venture inside a three-story contemporary-art gallery with a whimsical sensibility. Find them on Facebook.

Baladi
LEBANESE $$

(Map p78; ☑809-567-0070; Virginia de Peña 5, Naco; dishes RD$220-485; ☺noon-11pm Tue-Thu & Sun, to midnight Fri & Sat, closed Mon; ⓟ) Hidden away on a residential block in the hip Naco neighborhood, this tranquil Lebanese spot is the place to go when you're tiring of beans and rice and on the market for some Middle Eastern goodness. The humus, tabouleh and shawarma are all top-notch, and the friendly family that owns the place lives right upstairs.

Kogi Grill
KOREAN $$

(Map p64; ☑809-227-5577; Av 27 de Febrero 195; mains RD$385; ☺noon-4pm & 6-10pm Mon-Thu, to 11pm Fri & Sat; ❄) The mod design of colored mirror tiles and the informal vibe match the somewhat playful menu. Groups can choose to grill at their table, but regardless of the number of diners, every meal comes with a half-dozen delicious *banchan* (Korean side dishes). Not easily reached on foot, it's on a busy roadway at the corner of Ortega y Gasset.

★Samurai
JAPANESE $$$

(Map p78; ☑809-565-1621; Seminario 57; mains RD$850; ☺6:30am-4pm & 6pm-midnight Tue-Thu, noon-midnight Fri & Sat, noon-11pm Sun) One of the best Japanese restaurants in the city, with *yakinuku*-style tables (grill the meat and seafood at your table), a sushi bar and a large dining room. The outdoor area was recently revamped and is exceedingly tranquil.

Mijas Restaurante
SPANISH $$$

(Map p78; ☑809-567-5040; Max Henríquez Ureña 47; mains RD$900, tapas RD$150; ☺noon-midnight) Upscale and trendy Spanish restaurant serving some of the best tapas in the city. Live music Saturday nights.

Mitre Restaurant & Wine Bar
FUSION $$$

(Map p78; ☑809-472-1787; cnr Gustavo A Mejía Ricart 1001 & Av Abraham Lincoln 1005; mains RD$850; ☺11:30am-1am) This sleek restaurant, located in a nondescript building in an upscale business and residential district, serves a creative fusion of Asian, Italian and Dominican cuisines. The results are satisfying to both the eye and stomach; an outdoor patio and 2nd-floor wine and cigar bar are more casual than the stylish white-table-clothed dining room.

El Mesón de la Cava
DOMINICAN $$$

(Map p78; ☑809-533-2818; www.elmesondelacava.com; Av Mirador del Sur; mains RD$850; ☺noon-midnight) This is where Batman would take a date – this craggy stalactite-filled limestone cave is home to a unique and romantic restaurant. Formally clad waiters and soft merengue and salsa music add to the atmosphere, though the food, primarily grilled meats and fish, is ordinary. Live music some nights on the leafy terrace.

Drinking & Nightlife

Santo Domingo has the country's best nightlife scene, from glitzy nightclubs and casinos to small bars and dance spots, much of it located in the Zona Colonial. Restaurants and cafes along Plaza España and the eastern end of Calle El Conde are happening spots; that being said, most restaurants tend to be good places to linger with a few drinks.

★La Alpargatería
COCKTAIL BAR

(Map p58; ☑809-221-3158; Salome Ureña 59; margaritas RD$185; ☺10am-midnight Tue-Sun) At the entrance, guests step into a shoe shop where artisans craft espadrilles (light canvas shoes people started making in the Pyrenees in the 14th century). Continuing to the back, though, the store opens into a trendy cafe with comfy seating within intimate nooks and a leafy courtyard. The craft cocktails are standout here, especially the ginger-lemon margarita.

Mercado Colón BEER GARDEN
(Map p58; ☑ 809-685-1103; Arzobispo Nouel 105; ☺ noon-1am Tue-Sun) Channeling the Spanish *mercat* concept, this collection of artisanal food and alcohol vendors is housed under one Zona Colonial roof, with communal courtyard seating. Options include fresh sushi, piping-hot pizza and a variety of tapas, all assembled with local ingredients and innovative flavor combinations. It's a good place to drink craft beer and feel like part of a revolution.

Mamma Club CLUB
(Map p78; ☑ 809-868-8002; www.facebook.com/MammaClubRD; Av Gustavo Mejia Ricart 75; cover varies; ☺ 9pm-3am Thu-Sat) If the thickness of the bouncers' necks is any indication of how good the bar is, consider Mamma Club the hottest place in town. In the heart of the burgeoning Piantini neighborhood, it attracts the beautiful people with its epic light and sound systems, top-notch DJs and VIP bottle service. Ladies drink free on Thursdays. Just don't start any fights.

Parada 77 BAR
(Map p58; ☑ 809-221-7880; Isabel la Católica 255; ☺ 7pm-1am Sun-Thu, to 3am Fri & Sat) Thankfully, there's no dress code at this laid-back, grungy place with graffiti-covered walls. The vibe becomes decidedly high-energy on Sunday nights, when everyone heads here after the dance night at the nearby Monasterio de San Francisco (p72) winds down.

El Conde Restaurant CAFE
(Map p58; Hotel Conde de Peñalba, cnr El Conde & Arzobispo Meriño; ☺ 7am-midnight Sun-Fri, to 1am Sat) Hands down the best place for an afternoon drink. As much a restaurant as a cafe, El Conde's appeal isn't its varied menu of decent but overpriced food (pasta RD$350), but its commanding location at the busiest corner in the Zona Colonial, crowded with tourists and locals alike. Try cooling off with a *morir soñado* (RD$108).

G Lounge GAY & LESBIAN
(Map p58; ☑ 809-903-2345; Arzobispo Nouel 305; ☺ 9pm-4am Thu-Sat, to midnight Sun, closed Mon-Wed) A beloved gay bar in the Colonial Zone

that hosts regular drag shows. Find them on Facebook.

Cultura Cervecera CRAFT BEER
(Map p78; www.facebook.com/ccervecerard; Rafael Augusto Sánchez 96b; draft beer from RD$210; ☺ 4pm-midnight Mon-Thu, to 2am Fri & Sat, 3pm-midnight Sun; ☎) A place of refuge for hopheads both Dominican and foreign, this is the country's best bet – so far – to escape the Presidente stranglehold on beer geeks. Nearly 150 craft beers by the bottle along with six taps, often dedicated to local brews from Republica Brewing and Santo Domingo Brewery, among others.

It's 9km west of Zona Colonial and there's plenty of pub grub (mains RD$245 to RD$425) to wash down the IPAs! A second, bottles-only location has opened in the **Zona Colonial** (Map p58; Arzobispo Meriño 266; ☺ 11am-2am Tue-Sun; ☎) with a shotgun-style lounge area unfortunately sponsored by Corona – but the beers are still great!

Mandala Pub PUB
(Map p58; Sanchez 157; ☺ vaires) Also known as Proud Marys, this chill spot is one of the oldest bars in the Zona Colonial, defined by its exotic lamps and killer sangria.

Onno's Bar BAR
(Map p58; ☑ 809-689-1183; Hostos, btwn El Conde & Arzobispo Nouel; ☺ 6pm-midnight Sun-Thu, to 3am Fri & Sat) There's always something going on at this hot spot just off El Conde, with several flatscreen TVs, lasers, an illuminated bar, DJs and a smoke machine.

Double's Bar BAR
(Map p58; ☑ 809-688-3833; Arzobispo Meriño; ☺ 6pm-late) Good-looking 20-somethings grind away to loud pop and Latin music on weekend nights. Otherwise, groups can lounge around one of the couches or sidle up to the classic long wood bar.

Esedeku GAY & LESBIAN
(Map p58; ☑ 809-763-8292; Las Mercedes 341; ☺ 8pm-1am Tue-Sun, 9pm-3am Sat & Sun) Only a block from Calle El Conde, Esedeku is an intimate bar with a huge selection of cocktails. It's popular with local professionals; not for hustlers.

El Sarten BAR
(Map p58; Hostos 153; ☺ 7pm-late) A diverse mix of *capitañleos* get down to *son* (Afro-Cuban percussion), *bachata* and merengue at this old-school space.

Cacibajagua BAR

(Map p58; ☑809-333-9060; Las Mercedes; ⏰8pm-1am Sun-Thu, to 3am Fri & Sat) Also known as 'La Cueva' (the Cave), this small and dark spot favors good ol' rock music like Pink Floyd and Led Zeppelin. It recently relocated to Calle Las Mercedes.

Segazona Cafe BAR

(Map p58; ☑809-685-9569; El Conde 54; ⏰8:30am-1am Mon-Thu, to 3am Fri & Sat, to midnight Sun) Occupying separate spaces on either side of a cobblestoned alleyway, Segazona operates as an Italian-style cafe during the day and an Ibiza-like club on weekend nights, when DJs spin and dancers get off their feet and onto one of the day beds in the hangar-like backyard. Crepes, paninis and other morsels are also served inside and out.

Jet Set CLUB

(Map p78; ☑809-535-4145; Av Independencia 2253; ⏰8pm-late Fri, Sat & Mon) A trendy, good-looking crowd flocks to this disco where Justin Bieber's entourage tussled their way into the tabloids in late 2013. The club is often aglow with neon lights, and an oversized dance floor hosts salsa, merengue and *bachata* nights.

☆ Entertainment

Hotel nightclubs, especially those along the Malecón, are hugely popular, especially among Santo Domingo's rich, young and restless. Merengue and *bachata* are omnipresent, but house, techno, reggaeton and rock are popular as well. Newspapers are a good place to find out about upcoming concerts and shows, and if your Spanish is good, radio stations hype the capital's big events.

Estadio Quisqueya SPECTATOR SPORT

(Map p78; ☑809-616-1224; www.facebook.com/estadioquisqueya; 3456 Tiradentes Ave; tickets RD$250-1000; ⏰games 5pm Sun, 8pm Tue, Wed, Fri & Sat) One of the best places to experience Dominican baseball is at the home field of two of the DR's six professional teams, Licey and Escogido. You can get tickets to most games by arriving shortly before the first inning; games between the hometown rivals or Licey and Aguilas sell out more quickly.

Asking for the best seats available at the box office is likely to cost RD$1000 and put you within meters of the ballplayers and the between-innings dancers. Scalpers also congregate along the road to the stadium and at the entrance. A taxi back to the Zona Colonial should run around RD$200. The stadium has been the site of big-name concerts such as Justin Bieber and beloved Dominican singer/songwriter Juan Luis Guerra.

★ Colonial Gate 4D Cinema CINEMA

(Map p58; ☑809-682-4829; www.thecolonialgate.com; Padre Billini 52; adult/child RD$400/350; ⏰10am-11pm, closed Mon) Tucked away in the deep southeastern corner of the Zona Colonial, this hidden treasure is the country's first '4D' movie theater. The first three dimensions are what you'd expect, but fourth brings in the elements – mist, fog, wind, heat, smells, motion seats and bubbles. Admission includes three short films and headsets that translate them into nine languages.

The Great Wall of China and *Pirates 7D* are fantastic films for the thrills, but the most impressive (and award-winning) flick is *The Battle of Santo Domingo*, which the theater itself produced. During the film, which envisions the 1586 invasion of Sir Francis Drake, old Santo Domingo is brought to life as viewers feel they are flying over the city walls, getting slashed by pirate swords and dodging cannon balls.

Casa de Teatro CULTURAL CENTER

(Map p58; ☑809-689-3430; www.casadeteatro.com; Arzobispo Meriño 110; admission varies; ⏰9am-6pm & 8pm-3am Mon-Sat) Housed in a renovated colonial building, this fantastic arts complex features a gallery with rotating exhibits by Dominican artists, an open-air bar, and a performance space and theater that regularly host dance and stage productions.

El Teatro Nacional Eduardo Brito THEATER

(National Theater; Map p64; ☑809-687-3191; Plaza de la Cultura; tickets RD$150-500) Hosts opera, ballet and musical performances, from classical to Latin pop stars. Tickets for performances at this grandly ornate 1700-seat theater can be purchased in advance at the box office from 9:30am to 12:30pm and 3:30pm to 6:30pm daily. For show dates and times, call or check the weekend editions of local newspapers.

Centro Cultural Español CULTURAL CENTER

(Spanish Cultural Center; Map p58; ☑809-686-8212; www.ccesd.org; cnr Arzobispo Meriño & Arzobispo Portes; ⏰9am-9pm Mon-Sat) A cultural space run by the Spanish embassy, this institute regularly hosts art exhibits, film festivals and musical concerts, all with a Spanish bent. It also has 15,000 items in its lending library.

Casa de Italia
CULTURAL CENTER

(Italian House; Map p58; ☑809-688-1497; www.
casadeitaliard.org; Hostos 348; ⊙9:30am-9pm
Mon-Thu, to 6pm Sat) Hosts art exhibits in its
1st-floor gallery; also doubles as an Ital-
ian-language institute.

Casinos

After baseball, cockfighting and playing the
lottery, gambling is one of the DR's favorite
pastimes. Casinos generally open at 4pm
and close at 4am. Bets may be placed in Dominican pesos or US dollars. Las Vegas odds
and rules generally apply, though there are
some variations. All of the large hotels on
the Malecón have casinos, as do the Barcelo
Santo Domingo (p77) and **Hispaniola Hotel**
(Map p78; ☑809-221-7111; cnr Avs Independencia
& Abraham Lincoln; ⊙24hr), and all the dealers
speak English.

🛍 Shopping

More than anywhere else in the country,
shopping in Santo Domingo runs the gam-
ut from cheap tourist kitsch to high-end
quality collectibles. The easiest – and best
– neighborhood to shop in is the Zona Colonial, where you'll find rows of shops offering
locally made products at decent prices.

Casa Quien
ART

(Map p58; ☑809-689-0842; www.casaquien.com;
cnr Arzobispo Nouel & Sánchez; ⊙11am-7pm Wed-
Sun) Ensconced in an elegant, 16th-century
home in the Colonial Zone, Casa Quien exhibits and sells contemporary fine art, crafts,
books and other curios created by Dominican
artists in limited quantity. The artist-managed

space also hosts exhibitions and other events,
often in support of emerging talent, and has
received international praise for its mission
and works.

Felipe & Co
ARTS & CRAFTS

(Map p58; ☑809-689-5812; El Conde 105;
⊙10am-8pm Mon-Sat, to 6pm Sun) This shop
on Parque Colón, easily one of the best in
the Zona Colonial, is stocked with charming
high-quality handicrafts, including ceramics, jewelry and handbags, and also a good
selection of paintings.

Mapas Gaar
MAPS

(Map p58; ☑809-688-8004; 3rd fl, cnr El Conde &
Espaillat; ⊙8am-5:30pm Mon-Fri, 9am-1pm Sat)
Located on the 3rd floor of an aging office
building, Mapas Gaar has the best variety
and the largest number of maps in the Dominican Republic. Maps are designated by
city or region and include a country map, as
well as several city maps on the back of each
(RD$250).

Choco Museo
CHOCOLATE

(Map p58; ☑809-221-8222; www.chocomuseo.
com; Arzobispo Meriño 254; ⊙10am-7pm) More a
shop than museum, Choco Museo nonethe-
less has signs in Spanish and English that
explain the history of chocolate and manufacturing processes in the DR. It has a small
cafe and shop, as well as workshops where
you can make your own bars (organic and
fair-trade bars for sale US$6).

Cava Billini
WINE

(Map p58; cnr Padre Billini & Arzobispo Meriño;
⊙noon-2am Mon-Sat, from 11am Sun) The only

ART GALLERIES

Walking around Santo Domingo, you'll see sidewalk displays of simple, colorful canvases
of rural life and landscapes. This so-called Haitian or 'primitive' art is so prevalent that it's
understandable if you mistake it for the country's de-facto wallpaper. Most of what you
see on the street is mass-produced, low-quality amateur pieces with little value.

For unique and interesting Dominican pieces, there are a number of formal galleries
in Santo Domingo, such as the **Galería de Arte María del Carmen** (Map p58; ☑809-
682-7609; Arzobispo Meriño 207; ⊙7:30am-8pm) and the small **De Soto Galería** (Map
p58; ☑809-689-6109; Hostos 215; ⊙9am-noon & 2-5pm Mon-Fri). **Bolós Galería** (Map
p58; ☑809-781-1654; http://galeriabolos.blogspot.com; cnr Isabel la Católica & Padre Billini;
⊙7:30am-8pm) is stocked with imaginative, avant-garde sculptures and furnishings
(many of which are made of recycled materials).

Outside the Zona Colonial are dozens of other galleries that feature Haitian and
Dominican art, including **Galería de Arte El Greco** (Map p78; ☑809-562-5921; Av
Tiradentes 16, Naco; ⊙9am-noon & 2-6pm Mon-Fri, to 1pm Sat) and **Galería Arawak** (Map
p78; ☑809-565-3614; www.artearawak.org; Rafael Sánchez 53; ⊙9:30am-1pm & 3-5:30pm
Mon-Sat).

high-end wine shop in the Zona Colonial. It offers free tastings on Tuesdays (6pm to 8pm) and is a popular stop for those looking to enjoy a bottle at Lulú Tasting Bar (p80), which is under the same ownership, next door. Bottles run from RD$500, and a bottle of the priciest wine, Opus 1, is RD$2100.

El Catador WINE
(Map p78; ☑ 809-540-1644; www.elcatador.com; cnr Av Lope de Vega & Enrique Urena; ⊘10am-11pm Mon-Fri, to 7pm Sat) If in Piantini, this is the place to stock up on quality wine from around the world, as well as whiskey, gin, champagne and more. The elegant, brick-walled space has a back room with comfy couches where regular tastings are held.

Mercado Modelo MARKET
(Map p58; Av Mella; ⊘8am-6pm Mon-Sat, to 1pm Sun) Bargain hard at this crowded market, which sells everything from love potions to woodcarvings, jewelry and, of course, the ubiquitous 'Haitian-style' paintings. The more you look like a tourist, the higher the asking price. The market is housed in an aging two-story building just north of the Zona Colonial in a neighborhood of fairly rundown stores and souvenir shops.

Hombres de las Americas CLOTHING
(Map p58; ☑ 809-686-2479; hombresdelasmeri-cas@gmail.com; Arzobispo Meriño 255; ⊘10am-6pm Mon-Sat) A high-end boutique selling Panama hats and *guayabera* (also known as *chacabana*), traditionally white shirts worn on formal occasions. The former start at around RD$2300.

La Leyenda del Cigarro CIGARS
(Map p58; ☑ 809-682-9932; El Conde 161; ⊘9am-9pm Mon-Sat, 10am-8pm Sun) A good selection of premium cigars, but equal-ly importantly, the helpful staff are more than willing to answer the naive questions of cigar novices. Another location is several blocks away at the corner of Calles Hostos and Mercedes.

Librería Cuesta BOOKS
(Map p78; ☑ 809-473-4020; www.cuestalibros.com; cnr Av 27 de Febrero & Abraham Lincoln; ⊘9am-9pm Mon-Sat, 10am-7pm Sun) This modern, two-story Dominican version of Barnes & Noble is easily the nicest and largest bookstore in the city, and has an upstairs cafe (no wi-fi, though). Attached to the Supermercado Nacional.

Libreria de Cultura BOOKS
(Map p58; La Atarazana 2; ⊘9am-5pm Mon-Fri) An intellectual's collection of poetry, nonfic-tion and fiction, all in Spanish.

Librería Pichardo BOOKS
(Map p58; cnr José Reyes & El Conde; ⊘8am-6pm Mon-Fri) This store is squeezed into a cave-like space below a parking garage. Bargain for good prices on early and antique Span-ish-language books, mostly on colonial history and Latin American literature and poetry, plus some curios.

ℹ Information

DANGERS & ANNOYANCES
Pick-pocketing, especially on buses or in clubs, is the main concern.

➧ Be alert to the people around you and be careful with your wallet or purse (or use the safety deposit box back at the hotel).

➧ Never take out a phone on the street – thieves are known to run up and snatch them.

➧ The Zona Colonial is generally very safe to walk around, day or night. The Malecón is con-siderably less safe: be extra cautious if you've been drinking or you're leaving a club or casino especially late. Gazcue is a mellow residential area, but street lights are few.

➧ If you're unsure, play it safe and take a taxi.

EMERGENCY
For general police, ambulance and fire dial ☑ 911.

Cestur (☑ 809-222-2026; www.cestur.gob.do; cnr Jose Reyes & El Conde; ⊘8am-5pm) The Tourist Police can handle most situations;

Policia Nacional (☑ 809-682-2151)

INTERNET ACCESS
Internet cafes are scarce, whereas wi-fi is common at cafes and restaurants.

Cyberworld (☑ 809-606-3831; Av Dr Delgado 102, Gazcue; per hr RD$30; ⊘8am-6pm)

Internet Express Ciber Cafe (☑ 809-689-9264; El Conde; per 30 min RD$20; ⊘8am-9pm Mon-Fri, from 9am Sat & Sun) Inside small plaza on Calle El Conde

MEDICAL SERVICES
Centro de Obsetetricía y Ginecología
(☑ 809-221-7100; cnr Av Independencia & José Joaquín Pérez; ⊘24hr) Equipped to handle all emergencies.

Clínica Abreu (☑ 809-688-4411; http://clinicaabreu.com.do; Arzobispo Portes 853; ⊘24hr) Widely regarded as the best hospital in the city.

Farmacia San Judas (☑ 809-685-8165; cnr Av Independencia & Pichardo; ⊘24hr) Pharmacy that offers free delivery.

Farmax (☑809-333-4444; cnr Av Independencia & Dr Delgado; ☺24hr) Pharmacy that offers free delivery.

Hospital Padre Billini (☑809-333-5656; www.hdpb.gob.do; cnr Santomé 39 & Arzobispo Nouel; ☺24hr) The closest public hospital to the Zona Colonial; service is free but expect long waits.

MONEY

There are several major banks (Banco de Reserves, Banco Popular, Banco Leon, Banco Progreso and Scotiabank) with ATMs in the Zona Colonial. Gazcue also has a number of banks and others are scattered throughout the city, especially around major thoroughfares like Av 27 de Febrero and Av Abraham Lincoln. Large hotels, particularly those on the Malecón, all have at least one ATM.

POST

Both **Caribe** (p88) and **Metro** (p88) bus companies have package-delivery services based in their respective terminals; these are the best options for mailing anything within the country.

Federal Express (Map p78; ☑809-565-3636; www.fedex.com; cnr Av de los Próceres & Erick Leonard Ekman)

Post Office (Map p58; Isabel la Católica; ☺8am-5pm Mon-Fri, 9am-noon Sat)

TOURIST INFORMATION

Colonial Zone (www.colonialzone-dr.com) A detailed site with information and reviews on everything – historical sites, hotels, restaurants, bars – as well as discussions on Dominican history, superstitions and more.

Tourist Office (Map p58; ☑809-686-3858; Isabel la Católica 103; ☺9am-7pm Mon-Sat) Located beside Parque Colón, this office has a handful of brochures and maps for Santo Domingo and elsewhere in the country, as well as a half-dozen ones with a variety of Zona Colonial walking tours. Some English and French spoken.

TRAVEL AGENCIES

Colonial Tour & Travel (☑809-688-5285; www.colonialtours.com.do; Arzobispo Meriño 209) This long-running professional outfit is good for booking flights, hotel rooms, and any and all excursions from mountain biking to rafting to whale-watching. English, Italian and French spoken.

Explora Eco Tours (☑809-567-1852; www.exploraecotour.com; Gustavo A Mejia Ricart 43, Naco) Specializes in organizing customized tours, from a single day to a week, of national parks, nature preserves and rural communities. Website announces regularly scheduled trips open to general public.

Giada Tours & Travel (☑809-682-4525; www.giadatours.com; Hostal Duque de Wellington, Av Independencia 304) Friendly professional outfit arranges domestic and international plane tickets, and also conducts area tours.

Tody Tours (p72) Former Peace Corps volunteer who specializes in tropical birding tours all over the country.

❶ Getting There & Away

AIR

Santo Domingo has two airports: the main one, Aeropuerto Internacional Las Américas (p302), is 22km east of the city.

Most international flights use Las Américas. Direct connections include Antigua, Atlanta, Caracas, Havana, Miami, Newark, New York (JFK), Orlando, Pointpitre (Guadeloupe), Panama, San Juan (Puerto Rico) and St Maarten. The 3rd-floor food court and the one past arrivals are better bets than the limited, overpriced options beyond security by the gates. There are several ATMs in the arrivals area. Watch your bags. Cigar shops, cafes, pharmacy and gift shops are in the departures terminal.

The smaller Aeropuerto Internacional La Isabela Dr Joaquin Balaguer (p302), around 20km north of the Zona Colonial, handles mostly domestic carriers and air-taxi companies.

AeroDomca (www.aerodomca.com), Air Century (www.aircentury.com), Dominican Shuttles (☑809-931-4073; www.dominicanshuttles.com) and Aerolineas MAS (www.aerolineasmas.com) connect Santo Domingo, primarily Aeropuerto La Isabela, to Punta Cana, Samaná, Santiago and La Romana. Air Century also flies to San Juan in Puerto Rico and Port-au-Prince in Haiti, and Aerolineas MAS and Dominican Shuttles fly to Port-au-Prince in Haiti and to Aruba.

BOAT

The DR's only international ferry service, *Caribbean Fantasy*, run by America Cruise Ferries (p303) connects Santo Domingo with San Juan, Puerto Rico. The ticket office and boarding area are in the **Puerto Don Diego** (Map p58; Av del Puerto, Zona Colonial), opposite Fortaleza Ozama. The ferry departs Santo Domingo at 7pm on Sunday, Tuesday and Thursday, before returning from San Juan at 7pm Monday, Wednesday and Friday. The trip from Santo Domingo takes 12 hours (eight hours in the other direction; difference is because of prevailing currents) and costs around US$200 round-trip.

The other major terminal that handles cruise ships is the **Puerto Sans Souci** (www.sansouci.com.do/en/port/sansouci-port-of-santo-domingo) on the eastern bank of the Río Ozama, directly across from the Zona Colonial.

BUS

First-Class Buses

The country's two main bus companies – **Caribe Tours** (Map p64; ☑ 809-221-4422; www.caribe-tours.com.do; cnr Avs 27 de Febrero & Leopoldo Navarro) and **Metro** (Map p78; ☑ 809-544-4580; www.metroserviciosturisticos.com; Francisco Prats Ramírez) – have individual depots west of the Zona Colonial. Caribe Tours has the most departures, and covers more of the smaller towns than Metro does. In any case, all but a few destinations are less than four hours from Santo Domingo. Caribe Tours has a much larger terminal with a gift shop, though both have ATMs and a limited food selection.

It's a good idea to call ahead to confirm the schedule and always arrive at least 30 minutes before the stated departure time. Both bus lines publish brochures (available at all terminals) with up-to-date schedules and fares, plus the address and telephone number of their terminals throughout the country.

Expreso Bávaro Punta Cana (Map p64; ☑ Santo Domingo 809-682-9670; Juan Sánchez Ramirez 31) has a direct service between the Gazcue neighborhood (just off Av Máximo Gómez) in the capital and Bávaro. Departure times in both directions are 7am, 9am, 11am, 1pm, 3pm and 4pm (RD$400, three hours). Drivers are flexible and let passengers off at other stops in the city.

Another option is **APTRPA** (Map p58; ☑ 809-686-0637; www.aptpra.com.do; Ravelo), located amid the chaos of Parque Enriquillo, which services Higuey (RD$250), Bávaro and Punta Cana; there are six daily departures (on the hour) from 7am to 4pm for the latter two (RD$400).

Second-Class Buses

Four informal depots surround the smelly, exhaust-fume-filled Parque Enriquillo on the northern edge of the Zona Colonial. There are sections of the parque where you can catch a Bus to Bani, Higuey, Juan Dolio, San Cristóbal and San Pedro de Marcorís. Most buses make numerous stops en route. Because the buses tend to be small, there can be a scrum for seats. Since Metro and Caribe service the major destinations, especially those over several hours away, these should be avoided in the interest of comfort and sanity. *Caliente*, literally 'hot' buses, refer to those generally without air-con; *expreso* buses stop less often.

Buses to Haiti

Capital Coach Line (p304) and Caribe Tours (p88) offer daily services in comfortable, air-con buses to Port-au-Prince (US$40, six to eight hours). Capital Coach Line has one 8am departure daily that stops in Tabarre and ends in Pétionville, a neighborhood of Port-au-Prince, and another at 10am that goes only to Tabarre. Caribe Tours has daily departures at 9am and 11am to Pétionville; tickets are sold in a separate office marked Atlantic Travel Agency, at the entrance to the downtown terminal. If possible, make a reservation at least two days in advance.

CAR

Numerous international and domestic car-rental companies have more than one office in Santo Domingo proper and at Las Américas International Airport, including **Avis** (☑ 809-535-7191; Av George Washington 517; ⊗ 7am-6pm), **Dollar** (☑ 809-479-9806; Av Independencia 366; ⊗ 7am-6pm), **Europcar** (☑ 809-688-2121; Av Independencia 354; ⊗ 7am-6pm) and **Hertz** (☑ 809-221-5333; Av José Ma Heredia 1; ⊗ 7am-6pm).

❶ Getting Around

TO/FROM THE AIRPORT

A taxi into the city costs US$40, with little room for negotiation. An Uber to the Zona Colonial costs around US$30. The trip is a half-hour (26km). If other travelers arrive when you do, try sharing a ride. If flexible, carrying a light pack and prioritizing cost over comfort, you can walk around 100m to the right of baggage claim and grab a *motoconcho* (motorcycle taxi; RD$100) to take you to a *gua-gua* (minivan) stop on the highway.

Some taxis may be willing to take you from the city to the airport for less. Or grab any eastbound *gua-gua* from the city and get off at the airport turnoff (it's a regular stop on these routes); a pack of *motoconchos* will be waiting to ferry you the remaining kilometer or two.

The taxi fare from La Isabela is about US$15. There's no permanent taxi stand there, but at least one or two taxis meet every flight.

CAR

Driving in Santo Domingo can challenge the nerves and test the skills of even the most battle-hardened driver. Heavy traffic, aggressive drivers, especially taxis and buses, and little attention to, or enforcement of, rules means it's a free-for-all. Many of the city's major avenues are gridlocked during rush hour and you're better off walking.

Finding parking is not usually a problem, though if you are leaving your car overnight, ask around for a parking lot. Many midrange and top-end hotels have parking with 24-hour guards. In any case, be sure not to leave any valuables inside your car.

BUSES FROM SANTO DOMINGO
First-Class

DESTINATION	FARE (RD$)	DURATION (HR)	DISTANCE (KM)	FREQUENCY
Ázua	180	1¼	120	8 per day
Barahona	260	3½	200	4 per day
Dajabón	340	5	305	6 per day
Jarabacoa	270	3	155	4 per day
La Vega	200	1½	125	every 30min 6am-8pm
Las Matas de Santa Cruz	340	2½	250	4 per day
Monte Cristi	340	4	270	6 per day
Nagua	340	3½	180	11 per day
Puerto Plata	310	4	215	hourly 6am-7pm
Río San Juan	320	4½	215	8 per day
Samaná	310	2½	245	4 per day
San Francisco de Macorís	250	2½	135	every 30-60min 7am-7pm
San Juan de la Maguana	260	2½	163	4 per day
Sánchez	310	4	211	8 per day
Santiago	270	2½	155	hourly 6am-8pm
Sosúa	320	5	240	hourly 6am-7pm

Second-Class

DESTINATION	FARE (RD$)	DURATION (HR)	FREQUENCY
Baní	100	1½	every 15min 5am-9:30pm
Boca Chica	50	½	every 15min 6am-8pm
Higüey	275	2½	every 20min 5:30am-8pm
Juan Dolio	70	1	every 30min 5am-9pm
La Romana	160	1½	every 20min 5am-9:15pm
Las Galeras	350	3	3 per day
Las Terrenas	350	2½	5 per day
Paraíso	350	4	2 per day
Pedernales	400	6	2 per day
San Cristóbal	55	1	every 15-30min 5am to 10pm
San Pedro de Macorís	120	1	every 30min 5am-9:30pm
Santiago	200	2½	take any Sosúa bus

SANTO DOMINGO– SAMANÁ HWY

Considering its importance, it's strange that the turnoff to the two-lane, 102km Santo Domingo–Samaná Hwy (aka Juan Pablo II or DR-7; toll RD$412) is difficult to spot. To find it coming from Santo Domingo, drive east on the coastal road and past the toll booth for the airport; make a U-turn and continue slowly in the far right lane until you spot the small sign for Samaná.

PUBLIC TRANSPORTATION

Bus

The cost of a bus ride from one end of the city to the other is around RD$25 (6:30am to 9:30pm). Most stops are marked with a sign and the word *parada* (stop). The routes tend to follow major thoroughfares – in the Zona Colonial, Parque Independencia is where Av Bolivar (the main westbound avenue) begins and Av Independencia (the main eastbound avenue) ends. If you're trying to get across town, just look at a map and note the major intersections along the way and plan your transfers accordingly.

Metro

Caribbean islands and underground metros usually don't appear to go together, but in January 2009 Santo Domingo joined San Juan, Puerto Rico, as the second city in the region to have a commuter train system. Line 1 from La Feria (Centro de los Héroes) near the Malecón to the far northern suburb of Villa Mella is a 14.5km route with 16 stations running primarily north–south above and below ground along Av Máximo Gómez. In April 2013, Line 2, which runs east–west for 10.3km (entirely underground) along Av John F Kennedy, Expreso V Centenario and Av Padre Castellanos began operating. The master plan calls for six lines.

It's worth a trip for travelers to get a sense of Santo Domingo's size and sprawl, and on Line 1 for the rather stunning views over the rooftops, and scattered palm trees and mountains in the distance. The entrances, stations and subway cars are modern and clean, certainly a world away from New York City subways. The fact that stations are named after well-known Dominicans (and foreigners like John F Kennedy and Abraham Lincoln) rather than streets may be inconvenient, but it may also lead some to brush up on their history.

Each ride costs RD$20 or a 24-hour pass costs RD$80; however, it's best to purchase a card at one of the ticket booths for RD$60, which can then be refilled when needed. Place the card on top of the turnstile to enter the station (6:30am to 10:30pm).

Públicos

Even more numerous than buses are the *públicos* – mostly beaten-up minivans and private cars that follow the same main routes but stop wherever someone flags them down. They are supposed to have *público* on their license plates, but drivers will beep and wave at you long before you can make out the writing. Any sort of hand waving will get the driver to stop, though the preferred gesture is to hold out your arm and point down at the curb in front of you. The fare is RD$25 – pay when you get in. Be prepared for a tight squeeze.

Taxi

Taxis in Santo Domingo don't have meters, so you should always agree on the price before climbing in. The standard fare is around RD$250 from one side of the city to another; rates tend to be higher in the evening. Within the Zona Colonial it should be even cheaper. Taxi drivers don't typically cruise the streets looking for rides; they park at various major points and wait for customers to come to them. In the Zona Colonial, Parque Colón and Parque Duarte are the best spots.

You can also call for a taxi or ask the receptionist at your hotel to do so. Service is usually quick, the fare should be the same, and you don't have to lug your bags anywhere. Many of the top hotels have taxis waiting at the ready outside, but expect to pay significantly more for those. Reputable taxi agencies with 24-hour dispatches include **Apolo Taxi** (☑ 809-537-0000) and **Aero Taxi** (☑ 809-686-1212, 829-613-0713).

Uber

Uber is often cheaper and faster than getting a taxi in Santo Domingo.

Punta Cana & the Southeast

Best Places to Eat

➡ Las Palmas (p107)

➡ Passion by Martín Berasategui (p117)

➡ Ñam Ñam (p116)

➡ Balicana (p117)

➡ Restaurante Playa Blanca (p117)

Best Places to Sleep

➡ Zoetry Agua (p115)

➡ Paraíso Caño Hondo (p122)

➡ Paradisus Punta Cana (p114)

➡ Casa de Campo (p99)

➡ Ki-Ra (p105)

Why Go?

A Caribbean workhorse of sun and sand, the southeast is synonymous with go-big-or-go-home tourism and carries the weight of the Dominican Republic's most dramatic beaches and turquoise seas on its deeply tanned shoulders. Sprawling resort developments, some like city-states unto themselves, line much of the beachfront from Punta Cana to Bávaro, offering families, couples and the young and restless alike a hassle-free Caribbean holiday in some of the most idyllic environs in the region. But there is life beyond Punta Cana. Less-crowded beach towns like Bayahibe and Juan Dolio offer only slightly less dramatic seascapes but sands that go unshared with the masses. Isolated getaways like Playa Limón, beyond the sugar plantations and inland mountains to the north, showcase a different and worthwhile side of the southeast if you can tear yourself away from the buffets long enough to take the rewarding journeys required to make their acquaintance.

When to Go

➡ If you can hold off just past the winter holidays, January and February offer the same sun and sand as Christmas and New Year's Eve – but a whole lot less people.

➡ If you're looking for a fiesta, join North American spring breakers descending upon Punta Cana in March. If you're not on spring break, this is probably a bad time for that leisurely family vacation.

➡ For those pinching pesos, October bridges the gap between hurricane season and the preholiday onslaught. ¡Salud!

Punta Cana & the Southeast Highlights

1 **Punta Cana** (p110)
Throwing caution to the wind on an all-inclusive binge of pristine beaches and bountiful buffets.

2 **Parque Nacional Los Haitises** (p121) Ogling

mangrove-infested forests on a tranquil kayak excursion.

3 **Parque Nacional Cotubanamá** (p102) Dunking into crystal-clear waters on a snorkeling or diving trip.

4 **Montaña Redonda** (p120)
Gawking at the cinematic 360-degree views on this jaw-dropping hilltop.

5 **Cueva de las Maravillas** (p99) Plunging into a fascinating illuminated

ATLANTIC OCEAN

Reserva Científica
Lagunas Redonda
y Limón
*Laguna
Redonda*
Punta Gorda
**Montaña
Redonda** (4) (7) **Playa Limón**
La Mina
de Miches El Cedro • Las Lisas
• Sabana de Nisibón
Los Tosones • **Playa del Muerto**
• El Eslabón
Oriental (DR-4) **Playa Uvero Alto**
Lagunas **Playa del Macao**
de Nisibón • El Macao
El Seibo Cañada
Honda (DR-5) **Playa El Cortecito**
El Pintado Bonao • El Cortecito • **Playa Bávaro**
Otra Banda • • Bávaro
Batey Sabana • La Enea Chava de **Playa Cabeza de Toro**
de Chabón Bávaro **Playa Cabo Engaño**
El Guanito Veron •
Guayamate • • **Higüey** *Aeropuerto
Internacional* (1) **Punta Cana**
Guerrero • Magdelena *Punta Cana* **Playa Punta Cana**
La Altagracia
La Romana
(101) Juanillo • **Playa
Juanillo**
**La
Romana** (4) • San Rafael del Yuma
Altos de Chavón
Playa Minitas • Boca de Chavón Boca de Yuma
Bayahibe **Dominicus
Americanus** **Playa Blanca**
Cueva del Puente (9) *Bahía
de Yuma*
Playa Dominicus (3) Cabo
Guaraguao • **Parque
Nacional
Cotubanamá** • Martel San Rafael
El Peñon • • Granchorra
Paseo del Punta
Catuano Algibe
Punta Gorda • Isla Catalinita
Shark Point
Punta Roca
Mano Juan • Isla Saona
Punta Cana

underworld at this massive
underground museum.

(6) Juan Dolio (p94) Hiding
out for a few days on the best
beach near Santo Domingo.

History

Before sugar, it was cattle ranching and the cutting and exporting of hardwoods that drove the region's economy. But Cuban planters, fleeing war in their country, began to arrive in the southeast in the 1870s and established sugar mills with the Dominican government's assistance (this migration also explains baseball's popularity and importance in the region). Rail lines were built and La Romana and San Pedro de Macorís, formerly sleepy backwaters, began to prosper as busy ports almost immediately when world sugar prices soared. Hundreds of families from the interior migrated to the area in search of jobs. In 1920, after peasants were dispossessed of their land during the US occupation, many fought a guerrilla war against the marines in the area around Hato Mayor and El Seibo. Until the 1960s, the economy in the southeast was still strictly driven by sugar, despite fluctuations in the world market and agriculture in general. However, when the US company Gulf & Western Industries bought La Romana's sugar mill, invested heavily in the cattle and cement industries and, perhaps most importantly, built the Casa de Campo resort, tourism became the financial engine of the southeast, and remains so today.

ℹ️ Getting There & Away

The majority of international visitors to this region fly directly to the airport in Punta Cana and are then whisked away in private vehicles to their respective resorts. Otherwise, it's anywhere from a two- to three-hour drive, depending on your destination, from Aeropuerto Internacional Las Américas in Santo Domingo. La Romana has an airport as well, though. Meridiana, Neos Air, Blu-express and JetBlue fly in year-round, while American, Air Canada, Air Transat, Blue Panorama, Condor, Eurowings, Sunwing and Westjet offer seasonal flights.

Traffic between the resort centers can be surprisingly heavy and it's difficult to navigate much of the road system, which at the time of writing was being revamped and expanded. The distances aren't great, and the newly finished highway along the coast north of Bávaro all the way to Sabana de la Mar has greatly sped up transit times in the region.

Juan Dolio

POP 2488

Juan Dolio was once tipped as the Caribbean's next hot spot, and real estate speculators and investors flocked here when development began in earnest in the late 1980s, but these days you'll see more 'For Sale' signs and resorts left for dead than smiles and sunshine. Of course, the news isn't all bad: Juan Dolio is one of the few beach towns in the area that cater somewhat to independent budget travelers, and the laid-back feel around town makes losing a few days here far from difficult. Also, new investment such as the excellent Emotions by Hodelpha resort is doing its part to get Juan Dolio off life support.

◉ Sights & Activities

Los Delfines Water & Entertainment Park AMUSEMENT PARK
(☑ 809-476-0477; www.losdelfinespark.com; Autovia Del Este Km 15; adult/child RD$1300/1000; ⊙ 10am-6pm Wed-Sun; 🚼) This new water park between Juan Dolio and Boca Chica claims to be the Caribbean's biggest. With its 17 water slides and nine pools, it's indeed easy to get lost in here. If you're traveling with kiddos, this might just hit the spot.

Erika Cigua Tours ADVENTURE, CULTURAL
(☑ 829-863-8562; www.facebook.com/Erikaciguatours; Playa Real; ⊙ 10am-9:30pm Mon-Fri) This small beachside travel agency is located just west of Emotions by Hodelpha in the parking lot behind El Playero Gift Shop. It organizes day trips to Santo Domingo (per person US$40), Isla Saona (per person US$55), Isla Catalina (per person US$55) and Parque Nacional Los Haitises (per person US$65), as well as 4WD safaris to sugarcane plantations and waterfalls (per person US$55).

🛌 Sleeping

The intersection of Entrada a los Conucos and Carretera Local is the main area in town, with a number of small guesthouses, restaurants, bars, shops and services clustered nearby. Most of the proper hotels, including all of the resorts, are east of here, beyond walking distance if you're carrying baggage.

★ Hotel Fior di Loto GUESTHOUSE $
(☑ 809-526-1146; www.fiordilotohotels.com; Carretera Vieja; dm/s/d/tr from US$5/15/25/40; 🅿️ 🛜) This idiosyncratic place about 500m west of Juan Dolio's main intersection is for the traveler looking to mellow out in a backpacker-style hotel. That's not to say the rooms aren't comfortable: this little ashram in the Caribbean is worn

with character and has clean, tiled floors, high-power fans, tepid water and international cable TV. Rooms vary greatly, so take a look before committing.

There's meditation, yoga classes and massages (average at best, but relaxing for the price) and some proceeds from the hotel go to supporting a girl's foundation in India, where the good-hearted Italian owner, Mara, spends half the year.

Habitaciones Don Pedro
GUESTHOUSE $

(☏809-526-2147; juandolioarq@gmail.com; Carretera Local; r with fan/air-con RD$1000/1200; P ❂ ☎) This well-located and simple guesthouse is run by the extraordinarily friendly Antonio (Luís), who can usually be found across the street at the family's strategically placed beach bar (with good Dominican food from RD$100). The 22 rooms here are simple and uninspired, but are directly across the road from the town beach, 200m east of the main town intersection.

Emotions by Hodelpha
RESORT $$$

(☏809-338-9555; www.emotionsbyhodelpa.com; Carretera Local; all-incl s/d/tr from US$167/288/428; P ❂ @ ☲) Dominican hoteliers Hodelpha have swept into town and completely flipped a formerly struggling property into an all-inclusive millennial hot spot that's easily Juan Dolio's best. Opened in 2015, Emotions features a craft beer bar (11 on draft, 55 in bottles, including American legends Rogue Ales), a wine and cheese bar, and a gourmet coffeehouse – to name but a few standout amenities.

Add in four pools, a spa, a discotheque, three restaurants (Italian, Dominican, Mexican), a state-of-the-art Precor fitness center and an adults-only pool and leisure area and it all makes for quite an enticing package. Rooms are awash in muted greys and blues against a mostly white motif and are perfectly lovely for the price. If you're going to go all-inclusive, this is how it's done.

✕ Eating

Don't worry if you're staying at an all-inclusive with less than stellar buffet food – Juan Dolio has several decent restaurants, both in town near the main intersection and strung out along Carretera Nueva east of the main resort area.

★ Ristorante El Sueño
ITALIAN $$

(Carretera Local; pizza RD$320-500, pasta RD$300-520; ☺noon-11pm Tue-Sun; ☎) Italian owners and their Azurri cohorts sit around this casual open-air eatery *Godfather*-style, giving it a nod of authenticity it doesn't need – the real-deal pizzas do the job on their own. The lobster fettuccine also stands out, a favorite of local expats, as does the *all'amatriciana*, as does anything *alla criolla*, as does the whole menu.

It's one of this coast's most consistently great spots.

Paladart
STEAK $$

(☏809-526-1855; Calle Principal Primera; mains RD$300-1175, tapas RD$145-725; ☺10am-5pm Tue-Sun; ☎) This Argentine-Spanish grill kills your carnivorous cravings with juicy steaks (sirloin, tenderloin, rib eye), surf and turf, and chicken and jalapeño burgers. Otherwise, it can take you on a trip to Europe with authentic tapas like *manchego* cheese, *tortilla española* and Galician-style octopus. The outdoor patio is one of the town's most atmospheric for a meal and draws a healthy drinking crowd, too.

El Mesón
SPANISH, ITALIAN $$

(Carretera Nueva; mains RD$350-600; ☺11am-11pm Sun-Thu, to midnight Fri & Sat; ☎) If the waft of fresh-off-the-grill whole lobster doesn't suck you in, go for the spot-on paella (for two from RD$770) at this perennially popular Spanish restaurant across from Club Hemingway. You'll also find smoked chorizo, lamb, *morcilla* (blood sausage) and heaps of the usual suspects, all excellently prepared with little regard for your waistline. Don't skip the addictive aioli!

Guilia's Café
INTERNATIONAL, BURGERS $$

(Carretera Nueva; mains RD$200-550; ☺7am-5pm Thu-Tue; ☎) Juan Dolio's interpretation of a sports bar, the Welsh-Israeli Guilia's has 22 years under its apron. It's popular for English, American and Dominican all-day breakfasts, homemade burgers and fresh, English-cut fries, and the house lasagna, among a mishmash of other international treats. The flat-screen TVs are often tuned to the EPL, La Liga and American football. It's popular with foreigners, obviously.

Juan Dolio

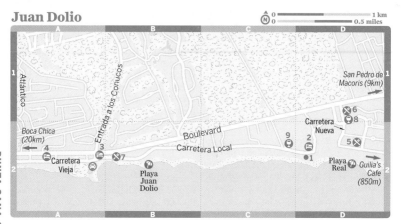

🍷 Drinking & Nightlife

There is no shortage of bars in Juan Dolio, though you'll need to be selective, depending on what you're looking for. On the western side, bars line the Boulevard de Juan Dolio around the main beach and intersection, but many cater to sex tourism. The best bars are on the eastern side of town, around Banco Popular and beyond along the Carretera Nueva.

Aguamarina Lounge COCKTAIL BAR
(☉6pm-3am Thu-Sun; 🛜) This small, outdoor bar, part of a hair salon, sits on a lively corner near Banco Popular and is a fine spot to knock back a couple of rounds of the classic rum cocktail of your choice (mojitos, piña coladas, mai tais; RD$250), mixed by Venezuelan bartenders, without constant propositions. Look for the blatantly sponsorial 'Brugal' signs.

Chocolate Bar BAR
(Plaza Chocolate, Carretera Local; ☉10am-late) Divey outdoor bar catering to all-inclusive escapists near Coral Costa Caribe Resort. There's DJs spinning house through the weekend. It almost never closes.

ℹ️ Information

DANGERS & ANNOYANCES

Cestur (Cuerpo Especializado de Seguridad Turística; ☏809-526-3211; www.cestur. gob.do; Boulevard; ☉24hr) Tourist police for emergencies; next to the National Police building.

Juan Dolio

⊙ Activities, Courses & Tours
1 Erika Cigua Tours................................D2

⊜ Sleeping
2 Emotions by Hodelpha......................D2
3 Habitaciones Don Pedro....................A2
4 Hotel Fior di Loto A2

⊗ Eating
5 El Mesón...D2
6 Paladart..D1
7 Ristorante El Sueño B2

⊜ Drinking & Nightlife
8 Aguamarina Lounge D1
9 Chocolate Bar.....................................C2

MEDICAL SERVICES

Farmacia Carol (www.farmaciacarol.com; Boulevard 56; ☉8am-11pm) A professional, well-stocked pharmacy.
Galmedical Internacional (☏809-526-2044; www.galmedical.net; Villas Del Mar 8; ☉24hr) Serious matters should be seen in San Pedro de Macorís, but otherwise the good doc here speaks English, German, French and Italian. It's off Carretera Nueva just north of Guilia's Café.

MONEY

Banco BHD León and BanReservas ATMs are located at the Total gas station on the boulevard west of Entrada a los Conucos, and are available between 7am and 9:30pm.
Banco Popular (Carretera Nueva; ☉9am-4pm Mon-Fri, to 1pm Sat) Has a 24-hour ATM; located 200m north of Barceló Capella Beach Resort.

Banco BHD León (Carretera Local) ATM in front of Coral Costa Caribe Resort.

ℹ Getting There & Around

Guaguas pass through Juan Dolio all day every day, going westward to Boca Chica (RD$35) and Santo Domingo (RD$70), and east to San Pedro de Macorís (RD$35) and La Romana (RD$100), among other destinations. No buses originate here, so there is no fixed schedule, but they pass roughly every 15 minutes from 6am to 7pm – stand on the boulevard at the corner of Entrada a los Conucos and flag down any one that passes.

Taxis can be found in front of any of the resorts in town and at the **Sitraguza Taxi Service stand** (☑ 809-526-3507). One-way fares for one to four people include those to Aeropuerto Internacional Las Américas (US$50), Santo Domingo (US$60), Bayahibe (US$90), Bávaro (US$140) and points further afield such as Las Galeras (US$260) and Lago Enriquillo (US$350). You can also call for door-to-door service.

La Romana
POP 130,426

This traffic-congested, bustling city is a convenient stop for those traveling between Santo Domingo, 131km to the west, and the beach resorts further east. Surrounded by vast sugar plantations, the in-dustry that bolsters its economy, and with the enormous Casa de Campo resort a few kilometers to the east, La Romana feels slightly more prosperous than neighboring cities. There isn't much beyond Casa de Campo, however, there are some great restaurants for refueling on cuisines and dishes you don't see on every other menu between here and Santo Domingo – almost worth a stop for that reason alone.

◉ Sights & Activities

Altos de Chavón   LANDMARK
(☑ 809-523-3333; US$25; ⊗ 8am-5:45pm) While a trip to a faux-15th-century Italian-Spanish village created by a Paramount movie-set designer won't exactly give you a window into Dominican culture, Altos de Chavón has some redeeming qualities, especially the excellent views of the Río Chavón (a scene from the film *Apocalypse Now* was filmed here). There's a handsome church, a small but well-done pre-Columbian museum and a 5000-seat amphitheater, which attracts big-name performers – Frank Sinatra did the inaugural gig here.

El Obelisco   MONUMENT
(Av Libertad, btwn Calles Márquez & Ducoudrey) Modeled after the George Washington monument in Washington, DC, the Obelisk is a much smaller version in central La Romana, painted on all four sides with

PUNTA CANA & THE SOUTHEAST LA ROMANA

LAYOVER: BOCA CHICA

Boca Chica, just 11km from Aeropuerto Internacional Las Américas, ends up being a good final stop for those wanting to take one last dip in the Caribbean before catching their flight home. Aside from its proximity to the capital and the airport, there's not a lot to recommend as it caters to a weathered crowd and is marred by in-your-face sex tourism.

There are over 25 dive sites in the area; the most recommended site is the shipwreck *Catuan*, a 33m-long troller sunk in 2006. The most recommended dive shop in town is **Caribbean Divers Asobuca** (☑ 809-854-3483; www.caribbeandivers.de; ⊗ 8am-5pm).

Neptuno's Refugio (☑ 809-523-9934; www.refugioneptunos.com; Calle Duarte; s/d from US$55/70, 1-bdrm apt US$75; 🅿 ❋ 🛜 🐾) is your best accommodation bet for comfort and a mainstream traveler atmosphere – a textbook testament to the definition of refuge, with chirping birds, friendly cats, lush common areas and Caribbean views.

Guaguas service Santo Domingo (*caliente/expreso* RD$60/70, 30 minutes, *caliente* every 10 minutes, *expreso* every 15 minutes, from 5:45am to 10pm), departing on the north side of Parque Central and along Av San Rafael.

You can find taxis in Boca Chica at **Taxi Turístico Boca Chica** (☑ 809-523-5325). For Aeropuerto Internacional Las Américas and Santo Domingo, you are much better off in an Uber, however, which costs under RD$300 to the airport from Boca Chica, a saving of nearly US$20 over inflated taxi prices.

La Romana

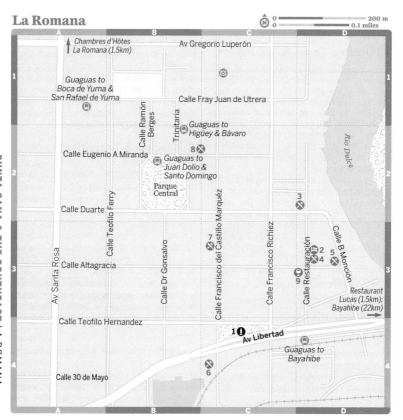

contemporary and historical depictions of Dominican life.

Isla Catalina ISLAND

In the 15th century, pirates including Francis Drake would lurk around Isla Catalina, waiting to pounce on Spanish ships sailing to and from Santo Domingo. Today, this island ringed by fine coral reefs teeming with fish in shallow water is a popular destination for groups from nearby Casa de Campo; the resort has frequent shuttles making the 2km trip, as do large cruise ships.

Golf GOLF

(www.casadecampo.com.do) Within the grounds of the Casa de Campo (p99) are four Pete Dye–designed golf courses, including 'The Teeth of the Dog,' open since 1971, which has seven seaside holes; and 'Dye Fore,' located in Altos de Chacon. Green fees for the former course in high season are US$250 for guests and US$395 for nonguests.

'Links' (high-season green fees guests/nonguests US\$150/175) also comes highly recommended.

You should make reservations as far in advance as possible. Tee times can be reserved by email (golfres@ccampo.com.do).

🛌 Sleeping

With the exception of the world-renowned Casa de Campo, sleeping in La Romana is far from a thrilling experience. The majority of basic hotels in and around the city center are utilitarian at best, but it's not a place anyone would likely spend more than one night in anyway.

Chambres d'Hôtes La Romana   B&B $$
(📱 809-349-4893; catherine.alquier@hotmail.fr; Calle Larimar 28; s/d incl breakfast from US\$30/50; 🛜☒) Upping the charm quotient in La Romana (not difficult), this five-room, French-run B&B sits in the quiet, vaguely Floridian-like residential Las Piedras neighborhood, 1.7km north of Parque Central. Rooms are well-appointed and feature quirky, semi-circular bathrooms due to an architectural quirk. Ogle the sea in the distance from the various patios, or take a dip in the funky, rhomboidal pool.

Hotel River View   HOTEL $$
(📱809-556-1181; hotelriverview@gmail.com; Calle Restauración 17; s/d/tr incl breakfast & dinner RD\$1900/2600/3600; 🅿☀🛜) One of La Romana's few hotels that has both a pleasant enough location and the right price, this multistory place is perched a block from the Río Dulce and is a solid choice for independent travelers. Don't expect a lot of smiles or faultless rooms, but you can have a coffee in the tiny patio area overlooking... the parking lot.

★ Casa de Campo   RESORT $$$
(📱800-877-3643; www.casadecampo.com.do; Av Libertad; r from US\$275, villas from US\$1530, all-incl supplement per adult/child US\$275/152; 🅿☀@🛜☒) Known as much for its celebrity guests (LeBron James, Beyoncé, Jay Z, Michael Jordan) and villa owners (Marc Anthony, Sammy Sosa, Pitbull) as for its facilities, Casa de Campo is an all-inclusive, super-sized place that remains discerning despite its enormity. The 185 or so hotel rooms have masculine hardwood furnishings, wonderful local art, 42-inch LCD TVs, Nespresso machines and a golf cart for all.

The enormous, 28-sq-km complex is home to 16 restaurants, an equestrian center, polo fields, an exclusive beach, a shooting range – the list goes on and on. It truly resembles a city-state, albeit one with G8 summit security and a disproportionate amount of 'beautiful people' per capita.

Catering mostly to celebrities, golf enthusiasts and families, Casa de Campo feels less like a resort than a tropical Beverly Hills, mainly due to the independent design of the 2000 or so extravagant luxury villas (of which 60 or so are in the rental pool, complete with personal chefs, butlers, maids and pools). All-inclusive rates include unlimited horseback riding, tennis, one round of skeet/trap shooting and nonmotorized water sports at the beach. Other available activities include kayak trips down the Río Chavón (per person US\$30) and buggy tours through sugarcane country (per person US\$87). Four Pete Dye–designed golf courses and Altos de Chavón, a Tuscan-style 'village', and a Mediterranean-style piazza overlooking a massive marina round out the resort's offerings.

Day passes (adult/child US\$75/45) are available for nonguests and can be purchased at the information office on the right before the entrance gates. Whether this is good value is debatable: you are allowed to enter the property, access the beach (towel and chaise lounge included) and have a meal and one drink (soda, beer or water). A property tour pass (US\$25)

WORTH A TRIP

CUEVA DE LAS MARAVILLAS

This enormous **cavern complex** (Cave of Wonders; adult/child RD\$300/100; ⊘9am-5:15pm Tue-Sun) is an on the highway some 20km west between San Pedro de Macorís and La Romana. Extending for 840m between Río Cumayasa and Río Soco, this massive underground museum is lighted and well marked. More than 500 pictographs and petroglyphs can be seen on the 45-minute guided tour (some English is spoken); the tour is included in the entrance fee so there's little reason to wander around on your own.

includes a visit to Altos de Chavón and the marina – no lunch or beach access.

Most guests arrive at the resort by air, either at the private landing strip or the airport that serves La Romana, and are then driven onto the property. If arriving by private vehicle, follow Av Libertad east across the river and stay in the right lane for 4km until you see the entrance on your right.

All of the resort's restaurants – the best in the region – are open to nonguests. You must email the concierge (a.concierge@ ccampo.com.do) for a reservation and be prepared to show identification at the security gate.

✖ Eating

Dining is the city's saving grace. Craving a bit of hummus and baba ghanoush? Maybe be some authentic Chinese? Handmade Italian tagliatelle rather than store-bought dry spaghetti? La Romana delivers, especially when it comes to cuisines and dishes that aren't exactly common in midsize Dominican towns.

Dom Ham   BURGERS $
(cnr Calle Altagracia & Benito Monción; burgers RD$175-300; ⊙5pm-midnight; 🛜) This festive, thatch-roofed open-air bar and grill is home to Carlos Pichardo, who got his start flipping burgers outside a baseball stadium. These days, though not made to order, his American-style Angus beef burgers have been called up to the big leagues, where his brick-and-mortar location is chock-full of international flags and nearly a beer to match each one.

DON'T MISS

PLAY BALL!

Estadio Tetelo Vargas on the north side of Hwy 3 in San Pedro de Macorís is home to the baseball team called the **Estrellas Orientales** (the Eastern Stars, (www.estrellasorientales.com.do).

During big games you'll get cheerleaders and marching bands through the stands – quite a contrast for those used to Major League Baseball in the USA!

Cinco   CAFE $
(Calle Restauración 15; 1/2/3 scoops RD$100/200/300; ⊙11am-9pm Mon-Wed, 10am-10pm Thu-Sun; 🛜) Cinco does Illy espresso, delicious beat-the-heat gelato, and creative panini (RD$210 to RD$495).

Trigo de Oro   CAFE, BAKERY $
(www.trigodeorodr.com; Calle Eugenio A Miranda 9; mains RD$160-300; ⊙7am-10pm Mon-Sat, to 1pm Sun; 🛜) Though it (oddly) had most of its shady courtyard renovated away in favor of a more modern look, this French bakery and cafe remains a welcome respite from *motoconcho* fumes. Located inside a historic mansion, the bakery side has freshly made pastries such as mini lime tarts and cheesecake, while the cafe does great sandwiches served on crusty baguettes and other light bites.

★ Restaurant Lucas   ITALIAN $$
(🖉809-550-3401; Plaza Buena Vista, Av Los Robles; mains RD$250-700, pizza RD$250-750; ⊙6-11pm Mon-Sat, 12:30-11pm Sun, closed Mon Apr-Dec; 🛜) This local's secret is buried inside a residential complex less than 2km from *centro*. Delectable fresh pastas (in-house-made ravioli, tagliatelle and gnocchi) are served on an atmospheric patio under a giant fig tree.

The jovial owner, from Liguria, greets everyone with his Italian enthusiasm. Try the black tagliatelle with lobster and tomato sauce (RD$700). Take note of the phone number, as you might have difficulty finding it, though it is better signed than it once was.

Chinois by Susana   CHINESE $$
(🖉809-550-5977; cnr Calle Duarte & Restauración; mains RD$300-675; ⊙11am-11pm; 🛜) Don't let the street noise steer you away from the atmospheric, Chinese-lantern-lit front courtyard of this high-quality Chinese hot spot serving up authentic, rarely seen dishes such as Peking Duck, spicy Malaysian chicken and seafood-stuffed potato nest, among other classics. Vegetarians could do worse than the tasty veg chow mein as well.

Shish Kabab Restaurant   MEDITERRANEAN $$
(Calle Francisco del Castillo Marquéz 32; mains RD$300-850; ⊙10am-10pm Tue-Sun; 🛜) The wall beside the bar is covered with photos of famous guests, attesting to the popularity of

this local *institución*. The Palestinian owners dish out limited Middle Eastern dishes like hummus, baba ghanoush and delectable shish kebabs (one should hope), but the menu also includes everything else, including perhaps the DR's coldest Presidente beer, served nearly frozen.

Punto Italia MARKET, ITALIAN $$
(Av Libertad; ☺9am-11pm Mon-Sat; ☝) Imports gourmet Italian and European brands; stocks fresh meat and cheeses and serves quick-fire pastas.

🍷 Drinking & Nightlife

Outside of the trendy bars and restaurants at Casa de Campo, La Romana doesn't have an enticing nightlife. There are plenty of rowdy discotheques and *colmados* (corner shops) favored by Dominicans, but it's really a workhorse of a town with simple options. Dom Ham (p100) has a decent selection of foreign beers, while El Corcho suits just fine for a *trago* (drink).

El Corcho COCKTAIL BAR
(cnr Calle Altagracia & Restauración; ☺3:30pm-midnight Mon, Wed & Thu, to 2am Fri & Sat; ☝) Notably trendy for La Romana, this small bar inside an upper-scale corner shopping plaza has cocktails, a decent selection of wine, a few rums and *bachata* aplenty. Best of all, there's a loungy patio in front to sip away an evening.

ⓘ Information

DANGERS & ANNOYANCES

Cestur (Cuerpo Especializado de Seguridad Turística; ☏809-813-9234; www.cestur.gob. do; Calle Francisco del Castillo Marquéz, near Av Gregorio Luperón; ☺24hr) The tourist police are located next to the post office.

MONEY

Banco BHD León (www.bhdleon.com.do; Calle Duarte) ATM located at the southeast corner of Parque Central.

BanReservas (www.banreservas.com; Calle Diego Avila) Has an ATM, also on Parque Central.

POST

InPosDom (www.inposdom.gob.do; Calle Francisco del Castillo Marquéz, near Av Gregorio Luperón; ☺8am-4pm Mon-Fri) Next to the tourist police.

MEDICAL SERVICES

Clínica Canela (☏809-556-3135; www. clinicacanela.com; Av Libertad 44) A private clinic with a 24-hour pharmacy and emergency room.

Farmacia Dinorah (Calle Duarte; ☺8am-9pm Mon-Sat, to 12:30pm Sun) Free delivery available.

ⓘ Getting There & Away

AIR

La Romana International Airport Casa de Campo (p302) is 8km east of town. There are a few regularly scheduled flights, but most of the traffic here is chartered. Carriers with year-round flights include Meridiana, Neos Air, Blu-express (from Italy) and JetBlue (from New York City). Air Canada, Air Transat, American Airlines, Blue Panorama, Condor, Eurowings, Sunwing and Westjet fly seasonally, among other charters.

BUS

Guaguas to Bayahibe (RD$60, 20 minutes, every 20 minutes, 6am to 7pm) depart from a stop on Av Libertad at Restauración.

Guaguas for other destinations leave from stops near or on Parque Central:

Bávaro (☏809-550-0880), RD$225, 1½ hours, 5:40am, 8:20am, 10:50am, 1:20pm, 3:50pm, 6:20pm)

Boca de Yuma (RD$100, 1¼ hours, every 30 minutes, 7am to 7pm)

Higüey (☏809-550-0880, *caliente/expreso* RD$100/110, 1¼ hours, every 30 minutes, 5:30am to 10pm)

Juan Dolio (RD$70, one hour, every 20 minutes, 5am to 9:35pm)

San Rafael del Yuma (RD$90, 45 minutes, every 30 minutes, 7am to 7pm)

Santo Domingo (RD$160, 1½ hours, every 20 minutes, 5am to 9:35pm)

ⓘ Getting Around

Motoconchos and taxis are typically found near the southeast corner of Parque Central. *Motoconcho* rides within the city normally cost RD$50. To rent a car, try **Avis** (☏809-550-0600; www.avis.com.do; cnr Calles Francisco del Castillo Márquez & Duarte; ☺8am-6pm). Taxis within town start from RD$100. Sample long-distance fares include those to La Romana airport (US$15), Altos de Chavón (US$30 return) and Cueva de las Maravillas (US$60 return). You can call **Santa Rosa Taxi** (☏809-556-5313; Calle Duarte) or **Sichotaxi** (☏809-550-2222) for a pick-up, or wait for the latter at a stop across the street from El Obelisco on Av Libertad.

Bayahibe & Dominicus Americanus

POP 2260

Bayahibe, 22km east of La Romana, was originally founded by fishermen from Puerto Rico in the 19th century. Today it's a tranquil beach village caught in a schizophrenic power play. In the morning it's the proverbial tourist gateway, when busloads of tourists from resorts further east hop into boats bound for Isla Saona. Once this morning rush hour is over it turns back into a sleepy village. There's another buzz of activity when the resort tourists return, and then after sunset another transformation. What sets Bayahibe apart is that it manages to maintain its character despite the continued encroachment of big tourism (and the arrival of paved roads, which now canvas the entire village).

A short drive from Bayahibe is Dominicus Americanus, an upscale Potemkin village centered on a terrific public beach with resorts, hotels, several shops and services, and a large Italian presence.

⊙ Sights & Activities

One advantage of staying in Bayahibe is that virtually every water-related activity is right outside your front door, so you avoid the long commute that most travelers make here daily from resorts further east.

Isla Saona   NATURE RESERVE
(RD$100) There's a reason why boatloads of tourists descend upon this island daily. The powdery, white-sand beach doesn't seem real from afar, and a dip in the aquamarine surf is a gentle restorative, like the waters of the most luxurious spa, while palm trees provide a natural awning from the intense sun.

**Parque Nacional
Cotubanamá**   NATURE RESERVE
(RD$100-300) More than simply Isla Saona, which is all that most people see on a group tour, the Parque Nacional Cotubanamá (formerly known as Parque Nacional del Este) includes eight emerged reef terraces, 400 or so caverns, some with pictographs and ceramic remains, and Islas Catalinita and Catalina, in addition to Saona. Designated a national park in 1975, it stretches over 310 sq km of territory, the majority of which is semihumid forest.

Bayahibe

Padre Nuestro CAVE
(Parque Nacional Cotumbanamá; snorkeling/
diving RD$250/300; ⊘8am-5pm) Located
deep inside Parque Nacional Cotubanamá
(p102), Padre Nuestro is a weaving 290m
tunnel flooded with freshwater that can
be dived by those with cave certification
and swum by the rest of us. It's not for the
faint of heart, but it's pretty spectacular for
those who take it on. Entry fees must be
paid at the park office in Bayahibe.

Cueva del Puente CAVE
(RD$100) Parque Nacional Cotubanamá has
more than 400 caves, many of which contain Taíno pictographs (cave paintings) and
petroglyphs (rock carvings). Archaeologists
have found several structures and artifacts
in and around the caves, including what
appears to be the remains of a large Taíno
city (perhaps the largest) and the site of a
notorious massacre of indigenous people
by Spanish soldiers. Only one of the caves
that contain Taíno pictographs, Cueva del
Puente, can be easily visited.

Isla Catalinita NATURE RESERVE
This tiny uninhabited island on the eastern edge of Parque Nacional Cotubanamá
is a common stop on snorkeling and diving tours. Arriving on the island's western
(leeward) side, it's about a half-hour hike
to the other side, where a lookout affords
dramatic views of powerful open-ocean
waves crashing on the shore. There is a
coral reef in about 2m of water that makes
for great snorkeling, and a good dive site
called Shark Point, where sharks are in fact
often seen.

Bayahibe SUP WATER SPORTS
(☑809-609-4045; www.bayahibesup.com) Swed-
ish-run outfitter offering one- and two-hour
stand-up-paddle tours to otherwise inac-
cessible beaches around Bayahibe. Tours
run US$30 or US$50 and there are rentals
for experienced paddlers as well (per day
US$40).

Snorkeling & Diving

Bayahibe is arguably the best place in the
country to dive or snorkel, with warm,
clear Caribbean water, healthy reefs and
plenty of fish and other sea life. The diving tends to be 'easier' (and therefore ideal
for beginners) than it is on the DR's north
coast, where the underwater terrain is less

flat, the water cooler and the visibility
somewhat diminished.

There are about 20 open-water dive
sites; some favorites include **Catalina Wall**
and an impressive 85m ship in 18m to 44m
of water, known as **St Georges Wreck** (after Hurricane Georges).

Casa Daniel DIVING
(Map p102; ☑809-833-0050; www.casa-daniel.
com; Calle Principal, Bayahibe; ⊘8am-6pm Mon-
Sat, to 4pm Sun) This German-run operator
offers one-tank dives with/without equipment rental for US$54/47. Packages of six
dives with equipment are US$290, 10-dive
packages are US$445. PADI certification
courses are available. Ask about accommodations packages as well. Day tours to Isla
Saona come with lobster (US$85) or with-
out (US$70). Half-day tours to Isla Catalina
run US$47.

Scubafun DIVING
(Map p102; ☑809-833-0003; www.scubafun.
info; Calle Principal 28, Bayahibe; ⊘8am-6pm) In
operation for over 20 years and located on
the main strip in the middle of town, this
American-run 5-star PADI dive center offers
two-tank dives in nearby reefs (with/without
equipment US$90/80) and day trips to Isla
Catalina and Isla Saona (both US$69). Be-
ginner and advanced PADI courses are also
offered.

🏖 Beaches

Playa Dominicus BEACH
(Map p105) The advantage of staying in
Dominicus Americana is being able to
walk to Playa Dominicus, a beautiful
stretch of thick, nearly white sand, with
good water for swimming. It does tend
to get crowded, especially because there's
easy public access via a parking lot at
the far eastern end of the enclave, which
means no cutting through hotels or restaurants for beach access.

Playa Bayahibe BEACH
(Map p102) Much of Playa Bayahibe, the
town beach to the right of the parking lot,
is occupied by dozens of motorboats waiting to ferry tourists to Isla Saona. There's
a relatively small, uninviting and narrow
stretch of sand between the last of these
and the start of the all-inclusive Dreams La
Romana – the beach here is restricted to
guests of the resort.

☞ Tours

Virtually every hotel in Dominicus Americanus offers a wide variety of tours. Most are more expensive than those arranged through one of the two dive shops in Bayahibe. These two major dive shops have multilingual guides and instructors, with Spanish, English, German, French and Italian spoken, and can accommodate groups of both snorkelers and divers.

One of the more enjoyable ways of spending a few hours exploring the coastline is to take a sail on a local's fishing boat. You won't have to ask many people before finding a taker; one particularly nice man who can read the winds like a soothsayer is **Hector Julio Brito** (☎829-285-4368), who charges RD$7000 per person for one to 10 people for a half-day trip. A longer outing, from 9am to 4pm to the *piscina natural* (natural pool), is the same price.

✦ Festivals & Events

Every year on the Saturday of Semana Santa (late March/early April), Bayahibe hosts a *regatta* of handmade fishing boats. The race runs from the town cove to Isla Catalina and back.

🛏 Sleeping

Bayahibe proper has several good budget hotels within walking distance of one another; locals can point you in the direction of a family willing to take on temporary boarders. Otherwise, small hotels, guesthouses and *cabañas* are the general rule.

Dominicus Americanus has several mid-range and top-end options – the advantage here is the short walk to an excellent beach. There's a string of all-inclusive resorts in Dominicus Americanus and along the road between here and Bayahibe.

Villa Baya HOTEL $
(Map p102; ☎809-833-0048; www.hotelvillabaya.com; Calle Tamarindo 1, Bayahibe; r with air-con from US$30, studio with/without air-con US$60/50; P❋🛜) Despite some irritating and unorthodox reservation policies (photocopies of credit cards required and such), the shaded *palapa*, floral-draped fringes and extra-large rooms are Bayahibe's best bang for the buck. The Italian-owned villas all come with patios and stone flooring, while the air-con rooms have kitchens and living-room spaces.

Cabañas Taíno CABAÑAS $
(Map p102; ☎829-924-9409; centralmico@yahoo.com; Calle Principal, Bayahibe; r with air-con US$58, cabaña with/without air-con US$31/22, 1-/2-bdrm apt US$68/100; P❋🛜) A perfectly doable budget choice located in the center of the action in town. Pop your head in before making a decision. It has simple rooms/apartments with basic furnishings, mini-bars, small porches, private bathrooms with hot water and working wi-fi in the rooms – the big advantage here over similarly priced options. There's also unembellished *cabañas* nearby. It's located above the supermarket.

Hotel Eden HOTEL $$
(Map p105; ☎809-833-0856; Av Laguna 10, Dominicus Americanus; r US$75; P❋🛜❄) A good choice for those seeking hotel-style comfort, amenities and service alongside peace and quiet (you can hear birds chirping here). Because it's located on the access road to the resort area, you might confuse the Eden for a hotel somewhere in Arizona or Florida, not necessarily on a Caribbean beach.

Cabaña Elke HOTEL $$
(Map p105; ☎809-833-0024; www.cabanaelke.it; Calle Eladia, Dominicus Americanus; d/q US$50/85; P❋🛜❄) Cabaña Elke is sandwiched between the road and a high fence marking the boundary of the Viva Wyndham Dominicus Beach property. Its rooms, arranged in two long narrow rows, are airy, especially the split-level doubles, and there's a nice pool area with lounge chairs, but unfortunately no view. There's also a cheap Dominican *comedor* and a highly rated Italian restaurant on premises.

Hotel Bayahibe HOTEL $$
(Map p102; ☎809-833-0159; www.hotelbayahibe.net; Bayahibe; s/d/tr incl breakfast US$45/86/111; P❋🛜) The staff are friendly but not particularly service-oriented, although Hotel Bayahibe has the some of best-value rooms in town. This three-story modern building is not hard to notice as it's the biggest around. Large, colorful rooms are very comfortable, with cable TV, balconies and small bathtubs; some even boast good views.

Villa Iguana GUESTHOUSE $$
(Map p102; ☎829-546-0400; www.hotelvillaiguanabayahibe.com; Los Manantiales 2, Bayahibe; d/tr from US$49/54, 1-bdrm apt US$99, all incl

Dominicus Americanus

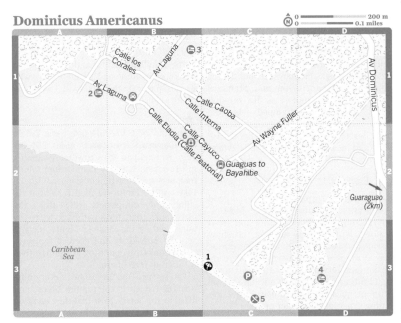

N · 0 — 200 m
0 — 0.1 miles

breakfast; P ❄ ☀) Under new Italian-Dutch ownership, this friendly 10-room flash-packer's hotel offers rooms on the simple but well-kept side (with extended, re-tiled bathrooms), to bigger offerings with mini-bars and flat-screen TVs (that oddly only work with Chromecast). A former penthouse suite has been converted into a bar and a pool for all guests' use and the vibe across the board is friendly.

★ **Ki-Ra** B&B $$$
(☎ 809-757-8661; www.ki-ra.com; Boca Chavón; r incl breakfast US$125; P ☀ ☀) About 6km down a dirt but passable road from the main highway between La Romana and Bayahibe sits this serene, holistic retreat run by UK expats Simon and Kira, the latter of whom is a certified homeopathic doctor. But it's anything but hokey; quite the contrary, the three rooms, housed in cutesy pastel-hued bungalows, make for tranquil escapes for all comers.

There's yoga, spa treatments (running the gamut from mud cleansing and Ayurvedic massage to reflexology and detoxification; medicinal herbs are grown on premises), and mostly vegetarian meals, served on request (from US$12). Guests can stay on the lovely property and sim-

ply hide away in the king- and queen-sized beds, or take on an initial consultation with immediately likable Kira (US$120) and have her plan your wellness getaway. Calm, composed and unique.

Iberostar Hacienda Dominicus RESORT $$$
(Map p105; ☎ 809-688-3600; www.iberostar.com; Playa Dominicus; all-incl s/d from US$174/220; P ❄ @ ☀ ☀) An impeccably maintained resort doused in soothing pastels, the Iberostar Hacienda Dominicus has beautifully landscaped grounds – most of the buildings surround quiet interior

courtyards with beautiful historic Spanish tiles, and there are duck-strewn ponds and tranquility-inducing fountains throughout.

Some big, gaudy art means the whole thing teeters precariously on the fortunate side of Vegas flamboyance, but it wins points for restraint in the end. Standard rooms aren't as grandiose as the common areas – they're even cramped – but the awesome pool (with its Jacuzzi island), huge beach (with a picturesque lighthouse bar) and newly renovated spa is where you'll be spending your time, anyway.

✖ Eating

Bayahibe has a surprising number of good restaurants for a town of its size. Most offer relaxing waterfront seating and fresh seafood, with Italians running the show in most cases. Dominicus Americanus has a number of modern tourist-ready restaurants serving a mix of international standards and fish, though few have views. Without question Las Palmas is the top dining experience in either place.

Mama Mia ITALIAN $
(Map p102; Plaza La Punta, Bayahibe; mains RD$150-300; ⊘12:30-3:30pm & 7:30-10:30pm Mon-Sat) It's very hard to eat this well for these prices in the DR, but this *spaghetteria* specializes in classic pasta recipes such as *all'amatriciana* (tomato sauce, bacon and chili – our fave), carbonara, *all'arrabiata* and *aglio, olio e peperoncino* (garlic, olive oil and chili powder), as well as local adaptations *(lambi,* or conch, in fresh tomato sauce).

It's yet another endlessly charming spot near Playa Bayahibe, overseen by a one-woman show in the kitchen. Dishes are palatably simple – concentrating on flavor nuance rather than huge portions or other gastro bells and whistles – and priced to please.

Comedor Mirabel DOMINICAN $
(Map p102; Calle Nuevo Bayahibe, Bayahibe; meals RD$150-250; ⊘noon-3pm Mon-Sat) Unsigned and off the beaten path, Mirabel serves up heaping plates of Dominican *platos del día* (beef, chicken, fish or pork along with rice, beans and a salad) and *sancocho* (on Friday) on a few picnic tables in front of her blue-walled house. Lunch hours only.

La Bodeguita SUPERMARKET, DELI $
(Map p102; Calle Principal, Bayahibe; ⊘8am-10pm) For those with more discerning taste, this small gourmet shop sells many Italian imports, including a slew of antipasti as well as cheese, charcuterie and wine for those who want to picnic on the sands with something besides conch.

★ Da Elio ITALIAN $$
(Map p105; ☑809-672-7614; Calle Eladia, Cabaña Elke, Dominicus Americanus; mains RD$350-900; ⊘noon-11pm; 🐾) Crowds are coming in droves since a new Lombardian family took over this cozy Italian staple at Cabaña Elke (p104). From the food (excellent Sicilian *caponata*, perfect grilled fish – the pizza looks great, too!) to the service to the house red by the glass (a Montepulciano actually served at the correct temperature), things are operating at comparatively different levels here.

Our server asked three times if everything was OK (which is three more times than usual at this level). Now that they mention it, things were fantastic! Reserve ahead in high season.

★ Saona Cafe CAFE $$
(Map p102; www.saonacafe.com; Calle La Bahia 1, Bayahibe; mains RD$125-1195, cocktails RD$150-400; ⊘10am-midnight Tue-Thu, to 2am Fri & Sat; 🐾) The French-Canadian owners of this excellent Bayahibe focal point surely scoured the coast to see what everyone else *wasn't* serving, then put it on their menu – bagels, French toast, excellent fries, fried chicken burgers, veggie stir-fries with tofu, lionfish – along with the best cocktail menu between Santo Domingo and Punta Cana (the passionfruit mojitos are insanely good!).

Mare Nuestro ITALIAN $$
(Map p102; www.marenuestro.com; cnr Calles Principal & La Bahia, Bayahibe; mains RD$250-1000; ⊘noon-11pm Tue-Sun; 🐾) Freezing red wine aside, this is the classiest restaurant in Bayahibe, a breezy, 2nd-story-patio affair overlooking beautiful views of the turquoise sea day and night. Lanterns and tablecloths add a romantic ambience and the food is equally impressive, offering excellent fresh-made pastas, salads, excellent fish dishes and melt-in-your-mouth risottos, among others.

There is a small but trendy lounge on the ground floor – a nice spot for a drink. Live music on Wednesdays.

⭐**Las Palmas**   SEAFOOD $$$
(Map p105; 829-850-2665, 809-972-5735; Playa Dominicus; prix-fixe from US$40; ⊙7:30-11pm Mon-Fri) This made-to-order fresh-lobster madhouse offers a meal to remember for crustacean lovers. Call ahead and make a reservation so they know to send a fisherman out to catch the right amount of lobsters, which will then be quickly thrown on the grill right in the middle of diners! The prix-fixe menu includes fresh fish, drinks and desserts.

As far as experiences go around here, it pretty much tops the list. They will open on weekends as well with reservations. It's sandwiched between the Wyndham and Iberostar resorts, near the public beach parking lot.

Drinking & Nightlife

Bayahibe has the best bar scene, though 'scene' is a bit of a stretch. The hidden Lost Bar is easily the best tradtional spot for a drink, while Saona Cafe (p106) teeter-totters between a bar and a restaurant and serves an extensive cocktail menu, mixed by properly trained mixologists, with sea views to boot. For the full-on disco experience, look for Byblos, halfway between Bayahibe and Dominicus Americanus on the latter's side.

⭐**Lost Bar**   BAR
(Calle Flor de Bayahibe, Bayahibe; ⊙7pm-midnight Mon-Thu, to 3am Fri & Sat) One of the best bars in the DR sits tucked away in a residential neighborhood less than five minutes' walk from the water. It's a favourite of local expats, who thought tourists would never find it. Think again! A hipster Italian bartender oversees the dark and sexy multiroom space with picnic and foosball tables, and a swing! Pizza is served.

To find it, head south on Calle Nuevo Bayahibe and hang a left at the third street on the left; it's about 300m on the left.

Super Colmado Bayahibe   BAR
(Map p102; Bayahibe; ⊙7am-noon & 3-9pm) Town square, town bar and town radio station (whether you want it or not) all rolled into one, this *colmado* is where locals gather to talk, drink and listen to music all day long. Nights always begin here.

Shopping

El Mundo   FOOD, GIFTS & SOUVENIRS
(Map p105; Calle Eladia, Dominicus Americanus; ⊙shop 9am-8pm Mon-Sat, 9am-1pm & 4-8pm Sun, restaurant noon-11pm) El Mundo can arrange day-old editions of world newspapers including the *New York Times*, *Le Monde* and *Corriere della Sera* with a day's notice, plus it has souvenirs, snacks and sundries.

It's also a bar, restaurant (mains RD$180 to RD$1000) and is a social gathering point.

ⓘ Information

DANGERS & ANNOYANCES
Cestur (Cuerpo Especializado de Seguridad Turística; ✆809-200-3500; www.cestur.gob.do; Calle Principal, Bayahibe; ⊙24hr) Tourist police at the entrance to Bayahibe.

LAUNDRY
Lavandaría Bayahibe (Calle Tamarindo, Bayahibe; ⊙8am-5pm Mon-Sat)
Lavandaría da Franco (Calle Cayuco, Dominicus Americanus; ⊙9am-5pm Mon-Sat) In Dominicus Americanus.

MEDICAL SERVICES
Centro Clinico Bayahibe (✆829-361-0903; Calle Tamarindo 15, Bayahibe; ⊙on call 24hr) English and Italian are spoken at this small home clinic run by friendly Dr Gustavo Brito Morel.
Farmacia Job (Calle La Bahia, Bayahibe; ⊙8am-9pm Mon-Sat, 8am-1pm Sun) Pharmacy across from Restaurant Capitan Kidd.

MONEY
BanReservas (www.banreservas.com) offers ATMs at both its **Bayahibe** (Calle Principal, Bayahibe) and **Domincus Americanus** (Calle Eladia, Dominicus Americanus) branches.
Banco BHD León (www.bhdleon.com.do; Bayahibe) Also has an ATM at Supermercado La Defensa in Bayahibe.

TOURIST INFORMATION
Parque Nacional Cotubanamá Park Office (Map p102; ✆809-833-0022; Bayahibe; ⊙8am-3pm) Located off the tour bus parking lot in Bayahibe. In addtion to park info, you pay the entrance fee here as well as for Padro Nuestro and Cuevo del Puente.

ℹ️ Getting There & Away

A single road of 7km or so connects the coastal highway with Bayahibe. The road splits about 1km south: the right fork heads to Bayahibe, the left on to Dominicus Americanus.

Guaguas to La Romana (Asodemirobam; Map p102; Calle Yinardy) leave from a new Asodemirobam station just off the tour bus parking lot on the north side of Bayahibe (RD$60, 20 minutes, every 20 minutes from 7:10am to 8:30pm). You can also catch a ride over to Dominicus Americanus (RD$25, five minutes, every 20 minutes) and back. For Higüey, it's best to connect in La Romana.

Bayahibe Taxi (Map p102; ☎ 809-833-0206) has a stand near the Super Colmado. Fares include Dominicus Americanus (US$10), La Romana Airport (US$30), Casa de Campo (US$35), Higüey (US$45) and Bávaro (US$110).

Sichotuhbared (Map p105; ☎ 809-833-0059; Dominicus Americanus) is the local taxi union in Dominicus Americanus, with a stop next to the Viva Wyndham Dominicus Beach. One-way rates for one to five people include La Romana Airport (US$30), Casa de Campo (US$35), Higüey (US$45), Aeropuerto Internacional Punta Cana (US$100) and Bávaro resorts (US$110). Be sure to agree upon a price before you get in the car.

To rent a car, look for **MTM** (☎ 829-471-6250; Calle Cayuco, Dominicus Americanus; ⏰ 8am-6pm Mon-Sat, to noon Sun) in Dominicus Americanus or **Joel Casa de Cambio** (☎ 829-204-7433; Calle Principal 10, Bayahibe; ⏰ 8am-7pm) in Bayahibe (who also rents scooters).

If driving to Playa Dominicus there's easy public access via a **beach parking lot** at the far eastern end of the enclave.

Higüey

POP 168,500

Higüey is a hectic, working-class hub kept in line by its giant concrete basilica, famous around the country and the lone needle worth visiting in this massive concrete haystack surrounded by sugarcane fields in all directions.

The basilica, rising from the center of town like an arched stone rocket set to launch, is both odd and beautiful and well worth a day trip or pit stop while passing through – in fact, you're bound to end up here at some point traveling around the southeast. If not, its prominence on the RD$50 note will have to do.

◎ Sights

Basilica de Nuestra Señora de la Altagracia CHURCH
(www.basilicahiguey.com; RD$40; ⏰ 6:30am-7pm) From the outside, this basilica is a strange mixture of the sacred and profane. A utilitarian concrete facade, not far removed from a military bunker, is topped by an elongated arch reaching high into the sky. But it's one of the most famous cathedrals in the country because of the glass-encased image of the Virgin of Altagracia housed inside amid a trippy kaleidoscopic altar of funky stained-glass glow.

According to the story, a sick child in Higüey was healed when an old man thought to be an Apostle asked for a meal and shelter at the city's original church, the Iglesia San Dionisio. On departing the following day, he left a small print of Our Lady of Grace in a modest frame. Since that day the 16th-century image has been revered by countless devotees, upon whom the Virgin is said to have bestowed miraculous cures. Originally housed in the handsome Iglesia San Dionisio, the image of the Virgin has been venerated in the basilica since the mid-1950s. Designed by Frenchmen Pierre Dupré and Dovnoyer de Segonzac, and completed in 1956, the long interior walls consist mostly of bare concrete and approach each other as they rise, connecting at a rounded point directly over the center aisle. The entire wall opposite the front door consists of stained glass and is quite beautiful, especially in the late afternoon when the sunshine casts honey-colored shadows across the floor.

Museo de la Altagracia MUSEUM
(www.basilicahiguey.com/museo/altagracia-museo.html; Calle Arzobispo Nouel; RD$200; ⏰ 8:30am-5pm Tue-Sat, 9am-5pm Sun) This extremely well-done and modern museum traces the history of religion and culture in the DR back to the 18th century. It is on the grounds of the Basilica de Nuestra Señora de la Altagracia, surrounded by an impressive sea of palm trees, and well worth a visit. It's supposed to have paid entry for tourists, but there was nobody taking money when we popped in.

🎊 Festivals & Events

Thousands of people travel to Basilica de Nuestra Señora de la Altagracia in a moving and intense homage to the Vir-

BOCA DE YUMA

The antithesis of big DR tourism, the ramshackle little town of Boca de Yuma plays the role of the end-of-the-road like a seasoned actor in an indie film. Off the beaten track in terms of mass tourism, the town sits at the southeast end of Hwy 4 and offers rough, unpaved roads and half-finished buildings leading to a quiet seaside promontory where waves crash dramatically into the rocky shore. Like a town forgotten, Boca de Yuma's slow-pace, near-apocalyptic crowdless feel is its appeal, along with cinematic sunrises and a wealth of fresh seafood, and it makes for a great little getaway from the grandiose resorts that are encroaching on the town in all directions.

Several kilometers west of town on the way toward the entrance of the national park is **Cueva de Berna** (RD$100; ⊘sunrise-sunset), a large cave with scattered Taíno pictographs (and graffiti) and stalactite and stalagmite formations. A caretaker usually sits outside the entrance and will gladly accompany you up the rickety ladder and deep into the cave (a small gratuity is appreciated). To find the cave, follow the paved road that runs along the ocean wall west (away from the mouth of the river) past the cemetery and follow the sign; you need no more than 15 minutes inside. Admission to the cave is supposed to be charged but it was deserted when we came through.

A few kilometers further west down the same road (4WD only), past several ranches with grazing cows and horses, is the eastern entrance to **Parque Nacional Cotubanamá** (RD$100). There's little formality or information as few people enter here. A long, easy-to-follow road hugs the coast for many kilometers and involves some hiking up a moderately steep slope to make it to the top of the rugged bluffs with beautiful views of the ocean. There is good bird-watching here if you're out early enough.

While Playa Blanca is a pretty, mostly deserted beach about 2km east of town on the other side of the river, the hassles of getting here may not make the trip worth it. The easiest and most expensive option is to hire a boat from one of the boatmen congregated at the mouth of the river on the east side of town (round trip RD$1500). One alternative is to have one ferry you to the other side of the river and walk to the beach; however, the path is hard to find and follow, and the sharp rocks are a hazard.

There are a few hotels along the road that hugs the fairly frantic seashore here. The best option is the five-room **El Arponero** (☑809-493-5522; www.elarponero.com; r incl breakfast from RD$2700; ⊘restaurant 10am-10pm; ▣), which offers Boca de Yuma's most expansive views from its wind-battered patio.

Several restaurants are lined up along the road overlooking the ocean, all serving similar menus focused on fresh seafood. **Restaurant La Bahia** (mains RD$350-750; ⊘8am-10pm) is a good option owned and operated by a friendly Dominican family.

gin every January 21. Pilgrims, dressed in their finest, file past the Virgin's image, seeking miracles and giving thanks. The church's bells chime loudly throughout the day. In August, the city's streets fill up with cowboys on horseback who ride in from all directions for the **Fiesta Patronal** (Festival of the Bulls).

🛏 Sleeping & Eating

Hotel Don Carlos   HOTEL **$**
(☑809-554-2344; cnr Calle Juan Ponce de León & Sánchez; s/d old bldg RD$1250/1490, s/d/tr new bldg RD$1490/1720/1900; ▣ ❊ ⊛) Only a block west of the Basilica de Nuestra Señora de la Altagracia, Don Carlos is a maze of rooms. It's friendly and professional for the most part, but deserving of only a night when passing through. Ask to stay in the newer annex, whose rooms are modern and larger; rooms in the older building are cramped and aged.

D'Yira   DOMINICAN **$$**
(Av Hermanos 61; mains RD$410-1300; ⊘8am-11pm; ⊛ ◢) If you're here for a night, this rustic Dominican choice is the way to go. The house specialty is *mofongos* (mashed plantains stuffed with seafood, vegetables and the like), which is even done here in a tasty vegetarian version (RD$375).

🍷 Drinking & Nightlife

Boka's Bar & Grill   COCKTAIL BAR
(cnr Calle Juan Ponce de León & Sánchez; ⊘3pm-midnight Mon-Thu, to 2am Fri & Sat; ⊛)

Near the Basilica de Nuestra Señora de la Altagracia, this cocktail bar does a lethal, vodka-laced sangria, which is lapped up by throngs of *Higüeyanos,* who pack in the wraparound outdoor patio for drinks even on a Monday. Cocktails cost RD$170 to RD$200.

ℹ Information

BanReservas (www.banreservas.com.do; Av La Altagracia) Has an ATM on the western end of the Av La Altagracia's leafy median.

ℹ Getting There & Away

Buses to Santo Domingo (☑ 809-554-2574; www.aptpra.com.do; cnr Av Laguna Llana & Colón, RD$260 to RD$285, two hours, every 20 minutes, 3:30am to 8:30pm) leave from the large Aptpra terminal. There are at least two *expresos* per hour.

Guaguas to La Romana (☑ 809-550-0880; Av La Altagracia; RD$100, 45 minutes, every 30 minutes, 5:30am to 10pm) leave from the small Sitraihr station on Av La Altagracia just west of Av Laguna Llana.

For Samaná, walk a few meters east to Asotraihs (it's hard to notice but the stop is in front of Banco La Dinamarca) and take one of the buses or *guaguas* to **Hato Mayor** (☑ 809-554-1177; Av La Altagracia 91) (RD$130, 1¼ hours, hourly, 4:40am to 8:10pm) and transfer to the bus for Sabana de la Mar, where there are ferries across the bay. Be sure to tell the driver that you are planning to connect to

another bus, as they will often drop you right at the next terminal.

Guaguas to **Bávaro** (☑ 829-554-4620; Av La Libertad 60) (RD$120 to RD$130, one hour, every 15 minutes, 4:55am to 10:30pm) leave from the Sitrabapu terminal 1.2km east of the basilica – about a RD$50 *motoconcho* ride.

Bávaro & Punta Cana

It wouldn't be out of line to equate the eastern coast of the Dominican Republic as a sort of sea and sun Disneyland – after all, it is here where the all-inclusive resorts snatch up broad swaths of cinematic beaches faster than the real estate agents can get the sun-soaked sands on the market. The beaches along the coastline from Punta Cana to El Macao rival those anywhere else in the Caribbean, both in terms of their soft, white texture and their warm aquamarine waters. Despite a lack of restraint on development in the area, the resorts and beaches here still manage to offer an idyllic Caribbean seascape for a seemingly endless crowd of sunseekers.

But it's not all buffet lines and bottomless *cuba libres*. Independent travelers can enjoy the sun and fun, too – even if it is slightly more challenging than flopping down on a resort beach-lounger for a week.

◎ Sights

Ojos Indígenas
Ecological Park & Reserve   NATURE RESERVE
(☑ 829-470-1368; www.puntacana.org; adult/child US$25/10, with guided tour US$50/30; ☺ 8:30am-5pm) ✐ Though development may eventually cover every inch of the Dominican coastline, for now there are still large areas of pristine coastal plains and mangrove forests. About 500m south of (and part of) the Puntacana Resort & Club (p115), this ecological park covers over 6 sq km of protected coastal and inland habitat and is home to some 100 bird species (27 of which are indigenous species native only to the DR), 160 insect species and 500 plant species.

Visitors can take very worthwhile three-hour **guided tours** in English, French or Spanish through a lush 30-hectare portion of the reserve, with 12 freshwater lagoons (three of which you can take a dip in) all fed by an underground river that flows into the ocean. Additional tours also include

ORIENTATION

Punta Cana, shorthand for the region as a whole, is actually somewhat of a misnomer. Punta Cana actually refers to the area just east and south of the airport. The majority of resorts are scattered around the beaches of Bávaro, a town established to house resort workers and really nothing more than a series of small, spread-out commercial plazas. Within Bávaro, El Cortecito is a short, grungy strip of shops along a 'town beach', and Los Corales is a nicer, more independently minded beach enclave just southeast of El Cortecito. Punta Cana (Grey-Haired Point), the easternmost tip of the country and where the airport is located, has some of the more luxurious resorts and Caribbean-hugging golf courses.

visits to the park's botanical and fruit gardens, iguana farm (part of a conservation program) and a farm-animal petting zoo.

The visitor center has a great collection of insects that was compiled by entomology students from Harvard, and interesting maps and photos of the area. The park is operated by the Puntacana Ecological Foundation, a nonprofit organization created in 1994 that works to protect the area's ecosystems – including 8km of coral reef along the reserve's shoreline – and to promote sustainable tourism and hotel practices. Nearly 4 hectares of the reserve are dedicated to the Center for Sustainability, a joint project with Cornell and other American universities to survey and study native plants, birds and insects. Guests of Puntacana Resort & Club get in free and can do self-guided tours; otherwise transportation from local hotels is included in the guided-tour prices.

Beaches

Ten or so beaches fall under the Punta Cana umbrella, stretching across over 50km of coastline. Public access is protected by the law, so you can stroll from less-exclusive parts like **Playa El Cortecito/Los Corales**, the former of which tends to be crowded with vendors, to nicer spots in front of resorts – but without the proper color wrist bracelet you won't be able to get a towel or chair.

North of El Cortecito is **Playa Arena Gorda**, lined with all-inclusive resorts and their guests on banana boats, parasailing or just soaking in the sun. A further 9km north of here is the best accessible surf beach, **Playa del Macao**, a gorgeous stretch of sand best reached by car. It's also a stop-off for a slew of ATV (all-terrain vehicle) tours that tear up and down the beach every day – there's less noise at the far northern end of the beach. The golden sands of **Playa Uvero Alto**, the area's northernmost beach, are 10km further north.

In the other direction, south of Bávaro and El Cortecito, is **Playa Cabo Engaño**, an isolated beach that you'll need a vehicle, preferably a 4WD, to reach. And then there's the furthest southern beach, the gorgeous, snaking stunner **Playa Juanillo**, whose sands are cleaned daily by Cap Cana staff – just maybe the fairest of them all!

Activities

Virtually every water activity is available but some involve a long commute to the actual site. Every hotel has a tour desk offering snorkeling, diving and boat trips to destinations such as Isla Saona (p102). Parasailing is done from the shoreline all over Punta Cana and Bávaro.

La Cana Golf Course
GOLF

(☑ 809-959-4653; www.puntacana.com/golf; Punta Cana Resort & Club, Punta Cana; ☉ 7:30am-5:30pm) Punta Cana's top golf course is located at the area's top resort. The 27-hole course, designed by Pete Dye, has some long and challenging par 4s and stunning ocean views. Green fees are US$135 for guests and US$175 (including cart) for nonguests for 18 holes, or US$80 (guests only) for nine. Club rental is US$50 for 18 holes or US$25 for nine.

Tee times may be booked online.

Also part of the Puntacana Resort & Club is the Tom Fazio–designed Corales Golf Course, with green fees for Puntacana Resort & Club homeowners and Tortuga Bay guests costing US$295, and nonguests for US$395.

Cap Cana
GOLF

(☑ 809-469-7767; www.capcana.com; Punta Cana) Cap Cana has one Jack Nicklaus Signature golf course, Punta Espada Golf Club, open for play since 2008 (nonguest greens fees from May to October are US$295, from November to May they're US$395), and two more on the way at the time of research. Punta Espada is considered one of the top courses in the Caribbean and in the world's top 100.

Happy Dive Center
DIVING

(☑ 809-589-2903; www.happydivecenterdr.com; Calle Pedro Mir, El Cortecito) This recommended Canadian/Dominican NAUI Pro Gold dive operator offers one-/two-tank dive excursions for US$50/90, night dives in Bayahibe (US$120) and NAUI and PADI certification courses (from US$300). All prices include equipment.

Hispaniola Aquatic Adventures
BOATING, SNORKELING

(☑ 800-282-5784; www.catamarantourpuntacana.com; from US$99) Runs highly popular party-boat catamaran tours for up to 25 people (or privately), taking in snorkeling at Cabeza del Toro as well a seafood lunch

PUNTA CANA & THE SOUTHEAST BÁVARO & PUNTA CANA

Bávaro & Punta Cana

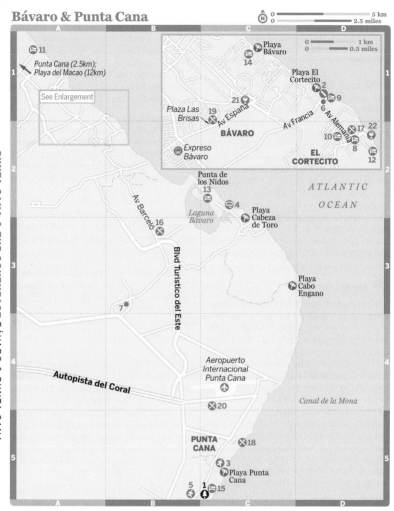

and lesser-known beaches and swimming holes. Prices include transportation and alcohol. They don't allow middleman sales and a portion of the price goes to a homeless children and dog charity in the DR.

X Bike   MOUNTAIN BIKING
(☎809-758-0113; www.mtbpuntacana.com) Need to shed some all-inclusive calories? The friendly Joaquin can get you out of the resorts and into the mountains, with half-day mountain-biking trips to Miches and Constanza and overnight trips to Jarabacoa. Prices start from US$75 per person.

Marinarium   SNORKELING
(☎809-468-3183; www.marinarium.com; adult/child 2-11yr US$106/53) A popular family outing is a snorkeling trip to the Marinarium, a natural offshore pool near Cabeza de Toro, which is arguably more ecofriendly than other excursions. Rays, nurse sharks, tropical fish and patches of coral are all on hand.

☞ Tours

Every resort has a separate tour desk that can arrange all manner of trips, from snorkeling and deep-sea fishing to the popular

Bávaro & Punta Cana

Isla Saona trip. A handful of locals set up on El Cortecito beach offer 2½-hour **snorkel trips** (per person US$25) and two-hour **glass-bottom boat rides** (per person US$35) to a nearby reef, as well as **parasailing** (15 minutes, per couple US$60). Most also offer **deep-sea fishing trips** (minimum four people, four hours, per couple US$120) for marlin, tuna, wahoo and barracuda. There are a few pushy kiosks near the north end of the beach, although the odds are that you'll be approached by touts anyway as soon as you set foot in town and on the beach. The most popular day tour by far is the trip to Isla Saona (p102) which costs US$50 to US$100. Keep in mind the cheaper prices on offer often mean a lack of license or insurance.

With the greatly improved highway, Tour Samaná with Terry (p128), based in Samaná, also now offers recommended days trip to the Península de Samaná with pick-ups in Punta Cana.

Runners Adventures   TOURS
(☑ 809-455-1135; www.runnersadventures.com; Av Barcelo; ☺ 7am-7pm) A well-established outfitter offering a range of adventure and cultural tours, including their most popular, Bávaro Runners, which takes in a sugarcane plantation, cigar museum, beach and horseback riding. Also offers city tours to Santo Domingo, a squirrel-monkey reserve and the longest zipline in the Caribbean.

RH Tours & Excursions   TOURS
(☑ 809-552-1425; www.rhtours.com; El Cortecito; ☺ 9am-2pm Mon-Sat) If you're looking to explore the region, this tour operator offers a number of decent day trips for tourists. Popular excursions include exploring Parque Nacional Los Haitises (US$138), boat trips to Isla Saona (US$99 to US$115) and tours of Santo Domingo's Zona Colonial (US$89). All full-day trips include lunch and drinks. English, German and Spanish are spoken.

🛏 Sleeping

For resorts in the area, walk-in-guests are about as common as snowstorms; if you can convince the suspicious security guards that your intentions are innocent and make it to the front desk, you'll be quoted rates that absolutely nobody staying at the resort is paying. Book all-inclusive vacations online or through a travel agent, as they can offer discounts of up to 50% off rack rates. Bear in mind that most resorts cater to a particular niche, whether it's families, honeymooners, golfers or the spring-break crowd.

There is finally a blossoming hostel scene in Bávaro, a refreshing alternative for independent travelers, and it's here where you will find the biggest bulk of independent restaurants and services in one place. El Cortecito is a scruffier beach enclave nearby.

Bávaro

★ **Macao Beach Hostel** HOSTEL $
(☎829-913-6267; www.facebook.com/macaobeachhostelpuntacana; El Macao; camping s/d without tent US$10/15, with tent US$15/20, dm US$14, r without bathroom US$35, all incl breakfast; P 📶) Friendly Colombian musician Andrés has cultivated a rural Dominican village experience at this new hostel spread among several colorful traditional Caribbean clapboard shacks. Despite being a mere 10 minutes' walk from Macao Beach, it feels worlds away, with cows and horses grazing in pastures across the road, and chickens, cats, dogs and a community donkey roaming freely.

There are four rustic private rooms with mosquito nets and a five-bed dorm along with simple, bamboo-walled bathrooms and a guest kitchen. Village kids hang around and a community chef whips up Dominican meals with advance notice (RD$150). Guests can take surf lessons, horseback rides or kick back in hammocks during the day, and sit around the fire at night with Andrés and fellow musicians providing the soundtrack.

Bávaro Hostel HOSTEL $
(☎809-931-6767; www.bavarohostel.com; Av Alemania, Edificio Carimar 4A, Bávaro; dm US$20, r US$30-50, 1-/2-bdrm apt $75/90; P ❄ 📶) A new Swedish owner has taken over this hostel mere meters from the beach, Bávaro's surefire independent traveler hub. It occupies several rooms in a four-story building in the heart of Los Corales. Private rooms come in pairs with shared kitchens and bathrooms; otherwise choose between four- and six-bed mixed dorms.

WORTH A TRIP

DOWN UNDER IN THE DR

Cueva Fun Fun (☎809-481-7773; www.cuevafunfun.com; Rancho Capote, Calle Duarte 12, Barrio Puerto Rico, Hato Mayor; adult/child US$155/110) runs spelunking trips to one of the largest cave systems in the Caribbean. Included in the day trip is a horseback ride, a walk through a lush forest, a 20m abseil and 2km walk through the cave, which involves a good deal of sploshing and splashing in the underground river.

Gava Hostel HOSTEL $$
(☎829-206-5583; gavahostel@gmail.com; Calle Russo, Edifico Dona Daliya, Apt B2; dm from US$20, r US$60; P 📶) A young and friendly Russian couple, Valentina and Andrey, run this tiny hostel with just four dorm beds and one private room set off on a quiet residential street between Los Corales and El Cortecito. It's small, but the hospitality is sweet, and the private room is large and welcoming – if you can manage to snag it.

Capri Beach House HOTEL $$
(☎809-994-2020; hotelcapribeach@gmail.com; Playa El Cortecito; r US$52-140; ❄ 📶) With Caribbean waves practically crashing right into its rooms, this eight-room beachfront hotel in the heart of El Cortecito is your best bet for a beach-bum hideaway. Three of the rooms offer sea views, front patios with hammock chairs and an extra loft bed above. There's a beachfront bar as well, which is decent enough for lazily drinking away an afternoon.

Hotel Cortecito Inn HOTEL $$
(☎809-552-0639; www.hotelcortecitoinn.net; El Cortecito; r incl breakfast US$80; P ❄ 📶 🏊) One of the few independent, reasonably priced choices in the area. Smileless service, confrontational staff and uninspiring breakfasts are the rule, but the rooms can be spacious and the pool and renovated grounds pleasant enough. Expect to leave your ID at reception.

★ **Paradisus Punta Cana** RESORT $$$
(☎809-687-9923; www.melia.com; Playa Bávaro; all-incl d from US$400; P ❄ @ 📶 🏊) Almost jungly and discerningly quiet, this resort feels nothing like most in the area. It attracts singles and families alike and takes appreciated steps to keep them separate where desired. Newly made-over standard rooms feature soft white and beige accents, an additional sitting area with sofa bed and sexy dual showers.

The 192 Reserve rooms feature lush courtyards, modern art, patios and Jacuzzi tubs for two. Both the large and winding main pool and the beach (full of day beds) are gorgeous, and the separate Royal Services pool feels like a Roman bath. Kids get a bungy swing and a climbing wall, adults 12 restaurants and 12 bars, including the new Winery, a cozy top-end wine bar; and Passion by Martín Berasategui (p117), considered the country's top restaurant. Everybody wins.

★**Zoetry Agua** RESORT **$$$**
(☏888-496-3879; www.zoetryresorts.com; Uvero Alto; s/d from US$426/692; [P][@][⊛][🖥][🏊]) The moment you walk into the intimate Zoetry, relaxation befalls you. Wooden accents and Balinese touches abound at this small property, with 96 suites that radiate out from the dramatic, cathedral-style lobby forged from bamboo and palm leaves. Spacious rooms deport you from typical all-inclusive fare to Asian-style luxury, with hardwood floors, stone showers and sink-in bathtubs.

Several rooms have direct access to the serpentine pool that snakes throughout the property. Wellness-focused daily activities (yoga, water spinning, pilates) rule here over party activities and drinking games, but guests who want a touch of nightlife can access any of the company's more hedonistic resorts nearby. The spa is predictably inviting and all food on premises is organic. Pretty perfect. Kids are allowed but are charged as adults, a clever way to keep their numbers low.

NaturaPark Beach
Ecoresort & Spa HOTEL **$$$**
(☏809-221-2626; www.blau-hotels.com; Cabeza de Toro; d from US$270; [P][⊛][@][🖥][🏊]) NaturaPark has a narrow beach outside the village of Cabeza de Toro, halfway between Bávaro and Punta Cana. From the Lincoln Logs–style recycled coconut-wood lobby furniture to the beautiful free-growing mangroves on the property, it's all got a sustainable edge and the 524-room resort has won awards for reducing its environmental impact.

It's extra popular with those who care more about reducing their carbon footprint than hopping in and out of bars and clubs at night. The pool is a bit small, but the beach is quite nice. Free-range swans, geese and flamingos and the Laguna Bávaro on its doorstep means nature is never too far away here.

Hard Rock Hotel Punta Cana RESORT **$$$**
(☏809-731-0099; www.hardrockhotelpuntacana. com; Playa del Macao; all-inclusive d from US$592; [P][⊛][@][🖥][🏊]) Imagine Las Vegas with a Caribbean sea. This den of decadence and cool sits atop Punta Cana's list of bold and beautiful resorts. The lobby feels like a rock-and-roll hall of fame, with memorabilia galore, including Madonna's sequined-covered limo. It caters to a diverse hipster crowd.

The gorgeous casino is the DR's largest (as is the spa) and there are 13 pools (seven oceanfront), 10 restaurants and 17 bars, so you're never far from the party on the sprawling grounds. But why not party in your room? They feature party-sized Jacuzzis at the foot of the beds. Nonguests can visit the casino, the happening Oro nightclub and Epik, one of the resort's trendier restaurants (mains US$22 to US$55). The latest bells and whistles include the revamped 18-hole Hard Rock Golf Club at Cana Bay and an app from which guests can pretty much do anything.

Los Corales Beach Village APARTMENT **$$$**
(☏809-552-1262; www.loscoralesvillage.com; Calle Los Corales, Los Corales; r from US$126; [P][⊛][🖥][🏊]) This small Italian-owned development has none of the grandiose ambitions of the nearby all-inclusives to be all things to all people. For those seeking more modest surroundings and a community feel, this longtime favorite offers 50 renovated suites, all with small private patios or balconies, some with oceanfront views. New bathrooms, floors and more spacious layouts debuted in 2016.

Punta Cana

Puntacana Resort & Club RESORT **$$$**
(☏809-959-2714; www.puntacana.com; Punta Cana; [P][⊛][🖥][🏊]) Famous for its part-time residents, like Julio Iglesias and Mikhail Baryshnikov, this discerning and huge resort is also notable for its environmental efforts, especially the associated ecological park across the street from the entrance to the resort. Unlike all-inclusives, however, lunch, dinner and drinks aren't included in the rates.

The resort's centerpiece property is the 200-room Westin near Playa Blanca (doubles including breakfast from US$460), opened in late 2013, where every room has at least a partial ocean view. The complex also includes the 124-room Four Points Sheraton (doubles from US$267), a 2012 opener, poised as a modern business hotel at Puntacana Village. But the real coup here is the luxurious and discerning Tortuga Bay (designed by the late Oscar de la

Renta; doubles from US$1323), a small enclave of one-, two- and three-bedroom villas that set the bar for luxury in Punta Cana. There are seven restaurants to choose from within the 60-sq-km complex, a Six Senses Spa, a modern PADI dive facility, a tennis center and a kiteboarding school, among numerous other distractions.

Eating

Resort buffets ensure most folks keep hunger pains at bay, but there are enough condos and villas and locals to support numerous independent eateries. Most are in shopping centers, easily reached by *motoconcho* or taxi.

The excellent **Super Mercados Nacional** (Puntacana Village, Punta Cana; ☺ 8am-9pm Mon-Sat, 9am-6pm Sun) is Punta Cana's best supermarket. In Bávaro, the best option is the new and huge **Jumbo** (www.jumbo.com. do; Downtown Mall, Bávaro; ☺ 8am-10pm Mon-Sat, 9am-9pm Sun). You'll find smaller supermarkets with daily essentials spread about many of Bávaro's plazas.

Solo Pollo　　　　　DOMINICAN $
(Plaza Brisas de Bávaro, Bávaro; meals RD$200-350; ☺ 11am-11:30pm Mon-Sat) A legion of locals flocks to this simple *comida criolla* restaurant serving – as the name implies – only chicken. Juicy, perfectly seasoned *pollo horneado* (baked chicken) is the specialty, going for RD$550 for the whole bird.

Kat's Corner　　　　　CAFE $
(Av Alemania, Los Corales; mains RD$175-425; ☺ 8:30am-midnight; ☎) Simple and social, Kat's is an open-air corner bar that hits the spot for American-style hangover cures – bacon, eggs, hash browns, breakfast burritos – and is a safe bet for fast-food drunken munchies (nachos, quesadillas, burgers) or a drink at any time of day. Live acoustic music on Wednesday and Thursday draws a festive crowd.

La Posada de Gladys　　　　　DOMINICAN $
(Av Alemania, Bávaro; meals RD$180-550; ☺ 8am-10pm) Get down with Dominicans at this pleasant, open-air *palapa* where the RD$200 plate of the day is the working man's staple in Bávaro. It's simple: a meat or fish dish accompanied by rice, beans and plantains, and made with local love. Don't let them charge extra over the menu price for a bigger piece of fish!

★ **Ñam Ñam**　　　　　CAFE $$
(www.nam-nams.com; Plaza Sol Caribe, Bávaro; mains RD$119-549; ☺ 11am-2:30pm & 6-11pm Tue-Sat, 7-10pm Sun; ☎ ☑) Ñam Ñam means 'yummy' in Serbian: that ain't no lie. The friendly Belgradian couple behind this tiny Los Corales kitchen – they do it all themselves – know a thing or two about making your belly happy. The now-famous burgers (RD$399 to RD$549), in regular, gourmet (minced with bacon and chili) and stuffed (with ham, cheese and mushrooms) versions, are superb.

But the menu of international comfort food doesn't stop there. There are also crepes, sandwiches, a wealth of veggie options and even Serbian *chevap,* a type of minced-meat kebab from the motherland. You can't go wrong dousing anything on the menu in the house-made pureed habanero-carrot hot sauce (serious burn), or the homespun mayo with parsley. You're welcome.

Little John　　　　　SEAFOOD $$
(☑ 809-469-7727; www.facebook.com/littlejohn-beach; Playa Juanillo; mains US$9-24; ☺ 9am-6:30pm; ☎) With its photogenic, colored-up VW van and pleasant open-air, white-washed setting on Playa Juanillo, Little John is the best spot to kick back with a wealth of properly mixed creative cocktails (RD$300 to RD$750) and a well-rounded, seafood-heavy menu on one of Punta Cana's prettiest beaches.

There's ceviche, oysters, burgers, sandwiches and a host of more creative mains than usual (goat confit risotto with avocado butter, for example). You can easily spend a day here and get up and come do it again at breakfast.

Wacamole　　　　　MEXICAN $$
(www.facebook.com/Wacamolepc; Av Alemania, Los Corales; mains RD$230-490; ☺ noon-midnight; ☎) Straight outta Cancún – Mexican hipsters lugged a tortilla machine from home and regularly smuggle in habanero peppers, all of which adds authenticity to this good-time, open-air *taqueria.* Fiery salsas are sure to make your nose run, while classic Mexican street tacos (*al pastor,* fish, *carne asada*), and wild cards like lobster ceviche, are made from scratch with organic ingredients.

It's a great bar as well, with top-shelf tequilas (Patrón, Herradura), though the bartending isn't quite up to snuff yet.

Balicana
FUSION $$

(www.balicana.com; Los Corales Beach Village, Los Corales; mains RD$420-550; ☺8am-midnight Mon-Sat; ☎) Give your taste buds a shock: this immensely pleasurable spot to eat – unbeknownst to most folks who don't wander into Los Corales Beach Village a(p115) – serves up Asian recipes normally missing in action in the DR. Thai (green curries, pad Thai), Indonesian (nasi goreng) and Malaysian (coconut curries) offerings are all devourable under a fan-cooled poolside *palapa* next to the pool.

Brot
CAFE $$

(Puntacana Village, Punta Cana; breakfast RD$255-375; ☺7am-10pm Mon-Sat, 8am-5pm Sun; ☎) Slammed at breakfast, this is where Punta Cana comes for its bagel fix. Fab *bagelwiches* (also available on baguettes) are the call, in such rarely seen flavors as Hummus Supreme and Montecristo, among others. There are also breakfast burritos, a wealth of salads and wraps, and scorching coffee. Homesickness cured!

★Passion by Martín Berasategui
BASQUE $$$

(Paradisus Punta Cana, Bávaro; 7-course prix-fixe guest/nonguest US$55/60; ☺6:30-10pm; ☎) Chef Martín Berasategui hails from San Sebastián in Spanish Basque country – not a bad place to eat for those who might not know – and he packed a few recipes in his gastro-luggage on his way to overseeing what is considered the best fine-dining experience in the Dominican Republic, at the Paradisus Punta Cana (p114).

The seven-course tasting menu is the way to go, where you might encounter dishes like a wonderful truffled ravioli; a fabulous crust-perfected salmon with fennel beads and fresh watercress, exploding chocolate olives and basil; a slow-cooked pressed veal cheek with romesco sauce; and a decadent little petit-four plate that's as pretty as it is sweet. You do need to temper your expectations a tad – despite seven Michelin stars amid various restaurants to Berasategui's name, he isn't over the stove here – but it's priced in your favor and the chef and line cooks have all worked under Berasategui's watch in Spain.

Restaurante Playa Blanca
FUSION $$$

(Puntacana Resort, Punta Cana; mains US$14-24; ☺11am-10:30pm; ☎) Flanked by an army of palms, this atmospheric open-air restaurant is within the Puntacana Resort complex but open to the public and worth the trip. The beach here (Playa Blanca) is spectacular, and you can eat on the sand for lunch.

The hip, white-on-white space reeks of cool, and the Dominican comfort menu is highlighted by some wild cards like spicy Dominican goat (US$16) as well as solid Dominican staples. It's atmospheric at night, but it's hard to skip the swirl of turquoise from across your plate at lunchtime.

☕ Drinking & Nightlife

Nightlife is big business in Bávaro. Many resorts have nightclubs and there are independent bars around the beaches near Los Corales and El Cortecito. Puntacana Village has vibrant nightlife as well – often quieter and more sophisticated than noisier Bávaro options. Of course, the hottest clubs of the moment change like baby's diapers. Coco Bongo, Oro, Vibe and Legacy Disco were the hot tickets during our visit.

Huracan Café
COCKTAIL BAR

(☎829-533-1300; www.huracancafe.do; Calle Mare, Los Corales; cocktails RD$200-280; ☺9am-11pm; ☎) This chill beach bar and sand lounge is quietly positioned out of street view in Los Corales and favored by hip expats, residents and trendier tourists. Circular love seats and hammocks facing the sea are perfect for wasting away a day at the beach, downing mojitos and caipirinhas and staring off at a parked pirate ship on the horizon.

Drink Point
BAR

(Av España, Bávaro; ☺10pm-5am Mon-Sat, to midnight Sun) If you'd like to avoid gaggles of tourists who funnel the free resort drinks before heading out of the hotels to around town, head straight to Drink Point at the corner of Av España and Av Francia, where Dominicans pack in nightly.

The *cuba libres* and Presidente cocktails flow freely amid a flurry of Caribbean chaos fueled by *bachata* and *merengue*. Be wary of distinctly aggressive 'sanky-pankys' here (the local term for women looking for visa love)!

Onno's
BAR

(www.onnosbar.com; Calle Pedro Mir, Bávaro; ☺5pm-late) This open-air bar right on El Cortecito beach is without question one of the area's best independent spots to catch a cocktail, which you can down to DJs spinning Haitian Creole jams one minute, Rihanna the next. Cool people, cool atmosphere.

ℹ Information

LAUNDRY

Laundromat Punta Cana (Plaza Arenal Caribe, Bávaro; ⊘ 8am-8pm Mon-Sat) Do-it-yourself laundry facility near Los Corales (wash/dry RD$150/200).

MEDICAL SERVICES

Centro Médico Punta Cana (☑ 809-552-1506; www.centromedicopuntacana.com; Av España 1, Bávaro) Name notwithstanding, this is the main private hospital in Bávaro, with multilingual staff, 24-hour emergency room and in-house pharmacy.

Farmacia Estrella (☑ 809-552-0344; Plaza Estrella, Bávaro; ⊘ 8am-11pm) Bávaro pharmacy offering delivery.

Hospitén Bávaro (☑ 809-455-1121; www. hospiten.es; Carretera Higüey-Punta Cana) Best private hospital in Punta Cana, with English-, French- and German-speaking doctors and a 24-hour emergency room. The hospital is located on the old Hwy 106 to Punta Cana, 500m from Cruce de Verón.

Pharmacana (Puntacana Village, Punta Cana; ⊘ 24hr) A good 24-hour pharmacy at Puntacana Village.

MONEY

There is always an ATM around until you need one, in which case they are always far away, despite nearly every Dominican bank having a branch in Punta Cana! Many resorts have their own, of course. Otherwise, the closest ATMs to the hostel scene around Los Corales are the **BanReserves/Banco Popular ATMs** (Av Alemania, Palma Real Shopping Village) at Palma Real Shopping Village, 2.2km southwest.

Banco Popular (Av España, btwn Plaza Brisas de Bávaro & Plaza Estrella) Has ATMs

Scotiabank Has ATMs at Puntacana Village (www.scotiabank.com; Puntacana Village) and Plaza Brisas de Bávaro (Plaza Brisas de Bávaro).

POLICE STATIONS

Cestur (Cuerpo Especializado de Seguridad Turística; ☑ 809-754-3082; www.cestur. gob.do; Av Estados Unidos, Bávaro; ⊘ 24hr) Headquarters is in Friusa, next to the bus terminal in Bávaro, with additional stations at the Punta Cana airport, Cabeza de Toro and Uvero Alto.

ℹ Getting There & Away

From the small village of El Cortecito, the road follows an endless cluster of strip malls to a Texaco gas station, where you'll find the bus station and the route to resorts further north and Higüey to the southwest.

AIR

Several massive thatched-roof huts make up the three terminals – Terminal A (Departures), Terminal A (Arrivals) and the new Terminal B – of the **Aeropuerto Internacional Punta Cana** (p302), located on the road to Punta Cana about 9km east of the turnoff to Bávaro. The arrival process, including immigration, purchase of a tourist card (US$10), baggage claim and customs, moves briskly.

Commercial airlines serving the Punta Cana airport year-round include the following: from Terminal A: Aerolineas Argentinas, Aeromexico, Air Canada, Frontier, JetBlue, LATAM, Southwest, Spirit, Sunwing and United; from Terminal B: Air Berlin, Air France, American Airlines, Avianca, British Airways, Copa, Delta Airlines, Edelweiss/Swiss and GOL. There are additional airlines and flights (including many charters), especially in high season.

There are Banco Popular ATMs located in the departure areas of Terminals A and B. Rental-car agencies at Terminal A (Arrivals), which generally open from 9am to 10pm, include:

AmeriRent (☑ 809-687-0505; www.amerirent.net; Aeropuerto Internacional Punta Cana)

Avis (☑ 809-688-1354; www.avis.com. do; Aeropuerto Internacional Punta Cana), **Budget** (☑ 809-466-2028; www.budget. com; Aeropuerto Internacional Punta Cana), **Europcar** (☑ 809-688-2121; www.europcar. com; Aeropuerto Internacional Punta Cana), **InterRent** (☑ 809-480-8188; www.interrent. com; Aeropuerto Internacional Punta Cana), **National/Alamo** (☑ 809-959-0434; www. nationalcar.com.do; Aeropuerto Internacional Punta Cana),

Payless (☑ 809-959-0287; www.paylesscar. com; Aeropuerto Internacional Punta Cana), **Sixt** (☑ 829-576-4700; www.sixt.com; Aeropuerto Internacional Punta Cana) and

Thrifty (☑ 809-959-0597; www.thrifty.com; Aeropuerto Internacional Punta Cana).

Also here is **Hertz** (☑ 809-959-0365; www. hertz.com; Aeropuerto Internacional Punta Cana).

Resort minivans transport the majority of tourists to nearby resorts, but taxis are plentiful – look for the Siutrataxi guys in pink shirts. Fares between the airport and area resorts and hotels range between US$30 and US$80 depending on the destination.

BUS

The 70km toll-road, Autopista del Coral, from La Romana to Punta Cana, was opened in 2012 to great fanfare, cutting the drive time from Santo Domingo to Punta Cana by two hours.

The bus terminal is located on Av Estados Unidos in Friusa, near the main intersection in Bávaro, almost 2km inland from El Cortecito. **Expreso Bávaro** (☑809-552-1678; www.expresobavaro.com; Cruce de Friusa) has direct 1st-class services between Bávaro and the capital (RD$400, four hours), with a stop in La Romana. Departure times in both directions are 7am, 9am, 11am, 1pm, 3pm and 4pm.

From the same terminal, **Sitrabapu** (☑809-552-0771; Av Estados Unidos), more or less the same company, has departures to La Romana at 6am, 8:20am, 10:50am, 1:20pm, 3:50pm and 6:20pm (RD$225, 1¼ hours); and to Higüey (RD$120 to RD$130, one hour, every 20 minutes, 3am to 10:30pm). To all other destinations, head for Higüey and transfer there. You can also get to/from Santo Domingo this way, but it's much slower than the direct bus.

For Sabana de la Mar (where you can catch the ferry to Península de Samaná), Miches-based Sitrahimi passes by the Sitrabapu station on its way to Miches (RD$250, 1¾ hours, 10:30am, 12:30pm and 5:30pm), from where you can switch for Sabana de la Mar; or you can transit via Higüey and Hato Mayor. A taxi from Punta Cana direct to Sabana de la Mar costs US$200.

GETTING AROUND

Local buses start at the main bus terminal, passing all the outdoor malls on the way to El Cortecito, then turn down the coastal road past the large hotels to Cruce de Cocoloco, where they turn around and return the same way. Buses have the local drivers' union acronyms – Sitrabapu or Traumapabu – printed in front and cost around RD$40, depending on distance. They generally pass every 30 minutes between 5am and 8pm, but can sometimes take up to an hour.

It is possible to take a local bus to the airport from Bávaro, but you will need to give yourself at least an extra hour to do so and you must change buses at Cruce de Cocoloco and/or Veron. Tell the driver you are going to the airport and he will drop you at the spot to switch buses. From the airport, don't count on any *guaguas* after 6pm.

Daytime traffic is sometimes gridlocked between the resorts clustered just north of Bávaro and El Cortecito. Despite the stop-and-go pace of driving, renting a car for a day or two is recommended if you prefer to see the surrounding area independently. Some agencies allow you to drop off the car in Santo Domingo, usually for an extra charge, but check in advance. Agencies outside the airport that are handy for Bávaro include:

5 Star Rentals & Excursions (☑829-917-7212; roberto.5starpuntacana@gmail.com; ⊗9am-7pm Mon-Sat, noon-7pm Sun) in Los Corales

Europcar (☑809-686-2864; www.europcar.com.do; Av España, Bávaro; ⊗8am-5pm) near Plaza Brisas de Bávaro

Avis (☑809-688-1354; www.avis.com.do; Av Barceló Km 6.5, Bávaro Car Rental Center; ⊗8am-5pm)

Budget (☑809-466-2028; www.budget.com; Av Barceló Km 6.5, Bávaro Car Rental Center; ⊗8am-5pm)

Payless (☑808-455-7113; www.paylesscar.com; Av Barceló Km 6.5, Bávaro Car Rental Center; ⊗8am-5pm)

National/Alamo (p118) all near Cruce de Cocoloco

Otherwise, there are numerous taxis in the area – look for stands at El Cortecito, Plaza Bávaro and at the entrance of most all-inclusive places. You can also call a cab – try **Siutratural**, in **Bávaro** (☑809-552-0617; www.taxibavaropuntacana.com) and **El Cortecito** (☑809-552-0617; El Cortecito), or **Taxi Turístico Beron** (☑809-466-1133; www.taxituristicoberon.com). Fares vary depending on distance, but some examples include US$10 (pretty much the minimum charge on a short trip within Bávaro), US$35 to the airport and US$40 to Playa Blanca. **Asobapuma** (☑829-638-5525; El Cortecito) water taxis can also be found on El Cortecito beach and cost between US$10 and US$20 per ride. *Motoconchos* congregate around Plaza Punta Cana in Bávaro and along the beach road in El Cortecito, and you can generally find one or two parked in front of the entrance to most resorts. Fares run around RD$100 to RD$200 within the El Cortecito/Bávaro area.

Playa Limón

Playa Limón, about 20km east of Miches and just outside the hamlet of El Cedro, is a 3km-long, isolated Atlantic beach lined with coconut trees leaning into the ocean – coveted property that you're likely to have to yourself for much of the time. Horseback-riding tours from Rancho La Cueva sometimes descend upon it a few hours a day, generally from late morning to early afternoon, but it's otherwise all yours.

The rugged area surrounding Playa Limón has two important wetland areas, including Laguna Limón, a serene freshwater body of water surrounded by grassy wetlands and coastal mangroves. The lagoon feeds into the ocean on the eastern end of Playa Limón and is known for bird-watching; tours are organized by Rancho La Cueva. The other lagoon – Laguna Redonda – is just 5km away, but is more commonly visited from Punta El Rey.

Sights

★ **Montaña Redonda** VIEWPOINT
(☑ 829-745-5182; www.facebook.com/montanaredondamiches; RD$100; ☺ 8am-6pm) This dramatic mountaintop viewpoint isn't new, but the selfie generation has discovered its value – *Dominicanos* flock here on weekends to take photos swinging in sky-high swing sets, hammocks and teeter-totters, or flying on broomsticks. The 360-degree mountain and sea views are jaw-dropping, among the DR's most cinematic. Transport from the parking lot is RD$700, but you can group together and pay RD$100 each. The bumpy, steep ride up is as wild as a roller coaster (some folks walk the 2.1km).

Once up, it feels as though you could see Haiti on a clear enough day! There is a small shop, restaurant (mains RD$250 to RD$375) and a professional photo company. You can even paraglide right off it as well (Dominicans pay RD$2500, foreigners anywhere between US$60 to US$80, for a 15-minute ride). The entrance is 6.5km west of the Playa Limón turnoff on the highway to Sabana de la Mar.

Sleeping & Eating

There are no services in Playa Limón beyond Rancho La Cueva (p120). If you want to eat beyond their menu or take a picnic at the beach, it's best to stock up on provisions before arrival. In theory you can also go to the market in El Cedro but you won't want to if the road is in bad condition.

Rancho La Cueva HOTEL $
(☑ 809-519-5271; www.rancholacueva.com; Playa Limón; s/d/tr with fan US$30/40/45; ℗ 🛜) Horses and pigs roam this out-of-the-way property that feels like a true find. The nine large spick-and-span rooms are sparsely furnished (but with colorful furniture) and there's hot-water showers.

An open-air restaurant hosts daily tour groups for a seafood buffet, but breakfast and dinner are taken from the restaurant, which sources mostly local seafood (mains RD$240 to RD$650).

The Austrian owner can arrange a trip that includes a visit to a coffee plantation, a seafood buffet and a boat ride across the lagoon (per person US$70), and trips to waterfalls (US$30), horseback rides (per hour US$10) and transportation to Montaña Redonda (p120) (US$50).

Getting There & Away

The turnoff to Playa Limón from the newly paved highway from Bávaro is on the very eastern edge of El Cedro and well signed. From the turnoff (teasingly paved for just 50m!), head north on a rough dirt road (a normal car can make it if it's dry; otherwise a 4WD is necessary). Rancho La Cueva is about 3km down this road – they can drag you out if you get stuck – and the beach only another 500m.

Keep in mind that the only gas stations between Otra Banda (the start of old Hwy 104) and Miches are in the town of Lagunas de Nisibón and El Cedro.

Guaguas running between Higüey (RD$150, one hour) and Miches (RD$85, 20 minutes) can be flagged down from the main road during daylight hours – just make sure you are on the right side of the street for where you want to go. If arriving, be sure to let the driver know that you want to get off in El Cedro; it's easy to miss. Then catch a *motoconcho* for the remaining 3km or so (RD$200).

Miches

POP 10,152

From the surrounding hills, Miches, on the southern shore of the Bahía de Samaná, is fairly picturesque. A slim 50m-high radio tower marks the geographic center of what appear to be well-ordered streets, and Playa Miches, just east of the town proper, looks inviting. Upon closer inspection, however, it's a fairly tumbledown place and the beach, though long and wide, is not very attractive. The water isn't good for swimming, mainly because the Rió Yaguada empties into the ocean here. Miches sometimes makes national headlines as the launching point for Dominicans hoping to enter the USA illegally, via the Mona Passage to Puerto Rico.

PARQUE NACIONAL LOS HAITISES

This 1375-sq-km park (caves RD$100; ⊙7am-8pm), whose name means 'land of the mountains', is at the southwestern end of the Bahía de Samaná, 9km west of Sabana de la Mar. It does indeed contain scores of lush hills, jutting some 30m to 50m from the water and coastal wetlands. The knolls were formed one to two million years ago, when tectonic drift buckled the thick limestone shelf that had formed underwater.

The area receives a tremendous amount of rainfall, creating perfect conditions for subtropical rainforest plants such as bamboo, ferns and bromeliads. In fact, Los Haitises contains over 700 species of flora, including four types of mangrove, making it one of the most highly biodiverse regions in the Caribbean. There are also 110 species of birds, 13 of which are endemic to the island.

The park also contains a series of limestone caves, some of which contain intriguing Taíno pictographs. Drawn by the native inhabitants of Hispaniola using mangrove shoots, the pictures depict faces, hunting scenes, whales and other animals. Several petroglyphs can also be seen at the entrance of some caves and are thought to represent divine guardians. Las Cuevas de la Arena, La Cueva del Templo and La Cueva de San Gabriel are three of the more interesting caves and shouldn't be missed.

Birders should keep an eye out for brown pelicans, American frigate birds, blue herons, roseate terns and the northern jacanas. If you're lucky, you may even spot the rare Hispaniolan parakeet, notable for its light-green and red feathers.

The most intimate way to see the park is on a kayak excursion. Whale Samaná (p127) and Flora Tours (p137) are excellent Samaná-based outfitters offering environmentally sensitive trips outside whale season (April to December). The Sabana de la Mar–based local guide association, Aguitusamar (p122), can also get you into the park as can several boatmen who mill about the park's entrance – try Joél (☑809-225-0517; Embadacero Caño Hondo) or Tin (☑809-225-0535; tinmauricio@hotmail.com; Embadacero Caño Hondo), who charge RD$2000 for two people, RD$3000 for up to five, for a 2½-hour tour that typically takes in the mangroves, Bahía de San Lorenzo, Muelle Antigua, Cuevas de la Arena and Cueva de la Línea.

🛏 Sleeping & Eating

Hotel La Loma   HOTEL $
(☑809-553-5562; www.hotellalomamiches.com; Miches; r/tr RD$1500/1800; P❋🛜🐕) Hotel La Loma is a comfortable place to stop for a night on your way to Sabana de la Mar, and it's certainly the best place to stay in town, even considering the management, which has quite a bit of attitude (at no extra charge, of course).

La Playita   DOMINICAN $$
(Calle Duarte 40; mains RD$300-650; ⊙9pm-midnight; 🛜) As good as it gets in Miches, this mini-complex along the town seafront does a good job with Dominican seafood and an even better job with drinking – the cold Presidentes go down quite nicely on the hardwood patio with seaviews, as does the rum at one of the two modern bars.

❶ Information

BanReservas (www.banreservas.com.do; cnr Calle Fernando Deligne & Gral Santana) is at the western end of town, one block from Calle Mella, with a 24-hour ATM.

❶ Getting There & Away

Sitrahimi (☑809-553-5042) has guaguas to Higüey (RD$180, 2½ hours, every 30 minutes, 4:25am to 6pm) and Bávaro (RD$250, 1¾ hours, 6am, noon, 5pm), leaving from a new terminal at the eastern entrance to town. **Asochosin** (☑849-214-6640; cnr Calles Mella & 16 de Agosto) has guaguas going to and from Sabana de la Mar (RD$120, 1½ hours, every 20 minutes, 6:30am to 6pm), leaving from the corner of Calles Mella and 16 de Agosto.

If you are simply passing through town, whether from Sabana de la Mar to Higüey or vice versa, let the driver know you want to catch an onward bus and he will most likely drop you at the next terminal, saving you a motoconcho or taxi ride between the two.

Sabana de la Mar

POP 13,723

The literal and figurative end of the road, this small, ramshackle and largely forgotten town is a gateway to Parque Nacional Los Haitises (though most folks generally visit from Península de Samaná). But with the long-awaited completion of Hwy DR-4 east to Miches, and plans for a car-ferry to Samaná in the works, Sabana is at a transition point to better capitalize on a slice of the economic pie from the growing number of tourists visiting the bay for whale-watching and Los Haitises tours. For now, Sabana remains the departure point for the passenger ferry across the bay to Samaná, as well as for the dangerous Mona Passage crossing to Puerto Rico, the first stop for many Dominicans hoping to make their way to the USA.

Tours

The Paraíso Caño Hondo is a highly recommended hotel 9km west of town and 1km past the Parque Nacional Los Haitises entrance, and offers good tours inside the park as well. **Boat excursions** range between RD$1250 and RD$4400 for groups of one to four depending on the extent of the tour, and **hiking trips** (RD$1500 for one to 20 people) through the park's *bosque húmedo* (rainforest) also can be arranged. During the humpback season, Paraíso organizes whale-watching tours (per person US$85) in the waters near Samaná.

Aguitusamar (☑ 809-868-4301; Calle Elupina Cordero; ☺ 8am-5pm), the local guide association, offers whale-watching tours in season (per person US$75), trips to Los Haitises (per person US$50) and Cayo Levantado (per person US$50), or combo trips for US$120 per person. There are five or so out of 26 guides that speak basic English (look for Rafael, Paulino, Roberto Jackson, Antonio Trinidad or Juan Julio Rodriguez). You'll find them in the small blue 'Tourist Information' office near the pier or hanging about the adjacent parking lot; or at the **Parque Nacional Los Haitises Office** (☑ 809-556-7333; Calle Elupina Cordero; ☺ 8am-3pm Mon-Fri, 24hr Sat & Sun), one block west of the town plaza. Both are on Calle Elupina Cordero, which parallels the seafront.

🛏 Sleeping & Eating

Hotel Riverside HOTEL $
(☑ 809-556-7465; Av de los Héroes 75; r with/without air-con RD$600/400; ❋) A block south of the Asotrasamar *guagua* station is this place to lay your head for the night; a family rents out 14 or so large rooms next door to their home.

★**Paraíso Caño Hondo** HOTEL $$
(☑ 809-696-3710; www.paraisocanohondo.com; s/d/tr incl breakfast RD$2040/3212/4437; 🅿 🛜 🌊) 🍴 Nothing good comes easy and this quirky and rustic retreat, one of the more special places to stay anywhere in the DR, and the antithesis of the all-inclusives for which the country is famous, won't persuade you otherwise. Coming upon Paraíso Caño Hondo so far out of the way after a long and rough road feels like an epiphany.

The Río Jivales, which runs through the 48-room property, has been channeled into 12 magical waterfall-fed pools, perfect for a soak any time of the day. Rooms are divided into the main area, which are large and rustic, and made mostly of wood, though extremely comfortable. Bathroom ceilings are made of aged dried palm fronds and energy-saving light fixtures are used throughout, giving the whole place a sustainable edge. A hilltop annex known as Altos de Caño has spectacular views, and the brand-new Bosque de Caño, best of all, has rooms built directly into the rock wall and featuring wonderful balconies with the most panoramic views. The *criolla* restaurant here is the best place to eat in the area (the hotel offers all-inclusive packages but it's cheaper to order from the menu à la carte). You can also visit on a day pass for RD$800 including lunch.

To find Paraíso Caño Hondo, follow the faded 'Parque Nacional Los Haitises' sign toward Caño Hondo one block south of the intersection of Hwys DR-3 and DR-4 in Sabana de la Mar – it's around 9km down a nasty but passable road.

El Caney DOMINICAN $
(mains RD$75-450; ☺ 7:30am-10pm) Location is everything and this thatch-roofed establishment just off the parking lot near the Aguitusamar guide association does a brisk business with folks heading out on excursions for the day. It serves simple but well-done Dominican breakfasts (best *mangú* we had on the trip!) and seafood,

with the menu relayed via the two friendly owners.

Restaurant Johnson SEAFOOD **$$**
(Calle Elupina Cordero 5; mains RD$225-650; ☺8:30am-midnight) Great seafood is offered at this simple Dominican place on the town square, walkable from the ferry pier.

ℹ Information

BanReservas (www.banreservas.com.do; Calle Duarte) is four blocks south of the ferry pier and has an ATM.

ℹ Getting There & Away

Hwy DR-3 from Hato Mayor descends from the hills straight into Sabana de la Mar, turning into Av de los Héroes before reaching a roundabout that leads to Av Duarte and Av Eliseo Demorizi (Calle Diego de Lira) to the east, the two one-way main streets, and eventually bumping right into the pier where the Samaná ferry leaves and arrives. DR-4 northeast from Miches intersects with the Higüey highway just south of town.

The turnoff to Caño Hondo and Parque Nacional Los Haitises is a short distance north of the Miches intersection – the sign is well-faded (and should be replaced by Paraíso Caño Hondo in the near future), but for now it's easier to spot Bodegon Hermanos Vasquez instead.

Guaguas leave from the entrance of town on or around Av de los Héroes, near the crossroads of Hwys DR-3 and DR-4. **Asotrasamar** (☑ 809-556-7343; Av de los Héroes) has *guaguas* heading to Santo Domingo (RD$285, 3½ hours, every 30 minutes, 4am to 4:30pm) that stop along the way in Hato Mayor (RD$100, one hour) and San Pedro de Macorís (RD$170, two hours). *Guaguas* with **Asochosin** (☑ 809-214-6640; Carretera Miches) also provide service to Miches (RD$120, one hour, every 20 minutes, 6:30am to 7pm).

Passenger ferries across the Bahía de Samaná to Samaná depart from the town pier (RD$200, 1¼ hours, 9am, 11am, 3pm and 5pm). From there you can catch *guaguas* to Las Galeras or Las Terrenas, or puddle-jump to other destinations on the north coast. Bad weather means rough seas and frequent cancellations, and some of the boats are rickety, making even a voyage under sunny skies a potentially seasickening experience for those with sensitive stomachs. Buy your ticket on the boat.

There are no taxi stops in Sabana de lar Mar but there are a few drivers. For trips with up to three passengers to Santo Domingo (RD$5500) and Bávaro (RD$5500), among others, contact recommended driver **Hector Hernandez** (☑ 809-920-1703).

PUNTA CANA & THE SOUTHEAST SABANA DE LA MAR

Península de Samaná

Best Places to Eat

➡ El Monte Azul (p135)

➡ Restaurante Luís (p141)

➡ La Terrasse (p142)

➡ El Lugar (p142)

➡ L'Hacienda (p130)

Best Places to Sleep

➡ Casa El Paraíso (p135)

➡ Dominican Tree House Village (p129)

➡ Eva Luna (p141)

➡ Todo Blanco (p134)

➡ Peninsula House (p141)

Why Go?

This sliver of land is the antithesis of the Dominican-Caribbean dream in the southeast, where resorts rule and patches of sand come at a first-class premium. Far more laid-back and, in certain senses, more cosmopolitan, Samaná offers a European vibe as strong as espresso; it's where escape is the operative word, and where French and Italian are at least as useful as Spanish. The majority of visitors come to gasp at the North Atlantic humpback whales doing their migratory song and dance from mid-January to mid-March, but the peninsula is no one-trick pony. Sophisticated Las Terrenas is the place for those who crave a lively social scene, and sleepy Las Galeras boasts several of the best and most secluded beaches in the Dominican Republic (DR).

When to Go

➡ North Atlantic humpback whales put on a show in the Bahía de Samaná from mid-January to late March. February is the best month.

➡ Crowds have thinned out by April, but weather remains pleasant.

➡ Enjoy drier days in early December after the autumn rains and before domestic holidaymakers descend.

History

Because of Bahía de Samaná's fortuitous geography – its deep channel, eastward orientation and easy-to-defend mouth, perfect for a naval installation – the Península de Samaná has been coveted, fought over and bought several times. At least six countries, including Haiti, France, Spain, the US and Germany, have occupied the Samaná area or sought to do so.

Founded as a Spanish outpost in 1756, Samaná was first settled by émigrés from the Canary Islands. It was deemed a prize as early as 1807, during the brief French possession of Hispaniola. France's commander in Santo Domingo proposed building a city named Port Napoleon in Samaná, but France lost the island before the plan could move forward.

After its independence from Spain, the DR was taken over by Haiti, which controlled Hispaniola from 1822 to 1844. During this period Haiti invited more than 5000 freed and escaped slaves from the US to settle on the island. About half moved to the Samaná area. Today, a community of their descendants still speaks a form of English.

During Haitian rule, France pressured its former colony to cede the Península de Samaná in return for a reduction in the debt Haiti owed it. (Haiti had been forced to pay restitution to France for land taken from French colonists in order to gain international recognition. Of course, France never paid restitution to former slaves for their ordeal.)

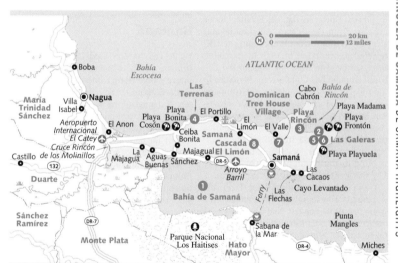

Península de Samaná Highlights

1 Whale watching (p127) Taking in the spectacular sight of majestic humpbacks breaching and diving in Bahía de Samaná.

2 El Monte Azul (p135) Dining precariously above a stupendous blue sea on the edge of the country in Las Galeras.

3 Playa Rincón (p133) Losing yourself for hours on gorgeous sun-toasted sands.

4 Las Terrenas (p136) Enjoying a sophisticated European atmosphere in cosmopolitan bars and restaurants.

5 Casa El Paraíso (p135) Gawking at postcard-perfect views from your bed at this cliff-hugging B&B in Las Galeras.

6 Las Galeras (p132) Lounging, snorkeling and lazing about isolated beaches in an end-of-the-road place,

one of the few independent-traveler-friendly locales in the DR.

7 Dominican Tree House Village (p129) Channeling your inner Tarzan or Jane in lush jungle tree houses in Samaná.

8 Cascada El Limón (p140) Navigating the rugged and wet mountain scenery of Samaná's interior on a trip to a 52m-high waterfall.

After independence from Haiti in 1844, the new Dominican government feared its neighbor would reinvade, so it sought assistance from France, Britain and Spain. The DR eventually resubmitted to Spanish rule in 1861, and Spain immediately sent a contingent of settlers to the Samaná area and reinforced the military installations on Cayo Levantado, a large island (and the site of a luxury resort today) near the mouth of the bay.

Even after independence in 1864, the Península de Samaná remained a tempting prize for other countries. Beginning in 1868, the US, under President Ulysses S Grant, sought to purchase the peninsula from the DR in order to build a naval base there. Dominican president Buenaventura Báez agreed to the sale in order to obtain the money and weapons he needed to stay in power. However, the US Senate, under pressure from Dominican exile groups and strong opposition from France and the UK, rejected the proposal in 1871. A year later, Báez arranged to lease the area to the US-based Samaná Bay Company for 99 years. To the relief of most Dominicans, the company fell behind on its payments and Baez' successor, Ignacio María González, rescinded the contract in 1874. The US revisited the idea of annexing Samaná in 1897 as the Spanish–American War loomed, but it decided to build its Caribbean base in Guantánamo Bay, Cuba, after it quickly defeated Spain.

German intentions toward the Península de Samaná were less clear, but US documents from the 1870s suggest that Germany was also seeking to establish a military base in the Caribbean. In 1916, during WWI, the US occupied the DR in part because it feared that Germany was seeking to establish itself there.

ⓘ Getting There & Around

Península de Samaná's Aeropuerto Internacional El Catey (p302; AZS; otherwise known as Aeropuerto Internacional Presidente Juan Bosch) is on the highway between Nagua and Sánchez. It receives international flights mainly from Canada (Ottawa on Air Canada, Toronto on Westjet, Montreal and Québec City on Air Transat, among others) and France (Paris on XL Airways). In high season, more cities in the US, Canada and Europe are serviced through charter flights. The airport has a lone car-rental agency, **Sixt** (☑ 809-541-7498; www.sixt.com).

One other airport – 'international' in name only – serves the peninsula. Domestic charter airlines serve Aeropuerto Internacional Arroyo Barril near Samaná, especially during whale-watching season.

Other than cruise ships, the only sea option is the regular ferry service between Samaná and Sabana de la Mar in the southeast. Cars are not allowed (though as the road to Sabana de la Mar nears completion, a car ferry is in the works) and the schedule is subject to the weather.

Journey time by car along the DR-7 highway from Santo Domingo to Samaná is less than two hours. The 102km stretch of highway begins at Autopista Las Américas DR-3 (30km east of Santo Domingo near the international airport) and ends at the Cruce Rincón de los Molinillos, 18km west of Sánchez. The toll road – practically an autobahn compared to most other roads in the country – costs RD$978 if you continue to Las Terrenas.

Caribe Tours (☑ 809-552-7434; www.caribetours.com.do) serves the peninsula by bus.

Samaná

POP 33, 200

While Las Terrenas and Las Galeras boast pristine swaths of sand and sophisticated international vibes, Samaná town – officially Santa Barbara de Samaná – is mostly content to trudge along as the peninsula's gritty and noisy workhorse. It would be worth little more than a glance in the rearview mirror for most tourists were it not for the whale-watching on offer here.

The first expedition to see North Atlantic humpback whales passing through the waters off the town was in 1985, and every year since then, from mid-January to mid-March, otherwise somnolent Samaná springs to life as an influx of tourists comes to catch glimpses of these magnificent aquatic mammals. Because North Atlantic humpbacks find the bay water particularly suitable for their annual version of speed dating, the commercialization of this natural spectacle has single-handedly catapulted the town's tourism status – for a few months each year, at least – to world-renowned.

◉ Sights

Cayo Levantado   ISLAND

A gorgeous public beach lies on the western third of this lush island, 7km from Samaná. It's the only section that's open to the public – a five-star hotel occupies the rest. Boatmen at Samaná's pier can get you there for RD$250 per person round-trip; groups of up to 15 people can negotiate a private full-day boat for RD$3000 round-trip.

Note that the idyll can be somewhat marred by the commercialization of the experience. Large cruise ships dock here regularly, and the facilities, including a few restaurants and bars, don't offer much peace and quiet. If you choose to visit, try to go in mid- to late afternoon, when most of the activity is winding down.

Playa las Flechas   BEACH

This small beach, around 5km east of Samaná, is easily accessible from town. It's thought by many historians to be the site of a small and short battle between Columbus' crew and the Ciguayos, a Taíno *cacique* (chiefdom), in which the Spaniards were driven back to their ship. A week later, their differences somehow reconciled, they formed an alliance against the rival *caciques*.

🏃 Activities

For sheer awe-inspiring, 'the natural world is an amazing thing' impact, seeing whales up close is hard to beat, and Samaná is considered to be one of the world's top 10 whale-watching destinations. Around 45,000 people travel here every year between January 15 and March 25 to see the majestic acrobatics of these massive creatures. February is peak season for humpback whales, but try to avoid the weekend of February 27 – the DR's Independence Day – as the associated Carnival makes it the busiest weekend of the winter and Samaná is packed.

Most of the whale-watching companies have a morning and an afternoon trip. There's little difference in terms of your likelihood of seeing whales, and although the water may be slightly rougher in the afternoon, it also tends to be less busy, with fewer boats out. The 43 vessels with legal permits belong to eight companies (two of them foreign owned – Canadian and Spanish – and the rest owned by Dominicans from Samaná) and around 12 independent operators. A co-management and self-regulation agreement was established in 1994 between the boat owners and various departments of the Dominican government, including the Ministry of Tourism and the Ministry of the Environment. A manual of rules and responsible behavior was created and every year all the stakeholders sign it to renew their commitment. One of the more important objectives is ensuring a minimum boat size of 8.7m: in big seas small boats are low

to the water and sometimes aren't aware of the whales until they're too close.

Private vessels can now obtain whale-watching permits once per season per boat for RD$2500 per passenger; this applies to yachts and boats of any size. Do your part by not patronizing illegal operators. Your vessel should have a registration number and a white-and-blue flag issued by the Ministry of the Environment.

★ Whale Samaná   WHALE WATCHING

(☑ 809-538-2494; www.whalesamana.com; cnr Mella & Av la Marina; adult/5-10yr/under 5yr US$59/30/free; ⊙ office 8am-1pm & 3-6pm Jan-Mar, 9am-1pm Mon-Fri Apr-Dec) 🌊 Samaná's most recommended whale-watching outfit is owned and operated by Canadian marine-mammal specialist Kim Beddall, the first person to recognize the scientific and economic importance of Samaná's whales way back in 1985. The company uses a large two-deck boat with capacity for 60 people.

Daily tours leave at 10am in January, 9am and 1:30pm from February to mid-March, and 10am from March 12 to March 25; they last three to four hours, including a stop at Cayo Levantado on the way back. The skilled captains religiously observe the local boat-to-whale distance and other regulations – most of which Beddall helped create – while on-board guides offer interesting information in five languages over the boat's sound system. Sodas and water are provided free of charge. The price does not include the admission fee to the marine sanctuary (RD$100, with a price hike consistently threatened). As a bonus, Whale Samaná allows you to reuse your ticket for a second trip if you don't see any whales – there is no expiration date for this offer. In low season, this is one of the few outfits taking kayaks into Parque Nacional Los Haitises (p121) – a definite highlight. Reserve in advance.

👉 Tours

Several agencies offer whale-watching excursions, as well as trips to Cascada El Limón (p140) (US$25) and Parque Nacional Los Haitises (p121) (US$65). For larger groups, most of these companies include a tour guide who can answer basic questions, but there are no naturalists associated with these operators.

PENÍNSULA DE SAMANÁ SAMANÁ

Samaná

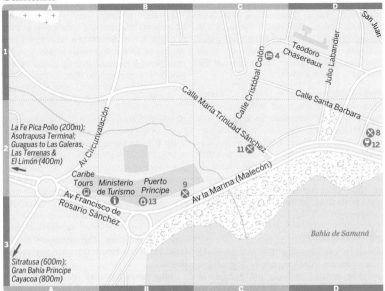

PENÍNSULA DE SAMANÁ SAMANÁ

Samaná

Tour Samaná with Terry ADVENTURE SPORTS
(☑809-538-3179; www.toursamanawithterry.com) This outfit offers recommended day trips to El Limón (p140), whale-watching (working alongside Whale Samaná (p127), adding transport and credit-card facilities to its services) and more adventurous horseback-riding/zip-lining and quad-biking/zip-lining combos starting from US$60. It also does a recommended four-beach trip to Las Galeras (p132) that includes a lobster lunch.

Terry can also arrange peninsula day trips for folks staying in Punta Cana.

Moto Marina BOATING
(☑809-538-2302; www.motomarinatours-excursionsamana.com; Av la Marina 3; ⊙8am-noon & 2-6pm Mon-Sat, 8am-noon Sun) A long-standing, dependable option for getting to Parque Nacional Los Haitises (p121).

🛏 Sleeping

There's little reason to stay in Samaná proper and most people booking whale-watching or Los Haitises trips do so from Las Terrenas, Las Galeras or further afield. Hotels here don't generally include breakfast, though coffee and tea are usually available.

clean, with cable TV, air-con and minibars, though the aging bathtubs aren't all that inviting.

★ Dominican Tree House Village
TREEHOUSE **$$$**

(☑ 800-820-1357; www.dominicantreehousevillage.com; El Valle; r without bathroom incl breakfast & dinner from US$235, VIP r with bathroom US$345; 🐜) 🅿 Tucked away discreetly in El Valle, this lush sustainable-ecotourism project is the spot to live out your dream of sleeping in a stilted cabin in the jungle. The 19 standard tree houses here are open on three sides and feature queen beds and hammock chairs, all with a dose of privacy and dramatic tropical-forest views.

The larger VIP cabins have outdoor shower and attached bathroom. Guests mingle over drinks and meals in the bar and lounge – like the tree houses, all constructed from 98% organic material and calling on a twisted climbing-root support system known as *bejuco* to help hold it all together – before heading down for a bit of rum in one of the property fire pits. Don't miss the 13-station zip line, either, one of the most thrilling in the Caribbean (guests/Dominicans/foreigners US$55/40/60). El Valle is 9.5km north of Samaná town.

Gran Bahía Principe Cayo Levantado
HOTEL **$$$**

(☑ 809-538-3232; www.bahia-principe.com; Cayo Levantado; all incl s/d from RD$19,520/24,400; 🐜 @ 🛜 🐜) This romantic five-star place has a lot going for it, including its 'private' beach on Cayo Levantado's idyllic sands. The 268-room hotel sits on extra-lush grounds and offers classic luxury á la the Ritz-Carlton (ie slightly stuffy). However, the excellent rooms, with hardwood floors and some with patio ocean views and vaulted ceilings, suffer from stuffiness less than the lobby.

There are two delightful pools, the best of which is accessed via an outdoor elevator, and four restaurants. Room service is available (unlike at its sister property in town). The downside is that it's on an island and you'll need to take a boat (provided by the hotel) to get there... Well, that's the upside, too. Cheaper rates are available when booked with tour packages.

Gran Bahía Principe Cayacoa
HOTEL **$$$**

(☑ 809-538-3131; www.bahiaprincipe.com; all incl s/d from RD$12,880/16,100; 🅿 🐜 @ 🛜 🐜) Perched on a cliff above the city with spectacular views

Aire y Mar
GUESTHOUSE **$**

(☑ 809-538-2913; aparthotel-aireymar@hotmail.com; Calle 27 de Febrero 4; r with air-con from RD$1300-2000; 🛜) A gold budget star goes to this six-room hilltop guesthouse. Rooms are bare bones (but clean!) and there's a nice communal kitchen, but the real highlight – and the reward for climbing the street from the *malecón* (waterfront path) and then a steep staircase – is the view from the hammock-strewn patio. The good-soul owner, Noelia, looks after guests with motherly care.

Samaná Spring Hotel
HOTEL **$**

(☑ 809-538-2946; samanaspring@hotmail.com; Cristóbal Colón 12; s/d RD$1500/2200; 🐜 🛜) The clean and extra-friendly Samaná Spring has 16 basic but well-maintained rooms with cable TV and hot water. It's close to much of the local nightlife (read: it can get noisy).

Hotel Blue View
HOTEL **$$**

(☑ 809-538-2215; hotelchino.samana@hotmail.com; San Juan 1; r/tr from RD$2650/4700; 🅿 🐜 🛜) Located above a nice international/Chinese restaurant (mains RD$165 to RD$950) on top of a hill, Hotel Blue View has rooms with balconies offering fantastic views of town and the waterfront. The rooms are shiny and

PENÍNSULA DE SAMANÁ SAMANÁ

of the bay (and maybe even of humpbacks during whale season), this 295-room resort is Samaná town's fanciest. Recently renovated standard rooms now boast vanilla accents, and there are three pools, three restaurants (Italian, French and seafood), a casino, a spa, a water-sports center, a discotheque and two beaches.

Eating

The majority of restaurants are located along Av Malecón, while cheaper eats can be found in converted wooden kiosks along the waterfront and along Av Francisco de Rosario Sánchez.

Café Italia   BAKERY $
(Av Malecón; items RD$50-90; ⊘ 7am-9pm; 🤙) The Península de Samaná in a nutshell: an Italian-owned cafe serving nothing but French pastries that aren't baked on premises but procured from the best French bakery in Las Terrenas and brought in daily! It's dead simple, little more than a display case of *pains au chocolat*, almond croissants and baguettes, and a few plastic tables.

Le Royal Snack   CAFE $
(Av Malecón 4; mains RD$140-350; ⊘ 7:30am-10pm; 🤙) Across from the ferry dock, this simple French-run cafe is a good bet for French-leaning quick meals throughout the day.

La Fe Pica Pollo   DOMINICAN $
(Av Francisco de Rosario Sánchez 15; meals RD$120-240; ⊘ 8am-11pm) A small hole in the wall close to the *guagua* terminal serving tasty fried chicken plus a few other Dominican dishes.

★ L'Hacienda Restaurant   STEAK, SEAFOOD $$
(Santa Barbara; mains RD$480-640; ⊘ 7pm-midnight Thu-Tue; 🤙) José, the friendly French chef-owner with a Spanish name – who comes from a family of nine, five of whom are chefs – has been running this intimate French-Caribbean spot since 1987. It's a small and simple nightly chalkboard menu of meat and seafood grills, served up in a soothing, baby-blue atmosphere fit for the Caribbean. Easily Samaná's best.

Expect a fresh fish or two (grilled or in *coco* sauce), a chicken and/or mixed-grill option and a couple of appetizers and desserts (a fresh *ceviche* here, a chocolate

mousse there, a green salad doused in perfect vinaigrette...).

Tierra y Mar   DOMINICAN $$
(cnr Avs María Trinidad Sánchez & Malecón; mains RD$150-600; ⊘ 8am-10:30pm; 🤙) Service can be an issue here, but there's no denying the food is tasty, especially the fish in Creole sauce (tomatoes, onions and peppers). There are North American/Dominican breakfasts and a variety of meat, seafood and pasta dishes as well. It's all served in an open-air thatched hut with bamboo furniture.

Taberna Mediterranea   SPANISH $$
(Av Malecón 1; mains RD$250-690; ⊘ 10am-11pm Tue-Sun; 🤙) The recently renovated front patio and neon-lit bar are definite ambience downgrades (though you can still opt for the older, stone-walled dining area), but the food at this Spanish tavern remains consistently good, with massive meat and fish *tablas* big enough for three or more (RD$1200 to RD$3800) leading the way, along with standard meat and fish dishes and pizza.

La Mata Rosada   DOMINICAN $$
(Av Malecón 5; mains RD$320-770; ⊘ 10am-3pm & 6:30-11pm) Malecón mainstay La Mata Rosada has an extensive menu of seafood and grills. The sophisticated front patio is the town's most formal, but that doesn't mean it's immune to *motoconcho* exhaust. The small bar is one of the classier ones in town. Vegans can go for the excellent white-bean salad by axing the bacon.

🍸 Drinking & Nightlife

Nightlife is no Samaná strong point. The wildest evenings take place along Av Malecón near Calle María Trinidad Sánchez, where locals gather in the evening at a line of makeshift bars pumping out reggaeton and merengue. You could also have a cocktail in one of the nicer restaurants along Av Malecón.

Cafe de Paris   BAR
(Av Malecón 6; cocktails RD$100-350; ⊘ 8am-midnight daily Jan-Mar, 10am-10pm Wed-Mon Apr-Dec; 🤙) Samaná's one welcoming bar, this French-owned mainstay offers more beers than most, a good selection of rum (including Nicaragua's excellent Flor de Cana) and standard cocktails in a makeshift, loungy environment. There's also an extensive menu of bar food, from salads

and sandwiches to crepes and pizza (mains RD$80 to RD$590).

Shopping

The expensive mini-market (Av Malecón; ☺9am-6pm) at Puerto Principe shopping center, which dominates the western end of Av Malecón, sells wine, cigars and kitsch souvenirs.

❶ Information

Banco Popular (Av Malecón 4; ☺8am-4pm Mon-Fri, 9am-1pm Sat) Across from the ferry dock.

BanReservas (Santa Barbara; ☺8am-5pm Mon-Fri, 9am-1pm Sat) One block north of Av Malecón.

Centro Médico de Especialidades Samaná (☑809 538-3999; www.cmes.com.do; Coronel Andrés Diaz 6; ☺24hr) Samaná's best hospital, run by Cuban doctors.

Cestur (Cuerpo Especializado de Seguridad Turística; ☑809-200-3500; www.cestur.gob.do; Av Francisco de Rosario Sánchez; ☺24hr) Tourist police; located behind Av Malecón on a small parallel street near the third traffic circle coming from the sea.

Clinic Assist (☑809-538-2481; Puerto Principe, Av Francisco de Rosario Sánchez; ☺24hr) Small, makeshift clinic.

Farmacia Carol (www.farmaciacarol.com; Puerto Principe, Av Francisco de Rosario Sánchez; ☺24hr) A professional, fully stocked 24-hour pharmacy.

Ministerio de Turismo (Ministry of Tourism; ☑809-538-2332; www.godominicanrepublic.com; Puerto Principe, Av Francisco de Rosario Sánchez 5; ☺8am-3pm Mon-Fri) Small national tourism office. Helpful for maps and other info, though not as well stocked with brochures as it should be.

❶ Getting There & Away

AIR

Aeropuerto Internacional El Catey (p302), 40km west of Samaná, receives international flights. The closest airstrip to Samaná, Aeropuerto Internacional Arroyo Barril, mostly receives domestic charter flights.

BUS

Caribe Tours (☑809-538-2229; www.caribetours.com.do; Puerto Principe, Av Francisco de Rosario Sánchez) offers services to Santo Domingo at 7am, 8am, 9am, 10am, 1pm, 2pm, 3pm and 4pm (RD$340, 4½ hours, daily), alternating between the faster highway route or the route via San Pedro de Macorís. Stops include Sánchez (RD$70, 30 minutes), Nagua (RD$100, one hour) and San Francisco de Macorís (RD$140, 1½ hours), but double-check the stops for your particular bus.

For direct services to Puerto Plata, 210km to the west, there are now three options. **Gingo** (☑829-376-8346) leaves from in front of the little park next to Banco Popular on Av Malecón at 8am. **Santo Canario** (☑829-944-3041) leaves at 11am beside Banco Popular on the park's western side. **Papagallo** (☑ask for Salvador 809-749-6415) offers a service at 1:45pm from under the mango tree on the eastern side of the park. If you miss him there, he waits at the municipal market until 2pm. All charge RD$300 and the trip takes about 3½ to four hours. Call ahead to double-check the day's departure. Arrive 30 to 45 minutes early to reserve a seat.

For service to towns on the peninsula, *guaguas* congregate haphazardly near the *mercado municipal*, 450m west of the Cestur station, near Calle Angel Mesina. From here, minivans head to Las Galeras (RD$100, one hour, every 10 minutes from 6:30am to 6pm), El Limón (RD$70, 50 minutes, every 15 minutes, 6:30am to 6pm) and Las Terrenas (RD$100, 1¼ hours, every 90 minutes, 6:30am to 4:45pm). Destinations further afield also leave from the same block at the more organized **Asotrapusa Terminal** (☑829-222-0368; Av Francisco de Rosario Sánchez). Destinations include Santo Domingo (RD$325, 2½ hours, every 45 minutes, 4:30am to 4:45pm) and Santiago (RD$325, three hours, every 45 minutes, 4:45am to 2:30pm). The Puerto Plata services also make a stop here on their way out of town, but seats may be full by then.

FERRY

Various operators run a **ferry service** – passengers only, no vehicles – across the Bahía de Samaná to Sabana de la Mar (RD$200, one hour plus, 7am, 9am, 11am and 3pm daily). Buy tickets on board. From there, it's possible to catch *guaguas* to several destinations in the southeast and then on to Santo Domingo.

TAXI

The **Sitratusa** (☑809-538-3131 ext 1246) taxi stand is operated by and sits just outside the entrance to Gran Bahía Principe Cayacoa resort. Fares are expensive. Samples include Las Galeras (US$45), Las Terrenas (US$55), Aeroporto El Catey (US$70), Caberete (US$170), Puerto Plata (US$190), Santo Domingo (US$190), Santiago (US$200) and Punta Cana (US$380).

GETTING AROUND

Samaná is walkable, but if you're carrying luggage, catch a *motoconcho* (motorcycle taxi) – they're everywhere. 4WD vehicles are your only option in terms of car rental – roads on the peninsula are bad enough to warrant the extra expense. Rates average around US$50 per day (tax and insurance included) and discounts are typically given for

PENÍNSULA DE SAMANÁ SAMANÁ

rentals of a week or longer. Try **Xamaná Rent A Motor** (☑809-538-2833; fabianking1812@ hotmail.com; Av Malecón; ⊙8am-6pm Mon-Sat, to noon Sun).

Las Galeras

POP 6930

The road to this small fishing community 28km northeast of Samaná ends at a shack on the beach. So does everything else, metaphorically speaking. One of the great pleasures of a stay here is losing all perspective on the world beyond – even the beautiful and isolated outlying beaches seem far away. By all means succumb to the temptation to do nothing more than lie around your bungalow or while the day away at a restaurant. But – if you summon the will to resist – Las Galeras offers a variety of land- and water-based activities.

The town's laid-back charms have not gone unnoticed, drawing a cosmopolitan mix of European and North American visitors, and it's one of the few independent-traveler-friendly locales in the DR.

There's one main intersection in town (about 50m before the highway dead-ends at the beach) and most hotels, restaurants and services are walking distance from there.

☉ Sights

Las Galeras has a number of natural attractions that can be visited by boat or car, or on foot or horseback. All can be reached on your own, provided you're in decent shape or have a sturdy vehicle.

Playa Frontón   BEACH
Playa Frontón boasts some of the area's best snorkeling. Apparently it's also popular with drug smugglers, Dominicans braving the Mona Passage on their way to Puerto Rico, and reality-show contestants – in 2002 *Expedición Robinson*, Colombia's version of *Survivor*, was filmed here. Trails lead to the beach, but it's easy to get lost, so hire a local guide (contact Karin at La Hacienda or,

---

ⓘ ROBBERIES

Tourists visiting Boca del Diablo and Playas Madama and Frontón on their own have frequently been robbed, especially in high season. Leave your valuables at your hotel or go with a local guide (RD$1000 per day).

---

preferably, come by boat: Asoldega (p136) charges about RD$3000 to Playa Frontón (RD$1000 per person with four or more).

Playa Madama   BEACH
Playa Madama is a small beach framed by high bluffs at the edge of the country; keep in mind there's not much sunlight here in the afternoon. Asoldega (p136) charges around RD$2500 to Playa Madama (RD$800 per person with four or more people).

Playita   BEACH
Better than the beach in town, Playita (Little Beach) is easy to get to on foot or by *motoconcho*. It's a stretch of tannish sand and mellow surf, backed by tall, dramatically leaning palm trees. On the main road just south of Las Galeras, look for signs to Hotel La Playita pointing down a dirt road headed west. Beach chairs rent for RD$100 per day.

Boca del Diablo   LANDMARK
'Mouth of the Devil' is an impressive vent or blowhole, where waves rush up a natural channel and blast out of a hole in the rocks. Car or motorcycle is the best way to get here – look for an unmarked dirt road 7km south of town and about 100m beyond the well-marked turnoff to Playa Rincón. Follow the road east for about 8km, then walk the last 100m or so.

⚡ Activities

Diving
Popular dive sites include **Piedra Bonita**, a 50m stone tower good for spotting jacks, barracudas and sea turtles; **Cathedral**, an enormous underwater cave opening to sunlight; and a sunken 55m container ship haunted by big morays. Several large, shallow coral patches, including **Los Carriles**, a series of underwater hills, are good for beginner divers.

For experienced divers, Cabo Cabron (Bastard Point, p137) is one of the north coast's best sites. After an easy boat ride from Las Galeras, you're dropped into a churning channel with a giant coral formation that you can swim around; you may see dolphins here.

Las Galeras Divers   DIVING
(☑809-538-0220; www.las-galeras-divers.com; Plaza Lusitania; ⊙8am-6pm) Las Galeras Divers is a well-respected, French-run dive shop at the main intersection. One-/two-tank dives including all equipment cost US$55/85 (US$10 less if you have your own gear). Discounted dive packages are offered. Various PADI-certification courses can also be arranged.

PLAYA RINCÓN

Pitch-perfect Playa Rincón, with soft, nearly white sand and multihued water good for swimming, stretches an uninterrupted 3km – enough for every day-tripper to claim their own piece of real estate. There's a small stream at the far western end, which is great for a quick freshwater dip at the end of your visit, and a backdrop of thick palm forest. Several restaurants serve seafood dishes and rent beach chairs, making this a great place to spend the entire day.

Most people arrive by boat; the standard option is to leave Las Galeras around 9am and be picked up at 4pm – it's around 20 minutes each way. Asoldega (p136) runs vaguely fixed-price return trips for RD$2500 (RD$800 per person with four or more people).

All but the last 2km of the road to the beach have been recently resurfaced, but even the unpaved section is passable in any vehicle, except after particularly heavy rain. The turnoff is 7km south of Las Galeras on the road to Samaná. A round-trip taxi, including waiting time (9am to 5pm), is RD$2000. *Motoconchos* will get you there for RD$1200 return.

One downside: an awful lot of flotsam and jetsam lies uncollected along the sands. Some historians say that it's here, not on Playa las Flechas, that Columbus and his crew landed.

PENÍNSULA DE SAMANÁ LAS GALERAS

Diving Scuba Libre DIVING
(🖉 809-958-9111; www.lasgaleras-scubadiving.com; Grand Paradise Samaná resort; ⏱ 8:30am-5pm) Scubalibre Diving Center is located at the far end of Grand Paradise Samaná's beach. In addition to diving, it offers snorkeling trips (from US$40) and windsurfer and catamaran rental and instruction (US$45 per hour), all available to guests and nonguests alike.

It's easy enough to walk to the dive shop by following the path along the beach from town; resort security will let you through. If you try to drive up, they won't let you in unless arrangements have been made.

Hiking

The spectacular **El Punto** lookout is a 5km walk from La Rancheta. To get there, simply continue past the turnoffs to Playas Madama and Frontón and keep climbing up, up and up. Allow at least an hour to get to the top.

Horseback Riding

Horseback Riding HORSEBACK RIDING
(🖉 829-939-8285; http://lahaciendahostel.com; per person 2hr/half-day/day US$35/55/75) Karin, the Belgian owner of La Hacienda Hostel, leads recommended horseback-riding tours to various spots around Las Galeras, including El Punto lookout, Playas Madama, Frontón and Rincón, and the surrounding hills. Her trips cater to all skill levels and range from two-hour excursions to half-day

and full-day trips. All-inclusive overnight trips are US$250.

Tours

It's possible to book all of the peninsula's standard tours with Las Galeras–based operators – day trips include whale-watching in Bahía de Samaná (US$50 with lunch) and boat excursions through Parque Nacional Los Haitises (US$65 per person) – but you're better off making your way to Samaná, where Whale Samaná (p127) and Tour Samaná with Terry (p128) have better reputations for eco-awareness and consistently churn out happy campers. A full-day boat excursion to all the beaches, including Rincón, is RD$6000 for up to four people round-trip.

Sleeping

Most of the hotels and bungalows in Las Galeras are within walking distance of the main intersection. The unimpressive Grand Paradise Samaná is the only resort in town.

La Hacienda Hostel GUESTHOUSE $
(🖉 829-939-8285; http://lahaciendahostel.com; dm/s/d US$14/28/35, 2-bedroom houses US$75; ⓟ @) Some 3km from the town intersection on the trail/rough road to Playas Madama and Frontón, Belgian expat Karin runs a one-woman show offering five rustic

rooms and a free-standing home (with cat!), a communal kitchen, and pleasant sea and mountain views. It's fairly basic, though – expect cold showers. Horseback riding with Karin is the big reason to stay here.

Sol Azul
BUNGALOW **$**

(☏ 829-882-8790; www.elsolazul.com; s/d incl breakfast from RD$2000/2500; P ☎ ⛱) A fun Swiss couple runs these four earthy, natural-hued and spacious bungalows, set around a manicured garden and pleasant pool area just 50m from the town's main intersection. Two of the bungalows feature mezzanine levels, and the breakfast buffet gets high marks from travelers – especially for the oranges and avocados straight from Sol Azul's own trees.

La Rancheta
BUNGALOW **$**

(☏ 829-889-4727; www.larancheta.com; s/d US$22/28; P) Buried in lush jungle 2.5km from the main intersection, this rustic guesthouse has four simple rooms in two-storied bungalows that can comfortably accommodate between four and six people (the top-floor rooms are less crude). Semi-outdoor rustic kitchens lend an eclectic cabin-in-the-woods feel to this *very* laid-back traveler favorite. Breakfasts are an extra US$4 to US$5 and are substantial.

★ Todo Blanco
BOUTIQUE HOTEL **$$**

(☏ 809-729-2333; www.hoteltodoblanco.com; r with/without air-con US$100/90; P ✳ ☎) Living up to its 'All White' name, this whitewashed, well-established inn sits atop a small hillock a short walk from the end of the main drag. Rooms are large and airy, with high ceilings, private terraces overlooking the sea, pastel headboards and new AC, while the multilevel grounds are nicely appointed with gardens and a gazebo.

Cheerful owner Maurizio is a fun guy to sip an espresso with, and he makes dedicated fresh-fruit runs to Samaná to supply guests' breakfasts (an extra US$9).

Plaza Lusitania Hotel
HOTEL **$$**

(☏ 809-538-0178; www.hotelplazalusitania.com; Plaza Lusitania, Principal; r with/without air-con incl breakfast from US$80/60; P ✳ ☎) Situated at the main intersection, on the 2nd floor of a tiny mall, complete with a decent Italian restaurant and a pleasant open-air atrium. Rooms are large and comfortable but nothing fancy.

El Monte Azul
B&B **$$**

(☏ 849-249-3640; www.restaurantsamana-monteazul.com; Loma del Monte Azul; r incl breakfast & spa treatment RD$4500; P ☎ ⛱) This boutique B&B attached to the stunning restaurant of the same name offers three modern rooms in the home of the Laotian-French owner-designer, Vanina, and her husband, Pierre, a French fisherman and the chef at the restaurant (p135). Done up with restrained trendiness, it's an artsy, turquoise-and-muted-grey-toned escape offering sky-high R&R with views that shock and awe.

Casa Por Qué No?
B&B **$$**

(☏ 809-712-5631; casaporqueno@live.com; s/d incl breakfast US$50/65; ☺ closed May-Oct; P ✳ ☎) Pierre and Monick, the charming French-Canadian owners of this B&B, are consummate hosts and have been renting two rooms on either side of their cozy home for nearly 30 years – each room has a separate entrance and hammock. It's only 25m or so north of the main intersection on your right as you're walking toward the beach.

The house is fronted by a long, well-maintained garden where tasty breakfasts (including delicious homemade bread) are served (RD$400 for nonguests). When you tire of DR's ubiquitous restaurant offerings, Monick can whip up her take on Asian cuisine for you. It's not the fanciest spot in town, but the hospitality is as warm as the sand.

Casa Dorado
B&B **$$**

(☏ 829-577-6777; www.casadoradodr.com; s/d from US$60/70; P ☎) This beautiful house, 1km from both the main intersection and Playita beach, features Mexican-influenced interiors styled by the American owner. Four rooms are available; the largest and most expensive comes with a Jacuzzi.

There are ample spots for relaxing, from expansive hammock-strung terraces to cozy living rooms – if the weather turns sour, this is where you want to be. If not, the excellent Dominican chef, Leonel, can guide you on a 90-minute trek to Playa Rincón. Breakfast in the gorgeously tiled kitchen is the real deal and guests from other hotels often find their way here, happy to pay US$8 for the pleasure.

Chalet Tropical
CHALET **$$**

(☏ 809-901-0738; www.chalettropical.com; Calle por La Playita; s/d/tr US$65/75/90, without bathroom US$55/65/80, chalets from US$185; P ✳ ☎) An Italian stylist is the big personality behind these wonderfully rustic-chic A-frame chalets, some broken up into rooms and others open plan. Boasting a striking range of colors and unique interior details like stone showers, coconut and bamboo wood accents, and all manner of creative combinations, everything here looks like a beautiful indigenous handicraft made to wow you.

⭐ **Casa El Paraíso**　　　　　　B&B $$$

(☏ 809-975-1641; www.facebook.com/CasaElParaisoRD; La Guázuma; r incl breakfast US$150-190; 🛜🐾) 🕊 Santo Domingo veterinarians Nora and José, a gourmet Italian chef named Mirko and a gaggle of Italian greyhounds are your hosts at this extraordinary six-room B&B in La Guázuma that practically tumbles out of the jungle into the whale-packed sea below. Room 5 (nicknamed 'Africa') is completely open on two sides, framing jungle, mountain and sea as you've never seen.

The other rooms, flush with Indonesian and Indian furniture, solar-heated showers and rustic recycled elements such as headboards from sunken ships and candle-lit coral walls, have similar views, so you can't go wrong – nor can you tear yourself away from the gorgeous pool and Jacuzzi, which also captures those vistas. With Mirko whipping up some of the best food in Las Galeras, excellent Dominican breakfasts that include local cheese and *mangu*, and a rainforest of lush hospitality around every corner, the name couldn't be more appropriate. It's 5.6km south of the main intersection in Las Galeras and reachable in a standard car.

🍴 Eating

Las Galeras has no shortage of decent grub, with many restaurants located within a stone's throw of each other on the main street. Note that many restaurants close outside high season. If you're after fruit and veg, try to flag down the produce guy, who combs the main drag around noon on Thursday and Sunday.

End of the Road　　　　　　FAST FOOD $

(Principal; mains RD$150-190; ⊙ 8am-9pm; 🛜) Right at the town intersection, this small traveler's hub serves gourmet Angus-beef burgers and massive burritos (including an awesome breakfast version) cooked by locals trained by the French chef of what was the town's choicest eatery.

Aux Délices de France　　　　BAKERY $

(Principal; mains RD$150-380, pastries from RD$60; ⊙ 7am-7pm) A good bet, this French bakery in a converted house on the main street serves salads, baguette sandwiches, *croque monsieurs/madames*, and pastries including almond croissants, lemon tarts and passion-fruit crumbles.

⭐ **El Monte Azul**　　　　　SEAFOOD, THAI $$

(☏ 849-249-3640; www.restaurantsamana-monteazul.com; mains RD$450-790; ⊙ 11am-2:30pm & 5-11pm Wed-Mon; 🛜) Clinging spectacularly to the edge of the DR, this rustic, postcard-perfect restaurant with amazing views offers some of the island's most dramatic dining. Go at sunset, when a kaleidoscopic flurry of hues melts into the sea as you nurse a signature passion-fruit libation and watch families of whales from a few small tables lining the cliff edge.

El Monte Azul offers two great-value menus (French-leaning seafood and Thai), the highlight of which is an excellent lionfish in a creamy white-wine, lemon and green-onion sauce. The rub is arriving (Google Maps is not your friend!): from town, head south on the main highway for 4km, then head east at the turnoff for La Guazama and follow the signs. Standard cars will struggle up the last 1km of the steep and rough road – they can come down and fetch you, or you could take a taxi from town (US$30 round-trip). Reservations are required and you can sleep here as well.

Restaurante Isabel　　　DOMINICAN, SEAFOOD $$

(La Playita; ⊙ RD$300-800) The simplest – and best – of the three restaurants at Playita beach sits right on the sand. Owner-chef Isabel has done little more than throw a steel grate over a clay oven to cook you whatever's fresh that day. Expect grilled fish, lobster or chicken and heaps of side dishes. Isabel's French-Canadian daughter-in-law whips up good cocktails as well.

El Pescador　　　　　　SPANISH $$

(www.restaurantpescador.com; Principal; mains RD$390-950; ⊙ 10am-11pm Dec-Apr, from 3pm May-Nov) Located across from BanReservas on the main road, this is an excellent seafood option, notably for its *paella* (the owner is Spanish), which could hold its own against any in the mother country. If you beg, they'll even serve it for one person (solo travelers, rejoice!).

Rincon del Marisco   DOMINICAN, SEAFOOD $$

(809-380-7295; Principal; mains RD$350-700; ⊙10am-10pm Wed-Mon) Local chef Rubi's gastronomic feats were previously the main event at a wonderful Playa Rincón beach restaurant. While she's traded in that dramatic setting for a simple open-air place in town, the food continues to shine: fresh fish, *langosta* (lobster), grilled chicken etc. Order anything in the wonderful coco sauce and douse your coconut rice in the excellent vinaigrette.

Drinking & Nightlife

Much of the nightlife involves drinks at one of the restaurants. The cinematic open-air space at the main intersection used to be home to the town's best watering hole, but it's now occupied by an Italian bar and grill called Gato Negro, which has yet to be embraced by the locals. There are also a few beach cocktail shacks.

Raquel Sun Set   BAR

(cocktails RD$150-300; ⊙generally 9am-9pm; 🛜) Feisty Raquel makes a mighty fine *mojito* at this new beach-shack bar, nuzzled in the sands of the town beach.

L'Aventura   BAR

(Principal; ⊙4pm-midnight Mon-Fri, 11am-3pm & 5pm-midnight Sat & Sun) A popular spot for a drink along the main road. It also serves what's considered to be the town's best pizza (RD$290 to R$540).

❶ Information

DANGERS & ANNOYANCES

Cestur (Cuerpo Especializado de Seguridad Turística; 849-452-5536; Principal; ⊙24hr) Tourist police.

MEDICAL SERVICES

Grand Paradise Samaná (www.grandparadise samana.com; ⊙24hr) The resort has a small clinic that nonguests can use in emergencies.

MONEY

BanReservas (www.banreservas.com; Principal) ATM one block north of the Malecón and another at Grand Paradise Samaná resort.

Clinica Bahia Azul A small, well-run clinic in town.

❶ Getting There & Away

The paved road coming from Samaná winds along the coast and through lovely, often forested countryside before reaching the outskirts of Las Galeras.

Guaguas head to Samaná (RD$100, one hour, every 10 minutes from 6:30am to 6pm) from the beach end of Calle Principal, and they also pick up passengers as they cruise slowly out of town. There are three daily buses to Santo Domingo (RD$375, three hours, 5:30am, 1pm and 3pm).

Taxis (809-481-8526) are available at a stand just in front of the main town beach (as well as a more expensive stand near the beach at Grand Paradise Samaná resort). Sample one-way fares are RD$3000 to Aeropuerto Catey, RD$2500 to Las Terrenas, RD$1000 to Samaná and RD$7000 to Santo Domingo. You may be able to negotiate cheaper fares, especially to Samaná.

Renting a car is an excellent way to explore the peninsula on your own. Prices are generally around RD$2700 per day with insurance; **RP Rent-a-Car** (809-538-0249; jreyes.jdrv@gmail.com; Principal; ⊙8am-5pm Mon-Fri, to 3pm Sat) is one option.

❶ Getting Around

You can walk pretty much everywhere in Las Galeras. *Motoconchos*, for trips to the beaches, congregate around the main intersection in town. For boat trips, try **Asoldega** (Asociación de Lancheros de Las Galeras), the local boat association; it doesn't have a fixed location, but boatmen congregate at the town beach.

Las Terrenas

POP 18,830

Once a rustic fishing village, Las Terrenas is now a cosmopolitan town and seems as much French (approaching a colony) and Italian as Dominican. Fashionable European women in designer sunglasses ride their personal ATVs with a bag of baguettes in tow, battling on roads with way too many *motos*. The balancing act between locals and expats has produced a lively mix of styles and a social scene more vibrant than that anywhere else on the peninsula. Walking in either direction along the beach road leads to a beachfront scattered with hotels, tall palm trees and calm, aquamarine waters.

Las Terrenas is well suited to independent travelers and a good place to hook up with fellow nomads.

◉ Sights

The beach is the main attraction in Las Terrenas. Playa Las Terrenas and Playa Casa Blanca flank the center of town, bookended by the calmer sands of Playa Las Ballenas (to the west) and Playa Punta Popy (to the east).

Las Terrenas might not be that close to the **Parque Nacional Los Haitises**, but since so few independent travelers make it to Sabana de la Mar, the closest entrance to the park, Las Terrenas has become a popular place to book trips there.

Flora Tours (p137) is a recommended operator, but virtually every company in town offers excursions to Los Haitises (though generally only twice a week unless you're part of a group of six or more, in which case you can arrange trips at your own convenience). There should be at least one company with a tour on offer five days a week, but schedules change, so it's best to book as soon as you arrive in town. Half-day tours typically cost US$75 including transport, lunch and guide.

Playa Bonita
BEACH

A getaway from a getaway, the appropriately named Playa Bonita (Pretty Beach) is only a few kilometers west of Las Terrenas. It's not without imperfections – the half-moon-shaped beach is fairly steep and narrow, and parts are strewn with palm-tree detritus. However, backed by a handful of pleasant hotels, this is an enticing, peaceful spot. By car, Playa Bonita is reachable along a paved road that turns off from Calle Fabio Abreu in Las Terrenas. A taxi here is US$15 each way, a *motoconcho* RD$200.

Playa Cosón
BEACH

The sand at Playa Cosón, 8km west along the main highway from Playa Bonita, is tan, not white, and the water greenish, not blue, but nevertheless it's a good place to lose yourself for the day while noshing at some excellent surf-sprayed restaurants. Two small rivers run through the thick palm-tree forest and into the ocean; the easternmost is said to contain agricultural runoff. A taxi to the beach is US$40 round-trip, a *motoconcho* RD$300.

🏃 Activities

Diving & Snorkeling

Las Terrenas has reasonably good diving and snorkeling and at least three shops in town to take you out. Favorite dive spots include a wreck in 28m of water and Isla Las Ballenas, visible from shore, with a large underwater cave. Most operators also offer special trips to **Cabo Cabrón** (Bastard Point) near Las Galeras and Dudu Cave near Río San Juan. Standard one-tank dives average

US$60 with equipment. A 10-dive package generally costs US$400. Two-tank day trips to Cabo Cabrón are US$160, including gear, lunch and transportation; one-tank day trips to Dudu Caves are US$130, also including gear, lunch and transportation. Open-water courses average US$480.

A popular full-day snorkel trip is to Playa Jackson, several kilometers west of town, reached by boat.

Dive Academy
DIVING

(📞 829-577-5548; www.diveacademy.co; 2nd fl, Beach Garden Plaza, Libertad; ⊙ 8am-9pm) This English-run NAUI outfitter, a Las Galeras transplant, offers a 10% discount for online bookings.

Turtle Dive Center
DIVING

(📞 829-903-0659; www.turtledivecenter.com; El Paseo shopping center, Paseo de la Costanera; ⊙ 10am-12:30pm & 4-7pm) A highly recommended SSI-affiliated shop, run by a safety-first Frenchman. Also runs snorkeling trips to Playa Jackson (full-day US$90) if booked in advance with five or more people, and daily trips to Isla Las Ballenas (snorkeling/two-tank dive US$35/100).

Kitesurfing & Windsurfing

Second only to Cabarete, Las Terrenas is a good place to try out a wind sport in the DR. The beach at Punta Popy, only 1km or so east of the main intersection, is a popular place for kitesurfers and windsurfers.

LT'Kite
WATER SPORTS

(📞 809-801-5671; www.lasterrenas-kitesurf.com; Calle 27 de Febrero; ⊙ 10am-6pm) Recommended kitesurfing school run by a friendly Frenchman who speaks Spanish and English as well. It rents surfboards (per day US$30) and kitesurfing equipment (per day US$70) and provides lessons and IKO certifications for the latter. Six hours of kitesurfing lessons (really the minimum needed to have a sporting chance of making it work) cost US$300.

👉 Tours

Flora Tours
ECOTOUR

(📞 829-923-2792; www.flora-tours.net; Principal 278; ⊙ 8:30am-12:30pm & 3:30-6:30pm Mon-Sat) 🏆 This French-run agency takes top honors in town for eco-sensitive tours to Parque Nacional Los Haitises and hard-to-access beaches, as well as more tranquil catamaran trips, culturally sensitive quad-bike tours to

Las Terrenas

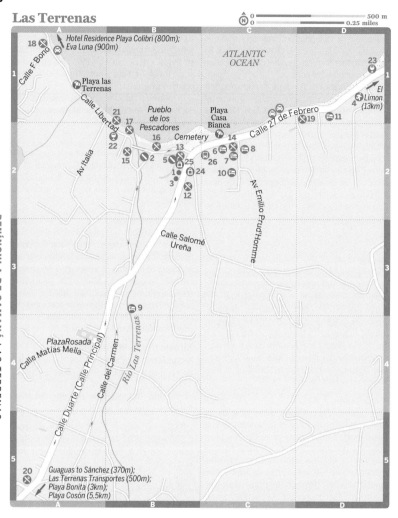

ATLANTIC OCEAN

Hotel Residence Playa Colibri (800m);
Eva Luna (900m)

Playa las Terrenas

Calle F Bono

Calle Libertad

Pueblo de los Pescadores

Playa Casa Bianca

Cemetery

Calle 27 de Febrero

El Limón (13km)

Av Italia

Calle Salomé Ureña

PENÍNSULA DE SAMANÁ LAS TERRENAS

Río Las Terrenas

PlazaRosada

Calle Matías Mella

Calle Duarte (Calle Principal)

Calle del Carmen

Av Emilio Prud'Homme

Guaguas to Sánchez (370m);
Las Terrenas Transportes (500m);
Playa Bonita (3km);
Playa Cosón (5.5km)

remote villages, mountain-bike excursions of varying levels and kayak tours through the mangroves at Playa Cosón.

Santí Excursiones
OUTDOORS

(☏829-342-9976; www.cascadalimonsamana.com; El Limón) Spanish-owned Santí, at the main intersection in El Limón, is a good choice for visiting El Limón waterfall (p140) (with/ without lunch RD$1200/900 on horseback, RD$900/600 on foot) but also the most expensive. The lunch is excellent (with a vegetarian option to boot), and the guides and staff (all adults) are better paid than elsewhere.

Parada la Manzana
OUTDOORS

(☏829-931-6964; www.facebook.com/Paradala manzanasaltodellimon; Carretera Principal, El Limón) Located 5km east of El Limón toward Samaná (and featuring the pleasant Apple cocktail bar), Parada la Manzana has the advantage of being much closer to El Limón waterfall (p140) than other tour operators. Its fees for the trip to the falls are RD$850 on horseback with lunch and RD$400 if you skip the meal.

Casa de las Terrenas
ADVENTURE

(☏809-666-0306; www.lasterrenas-excursions. com; Principal 280; ☺8:30am-noon & 3:30-6:30pm Mon-Sat) Small, friendly, French-run

Las Terrenas

PENÍNSULA DE SAMANÁ LAS TERRENAS

operation based in a little kiosk in front of Plaza Taína.

🛏 Sleeping

The majority of accommodations options are located along the beachfront roads to the east and west of the main intersection. Those to the east are across from the beach on the paved highway, while the cobble-stoned road to the west means the area is somewhat quieter and feels more secluded. Prices drop dramatically in low season, but at any time of year discounts are negotiable for long-term stays.

★ El Rincon de Abi   HOTEL $
(☎809-240-6639; www.el-rincon-de-abi.com; Av Emilio Prud'Homme; s/d/tr incl breakfast from RD$2000/2200/2400, bungalows with/without air-con RD$2500/2300, apt RD$4000-5000; P✳🛜⌖) This French-owned hotel is well maintained and full of cute colors, character and occasional pop-art surprises. Even better, there's a somewhat established independent-traveler vibe here. There's a nice communal outdoor kitchen, a Jacuzzi and a small pool.

Rooms are in either the main white-washed two-story building topped with a thatched roof (a tad sterile, but with high-pressure showers) or the roomy bungalows that have more vibrant colors, some with a nouveau-hippie vibe, others with a Warhol-esque aesthetic. Bonus points for high security: the owners have 24-hour video surveillance beamed to their iPhones.

Dan and Manty's Guesthouse   HOSTEL $
(☎849-873-5742; dm incl breakfast RD$800, r RD$1300; 🛜) It might be found via a trashy alleyway across a dirty creek and 950m from the sea, but Las Terrenas finally has a budget crash pad with a hostel-like vibe. Jovial American Dan and his Dominican partner, Manty, are the personalities behind the haphazard operation, which offers 10- and six-bed mixed dorms, fantastic-value private rooms and hot, made-to-order breakfasts.

Casa del Mar Neptunia   HOTEL $
(☎809-240-6884; www.casasdelmarneptunia. net; Av Emilio Prud'Homme; s/d incl breakfast RD$2100/2300; P🛜) It's a revolving door for owners and not the deal it once was, but this charming little oasis of hospitality and calm nurtures 10 large, airy rooms that have been spruced up (new security cameras, mosquito screens and bed linen, a fresh coat of paint) by the latest bosses, this round from Canada via Venezuela and Russia.

Casa Robinson   HOTEL $
(☎809-240-6496; www.casarobinson.it; Av Emilio Prud'Homme; r/tr RD$1300/2000; P🛜) Set in leafy grounds down a side street a block from the beach, this hotel offers privacy on the cheap. Fan-cooled rooms in the all-wood buildings are simple and clean and have little balconies and patios. Though Italian owned, it's run with a smile by Dominicans. It's a family-run place where any type of debauchery is not appreciated.

CASCADA EL LIMÓN

Tucked away in surprisingly rough landscape, surrounded by peaks covered in lush greenery, is the 52m-high El Limón waterfall. A beautiful swimming hole at the bottom can be a perfect spot to wash off the sweat and mud from the trip here, though it's often too deep and cold for a dip. The departure point is the small town of El Limón, only half an hour from Las Terrenas.

Just about everyone who visits does so on horseback, and almost a dozen *paradas* (horseback-riding operations) in town and on the highway toward Samaná offer tours; try **Santí** (p138) or **Parada la Manzana** (p138). (Don't hire someone off the street, as there's little difference in price and the service is consistently substandard.) All outfits offer essentially the same thing: a 30- to 60-minute ride up the hill to the waterfalls, 30 to 60 minutes to take a dip and enjoy the scene, and a 30- to 60-minute return trip, with lunch at the end. Your guide – whom you should tip – will be walking, not riding, which can feel a little weird but is the custom. Walking or on horseback, you will get wet, as there are several river crossings along the way – rubber sandals are a good idea.

If you book with a tour company in Las Terrenas, transportation to/from El Limón (*guagua* RD$50, taxi US$40 round-trip) may not be included. Typically the tour (horse, guide and lunch) costs per person from US$30 to US$55; try **Casa de las Terrenas** (p138) or **Flora Tours** (p137). Otherwise, it's a minimum 40-minute walk (from the main intersection in El Limón it's roughly 5.6km), up a sometimes very steep trail over rough terrain and with even a river or two to ford. It's not difficult to follow the path once you find it, though, especially if there are groups out on the trail. If you make the trip independently you'll need to pay the entrance fee (RD$50).

★ **Hotel Atlantis** HOTEL $$
(☑ 809-240-6111; www.atlantis-hotel.com. do; F Peña Gomez, Playa Bonita; s/d/q from $90/120/170; P❀🖰) This rambling and charming hotel is straight out of a fairy tale – all twisting staircases, covered walkways and odd-shaped rooms. The furnishings are comfortable, not luxurious, and each of the 18 rooms is different – some have balconies and fine ocean views.

There's a palm-tree-covered patio and the owner (a former private chef to French president François Mitterrand) handles the kitchen at the restaurant. Ask him to whip you up some lunch in the hotel's beach kiosk.

La Dolce Vita APARTMENT $$
(☑ 809-240-5069; www.ladolcevitaresidence. com; Calle 27 de Febrero; apt for 2/4 US$100/200; P❀🖰) The apartments at this aqua-trimmed Caribbean plantation–style seafront complex manicured to the nines are a good option for longer stays. Gourmands in the know consider the al fresco restaurant (mains RD$300 to RD$800) Las Terrenas' best Italian.

Hotel Residence Playa Colibrí HOTEL $$
(☑ 809-240-6434; www.hotelplayacolibri.com; Playa Las Ballenas; apt for 2/4/6 incl breakfast from US$109/209/315; P❀🖰) One of the last hotels along this stretch of Playa Las Ballenas, Playa Colibrí is a good option for those seeking peace and quiet. All 45 apartments are spacious and good value, with fully equipped kitchens; split-level ones are especially good for families. Each apartment has a terrace that overlooks a palm-tree-shaded pool area and meticulously manicured gardens.

Coyamar HOTEL $$
(☑ 809-240-5130; www.coyamar.com; cnr F Peña Gomez & Van der Horst, Playa Bonita; s/d/tr incl breakfast US$45/55/75; P🖰) Located at Calle Van der Horst and the beach road, Coyamar is the least luxurious of the Playa Bonita hotels. The casual, friendly vibe is especially good for families, and the restaurant occasionally dishes out Asian and Mexican dishes. Bright colors and good value rule the day here, and the four fan-cooled rooms are simple, spacious and comfortable.

Hotel Mahalo HOTEL $$
(☑ 809-240-1616; www.acaya-hotel-fr.com; F Peña Gomez, Playa Bonita; r with air-con incl breakfast US$100; P❀🖰) With a new Brazilian owner, Italian chef and Hawaiian name, the hotel formerly known as Acaya remains a dark horse, but it retains an

evocative feel of a more genteel era. The two-story colonial building sits back from the beach on a finely manicured lawn. It's an understated and tastefully furnished place, with a relaxing lounge-restaurant and a popular surf school.

★**Peninsula House**   GUESTHOUSE $$$
(☎809-962-7447; www.thepeninsulahouse.com; Playa Cosón; r US$650-800; P@🖥🗗) One of the Caribbean's most exquisite hotels, this Victorian B&B perched high on a hill overlooking Playa Cosón was previously the DR's hands-down top choice for utmost exclusivity and service. But plans by new owners were in the works in 2017 to construct a massive, 36-room expansion over the original six rooms, leaving to chance whether the place's soul can be salvaged.

To its credit, the investment team has kept one of the original owners and the manager on for the transition to ensure that the French chateau–style aesthetic is respected. A Venezuelan chef runs the kitchen (three-course dinner US$55), focusing on simple preparations of ingredients sourced locally and from the hotel's organic vegetable garden. Rooms are dressed head to toe in exquisite antiques, romantic four-poster beds and deep bathtubs – all staying – making the prospect of checking out agonizing. The average stay is five days, but you'll want to move in permanently.

★**Eva Luna**   VILLA $$$
(☎809-978-5611; www.villa-evaluna.com; Marico, Playa Las Ballenas; villas for 2/4 incl breakfast US$120/240; P🖥@🗗) A paragon of understated luxury, these five Mexican-style villas come with fully equipped kitchens, gorgeously painted living rooms, and terraces where a delicious gourmet breakfast is served. The bedrooms are a bit cramped, but the serenity and exquisite decor more than make up for it.

The romantic villas all face a quiet pool and a garden area and the whole show is overseen by the adorable Aude and her partner, Jérôme, a trained chef who has been known to throw a fish or two on the grill for special occasions if arranged in advance. It's west of town, tucked away in a residential neighborhood 300m from Playa Las Ballenas. Doubles are a steal in low season at US$100.

Albachiara Hotel   APARTMENT $$$
(☎809-240-5240; www.albachiarahotel.com; Calle 27 de Febrero; apt for 2/4/6 incl breakfast from US$155/225/325; P🖩🖥🗗) It suffers from a bit of street noise, but this 46-apartment hotel is well located, close to the beach and the center of Las Terrenas. It offers extra-large options, with king-size beds, big kitchens and cozy patios that look out on the grand columns that are a feature of the hotel's architecture.

✗ Eating

The most atmospheric restaurants in Las Terrenas are in Pueblo de los Pescadores, a cluster of fishing shacks that have become waterfront restaurants. Virtually every restaurant has an entrance facing the road and an open-air dining or bar area out the back that overlooks the ocean and narrow beach. For cheap Dominican fare (from RD$250), there's a line of beach shacks behind the cemetery in the center of town.

Boulangerie Française   BAKERY $
(Plaza Taína; items RD$45-160; ⊙7am-7:30pm Mon-Sat, to 7pm Sun) Transport yourself to Paris at this pleasant bakery serving fresh *pain au chocolat*, croissants, *beignets* and other traditional French pastries and desserts. The street-side patio practically feels like Montmartre, and it serves the best espresso on the peninsula by a long shot.

One Love Surfshack   BURGERS, BREAKFAST $
(www.onelovesurfshack.com; Pueblo de los Pescadores; mains RD$280-390; ⊙7am-1am Wed-Mon; 🖥) International tapas (samosas, quesadillas, bruchetta), decent burgers and breakfast are One Love's calling. It's equally popular as a great place to down a few cold ones (there's a two-for-one happy hour from 5pm till 8pm daily) to the tune of crashing waves – you could swing your life away here on the oceanside back porch.

New Canadian owners have taken over from old Canadian owners and it soldiers on as an English-friendly hangout.

★**Restaurante Luís**   SEAFOOD $$
(☎809-601-8772; Playa Cosón; mains RD$300-400, lobster per pound RD$650; ⊙10am-5pm) Practically a legend at this point, this ramshackle sea shack on Playa Cosón serves up some of Samana's best seafood. Dig your toes into the sand, shoot the breeze with the server over the daily catch (there's no menu), and sit back and wait for simplicity at its finest.

PENÍNSULA DE SAMANÁ LAS TERRENAS

French expats flock here at weekends for lobsters the size of Fiats.

But the fresh fish (filet or whole) is every bit as tasty. Seasoning ranging from salt, limes, oil and vinegar to house-made hot sauce in Gatorade bottles is all you'll see (or need) here. *Buen provecho!*

★La Terrasse
FRENCH $$
(Pueblo de los Pescadores; mains RD$380-730; ⏰11:30am-2:30pm & 6:30-11pm; 🕿) The Dominican chef at this sophisticated French bistro deserves a few Michelin stars for his steak *au poivre* (RD$550), one of the most perfect meals in the entire DR – you'll be genuflecting at his kitchen's door after it graces your lips.

The menu continues with lovely seafood like red snapper in garlic and parsley (RD$580), spicy Creole calamari (RD$430) and lobster with tarragon-butter sauce (RD$580). Like most spots along this gourmet promenade, the sea nearly steals back its wares every time a wave comes crashing in. But the best part of all might just be eating this for well under US$15 – a tall order anywhere in the world. Visa only.

El Lugar
STEAK $$
(🕿849-248-2580; www.facebook.com/ellugar. lasterrenas; Calle 27 de Febrero; burgers RD$340-750, steaks RD$600-2000; ⏰6:30-1:30am Wed-Mon; 🕿) Hands-on Belgian owner Bruno found a Las Terrenas niche: fulfilling carnivorous desires with juicy, rich burgers (go for the one with Reblochon cheese) and wood-fired steaks (both national and imported black Angus), lobster and fish, all served in a trendy, high-table atmosphere that lures the town's bold and beautiful for the complete package – ambience, service and excellent eats.

Good Food & Co.
CAFE $$
(Puerto Plaza; sandwiches RD$250; ⏰7am-midnight; 🕿✍) Vegetarians, rejoice! This quaint new Argentine-run cafe does healthy juices as well as gourmet sandwiches, burgers, bruschettas, salads and quiches, many vegetarian and all made from scratch. Popular sandwiches include serrano ham, Parmesan, pesto and arugula (rocket) or mozzarella, caramelized onion and arugula. Save room for the excellent *alfajors* (Argentine cookies filled with *dulce de leche*).

Le Tre Caravelle
ITALIAN $$
(Calle 27 de Febrero; mains RD$380-600; ⏰noon-11:30am; 🕿) A convivial little spot for risotto

(mushroom and red wine, saffron and sausage, shellfish) and fresh seafood, though the ambience won't floor you – waitresses in sailor hats (overly cutesy but extra friendly) and a questionable maritime-tiki motif might raise eyebrows.

Brasserie Bárrio Latíno Cafe
CAFE $$
(El Paseo shopping center, Principal; breakfast RD$50-180, mains RD$290-450; ⏰7:30am-9pm, hours vary; 🕿) Occupying the busiest corner in town – and milking that for all it's worth – this open-sided tropical brasserie has an eclectic menu of international standards including sandwiches, burgers, pastas and meat dishes. It's a popular breakfast spot for fresh pastries and the morning news from Paris.

La Casa Azul
ITALIAN $$
(Libertad; pizzas RD$250-520; ⏰11am-11pm; 🕿) Service leaves *mucho* to be desired, but the Italian owners turn out the best pizza in town, with a few tables right on the sand.

Beach
INTERNATIONAL $$$
(📞809-847-3288; www.thepeninsulahouse.com; Playa Cosón; mains RD$600-1200; ⏰noon-3pm; 🕿) The beach-club component of the Peninsula House hotel (p141) – open to nonguests as well – is a wonderful little plantation-style bungalow on a private lawn steps from Playa Cosón. A longstanding Dominican husband-and-wife chef team serves up a variety of eclectic gourmet dishes (fresh shrimp tacos, grilled lobster, BBQ pork ribs) from an often-changing menu scribbled on ceramic plates.

Le Thalassa
SEAFOOD $$$
(www.facebook.com/lethalassachezmarcet-valerie; Playa Las Ballenas; mains RD$570-980; ⏰3pm-midnight daily Jan-Apr, closed Mon May-Dec; 🕿) New French owners Marc and Valerie, fresh from a stint in Polynesia, are consummate hosts at this made-over, longstanding Playa Ballenas choice for a romantic evening out. Valerie eloquently and evocatively describes the nightly changing chalkboard specials (nothing frozen here!), a bounty of local seafood given a French culinary spin.

Wash back Polynesian tuna three ways or red snapper *al ajillo* (in garlic sauce) with choice international wines while the demure Dominican servers, trained above and beyond the island norm, restore your faith in hospitality.

Mi Corazon FUSION $$$
(☎ 809-240-5329; www.micorazon.com; Duarte 7; mains RD$860-1220; ☺ 7-11pm Tue-Sun Nov-Apr, closed Sun May-Oct; ☎) Las Terrenas may feel like a Franco-Italian enclave, but it's a Swiss-German trio that offers one of the area's top dining experiences. Daniel, Lilo and Flo ensure your culinary ride here is a doozy: everything is made fresh on the premises and served in a romantic white-washed colonial-style courtyard, open to the stars and complete with a trickling fountain.

Some molecular gastronomy creeps into the food here (in the deconstructed mojito, for example), but it's really all about fresh, simple flavors seasoned perfectly. A variety of menus is available to suit all appetites. The weekly changing chef's menu (three/five courses RD$1750/2250) is the way to go. No regrets.

Drinking & Nightlife

Most restaurants have bars and stay open well after the kitchen has closed. Barhopping could scarcely be easier, as it takes about 45 seconds to walk (or stagger, depending on the time of night) from one end of Pueblo de los Pescadores to the other. There are a few notable spots outside Pueblo de los Pescadores as well and a cluster of *discotecas* across the street.

★ **El Mosquito** COCKTAIL BAR
(Pueblo de los Pescadores; cocktails RD$250-400; ☺ 5pm-2am Mon-Thu, to 4am Fri & Sat, 6:30pm-2am Sun; ☎) The hottest bar in Las Terrenas by a landslide, this newly reopened, open-air lounge that was destroyed in the 2012 Pueblo de los Pescadores fire is a good-time juxtaposition of rustic lounge furniture, fairy-light-lit trees, exposed brick and local art that caters to a who's who of expats and tourists.

Standouts on the expansive – if not over-iced – cocktail list include the *caipi-chinola* (a passion-fruit caipirinha) and the frozen mojito.

Mojitos BAR
(Calle 27 de Febrero; ☺ 9.30am-9pm; ☎) The problem with mojitos is that they go down too fast. The ones at this upscale Punta Popy beach shack arrive in 14 flavors (with Cuban rum for an extra RD$50) in traditional *chinola* (passion fruit) and *tamarindo* varieties (from RD$200). You won't find better, even in Cuba.

Shopping

Calle Duarte (aka Calle Principal) and around are virtually wallpapered with the Haitian art found everywhere in the DR. The three shopping malls have several high-end boutiques, eating options and a few shops selling basic tourist kitsch.

Haitian Caraibes Art Gallery ART
(Principal 159; ☺ 9am-1pm & 4-7:45pm Mon-Sat) For a better selection of paintings than the ubiquitous cookie-cutter mass-produced ones, stop by this art gallery. It also sells interesting crafts, jewelry and typical batiks and sarongs.

La Casa de la Prensa BOOKS
(El Paseo shopping center, Paseo de la Costanera; ☺ 9am-7:30pm Mon-Sat, to 1pm Sun) Toward the rear of the El Paseo shopping mall, La Casa de la Prensa sells a variety of international newspapers and magazines, the majority in French and English.

ⓘ Information

DANGERS & ANNOYANCES
Cestur (Cuerpo Especializado de Seguridad Turística; ☎ 809-754-5042; Libertad; ☺ 24hr) The tourist police are located inside the Centro de Atención al Ciudadano at the Las Terrenas police station.

LAUNDRY
Lavanderia Las Terrenas (☎ 809-240-5500; per pound RD$70; ☺ 8am-noon & 2-7pm Mon-Fri, to 4pm Sat, to noon Sun) The most convenient laundry service, with 24-hour turnaround.

Super Farmacia del Paseo (El Paseo shopping center, Paseo de la Costanera; ☺ 9am-7pm Mon-Sat, to 1pm Sun) Well-stocked pharmacy.

MEDICAL SERVICES
Clínica Especializada Internacional (☎ 809-240-6701; www.ceiterrenas.com; Villa de Las Flores, Fabio Abreu; ☺ 24hr) An excellent private hospital run by Cuban doctors.

MONEY
There are handy ATMs at El Paseo shopping center, Pueblo de los Pescadores and Plaza Rosada.

Banco Popular (www.popularenlinea.com; Av Juan Pablo Duarte 52; ☺ 9am-4pm Mon-Fri, to 1pm Sat)

BanReservas (www.banreservas.com; Duarte 254; ☺ 8am-5pm Mon-Fri, 9am-1pm Sat)

TRAVEL AGENCIES
Colonial Tours (☎ 809-240-6822; www.colonialtours.com.do; Plaza Rosada; ☺ 9am-1pm & 3-7pm Mon-Fri, to noon Sat) The town's main full-service travel agency; helpful for bus info.

ⓘ Getting There & Away

AIR

International flights arrive at Aeropuerto Internacional El Catey (p302), located 8km west of Sánchez and a 35-minute taxi ride (US$70) to Las Terrenas. Air Canada, Westjet and Air Transat, among others, serve Canadian destinations; XL Airways goes to Paris. There's also a handful of charter flights.

BUS

For Santo Domingo, **Las Terrenas Transportes** (☑ 809-240-5302) operates direct coaches via the main highway (RD$375, 2½ hours, 5am, 7am, 9am, 2pm and 3:30pm), Puerto Plata (RD$325, three hours, 6:30am), Santiago (RD$320, three hours, 6:30am, 8:30am and 12:40pm) and Nagua (RD$150, 1¼ hours, 7am and 2pm). Buses leave from the Esso gas station on the outskirts of town, 2.5km south of the sea.

Guaguas to Samaná leave in front of Casa Linda at the corner of Calle Principal and the coastal road eight times daily (RD$100, 1¼ hours, 7:15am to 5pm). For those going to El Limón, 14km away, *guaguas* leave from the same stop (RD$50, 35 minutes, every 15 minutes from 7:15am to 7pm).

For Sánchez, **guaguas** (☑ 809-237-9550) leave from the Uchotesa depot on the outskirts of town (RD$70, every 20 minutes, 7am to 6pm).

CAR

Las Terrenas is easily accessible by road if you're motoring on your own. A portion of the US$150-million Blvd Turístico del Atlántico connects Las Terrenas with Aeropuerto Internacional El Catey, 24km to the west, avoiding the former need to transit through Sánchez.

The toll charges, relative to kilometers, are high (RD$528), and it hasn't exactly been embraced by locals, but it's a beautiful drive all the same.

TAXI

The local **taxi consortium** (☑ 809-240-6339) offers rides for one to six passengers to just about anywhere. Some sample one-way fares are Playa Cosón (US$25), El Limón (US$25), Samaná (US$70), Las Galeras (US$100), Santo Domingo (US$150) and Punta Cana (US$400).

GETTING AROUND

The two main roads in town are Calle Duarte (running one way south; also known as Calle Principal in town, and Av Juan Pablo Duarte or Av Duarte as it exits town) and the parallel Calle del Carmen (running one way north).

You can walk to most places in Las Terrenas, though getting from one end to the other can take half an hour or more. There are taxi and *motoconcho* stops in front of El Paseo shopping center and along the beach roads, and *motoconchos* are plentiful on Calle Principal and around Pueblo de los Pescadores – and are incessantly in your face practically everywhere else.

There are several local car-rental agencies in town. Rates start at US$50 per day and US$300 per week. One of the more established and reliable ones is **ADA Rental Car** (☑ 809-704-3232; www.ada-santodomingo.com; Plaza Taína; ⊙ 9am-1pm & 2:30-7pm Mon-Sat). At Aeropuerto El Catey, **Sixt** (p126) is the lone option. **Jessie Car** (☑ 809-240-6415; www.jessiecar.com; Pueblo de los Pescadores; ⊙ 8am-6pm Mon-Sat) is a recommended outfitter for quad bikes (US$60 per day) and scooters (US$25).

North Coast

Best Places to Eat

➡ Eze Bar & Restaurant (p170)

➡ Mares Restaurant (p151)

➡ Castle Club (p169)

➡ Restaurant Casa Veintiuno (p160)

➡ Taberna El Conde (p159)

Best Places to Sleep

➡ Casa Colonial Beach & Spa (p153)

➡ Punta Rucia Lodge (p176)

➡ Cabarete Surf Camp (p167)

➡ El Morro Eco Adventure Hotel (p178)

➡ Natura Cabañas (p168

Why Go?

From east to west on the Dominican Republic's north coast, you'll find world-class beaches, water sports galore and out-of-the-way locales evocative of timeless rural life. This long coastal corridor stretching from Monte Cristi and the Haitian border in the west to Río San Juan in the east has enclaves of condo-dwelling expat communities that have endowed some towns with a cosmopolitan air. There are forested hills, dry desert scrub, and jungly nature preserves. There are waterfalls to climb, sleepy little Dominican towns with laundry ubiquitously drying on clotheslines and mile after mile of sandy beaches. In the middle is Puerto Plata's international airport; nearby is the city itself and where most of the coast's all-inclusive resorts are located. Independent travelers will find accommodations of all stripes and several good places to base themselves for explorations further afield, especially Cabarete, where you can kitesurf, surf or just plain bodysurf.

When to Go

➡ Winds on the north coast pick up between December and March, making this an ideal time to try surfing and kitesurfing.

➡ Check out some of the best exponents in the Master of the Ocean competition in February.

➡ A jazz festival takes over Puerto Plata and Cabarete in October.

North Coast Highlights

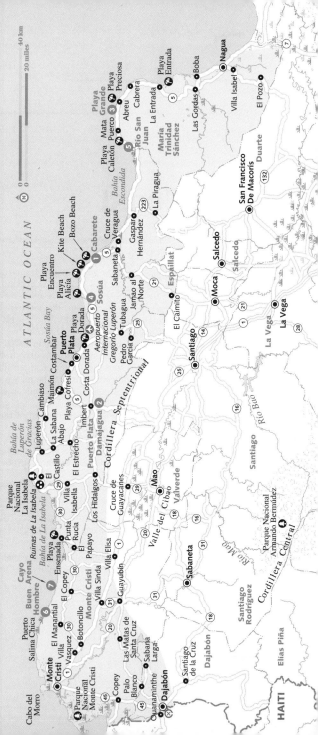

1 **Cabarete** (p161) Learning how to kitesurf or windsurf with the pros, and afterwards digging your toes into the sand, and feasting afterward on the beach.

2 **Twenty-Seven Waterfalls of Damajagua** (p150) Jumping and sliding down the *cataratas*.

3 **Playa Grande** (p173) Worshipping the sun or taking a surf lesson as the waves roll in.

4 **Sosúa** (p155) Exploring the underwater marine life or going on a catamaran trip.

5 **Río San Juan** (p171) Finding tranquillity in the typical small-town Dominican atmosphere.

6 **Buen Hombre** (p176) Learning to kitesurf in this seaside, end-of-the-road town.

7 **Cayo Arena** (p178) Spending the day on a tiny sandbar, snorkeling in clear turquoise waters and drinking Brugal rum.

ⓘ Getting There & Around

Aeropuerto Internacional Gregorío Luperón (p302) in Puerto Plata is within two hours' driving distance of almost everywhere on the north coast. You can rent a car there, although an SUV might be preferred if you're traveling to smaller communities inland or along the coast to the west of Puerto Plata. Cibao airport at Santiago and El Catey airport at Samana are secondary options worth considering.

Buses and *guaguas* (minivans) offer frequent service, although you may find the cost of the fare to be inversely proportional to your Spanish-language ability. Keep in mind the relatively small size of the country – Puerto Plata is only 215km from Santo Domingo.

Puerto Plata

POP 158,800

Squeezed between a towering mountain and the ocean is this working port town, the oldest city on the north coast. Wander the Malecón or the downtown streets surrounding the Parque Central and you'll see that significant revitalization efforts, meant to impress an influx of Carnival cruise ship passengers, have replaced what was until recently a palpable feeling of neglect. Intermingled with run-of-the-mill shops are the fading, once-opulent homes built by wealthy German tobacco merchants in the 1870s. Several restaurants are worth a visit, as are a few interesting museums, and the cable car ride to the nearby bluff, if not clouded over, offers panoramic views.

History

As Columbus approached the bay in 1493, the sunlight reflected off the water so brilliantly it resembled a sea of sparkling silver coins and so he named it Puerto Plata (Silver Port). He also named the mountain that looms over the city Pico Isabel de Torres (799m), in honor of the Spanish queen who sponsored his voyages. In 1496 his brother Bartolomé Colon founded the city.

An important port for the fertile north coast, Puerto Plata – and, indeed, the entire north coast – was plagued by pirates. It eventually became more lucrative for colonists to trade with the pirates (who were supported by Spain's enemies, England and France) rather than risk losing their goods on Spanish galleons. Such trade was forbidden and enraged the Spanish crown. In 1605 the crown ordered the evacuation of Puerto Plata – as well as the trading centers of Monte Cristi, La Yaguana and Bayajá – rather than have its subjects trading with the enemy.

The north coast remained virtually abandoned for more than a century, until the Spanish crown decided to repopulate the area to prevent settlers from other countries – namely the French from present-day Haiti – from moving in. Puerto Plata slowly regained importance, suffering during the Trujillo period, but eventually reinventing itself as a tourist destination. The early 1990s were golden years for the city, and for the first time tourism revenues surpassed those of its three main industries – sugar, tobacco and cattle hides – combined.

◉ Sights

Teleférico CABLE CAR
(☏809-970-0501; www.telefericopuertoplata.com; Camino a los Dominguez; round trip RD$350; ☉8am-5pm) A cable car takes visitors to the top of the enormous flat-topped Pico Isabel de Torres. On clear days there are spectacular views of the city and coastline – go early, before the mountain clouds up. The **botanical gardens** at the top are good for an hour's stroll. You'll also find a large statue of **Christ the Redeemer** (similar to but smaller than its counterpart in Rio de Janeiro), an overpriced restaurant and aggressive knick-knack sellers. Cable-car tickets are cash only.

Casa Museo General Gregorio Luperón MUSEUM
(☏809-261-8661; museogregorioluperon@claro.net.do; Calle 12 de Julio 54; adult/child RD$200/100; ☉9am-5pm, closed Sun) The life and times of native-born son and independence leader Gregorio Luperón are impressively fleshed out inside this beautifully restored, pale-green, Victorian-era building. Photographs and period artifacts trace Luperón's life, from humble beginnings to his role as provisional president during the 'Restoration,' as well as the story of Puerto Plata during the late-19th century.

Dominicans and Spanish speakers are charged only adult/child RD$100/50. At the time of research, the cafe was temporarily closed but was set to reopen under a new owner.

Fuerte de San Felipe HISTORIC SITE
(San Felipe Fort; RD$100; ☉9am-4:45pm, closed Sun) Located right on the bay, at the western end of the Malecón, the fort is the only remnant of Puerto Plata's early colonial days.

Puerto Plata

Puerto Plata

Built in the mid-16th century to prevent pirates from seizing one of the only protected bays on the entire north coast, San Felipe never saw any action. For much of its life its massive walls and interior moat were used as a prison.

Included in the price of admission is an audio tour (available in English, French, German, Russian and Spanish); however, it's disappointingly thin in terms of historical breadth and depth. There are short explanations of the objects displayed in the small museum – a few rusty handcuffs, a handful of bayonets and a stack of cannonballs. The views of the bay are impressive, though, and a large grassy area in front of the fort makes for a restful stop.

Also at the fort is Puerto Plata's lighthouse, which first lit up on September 9, 1879, and was restored in 2000. The white-and-yellow tower – 24.4m tall, 6.2m in diameter – is a melding of neoclassical style with industrial construction.

Museo del Ambar Dominicano   MUSEUM
(☑809-586-2848; www.ambermuseum.com; Duarte 61; RD$50; ☺9am-5pm Mon-Sat) The colonial-era building houses a collection of amber exhibits. These exhibits include valuable pieces with such rare inclusions as a small, 50-million-year-old lizard and a 30cm-long feather (the longest one found to date). Tours are offered in English and Spanish. A gift shop on the ground floor has a large selection of jewelry, rum, cigars, handicrafts and souvenirs.

Malecón   WATERFRONT
The completely paved Malecón (also known as Av General Luperón and Av Circun-valación Norte) runs along the shore. There are a handful of restaurants, as well as a half-dozen beachside shacks selling food and drinks on **Long Beach**, the main city beach around 2km east of downtown. A few experienced kitesurfers launch themselves into the waves here on windy days.

Casa de la Cultura   CULTURAL CENTER
(☑809-261-2731; Parque Central, Separación; ☺8am-noon) `FREE` In addition to dance and music workshops, the center often showcases work by Dominican artists in its 1st-floor gallery.

🏃 Activities

All the nearby all-inclusive resorts organize tours for their guests. For independent travelers, Mark Fernandez, the hardworking and personable owner of Freestyle Catamarans (p152), offers boat trips with snorkeling stops near Sosúa leaving from Playa Dorada, the entrance to which is about 4km east of Puerto Plata. Scuba divers looking to explore the north coast's reefs can contact **Sea Pro Divers** (www.facebook.com/seaprodiver). For big-game fishing trips contact **Gone Fishing** (☑829-728-6201). Though less renowned than Playa Encuentro near Cabarete, Puerto Plata's beach has decent conditions for surfing. Renowned surf school **Pau Hana** (☑809-669-0811; www.pauhanasurfcamp.com/surf-puerto-plata; behind Neptune Bar; surf board/paddleboard rental per hr US$20/30) recently opened an office here.

🧭 Tours

Brugal Rum Plant   TOURS
(☑809-261-1888; www.brugal.com.do; Carretera a Playa Dorada; US$5; ☺8am-4pm Mon-Fri) The country's most famous rum distillery offers 20-minute tours from a 2nd-floor gangway, during which visitors learn the history and

process, from sugarcane farming to bottling. At the end, everybody gets to sample the goods, and bottles are available for purchase.

★ Festivals & Events

Dominican Jazz Festival   MUSIC
(www.drjazzfestival.com; ☺Nov) Also held in Cabarete and Santiago, this long-running festival attracts top musical talent from around the country and abroad. Most of the visiting musicians run workshops for kids; one year Bernie Williams, former Yankee turned guitarist, taught both baseball and jazz.

Merengue Festival   MERENGUE
(☺early Nov) The entire length of the Malecón is closed to vehicular traffic, food stalls are set up on both sides of the oceanside boulevard and a stage is erected for merengue performances.

🛏 Sleeping

Unless you're after budget accommodations there's no real reason to spend more than a night in Puerto Plata, considering that there are better options everywhere else on the north coast. The new Hotel El Palacio is the best stay in town.

Villa Carolina   GUESTHOUSE $
(☑809-586-2817; www.villacarolina.hostel.com; Av Virginia Elena Ortea 9; s/d incl breakfast RD$1200/1600; P@🖨❄) This rambling old house with a leafy courtyard is easily the best place for independent travelers in Puerto Plata. Beyond the security gate at the end of a long driveway, several old cars, the family-occupied front house and the vine-covered pergola and pool area is the carriage-house-cum-villa where the tastefully furnished rooms are located.

The checkered tile floors add a touch of colonial elegance, both in the rooms and the large front lounge area. An old kitchen is available for guest use.

Hotel El Palacio   BOUTIQUE HOTEL $$
(☑809-261-0942; www.hotelelpalacio.com; Prof Juan Bosch 14; r from RD$2500; P❄🖨❄) This new option in Puerto Plata is housed within an exquisitely restored 1920s mansion originally inhabited by a sugar-cane baron. The expat owners are meticulous about upkeep and good service, and have adorned the hotel with attractive period furnishings and local art from the antique shop next door. The restaurant earns high marks for its elaborate breakfast (not included).

TWENTY-SEVEN WATERFALLS

Travelers routinely describe the tour of the **waterfalls** (☑829-639-2492; www.27charcos. com; Damajagua; highest waterfall RD$500, organized tour US$80-100) at Damajagua as 'the coolest thing I did in the DR.' We agree. Guides lead you up, swimming and climbing through the waterfalls. To get down you jump – as much as 8m – into the sparkling pools below. At the time of research, extreme flooding had taken out a suspension bridge visitors once used to cross a river and arrive at the attraction. In the meantime, guests were fording the river, but tour operators insisted that the bridge would be replaced promptly.

It's mandatory to go with a guide, but there's no minimum group size, so you can go solo if you wish. You can go up to the seventh, 12th or 27th waterfall, though most 'jeep safari' package tours only go to the seventh. You should be in good shape and over the age of 12. Foreigners pay RD$500 to the highest waterfall and less to reach the lower ones (US$1 of every entrance fee goes to a community development fund). Tour companies in Puerto Plata, Sosúa and Cabarete organize trips here for between US$80 and US$100. The falls are open from 8:30am to 3pm, but go early before the crowds arrive. A visitors center and restaurant are near the entrance.

To get to the falls, go south from Imbert on the highway for 3.3km (and cross two bridges) until you see a sign on your left with pictures of a waterfall. From there it's about 1km down to the visitors center. Alternatively, take a Javilla Tours (p152) *guagua* (bus) from Puerto Plata and ask to get off at the entrance. The big Texaco station at Imbert serves as a crossroads for the entire area. There is a frequent *guagua* service to Santiago (RD$80, one hour) and Puerto Plata (RD$40, 30 minutes).

✖ Eating

The supermarket **La Sirena** (Malecón; ⊙8am-10pm Mon-Sat, 9am-9pm Sun) is good for groceries and fast food, and **Mercado Municipal** (Cardenal Sancha; ⊙5am-7pm Mon-Sat, to noon Sun) has meat and vegetables.

Kaffe   CAFE $
(☑809-261-3440; www.kaffeweb.com; Profesor Juan Bosch 42; mains RD$150-450; ⊙8:30am-11pm; ☎) This homey, adorable cafe in downtown Puerto Plata is an ideal spot to chat with a friend over any number of elaborate coffee and chocolate drinks, including nutella frapuccinos, Bailey's iced coffees, and even hot chocolate with marshmallows. There's seating on the front and back patios as well as inside, and the menu is dominated by wraps, sandwiches and crepes.

El Bergantin   CARIBBEAN $$
(☑809-545-4912, 809-736-6496; http://elbergantin.com.do; Beller; mains RD$600; ⊙9am-11pm) Housed in a revamped Victorian-era building on Puerto Plata's central square, this new, nautical-themed Caribbean grill and pizzeria makes you feel fancy just walking in. From the gingerbread trim to the Victorian floor tiles to the saloon doors, the place feels infused with history and style, the wine list is extensive, and the food, though pricey, is up to snuff.

The fish'n'chips are getting talked about all over town, and are good. The lobster fondue is even better.

Tostacos & Sushito   MEXICAN, JAPANESE $$
(☑809-261-3330; cnr Presidente Vasquez & Francisco Peynardo; mains RD$280; ⊙4-11pm Tue-Thu & Sun, to midnight Fri & Sat) Offering tacos, burritos, sushi, sashimi and a few Dominican (tasty *mofongo*) and American options in between, this casual, outdoor eatery will appeal to a variety of tastes. And everything is above average, as you'd expect from the owner, Rafael Vasquez-Heinsen.

Kilometro Zero   DOMINICAN, ITALIAN $$
(☑809-244-4346; Av Luis Ginebra 6; mains RD$350; ⊙10am-11:30pm, closed Wed; ☎) A friendly open-air place where you can pull up a seat up at the bar or a picnic table to chow down on pasta (close to 20 varieties), surf and turf (RD$2500) or burgers and crepes. Several flatscreen TVs are usually tuned to sports.

Jamvi's   PIZZA $$
(☑809-320-7265; cnr Malecón & López; pizzas RD$400; ⊙10am-midnight) This gargantuan open-air pizza joint sits above street level on the Malecón, offering a pleasant sea breeze, great views and an elaborate playground. Good for a pizza and wine fix (there's a decent wine list); from 10pm till late it pumps merengue and reggaeton. Also delivers.

⭐**Mares Restaurant
& Pool Lounge**   DOMINICAN **$$$**

(809-261-3330; Francisco Peynado 6; mains RD$700; ⊗6pm-midnight Wed-Sat) Distinguished chef Rafael Vasquez-Heinsen has converted his elegant home into a candlelit destination for foodies. *Top Chef* and food channel fans won't be disappointed. The kitchen turns out what elsewhere might be defined as haute fusion cuisine – dishes that creatively combine Dominican ingredients with other culinary traditions: try the goat marinated with rum (RD$600). Reservations recommended.

🍸 Drinking & Nightlife

Along the beach on the eastern end of the Malecón are around a half-dozen informal bars that serve beer and cocktails, including **La Carihuela** (Malecón; ⊗10am-late). Regulars, both expats and Dominicans, head here for sundowners and simple meals (RD$200 to RD$300). National flags hang from a few kiosks, announcing the country of origin of their owners.

🛍 Shopping

Espigón Cigar Factory   CIGARS

(809-261-0178; www.espigoncigars.com; cnr Felipe 29 & Duarte; ⊗9am-5pm Mon-Fri, to 1pm Sat) Housed in a 1917 building that once stored tobacco, this new cigar store recently relocated from Moca to Puerto Plata to capitalize on the influx of cruise ship passengers to the area. The store offers short tours and manufactures its own blended and aged cigars, including the Espigón Corojo and the Espigón Maduro.

La Canoa   JEWELRY, SOUVENIRS

(809-586-3604; Av Beller 18; ⊗8:30am-6pm) La Canoa is a large, rambling store with a mini amber and larimar museum and work spaces where the stones are polished and set in jewelry. It also sells cigars (some are rolled on the premises), the usual acrylic Haitian paintings, postcards and other souvenirs.

ℹ **Information**

DANGERS & ANNOYANCES

Cestur (809-754-3101; cnr R Fernandez & Malecón) Tourist Police

MONEY

There are a few banks with ATMs in the blocks surrounding the Parque Central.

Banco BHD Leon (Prof Juan Bosch; ⊗9am-4:30pm Mon-Fri, to 1pm Sat)

MEDICAL SERVICES

Centro Médico Bournigal (🕿809-586-2342; Antera Mota; ⊗24hr)

Clínica Brugal Mejia Lopez (🕿809-586-2519; José del Carmen Ariza 15; ⊗24hr)

Farmacia Carmen (🕿809-586-2525; Calle 12 de Julio; ⊗8am-8pm Mon-Sat, 8:30am-12:30pm Sun) Pharmacy offering free delivery

ℹ **Getting There & Away**

AIR

Puerto Plata is served by Aeropuerto Internacional Gregorío Luperón (p302), 18km east of town along the coastal highway (past Playa Dorada), and just a few kilometers west of Sosúa. Numerous charter airlines, including several Canadian ones, use the airport, mostly in conjunction with the all-inclusive resorts. A taxi to or from the airport costs US$30 to US$35. Or walk 500m from the terminal to the main highway to flag down a *guagua* to Puerto Plata (RD$55, 45 minutes) or Sosúa (RD$15, 10 minutes).

Airlines with international service here include Air Berlin, Air Canada, Air Transat, Condor, Iberia, InterCaribbean Airways, American Airlines, Continental, Jet Blue, Lufthansa, Thompson, West Jet and United.

BUS

Eastbound Guagua

These leave from a stop on the east side of Parque Central, passing by the entrance of Playa Dorada and through Sosúa (RD$60, 30 minutes), Cabarete (RD$100, 45 minutes) and Río San Juan (RD$120, two hours).

NORTH COAST PUERTO PLATA

TOURS & BUS SERVICES FROM PUERTO PLATA

Caribe Tours (🕿809-586-4544; cnr Camino Real & Kounhart) and **Metro** (🕿809-586-6063; cnr 16 de Agosto & Beller) both serve Puerto Plata. Caribe Tours is cheaper, and all their buses leave hourly from 6am to 7pm.

DESTINATION	FARE (RD$)	DURATION (HR)
La Vega	170	2
Santiago	130	1¼
Santo Domingo	350	4
Sosúa	35	½

South & Westbound Guaguas

Javilla Tours (☑ 809-970-2412; cnr Camino Real & Av Colón; ⊘ buses every 15min 5am-7:30pm) serves Santiago (RD$130, 1½ hours) with stops along the way at Imbert (RD$40, 20 minutes) and Navarrete (RD$120, 50 minutes). To get to Monte Cristi, take Javilla's bus to Navarrete and tell the driver to let you off at the junction, where you can change for the Expreso Linieros bus (RD$140, 1½ hours).

CAR

Avis (☑ 809-586-4436, airport 809-586-0214; www.avis.com.do; Carretera Luperon Km 4; ⊘ 8am-6pm), **Budget** (☑ airport 809-586-0413; www.budget.com.do; Playa Dorada Plaza; ⊘ 7am-10pm), **Europcar** (☑ 809-586-7979; www.europcar.com.do; Av Luis Ginebra) and **National** (☑ 809-586-1366, airport 809-586-0285; www.nationalcar.com.do; Carretera Luperon Km 2.5; ⊘ 8am-5pm) all have offices at the airport (and in some cases outside the airport) where they are open 7am to 10pm and are usually on call overnight, but charge extra for late pickup or delivery.

❶ Getting Around

The old town and parts of the Malecón are walkable. Otherwise, you'll need to get comfortable taking *motoconchos* (motorcycle taxis) or *guaguas*, rent a car or shell out cash for taxis.

The main trunk roads in Puerto Plata are serviced by *guaguas* following lettered routes, which cost RD$20. Lines C and F will be of most interest to you: they run from as far west as Cofresí, through town and past Playa Dorada in the east. Line C runs direct; line F makes lots of twists and turns as it barrels through town.

Officially licensed drivers wear numbered, colored vests and tend to be only slightly more cautious in traffic than their unlicensed brethren. The in-town fare was RD$30 when we were there; to Playa Dorada it's RD$100.

You'll find taxi fares priced almost exclusively for tourists – the in-town fare is around RD$200. Taxis don't generally cruise the streets looking for customers, so try **Taxi Puerto Plata** (☑ 809-586-5335). There are several taxi stands around the city, including along the central park, along the Malecón and across the street from the Caribe Tours office

Playa Dorada & Costa Dorada

These two pretty, adjacent beaches, a few miles east of Puerto Plata, string together a handful of all-inclusive resorts and one five-star hotel. Both developments are marked by large archways – Playa Dorada is the much larger one and the first you come to on the highway from the airport. A prolonged downturn in Puerto Plata's mass-market tourism has led to the mothballing of many properties, reminders of developers' outsized ambitions and sub-par products, and of the national government's prioritizing of resort projects in the southeast. However, signs point to a small-scale revitalization with a renewed focus on quality.

🏃 Activities

Freestyle Catamarans   BOATING
(☑ 829-894-4636;   https://freestylecatamarans.com; Playa Dorada) These boating trips leave regularly from Playa Dorada and make snorkeling stops near Sosúa. They're a super fun way to spend a half-day, particularly because the crew is hilarious and there's an all-you-can-drink bar. If you want to get dropped off in Sosúa that can be arranged, but sailing back downwind is part of the fun.

Playa Dorada Golf Club   GOLF
(☑ 809-320-4262;   www.playadoradagolf.com; ⊘ 7am-7pm) This well-regarded 6218m, par-72 Robert Trent Jones course is the centerpiece of the Playa Dorada complex. The greens fee for nine holes is US$50, for 18 holes, US$75; caddies (US$9/18 for nine/18 holes) are obligatory, golf carts (US$15/25 for nine/18 holes) are not.

🛏 Sleeping

Most resorts offer day and night passes (US$45 to US$60), which entitle you to unlimited access to their facilities and a buffet lunch or dinner.

Suncamp   APARTMENT $
(☑ 809-320-1441; www.suncampdr.com; Principal; camp site US$10, r US$20; 🐾) Surrounded by lush jungle and set on a river near the village of Muñoz, 3km inland from Playa Dorada, thoroughly rustic Suncamp looks like a typical Dominican compound – concrete floors, corrugated-iron roof and makeshift furnishings. A stay here can be worthwhile if your standards of comfort are low and you have an interest in volunteering in a local community.

There's a variety of rooms, some with private bathroom (basically, a curtained-off toilet) and their own kitchen, though appliances are aged. Bring a flashlight and mosquito repellent. Diane, the expat owner, is friendly and welcoming and can help you plan trips in the region. Airport transfers are US$35. Popular with young backpackers as well as retirees looking for an inexpensive way to while away the days.

Viva Wyndham V Heavens RESORT $$
(☑ 809-562-6001; www.wyndhamhotels.com; Playa Dorada; all-incl s/d from RD$4100/$5740; P ❊ 🛜 ⛱) After a half-decade hiatus, this all-inclusive, adults-only resort has reopened with a new, modern look that channels – wait for it – heaven. The whole place is now sleek and white, with orange pillows thrown in for flair. And with five restaurants, a couple of bars and a swanky, recently remodeled pool area, the place does tap into something ethereal.

Sunscape Puerto Plata RESORT $$
(☑ 809-320-5084; www.sunscaperesorts.com/ puerto-plata; Playa Dorada; r from US$117; P ❊ @ 🛜 ⛱) Recently taken over by AM Resorts and turned from a Barceló into a Sunscape, this all-inclusive offers good value and has managed to remain vital at least in part because of its discounted internet deals enjoyed by a mix of Dominican families and guests from abroad. The tile-floored, attractive rooms have comfortable beds and the spa offers fish pedicures.

★**Casa Colonial Beach & Spa** LUXURY HOTEL $$$
(☑ 809-320-3232; www.casacolonialhotel.com; Playa Dorada; r US$660-1450; P ❊ 🛜 ⛱) This extraordinary hotel is one of the finest in the country. It offers 50 indulgent suites, each with marble floors, sparkling fixtures, canopied beds, ample balconies, a cedar-lined closet, and plush bathrobes and slippers. The grounds are set in a sprawling mansion and boast a tropical garden with orchids growing at seemingly every turn.

A fantastic bar and an infinity pool with four Jacuzzis are located on the roof, providing spectacular views of the ocean. A high-end spa and two elegant restaurants are also on site. It's important to note that rates are not all-inclusive.

Blue Bay Hotel & Resort RESORT $$$
(☑ 809-320-3000; www.bluebayresorts.com; Playa Dorada; per person all-incl RD$3200; P ❊ 🛜 ⛱) One of the few adults-only resorts on the north coast, Blue Bay styles itself as a boutique option for singles and couples looking for a holiday evocative of a Miami Beach hotel. The front lobby area is all flowing drapery, a super-high ceiling and blue pastel accents, though the try-hard minimalism

room design is slightly undermined by the lower-quality furniture.

Iberostar Costa Dorada RESORT $$$
(☑ 809-320-1000; www.iberostar.com; Costa Dorada; all-incl s/d US$156/234; P ❊ @ 🛜 ⛱) One of the better-value all-inclusives in the region, Iberostar receives its fair share of repeat customers. There is a certain Disneyland cheesiness about the place – you'll be greeted at reception by a porter wearing a pith helmet, for instance – but the grounds are enormous and well kept, the pool is immense, and the food better than average.

🍴 Eating

Le Petit Francois SEAFOOD $$
(☑ 809-320-9612; www.lepetitfrancois.com; El Pueblito, Playa Dorada; mains RD$400; ☺ 9am-11pm) This beachfront bar, liquor store (and okay it's a restaurant, too) seemingly has it all: lobster, booze, Dominican food, French food, poutine, the works. Patrons tend to sit in the plastic green chairs for hours drinking piña coladas and watching the kitesurfers. Sunday afternoons there's karaoke.

El Manguito Restaurant & Liquor Store SEAFOOD $$
(☑ 809-586-4392; mains RD$350; ☺ 11am-10pm) Nestled at the side of the highway just east of the Costa Dorada complex (and just west of Playa Dorada) is this good-value seafood joint. Beers here are only US$2, and the lobster (US$15) is great value. Service is excellent, and there's also a variety of desserts.

❶ Getting There & Away

The Playa Dorada taxi association charges many times the price you'd pay if you hailed a taxi on the street. Their taxis can be found at any of the hotel entrances and also in front of Playa Dorada Plaza. A ride to the airport will cost you US$45, to Sosúa US$45, to Cabarete US$50, and within the hotel complex US$15; to Puerto Plata it's US$15.

Or you can walk to hotel complexes' entrances on the highway and hail down a *guagua* to Puerto Plata (RD$25).

Costambar

Less a traveler's destination than an expat hideaway, Costambar is worth a visit for its beautiful, palm-shaded, white-sand beach with shallow water and patches of coral reef.

This is a private community that consists primarily of time-share units and vacation homes, some rundown, some half-built and many occupied for six months of the year by North Americans on the run from winter.

There's not much to do around here, other than hanging out at the beach or playing the occasional round of golf at **Los Mangos Golf Club** (☏809-970-3110, 829-679-5049; Cl Kennedy 2; 9 holes US$60), a nine-hole golf course with elevated greens, surrounded by tropical flora. It also offers massages at the country club.

🛏 Sleeping

Condo associations might rent by the week and occasionally by the night in low season, but the best bet for tourists is Villa L'Oase, a tranquil collection of villas just outside of town. A local monthly newsletter (www.costambarmonthly.com) can keep you up to date.

Villa L'Oase   GUESTHOUSE **$$**
(☏809-837-6845; www.loase.com; Playa Real 21; r incl breakfast $US60-95; ❄🛜💺) Costambar doesn't have many tourists, but all of them should stay at L'Oase. Tastefully adorned in Dominican art, the charming villas contain 12 bedrooms surrounding a relaxing pool and restaurant, and the whole thing is tucked away in a lush and private, well, oasis. Owners Joe and Vasthi are welcoming and knowledgeable, and regularly host missionary groups.

Fun surprise: there's a fully functional indoor racquetball court on the premises (and Joe is quite good).

🍴 Eating

Happy Hippo   CAFE **$**
(☏849-816-6113; www.hillvangogh.com; mains US$6; ⊙2pm-late) This bright and cheerful beach cafe is owned by Hill Van Gogh, an artist who claims to be a distant relative of Vincent Van Gogh. Her mamajuana is excellent, and the fried chicken's nothing to sneeze at either.

El Farolita   SEAFOOD **$$**
(☏809-970-7899; meal RD$300; ⊙9am-6pm, closed Tue) A standout beach restaurant, serving fish, burgers, fried chicken and more. The owner and staff members could not be nicer.

🍷 Drinking & Nightlife

El Catamaran   BAR
Local watering hole where tourists are frowned upon until enough rum is consumed, then welcomed with open arms. Then cursed at. Then welcomed again. Incredible drink specials on Saturdays starting at 5:30pm – US$3 for seemingly unlimited rum. Unless somebody else paid? Oh well. Find them on Facebook.

❶ Getting There & Away

A *motoconcho* from Puerto Plata will cost you RD$250, and a taxi US$17. If you're already in Costambar, try the local **taxi association** (☏809-970-7318). *Guagua* lines C and F from Puerto Plata pass on the highway (every 15 minutes from 6am to 6pm), although the village is a good kilometer from the highway, and the beach another kilometer past that.

Playa Cofresí

Five kilometers west of Puerto Plata lies the quiet, condo-dwelling hamlet of Cofresí. Around 6km west of the access road to Cofresí, three large resorts, all under the Riu banner, line the pretty Bahia Maimon. Next door, the large, Disney-like docking facility Amber Cove handles Carnival Cruise Line ships but is inaccessible to other travelers. The other draw is Ocean World, a Dominican version of Sea World.

◎ Sights

Ocean World   AMUSEMENT PARK
(☏809-291-1000; www.oceanworld.net; adult/child US$75/54; ⊙9am-6pm) With an enormous sign at the western end of the beach, it's impossible to miss Cofresí's main attraction, Ocean World, and its sea lions, dolphins, sharks, manta rays, aviary and show. You can swim with the dolphins or the sharks, but the practice of keeping dolphins in captivity, and especially interacting with them, has received sharp criticism from animal welfare groups in recent years. There are several restaurants, a disco, and a casino on site.

Lonely Planet does not condone activities that may harass animals.

🛏 Sleeping

Lifestyle Holidays Vacation Resort   RESORT **$$$**
(☏809-970-7777; www.lhvcresorts.com; all-incl per person US$150; 🅿❄@💺) At the heart of a sprawling resort village, this enormous all-inclusive complex offers some of the best deals on the north coast; as long as you don't expect glitz or panache you won't be disappointed. The rooms are well maintained and the buffet restaurant has enough

variety to satisfy, whereas the ambience of the 'specialty' restaurants is undermined by sub-par food.

Eating

Sandwiched between Ocean World and Lifestyle Holidays Vacation Resort is a tiny community of expats and condo dwellers, and a couple of decent restaurants.

Los Charos MEXICAN **$**
(mains RD$200; ⊙noon-9pm, closed Mon; 🖝) This warm, airy restaurant – with a motorcycle as decoration in the indoor dining room – has a menu full of Mexican fare like quesadillas, tacos and chili con carne. On the road to Ocean World.

Chris & Mady's SEAFOOD **$$**
(🖝809-970-7502; mains RD$350; ⊙8am-11pm; 🖝) Under an open-air thatched roof with tile floors and sturdy wooden tables, the restaurant has a wide-ranging menu with good seafood, including fettuccine with shrimp and the grilled catch of the day, at reasonable prices. The Sunday barbecue is popular with locals and expats alike. The owners also rent a couple of apartments on the property.

Le Papillon INTERNATIONAL **$$$**
(🖝809-970-7640; mains RD$550; ⊙6-11pm Tue-Sun) This fine restaurant, 100m east of Cofresí up a small hill, serves excellent meals in a large palapa-roofed dining area with dark-wood tables, a checkerboard floor and seafaring decor, including fish tank. Favorites include leg of rabbit, smoked yellowtail or dorado, pepper steaks and vegetable curry.

🍷 Drinking & Nightlife

Hotel guests in Cofresí will find plenty to do after-hours, particularly at the Ibiza-like lounge **Café del Mar** (🖝809 97 0777 ext 21877; www.facebook.com/pg/cafedelmarpuertoplata; ⊙9am-1am) and the chill **Ocean World Terrace** (🖝809-291-1111; ⊙8am-late) bar. Lifestyle also has a casino and cigar bar in the same building that used to house the Vegas-style Bravissimo show, which was wildly popular for years but came to an end in late 2016.

ⓘ Getting There & Away

Take *guagua* C or F (RD$20) from Puerto Plata. Going back to town take only the C – the F does lots of twists and turns in the city and takes twice as long to get you to the center. It's a steep downhill walk of about 700m to the main beach area. There's *guagua* service until

---

OFF THE BEATEN TRACK

TUBAGUA PLANTATION ECO-VILLAGE

Twenty minutes from Puerto Plata, this rustic but well-constructed mountain-top **eco-retreat** (🖝809-696-6932; www.tubagua.com; El Descanso; r incl breakfast from US$30; 🅿🖝) is where guests can get a taste of rural DR life, eat delicious meals (US$10 to US$15), and visit a nearby coffee farm, an amber mine and a system of waterfalls. Owner Tim Hall doubles as the Canadian consul, and he has a wealth of knowledge about the DR and sustainable tourism.

---

about 7pm. If you're driving, simply follow the main highway west.

There's also a taxi stand (US$25 to Puerto Plata and US$100 to the airport) located just outside Lifestyle Holidays.

Sosúa

POP 49,600

Sosúa by day and Sosúa by night are two different creatures. When the sun is out, the beach and calm bay are ideal for swimming and attract a broad swath of Dominicans, foreigners and families alike. When evening comes, the place becomes what expats refer to as 'so-sewer.' The inescapable fact, despite the mayor's efforts otherwise, is that Sosúa is known for sex tourism. Bars fill up with Dominican and Haitian sex workers, and men can expect to be accosted and propositioned.

Regardless, Sosúa is the base for the area's scuba-diving operations and conveniently located for exploring the north coast. The town's curious status as the cheese and dairy capital of the DR was established by around 350 families of Jewish refugees who fled Germany and other parts of Europe in 1940. Since few were farmers, most left after a couple of years, but not before building many fine homes.

◉ Sights

Museo de la Comunidad Judía de Sosúa MUSEUM
(Jewish Community Museum of Sosúa; 🖝809-571-2633; Dr Alejo Martínez; RD$150; ⊙9am-1pm & 2-4pm Mon-Fri) This museum has exhibits with Spanish and English text describing the

Sosúa

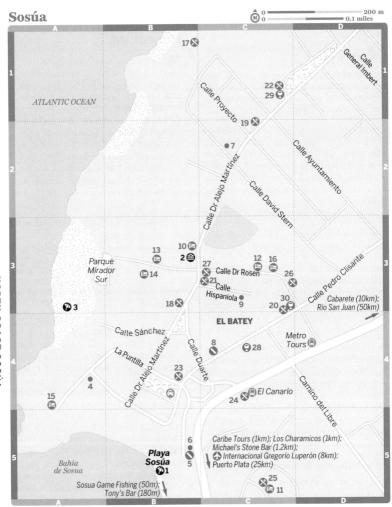

Jewish presence in the DR. At the multinational Evian conference in 1938 the DR was the only country to officially accept Jewish refugees fleeing Nazi repression in Germany. If the gate is locked during opening hours, ring the number listed above – but don't get your hopes up.

🦪 Beaches

★ Playa Sosúa   BEACH

Playa Sosúa is the main beach, and practically a city within a city. Located on a crescent-shaped bay with calm, turquoise waters, this narrowing (due to erosion)

stretch of sand is backed by palm trees and a seemingly endless row of souvenir vendors, restaurants, bars and even manicurists. The crowds of Dominican families and long-term visitors staying in local hotels and condos make this lively beach a great place for people-watching.

Snorkel gear is available for rent (two hours RD$400, includes life jacket and bread for the fish).

Playa Alicia   BEACH

An ordinary and wide patch of brownish-yellow sand (no shade) lapped by calm

Sosúa

waters, Playa Alicia has steadily grown and been 'replenished' since its creation nearly a decade ago. Whether this has been done in an environmentally sound manner is disputed. Steps leading down to the beach can be found at the end of Calle Dr Rosen in Parque Mirador Sur, a small paved plaza with benches and a cafe kiosk.

Activities

Diving & Snorkeling

Sosúa is generally considered the diving capital of the north coast. In addition to the 18 dive sites within boating range of Sosúa Bay, dive shops also organize excursions as far afield as Río San Juan (through mangroves and freshwater Dudu Cave), Cayo Arena and even Haiti. There's a good variety of fish plus hard and soft corals (several projects to restore depleted coral are in the works), drop-offs and sponges.

Among the popular dive spots nearby are **Zíngara Wreck**, an upright 45m ship sunk in 1993 as an artificial reef in around 35m of water; and **Coral Gardens** and **Coral Wall**, both offering coral formations in depths ranging from 14m to 53m.

Prices are generally US$100 for two dives with gear, around US$10 less if you have your own equipment, and slightly more for dives further afield. Booking a dive package brings the price down considerably – with a 10-dive package, the per-dive price can be as low as US$30 if you have your own gear. All of Sosúa's shops offer certification courses. Snorkeling trips are available at all shops, and cost US$30 to US$45 per person, depending on the length and number of stops; equipment is always included.

One big difference about the shops is that the predominant language among the staff is German, though English and Spanish are spoken by all.

Northern Coast Diving   DIVING
(☑ 809-571-1028; www.northerncoastdiving. com; Pedro Clisante 8) This well-respected dive shop is one of the best, and the most willing to create customized excursions to little-visited dive sites. It also sells gear, repairs equipment and fills tanks.

Dive Center Merlin   DIVING
(☑ 809-571-4309; www.divecenter-merlin.com; Playa Sosúa) At the end of the road to Playa Sosúa.

Fishing

Alberto Fishing Tour   FISHING
(☑ 829-212-3657; captainrony_julye2@hotmail. es; Playa Sosúa) A super nice and knowledgeable fishing guide. Get in touch for prices.

Sosua Game Fishing FISHING

(☑829-810-8799; www.sosuagamefishing.com) Half- and full-day fishing tours. Has an informal office at El Pescador, a restaurant on Playa Sosúa.

Zip-Lining

Monkey Jungle OUTDOORS

(☑829-554-2425; www.monkeyjungledr.com; zipline adult/child US$50/30; ⊙9am-5pm) Follow the access road to El Choco a further 9km for Monkey Jungle, a working organic farm with a sanctuary for rescued squirrel and capuchin monkeys and a thrilling 4400ft zip line. All proceeds go to the on-site medical and dental clinic which provides free care to the surrounding communities. In what might seem like a disconcerting clash to some, a handgun firing range shares the property.

🐾 Tours

There are a lot of cheesy package tours on offer at numerous agencies along the north coast. Many involve spending the majority of your day on a gaudily painted 'safari' bus getting to and from your destination. Be wary of any tour purporting to show you 'Dominican culture' – the 'local school' you'll visit will be more a Potemkin village than an authentic place of learning.

Tours that are most worth doing include rafting in Jarabacoa (four hours each way, US$60 to US$80), Cayo Arena for snorkeling (three hours each way, US$55 to US$65), whale-watching in Samaná (from mid-January to mid-March, four hours each way, US$120 to US$140), and anything involving a boat – catamaran tours (US$55 to US$90) and deep-sea fishing (US$50 to US$100) are hard to fake, and are generally good value. Try checking in with **Eric Tours** (☑809-710-0503, 809-571-3434; http://erictoursinternational.com; Beach Way 18; ⊙8am-5pm), **Mel Tours** (☑809-571-4002; www.mel-tour.com; David Stern) and Sosua Game Fishing.

🍳 Courses

Spanish Center LANGUAGE

(☑809-571-4630; www.the-spanish-center.com; Hispaniola; per hr US$15, per 15hr week US$150; ⊙8am-6pm Mon-Fri, 9am-1pm Sat) Spanish language courses, and one- or two-week packages that include airport transport, lodgings and food.

Casa Goethe LANGUAGE

(☑809-571-3185; www.edase.com; La Puntilla 2) This German-run outfit has private and group Spanish classes in the mornings, and the center can organize activities including scuba diving or salsa-dancing classes in the afternoon. Long-term housing arranged either at the center itself or in area hotels.

🛏 Sleeping

There are a number of good hotels; just keep your wits about you and be sure you aren't checking into a flop house.

Hotel El Rancho HOTEL $

(☑809-571-4070; www.hotelelranchososua.com; Dr Rosen 36; r from US$50; [P][❄][🌐][🏊]) The rather pleasant leafy pool and garden area is the centerpiece of this small centrally located hotel only a block from Playa Alicia. A three-story modern concrete building decorated with vaguely Mexican murals and topped with a palapa-style roof for show, El Rancho has clean, well-kept rooms.

Hotel Casa Valeria HOTEL $$

(☑809-571-3565; www.hotelcasavaleria.com; Dr Rosen 28; s/d incl breakfast US$58/68; [❄][🌐][🏊]) All 11 rooms at this cozy hotel are slightly different, whether in size, furnishings or decor, but all feature comfortable beds, attractive furnishings and ceramic-tiled bathrooms. Rooms are set around a leafy courtyard with a kidney-shaped pool in the middle; at the time of research a chic new bar and restaurant were under construction.

Hotel Sosúa Sunrise HOTEL $$

(☑809-571-2429; www.hotelsosuasunrise.com; Dr Rosen 25; s/d incl breakfast & dinner US$65/75; [P][❄][🌐][🏊]) This well-managed hotel contains 24 rooms on two floors, connected by broad breezy corridors. All rooms have red-tile floors, clean modern bathrooms with hot water, cable TV and security boxes. There's a nice pool area, and Playa Alicia is just down the street. A small outdoor restaurant serves breakfast.

★Casa Veintiuno BOUTIQUE HOTEL $$$

(☑829-342-8089; www.casaveintiuno.com; Piano 1; r incl breakfast US$175-200; [❄][🌐][🏊]) Two whitewashed, modernist homes on a hill just outside town have been transformed into a comfortable and intimate B&B, both a quiet refuge and a base for exploring the area. The owners Saskia and Mark – and their three dogs – provide personable and attentive service, even shuttling every guest into town for a private tour.

Many guests, however, choose to spend much of their time lounging around one of two courtyard pool areas or in the upstairs lounge, which has a telescope, treadmill, Wii game system and a 'library' of DVDs, books and boardgames. Breakfast and lunch are for guests only, and the best dinner in town is available here Wednesday through Sunday to nonguests who make reservations.

Casa Marina Beach and Reef Resorts
RESORT **$$$**

(☑ 809-571-3535; www.amhsamarina.com; Dr Alejo Martínez; all-incl s/d US$123/205; P ❄ @ ☀) This large complex with three pools, five restaurants and more than 600 rooms is arranged in three-story buildings with direct access to Playa Alicia. The rooms are classic all-inclusive: clean and comfortable but not memorable, with cable TV and a balcony, and most look onto the pool. Four sweet new hot tubs were recently built into the shoreline's rocky natural sundeck.

Terra Linda Hotel Spa & Resort
HOTEL **$$$**

(☑ 809-571-2220; www.terralindaresort.com; Dr Rosen 22; s/d US$79/85; P ❄ 🛜 ☀) Three stories of well-kept and comfortable rooms with small flatscreen TVs surround Terra Linda's large inner courtyard, which has an Olympic-sized pool – it feels like an oasis from the noisy street. Look for the entrance below street level, concealed behind the Scotch 'n' Sirloin restaurant.

Piergiorgio Palace Hotel
HOTEL **$$$**

(☑ 809-571-2626; www.hotelpiergiorgio.com; La Puntilla; r incl breakfast US$95; P ❄ ☀) Popular with wedding planners, the Piergiorgio is built on a rocky cliff overlooking the ocean, ornately constructed with a white gingerbread facade and a grand red-carpeted staircase that spirals to the top floor. The room furnishings are aging and don't match the magnificent sea views – ask for a room on the 3rd floor. The cliffside restaurant (mains RD$600) is an undeniably romantic spot.

Eating

A handful of restaurants are within a block of Parque Central and most hotels have their own. Pedro Clisante is lined with informal bars and restaurants, as is the path along Playa Sosúa – head to Tony's Bar (p159) for great seafood and cocolocos. **Playero Supermarket** (☑ 809-571-1821; ☺ 8am-9pm Mon-Sat, from 8:30am Sun) on the main highway has a good selection of local produce and imported delicacies.

★ Taberna El Conde
TAVERNA **$$**

(☑ 829-868-0909; www.tabelconde.com; cnr Dr Alejo Martinez & Dr Rosen; mains RD$265-555; ☺ 11:30am-11:pm) This casual but enchanting establishment is constantly raising the culinary bar in Sosúa with its craft cocktails and innovative gastromony. The incredible honeysucklesmoke cocktail is made with rum, lime, orange and a cinnamon-smoked glass (tastes just like honeysuckle!) and dishes are things like Tandoori mahi mahi with mango chutney. Also, everything is totally under-priced (don't tell the owner/chef).

Tony's Bar
SEAFOOD **$$**

(☑ 829-701-8789; Playa Sosúa; mains US$7-10; ☺ sunrise-sunset; 🛜) The best bar on Playa Sosúa is Tony's, for it's seafood but also for the incredible coco locos. Tony, who is Dominican but speaks German, English, French and Spanish, also offers wi-fi and a free bathroom. If you want to order something that doesn't appear on his menu, he will go get it. Find him on Facebook.

La Terrassa
INTERNATIONAL **$$**

(☑ 829-661-2368; Dr Alejo Martinez; mains RD$350; ☺ 7am-11pm; P 🛜) Housed in a corner of a luxury condo development is this contemporary restaurant. Equally recommended for its extensive breakfast menu, especially its fresh croissants, as it is for its lunch and dinnertime menu featuring kebabs, seafood and risotto. The exceedingly cute cafe attached serves loose-leaf tea, fanciful pastries and cakes, and hosts a popular jazz and blues brunch on Sunday.

There's also a children's area with cute mini-furnishings.

Michael's Stone Bar
SEAFOOD **$$**

(☑ 809-804-3666; Julio Arzeno; mains RD$330; ☺ 10am-9pm) Perched on a cliff at the very southern end of Playa Sosúa, this simple, traditional eatery combines million-dollar views with freshly prepared crab, fish and lobster. Diners are mostly locals, but it's welcoming to newcomers and definitely worth seeking out. Accessed only by following the road (through the 'neighborhood' of Los Charamicos) down from the highway.

Bourbon Street Grill
CAJUN **$$**

(☑ 849-251-1561; Pedro Clisante 20; mains RD$350-450) This Cajun place changed locations recently, and is now (deservedly) in a prime spot along Pedro Clisante. Ribs, po' boys, shrimp gumbo and bottomless sweet tea (that comes in a mason jar) are all on the menu, and there's also a cigar lounge at the back of the restaurant.

Rocky's Rock & Blues Bar Hotel   DOMINICAN, AMERICAN $$
(☑809-571-2951; Dr Rosen 24; mains RD$250; ⊙8am-midnight; ☎) The sign outside says 'World Famous Ribs,' but that's just the beginning – the breakfasts, served until 3pm, are great value, the steaks are Dominican beef (not imported), and the beers are some of the cheapest in town. Pizza is served after 5pm and the music is pure rock and blues.

Bailey's   INTERNATIONAL $$
(☑809-571-3085; Dr Alejo Martínez; mains RD$600-800; ⊙8am-midnight) A favorite among expats, this quirky restaurant offers specialties such as chilli burgers and enormous schnitzel sandwiches. The decor includes lots of rattan furniture and potted plants, as well as a welcome continually spraying mist of water to keep things cool. A new hotel and playground were under construction here when we visited.

Marua Mai   DOMINICAN $$
(☑809-571-3682; cnr Pedro Clisante & Arzeno; mains RD$450; ⊙8am-11pm) This Dominican/German–owned restaurant has been a solid midrange choice – with great burgers, seafood and lobster by the kilo – for several decades now. There's a pleasant bar for a quiet drink before or after. Good breakfasts, too.

Bologna   ITALIAN $$
(☑809-571-1434; Dr Alejo Martínez 33; mains RD$300-600; ⊙8am-11:30pm; ❋☎) Locals and expats rave about the quality of the pizza and pasta, not to mention the oreo cheesecake, at this family-friendly place just north of the town center. The vibe, encouraged by regulars, is of a small-city neighborhood joint with a diner feel. Delivers.

Scotch & Sirloin   STEAK $$
(☑809-571-2220; Dr Rosen; mains RD$500; ⊙7:30am-11:30pm; ☎) Scotch & Sirloin is housed in an attractive open-air pavilion above Sosúa's Terra Linda Hotel, specializing in burgers, steaks and baby back ribs (RD$795). It shares the space with Pizza Uno, which offers wood-fired brick-oven pizza, and El Batey Grill, with an extensive menu of Dominican dishes.

★ Restaurant Casa Veintiuno   ITALIAN $$$
(☑829-341-8551, 829-342-8089; www.casaveintiuno.com; Piano 1; mains US$15-32; ⊙6-10pm Wed-Sun) A bit out of town and tucked into an eponymous guesthouse up a hill, this poolside, a la carte Italian restaurant serves the finest meals in all of Sosúa. The menu changes daily depending on what's available, but you can count on juicy filet mignon, steak tartar, fresh seafood and a vast selection of international wines and craft cocktails.

Be sure to call a couple of days ahead to reserve your table; this place fills up and prioritizes its overnight guests.

Baia Lounge   SEAFOOD $$$
(☑849-816-2436; Bruno Philips; ⊙7:30-11am, noon-3pm & 6:30-11pm) This beachfront space is part of Gansevoort Dominican Republic, an ultramodern condo development on a tranquil beach at the end of town. The Mediterranean and international menu involves freshly caught seafood and wine pairings. Lunch is considerably less spectacular.

La Finca   INTERNATIONAL $$$
(☑809-571-3925; cnr Dr Rosen & Dr Alejo Martínez; mains from RD$600; ⊙5:30-11:30pm; ☎) This longtime Sosúa culinary landmark with a colonial-era design scheme takes its cuisine seriously, both in its presentation and price. Steak and seafood are the rock stars here – there's chateaubriand, surf and turf, and a mixed seafood platter for two (US$50). It has an amazing cocktail list, and the menu is in five languages, including Russian.

🍷 Drinking & Nightlife

Sosúa's nightlife – the epicenter is along Calle Pedro Clisante – is packed with bars and clubs, many catering to prostitutes and their customers. A mayoral initiative to enclose every open-air place with walls and windows to make prostitution less visible didn't work (and didn't last).

Cocktail Hall   BAR
(Bruno Philips; ⊙noon-11pm; ☎) Beside Sosúa's La Terrassa restaurant is this smart and fashionable sliver of a bar. It's a good place for watching sports while sipping craft cocktails, particularly the old fashioned or the Moscow mule.

Prantium   BAR
(cnr Pedro Clisante & Dr Rosen; ⊙10am-3am) Dominicans come here for merengue, *bachata*

and the occasional reggaeton, as well as the cheap beer. Especially crowded on Friday from 4pm.

Britannia Pub BAR
(☑ 809-571-1959; Pedro Clisante 13; ☺ 8am-11pm) Popular with expats, this is a pleasant spot for a quiet drink. There's a good book exchange at the back, and the cheap bar food, like burgers and wings, isn't bad.

❶ Information

DANGERS & ANNOYANCES
Cestur (☑ 809-754-3274) Tourist police

LAUNDRY
Family Laundry (☑ 809-324-7922; cnr Calles Dr Rosen & Dr Alejo Martínez; per kilo RD$55)

MONEY
Banco Popular (cnr Dr Alejo Martínez & Sánchez; ☺ 9am-4pm Mon-Fri, to 1pm Sat)
Banco Progreso (Pedro Clisante; ☺ 9am-4:30pm Mon-Fri, to 1pm Sat)

MEDICAL SERVICES
Centro Medico Cabarete (CMC; ☑ 809-571-4696; www.centromedicocabarete.com; ☺ 24hr) This private hospital is on the main highway only 1km east of Sosúa.
Farmacia KH3 (☑ 809-571-2350; Pedro Clisante; ☺ 8am-9pm Mon-Sat, 9am-6pm Sun)

❶ Getting There & Away

AIR
Sosúa is much closer to the **Aeropuerto Internacional Gregorio Luperón** (POP; ☑ 809-291-0000; www.puerto-plata-airport.com) than Puerto Plata, although it's commonly referred to as 'Puerto Plata airport.' A taxi from the airport to Sosúa is US$25. You can also walk 500m from the terminal to the highway and flag down a passing guagua (RD$20, 10 minutes).

BUS
Metro Tours (☑ 809-571-1324; cnr Av Luperón & Dr Rosen) has its depot on the highway in the middle of town. It runs services to Santiago (RD$220, two hours) and onward to Santo Domingo (RD$425, five hours; 6:20am, 8:20am, 10:20am, 1:20pm, 3:20pm and 5:50pm; also 2:20pm and 4:20pm Sundays). **Caribe Tours** (☑ 809-571-3808) has a depot on the highway at the edge of Los Charamicos neighborhood, 1km southwest of the city center. It offers a service from Sosúa to Santo Domingo (RD$350, hourly from 4:30am to 6:30pm). Grab the same bus for Puerto Plata (RD$35, 30 minutes), Santiago (RD$160) and La Vega (RD$250). Bring warm socks, a sweatshirt (the air-con is on high) and earplugs (the sound from pirated DVDs is on full blast).

El Canario (☑ 809-291-5594) is a Puerto Plata–based bus that leaves daily to Samaná (RD300, three hours) at 6:30am from the main parada (bus stop). Be sure to call the day before to reserve your seat.

GUAGUA
For eastbound destinations along the coast, go to the highway and flag down any passing guagua. They pass every 20 minutes or so, with services to Puerto Plata (RD$35, 30 minutes), Cabarete (RD$25, 20 minutes) and Río San Juan (RD$75, 1½ hours).

❶ Getting Around

You can walk just about everywhere in Sosúa, except to the hotels east of the center, which are better reached by motoconcho or taxi. The former are easy to find around town, while shared and private taxis for intercity travel along the coast can be located at a **taxi stand** (☑ 809-571-3093; cnr Pedro Clisante & Dr Rosen). A trip to Cabarete should run around RD$600.

To rent a car, make your way to the airport (8km away).

Cabarete

POP 14,600

This one-time fishing and farming hamlet is now the adventure-sports capital of the country, booming with condos and new development. You'll find a sophisticated, grown-up beach town, with top-notch hotels, and a beach dining experience second to none (not to mention the best winds and waves on the island). Cabarete is an ideal spot to base yourself for exploring the area – you're within two hours' drive of the best that the coast has to offer, and if you want to go surfing, or windsurfing, or kitesurfing, heck, you don't even need to leave town. You'll hear a babble of five or six languages as you walk Cabarete's single street, where the majority of the hotels, restaurants and shops are located.

🏃 Beaches

Cabarete's beaches are its main attractions, and not just for sun and sand. They're each home to a different water sport, and are great places to watch beginner and advanced athletes alike.

Cabarete

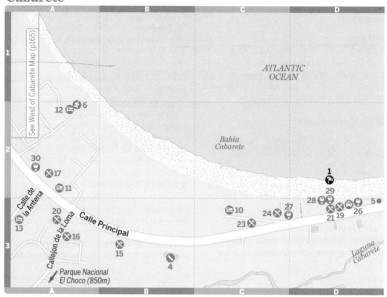

Cabarete

Playa Encuentro   BEACH

Four kilometres west of town. The place to go for surfing, though top windsurfers and kitesurfers sometimes come to take advantage of the larger waves. The beach itself is a long, narrow stretch of sand backed by lush tropical vegetation; strong tides and rocky shallows make swimming here difficult. To find the beach, look for the fading yellow archway and sign that says 'Coconut Palms Resort.' Definitely not safe to walk around here at night.

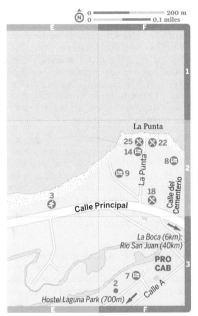

though December is crowded, the winds aren't the most consistent.

Whether you spend your day lounging on the beach or pursuing a more athletic endeavor, it's worth considering a therapeutic visit to one of several local spas for a relaxing massage.

Parque Nacional El Choco   NATIONAL PARK
(☑ 829-779-1975; entry incl cave tour US$20; ⊙ 9am-3:30pm) The famous caves of Parque Nacional El Choco are ensconced in the foothills of the Cordillera Septentrional, among 77 sq km of pastureland, lagoon, jungle, freshwater springs and rolling hills. The stunning, privately managed caves are walking distance from town, and can be visited during a 1½-hour tour. Bring a swimsuit – the crystal-stalactite caves 25m below the surface offer two opportunities to swim in small clear pools, provided the guide can still see you with his flashlight.

The park has recently added new excursions, including a boat ride on the lagoon (US$20 per person) a 2½-hour guided hike (US$40 per person), horseback riding (US$40 per person) and birdwatching treks (US$40) and various combinations of these activities.

Kitesurfing

Cabarete is one of the top places in the world for kitesurfing, which long ago eclipsed windsurfing as the town's sport *du jour*. Kite Beach, 2km west of town, has ideal conditions for the sport, which entails strapping yourself to a modified surfboard and a huge inflatable wind foil, then skimming and soaring across the water. Bozo Beach at the west end of the city beach is also a good spot and typically less crowded. A number of kitesurfing schools offer multiday courses for those who want to learn – just to go out by yourself you'll need at least three to four days of instruction (two to three hours' instruction per day). Lessons generally don't begin until after 11:30am when winds pick up, though if the wind is too strong, say about 25 knots, they may be canceled. The learning curve for the sport is quite steep – you'll need several weeks to get good enough to really enjoy yourself.

Expect to pay US$200 to US$280 for four hours of beginner lessons, or anywhere from US$400 to US$500 for a three- to four-day course (around 10 hours total). Small groups are charged less per person; however, because newbies pick things up at different

Kite Beach   BEACH
(Map p165) Two kilometers west of town. A sight to behold on windy days, when scores of kiters of all skill levels negotiate huge sails and 30m lines amid the waves and traffic. On those days there's no swimming here, as you're liable to get run over.

Playa Cabarete   BEACH
(Map p162) Main beach in front of town. Ideal for watching windsurfing, though the very best windsurfers are well offshore at the reef line. Look for them performing huge high-speed jumps and even end-over-end flips.

Bozo Beach   BEACH
(Map p165) On the western downwind side of Playa Cabarete, and so named because of all the beginner windsurfers and kitesurfers who don't yet know how to tack upwind and so wash up on Bozo's shore. There are more kiteboarders at Bozo than at Playa Cabarete, and the surf here is better for boogie boarding.

⊙ Sights & Activities

The surfing high season is the kitesurfing low season. While there are winds year round, the best months for the latter are July, August and the beginning of September. February can be a good month, and

NORTH COAST CABARETE

speeds, this can be frustrating for some. Schools and instructors vary considerably, so spend time finding one where you'll feel comfortable.

Kitesurfing is a potentially dangerous sport, and it is extremely important that you ask questions and voice fears or concerns, and that you receive patient, ego-free answers in return. The International Kiteboarding Organization (www.ikointl. com) has a feature listing student ratings for schools and instructors.

About half of the schools are located on Kite Beach. You can check conditions on www.windalert.com or www.windguru. com. Most shops rent complete gear if you already know the ropes (around US$60 for a half day or US$80 per day in low season).

Dare2Fly   KITESURFING

(Map p165; ☑ 809-571-0805; www.dare2fly.com; Kite Beach) Owned by Vela Windsurf Center, Dare2Fly, which has mainly European instructors, is located at Agualina Kite Resort (p168).

Laurel Eastman Kiteboarding   KITESURFING

(Map p162; ☑ 809-571-0564; www.laureleastman. com; Millennium Luxury Beach Resort & Spa) Run by one of the world's top kiteboarders, this is a friendly, safety-conscious operation located on the beach at the high-end Millennium Resort. High-quality equipment and lessons offered in five languages. Nifty-looking bags made by local tailors from donated kites are sold in the shop – profits go to Kiters 4 Communities (www.kiters4communities.org), an organization in a nearby Haitian community school.

Kite Club   KITESURFING

(Map p165; ☑ 809-571-9748; www.kiteclubcabarete.com; Kite Beach) This well-run club is at the top of Kite Beach, and has a fantastic atmosphere for hanging out and relaxing between sessions. The tiny kitchen delivers delicious fresh ahi tuna salads and sandwiches.

Kitexcite   KITESURFING

(Map p165; ☑ 829-962-4456; www.kitexcite.com; Kite Beach) This school was one of the first in Cabarete. Several of its instructors are Dominican, and the school uses radio helmets, video-based learning and optional offshore sessions to maximize instruction.

Paddleboarding

Increasing in popularity is this somewhat meditative, less adrenaline-inducing method of boarding. All-around ocean sport athlete, trainer and colorful storyteller John Holzall (methodlodge@gmail.com) will take you on a paddle around the lagoon near Kite Beach. Laurel Eastman Kiteboarding rents boards for US$20 per hour; only on mornings when the ocean is calm.

Kayak River Adventures   OUTDOORS

(☑ 829-305-6883; www.kayakriveradventures. com) Helmut, the German man who runs this highly recommended operation, is enthusiastic and professional and will tailor canyoning, kayaking and stand-up paddleboarding trips to your needs (including late morning start times).

Surfing

Waves of up to 4m, among the best waves for surfing on the entire island, break over reefs 4km west of Cabarete on Playa Encuentro. The waves break both right and left and are known by such names as Coco Pipe, Bobo's Point, La Derecha, La Izquierda and most ominously, Destroyer. Several outfits in town and on Playa Encuentro rent surfboards and offer instruction. Surfboard rental for a day is around US$20; a two-hour course costs US$45 to US$50 per person, and a five-day surf camp costs US$250 per person. All the surf schools have small offices on Playa Encuentro.

Newbies should keep in mind that surfing is generally an early morning sport and most people stop in the early afternoon before the wind picks up (some will head out again around 5pm).

Kele Surf School   SURFING

(☑ 829-846-6930; www.kelesurf.com; group lesson per hr US$40, board rental per day $US25; ☉ 7am-4pm) Owned by an inspiring young woman who grew up in Encuentro and works as a fashion model, Kele Surf School is hands down the best choice for aspiring female surfers. Unlike some of the smarmy instructors known to populate Encuentro, Kele's won't try any 'hanky panky.' Also her equipment is top quality and her prices are competitive.

Pau Hana Surf Camp   SURFING

(☑ 809-884-2828; www.pauhanasurfcamp.com; Playa Encuentro) One of the first schools on the beach, Pau Hana has a good reputation and primarily employs local kids.

Cabarete Surf Camp SURFING
(Map p162; ☑ 829-548-6655; www.cabaretesurf-camp.com) One of the most popular camps in Cabarete, with fantastic accommodations and instructors. Also offers kitesurfing lessons.

Swell Surf Camp SURFING
(Map p162; www.swellsurfcamp.com) A recommended surf camp located in the middle of Cabarete with well-maintained accommodations and a very social atmosphere.

Bobo Surf's Up School SURFING
(☑ 809-882-5197; www.bobosurfsup.com; Playa Ecuentro) Offers a number of packages with varying hotel and meal options to suit different budgets.

Take Off SURFING
(☑ 809-963-7873; www.321takeoff.com; Playa Encuentro) The owner also organizes the Master of the Ocean (p166) competition.

Windsurfing

Cabarete's 'discovery' by French Canadians in the late 1980s as one of the best places for windsurfing in the Caribbean – strong, steady winds, relatively shallow water and a rockless shore – was what put the village firmly on the international tourists' radar. Once high profile, the sport's popularity has been waning.

Board and sail rentals average US$20 to US$30 per hour, US$60 to US$75 per day or US$280 to US$300 per week. Renters are encouraged to purchase damage insurance for an additional US$50 per week. Private lessons cost around US$60 for an hour, US$200 for a four-session course, with discounts for groups.

If you prefer an actual boat attached to your sail, head to the Israeli-owned **Carib Wind Center** (Map p162; ☑ 809-571-0560; www.caribwindcabarete.com; Principal). It also rents Lasers and catamarans and provides instruction.

Vela Windsurf Center WINDSURFING
(Map p162; ☑ 809-571-0805; www.velacabarete.com) Vela Windsurf Center, on the main beach, uses excellent gear and works in conjunction with kitesurfing school Dare2Fly. It also rents sea kayaks (per hour US$10).

West of Cabarete

See Cabarete Map (p162)

West of Cabarete

◎ **Sights**
1 Bozo Beach A1
2 Kite Beach A1

🔵 **Activities, Courses & Tours**
Cabarete Coffee Company .... (see 11)
Dare2Fly .... (see 5)
Dominican Fisherman .... (see 11)
3 Kite Club A1
4 Kitexcite A1

🛏 **Sleeping**
5 Agualina Kite Resort A1
6 Cabarete Beach Houses at Nanny
Estates B2
7 Extreme Hotel A1
8 Kite Beach Hotel A1
9 Kite Beach Inn A1
10 Ultravioleta Boutique Residences B2

🍴 **Eating**
11 Cabarete Coffee Company B2
12 Vagamundo Coffee & Waffles B3

Diving

Northern Coast Diving DIVING
(Map p162; ☑ 809-571-1028; www.northerncoast-diving.com) Well-respected Sosúa-based dive shop with a representative in Iguana Mama. Organizes excursions from Laguna Dudu in the east to Monte Cristi in the west.

Dive Cabarete

DIVING

(Map p162; ✆809-915-9135; www.divecabarete. com; Plaza Hotel Kaoba, Principal) The only PADI dive center in the town of Cabarete.

Mountain Biking

Max 'Maximo' Martinez

BICYCLE TOUR

(✆809-882-5634; maxofthemt@gmail.com; full day incl rental per person US$70) If strapping a GPS and a machete to your bike and going out bush is your idea of a good time, hook up with Max 'Maximo' Martinez, a passionate and experienced mountain-bike guide. Maximo can tailor trips to any length and stamina level.

Horseback Riding

Rancho Luisa

HORSEBACK RIDING

(✆809-986-1984) A kind, young expat runs this horse ranch out near Sabaneta de Yasica. A 2½-hour ride ($45 including transport to/from Cabarete) takes you through beautiful mountain scenery and past waterfalls and rural villages. There's also on overnight trip available (US$200), which includes a stay in an all-inclusive.

🧭 Tours

★ Iguana Mama

OUTDOORS

(Map p162; ✆809-571-0908, cell 809-654-2325; www.iguanamama.com; Principal) This professional and family-run adventure-sports tour operator is in a class of its own. Its specialties are mountain biking (from easy to insanely difficult, from US$50) and canyoning. Trips to Damajagua (US$89) go to the 27th waterfall, and Iguana Mama pioneered a canyoning tour to Ciguapa Falls, which only this operator offers. The highest jump is over 10m.

There's also a variety of hiking trips, including a half-day walk (US$35) into Parque Nacional El Choco, and its Pico Duarte trek is handy if you want transportation to and from Cabarete (per person US$450). Iguana Mama can also arrange a number of other half-day and full-day canyoning trips in the area (US$89 to US$195). Action and adventure junkies should ask about the one-week 'Mama Knows Best' tour – seven days of nonstop adrenaline.

Cabarete Coffee Company

TOUR

(Map p165; ✆809-571-0919; www.cabareteco ffeecompany.com; Principal) Small groups (up to 10 people) can take half-day cacao tours (US$75 per person), essentially 'cultural' tours where you lunch in a local's home and hike to a small village in the foothills of the Cordillera Septentrional. They're great for kids, photographers and kitesurfers, since you're back in town by 2pm when the winds pick up. Tours of a coffee plantation around Jarabacoa are by reservation with groups of six or more (US$200 per person).

Dominican Fisherman

FISHING

(Map p165; ✆809-613-4177; Principal, Cabarete Coffee Company) This particular 'Dominican Fisherman' takes small groups out deep-sea fishing (in a self-described 'rustic' boat; four hours, US$105 per person) or on the *Rio Yásica* (three hours, US$45 per person) and nearby reef (four hours, US$95 per person). You can arrange to have your catch cleaned and cooked.

🎓 Courses

Cabarete Language Institute

LANGUAGE

(Map p162; ✆809-713-5002; www.cabaretelan guage.com; Pro Cab Calle B) Conversational Spanish lessons for all levels. Expect to pay around RD$1100 per hour for private lessons, and cheaper group courses are also available.

🎉 Festivals & Events

Dominican Jazz Festival

MUSIC

(www.drjazzfestival.com; ☉Nov) Held in Puerto Plata and Santiago, this long-running festival attracts top musical talent from around the country and abroad. Most of the visiting musicians run workshops for kids; one year Bernie Williams, former Yankee turned guitarist, taught both baseball and jazz.

Master of the Ocean

SPORTS

(www.masteroftheocean.com; ☉last week Feb) A triathlon of water sports – surfing, windsurfing and kitesurfing. From the beach you can watch some spectacular performances.

🛏 Sleeping

In low season you can pick up deals on long-term rentals, but in high season – when condo owners return – rooms are hard to find. **L'Agence** (Map p162; ✆809-571-0999; www.agencerd.com) and **El Magnifico** (Map p162; ✆809-571-0868; www.hotelmagnifico.com; Cementerio; r from US$116, apt for 4 from US$250; ❉ 🛜 🏊) can help you find a condo. Others worth looking into are **Ultravioleta Boutique Residences** (Map p165; ✆829-931-5555; http://ultravioletacabarete.com; 1-/3-bedroom apt US$215/545; 🅿 ❉ 🛜 🏊) and **Cabarete**

Beach Houses at Nanny Estates (Map p165; ☏809-571-0744; www.cabaretebeachhouses.com).

New developments are constantly emerging, and the one all-inclusive here is Viva Wyndham Tangerine. It was undergoing renovations when we visited.

★**Surf Break Cabarete**　　　　B&B **$**
(☏829-921-4080;　　www.surfbreakcabarete.com; Playa Encuentro; s/d incl breakfast from US$35/42; P❋☎☀) The best value stay in Playa Encuentro offers both surf and yoga packages, along with a range of darling, palapa-topped accommodations in two lush complexes. The pool area and yoga studio are superbly tranquil, and the owner is friendly and helpful. This is the hotel of choice for women traveling alone (and anybody else, really).

★**Cabarete Surf Camp**　　　　HOSTEL **$**
(Map p162; ☏829-548-6655; www.cabaretesurfcamp.com; s incl breakfast & dinner US$25-44, d US$33-66, apt US$75-120; P❋☎☀) On the edge of a lagoon a five-minute walk inland, this lushly landscaped property has small, colorful and rustic backpacker-style cabins; larger, modern rooms with kitchenettes in a two-story, Victorian-style building; and, best of all, two colonial-style, all-wood rooms with louvered windows in a 'tower' above the kitchen and dining area.

During the high season, Cabarete Surf Camp has a fun social scene with great barbecue dinners – nonguests should consider heading here, especially for the churrasco. A nice pool and surfing and kitesurfing packages are offered – in fact, it's ideal for those looking for a laid-back base from which to learn how to surf or kitesurf.

Hotel Alegría　　HOTEL, APARTMENTS **$**
(Map p162; ☏809-571-0455; www.hotel-alegria.com; Callejón 2; r from US$27, studio/apt US$65/120; P☎) Hidden down one of Cabarete's few side streets, the Alegría has beach access, along with a wooden deck at the top of the hotel with a Jacuzzi and good ocean views. The studios and apartment each have kitchens, but more importantly the owner and staff are friendly, informative and professional.

Hostel Laguna Park　　HOSTEL **$**
(☏809-571-9263; www.facebook.com/HostelCabarete; Castillo 1, Pro Cab; dm US$12, r US$35; ☎☀) The rather anomalous facade of this large brick building, converted by its gregarious owner into a cavernous hostel, resembles a suburbanite's version of a castle replete with a turret. It's a conventional-looking space inside with concrete floors, spare and second-hand furnishings, a common room with a pool table and a mix of dorm and private rooms.

Kite Beach Inn　　HOTEL **$**
(Map p165; ☏809-490-5517; www.kitebeachinn.com; r with fan/air-con US$40/45; P❋☎☀) Budget-minded kitesurfers should consider this place, opened in 2013 by an expat couple. Clean and simply furnished rooms with new flatscreen TVs are in a building set just off the road. While the inner courtyard and small pool are ordinary, the beachfront deck is delightful.

Extreme Hotel　　HOTEL **$$**
(Map p165; ☏809-571-0330; www.extremehotels.com; Kite Beach; r US$60; P☎☀) ✈ Trapeze, kickboxing, physical therapy camp, a half pipe for skateboarders – certainly not your standard hotel offerings. Then again, this ecologically minded, solar-powered and self-described 'upscale hostel' is meant for those seeking an unconventional beach holiday. No TVs and no air-con in the spacious and simply furnished fan-cooled rooms.

Families and groups should consider the huge three-bedroom, three-bathroom penthouse. All of the produce at La Mesa Taina, the newly opened restaurant and sushi bar, is either grown on the property (using aquaponics) or on an organic farm near Sabaneta de Yasica. Attached and affiliated with the hotel is the kitesurfing school Go Kite Cabarete.

El Encuentro Surf Lodge　　LODGE **$$**
(☏809-669　0811;　http://elencuentrosurflodge.com; r US$90; P❋☎☀) A new, boutique surf lodge in walking distance of Playa Encuentro. It has only nine rooms, a snack bar open from 7am to 2pm for breakfast and lunch and a nice lap pool.

Swell Surf Camp　　HOTEL **$$**
(Map p162; ☏809-972-2406; www.swellsurfcamp.com; weekly incl breakfast & 4 dinners dm/s/d US$425/635/1000; P❋☎☀) Designed with the discerning surfer in mind, Swell is far from a crash pad. The spare clean lines, plush bedding, modern photographs and funky furniture say 'boutique,' but the pool, ping-pong and foosball tables and social vibe suggest otherwise. A huge wood communal table is the center of the hanging-out action.

Hooked Cabarete
BUNGALOW **$$**

(☑809-935-9221; www.hookedcabarete.com; Playa Encuentro; s/d/tr US$60/82/100; P❋☎☲) If a beachfront location isn't a priority, then this small property down a dirt road 200m or so from Playa Encuentro is a nice place to ensconce yourself – especially if you're a surfer. A handful of modern, bungalow-style studio apartments with kitchenettes and attractive wooden porches surround a quiet garden courtyard and small pool.

The new owners have, if anything, improved upon the original. It also features a ping-pong table and rents scooters and bicycles, so you can get into town easily.

Agualina Kite Resort
HOTEL **$$**

(Map p165; ☑809-571-0787; www.agualina.com; Kite Beach; r US$107; P❋☎☲) Opened in 2004, this is the most comfortable lodging on Kite Beach. Studios and apartments have stylish, well-equipped kitchens – stainless-steel refrigerators are an especially nice touch – and large modern bathrooms with glass showers and gleaming fixtures. There's free wi-fi throughout the building.

Kite Beach Hotel
CONDO **$$**

(Map p165; ☑809-571-0878; www.kitebeach hotel.com; Kite Beach; s/d incl breakfast US$59/69; P❋☎☲) This oceanfront hotel boasts well-appointed rooms with gleaming tile floors, good-sized bathrooms and satellite TV. All suites and apartments have balconies that afford at least partial ocean views. The laid-back pool area makes a great place to watch the action in the sky and on the water.

★ Natura Cabañas
RESORT **$$$**

(☑809-571-1507; www.naturacabana.com; r incl breakfast US$236; P@☲) Owned and designed by an expat husband-wife team, this collection of marvelously designed thatched-roof bungalows about halfway between Cabarete and Sosúa is the epitome of rustic chic. Everything is constructed from natural materials – mahogany, bamboo and stone – and a gravel path leads to a secluded beach. Two open-air restaurants serve exquisitely created dishes (US$15 to US$30).

The hotel also features a spa and an incredibly tranquil yoga deck.

Millennium Luxury
Beach Resort & Spa
BOUTIQUE HOTEL **$$$**

(Map p162; ☑809-571-0407; www.cabaretemillennium.com; r US$177, apt from US$472; P❋☎☲) Ultra-modern, quintessential Miami Beach (now in vogue in Cabarete), the Millennium is a swanky beachfront property with a cool, if somewhat chilly, ambience. The spacious rooms are furnished in a minimalist style and the infinity pool is especially nice.

Velero Beach Resort
HOTEL **$$$**

(Map p162; ☑809-571-9727; www.velerobeach.com; La Punta 1; r from US$175; P❋@☲) Distinguished by boutique-style rooms and its location down a small lane at the relatively traffic-free eastern end of town, Velero is an excellent choice. True to its four-star rating in service, professionalism and property maintenance, the Velero has recently opened a new restaurant, and the pool and lounge area are also top notch.

Hotel Villa Taína
HOTEL **$$$**

(Map p162; ☑809-571-0722; www.villataina.com; r/apt incl breakfast from US$109/148; P❋@☎☲) This appealing boutique-y hotel at the western end of town has 61 tastefully decorated rooms, each with balcony or terrace, air-con, comfortable beds and modern bathroom. It has a small, clean pool and a nice beach area fringed by palm trees. Suites and deluxe suites are also available.

✖ Eating

Dining out on Cabarete's beach is the quintessential Caribbean experience – paper lanterns hanging from palm trees, a gentle ocean breeze and excellent food (even if it does cost the same as you'd pay back home). Many of the bars on the beach serve good food, but note that many close up for part of October.

The best supermarket is **Janet's** (Map p162; ☑809-571-9770; Principal; ⊙8am-8pm Mon-Sat, to 1pm Sun) at the east end of town.

★ Mojito Bar
SALADS, SANDWICHES **$**

(Map p162; mains RD$170; ⊙11am-2am, closed Tue; ☎☲) One of the few reasonably priced beachfront places, Mojitos has an excellent selection of natural juices, healthy salads, Dominican food and sandwiches (some vegan and vegetarian). It's a sliver of a space near the middle of the beach. Happy hour is from 4pm to 8pm (two mojitos RD$200).

Vagamundo Coffee & Waffles
CAFE **$**

(Map p165; www.vagamundocoffee.com; across from Supermercado La Rosa; latte RD$145, waffles RD$100-250; ⊙7am-4pm; P☎) Just outside of town, this new third-wave coffee shop offers all the latest in coffee technology, including cold brew and Chemex coffee-makers. It's a super relaxing place to work or hang out with a friend, and the Belgian waffles are delicious (try the Uluatu, with passionfruit, mint and ricotta).

Cabarete Coffee Company   CAFE $

(Map p165; ☑809-571-0919; www.cabaretecof-fee.com; Principal; mains RD$150; ☺7am-3pm Dec-Jul; ❄🕏) 🍴 A tiny spot with all-day breakfast menu (waffles, omelets and even bagels), healthy paninis, fresh smoothies, organic and locally sourced ingredients and, as you'd expect, excellent coffee. Owned and operated by Patricia Suriel of the **Mariposa Foundation** (☑809-571-0610; www.mariposadrfoundation.org). All proceeds go to the Mariposa DR Foundation, which educates and empowers girls in the community to help end poverty.

Panadería Repostería Dick   BAKERY $

(Map p162; ☑809-571-0612; Principal; set break-fasts RD$150; ☺7am-5pm, to 1pm Sun) A morning destination for its large set breakfasts with juice and strong coffee. The bakery does wholewheat bread and tasty vanilla-cream Danish pastries.

Belgium Bakery   BAKERY $$

(Map p162; ☑809-571-0637; Plaza Popular Cabarete, Principal; mains RD$260; ☺7am-7pm; 🕏) Hands down *the* place for breakfast in Cabarete: strong coffee, delicious bread and pastries and large omelets. Though it fronts a parking lot and not the beach, the outdoor patio seating is an ideal spot to while away several hours. Burgers, paninis and salads are served throughout the day.

La Parilla de Luis   BARBECUE $$

(Map p162; ☑809-857-5527; Callejon de la Loma; mains RD$220; ☺4-11pm) Ignore the noise and fumes from idling *motoconchos* and pull up a plastic chair to enjoy delicious plates of barbecue chicken and yucca.

La Casita de Papi   SEAFOOD $$

(Map p162; ☑809-986-3750; mains RD$650; ☺noon-11pm, closed Mon; 🕏) An institution in Cabarete, this cozy beachfront restaurant does a great garlic shrimp paella dish as well as lobster and grilled fish.

Otra Cosa   FRENCH $$

(Map p162; ☑809-571-0607; edcoll13@gmail.com; La Punta; mains RD$600; ☺6:30-10:30pm, closed Tue; 🕏) Located at a secluded spot with marvelous sea breezes at dusk, this French-Caribbean restaurant guarantees a pleasant dining experience. You can listen to the surf and watch the moon rise over the water while sipping wine and feasting on seared tuna in ginger flambéed in rum (RD$825).

An *amuse-bouche* of eggplant caviar and a shot of *mamajuana* (rum, red wine and honey drink), both complimentary, serve as bookends to the meal. Reservations recommended and cash only.

Gordito's Fresh Mex   MEXICAN $$

(Map p162; www.gorditosfreshmex.com; Ocean Dream Plaza, Principal; mains RD$375; ☺11:30am-9pm; 🕏) California transplants opened this immediately popular Dominican version of Chipotle, and they're now discussing plans to expand to new locations in the DR. Gordito's goes beyond burritos, though, offering things like chicken yucatan (honey buttermilk marinated chicken with corn sauce, *queso fondito*, avocado and *pico de gallo*), along with fish tacos and empanadas.

NORTH COAST CABARETE

OUT OF TOWN EATS

If you should ever grow tired of the beachside scene in Cabarete, the following restaurants are wonderfully unique options. Even if it weren't for the excellent food, they would be worthy destinations simply for the chance to get out into the countryside.

Castle Club (☑809-357-8334; www.castleclubonline.com; Los Brazos; per person excl drinks US$40; ☺vary) Memorable meals a half-hour dive away in the mountains.

Blue Moon Hotel & Restaurant (☑809-757-0614; www.bluemoonretreat.net; Los Brazos; per person US$20; ☺dinner) Just 200m before Castle Club, this bungalow-style hotel and restaurant serves quality Indian-Caribbean fusion.

Wilson's at La Boca (☑809-667-1968; mains RD$200) A little BBQ shack on the Yasica River in Islabon, around 8km southeast of town.

Restaurante Chez Arsenio (☑809-571-9948; restaurantechezarsenio@hotmail.com; Hideaway Beach Resort; mains RD$500; ☺11am-10pm Mon-Fri, from 9am Sat & Sun) On the western end of Playa Encuentro, Hideaway Beach Resort's restaurant serves up excellent Dominican, Italian and seafood dishes.

Pomodoro

ITALIAN $$

(Map p162; ☏ 809-571-0085; mains RD$380; ⏱11am-11pm; ☏) Pomodoro serves the best crispy-crust pizza on the beach. A new owner has introduced a side operation of delicious gelato, and kept the live jazz performances on Thursday nights (8pm to 10pm). Delivers.

★ Eze Bar & Restaurant

ITALIAN $$$

(Map p162; ☏ 809-571-0586; www.ezerestaurant. com; Plaza Carib Wind; mains US$15-25; ⏱8am-11pm) Eze Bar is not visible from the main drag, and unless you approach it from the beach, to get there you must walk through a windsurfing shop. The place is small but chic, with a fairly unoriginal Miami Beach vibe, so it's a bit of a shock when the Italian food arrives and blows your mind.

The tuna tartar might be the best in all the Caribbean, with mouthwatering morsels of fresh fish, avocado and an unusual ingredient – black olives. The dorado is a flaky dream, and the menu also features exquisite salads, healthy wraps, homemade pastas and meat dishes. The Italian chef is known around town for opening ambitious restaurants but this is his first home-run. It's pricey but worth it, and happy hour is every day from 5pm to 7pm.

Sunset Grill

DOMINICAN $$$

(Map p162; ☏ 809-571-9727; Velero Beach Resort; mains US$18; ⏱8am-10pm) This restaurant is the best spot in town to watch the sunset, and serves up Dominican cuisine along with fresh seafood, steaks, pasta and juicy burgers. Top dishes include the shrimp à la Victor and the seared fresh tuna.

Bliss

MEDITERRANEAN $$$

(Map p162; ☏ 809-571-9721; Callejon de la Loma; mains RD$750; ⏱6pm-midnight, closed Wed) It may not be on the beach, but sitting around the small, crystal-blue pool with a top-shelf cocktail in your hand, you can be forgiven for not caring. By all accounts, the new owners have not only maintained the kitchen's high standards but introduced homemade pastas as well – the seafood risotto and linguini with lobster can be especially recommended.

🍷 Drinking & Nightlife

Cabarete nightlife is centered on the bars and restaurants that spill out onto the beach – it's a fun and vibrant scene. Most are open to around 3am. 'Subtle' prostitution exists at some nightspots, but most importantly keep an eye on your valuables and do not walk on the beach at night east of Villa Taina, essentially the stretch between Cabarete Beach and Punta Goleta.

Wineyard

WINE BAR

(Map p162; ☏ 809-571-0165; Plaza Ocean Dream; tasting RD$500; ⏱11am-10pm Mon-Sat) The first wine store to open in Cabarete has an incredible selection of fine wines primarily from Australia, California, New Zealand and Argentina, and also a small menu of tasty cheeses, ceviche and carapaccio (the owner will help you pair these). The affable owner holds tastings and special theme nights, for example, wine-themed movie nights. RD$500 tastings include four wines.

Kahuna

BAR

(Map p162; ☏ 809-571-0064; Cabarete Beach; ⏱9pm-3am) An excellent sports bar with NFL, NHL, NBA and games from many other league acronyms on the big screen, along with regular food and drink specials. Late nights here are especially fun, with lots of dancing and two beer-pong tables.

Leaf

LOUNGE

(Map p162; ☏ 829-908-2810; Cabarete Beach; ⏱10:45am-3am) This lounge is the only place on the beach to hear house and techno music, and DJ/owner Christian Azar makes sure it's the good stuff. Dancing goes 'til late.

Voy Voy

BAR

(Map p162; ⏱6pm-late) Vela Windsurf Center by day, bar by night, this small, hip cafe also serves sandwiches and snacks. Monday karaoke is a mandatory part of Cabarete beach life, as are the regular open mic and dance nights.

Onno's

CLUB

(Map p162; ⏱9am-3am) This edgy, Dutch-owned restaurant and nightclub is a European and hipster hangout and serves good-value food on the beach. At night a DJ spins a decent set.

Lax

BAR

(Map p162; www.lax-cabarete.com; ⏱9am-1am) This mellow bar and restaurant serves food until 12:30pm, when the DJ starts to spin.

🛈 Information

DANGERS & ANNOYANCES

Cestur (Tourist Police; ☏ 809-571-0713, 809-754-3036; Principal) At the eastern entrance to town.

INTERNET ACCESS

Fujifilm Digital (☑ 809-571-9536; Principal; per hr RD$30) Fast internet connection and headphones.

LAUNDRY

Lavandería Janko (Principal; per kg RD$30; ⊘ 9am-6pm Mon-Sat) Eastern end of town, opposite Janet's Supermarket.

MEDICAL SERVICES

Servi-Med (☑ 809-571-0964; Principal; ⊘ 24hr) English, German and Spanish are spoken, and travel medical insurance and credit cards accepted.

MONEY

There's a **Banco Popular** (Principal; ⊘ 9am-4:30pm Mon-Fri, to 1pm Sat) and **Scotiabank** (Principal; ⊘ 9am-5pm Mon-Fri, to 1pm Sat) on Calle Principal.

ⓘ Getting There & Away

BUS

None of the main bus companies offer service to Cabarete – the closest depots are in Sosúa. They zip through town without stopping on their way to Nagua before turning south to Santo Domingo.

A large, white bus with air-con on its way from Puerto Plata to Samaná stops at the gas station just east of town every day at 1:30pm. From Cabarete, the three-hour trip costs RD$250.

CAR

If you want to rent a car, you can do so at the airport or in town. One fantastic option is **Easy Rider** (☑ 849-863-9560; www.facebook.com/easyridercabarete; ⊘ 8am-7pm), where prices are reasonable and full insurance coverage is provided (you will not be held responsible for damaged windows, tires or anything else). If you're in town and prefer to rent at the airport, you can take a *guagua* (30 minutes) to the airport road (just past Sosúa), walk 500m to the terminal and shop around at the numerous car-rental agencies there.

It's around a 2½-hour drive in your own vehicle from Cabarete to Samaná.

GUAGUA

Heaps of *guaguas* ply this coastal road, including east to Sabaneta (RD$25) and Río San Juan (RD$80, one hour) and west to Sosúa (RD$25, 20 minutes) and Puerto Plata (RD$50, 45 minutes). Hail them anywhere along Cabarete's main drag.

A *guagua* to Santo Domingo is RD$280, but you're better off catching a bus in Sosúa.

MOTOCONCHO

Transportation in town is dominated by *motoconchos*, who will attempt to charge you two

ROUTE 21
....

The quickest way from Cabarete to Santo Domingo is to take Rte 21, a 'shortcut' through the mountains that heads inland from the coastal highway near Sabaneta de Yasica. It passes through beautiful mountain scenery and small villages before hitting Moca and then empties into Hwy 1 at La Vega. Depending on your driving skill and weather conditions, the trip can be made in around three hours.

to three times the price you'd pay for a similar ride in Puerto Plata. Don't be surprised if you can't haggle them down. A ride out to Kite Beach should cost RD$50 and Playa Encuentro RD$100.

SCOOTER

A popular option is to rent a scooter or a motorcycle. Expect to pay around US$20 per day, less if you rent for a week or more. There are lots of rental shops along the main drag, and some hotels rent two-wheeled transportation too. Be aware that helmets aren't always available, so if that's important to you consider bringing your own.

TAXI

The motorcycle-shy can call a **taxi** (☑ 809-571-0767; www.taxisosuacabarete.com), which will cost RD$500 to Encuentro, US$45 to Aeropuerto Internacional Gregorio Luperón 18km west, and US$35 to Puerto Plata. For the Santiago airport it's around US$100, and for Santo Domingo its US$200. There's also a taxi **stand** (Map p162) in the middle of town.

Río San Juan

POP 9000

Only an hour east of Cabarete, this sleepy town is distinctive because of its location on a mangrove lagoon and its business-owning French expat community. Several of the north coast's best beaches are within easy driving distance, and diving and snorkeling are nearby.

Laguna Gri-Gri, which shares the same ecosystem as Los Haitises south of Península de Samaná, was once Río San Juan's claim to fame. Unfortunately, overuse and pollution mean the lagoon is no longer pristine and swimming is not recommended.

Headed east you'll hit two of the country's most beautiful beaches, Playas Grande and Preciosa, and continuing further you'll come to Cabrera, a sleepy town of stone houses with colorful shutters, flower boxes and well-kept gardens, as well as lavish vacation homes owned by Dominicans and expats.

⛱ Beaches

Other than the small **town beach** on the bay, which is good for swimming, **Playa Caletón** is the closest beach.

Around Cabrera are **Playa Diamante**, **Playa El Breton** and **Playa Entrada**. Entrada is the most spectacular of the three, but all are worth checking out.

👁 Sights

Laguna Gri-Gri LAGOON
(Duarte) This lagoon at the northern end of Calle Duarte is fairly picturesque, with a dozen or more boatmen offering hour-long tours (US$50 for up to seven people) through tangled mangrove channels, including interesting rock formations and a cave populated by hundreds of swallows.

Look for a small shack next to the public bathrooms down by the Laguna – you'll find it easier to join a group on weekends, when Dominicans come to take this trip. You can also visit the lagoon on foot – there's a path on the far side of the Hotel Bahía Blanca along the water's edge into the mangroves.

🏃 Activities

Playa Grande Surf School SURFING
(☎829-705-1416; Playa Grande; lessons US$45) Offers surf lessons on Playas Grande and Preciosa, and also rents surfboards for US$25, kayaks for US$15 and snorkel gear for US$12.

Playa Grande Golf Course GOLF
(☎809-582-0860; www.playagrande.com; Carretera a Nagua; 9/18 holes US$80/140; 🕐7am-4:30pm) Aman resorts now controls this par-72 course built on a verdant cliff before Playa Grande. At the time of research, only members and Amanera guests had access to the course, but that could change. Be sure to call ahead.

Diving & Snorkeling

Río San Juan has a great variety of nearby dive sites, including **Seven Hills**, a collection of huge coral heads descending from 6m to 50m, and **Crab Canyon**, a series of natural arches and swim-throughs. Twenty minutes east of Río San Juan is **Dudu Cave**, one of the best freshwater cavern dives in the Caribbean, where the visibility is almost 50m. Most dive shops require an advanced diver certificate or at least 20 logged dives to do these trips. **Happy Dive Center** (☎809-589-2903; www.happydivecenterdr.com; per tank incl equipment US$50, open-water course US$380, snorkeling US$35), a shop based by Laguna Gri-Gri in Río San Juan, can arrange the trip for US$50 per dive, or you can organize something from Sosúa.

Near the dive sites, a water-filled limestone cave runs all the way to the ocean. Non-divers can access the landscaped picnic area (RD$100) for cliff jumping and rope swinging.

🛏 Sleeping

Vista Linda VILLA **$**
(☎829-508-9855; villa.esperanza@icloud.com; Principal Bejuco Alhambre; villa incl breakfast from US$45; Ⓟ❄📶🏊) Just out of town from Río San Juan, this cute collection of seven newly constructed villas offers striking views of the countryside. The meticulous expat owners prepare delicious breakfasts in their home at the top of the complex, and will also make dinner if you ask in advance. Discounts are available for long-term stays.

Bahía Blanca HOTEL **$**
(☎809-589-2563; bahia.blanca.dr@claro.net.do; Gaston F Deligne; r RD$1500; 📶) Perched on a rocky spit over turquoise-blue waters and marking the eastern end of the town beach, the long-running Bahía Blanca has undeniably beautiful ocean views. Rooms are basic – with clean, tile floors and private bathrooms – but show their age. All but two have at least partial ocean views and wide balconies.

Flooding in late 2016 caused considerable damage to this property, but it remains open.

Amanera RESORT **$$$**
(☎809-589-2888; www.aman.com/resorts/amanera; Playa Grande; r from US$1536) You probably won't stay at this resort, but just knowing about it (and maybe calling ahead to try to eat or golf there) is worth it. In fact, we're fairly certain they let us in because the staff was getting bored. Anyhow, this is the latest masterpiece of the international hotel chain Aman, and it is absurdly opulent.

The 25 sumptuous casitas set back from Playa Grande are all constructed of teak and caliche, with amazing views and remote control everything. The lobby and restaurant are even more ridiculous, with floor-to-ceiling windows overlooking all of Playa Grande and infinity-pools everywhere. If they do let you on the property for lunch, order the lobster.

PLAYAS GRANDE & PRECIOSA

Just 8km east of Río San Juan is **Playa Grande,** one of the most beautiful beaches in the DR. The long, broad, tawny beach has aquamarine water on one side and a thick fringe of palm trees on the other, with stark white cliffs jutting out into the ocean in the distance. A **surf school** (p172) here offers lessons.

Facilities at the eastern end of the beach include a little 'village' of pastel-colored clapboard shacks selling freshly caught seafood including lobsters, prawns and grilled snapper served with rice and plantains, and piña coladas made with real pineapple and coconut juice. Plastic tables and chairs are usually available so you can chow down on the beach in comfort. Facilities also include souvenirs, and bathrooms with outdoor showers. These amenities and the newly paved access road have diminished the previously remote and wild feel of the area. Vendors rent beach chairs (per day RD$150), umbrellas (per day RD$175), snorkel equipment (full day RD$500), body boards (per hour RD$150) and surfboards (per hour RD$500). If seeking solitude, walk west along the beach, away from the entrance.

Only 25m down a path leaving from just in front of Playa Grande's bathrooms is another spectacular stretch of sand called **Playa Preciosa**. The waves are enormous, and tend to attract surfers at dawn.

A word about safety: these beaches have heavy surf and a deceptively strong undertow. Riptides – powerful currents flowing out to sea – form occasionally, and people have drowned here. Be conservative when swimming, and children and less-experienced swimmers should probably not go in at all unless the surf is low. If caught in a riptide, swim parallel to the shore until out of the current and then swim in.

If you take a *guagua* from town, drivers will let you off just before the security gate marking the entrance to the beaches. You can also hire a *motoconcho* (RD$100) or a taxi (RD$300) to take you directly there.

NORTH COAST RÍO SAN JUAN

Balaji Palace VILLA **$$$**
(☑ 809-722-2275, in USA 978-409-2739; info.balaji@ warwickhotels.com; Playa Grande; all-incl s/d from US$175/350; P❄☎☀) Built into the cliffs above Playa Grande, this exquisite Warwick hotel looks like it was designed by the Moors, and is replete with palatial details such as stately columns, abundant marble and bright-red cuppolas. The 18 rooms offer four-poster beds and antique furnishings, and some boast incredible ocean views. The romantic property also features a pool and a helipad.

✖ Eating

La Casona DOMINICAN **$**
(☑ 809-589-2597; Duarte 6; mains RD$200; ◷9am-9pm) This friendly restaurant serves extra-good empanadas.

Café de Paris FRENCH **$$**
(☑ 809-589-2405; Laguna Gri-Gri; mains US$5-10) This hot-pink-and-white Parisian cafe sits right on Laguna Gri-Gri and is an excellent spot for fresh juice or a cocktail. The conch and shellfish are favorites, but save room for the passionfruit mousse.

Estrella Bar
& Restaurant DOMINICAN, FRENCH **$$**
(☑ 809-753-9062; Duarte; mains RD$300-700; ◷8am-11pm; ☎) A few blocks up from the lagoon, Estrella serves up a standard French/ Dominican menu, with especially good seafood specials.

❶ Information

There's a **Banco Progreso** (☑ 809-589-2393; Duarte 38; ◷8:30am-4pm Mon-Fri, 9am-1pm Sat) just off the main coastal highway

The **Cestur** (tourist police; ☑ 809-754-3034) office is located across the street from Bahía Blanca.

❶ Getting There & Away

It's only about a 1½-hour drive from here to Samaná.

BUS

Caribe Tours (☑ 809-589-2644), just west of Calle Duarte on the coastal highway just outside town, provides bus service between Río San Juan and Santo Domingo (RD$350, 3½ hours) and stops along the way at Nagua (RD$80, one hour) and San Francisco de Macorís (RD$220, 2½ hours). Buses depart at 6am, 8am, 10:30am, 2:30pm and 3:30pm.

WESTBOUND GUAGUA

Westbound *guaguas* come and go along the coastal highway. Departures occur nearly every 30 minutes from 6am to 5pm to Cabarete (RD$80, 1½ hours), Sosúa (RD$100, 1½ hours) and Puerto Plata (RD$125, two hours).

EASTBOUND GUAGUA

Eastbound *guaguas* line up on the coastal highway and leave every 10 minutes from 6:30am to 6pm for Playa Caletón (RD$30, 10 minutes), Playa Grande (RD$50, 15 minutes) and Nagua (RD$125, 1¼ hours). From Nagua you can catch *guaguas* to Samaná.

TAXI

There's a **taxi stand** ([☑ 809-589-2501) on Calle Duarte between Calles Luperón and Dr Virgilio García. Some sample fares are Playa Caletón RD$250, Playa Grande RD$400, Cabarete RD$2500, Aeropuerto Puerto Plata RD$3500 and Las Terrenas on the Península de Samaná RD$5000.

Luperón

POP 9300

Luperón is famous as a 'hurricane hole' – a safe haven from rough seas for boaters (treasure hunters suspect several Spanish galleons foundered and sunk just before reaching safety here). There are two fairly rundown marinas and on average anywhere from 100 to 150 craft in the harbor. Unless you're a boater, though, the town has little appeal. Deeply rutted and dusty streets are quiet during the day and in near total darkness at night. However, nearby Playa Grande is a beautiful long strip of palm-backed white sand with wavy blue waters. The shabby all-inclusive resort fronting the beach has closed (mercifully for guests but an unfortunate blow to Luperón's economy); however, the property's buildings remain, abandoned and dilapidated. The easiest access is down a dirt and gravel road running beside the former resort. A *motoconcho* ride from town is about RD$75.

🏃 Activities

With enough time and patience, it's possible to arrange a boat trip at Marina Puerto Blanco. There are no official tours, but if you put the word out that you're interested someone is bound to turn up sooner or later. Prices vary widely depending on the captain, but expect to pay US$40 to US$60 for a half-day trip, or US$70 to US$120 for a full day.

🛏 Sleeping

There's really no reason to stay around here, unless you're on a boat. If you get stuck, the best place is **Estancia Principe Aparthotel** ([☑ 809-571-8373; www.estanciaprincipe.com; Principal 4; apt RD$1300;).

🍴 Eating

Las Velas Restaurant   SEAFOOD $
([☑ 809-739-2010; Marina Puerto Blanco; mains RD$300; ⊙ 8am-11pm) This waterfront establishment at the marina is a great place to kick back with a Presidente and meet some boaters and fishermen. It's a pretty relaxing place to eat, with a good view of the water and a decent chicken Caesar salad.

ℹ Information

Thornless Path (www.thornlesspath.com) is Caribbean cruiser and Luperón resident Bruce Van Sant's website tribute to the town.

Luperon's sole ATM, a Banreservas on Calle Duarte across the street from Cestur, is notorious for being frequently out of cash or not functioning.

ℹ Getting There & Away

Guaguas to Imbert (RD$50, 30 minutes, every 15 minutes 5am to 6:30pm) leave from a stop on Calle Duarte at 16 de Agosto, four blocks south of Calle 27 de Febrero. From Imbert you can pick up *guaguas* headed south to Santiago or north to Puerto Plata.

A taxi from Puerto Plata should cost around RD$3800. From Luperón to Punta Rucia costs around RD$2000.

Punta Rucia

POP 500

Punta Rucia a pleasant little town with a gorgeous strip of ivory-sand beach. The only real trouble is that sand flies are ubiquitous and bite with abandon.

The other problem used to be getting there, but with an improved access road, this beachfront village has grown considerably, and feels only a little less remote than in the past. That said, heavy rains can still restrict road travel in the region, and most people who venture out this way come from Puerto Plata area all-inclusives on day trips to Cayo Arena (aka 'Paradise Island'). Around 9km northwest of Punta Rucia, the picturesque sandbar is surrounded by crystal-clear water and pristine corals, which makes the snorkeling incredible.

PARQUE NACIONAL LA ISABELA

This historically significant **national park** (RD$100; ⊙8am-5pm) near the town of El Castillo marks Columbus' second settlement on Hispaniola. When he arrived at the first settlement at Cap-Haïtien in Haiti on his second voyage to the New World, he found it destroyed, so he shifted 110km east and set up a new camp here; the foundations of several oceanfront buildings are all that remain. A small, fairly lackluster **museum** visited frequently by groups of Dominican primary-school students marks the occasion. Exhibits in Spanish include sociopolitical explanations of the Taíno communities encountered by Columbus, some old coins, rings, arrowheads and a small-scale replica of Columbus' house. Across the road from the park is the **Templo de las Américas**, a loose and much larger replica of La Isabela's original church built as part of the settlement's 500th anniversary celebrations.

Near the park is **Playa Isabela**, a broad outward-curving beach with coarse sand and calm water. There are a couple of small beach restaurants, and sometimes they serve sea urchins (be careful not to step on these in the shallows). Rancho del Sol, a rambling, idiosyncratic hotel near the entrance to the national park, might be open in the near future.

A taxi from Luperón, 11km to the east, will set you back US$50 return (if the driver waits) and a *motoconcho* (motorcycle taxi) around RD$200 one way. It's possible, but somewhat harder, to get to La Isabela from the main highway between Santiago and Monte Cristi. Turn off at Cruce de Guayacanes and head north 25km to Villa Isabella, passing through Los Hidalgos on the way. The signs can be confusing, so ask for 'El Castillo' – the town where the park is located – as you go. The park is 7km from Villa Isabella.

However, throngs of visitors in the water can detract from the experience.

🏃 Activities

The VIP catamarans and speedboats of El Paraíso Tours (p175) shuttle groups to the Cayo Arena sandbar for several hours before returning via **Estero Hondo**, the mangrove lagoon just to the west (you could spot a manatee). If you want to avoid the crowds, contact **Martinez** (☎829-262-0073), a local Spanish-speaking fisherman offering a more customized experience.

On weekends hundreds of people, primarily Dominicans from Santiago, occupy **Playa Ensenada**, a narrow strip of sand with calm, shallow water 3km east of Punta Rucia. Don't expect quiet or privacy, but with coastal mountains within view to the northwest, water like a bathtub and a seafood meal from one of the nearly two-dozen shacks (lobster RD$300; open till 6pm) lining the beach behind a row of palm trees and picnic tables, it's easily worth a long afternoon visit.

👉 Tours

El Paraíso Tours BOATING
(☎809-320-7606; www.paradiseisland.do; speedboat/VIP incl drinks & lunch US$90/150) Lots of agents sell the Cayo Arena tour, but the actual operator is El Paraíso Tours. If you're coming from Puerto Plata be prepared to spend

a few hours each way on a bus to Playa Ensenada. From there speedboats and a VIP catamaran shuttle everybody to the tiny, scenic sandbar of an island for excellent snorkeling and all-you-can-drink rum.

After a couple of hours, tourists return through the mangroves, and VIP clients also visit Paraiso Ecolodge in Punta Rucia to feast at a buffet that includes grilled lobster.

🍽 Sleeping & Eating

A bunch of rental homes and villas populate the beachfront areas, and new hotels have sprung up in recent years, including the new Paraiso Ecolodge.

For food, you can join one of the tour-group buffets at Paraiso Ecolodge for US$15, including drinks. There is also a bunch of casual restaurants (mains RD$200) and beachside fish stands that serve basic, cheap meals. The pizza at Beicaraibi Rincón Italiano (p176) is outstanding.

Villa Rosa B&B $
(☎809-801-8160; d/tr/q incl breakfast RD$1900/2300/2700; ❋🛜🏊) The cafe and lounge area of this intimate, three-room, French-owned place is on the village's sandy beachfront. Other standout features include an above-ground plunge pool and a small thatch-roofed building with tastefully furnished rooms containing rainwater shower heads and cable TVs. Pasta and seafood are

WORTH A TRIP

BUEN HOMBRE

Remember how in *The Beach* Leonardo DiCaprio hears about a super secret island in Thailand and then goes on a crazy adventure to get there? This is what is now happening on the north coast of the Dominican Republic, with Buen Hombre.

Rumors of wind-whipped shallows in this new, off-the-grid kitesurfing paradise are circulating in the bars of Cabarete, luring away some of its most intrepid adrenaline junkies. If half of what they hear of Buen Hombre is true, they want to see it for themselves, and so they zip out into the DR's northwestern desert past gnarled cacti and herb-eating goats in search of a new thrill. At the end of the road they find a tiny fishing village, eight beachfront bungalows, a simple restaurant and a hut full of kiteboarding equipment. Oh, and a former pro tennis player and Estonian-Swedish filmmaker who speaks eight languages and built the place.

That's Riin Urbanik. She came to the area first as a traveler, and when she beheld Buen Hombre's arid, undulating landscape and felt the wind's strength, she dropped everything and started a **Kite School Buen Hombre** (☑829-521-2367; www.kitebuenhombre.net; Buen Hombre; s/d bungalow US$30/35, week-long kitesurfing course US$900). She soon came to know the community of Buen Hombre, which means 'good man' and comes from kind villagers who risked their lives attempting to save passengers from ships that centuries ago wrecked in the area. The good men of Buen Hombre also helped Riin build her dream, and one of its good women was hired as the chef.

Today people come from around the world to stay at Buen Hombre, where they take up kitesurfing or perfect their skills, bond with a group of like-minded travelers (often including diplomats, tech nerds and NGO types) and go on excursions to nearby mangrove islands and sandbars. In the evenings, when there's a full moon, they kitesurf in its glow and throw parties. On darker nights, they sit around a bonfire telling stories, drinking rum and preparing for another day in the wind.

Unlike *The Beach*, Buen Hombre is accessible via a recently-paved road. Many visitors rent cars or catch a ride out with Riin, traveling west on Autopista Duarte until they reach Botoncillo, and then hanging a right and winding out over the mountains, toward the coast. The drive itself is worthwhile, and even non-kitesurfers have been known to show up in Buen Hombre for the night, just to see it for themselves.

served up upon request, and kayaks and paddleboards are available for rent next door.

Paraiso Ecolodge HOTEL **$$**
(☑809-320-7606; www.paradiseisland.do/en/paraiso-ecolodge-2; s/d incl breakfast US$90/110; P❀☂) This newcomer to Punta Rucia may be the only self-proclaimed ecolodge to also contain a VIP area with Miami-style lounge beds. And while the austere concrete structure set back from the ocean may be less than inspiring, the point is this: sleeping meters from one of the most serene beaches on the DR's north coast is now possible.

Ocean toys like kayaks and a water trampoline are included with a stay, and the restaurant is excellent, but be sure to let somebody know in advance if you plan on eating there; the chef isn't always around.

★Punta Rucia Lodge LODGE **$$$**
(☑849-858-8400; www.puntarucialodge.com; r incl breakfast from US$253; P☂☒) 🍴 An expat

couple runs Punta Rucia Lodge, a handful of colorfully painted cabins wonderfully situated on a bluff overlooking the ocean just east of town. Though the grounds are nearly concealed and overrun by a tangle of flowering trees, you can settle into one of the three cabins' front-porch hammocks or a dining-area perch for mesmerizing, unobstructed views.

This is a place to unwind and disconnect – no locks and no wi-fi. A stairway leads down to what is, for all intents and purposes, a private white-sand beach. Dinner can be prepared upon request and ocean kayaks are available for guests' use. The hotel can arrange for transport from Isabela (RD$250 per person). Call to reserve a room in advance, lest you risk coming all this distance only to be turned away.

Beicaraibi Rincón Italiano PIZZA **$**
(☑809-704-3045; Principal; pizza US$5; P) This palapa-topped, beachfront hut serves up incredible pizzas with a variety of fresh local

toppings, and also Italian dishes like *pulpo carpaccio* (thin-sliced raw octopus). In the evenings, the place is lit up with Tiki torches and hundreds of stars are often visible – just bring bug spray with DEET to keep the sand flies at bay.

The owner also rents out five apartments nearby, and allows pets.

ⓘ Getting There & Away

A recently paved road connects Punta Rucia to Villa Isabella 25km to the east and even further to Luperón. The other route is from Villa Elisa, 20km west of Laguna Salada on Hwy 1. From there, the road north is a patchwork of dirt, rocks and pavement – take it slow in a compact vehicle and don't use this route if it has rained recently.

Monte Cristi

POP 25,000

A dusty frontier town originally founded by the Spanish crown in 1750, Monte Cristi's allure, if it can be said to have one, lies in its end-of-the-road feel. Most travelers are passing through on their way to or from Haiti. Its formerly prosperous incarnation as the base of the Grenada Fruit Company can be seen in the wide streets and dilapidated Victorian homes in the immediate vicinity of the Parque Central. Some have been restored enough to appreciate their one-time glory. Residents continue to make their living fishing and tending livestock, just as they've done for generations; another source of revenue is salt harvested from evaporation ponds north of town and sold in the US by Morton Salt.

In February Monte Cristi celebrates what is considered the most brutal Carnival in the country – participants carry bullwhips and crack each other as they walk through the streets.

◉ Sights & Activities

El Morro   MOUNTAIN

(The Hill; ⊘8am-5pm) FREE Part of the 1100-sq-km Parque Nacional Monte Cristi that surrounds Monte Cristi on all sides, El Morro sits 5km northeast of town – follow Av San Fernando north to the beach and continue to your right until the road dead-ends. Opposite the ranger station, 585 wooden stairs lead to the top (239m). If you manage to safely scramble over the rotting planks and loose gravel, you'll be rewarded with excellent views. It's about an hour return.

Parque Central   PARK

Notable solely for the 50m clock tower designed by French engineer Alexandre Gustave Eiffel. Imported from France in 1895, the tower deteriorated until 1997 when the Leon Jimenez family, of Aurora cigar and Presidente beer fortune, financed its restoration.

Diving, Snorkeling & Boating

Fortune-hunting wreck divers work this coastline, but the many wooden galleons that sank here have long since rotted away, leaving little for recreational divers to see. Still, the corals here make excellent diving, and tour operator **Galleon Divers** (☑809-654-3924; Costa Verde) runs trips to all the best sites.

Most of the hotels in town, or the tour operator **Soraya & Leonardo** (☑809-221-0450, 809-961-6343; http://sorayayleonardotours.com; Bugalu 3; ⊘7am-7pm), organize snorkeling tours, trips to the isolated beach at **Isla Cabra** (RD$2000), and boat trips to **Los Cayos de los Siete Hermanos** (RD$12,000), a collection of seven uninhabited islands inside the national park (usually up to eight people). Your best bet is to come on weekends in the high season (November to March) or expect high prices and the possibility of not finding an available boatperson.

🛏 Sleeping

Most of the town's options are along Playa Costa Verde west of town, but there's one good option in the center and another up by El Morro.

El Cayito   HOTEL $

(☑809-579-3120; www.hotelelcayito.com; Costa Verde; r incl breakfast from US$50; ☀) This new place on the Costa Verde offers cozy, inexpensive accommodations in brightly painted containers with thatched roofs, along with plusher, pricier rooms (US$80) in a separate building. The well-kept property features a pool, an open-air, 2nd-floor restaurant and an aviary that's home to 200 parakeets.

Chic Hotel   HOTEL $

(☑809-579-2316; Benito Monción 44; r with fan/air-con RD$650/1100; 🅿❄🛜☀) The front-desk person is dressed sharply and the entryway is marked by columns, and yet this hotel is a far cry from chic. However, the 46 rooms are kept clean and you can pop out for a bite to eat at its restaurant and ice-cream store with streetside seating.

Many of the rooms are windowless and street noise can be a problem in front. Check out the mango tree the hotel was built around – you'll pass the trunk in the hallway.

Hotel Los Jardines
BUNGALOW $

(☑ 829-930-7110; hoteljardines@gmail.com; Playa Costa Verde; r with fan/air-con RD$1380/1840; P ❄ ☎) The perfectly manicured grounds punctuated with a towering palm tree or two feel like a sanctuary from the dusty streets. The four basic rooms are something of a letdown but each has a porch with chairs. Head north out of town toward El Morro and turn left onto the waterfront dirt road.

★ El Morro Eco
Adventure Hotel
BUNGALOW $$$

(☑ 849-886-1605; www.elmorro.com.do; El Morro; r incl breakfast US$115; ❄ ☎ ☎) Fairly remote, though only a short walk from the base of El Morro, this collection of high-end boutique bungalows, easily the choicest accommodation from Monte Cristi to Puerto Plata, is worth the journey. Contemporary design touches such as flatscreen TVs and large, black-and-white photos of Monte Cristi are seamlessly integrated into the property's natural design aesthetic.

Dinner is served in an attractive nautically themed dining area and the pool area is a fantastic place to lounge the day away.

Cayo Arena
APARTMENT $$$

(☑ 809-579-3145; www.cayoarena.com; Playa Costa Verde; ste RD$6400; P ❄ ☎) A two-story modern building with a handful of two-bedroom suites with full kitchens, living rooms and balconies, especially recommended for families or small groups. A small pool and restaurant are on site. Head north out of town toward El Morro and turn left onto the waterfront dirt road.

✗ Eating

A result of the fact that goats feed on oregano plants, the *chivo* here is renowned for its spiciness. Ask to try different varieties: *ripiado* (pulled goat), *horneado* (partly blackened, firm on the inside) and *picante* (traditional stew).

Lilo Supermercado (Juan de la Cruz Alvarez), one block south of Duarte, is the place to stock up on drinks and other supplies.

★ Restaurant Coco Mar
SEAFOOD $$

(☑ 809-579-7354; mains RD$250-800; ☺ 8am-10pm) Look for this restaurant with oceanfront outdoor seating just before the green monstrosity of the Hotel Montechico. Buoys and fishing nets hang from the indoor dining room ceiling, befitting its maritime theme and seafood-focused menu.

Lilo Cafe & Restaurant
DOMINICAN $$

(☑ 809-579-3169; Juan de la Cruz Alvarez 27; mains RD$300; ☺ 7am-midnight; ❄ ☎) Businesspeople and office workers popularize this sleek, contemporary place across the street from the grocery of the same name. The menu is fairly typical with grilled fish, chicken and meat dishes as well as crab, *lambi* (conch) and four types of *mofongo* (mashed plantains with meat). Shaded outdoor patio seating is available.

🍷 Drinking & Nightlife

There are lots of bars scattered around town, though none stand out much. On weekends, locals head for **Diamond Club** (☑ 829-346-0026; 30 de Mayo & Carretera Castañuelas; ☺ 9pm-4am Fri-Sun) for live music and dancing.

ℹ Information

Everything you'll need is on or within a block or two of Calle Duarte, including a pharmacy, ATM and the post office.

The modest **Hospital Padre Fantino** (☑ 809-579-3073; Av 27 de Febrero; ☺ 24hr) is two blocks north of Calle Duarte.

Cestur (Tourist Police; ☑ 809-754-2996)

ℹ Getting There & Away

Hwy 1 enters Monte Cristi from the east, where it turns into Calle Duarte and becomes the main east–west road through town. Av Mella becomes Hwy 45 to Dajabón, which is now completely paved.

Caribe Tours (☑ 809-579-2129; cnr Mella & Camargo) has a depot a block north of Calle Duarte. Buses to Santo Domingo (RD$350, 4½ hours) leave at 7:30am, 8:30am, 10am, 1:45pm, 3pm and 4pm, with a stop in Santiago (RD$190, 2¼ hours).

The Expreso Liniero *guagua* terminal is on Calle Duarte near the eastern entrance to town; it goes to Dajabón (RD$60, 40 minutes, every 20 minutes from 7:30am to 10pm). For Puerto Plata, take any Santiago-bound *guagua* and get off at the junction in Navarrete (RD$180, 1½ hours, every 20 minutes) to change to another *guagua* (RD$140, one hour, every 20 minutes).

Dajabón

POP 25,200

Most foreigners in this dingy border town are on their way to or from Haiti, and it's likely they won't stick around longer than it takes to get that passport stamped and find suitable transport.

That changes on Monday and Friday, when the border bridge opens and Haitians pour across for the lively Haitian market (⊙7am-7pm Mon & Fri), a bustling market held on the DR side of the border. Haitians come come over to buy and sell fruit, vegetables and everything else, as well as contraband (including donations from international organizations, which are sold here wholesale and then shipped elsewhere in the country). Crowds push and shove wheelbarrows, motorcycles burrow through the throng and crates of goods are piled high on women's heads.

🛏 Sleeping & Eating

An acceptable option for the night is the unfortunately named Hotel Masacre (✆809-579-8727; www.hotelmasacredr.com; Cl Sánchez 89; r from US$27; P ❄ 🛜), which is actually a tidy and well-managed establishment.

Vendors sell grilled corn and hot dogs on the main park, and there are a few undistinguished eateries on the main road coming into town.

❶ Information

Several major banks with ATMs are located around a circle at the northern entrance to town.

DAJABÓN TO HWY 1

If you're making the trip out west you might as well drive in a loop so as not to retrace your steps. Take Hwy 1 from Santiago out to Monte Cristi, spend the night and head to Dajabón the following day, preferably a market day (Monday or Friday). On the return, head south on 18, which takes you through small villages, country towns and pastoral scenery. You pass through Sabaneta and Mao before meeting up again with Hwy 1 – from there you can head to the north coast or south.

❶ Getting There & Away

Reaching the border is simple; coming from Monte Cristi on Hwy 45, as most people do, you'll come to a huge arch (the formal entrance to town) and a short distance afterward the Parque Central on the east side of the street. Just past the park is Calle Presidente Henriquez; turn right (west) and the border is six blocks ahead. If you're arriving by Caribe Tours bus, the bus station is on Calle Presidente Henriquez. Just walk west from the bus station five blocks to get to the border. The border is open 9am to 5pm, except Monday and Friday market days 8am to 4pm.

Caribe Tours (✆809-579-8554; cnr Carrasco & Henríquez) buses to Santo Domingo (RD$350, five hours) with stops in Monte Cristi and Santiago (RD$190, 2½ hours) leave at 6:45am, 7:45am, 9:30am, 1pm, 2:15pm and 3:15pm.

Expreso Liniero (✆809-579-8949) *guaguas* go to Monte Cristi (RD$60, 40 minutes) and Santiago (RD$190, 2½ hours). The terminal is just beyond the arch at the entrance to town on the east side of the road.

Central Highlands

Best Places to Eat

➡ Aroma de la Montana (p195)

➡ Il Pasticcio (p185)

➡ Camp David (p185)

➡ La Baita (p194)

➡ De Parrillada (p195)

Best Places to Sleep

➡ Rancho Baiguate (p194)

➡ Tubagua Plantation Eco-Village (p155)

➡ Alto Cerro (p200)

➡ Camp David (p184)

➡ Jarabacoa Mountain Hostel (p193)

Why Go?

Even die-hard beach fanatics will eventually overdose on sun and sand. When you do, the cool, mountainous playground of the Central Highlands is the place to come: where else can you sit at dusk, huddled in a sweater, and watch the mist descend into the valley as the sun sets behind the mountains? Popular retreats, roaring rivers, soaring peaks and the only white-water rafting in the Caribbean beckon. Down below in the plains of the Valle del Cibao is where merengue spontaneously erupted onto the musical landscape, and where you'll find some of the best Carnival celebrations in the country. Economic life in the Central Highlands revolves around Santiago, the Dominican Republic's second-largest city and the capital of a vast tobacco- and sugarcane-growing region. So it goes without saying that a visit here requires sipping rum and puffing a local cigar.

When to Go

➡ Some of the DR's most raucous Carnival celebrations take place in Santiago and La Vega in February and March.

➡ It is dry in the area around Santiago in January to March and June to August

➡ Mountain towns such as Jarabacoa and Constanza are cooler year-round; temperatures can fall below freezing at night.

ℹ Getting There & Away

Santiago's Aeropuerto Internacionál del Cibao (p302) is the third-largest airport in the country and offers frequent international service to major destinations. There's a good selection of car-rental agencies at the airport.

Santiago sits on the main trunk highway that runs north from Santo Domingo to Puerto Plata,

and it has bus services to all points of the compass. First-class buses service all major destinations, except Constanza – for that you'll need to hop on a *guagua* (local bus). Renting a car, preferably an SUV, will give you more freedom to explore the countryside.

CENTRAL HIGHLANDS GETTING THERE & AWAY

Central Highlands Highlights

❶ White-water rafting (p191) Riding the Caribbean's only raftable river, the turbulent Río Yaque del Norte near Jarabacoa.

❷ Pico Duarte (p196) Scaling the Caribbean's highest peak and lingering at the top to take in the views.

❸ Constanza (p199) Watching the sunset as the mist descends into the high-altitude valley surrounding the town.

❹ Santiago (p181) Dancing merengue till the wee hours at one of the bars near the Monument.

❺ Carnival (p189) Partying with the locals in little La Vega in February, when the town throws the country's biggest party.

❻ Cigar factory tour (p186) Head to Tamboril, just outside Santiago, to check out a factory and learn where stogies come from.

Santiago

POP 691,000

One of the oldest settlements in Spain's New World empire, Santiago is the country's second-largest city, spilling over its original border, the Río Yaque del Norte. This sprawling place churns out rum and cigars, feeding off the large-scale tobacco and sugarcane plantations that dominate the valley floor. The Cordillera Central to the west and Cordillera Septentrional to the north hem in the city, which is divided by Hwy Duarte.

Overlooked by most travelers, Santiago is a good place to contemplate ordinary Dominican life. Typical of poor barrios countrywide, Santiago's are a maze of haphazardly constructed homes with corrugated-iron roofs. Meanwhile, just east of downtown is Cerros de Gurabo – surely one of the wealthiest neighborhoods in the DR – where roads are lined with mansions concealed behind high walls. But all strata of society cheer for the hometown baseball team and come together around the Monument, the city's raucous nightlife center.

History

Santiago was founded in 1495 by Christopher Columbus' elder brother, Bartholomew. But the earthquake of 1562 caused so much damage to the city that it was rebuilt on its present site beside the Río Yaque del Norte. It was attacked and destroyed several times by invading French troops as part of long-simmering tension between Spain and France over control of the island. Santiago also suffered terribly during the DR's civil war in 1912.

The years immediately following the civil war were some of the city's best. WWI caused worldwide shortages of raw tropical materials, so prices soared for products such as sugar, tobacco, cocoa and coffee – all of which were being grown around Santiago. From 1914 until the end of the war and into the 1920s, Santiago's economy boomed. Lovely homes, impressive stores, electric lighting and paved streets appeared throughout town. In May 1922, Hwy Duarte opened, linking Santiago with Bonao, La Vega and Santo Domingo to the south.

◉ Sights

The center of town is Parque Duarte, a usually crowded, leafy park with a gazebo, the cathedral to its south and Palacio Consistorial to its west.

★ **Centro León**　　　　　　　　MUSEUM

(☏809-582-2315; www.centroleon.org.do; Villa Progreso, Av 27 de Febrero 146; adult/child RD$150/100, Tue free; ⊙10am-7pm Tue-Sun) This large, modern museum, built with the tobacco wealth of the León Jimenez family, is a world-class institution with an impressive collection of paintings that trace the evolution of Dominican art in the 20th century. There are three exhibition rooms in the main building: one focuses on the island's biodiversity, Taíno history and cultural diversity; a second displays a permanent collection of Dominican art; and an upstairs room houses temporary art exhibits. The aviary and photography exhibition are out the back.

An excellent gift shop sells books on Dominican history, art, culture and food, and there's an appealing cafeteria serving sandwiches and drinks. During the evenings, the center offers an ever-changing schedule of art-appreciation classes, arthouse cinema and live music.

The Centro León is a few kilometers east of downtown. A taxi there will cost around RD$150, or pick up a Ruta A *concho* (private car that follows a set route; RD$20) along Calle del Sol – not all Ruta A *conchos* go as far as the Centro León, though, so be sure to ask.

Monumento a los Héroes de la Restauración de la República　　MONUMENT

(Monument to the Heroes of the Restoration of the Republic; Av Monumental; museum RD$60; ⊙9am-5pm Tue-Sat) On a hill at the eastern end of the downtown area, this monument is Santiago's most recognizable sight, featuring a large bronze Angel de La Paz statue at the very top. The boxy, eight-story edifice was originally built by dictator Rafael Trujillo to celebrate himself, but it was rededicated after his assassination to honor the Dominican soldiers who fought the final war of independence against Spain.

Large bronze statues of the generals gaze down upon Santiago from the steps, and the site's upper floors offer life-size museum exhibits of Dominican history. Large groups of uniformed primary-school kids visit often, and joggers train on the steps around dusk.

Catedral de Santiago Apóstol   CHURCH
(cnr Calles 16 de Agosto & Benito Monción; ⊘ 7-9am Mon-Sat, to 8pm Sun) Santiago's cathedral, opposite the southern side of Parque Duarte, was built between 1868 and 1895 and is a combination of Gothic and neoclassical styles. The cathedral contains the marble tomb of late-19th-century dictator Ulises Heureaux, an elaborately carved mahogany altar and impressive stained-glass windows by contemporary Dominican artist Dincón Mora.

**Centro de la Cultura
de Santiago**   NOTABLE BUILDING
(🖉 809-226-5222; Calle del Sol; ⊘ 9am-4pm Mon-Sat, performance times vary) Though not much to look at from the outside, the Centro de la Cultura de Santiago, a half-block from Parque Duarte, offers a regular program of musical and theatrical performances, including plays, choral singing, children's theater and holiday concerts. There's also a rotating exhibition of Dominican painting in the small gallery. Pass by for a copy of the monthly schedule.

Fortaleza San Luis   MUSEUM
(🖉 809-226-2029; cnr Boy Scouts & San Luis; ⊘ 10am-5pm Mon-Sat) Built in the late 17th century, the Fortaleza San Luis operated as a military stronghold until the 1970s, when it was converted into a prison. Today it houses a small museum, with an emphasis on Dominican military history, including ancient rusty weapons and a collection of 20th-century tanks and artillery.

Casa del Arte   GALLERY
(🖉 809-471-7839; Benito Monción 46; ⊘ 9:30am-12:30pm & 2:30pm-late Mon-Sat) `FREE` This small gallery displays Dominican painting, photography and sculpture. Some nights of the week a film club meets to screen arthouse and good-quality Hollywood flicks (with free admission). There's sometimes live music (from RD$100) and, on Saturday, live theater (RD$100).

☞ Tours

Camping Tours   ADVENTURE
(🖉 809-583-3121; www.campingtours.net; Villa Olga, Calle Two 2) Offers the cheapest trek to Pico Duarte (p196). Expect Spanish-speaking guides and groups of 20 to 25 people. Prices per person are US$220 on foot and US$255/290 with a shared/private mule.

LOVE MOTELS

Not what the name might suggest! If you're travelling with a partner and are up for something out of the ordinary, the garishly designed couples motels (*cabaña turisticos*) on Autopista Duarte are pretty hilarious. You pay by the hour, nobody sees your face, and some rooms even offer stripper poles and disco-party ball lights. **Bora Bora Apart Hotel** (www.borabora.com.do; Autopista Duarte Km 51/2; r from RD$2215; P ❀ 🔊) is the best one.

★ Festivals & Events

Carnival   CULTURAL
(⊘ Feb) Santiago is famous for its fantastical Carnival *caretas* (masks) and hosts an international *careta* competition in the lead-up to the big event. Rival neighborhoods La Joya and Los Pepines make up the bulk of the parade, with onlookers watching from overpasses, apartment buildings and even the tops of lampposts. The costumes – colorful, baggy outfits with capes and masks – are always the highlight.

🛏 Sleeping

Options in Santiago aren't particularly inspired, but they're also relatively affordable. If you decide to come to town for Carnival (p183), be sure to make reservations – rooms fill up fast at this time of year.

Via Emilia   B&B $
(🖉 809-820-6609; www.viaemiliasantiago.com; Estado de Israel 16; s/d/tr incl breakfast US$30/35/40; ❀ 🔊) The best budget option in the northeastern outskirts of town is this three-room B&B, which offers basic private rooms and excellent Italian meals just for guests (think homemade ravioli and decadent tiramisu). Because it's so small, the whole place is often booked – be sure to reserve well in advance.

Sana El Jardin Secreto   HOSTEL $
(The Secret Garden; 🖉 585-451-8239; www.sana-villa.com; Espalliat 48, Tamboril; dm US$12, r from US$25; P 🔊) A weird and wonderful compound based near Tamboril's tobacco factories, this expat-owned property is secure and affordable, offering the only dorm beds in the region. Tidy rooms are named after the owner's

Santiago

grandchildren, and the expansive gardens surrounding the hotel feel like a Dominican version of *Alice in Wonderland*. A local chef prepares tasty Dominican meals.

Hotel Platino
HOTEL **$$**

(☑809-724-7576; www.hotelplatinord.com; Av Estrella Sadhalá; s/d incl breakfast from RD$1900/2400; P❋☎) At the back of a strip mall a short drive from town, this is an excellent-value option. While standard rooms, especially the small basement rooms, lack natural light, the beds are comfortable and the rooms have small desk, TV and mini-fridge; executive-floor rooms have plasma TV and attractive wooden floors. A large gazebo marks the entrance.

To get your bearings on a map, the hotel is across the street from an entrance to the Pontifica Universidad Catolica Madre y Maestra (PUCMM).

Hodelpa Centro Plaza
HOTEL **$$**

(☑809-581-7000; www.hodelpa.com; cnr Calles del Sol & Mella 54; r incl breakfast US$100; P❋☎) The fact that this business-class hotel, part of the Hodelpa chain, is located only a block from the primary commercial artery in the heart of the city means that lower floors suffer from street noise.

Expect courteous, professional service but fairly plain rooms, some dimly lit. There's a restaurant, tapas bar, lounge and small casino attached.

Aloha Sol Hotel
HOTEL **$$**

(☑809-583-0090; Calle del Sol 50; s/d incl breakfast from RD$2300/3000; P❋@☎) This central hotel is a good deal if you don't mind the mildly stale quality of the furnishings in the rooms and common areas. Be sure to ask for a room with window exposure and check out several before committing – the lighting situation varies. The breakfast buffet is better than average and there's a casino attached.

★ Camp David
HOTEL **$$$**

(☑809-276-6400; www.campdavidranch.com; Carretera Luperón Km 7½; r incl breakfast US$115; P❋☎) On a 923m mountain ridge about 30 minutes northeast of Santiago, Camp David offers sweeping vistas over the city and valley below. The extremely large rooms, with high-end boutique-style features such as marble sinks and porcelain-tile floors, have private balconies. There's also a top-notch restaurant.

Ask for room 2203 for fantastic city views and room 2205 for comparable mountain ones. The property was founded by an admirer of Rafael Trujillo, which explains why the

former dictator's 1956 Cadillac is displayed in front of the central office. As the hotel's several kilometers off the main road, you'll need a car to get here, or take a taxi (RD$500).

Hodelpa Gran Almirante   HOTEL **$$$**
(☑ 809-580-1992; www.hodelpa.com; Av Estrella Sadhalá; r/ste US$215/364; P ❉ @ 🛰 ☎) The obvious choice for business travelers, the Gran Almirante also entices tourists looking for extra comfort: there are top-notch rooms and a sundeck, spa and gym. A casino and a variety of restaurants and bars round things off. It's several kilometers from downtown, but the neighborhood has a handful of good restaurants within walking distance.

✗ Eating

Quality dining options in the downtown area are few and far between. There's a handful of decent Dominican and international fast-food joints on and around Calle del Sol and hole-in-the-wall *comedors* in the surrounding blocks. Many of the bars and lounges around the western and southern side of the Monument serve food as well.

Naturalis Té   TAIWANESE **$**
(☑ 809-241-0809; www.facebook.com/pg/Naturalis-Te-143849088973415; Estado de Israel; plato del día RD$$150; ☉ 11am-7:30pm Tue-Fri, 11:30am-7pm

Sat & Sun; 🛰 ✈) This adorable Taiwanese cafe offers tasty, nutritious vegetarian food, along with natural juices and cold flavored teas. The *plato del día* is a steal, and includes soup, salad, tortillas and a selection of cooked vegetables. There's nothing else like this in all of Santiago.

★**Camp David**   DOMINICAN **$$**
(☑ 809-276-6400; www.campdavidranch.com; Carretera Luperón Km 7½; mains RD$550-1300; ☉ 7am-midnight) Sit outside on the restaurant's balcony, with piano music on the stereo and the city spread out at your feet... This is easily the most romantic spot around, though you'll need a car to make it up the mountain to where it's perched outside town. Beef is the specialty here – go for the *filete de res* (225g of Angus beef).

★**Il Pasticcio**   ITALIAN **$$**
(☑ 809-582-6061; www.ilpasticciord.com; Calle 3 & Av Del Llano, Cerros de Gurabo; mains RD$375; ☉ noon-4pm & 7-11pm Tue-Sun; P ❉) Paolo, the Italian owner here, is full of character and style, and he's been welcoming Santiago's powerful and bohemians since 1995. Curiously decorated with a range of objets d'art, the restaurant is a reflection of his personality,

CIGAR FACTORY TOURS

Many of the world's top cigar brands make their wares in and around Santiago – La Aurora, Montecristo and Arturo Fuente, to name a few. Many of those name brands contract the work to local Dominican cigar makers, who then offer the 'label-less' cigars to locals and travelers at half price. It's critical when buying cigars to test whether they've been made well and stored properly. Pick up the cigar: it should have a springy tightness, indicating solid construction. If it's too soft or too hard, it won't draw well. It shouldn't crackle under your fingers, either; that means it's too dry and will smoke like kindling.

Many of the factories are located northeast of Santiago at the foot of the Cordillera Septentrional in the village of Tamboril (27 de Febrero turns into Carretera Tamboril), where you can spend a night at **Sana El Jardin Secreto** (p183). The easiest and best factory to visit is **La Aurora Parque Industrial** (☑809-734-2563; Tamboril; ⊗8am-noon & 2-3:30pm), affiliated with the Centro León museum, which used to have a small La Aurora workshop. Many of the producers, including **La Flor Dominicana** (☑809-580-5139, 829-898-6214; tabacaleraflordetamboril@hotmail.com; Calle Real Tamboril, Tamboril; ⊗7am-5pm Mon-Fri) FREE, offer free tours; most are open Monday to Friday, and reservations are preferred. If you're keen to puff cigars in a classier setting, head for the **Las 3 Reinas** (☑809-390-0529; Aquiles Ramirez; ⊗10am-8pm Mon-Fri, to late Sat) cigar shop.

and the menu of fresh pasta, meat and seafood is truly satisfying. Don't miss the salmon carpaccio.

Marisco Caribeño   SEAFOOD $$
(☑809-971-9710; cnr Calle del Sol & Av Francia; mains RD$425; ⊗10am-midnight Sun-Thu, to 2am Fri & Sat; P❋) This long-running restaurant serves grilled fish and seafood in an elegant indoor dining room, a breezy outdoor garden or a more ordinary, brightly lit back room. There are sushi specials on Wednesday night, live music on Friday and a Sunday buffet brunch (adult/child RD$695/395).

La Campagna   SANDWICHES $$
(☑809-581-5056; Av Juan Pablo Duarte; mains RD$300; ⊗8am-midnight; ❋🛜✏) This charming cafe features a patio beneath a thatched roof and an extensive, healthy menu including smoothies, salads, burgers and soups. Sunflowers on every table, decorative lights and quaint latticework give the place a very homey vibe.

La Picola Amaia   ITALIAN $$
(☑809-724-8831; cnr Valverde & Av Metropolitana; mains RD$220-400; ⊗11am-11pm Sun-Thu, to midnight Fri & Sat; ❋) More than a dozen varieties of pizza and pasta are on the menu at this modern, postage-stamp-sized restaurant in the Jardines neighborhood. A surprising bonus if you want to mix things up is that you can also order sushi (rolls RD$185) and other Japanese fare from the even smaller, attached Sushi Ya.

El Carrito de Marchena   DOMINICAN $$
(☑809-583-6355; Av Estrella Sadhalá; mains from RD$250; ⊗noon-midnight; P❋🛜) This open-air pavilion is where groups of friends roll up after a night of dancing and boozing. A few large-screen TVs are tuned to sports and the extensive menu includes tacos (RD$125), burritos (RD$275) and *mofongo* (fried plantains mashed together and mixed with a variety of meats or other fillings; RD$250).

Noah Restaurant & Lounge   DOMINICAN $$$
(☑809-971-0550; Calle del Sol 4; mains RD$600; ⊗noon-midnight Mon-Thu, to 1am Fri & Sat; P❋) Possibly downtown's and the Monument's most upscale restaurant, stylish Noah does pasta, fish and meat dishes, plus more than a dozen varieties of pizza and sushi rolls.

🍷 Drinking & Nightlife

Clustered around the Monument (especially on Calle Beller) are a dozen or so bars, restaurants and late-night eateries, making this Santiago's best place for general revelry.

The city center gets dodgy late at night; take a taxi home.

New Monte Bar   CLUB
(☑809-575-0300; Av 27 de Febrero 18; ⊗6pm-late Wed-Mon) A diverse mix of locals, dom-yors (Dominicans living in New York City) and even a celebrity baseball player or two come here for serious merengue music and dancing. Cover charges vary. It's set amid a series

of auto-repair shops in the Las Colinas neighborhood north of the center; you'll want a cab there and back (RD$200 each way).

Lazotea
BAR

(☑ 809-980-3789; 5th fl, Plaza Bella Terra, Av Pablo Duarte; ☺ 6pm-late) This bar atop the Plaza Bella Terra shopping mall has great views and a good after-work scene.

Kukara Macara Country Bar & Restaurant
BAR

(☑ 809-241-3143; www.kukaramacara.net; Av Francia 7; ☺ 10am-2am) Customers enter through old saloon doors and are welcomed by servers dressed like cowgirls and cowboys at this kitschy but fun western-themed restaurant (mains RD$475). The walls and ceiling are decked out in saddles, lassos and sheriff signs, and the tasty margaritas arrive in massive fishbowl glasses.

Ahi-Bar
BAR

(☑ 809-581-6779; cnr RC Tolentino & Av Restauración; ☺ 4pm-late) The best of a string of bars on Calle RC Tolentino, Ahi has a modern open-air patio set above street level. Most people come to drink, but the food's pretty good too. A sister dance club across the street attracts the young and stylish with karaoke on Thursday night and merengue and *bachata* most other nights.

Puerta del Sol
LOUNGE

(cnr Calle del Sol & Calle 6; ☺ 11am-2am; 🛜) A cross between VIP airport lounge, sports bar and stylish Miami nightclub, this sleek establishment stretches along the southern side of the Monument. Large-screen plasma TVs cover the back wall, and the other sides are open to the street. There's a large menu of drinks and Dominican and international fare (mains RD$375), and a wine and cigar store.

☆ Entertainment

Dao al Pescao
LIVE MUSIC

(☑ 829-919-0055; www.facebook.com/pg/DaoAlPecaoBar; Benito Monción 41; ☺ 6pm-midnight) This Caribbean tapas bar occupies a refurbished mansion filled with trippy art and tropical plants – it's the kind of place you'd come Saturday night to drink a few cocktails, hear some DJs and feast on innovative Caribbean fare. Unique dishes include pork and *mamajuana* (a beverage made with herbs, dried bark, rum, wine and honey) empanadas and artisanal *chorizo* (mains RD$150).

Estadio Cibao
STADIUM

(☑ 809-575-1810; Av Imbert) Santiago's Águilas baseball team is one of six in the country and the most successful in the league's history. Watching local fans root for the home side is almost as fun as the games themselves, held two to three times a week in winter. The 18,000-seat stadium is northwest of the city center and tickets start at RD$50 for the bleachers; it's wise to book in advance.

To get there, take a taxi or hop on any Ruta A *concho* westbound on Calle del Sol.

🛍 Shopping

Calle del Sol, downtown's primary commercial artery, is lined with unremarkable clothing shops, banks, hair salons and department stores. The city has several shopping malls, all with food courts and movie theaters.

Outdoor Market
MARKET

Behind the indoor market, this covered shopping area spans a couple of blocks, with clothing, shoes and miscellaneous items for sale.

Calle del Sol Indoor Market
MARKET

(btwn España & Av 30 de Marzo) A two-story complex with booths containing basic souvenirs like cigars, paintings, jewelry and *mamajuana*.

ℹ Information

DANGERS & ANNOYANCES

Cestur (☑ 809-754-3038) Tourist Police

INTERNET ACCESS

Centro de Internet Yudith (☑ 809-581-4882; Calle 16 de Agosto; per hr RD$30; ☺ 8am-7pm Mon-Fri, to 5pm Sat) Near Calle Mella.

MEDICAL SERVICES

Farmacia Jorge (☑ 809-582-2887; cnr España & Av Gómez; ☺ 8am-6:30pm Mon-Sat)

Hospital Metropolitano de Santiago (☑ 809-947-2222; www.homshospital.com; Autopista Duarte Km 2.8; ☺ 24hr)

MONEY

BanReservas (Calle del Sol 66; ☺ 9am-5pm Mon-Sat) Has an ATM.

ℹ Getting There & Away

AIR

Santiago's airport (p302), around 12km south of downtown, is serviced by several major airlines, including Delta, United, Copa, JetBlue, American

Airlines, Spirit, InterCaribbean Airways and Tropical Aero Servicios.

Taxis (US$15 to US$20 one way) are your only option to and from town.

BUS

Caribe Tours (☑ 809-241-1414) has two terminals in Santiago: in Las Colinas on Av 27 de Febrero about 3km north of the center, and more conveniently in the Jardínes neighborhood at Maimon and 27 de Febrero, just steps from the competing **Metro Buses terminal** (☑ 809-227-0101; www.metroserviciosturisticos.com). All Caribe buses stop at both stations, except for the service to Haiti, which stops at Las Colinas only. All three bus terminals are on or near the Ruta A concho line; otherwise, take a taxi.

CAR

The airport has a good selection of reliable international car-rental companies, including **Avis** (☑ 809-582-7007; www.avis.com; Carretera Santiago-Licey Km 2; ⊙ 7am-11pm), **Europcar** (☑ 809-233-8150; www.europcar.com; ⊙ 7am-11pm) and **Hertz** (☑ 809-233-8555; www.hertz.com; ⊙ 7am-11pm). Have RD$25 on hand for the toll to leave the parking lot. Close to a dozen local companies line the access road between the terminal and the highway – most will arrange pickup from the airport.

ⓘ Getting Around

Conchos are private cars (up to six passengers per vehicle) that follow set routes around town, charging RD$12 to RD$20. *Concho* drivers pay a weekly fee for a permit to slap a letter on their windshield and drive the route. After dark, however, the unlicensed *piratas* take over, so exercise caution before hopping into an unknown person's car.

Guaguas to La Vega leave from near the Fortaleza San Luis.

Though it's pricier than *conchos*, Uber is a relatively easy way to get around.

San José de las Matas

POP 38,600 / ELEV 518M

This small mountain town 45km southwest of Santiago is a jumping-off point for two major hiking trails in the Parque Nacional Armando Bermúdez. It's a pleasant enough town, with nice mountain views, and several rivers and *balenarios* (swimming holes) to swim in – a place to linger before or after a long hike.

🛏 Sleeping & Eating

Hacienda Campo Verde　　　　RESORT **$**
(Ventana Rio Lindo; ☑ 809-626-7777, 829-635-8000; www.campoverdeoficial.com; Inoa; r incl breakfast RD$2000; ⓟ 🛜 ⛱) Tucked in the hills a few kilometers from San José de las Matas, this sprawling, riverfront aquatic compound is a huge draw for Dominican families. The massive property offers two sleeping options: Hotel Rio Lindo's rooms are affordable and decent, overlooking the water, and Villas Macadamias' colonial-style rental homes are suitable for larger groups or families.

The main draws here are the swimming areas, which include a natural river and an elaborate system of pools. An associated restaurant serves Dominican food from 9:30am to 6pm, including decent *mofongo* (mashed plantains with pork rinds) and sandwiches. The place seems entirely wholesome, with one odd exception: the pink, diamond-studded headboards in Hotel Rio Lindo look like they're straight from a '70s adult film.

The restaurant at Hacienda Campo Verde serves decent *mofongo* and sandwiches.

🍷 Drinking & Nightlife

This is the kind of town where any partying will be DIY. Head to Santiago for night-time thrills.

BUS TIMETABLE

DESTINATION	FARE	DURATION	FREQUENCY
Cap-Haïtien (Haiti)	RD$1152	8hr	noon daily
Dajabón	RD$200	2½hr	take Monte Cristi bus
La Vega	RD$80	30min	take Santo Domingo bus
Monte Cristi	RD$190	1¾hr	6 times daily, 8:45am-6pm
Puerto Plata	RD$120	1¼hr	hourly, 8:15am-9:15pm
Santo Domingo	RD$270	2½hr	26 times daily, 5:45am-8:15pm
Sosúa	RD$160	2hr	take Puerto Plata bus

ℹ Getting There & Away

Guaguas for Santiago (RD$100, one hour, 6:15am to 7pm) leave from opposite the Texaco station at the town entrance. Buses leave roughly every 15 minutes in the morning, but you may have to wait an hour or more in the middle of the day. By car it's only 45 minutes to Santiago.

La Vega

POP 248,000

Pressed up against the highway halfway between Santo Domingo and Santiago, La Vega is known primarily as a transportation hub and the site of the country's most boisterous Carnival celebrations. And while in most respects it's a lackluster town – dusty and noisy during the day – La Vega's origin is interesting.

In the 1490s, Christopher Columbus ordered a fort built in the area to store gold mined nearby. Over the next 50 years, the first mint in the New World was established, the nation's first commercial sugar crop was harvested, and the first royally sanctioned brothel in the western hemisphere opened for business in La Vega. The prosperity ended in 1562, when an earthquake leveled the city, causing so much damage that the settlement was moved several kilometers to its present site on the Río Camú. You can visit what remains of the old city near the town of Santo Cerro.

◉ Sights

Make your way to La Vega during Carnival (p189) if at all possible. Otherwise, a few worthwhile sights lie outside the city, only really easily accessible in a private vehicle.

Santo Cerro CHURCH

Legend has it that Christopher Columbus placed a cross he received as a bon-voyage gift from Queen Isabella atop this hill, which commands fantastic, sweeping views of the Valle del Cibao. During a battle between Spaniards and Taínos, the latter tried to burn the cross, but it wouldn't catch fire. The Virgen de las Mercedes appeared on one of its arms and the Taínos are said to have fled in terror.

Today the cross is gone – supposedly it's in private hands – but you can still see the Santo Hoyo (Holy Hole) in which the cross was allegedly planted. The hole is inside the Iglesia Las Mercedes, covered with a small wire grille and tended by nuns and

Jesuit priests. The beige-and-white church is a major pilgrimage site, drawing thousands of believers every September 24 for its patron-saint day. Be sure to look for a fenced-off tree near the steps leading to the church – it's said to have been planted in 1495.

Santo Cerro is northeast of La Vega, several kilometers east of Hwy Duarte, up a steep, winding road. It's somewhat confusing to find your way as you're leaving the city, so ask for directions.

La Vega Vieja HISTORIC SITE

(RD$100; ☉ 8am-5pm) What's left of the original site of La Vega are the ruins of the fort Christopher Columbus ordered to be built and a church. After the great earthquake of 1562, most of what remained of the structures was taken to the latter-day La Vega, where it was used in construction. With some imagination and the help of a guide (Spanish speaking only), it's possible to begin to grasp the historical implications of what you're seeing.

A small museum at the back of the site contains Taíno and Spanish tools, weapons and ceramics. Admission and guide fees seem open to negotiation and depend on the number in your party.

To get here, continue around 4km past the turnoff for Santo Cerro and look for an old, battered sign on the left-hand side of the road.

Catedral de la Concepción CHURCH

(cnr Av Guzman & Adolfo; ☉ varies) La Vega's infamous cathedral, facing the main plaza, is a fascinating eyesore that looks like a cross between a medieval fortress and a coal plant. It's an odd mixture of Gothic and neo-industrial styles, though the large, contemporary interior is easier on the eye.

✦ Festivals & Events

Carnival CULTURAL

(☉ Feb) La Vega hosts the DR's largest and most organized Carnival celebrations. Townspeople belong to one of numerous Carnival groups, which range from 10 to 200 members and have unique names and costumes. The costumes (which can cost up to US$1000) are the best part of Carnival here, featuring colorful baggy outfits, capes and diabolical masks with bulging eyes and pointed teeth.

Groups march on a long loop through town, and spectators watch from bleachers

CENTRAL HIGHLANDS LA VEGA

set up alongside or march with them. The latter do so at their own risk – the costumes include a small whip with an inflated rubber bladder at the end, which is used to whack passersby on the backside.

🛏 Sleeping & Eating

Unless you're in La Vega for Carnival, there's no real reason to stay overnight. For some better options, head to Santiago or Jarabacoa.

Food stands serving fried chicken and *pastelitos* (flaky fried dough stuffed with meat, cheese or veggies) can be found in front of the cathedral. There are several open-air *comedors* and Dominican fast-food restaurants along the highway.

Hotel Rey HOTEL $$
(☑ 809-573-9797; Don Luis Despradel; r from RD$2000; P ❋ 🛜) The most respectable choice in the city, Hotel Rey is close to the highway and half a dozen blocks from the cathedral. It caters to business travelers, so expect clean rooms and friendly and attentive service; the deluxe rooms, with king-size beds, flat-screen plasma TVs and better lighting, are definitely worth the extra RD$500.

There's an on-site restaurant (mains RD$200) that serves uninspiring if decent Dominican fare – a good thing if you pull in after dark and don't want to wander the streets looking for a meal. A new casino and *discoteca* have recently opened on the 1st floor.

Macao Grill PIZZA, DOMINICAN $$
(☑ 809-573-2020; Don Antonio Guzman 82; mains RD$150-300; ⊙ 8am-9pm, pizza served 11am-midnight; ❋ 🛜) This decent restaurant near the cathedral serves good deep-dish pizza, along with burgers and burritos.

Drinking & Nightlife

There's a new casino and *discoteca* at Hotel Rey. Apart from that, you'll have to wait for Carnival for any sign of a pulse.

❶ Getting There & Away

La Vega is a regular stop on the well-traveled Santo Domingo–Santiago route. Caribe Tours (p188) has its terminal on the main highway, 1.5km from the center of La Vega. The main street, Av Antonio Guzman, runs north–south and intersects Hwy Duarte on the northern side of town.

Another option for the trip to Santiago is to catch a guagua (RD$80, 50 minutes) leaving from a terminal on the main road into town. Alternatively, guaguas and pickups for Jarabacoa (RD$90) leave when full from a stop called Quinto Patio (about 1km from the center, RD$200 in a taxi) from 7am to 6pm.

To Constanza, direct 2nd-class buses (RD$150, two to three hours) leave from the mercado público (public market) at around 8am and 2pm, though departure times can vary.

Jarabacoa

POP 40,550 / ELEV 488M

Nestled in the low foothills of the Cordillera Central, Jarabacoa maintains an under-the-radar allure as the antithesis of the clichéd Caribbean vacation. Nighttime temperatures call for light sweaters, a roiling river winds past forested slopes that climb into the clouds, and local adventurers share stories of their exploits over a beer in the handful of bars near the town's Parque Central. The fact that thousands of well-to-do Dominicans from Santo Domingo and Santiago have built summer homes here is a testament to Jarabacoa's laid-back charm as the 'City of Eternal Spring.' With a number of good hotels outside town, this is the

BUSES FROM LA VEGA

DESTINATION	FARE	DURATION	FREQUENCY
Jarabacoa	RD$90	1hr	buses from Santo Domingo pass by at 7am, 10am, 1:30pm & 4:30pm
Puerto Plata	RD$160	2hr	take the Sosúa bus
Santiago	RD$80	40min	take the Sosúa bus
Santo Domingo	RD$200	1½hr	every 30-60min 6:45am-8:15pm
Sosúa	RD$200	2½hr	hourly 7:30am-8:30pm

place to base yourself if you want to raft, hike, bike, horseback ride, go canyoning or simply explore rural life. At weekends, locals head 4km north of town to the Balneario la Confluencia, where the Río Yaque and Río Jimenoa meet, to swim and picnic.

◉ Sights

Waterfalls

The three waterfalls near town are easy to visit if you've got your own transportation. If not, a *motoconcho* tour to all three will set you back around RD$1000, a taxi US$80 to US$100.

Salto de Jimenoa Uno WATERFALL
(RD$100) So picturesque are the falls that an opening scene of the movie *Jurassic Park* was filmed here. Of the three waterfalls near Jarabacoa, it's definitely the prettiest – a 60m cascade pouring from a gaping hole in an otherwise solid rock cliff. There's a sandy beach and an appealing swimming hole, but the water is icy cold and potentially dangerous; if you do swim, stay far away from the swirling currents.

The trailhead to the waterfall is 7km from the Total station in Jarabacoa along the road to Constanza. Look for the small shed housing the 'office' for this community project – admission includes a bottle of water. The steep path down is slippery after rain and sweat-inducing at all other times (expect each way to take between 20 minutes and half an hour).

Salto de Baiguate WATERFALL
FREE In a lush canyon, Baiguate is not as visually impressive as the others, but it's the most accessible for swimming. A lovely 300m trail cut out of the canyon wall leads from the parking lot to the *salto* – canyoning (p193) trips end here with a rappel down the falls.

To get there, take Calle El Carmen east out of Jarabacoa for 3km until you see a sign for the waterfalls on the right-hand side of the road. From there, a badly rutted dirt road, which at one point is crossed by a shallow creek, leads 3km to a parking lot.

Salto de Jimenoa Dos WATERFALL
(RD$50) Generally referred to as Salto Jimenoa, this waterfall's appeal consists in the views only, as the bathing pools at the foot of the 40m cascade are fenced off. From the parking area, it's a 500m walk over a series

of suspension bridges and trails flanked by densely forested canyon walls. The turnoff to the falls is 4km northwest of Jarabacoa on the road to the Duarte Hwy.

You'll reach a major fork in the road with a large bank of signs; the falls are to the right. From there, a paved road leads 6km past a golf course to the parking lot.

🏃 Activities

Jarabacoa is an adventure capital, with popular excursions for canyoning, hiking and white-water rafting.

White-Water Rafting

Promising and delivering thrills, chills and, for the unlucky, spills, a rafting trip down the Río Yaque del Norte is an exhilarating ride. A typical excursion begins with breakfast, followed by a truck ride upriver to the put-in. You'll be given a life vest, a helmet and a wet suit, plus instructions on paddling and safety. You're usually only asked to paddle part of the time: in the rapids to keep the boat on its proper course, and occasionally in the flat-water areas to stay on pace. You'll stop for a small snack about two-thirds of the way downriver, and then return to Jarabacoa for lunch.

The rapids are rated Class II and III (including sections nicknamed 'Mike Tyson' and 'the Cemetery'), and part of the fun is the real risk of your raft turning over and dumping you into a rock-infested, surging river. A videographer leapfrogs ahead of the group along the riverbank, so you can watch (and purchase) the instant replay afterwards over a beer.

The Río Yaque del Norte has Class IV and V rapids much further up in the mountains. No official tours go that far, but some intrepid guides raft it for fun on their own time. Ask around at Rancho Baiguate (p194) – if you don't mind paying a premium, you might be able to organize something.

A lot of people come from the north coast to raft and then head straight back, which involves at least three hours each way on a bus. Consider spending a couple of nights in Jarabacoa – you'll enjoy your trip much more if you do.

Hiking

The area's big trek is to Pico Duarte (p196), but there are several shorter half-day and full-day walks you can take in the area.

Jarabacoa

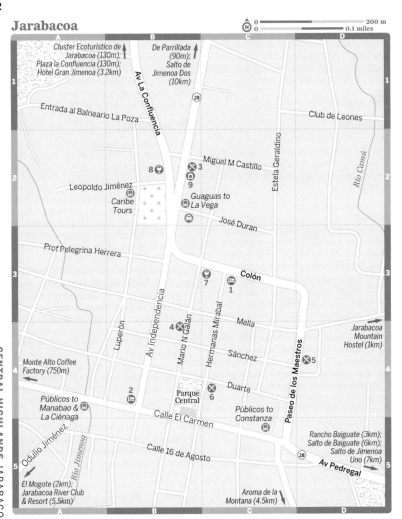

You can get a taste of the ecology of Parque Nacional Armando Bermúdez with a day hike to **Los Tablones** (seven hours, about 10km). The trail is not especially well marked and it's highly recommended to go with a local guide. Rancho Baiguate can arrange the trip (US$150 per person including meal, minimum two people), which involves a four-hour walk up and another four hours back down, or you can make your way to the park yourself, pay the entrance fee of RD$200 and negotiate with guides there. It's a 10-minute drive southwest of La Ciénaga on a very rough road to the Los Tablones trailhead.

A challenging steep hike is to **El Mogote** (1573m), west of town; to get to the trailhead 5km away, hop in a taxi (one way RD$200). Along the way you'll encounter a Salesian monastery where the monks have taken a vow of silence. From here it's a stiff five-hour hike to the summit, so the route's only for the very fit. Start early, wear boots if you have them, and bring plenty of water. It's a slippery walk (or slide) down from the top (at least the first half).

La Jagua (four hours, about 6km), a shorter walk in the area, can also be arranged by

Jarabacoa

Sleeping
1 Hostal Montaña Verde C3
2 Hotel Brisas del Yaque II B4

Eating
3 Jarapan B2
4 Mercado Modelo B4
5 Pizza & Pepperoni............................. D4
6 Restaurant del Parque Galería.......... C4

Drinking & Nightlife
7 Entre Amigos.......................................C3
8 Venue Bar & Lounge...........................B2

Shopping
9 Galeria el Punto del Arte B2

Rancho Baiguate (US$50 per person including meal).

Canyoning

A few hours rappelling, jumping, sliding, zip lining and swimming down a mountain river will have you feeling like a Navy SEAL or Hollywood stunt person. Contact Rancho Baiguate.

Paragliding

Flying Tony　　　　ADVENTURE SPORTS
(☎809-854-5880, 809-848-3479; www.flyindr.com; tandem flights US$60, course US$800) Antonio Rosario Aquino is the proprietor of this long-standing paragliding operation and one of the most experienced pilots on the island. The outfit offers tandem flights and courses to prepare the bold for solo flights. After take-off, paragliding only requires an ability to sit in a comfortable contraption (and endure a 360-degree whirl or two). Remember to bring your camera.

☞ Tours

Rancho Baiguate　　　　TOURS
(☎809-574-6890; www.ranchobaiguate.com; Carretera a Constanza) Rancho Baiguate is recommended for safety and reliability. Its main clientele are Dominican groups from the capital and foreign guests from the all-inclusive resorts near Puerto Plata, but independent travelers can join any of the trips, usually by calling a day or two ahead (except for Pico Duarte trips, which should be arranged weeks in advance).

Activities (prices include breakfast and lunch) range from rafting (US$50) to canyoning at Salto de Baiguate (p191) (US$50

including all gear) to mountain biking (US$25 to US$40); there are also waterfall tours (from US$9 without lunch). Pico Duarte trips range in price depending on number of people and side trips; a three-day trip for four people with no side trips costs US$365 per person.

Monte Alto Coffee Factory　　　　TOURS
(Ramirez Coffee Factory; ☎809-574-2618; Altos del Yaque; ⊙8am-1:30pm & 2-4pm) The family-run Monte Alto coffee farm is near Manabao, but the processing factory is just outside Jarabacoa – to get there, cross the bridge over the river. You can sample a cup of Monte Alto brand coffee in a little cafe-shop in the parking lot.

🛏 Sleeping

Most of the best high-end and midrange sleeping options are just outside town and along the Río Yaque del Norte. Budget travelers will be pleased to know that one of the country's best hostels is just a short walk north of town.

★Jarabacoa Mountain Hostel　　　　HOSTEL $
(☎809-574-6117; www.jarabacoahostel.com; s/d/tr/q from US$25/32/42/48; P❄🛜) About 15 minutes' walk from town, this 'hostel' is actually a modern, two-story home, with a state-of-the-art, fully equipped kitchen and a variety of plush rooms, the best of which offer a balcony and a Jacuzzi (including bath salts!). The friendly, knowledgeable owners help guests plan their trips and provide complimentary coffee, laundry machines and bicycles.

For those who plan to hike Pico Duarte, a stay here after the trek makes good sense, as you can relax, wash your clothes and even watch Netflix. The shared living room and kitchen is a great space for travelers to cook meals and swap adventure tales.

Hotel Brisas del Yaque II　　　　HOTEL $
(☎809-574-2100; hotelbrisasdelyaque@hotmail.com; Av Independencia 13; r from RD$1870; P❄🛜) The Yaque II has large, comfortable, modern rooms and front-desk staff able to answer travel-related questions. The twin rooms are distinctive in having two bathrooms, one for each guest. Ask for a 'mountain-facing' room, if only to avoid street noise.

Hostal Montaña Verde　　　　HOTEL $
(☎809-574-4108; Hermanas Mirabal; r with fan/aircon from RD$1400/1700; P❄🛜) A good-value choice if staying in town is a priority. There's

a small lobby leading to a long, hospital-like hallway lined with 13 basic, clean rooms that feature small bathrooms and TVs. There's no restaurant or breakfast, but the location in the town center puts you close to plenty of options for meals. The owners are friendly and welcoming.

★ **Rancho Baiguate** RESORT $$
(☏809-574-6890; www.ranchobaiguate.com; Carretera a Constanza; all-inclusive s US$65-72, d US$103-135, tr US$158, q US$198; P 🛜 ⚐) 🏊 A wonderful base for exploring the mountains, Baiguate is a rustic resort set in an enormous 72-sq-km compound. Ask for a room in the building beside the river that runs through the complex – its large, comfortable, tile-floored rooms have patios with wicker chairs. For fun, there's a pool, beach volleyball, ping pong, zip lining, miniature horses and a trout pond.

Large groups of students pack the place at weekends and during holidays, but midweek in low season you might have it all to yourself. An on-site veggie garden and permaculture farm supplies the competent Dominican cook, and a worm farm and a gray-water treatment plant reduce the resort's impact on the environment.

The friendly staff speak English and the area's best adventure-tour company (p193) is here. The hosts can pick you up from town.

Hotel Gran Jimenoa HOTEL $$
(☏809-574-6304; www.granjimenoahotel.com; Av La Confluencia; s/d/tr incl breakfast from RD$2475/3110/3790; P 🛜 @ 🛜 ⚐) Set several kilometers north of town right by the roaring Río Jimenoa, this is the Cordillera Central's most upscale hotel. It's neither on the beach nor an all-inclusive hotel, but you could easily spend a week here without leaving the extensive grounds, which include a footbridge to a bar on the far riverbank.

Rooms were recently revamped and some offer incredible river views, as do tables at the hotel's fine restaurant. Dishes (mains RD$550) include Dominican, Italian and French standards, as well as guinea hen and rabbit in wine sauce.

Jarabacoa River Club & Resort HOTEL $$
(☏809-574-2456; s/d incl breakfast RD$2935/3910; P 🛜 @ ⚐) This rambling, multi-level, fun-for-all-ages complex sits on both sides of the Río Yaque del Norte, around 26km south of town on the way

to Manabao. The two-story building has spacious, clean rooms, but it's the terrace views that are special.

White-water-rafting trips begin just north; you can hang out at the riverside restaurant or cafe, or at one of the pools, and see the groups pass below.

Villa Celeste Estate B&B $$$
(☏829-766-3524, 829-766-3524; www.villacelesteestate.com; Los Pinos; s/d incl breakfast from US$99/159; P 🛜 🛜 ⚐) About 14km north of Jarabacoa, this divine eight-room guesthouse is tucked away in a private and verdant gated community designed to mimic the Swiss Alps. The well-constructed, multi-level home features contemporary furnishings, colonial details and a classy rooftop gazebo that looks over the backyard swimming pool and the surrounding greenery, which can also be viewed from the rooms' terraces.

Guests spend their days relaxing and feasting on *prix fixe* meals prepared with fresh ingredients from local farmers.

🍴 Eating

All accommodations have their own restaurants, but be sure to venture out and try local eateries. Several modern supermarkets are in the center of town.

Mercado Modelo MARKET
(Av Mario N Galán; ⊙9am-6pm Mon-Sat) The Mercado Municipal sells fresh fruit, vegetables, meat and other foodstuffs.

Jarapan BAKERY $
(☏829-273-8543, 809-574-6724; Federico Basilis & Miguel M Castillo; baguettes from RD$50; ⊙7am-10pm; 🛜) This Spanish-style bakery across from the Esso gas station at the northern end of town serves excellent espresso and lots of baked treats, both sweet and savory. It's the only place in town to find decent, freshly baked bread.

La Baita ITALIAN $$
(☏809-365-8778, 829-451-0379; marco.brand@hotmail.it; Av La Confluencia 74; mains RD$390-650; ⊙11am-11pm, wood-fired oven 11am-3pm & 5-11pm Mon-Fri, 11am-11pm Sat & Sun) A newcomer to Jarabacoa's restaurant scene, this little Italian place north of town nails it with homemade pastas, wood-fired pizzas and imported meats and cheeses. The affable owner-chef helps guests select the perfect glass of Italian wine to go with

any main dish, be it the mouthwatering linguine with *langostinos* (little lobsters) or a tender slab of Argentine beef.

As if the food weren't enough, the restaurant is set in a quaint log cabin in the hills, surrounded by greenery. There's also a small outdoor seating area.

De Parrillada   INTERNATIONAL **$$**
(☑809-574-7656; Dambury Conn 3; steak RD$695; ◷noon-10pm Mon-Fri, to midnight Sat & Sun) Set back from town on a quiet side street, this rustic and charming establishment is candlelit by evening, and serves up adventurous dishes combining imported meats with local produce and flavors – for example, rosemary pork stuffed with mozzarella and drizzled with homemade passion-fruit sauce. The friendly owner-chef often emerges to socialize with guests.

Pizza & Pepperoni   PIZZA **$$**
(☑809-574-4348, 809-574-4079; Paseo de los Maestros; pizza RD$200-500; ◷11am-11pm; 🛜) The straightforward name isn't entirely accurate. Yes, excellent pepperoni pizzas are on the menu here, along with more than a dozen other varieties, but so too are calzones, burgers, pasta, grilled meat and fish dishes. There's a modern outdoor dining area with TVs tuned to sports. Delivers.

Restaurant del Parque Galería   DOMINICAN **$$**
(☑809-574-6749; Hermanas Mirabal; mains RD$200-800; ◷11am-10pm; 🛜) This long-standing two-story restaurant has a wrap-around bar on a balcony overlooking Parque Central. The large menu includes Dominican specialties like *chivo* (goat; RD$450) and *churrasco* (grilled meat; RD$850), as well as international favorites.

★ Aroma de la Montana   INTERNATIONAL **$$$**
(☑829-452-6879;   http://aromadelamontana. com; mains RD$600-1500; ◷noon-10pm Mon, 10am-10pm Tue-Thu, 9am-11pm Fri-Sun, top fl 1-11pm Sat, 12:30-6pm Sun; 🅿🛜) Sweeping, practically aerial views of the entirety of the Jarabacoa countryside are available from the balcony seating at this sophisticated mountaintop restaurant. Lunchtime has a family atmosphere, but there's a distinctly romantic candlelit vibe on weekend nights, particularly on the top floor, which rotates 360 degrees at weekends. The menu includes rib-eye steak, chicken, salmon, and a *parrilla* for two.

SONIDO DEL YAQUE

This **community-tourism project** (Cabanas Cazuelas de Dona Esperanza; ☑809-727-7413; sonidodelyaque@gmail. com; Los Calabazos; all-incl per person RD$1000) consists of wood and concrete cabins, each with bunks and a porch, set amid lush jungle above the roaring Río Yaque del Norte. There's electricity, hot showers and mosquito nets. Meals are available with notice. It's not signposted, so, coming from Jarabacoa, look for a tiny shop at the right-hand side of the road.

The project was initiated by the women of the village of Los Calabazos, around halfway between Jarabacoa and Manabao.

The road to the restaurant, part of a large property development called Jamaca de Dios, winds its way up between the Pinar Quemado and Palo Blanco mountains south of town. In its original incarnation, an informal spot serving free hot dogs and hamburgers, it was meant to encourage potential vacation-home buyers to stop and take in the fresh air and views. Have ID on hand for the guards at the development's security gate. Because of noise, motorcycles aren't allowed at weekends.

🍷 Drinking & Nightlife

Social life in Jarabacoa revolves around Parque Central: the church and restaurants are all here. At night the numerous *colmados* (a combination of corner store, grocery store and bar) pump loud merengue and beery customers onto the sidewalk, where the party really gets going.

Entre Amigos   CLUB
(☑809-574-7979, 809-574-2828; Colón 182; ◷9pm-late Fri-Sun) This thumping bar is the best party in town – expect merengue, salsa and reggaeton, and elbow-to-elbow service at the bar. There's often karaoke early in the evening, ending at 11pm.

Venue Bar & Lounge   BAR
(Av La Confluencia) A swanky lounge where velvet ropes cordon off VIP areas and neon lights illuminate the beautiful people.

🛍 Shopping

Galeria el Punto del Arte   ART
(📞809-574-6724; Federico Basilis; ⏰7am-10pm)
Opened recently by a long-time Dominican
art collector, this imaginative gallery features more than 150 works by local artists
and a library of about 50 art books. The
space doubles as a bar and bistro, hosting
regular jazz concerts and classes in drawing
and painting. Don't miss the crepes.

ℹ Information

DANGERS & ANNOYANCES

Cestur (Tourist Police; 📞809-754-3072, 809-
754-3068; Miguel Castillo) Behind the Caribe
Tours terminal.

MEDICAL SERVICES

Clínica Dr Terrero (📞829-460-1691; Av
Independencia 2A)

MONEY

Banco Popular (📞809-544-5555; Av La
Confluencia; ⏰9am-5pm Mon-Fri, to 1pm Sat)
In Plaza La Confluencia.

BanReservas (📞809-960-7100; cnr Sanchez
& Marío N Galán; ⏰8am-5pm Mon-Fri, to 1pm
Sat)

TOURIST INFORMATION

Cluster Ecoturístico de Jarabacoa (📞809-
574-6810; http://jarabacoard.com; Plaza La
Confluencia; ⏰8am-noon & 2-6pm) Small shop
with a few locally produced ceramic pieces for
sale and information on activities and tours
(Spanish only); there's also an excellent map of
the town and surrounding area (RD$150).

ℹ Getting There & Away

Públicos to Constanza (RD$150, 40 minutes,
about 9am, 11:30am and 1:30pm) leave from
diagonally opposite the Shell petrol station (at
the corner of Duverge and Calle El Carmen).
Publicos to **La Ciénaga** (RD$100, 1½ hours,
about every two hours) leave from Calle Odulio
Jiménez near Calle 16 de Agosto. The road is
42km long, of which the first 33km is mostly
paved. (Returning can be a challenge, especially if you're coming back from an afternoon
hike. Hail any truck heading towards Jarabacoa;
chances are the driver will let you hop aboard.)

Guaguas provides frequent service to La Vega
(RD$85, 30 minutes, every 10 to 30 minutes
6am to 6pm) leaving from the **terminal** (cnr Av
Independencia & José Duran).

Caribe Tours (📞809-574-4796; Leopoldo
Jiménez) offers the only 1st-class bus service
to/from Jarabacoa. It has four daily departures

to Santo Domingo (RD$270, 2½ hours, 7am,
10am, 1:30pm and 4:30pm), which stop in La
Vega (RD$75, 45 minutes).

ℹ Getting Around

To get to outlying hotels and sights you can easily flag down a *motoconcho* during the day. If you
prefer a cab, try **Jaroba Taxi** (📞809-574-4640)
near the Caribe Tours terminal or hail one at the
corner of José Duran and Av Independencia.

There are several car-rental agencies in Jarabacoa, but it's best to bring a car with you if you
need one.

Parques Nacionales Bermúdez & Ramírez

In 1956 the Dominican government established Parque Nacional Armando Bermúdez
with the hope of preventing the kind of deforestation occurring in Haiti. The park en-
compasses 766 sq km of partly tree-flanked
mountains and pristine valleys. Two years
later, an adjoining area of 764 sq km to the
south was designated Parque Nacional José
del Carmen Ramírez. Between them, the
parks contain three of the highest peaks
in the Caribbean, and the headwaters of 12
major rivers, including the Río Yaque del
Norte, the country's only white-water river
and its most important watercourse.

🏃 Activities

Climbing Pico Duarte

Pico Duarte was first climbed in 1944, as
part of a celebration commemorating the
100th anniversary of Dominican independence. During the late 1980s, the government
began cutting trails in the parks and erect-
ing cabins, hoping to increase tourism to the
country by increasing the accessibility of its
peaks.

Up to around 2000m the mountain is
covered in rainforest, with foliage thick
with ferns and some good bird life. Above
this elevation it's mostly *pino caribeño* – a
monoculture plantation that looks suspi-
ciously like Monterey pine (the stuff loggers
like because of its spindly, knot-free branches). Forest fires have left the landscape a bit
barren in some spots, and the wildlife consists mostly of bands of crows and a wild
boar or two. There's the occasional colorful
epiphyte amid the bleakness.

Parque Nacionales Bermúdez & Ramírez

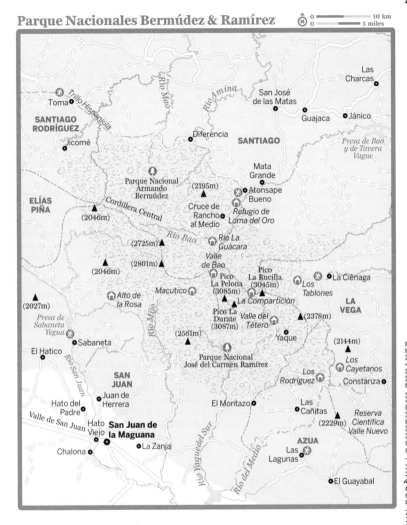

Tours & Guides

The easiest way to get to the summit is to take an organized tour. Prices vary widely and depend on how many people are going and for how long. Expect to pay roughly US$100 to US$200 per person per day. It's best to book as far in advance as possible.

➡ Rancho Baiguate (p193) is the best overall choice for non-Spanish speakers, as it's based in Jarabacoa and also offers a detour through Valle del Tétero. Its three-day, two-night 'Pico Express' trip is around US$380 per person.

➡ Iguana Mama (p166) in Cabarete is good if you want transportation to and from the north coast. It has only four officially listed dates a year but can likely arrange customized group trips, which cost around US$450 per person.

➡ Camping Tours (p183) in Santiago is the cheapest choice, as it caters primarily to Dominicans, but the guides speak only Spanish. This is your only option if you want to walk Mata Grande to Pico Duarte and exit at La Ciénaga.

Self-Organized Tours

Your other option – assuming you speak good Spanish and you're not in a hurry – is to go to La Ciénaga in person and organize mules, food and a guide on your own. Keep in mind, however, that no matter what time of day you show up you won't be ready to leave until the following morning. Travelers with their own camping gear can spend the night in a tent at the park entrance. Mules and muleteers go for around RD$700 per day each, and the lead guide around RD$1000 per day (there's a minimum of one guide for every five hikers). Be aware also that, if you leave via a different entrance from the one where you came in, you'll have to pay several days' extra wages for your guides to get back to the starting point (where they live). Guides can organize basic provisions for you. There's a small spring of drinking water halfway up the trail from La Ciénaga, but you're well advised to pack your own water (in water-cooler-sized bottles, which the mules carry).

Attempting to climb Pico Duarte without mules is neither possible nor desirable – you can't enter the parks without a guide, and a guide won't go without mules. And walking with a full pack in the heat would likely drain whatever enjoyment you might get from the walk. Mules are also essential in case someone gets injured.

WHAT TO BRING

➤ Cold- and wet-weather clothing (at all times of year)

➤ Sturdy boots

➤ Raincoat

➤ Flashlight (torch)

➤ Sunscreen

➤ Insect repellent

➤ Dry bag (for packing your gear in)

➤ Extra dry bag (to protect the sleeping bag and mattress your outfitter will supply you with)

➤ Energy bars

Routes to the Top

There are two popular routes up Pico Duarte. The shortest and easiest (and by far the most used) is from La Ciénaga. It's 23km in each direction and involves 2275m of vertical ascent en route to the peak. It's strongly recommended to do this route in three days: one long slog of a day to arrive at the La Compartición campground (2450m), one easy day to hike up and enjoy the views (and, if you're an early riser, the sunrise), and one long day back out again. The trip can be done in two days by getting up at 4am for a dawn summit, but afterward it's a grueling, hot slog down the mountain. Consider adding a fourth day to do a side trip to the Valle del Tétero, a beautiful valley at the base of the mountain.

The second most popular route is from Mata Grande. It's 45km to the summit and involves approximately 3800m of vertical ascent, including going over Pico La Pelona, a peak only slightly lower than Pico Duarte itself. You'll spend the first night at the Río La Guácara campground and the second at the Valle de Bao campground. You can walk this route in five days (return), but it's far more interesting to walk out via the Valle del Tétero and La Ciénaga (also five days). Camping Tours (p183) offers the hike from Mata Grande, which tends to begin from the town of San José de las Matas.

It's also possible to reach the peak from Sabaneta, Las Lagunas and Constanza. These routes are little traveled, significantly more difficult, and not offered by any tour companies – you'll need to organize a guide and mules yourself.

🛏 Sleeping & Eating

There are approximately 14 campgrounds in the parks, each with a first-come, first-served cabin that hikers can use for free. Each cabin can hold at least 20 people and consists of wooden floors, walls and ceiling, but no beds, cots, mats or lockers of any kind, and latrines are outside. If you have a tent, consider bringing it along.

Most of the cabins have a stand-alone 'kitchen': an open-sided structure with two or three concrete wood-burning stoves. Fallen deadwood is usually abundant near the campgrounds – be sure you or your guide brings matches and some paper to get the fire started.

D'Mari Cafeteria
CAFETERIA $

(mains breakfast/lunch RD$100/150; ⊙9am-close)
Before you climb Pico Duarte, fuel up on eggs and ginger-flavored coffee at this yellow wooden house on the way to La Ciénaga.

ℹ Information

There are ranger stations near the start of the major trails into the parks, including at **La Ciénaga** (park RD$100; ⊙7am-5pm). As a safety precaution, everyone entering the parks, even for a short hike, must be accompanied by a guide.

ℹ Getting There & Away

Ordinarily, transportation to and from Pico Duarte is arranged entirely through tour companies. Self-guided hikers can take *públicos* to La Ciénaga from Jarabacoa for around RD$100.

Constanza

POP 34,700 / ELEV 1097M

There's a saying here in the mountains: 'God is everywhere, but he lives in Constanza.' And you can see why: set in a fertile valley and walled in by towering mountains, it's a breathtaking spot. Dusk, especially, is awesome – as the sun sets behind the peaks, a thick mist sinks into the valley floor. This is the capital of industrialized agriculture: 80% of fruit and vegetables (mainly potatoes, strawberries, apples, lettuce and garlic) and 75% of flowers are grown on farms around here.

The agricultural tradition dates back to the 1950s, when Constanza was home to Japanese farmers who arrived at the invitation of dictator Rafael Trujillo. Trujillo hoped that, in return for receiving superior farmland at dirt-cheap prices, the 50 Japanese families would convert the fertile valley into a thriving agricultural center, which they did.

◉ Sights & Activities

Other than biking and paragliding, there isn't a whole lot to do around Constanza, though Dominicans from the lowland cities journey here for weekend getaways, drawn by the cooler climate and the feeling of remoteness.

Most hotels in the area can organize tours to the main sites outside town, which are all quite distant and require a 4WD.

Reserva Científica
Ebano Verde
NATURE RESERVE

Look for the entrance to this 23-sq-km reserve on the road to Constanza from Santiago. If time is limited, there's an easy 2km nature trail through tropical forest where you might spot Dominican magnolias, the green ebony tree and red-tailed hawks. A more difficult 6km path leads to a pool you can swim in at the base of a small waterfall.

Aguas Blancas
WATERFALL

This breathtaking waterfall, reputedly the largest in the Greater Antilles, is a scenic but extremely rough 16km drive from Constanza (you'll need a 4WD). The falls – one cascade in three sections – crash 135m down a sheer cliff into a pool of clear blue and extremely cold water. Because you don't get a full view until you're close up after a walk through a tight canopy of jungle, the approach feels dramatic.

Turn north at the Isla gas station and continue past Colonia Japonésa. If you haven't got your own vehicle, many hotels can take you there for around RD$2500 (for up to five people). The way through the mountains passes by a couple of extremely poor communities of Haitian and Dominican farm workers.

Reserva Científica
Valle Nuevo
NATURE RESERVE

(Parque Nacional Juan Pérez Rancier) This remote park begins around 17km southeast of Constanza. Las Pirámides, a monument marking the geographic center of the DR, is 46km away. The area records the coldest temperatures in the country, sometimes reaching -8°C during the night, and at 2438m it's the highest plain in the Caribbean. In theory, you can drive all the way from here to San José de Ocoa, around 90km south (though you might need a military vehicle).

Piedras Letradas
CAVE

Meaning 'Inscribed Stone,' Piedras Letradas is a shallow cave containing scores of Taíno petroglyphs and pictograms, mostly depicting animals and simplistic human-like figures. The site is a good 30km northwest of Constanza via the town of La Culeta. The road to La Culeta is paved, but it deteriorates quickly after that – you'll need a 4WD.

Flying Sky
PARAGLIDING

(☑829-559-5283, 829-906-5106; www.facebook.com/flyingskyconstanza.rd/) This operation scoops visitors up from their hotels, drives them up a mountain and launches them over

Constanza, tandem or solo (with a license). The flight lasts around 15 minutes, and the adrenaline rush and the view are equally spectacular.

Cicloruta
CYCLING

(☑ 849-957-1319, 809-539-1022; Constanza airport; rentals RD$300) Based at the airport, this place rents bicycles, and offers guided group rides 9am to 11am and 3pm to 5pm weekends.

⭐ Festivals & Events

Fiestas Patronales
CULTURAL

(☺ Sep) Every September – the exact date varies – Constanza goes nuts during Fiestas Patronales, a nine-day-long party that's nominally in honor of the Virgen de las Mercedes, the town's patron saint. There are live music events and beer tents in the park, and the whole shebang culminates in the crowning of the new *reina* – a Miss Constanza pageant, of sorts.

🛏 Sleeping

Constanza fills up at weekends and during holidays and empties during the week. The center of town is noisy, with a constant din of motorcycles and scooters.

Hotel Bohío
HOTEL $

(☑ 809-539-1645; www.facebook.com/hotelbohio constanza/; Rufino Espinosa 15; r RD$600; ☏) If you're keen to stay in town, Hotel Bohío is a great option, with its tall stone chimney and funky interior artwork. The rooms are adequate, with fans and hot water.

⭐ Alto Cerro
HOTEL $$

(☑ 809-539-6192; www.altocerro.com; Guarocuya 461; s/d/tr incl breakfast RD$2300/2500/2850, villas for 2/5/7 people RD$3300/5200/7800, camping per person RD$250; ℗ ☏) Easily the best option near Constanza, this large, family-owned complex is 2km east of town off the road towards Hwy Duarte (the turnoff is just past the airport on your left). The quaint accommodations line a hillside perched partway up a high bluff, offering balconies with terrific views of the whole valley. The two-story villas also have kitchens.

The hotel's restaurant (mains RD$340), probably Constanza's best, has breathtaking views from the 2nd-floor balcony and well-dressed waitstaff serving Dominican and European-style dishes. There's a small store with basics for a simple meal as well. Behind the main building is a well-maintained camp-

ground, for which guests must bring their own tents.

🍴 Eating & Drinking

The town offers several good restaurants serving local specialties. The best dining option is just out of town at Alto Cerro. At weekends Constanza's Parque Central comes alive with locals drinking at the end of the day – it's a sociable place to hang out for an hour or two. Softball games are held almost every night at 7pm on the field a few blocks west of the park.

Mercado Municipal
MARKET $

(cnr Gratereaux & 14 de Julio; ☺ 7am-6pm Mon-Sat, to noon Sun) For locally grown produce, try this market.

Restaurant Aguas Blancas
DOMINICAN $$

(Espinosa 54; mains RD$200-450; ☺ 9am-10pm; ☏) The cozy (chilly at night, so bring a sweater) log-cabin-like dining room here qualifies as fine dining in Constanza. Along with the usual Dominican fare are a few simple pasta dishes and the specialty: *guinea guisada* (guinea-fowl stew). The place also makes its own delicious array of hot sauces.

Lorenzo's Restaurant
DOMINICAN $$

(☑ 809-539-1561; Luperón 83; mains RD$250; ☺ 11am-10pm) You'll find solid Dominican fare and heaping portions at this restaurant at the western edge of town. Crowded at lunchtime – especially on Sunday, when few other restaurants are open – Lorenzo's doles out sandwiches, pasta, pizza, fish and hearty *sancocho* (a stew of meat, sausage, plantain and potato; RD$150).

Dilenia
DOMINICAN $$

(☑ 849-806-9995; Gastón F Deligne; mains RD$320-420; ☺ 11am-6pm Mon-Thu, to 10pm Fri & Sat, to 6pm Sun) Tucked down a residential side street at the entrance to town, Dilenia has a small all-wood dining room and an even smaller Spanish and English menu with dishes like shrimp in garlic sauce, guinea in wine and good ol' chicken fingers.

ℹ Information

DANGERS & ANNOYANCES
Cestur (Tourist Police; ☑ 809-754-2994)

INTERNET ACCESS
Copy Centro (Sanchez 9; per hr RD$30; ☺ 8am-10pm Mon-Fri, to 5pm Sat)

MEDICAL SERVICES

Farmacia San José (☎809-539-2516; Miguel Abreu 87) At the northeastern corner of the park.

Hospital Pedro Antonio Cespede (☎809-539-3052; Av General Luperón; ⊙24hr) Fully equipped emergency room. On your right as you come into town, just past the airport.

MONEY

Banco Léon (Luperón 19)

BanReservas (Abreu 48; ⊙8am-5pm Mon-Fri, 9am-1pm Sat)

Getting There & Away

CAR

The road between Jarabacoa and Constanza, once jaw-rattlingly bad, has been completely paved. Compact cars can make the trip in 45 minutes to an hour, depending on how many slow-moving trucks are navigating the switchbacks. If you're coming from Hwy Duarte, the turnoff at El Albanico is 89km north of Santo Domingo, and from there it's 51km on a well-paved, twisty mountain road that passes through lush scenery and a handful of small villages. Keep in mind, however, that you'll need an SUV to venture anywhere outside town.

GUAGUAS

Linea Junior (☎809-539-2177; Calle 14 de Junio, btwn Rufino Espinoza & Gratereaux) services La Vega (RD$250, 1½ hours), Santiago (RD$375, two hours) and Santo Domingo (RD$375, 2½ hours). Other *guaguas* travel to Jarabacoa (RD$175, 40 minutes). *Guaguas* also regularly service El Albanico (RD$175, 40 minutes), where you can change for a *guagua* to Santo Domingo and La Vega.

East of Santiago

San Francisco de Marcorís

POP 188,000

San Francisco de Macorís is a bustling, relatively prosperous city surrounded by cocoa and rice fields in the heart of the Valle del Cibao. It has a number of colonial buildings, a large, pretty plaza, and the stadium for the Gigantes (Giants), one of the DR's six professional baseball teams.

The best reason to venture out this way is to take a day trip to Loma Quita Espuela national park. Another good reason is to tour a chocolate farm: the DR is the number-one producer of organic cacao worldwide.

Tours

Sendero del Cacao TOURS

(☎809-547-2166; www.cacaotour.com; tours US$45) Sendero del Cacao offers excellent two-hour tours (in Spanish, English and French) of its picturesque working plantation, including explanations and demonstrations of the entire process; tours end with a large lunch. With your own vehicle, it's only a 15-minute drive from Parque Duarte.

Sleeping & Eating

There aren't many options around San Francisco de Marcorís. Head back to Santiago for more choice.

There are some adequate eateries in town that serve local food, but there's nothing mind-blowing.

Hotel Las Caobas HOTEL $

(Mahogany Hotel; ☎809-290-5858; lascaobas.reservas@gmail.com; cnr Carrón & Av San Diego; s/d RD$2300/2700; P ❄ ☏ ≋) The 'Mahogany Hotel' lives up to its name, with furnishings constructed of the hardwood in the lobby and the on-site restaurant. The rooms are pungent with air freshener, but all have safe, fridge and TV. The restaurant is open all day, and a pleasant pool beckons out the back.

It's conveniently located just a few hundred meters from the Fundación Loma Quita Espuela offices.

Buffalo Steak House DOMINICAN, BARBECUE $$

(☎809-290-3444; San Francisco 63; mains RD$280; ⊙noon-11pm Sun-Thu, to 1am Fri & Sat) On the southern side of Parque Duarte, this western-themed restaurant has a relatively upscale open-air dining area and excellent burgers, seafood and, of course, steaks.

Getting There & Away

The turnoff from Hwy Duarte is about 15km (10 minutes) south of La Vega. It's possible but more difficult (and involves much worse roads) to come south from the coast via Nagua. **Caribe Tours** (☎809-588-2221; cnr Castillo & Hernández) runs more than a dozen buses daily to Santo Domingo (RD$250, 6am to 6:30pm).

Moca & Around

POP 95,000

The country town of Moca has prospered in recent decades as a result of its production of coffee, cocoa and tobacco. During the 18th century the town was one of the Spanish colony's chief cattle centers. In 1805, an in-

RESERVA CIENTÍFICA LOMA QUITA ESPUELA

Loma Quita Espuela (the Mountain of the Missing Spur) – a reference to the dense underbrush that ripped boot spurs from cowboys – is a remote and lovely national park that contains the island's largest rainforest. It's full of endemic species that are on the point of extinction. The NGO **Fundación Loma Quita Espuela** (☑809-588-4156; http://fundacion-loma-quita-espuela.jimdo.com; Urbanización Almánzar, cnr Luis Carrón & Av del Jaya; ☺8am-4pm) is actively involved in developing sustainable ways for local farmers to use this natural resource.

The foundation offers a hike to the top of Loma Quita Espuela (942m; RD$700 for up to five people, plus RD$100 per person park-entrance fee), where an observation tower commands excellent views of the Valle del Cibao. A guide (Spanish speaking only) is mandatory.

There's also a shorter walk that tours several cocoa plantations, where you can buy *bola de cacao* – crude-chocolate balls that are used to make hot chocolate. The tour ends at a local *balenario* (swimming hole), where you can take a dip; there are several Taíno caves nearby, too.

Simple accommodations are available at **Rancho Don Lulú** (☑809-863-8929; www.ranchodonlulu.com; r RD$350), just 1km from the Loma Quita Espuela trailhead. There are eight rooms in a rustic cabin a couple of hundred meters from the owners' home, where you eat (meals RD$200).

The entrance to Loma Quita Espuela is 15km (30 minutes) northeast of San Francisco de Macorís on a rough road that gets progressively worse; don't try it without a good 4WD.

---

vading army took Moca, killed virtually the entire population and burned the town to the ground. Moca struggled back, and in the 1840s began to raise tobacco as a commercial crop; now, some of the world's finest cigars contain tobacco grown on the hillsides around the town.

◉ Sights

Museo de Hermanas Mirabal   MUSEUM
(☑809-587-8530; RD$100; ☺9am-5pm Tue-Fri, to 6pm Sat & Sun) The home of Patria, Minerva and María Mirabal, sisters who were assassinated by agents of dictator Rafael Trujillo in 1960 because of their opposition to his regime, has been turned into a time-capsule museum. Everything in the rooms is presented as if the sisters just left; even the garments they were wearing when they were killed are displayed. Admission includes a guided tour (in Spanish only). The house is east of Moca and around 4km east of the town of Salcedo.

Iglesia Corazón de Jesus   CHURCH
(Moca; ☺varies) FREE The Iglesia Corazón de Jesus has a panel of beautiful stained glass imported from Turin, Italy.

✗ Eating

Juan Pablo   DOMINICAN $
(☑809-578-2024; cnr Corazon de Jesus & 26 de Julio; mofongo RD$225; ☺8am-midnight Mon-Sat, from 11am Sun) This casual restaurant sits below a tall, thatched roof and offers heaping plates of yummy *mofongo*, with a choice of cheese, *chicharrón* (fried pork), *chorizo* (sausage), chicken and combinations thereof. Fruit juices and desserts are also available.

ⓘ Getting There & Away

There's not much point coming out this way if you haven't got your own car.

The Southwest & Península de Pedernales

Why Go?

Talk about criminally undervisited. Few travelers make it to the southwest of the Dominican Republic: it's remote, and its little-known highlights take some effort to uncover – but that's exactly the reason to visit. Heading west from Santo Domingo takes you not only in the opposite direction to the eastern beach resorts but also to a different DR – one whose landscape isn't defined by tourism but by scenes of everyday life. You can explore the cloud forests of the mountains with their soundtrack of birdsong, or the cactus-studded desert that stretches all the way to the Haitian border. Then there's the stunning coastline of the Península de Pedernales, which offers miles of pristine, empty sands and clear turquoise sea. When you reach the Bahía de Las Águilas, a deserted 10km stretch of postcard-perfect beach, you'll feel as though you've hit the traveler's jackpot.

Best Places to Eat

➡ Rancho Tipico (p221)
➡ Casa Bonita (p215)
➡ Rincón Mexicano (p207)
➡ El Meson Suizo (p206)

When to Go

➡ The best time to see the birds and wildlife of the biodiverse Laguna Oviedo is in March and April.

➡ With sunny skies and endless fiestas, December to February is the DR's busiest time.

➡ Caffeine fiends should make a beeline for Polo's organic-coffee festival (p219) in October.

Best Places to Sleep

➡ Casa Bonita (p215)
➡ Eco del Mar (p221)
➡ Hotel Casablanca (p214)
➡ Salinas Hotel (p205)
➡ Ecoturismo Comunitario Cachóte (p212)

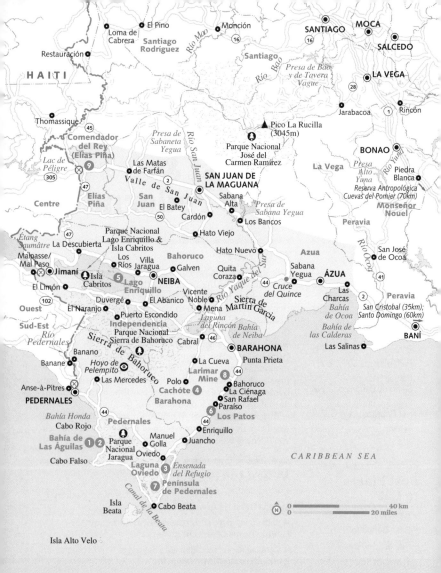

The Southwest & Península de Pedernales Highlights

1 **Bahía de Las Águilas** (p221) Taking a spectacular boat ride to the most remote and beautiful beach in the DR.

2 **Eco del Mar** (p221) Drinking in paradise at the DR's most blissful beach bar.

3 **Laguna Oviedo** (p216) Spotting flamingos and turtles on a boat tour to a salty lagoon.

4 **Ecoturismo Comunitario Cachóte** (p212) Staying in a remote cabin in a tranquil cloud forest.

5 **Lago Enriquillo** (p219) Spotting beefy iguanas at an inland saltwater lake.

6 **Los Patos** (p214) Cooling off in an idyllic freshwater pool near Paraíso.

7 **Península de Pedernales** (p210) Driving along one of the most beautiful and little-known coastal routes in the DR.

8 **Larimar Mine** (p216) Sourcing semiprecious stone at a one-of-a-kind mine.

9 **Haitian Market** (p210) Exploring the commercial spectacle at the border.

ℹ Getting There & Away

Although there's one nominally international airport just outside Barahona, no commercial airlines were flying there in early 2017 and the only way to get here was by bus or car. Caribe Tours (p208) has regular service to Barahona and San Juan de la Maguana, but after that only *guaguas* (small buses) transit the rest of the region. Because of union agreements, *guaguas* plying the coastal highway do not stop at every town along the way, even though they pass right through them. Be careful to get on the right bus, or you'll be let off outside town and will have to walk or catch another ride in.

WEST OF SANTO DOMINGO

From Santo Domingo, Hwy 2 cuts inland to the provincial capital of San Cristobal and from there it continues south to the city of Baní. Hwy 41, north to San José de Ocoa, takes you into the foothills of the Cordillera Central.

Baní

POP 92,000

Notable mainly as a convenient stopping point for those driving between Santo Domingo and Barahona, Baní also marks the turnoff for the beach and sand dunes of Las Salinas, 25km to the southwest.

◎ Sights

Monumento Natural Dunas de las Calderas
NATURE RESERVE

(RD$50, guide per groups of 10 RD$300; ⊘ 8am-5pm Mon-Fri, to 6pm Sat & Sun) This protected reserve, part of the Península de las Salinas, is 20 sq km of gray-brown sand mounds, some as high as 12m. A guided tour offers views of the dunes and beaches beyond and is well worth a look if you want to see a unique landscape in the Caribbean. The brown, sandy beach nearby gets crowded at weekends and is particularly popular with windsurfers. Weekdays it's all yours.

To get to Las Salinas, take Av Máximo Gómez 400m west of Parque Duarte and turn left at the Isla gas station onto Av Fernando Deligne; this eventually bears right onto a single paved road that passes through several small 'towns,' at least one of which has an ATM. There's a naval station at the end of the road; continue past the guard's pillbox and turn left. Follow this road into town. The entrance to the dunes is 1.5km east of Salinas Hotel & Restaurant a great place to bed down if you come.

🛏 Sleeping & Eating

Hotel Caribani
HOTEL $

(☑ 809-522-3871; hotelcaribani@gmail.com; Sánchez 12 Oeste; s/d RD$1600/1800; ※ �î); Conveniently located only a block from the northwestern edge of Parque Duarte. Each basic room has cable TV, air-con, some tropical art and perhaps a standard safe box in the bathroom.

There's a restaurant as well (mains RD$100 to RD$700).

★ Salinas Hotel & Restaurant
RESORT $$$

(☑ 809-866-8141; www.facebook.com/Hotel salinas; Puerto Hermosa 7; d RD$4000, all-inclusive RD$7000; P ※ ⎌ ⊠) This lovely thatched-roof hotel is located at the near-literal end of the road 20km southwest of Baní, amid semi-arid desert, striking mountains and a postcard-blue bay. The large, comfortable rooms have shabby-chic, rustic furnishings and stunning mountain views. The extra-large top-floor suites cost no extra, so it pays to ask for them specifically. Note that there's no beachfront.

The restaurant – easily the best place to eat in town – shares the amazing views and serves up lobster (RD$800), fresh fish (from RD$395) and chicken (RD$425).

Sailboats are docked at the attached marina and the hotel has its own helipad and yacht; the latter sails with groups of 40 or more for RD$500 per person. Otherwise, Salinas is most easily reached by car, but there are *guaguas* to Baní (RD$60, 45 minutes) that pass it hourly from 7:30am to 7:15pm.

Pala Pizza
ITALIAN $$

(www.palapizza.com.do; cnr Duarte & Sánchez; mains RD$196-418, pizzas RD$223-1266; ⊘ 11am-11pm; ⎙) Yes, it's a chain, but this is Baní and locals swear it's better than anything else nearby. Think of it as a Dominican Pizza Hut: there's perfectly decent pizza (think Chicago style, wheat crust, stuffed crust – it has it all), plus tacos, salads, calzones, wraps, pasta, burgers and decent brownies with ice cream.

ℹ️ Information

MEDICAL SERVICES

Centro Médico Regional (☎809-346-4400; Presidente Billini 43; ⊙24hr) A recommended hospital three blocks east of Parque Duarte.

Farmacia Santa Ana (☎809-380-2525; cnr Presidente Billini & Mella; ⊙8am-11pm) At the southeastern corner of the park. Also delivers.

MONEY

Banco BHD León (www.bhdleon.com.do; cnr Hwy Sánchez & Señora de Regla)

Banco Progresso (Presidente Billini, btwn Señora de Regla & Av Fabio Herrara) One block east of the park.

ℹ️ Getting There & Away

Asomiba (☎809-522-7347) express *guaguas* to Santo Domingo (RD$110 to RD$130, 1¼ hours, every 10 minutes 4am to 9:30pm) leave from a terminal half a block west of the main park. **Guaguas to Salinas** (cnr Presidente Billini & Mella, RD$60, 45 minutes) depart every 30 minutes from 8:50am to 7:50pm.

Passengers wait for *guaguas* to Barahona (RD$200, two hours, every 30 minutes 7:30am to 7pm) and Jimaní (RD$450, 3½ hours, every 40 minutes 8am to 6pm) at the corner of a small, orange food stall called **La Paradita del Sur** (Av Máximo Gómez), about 650m west of the park. They're coming from Santo Domingo and don't have a fixed schedule for Baní. They don't linger long, so be alert.

Ázua

POP 88,000

Ázua is the first and largest town you'll encounter as you approach the Southwest from the east, but unless you're incapacitated, sleeping here would be a quirky choice. For those on a trajectory to or from the Haitian border at Comendador del Rey (Elías Piña), Ázua might be a transit hub for buses to the interior west. Otherwise, Baní is a much more pleasant place to spend the night.

🍴 Eating

Dining in Ázua doesn't offer a whole lot beyond fast-food *pica pollo* (fried chicken), and Chinese and simple Dominican places that throw protein on a plate with rice and beans. That said, there's one exception that almost warrants a special stop here just to eat.

⭐**El Meson Suizo**   DOMINICAN **$$**
(Calle 19 de Marzo 121; mains RD$225-800; ⊙7am-midnight; ☎) This slightly upscale place is one of the Southwest's better spots to eat, so getting stuck in Àzua isn't a total loss. Excellently prepared *mofongos* (mashed plantains with meat or seafood), pasta, meat and fish – try the lovely fish in garlic sauce *(al ajillo)* – are delivered by shirt-and-tie staff to an atmospheric outdoor patio with chirping birds and squawking chickens.

ℹ️ Getting There & Away

Caribe Tours (☎809-521-5088; www.caribe tours.com.do; cnr Nuestra Señora de Fatimas & Emilio Prud-Homme) buses between Santo Domingo and Barahona stop in Ázua, arriving at and departing from a small office three blocks northeast of Parque Central. Buses from Ázua to Santo Domingo (RD$200, two hours) depart at 7:15am, 7:30am, 10:45am, 11:15am, 2:30pm, 2:45pm and 6:15pm. To Barahona (RD$150, 1½ hours), the opposite way, buses leave at 8am, 11:30am, 3:30pm and 7pm.

Asodema (☎809-683-6046) express (RD$210) and regular *guaguas* (RD$190) go to Santo Domingo (two hours, every 10 minutes 4:20am to 7pm) from a terminal on Av Duarte, on the corner opposite the park. For San Juan (RD$130, 1½ hours, every 15 minutes 5am to 5:30pm) and the path to the Haitian border, Asodumas *guaguas* depart from in front of Panadería Doña Petra near Parque 19 de Marzo, three blocks from Parque Central. *Guaguas* to Barahona (RD$100, one hour, every 30 minutes 6:30am to 4pm) also pass by here. It's infinitely better to pick up a *guagua* for Barahona at points east of here.

INLAND

Three highways lead west to the Haitian border. Fifteen kilometers west of Ázua the highway branches west to San Juan de la Maguana and the border at Elías Piña, and south to Barahona. At Barahona the road splits again -- the interior road runs past Lago Enriquillo to the busy Jimaní border post, and the southern road hugs the coast before dead-ending at Pedernales and the residential border crossing to Haiti.

San Juan de la Maguana

POP 78,000

Monument heavy and kind of quirky, San Juan de la Maguana is a pleasant place to kill a night in transit. Haitians are increasingly moving in as Dominicans move away, bringing a Vodou influence to the city's Dominican Catholic culture. San Juan's also known as La Ciudad de los Brujos (the City of Shamans), but most shamans live in the hills outside the city and are definitely not tourist attractions.

◉ Sights

El Corral de los Indios   HISTORIC SITE

Despite being referred to as 'the Stonehenge of the Dominican Republic,' this pre-Colombian site – one of the few in the Antilles – doesn't quite live up to the hype. El Corral de los Indios is composed of a large, circular clearing containing a 1.5m-long gray stone with a face carved on one end. Research here is thin, but the site is said to have originally consisted of two rows of block stones forming two concentric circles around the center.

One theory is that this was a ceremonial place for the Caonabo and Anacaona Indians as well as an astronomical instrument. Today the only thing surrounding the center is a football field with some grazing horses. The site is 5km north of Calle Independencia.

🛏 Sleeping & Eating

Hotels in San Juan are generally full of Dominican business travelers and for this reason are often good value. There's no shortage, either, as this is a popular stop for those heading to and from the Haitian border at Elías Piña. The best concentration tends to be within a few blocks of the town arch.

Hotel Maguana   HOTEL $

(☑ 809-557-2244;   hotelmaguana@outlook.es;   Av Independencia 72;   s/d/tr from RD$1534/1770/2596; P✱🛜) Built at dictator Trujillo's request in 1947, the Maguana has an imposing facade and interior courtyard that suggest a grandeur that has now faded, but that doesn't mean it's not interesting. All rooms have hot water and TV, although some lack windows, and the singles are cramped.

There's a great (but noisy) alfresco bar in the parking lot and a quieter interior bar. If you can afford it, ask for the Trujillo suite, where Rafael himself used to lay his head. No breakfast is included, but there's a restaurant on premises.

Hotel Nuevo Tamarindo   HOTEL $

(☑ 809-557-7002;   hoteltamarindosjm@hotmail.com;   Dr Cabral 26;   s/d/tr with air-con RD$1000/1500/1800, s without air-con RD$700; P✱🛜) Clean and simple rooms, international cable TV, normally reliable wi-fi and a small restaurant all feature at this perfectly located hotel right across the street from Caribe Tours.

Hotel y Supermercado
El Detallista   SUPERMARKET $

(cnr Trinitaria & Puello; 8am-9pm Mon-Sat, to 1pm Sun; P✱) For groceries, Hotel y Supermercado El Detallista is one-stop shopping: the best grocery store, an ATM and a Western Union branch.

★ Rincón Mexicano   MEXICAN $$

(cnr Calles 27 de Febrero & Capotillo; mains RD$110-690; ⊗6pm-midnight) Owned by a real live *mexicana* (who does the cooking) and her Dominican husband, this airy, immeasurably pleasant restaurant pumps out authentic Mexican tacos (RD$110), as well as enchiladas, fajitas and the like. Chase it all with excellent margaritas and toast to your good fortune that a place like this exists in San Juan.

The lack of wi-fi and menu prices is irritating, however.

La Galeria del Espía   DOMINICAN $$

(Av Independencia 5 & 7; mains RD$150-495; ⊗11am-4pm & 6:30pm-1am; 🛜) Don't let the tinted facade just opposite Parque Central deter you: this is a friendly, mega-popular spot for simple and quick Dominican food. The plate of the day goes for RD$280 and there's an often-changing menu of fresh and filling traditional food. If you're coming from Haiti, it's the perfect introduction to DR dining.

🍷 Drinking & Nightlife

The Hotel Maguana has a rowdy outdoor bar in its parking lot that's popular for *bachata* (Dominican music) and karaoke at weekends. Nearby, the awesomely named Super Fría Los Freezer is the liquor store–bar of choice. Don't miss the margaritas at Rincón Mexicano (p207)!

RAFAEL TRUJILLO'S SAN CRISTOBAL

Most visitors heading west from the capital pass right through San Cristobal, the home town of dictator Rafael Trujillo just 30km from Santo Domingo. Trujillo erected all sorts of monuments to himself here and built extravagant buildings, but today little evidence of his regime remains and the city is a traffic-clogged provincial capital.

San Cristobal's strangest sight, the **Castillo del Cerro** (Escuela Nacional Penitenciaria (ENAP); http://enap.pgr.gob.do; Prolongación Luperón s/n; ⊙ 9am-4pm Mon-Fri) FREE, is currently used as the National Penitentiary School. It was built on Trujillo's orders for himself and his family in 1947 (at a cost of US$3 million), but Trujillo reportedly hated the finished product and never spent a single night there. The name means 'Castle on the Hill,' which is pretty accurate – it overlooks the city – but the concrete-and-glass structure looks more like an office building than a castle.

Inside, however, huge dining rooms, ballrooms and bedrooms have fantastic ceilings and wall decorations painted in gaudy colors. The bathrooms – of which there must be 20 – have tile mosaics in reds, blues and gold leaf. There are six floors in all, and you can spend half an hour or more just wandering through the once-abandoned structure. There's also a small museum detailing some of Trujillo's atrocities, including a few original instruments of torture and murder, a replica electric chair and – huh? – loads of exquisite bed frames. All visitors are escorted by ENAP employees.

Any taxi driver or *motoconchista* (motorcycle taxi driver) can take you there – it probably makes sense to ask the driver to come back in 30 to 60 minutes to pick you up. If you've got a vehicle, from Parque Independencia take Calle María Trinidad Sánchez west for 700m. Take a left onto Calle Luperón and follow it up the hill 500m until you reach a fork in the road. There, veer right and head up the hill another 700m to the entrance gates. Visitors must adhere to the dress code of shirts and closed-toe shoes.

In the home of local resident José Miguel Ventura Medina, known to some as 'El Hippi,' the informal **Museo Jamas El Olvido Será tu Recuerdo** (✆ 809-474-8767; General Leger 134; adult/child RD$200/100; ⊙ 24hr) FREE has a name translating literally to 'Forgetfulness will never be your remembrance' or simply 'You will never be forgotten.' The 'you' in this case is none other than Generalísimo Trujillo, who, along with John F Kennedy, was Ventura's favorite world leader. Most will not agree with Ventura's assessment of Trujillo as a 'good dictator,' but the extensive collection is worth poking around.

❶ Information

DANGERS & ANNOYANCES

Policia Nacional (National Police; ✆ 809-557-2380; www.policianacional.gob.do; cnr Av Independencia & Dr Cabral; ⊙ 24hr) A block west of the large white arch at the eastern entrance to town.

MEDICAL SERVICES

Centro Médico San Juan (✆ 809-557-5345; Trinitaria 55) Your best bet for private medical attention.

Farmacia Iguamed (cnr Trinitaria & Dr Cabral; ⊙ 8am-10pm Mon-Sat, 9am-1pm Sun) Centro Médico San Juan's affiliated pharmacy.

MONEY

Banco León ATM (www.bhdleon.com.do; cnr Av Independencia & Mella)

BanReservas ATM (www.banreservas.com; cnr Carretera Sánchez Km 1 & Joaquín Balaguer)

POST

InposDom (www.inposdom.gob.do; Mella 31; ⊙ 8am-4pm Mon-Fri) No Dominican flag and no sign whatsoever, but this is the post office, next to Defensa Civil.

❶ Getting There & Away

When the highway hits town it splits into two one-way streets – the westbound street is Calle Independencia and the eastbound is Calle 16 de Agosto. A large white arch modeled on Paris' Arc de Triomphe stands dramatically at the eastern entrance to the city. At the western end of town is San Juan's large plaza, with a pretty cream-colored church on one side and a school of fine arts on the other.

Caribe Tours (✆ 809-557-4520; www.caribe-tours.com.do) has a terminal 75m west of Hotel Maguana next to Pollo Rey. Buses to Santo Domingo (RD$300, three hours) depart at 6:30am, 10:15am, 1:45pm and 5:30pm.

Guaguas for Santo Domingo (RD$300, three hours, every 30 minutes 4am to 7pm) leave from

Ventura, who speaks Spanish and English, has plenty of stories to go along with his collection, which includes photos and other memorabilia, plus a slew of random antiques from old corn and coffee grinders to early typewriters. The museum is open whenever Ventura is home; if he's not there, give him a call. It's 6½ blocks north and one block east of Parque Colón – look for a small white car perched on the rooftop. Ventura also rents a very rustic room (RD$500).

The area's most impressive attraction, however is the **Reserva Antropológica El Pomier.** (☑829-354-5900; RD$100, guide RD$300; ☺8am-4pm) Visiting is like reading a history book written in stone. There are 57 limestone caves in the area 10km north of San Cristobal, five of which (containing almost 600 paintings) are open to the public – though note that they're frequently closed for renovations. The caves contain thousands of drawings and carvings that constitute the most extensive example of prehistoric art yet discovered in the Caribbean, including works by Igneri and Caribs as well as the Taínos.

Because of its proximity to Santo Domingo and its dearth of quality accommodations, San Cristobal is not a popular choice for staying overnight. The nearby Rancho Ecológico El Campeche, however, offers one of the country's few opportunities to camp.

San Cristobal's culinary claim to fame is the *pastel en hoja* (literally 'pastry in paper'), basically a doughy empanada stuffed with cheese or meat and wrapped in a piece of butcher paper. They cost around RD$90 apiece and can be found at most eateries, including **Pasteleria Chichita** (General Leger 58; pasteles RD$70-120; ☺7am-11pm).

Buses for San Cristobal leave Santo Domingo from Parque Enriquillo (RD$55 to RD$75, one hour). In San Cristobal, **guaguas for the capital** (RD$85, 45 minutes, every 20 minutes 6am to 8pm) leave from a stop at the southeastern edge of the park. **Guaguas to Baní** (RD$90, 45 minutes, every 25 minutes 7am to 7pm) leave from beside the Isla gas station on Carretera Sánchez (Calle Padre Borbón) that's 600m west of Parque Colón. For towns further west, such as Azua (RD$190, 1½ hours) and Barahona (RD$250, 3½ hours), you have to go out to the further-flung **Isla gas station** (Carretera Sanchez), 4.3km north of Parque Colón on the main highway, and flag down a passing bus.

the **Terminal Tenguerengue** (☑809-557-3854; cnr Independencia & Eusebio Puello), three blocks east of the arch. There are three express buses (RD$300, 6:30am, 9:30am and 3pm), which make the trip half an hour faster because they don't make a food stop along the way.

If you're going to Barahona, you can take any of the four Caribe Tours buses to Azua, or catch an **Asodumas** (☑829-761-5693; Eusebio Puello) *guagua* from its small terminal half a block south of the Tenguerengue terminal (RD$130, 1½ hours, every 20 minutes 5am to 6:15pm), and catch a Barahona-bound bus there. Alternatively, take a Santo Domingo *guagua* and get off at Cruce del Quince (RD$130, one hour), the main highway intersection, 15km west of Azua, and catch a southbound *guagua* from there.

Guaguas to Comendador del Rey (Elías Piña; RD$130, one hour, every 20 minutes 7am to 6pm) depart from the small Fenatrano (Caonabo) terminal at the far western end of town, just before the Mesopotamia bridge. You can walk with a pack, but probably not with luggage. Head out of town

west on Calle Caonabo, four blocks north of Calle Independencia. Additionally, make absolutely sure your bus is going all the way to Elías Piña: if there aren't enough passengers, it may dump you halfway (at Las Matas) and you'll have to wait for another bus to come through (or pay a premium for a taxi). A taxi direct to the border for up to four passengers costs RD$1800.

Taxis and *motoconchos* may be found near Parque Central; or phone **Taxi del Sur** (☑809-557-6400).

Comendador del Rey (Elías Piña)

POP 19,300

Comendador del Rey, or Comendador for short, is the official name of the border town west of San Juan. However, almost everyone who doesn't live there calls it Elías Piña, which is the name of the province, and you'll have more luck using that name anywhere but in town. Comendador is best known for its twice-weekly Haitian market, when hundreds of Haitians arrive on donkeys and on foot to sell their wares.

Comendador also has a major military base and a police headquarters, and security (aimed at preventing illegal Haitian immigration) is tight. Even foreign travelers may find themselves detained and questioned if they're not carrying their passport.

◉ Sights

Haitian Market   MARKET
(Av 27 de Febrero, btwn Las Mercedes & Ramon Matias Mella; ☻6am-4pm) The Haitian market is impossible to miss: just stay on the main road through town until you run into it. Vendors lay their goods out on the ground, shaded by tarps suspended from every available tree, road sign and telephone pole. Cooking utensils, clothing, shoes, fruit and vegetables are the primary items, sold for discounts of as much as 50%.

There's not much in the way of handicrafts, since few tourists attend the market, but just wandering around and taking in the scene is worthwhile. Of most interest to tourists might just be a bottle of Barbancourt Haitian rum (and who knows – maybe you'll see a colander you like). The market's at its biggest on Monday and Friday.

🛏 Sleeping & Eating

Casa Teo Hotel y Ferretería   HOTEL $
(☎809-527-0392; Eusebio Puello; s/d/tr with fan RD$400/800/1200; ❄) Every border town should have one of these places – for all your holiday hardware needs! A hotel that doubles as a hardware store, it faces the park and is predictably prison-cell-like, with barren walls and rather gruff service.

D'Melkin   FAST FOOD $
(Av 27 de Febrero 1; mains RD$100-150, pizza RD$100-650; ☻8am-midnight) Don't get too excited – the title of 'best restaurant in town' doesn't mean much in Comendador. But D'Melkin is a quick and easy stop for sandwiches and pizza, with a pleasant enough patio overlooking the prettiest thing in town: the circular Parque Central.

ℹ Information

There's a public hospital at the eastern entrance to town, near the military base, but you're better off moving on to San Juan unless you're at death's door.

Policía Nacional (☎809-527-0290; www.policianacional.gov.do; cnr Calles 27 de Febrero & Las Mercedes; ☻24hr) For emergencies.

ℹ Getting There & Away

The highway splits into two one-way streets when it enters town. The westbound street is Calle Santa Teresa and the eastbound is Calle 27 de Febrero. Almost everything you need is on or near those two streets. The park is at the eastern end of town, between Calles Las Carreras and Las Mercedes. There's a large traffic circle at the western end of town, at which point the roads merge again and lead to the Haiti–DR border, about 2km away.

The main guagua terminal (Av 27 de Febrero) is at the eastern end of the main park. Buses leave from here for Santo Domingo (RD$400, four hours, every 30 minutes 3am to 6pm). If you're just going to San Juan (RD$130, one hour, every 30 minutes 6am to 8:40pm), take one of the guaguas parked just outside the terminal, as the Santo Domingo bus doesn't officially stop in San Juan. For Barahona, take a Santo Domingo bus to Cruce del Quince (the main highway intersection 15km west of Ázua; RD$250, 1½ hours) and then catch a southbound bus from there. Or use Caribe Tours (p208).

PENÍNSULA DE PEDERNALES

The Península de Pedernales contains some of the DR's most outstanding attractions: the sublime beach at Bahía de Las Águilas, super-salty Laguna Oviedo, Parque Nacional Jaragua, the cloud forest of Cachóte and world-class bird-watching in the Parque Nacional Sierra de Bahoruco. Despite all this, tourism in this part of the country is surprisingly low.

The peninsula was originally a separate island, but tectonic movement pushed it north and upward into Hispaniola, closing the sea channel that once ran from Port-au-Prince to Barahona and creating many of the unique geographical features you see today.

The Southwest is the best place on the island to go bird-watching, as you can see nearly all Hispaniola's endemic species here. At last count, there were roughly 310 known species of bird in the DR and 32 endemic bird species on the island. Half of these are migratory, making winter the best time to spot them.

Parque Nacional Jargua

This park (RD$100; ☉8am-5pm) is the largest protected area in the DR. Its 1400 sq km includes vast ranges of thorn forest and subtropical dry forest, and an extensive marine area that spans most of the southern coastline, including Laguna Oviedo, Bahía de Las Águilas and Islas Beata and Alto Velo.

Barahona

POP 62,000

Full of industrial smokestacks and of little interest to travelers, Barahona is an eyesore on an otherwise dramatically beautiful coast. A growing number of quality, good-value accommodations sit along the coastal road between here and Paraíso, though, making the city somewhat unavoidable when you're exploring the region. It's home to one of the few ATMs until you reach Pedernales (there's also one in Enriquillo), so you'll likely need to come here to get cash, and it's also a necessary transfer point if you're traveling by bus.

History

By Dominican standards, Barahona is a young city, founded in 1802 by Haitian general Louverture as a port to compete with Santo Domingo. For over a century, residents mostly made their living taking what they could from the Caribbean Sea, but today fishing accounts for only a small part of Barahona's economy. Dictator Rafael Trujillo changed everything when he ordered many square kilometers of desert north of town to be converted to sugarcane fields for his family's financial benefit. More than three decades after his assassination, the thousands of hectares of sugarcane continue to be tended, only now they're locally owned and benefit the community.

☞ Tours

★**Ecotour Barahona** ECOTOUR
(☎849-856-2260, 809-856-2260; www.ecotour barahona.com; Apt 306, Carretera Enriquillo 8, Paraíso; ☉9am-6pm) This professional French-run tour company has been pioneering tourism in the Southwest since 2004. It offers good day trips to Bahía de Las Águilas, Lago Enriquillo, Laguna Oviedo and Cachóte, among others. It also offers a handful of day hikes

> **ⓘ WARNING: CESFRONT!**
>
> If you'll be leaving any of the border towns by personal vehicle, note that CESFRONT (Cuerpo Especializado de la Seguridad Fronteriza Terrestre), the Dominican border patrol, has set up numerous checkpoints on the highways out of Jimaní, Comendador del Rey (Elías Piña) and Pedernales. Make sure your documents (car registration, passport, visa/tourist card etc) are in order, as there have been some reports of officers extorting money from those passing through. Travelers have been asked for US$20 in order to get their passport back – even when nothing was amiss with their documents.

in the hills around Paraíso, and can organize multiday trekking and bird-watching tours.

Most day trips cost US$119 for two people and go down in price as groups get larger; prices include an excellent three-course picnic lunch.

⨭ Sleeping

Unless you're after dirt-cheap accommodations, there's no reason to stay in the city itself. A far better plan is to use Barahona for services only and stay in one of the numerous hotels strung along the coast south of town on the road to Paraíso.

★**Hotel Loro Tuerto** GUESTHOUSE $
(☎809-524-6600; www.lorotuerto.com; Av Del Monte 33; s/d RD$1500/1800; ❄️🛜) This charming nine-room guesthouse on noisy Av Del Monte has far more character than any of its competitors. Frida Kahlo reproductions dot the walls and simple rooms surround a peaceful courtyard with hammocks. There's a cafe (mains RD$250 to RD$280) up the front that does breakfast, too.

Hotel Las Magnolias HOTEL $
(☎809-524-2244; magnolia.cdm@hotmail.com; Aracoana 13; s/d/tr RD$1200/1400/2000; 🅿️❄️🛜) This 15-room hotel wins a star for its hands-on, friendly owner and equally simpatico staff, who make sure the place runs smoothly. Rooms are simple, and bathrooms need a bit of renovating, but it's a comfortable spot with slightly more personality than average. There's wi-fi in the lobby and nearby rooms 1 and 2.

There's free coffee (unsweetened, and made with an Italian Moka!) and water. If you're driving, note that a nearby radio tower kills electronic key fobs.

Hotel Cacique HOTEL $

(☑809-524-4620; Peña Gómez 2; s with fan RD$600, s/d with air-con RD$850/1300; ❋@🐾) A good-value option, especially if you opt for a room without AC. Some rooms are better than the aged common interiors suggest, with renovated bathroom, cable TV, hot water and nicely tiled floor. There's a simple restaurant, (wickedly sweet) free coffee, wi-fi in the lobby and a small internal patio.

Although there's a fair bit of local foot traffic, it's surprisingly quiet. There's no parking, but a night security guard keeps an eye on cars in front of the hotel. The front desk can be a riot when they're hitting the *cerveza*!

Ecoturismo Comunitario Cachóte CABIN $$

(☑829-863-8833; soepa.paraiso@yahoo.com; per person incl meals from RD$3000) 🍴 Bed down in a Caribbean cloud forest at the rustic cabins that make up Ecoturismo Comunitario Cachóte, each housing one large queen-size bed and a triple-decker dormitory-style bunk. There are excellent hiking and bird-watching right outside your door and you'll feel about as far removed from a Caribbean island as you can be!

Eating

Barahona has a few decent restaurants scattered about town and along the *malecón* (waterfront), but you won't stretch your taste-bud limits here.

POLO MAGNÉTICO

Twelve kilometers west of Barahona is the town of Cabral and the turnoff south for nearby Polo. About 11km south of the turnoff you'll encounter a famous mirage. Put your car in neutral, let go of the brake and watch your car get 'pulled' uphill. The effect is best between the towns of El Lechoso and La Cueva, and it works on a smaller scale, too: if you get out of the car and put a water bottle on the road, it will also show a mysterious desire to climb uphill. The effect is known as a 'gravity hill,' an optical illusion caused by the slope's shape and its relation to the surrounding landscape.

Super Jacobo SUPERMARKET $

(cnr Padre Billini & Anacaona; ⊙7am-9pm Mon-Sat, to 2pm Sun) Stock up on rations for travels further south.

Junior's FAST FOOD $

(Nuestra Señora del Rosario 2; sandwiches RD$80-260; ⊙10am-midnight Sun-Thu, to 2am Fri & Sat) Among the best value in town for size, taste and price. Enjoy sit-down service at picnic tables on a pleasant outdoor patio or order hefty grilled sandwiches (serious business in Barahona) from a stand-alone to-go shack. You'll find tacos, quesadillas and burritos as well.

As it's open till the wee hours in the middle of the *malecón* madness, this is the epicenter of drunken munchies.

Restaurant Pizzería D'Lina DOMINICAN $

(Av 30 de Mayo 11; mains RD$175-450; ⊙8am-11pm; 🐾) This is your requisite Dominican cheapie, catering to a loyal clientele who come for simple, home-style food. It's certainly not friendly, but cheap sandwiches (RD$80 to RD$250), *platos del día* (RD$200), decent pizza, and various meat, chicken and seafood dishes – try the *lambi* (conch) *a la vinagreta* – are served on a pleasant and breezy palapa-topped patio.

★ Brisas del Caribe SEAFOOD $$

(☑809-524-2794; Carretera Batey Central; mains RD$300-960; ⊙9am-11pm daily, bar 5pm-midnight Thu-Sun; 🐾) The kitchen here dishes out fresh seafood as the seasons dictate (though the seasons sometimes affect consistency as well). The perfectly sized seafood-soup appetizer (RD$190) has more seafood than broth, and the zesty fish medallions *al coco* (RD$450) are tasty (though they're not medallions). A terrace bar has recently been added.

ℹ Information

DANGERS & ANNOYANCES

Cestur (Cuerpo Especializado de Seguridad Turística; ☑809-754-3035; Carretera Batey Central) Tourist police; along the waterfront, 550m north of Av Del Monte.

MEDICAL SERVICES

Centro Médico Regional Magnolia (☑809-524-2470; Peña Gómez 71; ⊙24hr) The best private clinic.

Super Farmacia Y/C (cnr Av Del Monte & Duvergé; ⊙8am-9pm Mon-Sat, 9am-2pm Sun) Well-stocked pharmacy.

MONEY

Stock up on cash in Barahona – the nearest ATMs are in Enriquillo (50km away) and Pedernales (122km away). There's a **Banco Popular ATM** (cnr Jaime Mota & Padre Billini) at Parque Central. If you have to return from the south for cash, you don't have to come all the way into town: there's a **BanReservas ATM** (cnr Peña Gómez & Padre Billini) at the Isla gas station at the town's southern entrance.

POST

InposDom (www.inposdom.gob.do; Parque Central; ⊗8am-4pm Mon-Fri)

TOURIST INFORMATION

Ministerio de Turismo (☑809-524-5130; 2nd fl, Av Enriquillo 27; ⊗8am-3pm) This small, regional Ministry of Tourism office is good for a map and a bit of local info. It's inside the Fedomu building next to Cestur.

ⓘ Getting There & Away

AIR

Aeropuerto Internacional María Móntez (p302) is located 7km north of town. It receives charter flights only.

BUS

There's frequent *guagua* service to all points of the compass during daylight hours. You can also pick up south-bound *guaguas* at a stop on the highway at the southern end of town. *Guaguas* generally leave every 15 to 30 minutes during daylight hours.

A frequent express service to Santo Domingo (RD$280, three hours, hourly 6am to 7pm) leaves from the **Sinchomiba** (☑809-524-2449; cnr José D Matos & Av Casandra Damirón) terminal at the corner of Av Casandra Damirón and Calle José D Matos near the northwestern entrance to town. Regular services (RD$250, three hours, every 20 minutes 6am to 7pm) also depart from here.

Guaguas to Paraíso (cnr Calles 30 de Mayo & Peña Gómez, RD$100, 40 minutes) depart every 20 minutes from 6am to 6pm. *Guaguas* to Pedernales (Peña Gómez, RD$250, 2½ hours), depart every 30 minutes from 6:30am to 11pm.

Guaguas heading west to the Haitian border at Jimaní call at Calle María Móntez just north of Calle Colón (RD$240, two hours, every 40 minutes 7am to 6:20pm). It's also possible (but difficult) to visit Isla Cabritos via *guagua* – take any guagua to Neiba (Av Del Monte, RD$130, 1¼ hours, every 20 minutes 6am to 7pm) from the corner of Calle Padre Billini and Av Del Monte and then transfer to a La Descubierta–bound bus (RD$100, one hour, every 20 minutes 6:10am to 6pm).

WORTH A TRIP

RESERVA ANTROPOLÓGICA CUEVAS DEL POMIER

Visiting the **Reserva Antropológica El Pomier** (☑829-354-5900; RD$100, guide RD$300; ⊗8am-4pm) is like reading a history book written in stone. There are 57 limestone caves in the area 10km north of San Cristobal, five of which (containing almost 600 paintings) are open to the public – though note that they're frequently closed for renovations. The caves contain thousands of drawings and carvings that constitute the most extensive example of prehistoric art yet discovered in the Caribbean, including works by Igneri and Caribs as well as the Taínos.

For San Juan de la Maguana, take any non-*expreso* Santo Domingo–bound *guagua* and get off at the Cruce del Quince intersection (15km west of Ázua; RD$100, one hour), and wait there for a west-bound bus to San Juan (RD$150, one hour).

Caribe Tours (☑809-221-5318; www.caribetours.com.do; cnr Peña Gómez & Apolinar Perdomo) has 1st-class services to Ázua (RD$150, one hour) and Santo Domingo (RD$300, three hours) departing at 6:15am, 9:45am, 1:30pm and 5:15pm.

ⓘ Getting Around

Barahona is somewhat spread out, though the area around the center is navigable by foot. For points further afield, taxis and *motoconchos* can be found beside Parque Central and along Av Del Monte, or call the local **taxi association** (☑809-524-3003; Av Del Monte).

It's unwise to take *motoconchos* along the coastal road after dark.

South of Barahona

Once you pass Barahona's southernmost military checkpoint on the highway heading towards Pedernales, things begin to feel a bit more wild: the road hugs the peninsula on the right and there's a deep-blue, highly underrated sea on the left. Some of the best hotels and resorts in the southwest sit on rocky outcrops along this route, all within 20km of Barahona and all with stupendous views. Eventually the adjoining seaside villages of Bahoruco and La Ciénaga emerge: two typical small communities in the heart of larimar-mineral

---

ⓘ GAS STATIONS

Gas (petrol) is somewhat scarce along the Península de Pedernales. Leaving Barahona, you'll find stations in La Ciénaga, Paraíso and Enriquillo (54km south of Barahona), the last gas before Pedernales, 75km away. Be sure to fill up your tank!

---

country, with friendly locals and gravelly beaches used for mooring boats rather than swimming. From there things take a dramatic turn as the highway crests at one of the most beautiful landscapes in the southwest. An impossible swirl of cerulean-turquoise sea commands your attention as the road rolls into tiny, aptly named Paraíso, and Los Patos beyond, home to a heavenly beach.

🏃 Activities

★ Playa Los Patos   BEACH, SWIMMING

(Carretera Barahona-Paraíso, Los Patos) Playa Los Patos, a pretty white-stone beach, and its adjacent *balneario* (swimming hole) are idyllic traveler finds. Water flows clear and cool out of the mountainside, forming a shallow lagoon before running into the ocean. Shacks serve good, reasonably priced food and cold *cerveza*. At weekends it's crowded with Dominican families, but it's much quieter midweek.

You can visit newly opened caves housing Taíno petroglyphs across the street from the *balneario*.

🛏 Sleeping

The stretch of hotels along the Barahona–Paraíso coastal highway are some of the best in the Southwest. All feature stunning sea views and great restaurants. The town of Paraíso is a good budget alternative to Barahona.

Hotel Comedor Kalibe   HOTEL $

(☑ 809-243-1192; Arzobispo Meriño 16, Paraíso; s/d with fan RD$1500/1800, with air-con RD$2000/2500; P ❄ 🔊 ☀) This small, welcoming hotel is two blocks from the beach. There's a pleasant poolside courtyard, and the top-notch rooms have cable TV.

The simple but decent restaurant (mains RD$200 to RD$350) serves plenty

of seafood dishes, but check ahead to be sure it's open.

Hotelito Oasi Italiana   HOTEL $

(☑ 829-926-9796; www.lospatos.it; Hacia la Culebra 6, Los Patos; r weekend/weekday from RD$1300/1600; P ❄ 🔊 ☀) Set on a rise a few hundred meters from the beach, this Italian-owned hotel offers spacious but sometimes stuffy rooms, though the real star of the show is the food at the guest-only restaurant (mains RD$250 to RD$400). There are no gastro-gimmicks here – just simple, well-prepared pizza and pasta served up by the Veronese chef-owner.

Hotel Casablanca   B&B $$

(☑ 829-740-1230; www.hotelcasablanca.com.do; Km 10, Carretera Barahona-Paraíso; s/d/tr incl breakfast US$60/70/90; P 🔊) A Swiss-owned B&B, the Casablanca offers the coast's most personal experience in this price range. Six simple but comfortable rooms, with fan and either king-size bed or queen and twin, are set in a well-tended garden. Just 50m away a beautiful curving cliff provides a dramatic view of the Caribbean.

Stairs lead to a narrow beach that's mostly rocky but has some nice sandy spots. The breakfast is one of the best you'll have in the entire country. Ditto for dinner – even if you aren't staying here, consider phoning ahead in the morning to reserve a spot, as the owner is one of the peninsula's best cooks. Anything she does with *lambi* (conch) or octopus will knock you out!

Playazul   RESORT $$

(☑ 809-454-5375; www.playazulbarahona.com; Km 7, Carretera Barahona-Paraíso; s/d/tr incl breakfast RD$1900/2900/4000; P ❄ 🔊 ☀) This French-run, 21-room mini resort offers good value in its tastefully decorated rooms, most of which face the pool and sea and offer a bit of privacy on their palapa-roofed patios. The resort's built on a bluff with great ocean views, and you'll be dodging free-roaming peacocks along the concrete slabs leading down to a pretty (though rocky) private beach.

Breakfast is served in the French-influenced restaurant (mains RD$220 to RD$980), which is also popular with nonguests.

★ **Casa Bonita** HOTEL $$$

(☎809-476-5059; www.casabonitadr.com; Km 17, Carretera Barahona-Paraíso; r incl breakfast Dominicans/foreigners from US$217/280, 2-bedroom villas US$500; P❄@🖥🌊) 🚶 Formerly the vacation retreat of a Dominican family – and now run by siblings as a discerning boutique accommodation – Casa Bonita is set on a hill with stunning Caribbean and mountain views in all directions. It's easily the Southwest's most remarkable hotel. The 14 older rooms, a short walk from the stunning freshwater infinity pool, Jacuzzi and hammock-strung gardens, are modestly stylish.

Sixteen new rooms – all stunningly furnished and with private plunge pools – are on the way. The restaurant is steeped in sustainability, with everything coming from its own organic vegetable garden or sourced locally. Specialties include a remarkable baked artisanal cheese (RD$600) from Polo. You won't soon forget the Tanama spa, built into the forest, where you can be massaged on a bed *in the river*. A 10-platform canopy/zip-line tour and mountain-biking trails have been added, giving the hotel an adventure edge. It's refined, personal and close to perfect.

Piratas del Caribe HOTEL $$$

(☎809-243-1140; www.hotelpiratasdelcaribe.com; Arzobispo Nouel 1, Paraíso; r/ste incl breakfast from US$99/179; P❄🖥🌊) Passing through the gates of this boutique oasis in the heart of Paraíso feels like an epiphany. You'll be greeted with just five rooms, all with large private patios (four offering 2nd-floor sea views) that are idyllic spots to have breakfast. It's Spanish-French owned and Spanish-German managed, so there's a European feel to the place.

Its location near to the town's drinking square means it suffers from a fair bit of noise pollution.

🍴 Eating

Most hotels along the coastal highway have their own restaurants, which are generally excellent and open to nonguests. Further south, Paraíso is a dead-end for food, but nearby Los Patos boasts a few expat-run Italian spots that are both cheap and tasty.

Pizzeria California ITALIAN $$

(Carretera Principal de Los Patos, Los Patos; pasta RD$250-500, pizza RD$450-1100; ⊙10am-10pm) The simple pastas and pizza here outclass the plastic tables on which they're served. Prices include a cinematic sea view.

Restaurante Luz SEAFOOD $$

(Carretera Baharona-La Ciénaga; mains RD$250-600; ⊙8am-9pm) On the coastal road in the adjoining villages of Bahoruco and La Ciénaga, this good option has a tidy 2nd-floor dining room overlooking the shore and crashing waves, and a nice ocean breeze. It's old-school Dominican, serving mainly grilled fish and *lambi* (conch) on tables dressed with crocheted tablecloths.

VISITING CACHÓTE'S CLOUD FOREST

About 25km (1½ hours' drive) west of Paraíso on an impressively bad road – you ford the same river half a dozen times – sit the remote cabins of Ecoturismo Comunitario Cachóte (p212). At 1400m, the cabins are at the heart of a Caribbean cloud forest, where a low mist hangs heavy over the trees. It's here that seven rivers spring from the ground to supply the coastal towns below.

In order to protect the water supply, coffee growing was ended in the 1990s, and, with the help of Peace Corps volunteers, cabins have been constructed and short trails built in the regenerating forest.

The cabins are rustic but comfortable, and each has a large queen-size bed and a triple-decker dormitory-style bunk. Prices per person get cheaper the larger the group, and all-inclusive packages are also available. Transportation is not included in the price. Hiring a 4WD and driver can run upwards of RD$5000 for up to 10 people, but it's more economical (and less comfortable!) to catch the local transport for folks living in the mountains (RD$500 per person return) in La Ciénaga or Barahona.

Book at least two weeks in advance. Ecotour Barahona (p211) also runs a day trip to Cachóte (US$119), stopping at the small communities along the way, and can arrange overnight stays.

Hikes in the area offer great bird-watching (31 species of endemic bird have been identified here, including the Dominican parrot) and visits to a traditional mountain village. Guides can point out plants used in medicine and even in local Haitian Vodou.

BUYING LARIMAR

There are a few small shops selling handmade larimar jewelry along the coastal road. This rare stone, unique to the DR, is a great memento of the remarkable color of the sea along this coast. Stones range in price from RD$200 to RD$6000 depending on the size of the raw piece. Two of the best spots are the new **Museo Larimar** (☑ 829-470-6526; museolarimar@gmail.gob.com; Carretera Barahona-Paraíso, Bahoruco; ◷ 9am-5pm Mon-Fri, to 4pm Sat, to 3pm Sun), on the coastal highway, and the smaller, more rustic **Gift Shop Noelia** (☑ 829-816-2433; Carretera Baharona-La Ciénaga; ◷ 8am-7:30pm) along the beachside road that goes through Bahoruco and La Ciénaga (it's next door to Restaurant Luz and run by the same family).

The former is well signposted along the main highway. To reach the latter once you've entered Bahoruco on the main highway, pass the baseball 'diamond', cross a bridge and look for an unsigned road that goes to your left along the beach. Follow that road to the beach for about 800m, and you'll see Restaurant Luz on your left and Noelia on your right.

❶ Information

Paraíso is one of the few reliable places for internet access between Barahona and Pedernales, though the wi-fi is still slow. Try **Paradi.Net** (cnr Deligne & Jesiaca, Paraíso; per hour RD$25; ◷ 8am-7pm); no computers – bring your own device!

For medical emergencies, there's the **Clínica Amor el Prójimo** (☑ 809-243-1401; Arzobispo Merino & Arzobispo Nouel, Paraíso), or head to Enriquillo.

❶ Getting There & Away

The **guagua stop in Paraíso** (cnr Carretera Barahona-Paraiso & Enriqullio, Paraíso) is 1km uphill from the beach. From here you can get buses north to Barahona (RD$100, 45 minutes, every 20 minutes 6:30am to 5pm). Southbound *guaguas* to Enriquillo (RD$50, 20 minutes, every 20 minutes 8am to 7pm), Laguna Oviedo (RD$100, one hour, every 30 minutes 9am to 4pm) and Pedernales (RD$250, 1½ hours, every 30 minutes 8am to 5pm) pass by here as well. You can also flag down southbound *guaguas* where the highway intersects with the town's main road south of the village.

Santo Domingo–bound express buses from Pedernales pass through here around 5am (RD$350, four hours). If you want a guaranteed seat, you'll need to put your name on a list at the office of **Transportes Cuchi** (☑ 809-243-1279; Arzobispo Nouel 41, Paraíso) in town. (Most folks just catch a *guagua* to Barahona and move on to Santo Domingo from there.)

Larimar Mine

All larimar in the DR – and, indeed, the world – comes from this one mine. The mineral was discovered in 1974 by Miguel Méndez, who named it after his daughter, Larissa, adding *mar* (sea). Its scientific name is blue pectolite.

The mining operations are carried out not by a large company but by a collective of individual miners. You can visit the mines and even go down some of the shafts. A small group of basic shacks sells cut-rate larimar jewelry, and a few no-name eateries sell food and drink to the miners.

To get there, look for the turnoff in the hamlet of El Arroyo, 13km south of Barahona (3km north of Bahoruco). There's no specific sign, but there's a European Commission sign referring to the mine. It's an hour's drive on a rough road (4WD absolutely required). Ecotour Barahona (p211) offers a tour here (US$119).

Laguna Oviedo

Hypersalinic Laguna Oviedo, separated from the ocean by an 800m-wide strip of sand, is a popular bird-watching destination and home to a small colony of flamingos, which swells in size during winter. You're also likely to spot ibises, storks and spoonbills, especially in late spring and early summer. The enormous, one-ton *tinglar* (leatherback) turtle comes here from April to August to lay and hatch its eggs, but it can usually be seen only very late at night.

You can take a boat tour from the well-organized **visitor center** (◷ 6am-6pm). A three-hour tour costs RD$3500 per boat (for up to five people), including a Spanish-speaking guide. You'll also need to pay the national-park entrance fee (RD$100). The tour includes a brief visit to a small Taíno cave, plus a short walk across the dividing strip to the ocean and the beach, a beautiful yellow strand marred by an unbelievable quantity of plastic flotsam and jetsam – broken buckets, empty bleach bottles and the occasional light bulb. Wear shoes.

If you're especially interested in turtles, arrange a tour with **Francisco Saldaña Cuevas** (☑829-808-8924). **Saturnino Santana** (☑829-810-7989) and **Melvin González** (☑829-306-1686) are also good bets for guiding in basic English.

Ecotour Barahona (p211) offers a day trip here (US$119).

There are two viewing platforms – one on the shore behind the visitor center, another on the largest of the lake's 24 or so islands, where you'll also find lots of big iguanas. The lake is so salty that in the dry season you'll see crystallized salt mixed with sand on the islands.

There's a well-marked entrance to the park and lagoon off the coastal highway about 3km north of the town of Oviedo. Oviedo and Pedernales buses can drop you at the park entrance. The last bus back to Barahona passes by around 4pm.

Most visitors aren't around after sunset and lodging options are scarce. If you get stuck, stay in one of the five basic rooms at **Hotel Begó** (☑829-720-4934; Carretera Pedernales; s/d with fan RD$500/600, with air-con RD$700/1200; ⓟ❄), located just up the highway from the visitor's center.

Islas Beata & Alto Velo

Islas Beata and Alto Velo are end-of-the-world spots, difficult to access but seductive because of their remoteness. They're challenging for independent travelers to visit, and can be enjoyed more fully by taking a tour.

Isla Beata, once home to a prison for political dissidents under the dictatorship of Rafael Trujillo in the 1950s, is now jointly managed by the military and the Parque Nacional Jaragua. The small fishing village of Trudille sits directly on Playa Blanca, a 40km-long white-sand beach full of iguanas. The prison was destroyed after Trujillo's assassination, but you can still visit the ruins.

Isla Alto Velo is a smaller, uninhabited island 1½ hours south of Isla Beata. It's the southernmost point in the DR. Windswept and covered in bird droppings (from the swarms of seagulls that live there), the island has a lighthouse at its highest point (250m). It's a two-hour (5km) return walk to the lighthouse, with amazing views along the way. There's no beach, though.

The best way to visit the islands is to take a tour with Ecotour Barahona (p211), which offers a day trip to Isla Beata (US$140 per person, minimum six), with the option of adding a night in Las Cuevas, and trips to Alto Velo on a private basis.

Pedernales

POP 14,600

The coastal highway dead-ends in Pedernales, which is quite a friendly and pleasant place to spend an evening – as far as border towns go. Haiti can be reached via a residential street and border post about 1.5km from the center. Otherwise, the town is principally of interest to those who want to linger at Bahía de Las Águilas or in the national parks nearby, and those who want to take in the town's well-organized Haitian market on Monday and Friday.

Although it's rarely used by foreigners, this is by far the least chaotic and easiest-to-navigate border crossing. There's very little traffic and a minimal police and military presence.

🛏 Sleeping & Eating

Hostal Doña Chava HOTEL $
(☑809-524-0332; hostalchava069@gmail.com; PN Hudson 5; s/d/tr with air-con RD$1200/1450/1650; ⓟ❄@ⓦ) 🌿 A little traveler oasis, Hostal Doña Chava offers clean, simple rooms with tidy bathrooms and cable TV. There's a pleasant patio that doubles as a lush hangout area. It's often frequented by aid workers, NGO employees and travelers. Rates including breakfast are available for RD$300 or so extra per person.

King Crab SEAFOOD $$
(Dominguez 2; mains RD$350-575; ⊙9am-11pm; ⓦ) Top eats in Pedernales are had in this seafood-centric restaurant that does an immensely satisfying job with classic Dominican preparations: *a la vinagreta, a la criolla* etc (try the former with the tasty conch). It's friendly, the owner speaks English, and the kitchen procures a Colombian habanero hot sauce from the Haitian market that puts domestic hot sauces to shame.

Restaurante Ibiza DOMINICAN $$

(Calle 27 de Febrero 35; mains RD$275-575; ⊘8am-11pm; 🐾) Not all dishes are available at all times, but this friendly Dominican spot serves the gamut of Dominican *comida típica*, all manner of fish and seafood (crab, shrimp, conch), and a few pasta and meat options.

Drinking & Nightlife

Cafeteria Daniel BAR

(cnr Av Libertad & Pérez Rocha) Very simple but marginally friendly bar with ice-cold Presidentes.

Information

DANGERS & ANNOYANCES

Policía Nacional (📞809-524-0362; www. policianacional.gob.do; Pérez Rocha)

MONEY

Banco Popular ATM (Duarte) In the Supermercado Pedernales.

BanReservas ATM (cnr Calle 27 de Febrero & Av Duarte)

BanReservas ATM (Av Libertad) On the road into town.

Getting There & Away

Sinchomipe (📞809-524-0117; cnr Calles 27 de Febrero & Santo Domingo) *guaguas* for Santo Domingo (RD$500, seven hours) depart hourly from 6am to 4:40pm; its *guaguas* to Barahona (RD$250, two hours) depart every 30 minutes from 8am to 3pm.

A quick *motoconcho* ride (RD$50) along Calle 27 de Febrero leads to the Haitian border and the small village of Anse-à-Pitres, 1.5km from the intersection of Calle 27 de Febrero and Av Duarte near BanReservas.

ⓘ ENTRY & EXIT

If you are exiting the DR here, look for the **Dirección General de Migración** (www.migracion.gob.do; ⊘8am-6pm) inside the small blue customs (Dirección General de Aduanas) building on your left 75m before the border. If you have trouble finding it, look for uniformed CESFRONT border-patrol officers, who can point it out to you. The border is open from 8am to 6pm.

Parque Nacional Sierra de Bahoruco

Together with Parque Nacional Jaragua and Lago Enriquillo, **Parque Nacional Sierra de Bahoruco** (RD$100; ⊘8am-5pm) – located directly west of Barahona – forms the Jaragua-Bahoruco-Enriquillo Biosphere Reserve, the first Unesco Biosphere Reserve in the country.

This national park, replete with orchids and birds, covers 800 sq km of mostly mountainous terrain and is notable for the rich variety of vegetation that thrives in its many climates, ranging from lowland desert to cloud forest. Its valleys are home to vast areas of broad-leafed plants, which give way to healthy pine forests at higher elevations. Hoyo de Pelempito (p218), offering spectacular views, is in the southern part of the park.

Within the national park are 166 orchid species, representing 52% of the country's total. Around 32% of those species are endemic to the park. Flying about among the park's pine, cherry and mahogany trees are over 75 species of bird, including 28 of Hispaniola's 32 endemic species. The high mountain habitat is home to the La Selle thrush, white-winged warbler, Hispaniolan spindalis, emerald hummingbird, Hispaniolan trogon, broad-billed and narrow-billed tody, western chat-tanager and Hispaniolan parrot. At lower elevations you'll see white-necked crows, flat-billed vireos and the elusive bay-breasted cuckoo.

In the mountains the average temperature is 18°C, and annual rainfall is between 1000mm and 2500mm.

Hoyo de Pelempito GORGE

Part of Parque Nacional Sierra de Bahoruco (p211), the 'hole' at Pelempito is actually a deep gorge formed when the Península de Pedernales rammed into Hispaniola umpteen million years ago. The tourist office, perched at the edge of a cliff at 1450m, offers breathtaking views, north and east, of completely untouched national park. It has information (in Spanish) on the area's flora and fauna, and a number of short nature walks have small signs identifying the various plants.

Serious bird-watchers scoff that this is a poor bird-watching location, but for the casual tourist the views make it worth the drive.

THE POLO ORGANIC COFFEE FESTIVAL

Held in the small town of Polo, nestled on the southern slopes of the Sierra de Bahoruco, this **festival** (Festicafé; ☑809-682-3386; www.festicafe.blogspot.com; Polo; ☉Oct) sees local coffee growers celebrate the end of the coffee-harvesting season. There's a 'coffee parade,' lots of (decaffeinated) games for the kids, stands selling coffee and southwestern arts and crafts, and, in the evenings, live merengue and *bachata* (Dominican music).The organizers also lead hiking trips to remote coffee plantations in the mountains.

There's no real hotel in town, but during the festival the organizers can put you up in a spare room in someone's house – be sure to call several weeks ahead, as rooms fill up fast. Even if the festival's not on, various shops around town sell the coffee packaged to go – it's excellent if you take your caffeine seriously and worth the side trip if you have wheels.

From Barahona, drive 12km west to Cabral and look for the marked southbound turnoff in the middle of town (there's a flashing traffic light). From there it's about a 20km (30-minute) drive to Polo.

Pelempito sits on the southern side of the Sierra de Bahoruco. The turnoff is about 12km east of Pedernales. Shortly after the turnoff to Bahía de Las Águilas, you'll cross a small bridge. Immediately afterwards, turn left onto a dirt road that swings around to the paved road north to Hoyo de Pelempito (it ends up being same road that leads to Bahía de Las Águilas, but you'll go in the opposite direction). Around 13.5km later, you'll come to a ranger station. From here, the paved, highway-like road continues for 16km, and then turns into a rutted dirt track for the last 7km. Rains frequently destroy this part of the road, so you'll need a 4WD or a very high vehicle.

There are no formal lodgings in the park, but bird-watching camp **Villa Barrancoli** (☑809-686-0882; www.todytours.com; cabins per person incl dinner US$35) may be available. When the camp is not otherwise in use, independent travelers are welcome – be sure to email for a reservation several days in advance. It's run by **Tody Tours** p72.

You'll want a good 4WD, and some experience of driving one. To get to the park from Barahona, head to the town of Duvergé along the southern side of Lago Enriquillo. In town, look for the mural of the cuckoo and the parrot on the left-hand side a few blocks past the gas station. Turn left here and drive for about half an hour to reach Puerto Escondido. You'll see the park office on your right as you enter. Continue to a T-intersection, then turn left, following the sign to Rabo de Gato. Turn right

and cross the canal. At the next fork turn right again and follow the signs to Rabo de Gato until you come to the Villa Barrancoli campsite.

NORTH OF PEDERNALES

Lago Enriquillo & Isla Cabritos

Lago Enriquillo is the remains of an ancient channel that once united the Bahía de Neiba to the southeast (near Barahona) with Port-au-Prince (Haiti) to the west. The accumulation of sediments deposited by the Río Yaque del Sur at the river's mouth on the Bahía de Neiba, combined with the upward thrust of a continental plate, gradually isolated the lake. Today it's a 200-sq-km inland sea with no outlet, the island of Isla Cabritos marooned within it. In recent years the lake's recession has revealed a sunken forest that gives the whole region an even more otherworldly appeal.

◉ Sights

Parque Nacional Lago Enriquillo & Isla Cabritos   NATURE RESERVE
(☑809-880-0871;   Dominican/foreigner RD$30/50; ☉8am-6pm) This park comprises Lago Enriquillo, an enormous saltwater lake 40m below sea level, and Isla Cabritos, the island at its center. Varying from 40m to 4m below sea level, the island (closed to visitors indefinitely) supports a variety

of cacti and other desert flora. In summer, temperatures of 50°C have been recorded. The lake's residents include an estimated 200 American crocodiles, and Ricord's and rhinoceros iguanas, some more than 20 years old and considerably bigger than most house cats.

There's a blooming of cactus flowers from March to June, and June also sees a small swarm of butterflies. From December to April you'll see flamingos and egrets.

The park entrance and visitor center (Carretera Jimaní-Neiba; ⊙8am-5pm) are about 3km east of La Descubierta.

Las Caritas   CAVE
(The Masks; Carretera Jimaní-Neiba; RD$100) A short distance east of the park entrance, on the northern side of the highway, look for Las Caritas, a small rock formation with what are believed to be pre-Taíno petroglyphs. Bright-yellow handrails guide the short but somewhat tricky climb up the hillside – you'll need shoes or decent sandals. You'll be rewarded at the top with a close look at the pictures and a fine view of the lake. Very little is known about the meaning of the figures.

Note that much of the rock here is petrified coral, a remnant of the time the entire area was under the sea.

🕝 Tours

The local guide association (🕿829-265-8560; Carretera Jimaní-Neiba) offers boat tours of the park for RD$2500 for up to 10 people – expect a sore, wet bum (and salt stains). Boats leave at 7:30am, 8:30am and 12:30pm, but that doesn't seem set in stone. Be sure to call ahead – if a tour group has the boat reserved, you might be out of luck. Additionally, these guys don't seem to hang around – you must call them in advance. The boat will take you to the mouth of the Río de la Descubierta – where the most crocodiles (and, from December

to April, flamingos) are visible – but not Isla Cabritos, which has been closed for a few years and will remain so indefinitely to allow some of the negative environmental effects of tourism to subside. Due to the island's exclusion, the tour now lasts one hour (instead of two) and is considerably cheaper. Bring a hat and plenty of water.

Tours leave from the park visitor center.

🛏 Sleeping & Eating

Nearby La Descubierta (popular for its large swimming hole right in the middle of town) has food shacks but not much to feast on. Everyone who comes here prefers the excellent home-cooked meals at Hotel Iguana.

Hotel Iguana   GUESTHOUSE $
(🕿809-958-7636, 829-258-7823; Padre Billini 3, La Descubierta; r per person RD$400; 🅿) There's not much reason to spend the night here, but Hotel Iguana, on the main road west of the park, will do in a pinch. Rooms are small and simple but also clean and quiet, with private bathrooms and better-than-expected beds. Call ahead to arrange excellent home-cooked meals (RD$300 to RD$350).

🛈 Getting There & Away

You're better off driving yourself if you're coming this far north of Pedernales, but you can also grab a guagua from Barahona to Neiba, then switch there for La Descubierta (RD$100, one hour). Tell the driver to drop you at the visitor center.

Ecotour Barahona (p211) offers a popular day trip to Lago Enriquillo (US$139), including lunch in La Descubierta, a visit to Las Caritas and a quick dip in the Las Marias swimming hole in Neiba.

Jimaní

POP 10,034

This dusty border town is on the most direct route from Santo Domingo to Port-au-Prince, and is therefore the busiest of the four official border crossings. Dominicans from as far away as Santo Domingo come here for the daily market. There are also a few tiendas (stores) selling Haitian beer (Prestige) and rum (Rhum Barbancourt), both arguably better than their Dominican counterparts. The market is just past the

---

🛈 ENTRY & EXIT

For exit procedures, the Dirección General de Migración (🕿809-508-2555; www.migracion.gob.do; ⊙8am-6pm) is in the small green trailer, the last building on your left, just next to the border. Knock on the door.

BAHÍA DE LAS ÁGUILAS

Bahía de Las Águilas is the kind of beach that fantasies are made of. This pristine utopia is located in the extremely remote southwestern corner of the DR, but those who make it here are rewarded with 10km of nearly deserted shore, forming a gentle arc between two prominent capes. It's reachable mainly by boat from Playa Las Cuevas – the ride weaves in and out of rocky outcrops and past gorgeous cliffs with cacti clinging to their craggy edges and sea-diving pelicans nearby. Paradise found.

To get to the beach, take the paved (and signposted) road to Cabo Rojo, about 12km east of Pedernales. You'll reach the port of Cabo Rojo after 6km. Here things get a little trickier thanks to Hurricane Matthew, which mucked up the sand at Playa Cabo Rojo so that only 4WDs can now pass. If you're in a standard car, you'll need to follow the sign (turning left instead of continuing straight) to Cementos Andino Domincanos instead, a 2.2km detour around the back of Cabo Rojo. When you see the massive gated cement factory ahead, turn right again and follow the road around until you're back on the normal signed path on the other side of Playa Cabo Rojo.

Continue following the signs to Bahía de Las Águilas (the road turns nasty after Cabo Rojo, but it's manageable – slowly – in a normal car) to a tiny fishing community called Las Cuevas 6km after that. Note the namesake cave in the middle of the settlement – fishing folk used to live inside it. There are two ways to get to Las Águilas from here. One is to have a really good 4WD (and a driver with significant off-road experience) and attempt to drive there on a steep, pockmarked 2.6km track through the coastal cactus forest. The far more spectacular alternative is to take the scenic route by boat.

Fancy glamping in paradise? Professional-style camping tents at **Eco del Mar** (☑ 829-576-7740, 809-906-8170; www.ecodelmar.com.do; Playa Las Cuevas; camping per person incl breakfast RD$900-1500) are strewn about the sands of Playa Las Cuevas, and the nearby **Rancho Tipico** (☑ 809-753-8058; cuevasdelasaguilas@hotmail. com; Playa Las Cuevas; mains RD$250-750; ☺ 8am-7pm) restaurant offers tours. Prices are RD$2000 per boat for groups of one to five, RD$2500 per boat for six people, RD$375 per person for seven to 10 people, RD$350 per person for 11 to 15 people and RD$325 per person for 16 to 20 people. The owner rents snorkeling kits for RD$600.

You can also negotiate with the guides and boatmen who gather around the national-park ranger station just off the parking lot in Las Cuevas and mill about the small pier a few meters past Rancho Tipico. Snorkeling gear is included in their prices, but they don't always have it, so bring your own if you can. If you arrive here solo, the best option is to form a group to share the boat ride – easier at weekends, when it's busy.

With all choices you'll also need to pay the national-park entrance fee (RD$100) at the ranger station.

Ecotour Barahona (p211) runs a day trip here (US$119). It organizes all the logistics, picks you up and drops you off at your hotel, supplies lunch, and can show you where the best corals are to go snorkeling.

Dominican border post in no-man's-land. This area – including immigration posts and other border-control facilities – was prone to flooding from the alarmingly expanding shoreline of Etang Saumâtre (also known as Lake Azuéi), Lago Enriquillo's twin lake on the Haitian side, but this threat has subsided in recent years as the lake is now receding. Its southeastern end sits just 1km from the border post under normal conditions.

🛏 Sleeping & Eating

Hotel Taíno Frontera ⠀⠀⠀⠀⠀⠀HOTEL $
(☑ 809-248-3208; www.hoteltainofrontera.blogspot. com; Calle 19 de Marzo 4; r RD$1000; P ✳ 🛜) This hotel has suffered some serious decline since its promising opening a few years ago (apparently the owners are in Santo Domingo now). It's still the best of a bad crop of options, though, offering rooms decked out with nice furniture and big, modern bathrooms.

It's a straight 2.5km shot from the border next to the road to La Descubierta.

Hotel Jimaní   HOTEL $

(☎ 808-248-3619; Calle 19 de Marzo 2; r with/
without air-con RD$1000/800; [P] [❄] [📶] [❄]) A
vaguely institutional 10-room hotel on
the road to the border. Rooms are basic,
the coffee is free and there's a small rum
bar and pool. What more can you ask for
at a border hotel? All rooms are not created equal, so take a look at a few before
committing.

❶ Information

ENTRY & EXIT FORMALITIES

The border is open from 8am to 6pm. Immigration
formalities are handled by **Dirección General de
Migración** (www.migracion.gob.do; ⊙ 8am-6pm).

DANGERS & ANNOYANCES

If you run into any trouble, head to **Policía Nacional** (☎ 809-248-3043; www.policianacional.
gob.do; Calle 19 de Marzo 1).

MEDICAL SERVICES

Medical emergencies can be handled at the
new **Hospital General Melenciano Jimaní** (cnr
Duarte & Gaspar Polanco).

MONEY

There is a BanReservas ATM at the western
end of Calle 19 de Marzo, the main road
from Neiba just before it leaves town for the
Haitian border.

❶ Getting There & Away

Jimaní is served by *guaguas* from Santo
Domingo, which pass Baní, Neiba and La De-
scubierta along the way, and by those from
Barahona via Duvergé and the southern side of
Lago Enriquillo.

For Santo Domingo (RD$500, five hours,
every 30 minutes 1am to 5pm), **Asodumichoc-
oji** (☎ 809-248-3025; cnr Calles 27 de Febrero
& Duarte) has a proper terminal near the
bottom of the hill. (For La Descubierta, the fare
is RD$100 and the journey takes 30 minutes.)
Guaguas to Barahona (Calle 27 de Febrero)
(RD$300, 2½ hours, every 40 minutes 4am to
3pm) leave from a shady corner about 200m
up the hill, across from a small Chinese store.
Caribe Tours has a direct service from Santo
Domingo to Port-au-Prince, with a stop in
Jimaní.

Haiti

Best Places to Eat

→ Papaye (p234)

→ Lakou Lakay (p246)

→ L'Estaminet (p233)

→ Sesanet (p239)

→ Café 36 (p233)

Best Places to Sleep

→ El Rancho (p230)

→ Habitation des Lauriers (p244)

→ Royal Decamero Indigo Beach Resort & Spa (p241)

→ Abaka Bay Resort (p255)

→ Chic Chateau (p254)

Why Go?

The most common phrase in Haiti might surprise you. It's *'pa gen pwoblem,'* and it translates to 'no have problem.' Haitians use it in a dizzying array of contexts: responding to thank-yous, asserting well-being, filling awkward silences. Despite Haiti's well-documented struggles, exacerbated lately by natural disasters, proud Haitians use the phrase sincerely, conveying an uncanny ability to live in the moment and appreciate what they do have, which is quite a lot.

Tranquil beaches, tumbling waterfalls and pine-tree-capped mountains dot the varied and striking landscape, easily rivaling the natural beauty found anywhere else in the Caribbean. The world's only successful slave rebellion happened here, and the music, art and culture that came with it make Haiti entirely unique. As those who come to assist Haiti often learn, an encounter with the soul of this fascinating, beautiful country often benefits a traveler far more than one could ever hope to help it.

When to Go

→ November to March sees the hottest, driest days in most of the country (with the exception of some rain in the north); these months are also ideal for travel due to attractions such as the countrywide Fet Gédé Vodou festival (November), and Carnival in Port-au-Prince and Jacmel (February).

→ The shoulder season (April to June) sees quite a bit of rain in the south, as well as in Port-au-Prince.

→ Hurricane season stretches from August to October, and many days are humid with considerable rainfall. Still, travel is perfectly feasible if there are no big storms.

Haiti Highlights

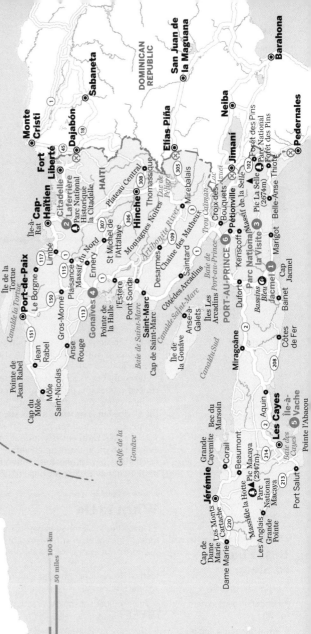

1 **Jacmel Carnival** (p252) Joining the country's most theatrical parade and street party, which celebrates Vodou, sex, death and revolution.

2 **Citadelle Laferrière** (p246) Discovering a mountain fortress above a ruined palace – a symbol of the world's first black republic.

3 **Parc National la Visite** (p238) Hiking past weird broken rock formations with views out to the Caribbean Sea.

4 **Vodou Ceremony** (p248) Plugging into Haiti's subconscious by attending a Souvenance or Soukri with drums, sung prayers and imagery.

5 **Île-à-Vache** (p255) Kicking back on this white-sand sliver of paradise, splashing around in turquoise shallows and feasting on fresh lobster.

6 **Port-au-Prince** (p225) Exploring the soul of the buzzing capital via thriving art, music and cultural scenes.

PORT-AU-PRINCE

POP 978,000

Let's admit the obvious: Port-au-Prince doesn't have the image of somewhere you'd visit for fun. A true city of the developing world, just a couple of hours by air from Miami, the city was preceded by a reputation for impoverished chaos even before the 2010 earthquake shook it to its foundations. Years later the recovery is still slow going, the gulf between rich and poor remains as wide as ever, and the streets remain cluttered with trash and rubble.

And yet the city remains one of the most vibrant and exciting in the Caribbean. Like a bottle of local *klerin* liquor, Port-au-Prince takes the raw energy of Haiti and distills it into one buzzing shot, and witnessing the self-sufficient spirit of its people might be the most life-affirming experience you have on your travels. It's a chaotic, exhilarating, compelling place, and if you're not careful, it may well capture your soul.

History

Port-au-Prince was founded in 1742 during the boom years of French rule, and was given its royal charter as capital seven years later. Its name is taken from the French ship *Prince,* which had first moored there in 1706.

During the slave revolution, Port-au-Prince was a key strategic target, although the slave armies saw it as a mulatto stronghold. When Haiti was reunited in 1820, Port-au-Prince regained its capital status and has dominated the country ever since.

The initial site of the city was confined to the modern Bel Air district. During the 19th century Port-au-Prince grew rapidly, its expansion only occasionally halted by the periodic fires that burnt it to the ground. Wealthier residents created the suburbs of Turgeau and Bois Verna, where many of Port-au-Prince's best 'gingerbread houses' are found. The poor found themselves pushed to the less salubrious marshy areas of La Saline in the north.

The US occupation of 1915 improved the city's infrastructure and there was further modernization in the 1940s, to celebrate the city's bicentennial. During the Duvalier period (1957–1986), anarchic growth was more the order of the day. The model development of Cité Simone (named for 'Papa Doc' Duvalier's wife) lapsed into slums, and was subsequently renamed Cité Soleil.

When the 2010 earthquake struck, a third of Haitians were living in Port-au-Prince and the uncontrolled expansion of poor-quality buildings had left the city egregiously imperiled. Vital infrastructures – as well as a number of notable buildings, including the National Palace and the Cathedral of Our Lady of Assumption – were damaged or destroyed. Today in Port-au-Prince, construction fences still surround some collapsed buildings and piles of rubble remain, and many thousands of people left homeless have been relocated to tent cities outside of the capital.

Rebuilding and clean-up efforts have been conducted at a snail's pace, and recent political instability in Port-au-Prince certainly hasn't helped. President Jovenel Moïse won an election in October of 2015, but violent protests and dubious voter fraud accusations by opponents prevented him from taking office for more than a year. (He was finally declared the winner after a second election, which was further delayed by Hurricane Matthew, in early 2017). Unemployment remains one of Port-au-Prince's greatest challenges, with much of the population trying to make ends meet selling goods and services in the street.

◉ Sights

Champs de Mars   PARK
(Map p228; Port-au-Prince) A series of parks split by wide boulevards that collectively make up the Place des Héros de l'Independence, with the former site of the demolished Palais National at its center, this broken heart of Port-au-Prince suffered greatly in the 2010 earthquake and is no longer a place to linger. A tall fence has been constructed around the parks, but intrepid travelers may ask permission from guards to enter; a guided city tour with Voyages Lumière (p226) also takes you in.

Several statues of Haiti's founding fathers dot Champs de Mars: Toussaint Louverture, Jean-Jacques Dessalines (on horseback), Alexander Pétion and Henri Christophe. The Marron Inconnu, the iconic statue of the unknown slave blowing a conch-shell trumpet, is also found here. It's odd to wander among the city's former main attraction, imagining it as a tent camp for thousands after the earthquake, and beholding it in its new state as a ghost town. Supposedly, once the last of the rubble is cleared and what's left of the place is thoroughly cleaned up, the site will reopen to the public.

HAITI PORT-AU-PRINCE

Musée du Panthéon National MUSEUM
(Mupanah; Map p228; ☑ 3417-4435; Pl du Champs de Mars, Port-au-Prince; US$5; ⊘ 8am-4pm Mon-Thu, to 5pm Fri, 10am-4pm Sat, noon-5pm Sun) This modern, mostly subterranean history museum, set below gardens, hosts a permanent exhibition chronicling Haiti's history, from the Taínos and slavery to independence and the modern era. Fascinating exhibits include exquisite Taíno pottery; the rusting anchor of Columbus' flagship, the *Santa María;* a copy of the fearsome Code Noir that governed the running of the plantations; the silver pistol with which Christophe took his own life; Emperor Faustin's ostentatious crown; and 'Papa Doc' Duvalier's trademark black hat and cane.

Architecturally, the design of the museum echoes the houses of Haiti's original Taíno inhabitants. This design ethos is also visible internally, whereby a conical central light well illuminates a gold monument that recreates the cannons and banners found on the national flag. The bodies of Haiti's founding fathers are interred below this tribute, and the names of other independence heroes are marked on surrounding walls.

★**Grand Rue Artists** ARTS CENTER
(Map p228; www.atis-rezistans.com; 622 Grand Rue, Port-au-Prince; ⊘ 8am-8pm) While most of Haiti's artists are represented in the rarefied air of Pétionville's galleries, a collective of sculptors and installation artists produces spectacular work in an unlikely setting, squeezed into the cinder-block houses among mechanics and body workshops on Grand Rue. In this Caribbean junkyard gone cyberpunk, the artists turn scrap and found objects into startling Vodou sculpture, exploring a heady mix of spirit, sex and politics, all grounded in the preoccupations of daily Haitian life.

André Eugène is the founder and elder member, sculpting in wood, plastic and car parts to produce his vision of the *lwa* (Vodou spirits). Dolls' heads and human skulls abound, alongside the earthy humor of highly phallic Gédé pieces. Jean Hérard Celeur, another of the artists, trained as a sculptor, and has done many of the largest pieces: life-sized statues of twisted wood and parts of car chassis, hubcaps, old shoes and a liberal application of twisted nails.

Local children are also involved in making art, through the spin-off organization Ti Moun Rezistans.

This hub of creativity is near Ciné Lido, set slightly back from the road. Look for the giant Gédé statue made from car parts and with a giant spring-loaded penis guarding the way. Just beyond this, Eugène's house-museum is surrounded by statues, with the motto 'E Pluribus Unum' ('out of many, one') hung over the door.

Barbancourt Rum Distillery DISTILLERY
(☑ 2816-7110, 2816-3090; info@barbancourtrhum. com; off Rte de Blanchard, Mouline; ⊘ hours vary) **FREE** North of the airport and tucked among sugarcane fields, this famous rum distillery welcomes visitors on Fridays from November to May. The enlightening tour highlights the history of rum in the region and includes an explanation of the aging and distillation processes. The company's beloved Estate Reserve rum, aged 15 years, is on-hand for sampling and purchase. Reserve ahead.

☞ Tours

The vast majority of people who visit Haiti will be better off exploring the country with a knowledgeable guide, as getting around on one's own, particularly without speaking French or Creole, is very challenging.

Voyages Lumière TOUR OPERATOR
(☑ 3607-1321; www.voyageslumiere.com/haiti) Long-standing and reputable tour agency owned by expat Jacqui Labrom, who has spent decades in Haiti and arranges excellent cultural, historic and adventure trips all over the country.

Pale Dlololo Creole Institute and Tours LANGUAGE
(☑ 4608-3366; www.paledlololoinstitute.com; 1 week US$200, private tutoring per hr US$20, online Skype classes per hr US$30) Owned by local tour guide Soulouque Anderson, a direct descendant of the Emperor Soulouque, this language school and tour company has guests speaking Creole on exotic Haitian getaways in no time. A one-week course includes 20 to 25 hours of small-group instruction and field trips to cultural and historical destinations in Port-au-Prince.

Soulouque travels to his students for Creole courses, and also arranges transport, lodgings and all-you-can-drink-Prestige for group trips he plans to charming mountain destinations and secluded, little-known beaches.

Tour Haiti TOURS
(Map p232; ☑2813-2223, 2812-2223; www.tourhai
ti.net; 38 Bis Rue Darguin, Pétionville; ⊙8am-4pm
Mon-Fri, to 1pm Sat) A reputable tour agency
that does custom trips all over Haiti.

🛏 Sleeping

There's one main decision to make when
choosing a bed for the night: whether to
stay downtown or above it all in Pétionville.
In both areas you'll find plentiful midrange
and high-end accommodations; budget options are tougher to come by.

Port-au-Prince

★St Joseph's Home
for Boys Guest House GUESTHOUSE $
(☑3892-6071; www.sjfamilyhaiti.org; Delmas 91, Delmas; r shared per person incl full board US$55; 🛜)
Rebuilt with great fortitude after the original
house collapsed in the earthquake, this home
for ex-street boys offers a fantastic Haitian experience. The tall, sleek new building includes
a rooftop lounge offering amazing city and
mountain views, and well-kept shared rooms
include bunk beds and pristine bathrooms.
Delicious meals are taken communally. The
guesthouse is opposite Radio Haiti-Inter.

Hôtel Oloffson HOTEL $$
(Map p228; ☑3810-4000; www.hoteloloffson.
com; 60 Ave Christophe, Port-au-Prince; r/ste
from US$100/200; 🅿❄@🛜🏊) If Haiti has
an iconic hotel, it's the Oloffson. Immortal-
ized as Hotel Trianon in Graham Greene's
The Comedians, the elegant gingerbread
building is one of the city's loveliest, further tricked out with paintings and Vodou
flags. There's a very sociable bar for your
rum punches, and every Thursday the house
band RAM plays until the small hours.
    Sadly, the Oloffson isn't beyond trading
on its name, and the rooms, fixtures and service don't quite live up to the tariff. Still, it
remains a lively scene.

Le Plaza HOTEL $$
(Map p228; ☑2814-6000, 2814-6027; www.plaza-
haiti.com; 10 Rue Capois, Port-au-Prince; r incl breakfast US$104; 🅿❄🛜🏊) The unobtrusive main
entrance opposite Champs de Mars (you'll
walk past it twice) hides the fact that this
is downtown's largest and most high-class
hotel. Rooms have balconies facing inward
to a central quadrangle and, while well fitted
out with all the mod-cons, are best described
as business-class bland. A second home for
visiting international media.

Park Hotel HOTEL $$
(Map p228; ☑2227-6814; 23 Rue Capois, Port-au-
Prince; s/d incl breakfast US$59/88; 🅿❄🛜🏊)
An old townhouse-hotel facing Champs de
Mars, the Park aspires to faded grandeur, but
ends up just feeling a bit sleepy. Rooms are
simple but well turned out, set around the
empty pool at the back or in the block alongside. The gardens are shady, adding to the
quiet atmosphere. Good value for downtown.

★Inn at Villa Bambou BOUTIQUE HOTEL $$$
(Map p228; ☑3702-1151; www.villabambouhaiti.
com; 1 Rue Marfranc, Pacot; r incl half board from
US$250; 🅿❄🛜🏊) A 1920s house rebuilt
since the earthquake, this is a truly gorgeous boutique hotel. There are half a dozen
rooms, each named for a herb and beautifully decorated. The quality of the food is a
particular selling point, along with the leafy
garden – and if there's a guesthouse offering
better views of Port-au-Prince, we'd like to
know about it.

Karibe Hôtel HOTEL $$$
(☑2812-7000; www.karibehotel.com; Juvenat 7,
Juvenat; s/d from US$174/191, ste from US$285;
🅿❄@🛜🏊) One of the fanciest big hotels
in Haiti, this hotel-cum-conference-center is
where you'll find the richest businessfolk, international consultants, and even presidents
putting their bills on expenses (Bill Clinton
and 'Baby Doc' Duvalier have been guests).
Rooms and service are impeccable, and the
posh rooftop bar gets packed on Friday nights.

Servhotel BUSINESS HOTEL $$$
(☑2812-7500; www.servotelhaiti.com; Route
de l'Aéroport; s/d incl breakfast US$142/164;
🅿❄🛜🏊) This modern hotel right near the
international airport is a good place to rest
post-arrival or pre-departure. Constructed
of paraseismic steel, Servotel went up just
after the earthquake to provide a place
where guests could feel safe, and the sleek
design, cushy rooms and friendly service
don't hurt either. The airport shuttle is free.

Marriott Port-au-Prince HOTEL $$$
(☑2814-2800; www.marriott.com; 147 Ave Jean-
Paul II, Turgeau; r US$187; 🅿❄🛜🏊) When the
Marriott opened near downtown Port-au-
Prince in 2014, it set a new bar (and price
point) for hotels in its class. The ceilings are
a bit higher, the counter tops glisten whiter,
and the staff is a touch more professional.
When expats grow weary of daily struggles
in Haiti, they make for the Marriott and its
potent rum sours.

Port-au-Prince

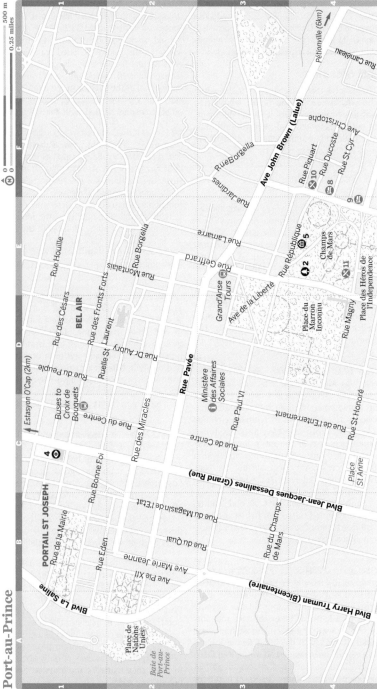

HAITI

Baie de
Port-au-
Prince

Place de
Nations
Uniès

PORTAIL ST JOSEPH

BEL AIR

Blvd La Saline

Rue de la Mairie

Rue Eden

Rue Bonne Foi

Ave Marie Jeanne

Ave Pie XII

Rue du Quai

Rue du Magasin de l'État

Rue du Champs
de Mars

Blvd Harry Truman (Bicentenaire)

Blvd Jean-Jacques Dessalines (Grand Rue)

Rue des Miracles

Rue du Centre

Rue de Centre

Ruelle St Laurent

Rue des Fronts Forts

Rue du Peuple

Rue des Césars

Rue Houille

Rue Montalais

Rue Borgella

Rue Dr Aubry

Rue Pavée

Estasyon O'Cap (2km)

Buses to
Croix de
Bouquets

Place
St Anne

Ministère
des Affaires
Sociales

Rue Paul VI

Rue de l'Entrerrement

Rue St Honoré

Grand'Anse
Tours

Ave de la Liberté

Place du
Marron
Inconnu

Place des Héros de
l'Independence

Rue Magny

Champs
de Mars

Rue Geffrard

Rue Lamarre

Rue République

Rue Borgella

Rue Jardines

Ave John Brown (Lalue)

Rue Borgella

Rue Piquart

Rue Ducoste

Rue St Cyr

Ave Christophe

Rue Cameau

Pétionville (6km)

2

4

5

8

9

10

11

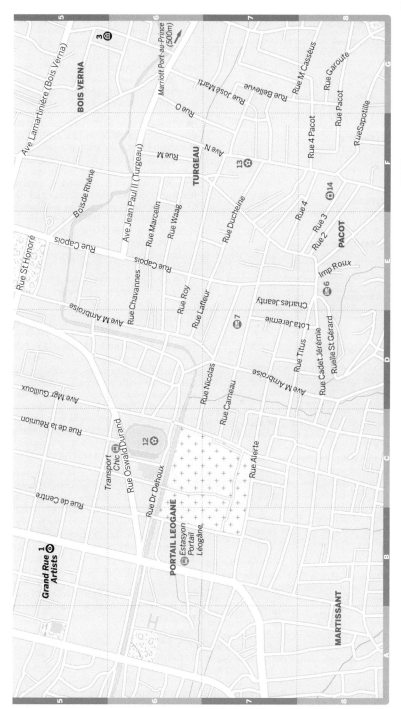

HAITI

BOIS VERNA

TURGEAU

PACOT

MARTISSANT

PORTAIL LEOGANE

Grand Rue 1 Artists

Ave Lamartinière (Bois Verna)

Marriott Port-au-Prince (500m)

Rue M Casséus
Rue Garoute
Rue Bellevue
Rue José Marti
Rue Pacot
Rue O
Rue 4 Pacot
Rue Sapotille
Rue N
Ave N
Rue M
Bois de Rhêne
Ave Jean Paul II (Turgeau)
Rue St-Honoré
Rue Capois
Rue Marcelin
Rue Waag
Rue Ducheine
Rue 4
Rue 3
Rue 2
Imp Roux
Rue Capois
Rue Chavannes
Rue Roy
Rue Lafleur
Charles Jeanty
Ave M Ambroise
Lota Jeremie
Rue Titus
Rue Cadet Jérémie
Ruelle St Gérard
Ave Mgr Guilloux
Rue de la Réunion
Rue de Centre
Transport Chic
Rue Oswald Durand
Rue Nicolas
Rue Cameau
Ave M Ambroise
Rue Dr Dehoux
Estasyon Portail Léogâne
Rue Alerte

3
13
14
6
7
12

Port-au-Prince

◎ **Top Sights**
  1 Grand Rue Artists B5

◎ **Sights**
  2 Champs de Mars....................................E4
  3 Maison Dufort..G5
  4 Marché de Fer C1
  5 Musée du Panthéon National E4

◎ **Sleeping**
  6 Hôtel Oloffson E8
  7 Inn at Villa Bambou D7
  8 Le Plaza..E4
  9 Park Hotel E4

◎ **Eating**
  10 Café Terrasse...F4
  11 Les Jardins du Mupanah.....................E4

◎ **Entertainment**
  Hôtel Oloffson ....(see 6)
  12 Sylvio Cator Stadium C6
  13 Yanvalou F7

◎ **Shopping**
  14 Comité Artisanat Haïtien F8

Pétionville

An influx of new hotels and improvements to old ones has made Pétionville more glamorous than ever.

Ibo Lele   HOTEL **$$**
(Map p232; ☑ 2940-8503, 2940-8502; Rue Ibo Lele, Pétionville; s/d incl breakfast US$88/121; ⓟ❋ 🛜 ☒) The Ibo Lele was a big player in the 1960s tourist-heavy years, and it remains a stunning, albeit quieter, option. Rooms still maintain quality, and the huge pool and delicious restaurant are draws for nonguests to use (if you have transportation to get here). There are also breathtaking views, as the hotel is perched high on the slopes above Pétionville proper.

★ **La Lorraine**   BOUTIQUE HOTEL **$$$**
(Map p232; ☑ 2816-8300; www.lalorrainehaiti. com; 36 Rue Clerveaux, Pétionville; r/ste incl breakfast $125/143; ⓟ❋ 🛜) This newly restored 1950s home-turned-boutique-hotel is perhaps the most relaxing stay in all of Pétionville. Apart from the high-arching door frames, each room is uniquely arranged with contemporary furnishings and fine Haitian art, with some rooms featuring balconies and hammocks and others containing mini gardens. The owner's

meticulous attention to detail is apparent at every turn; service is impeccable.

The beloved hotel restaurant, Café 36 (p233), features a daring and delicious international menu and backs up to an art gallery, with the chic space frequently hosting events, including a regular Monday-night trivia game. The rum sours here really do the trick.

★ **El Rancho**   BOUTIQUE HOTEL **$$$**
(Map p232; ☑ 2815-1000, in USA 212-219-7607; www.nh-hotels.com; 5 Rue Jose Martin, Pétionville; r from US$165; ⓟ❋ 🛜 ☒) In 2013 the Spanish hotel Chain NH took the reins at this upscale Pétionville hotel and casino, revamping the snazzy, fountain-lined entryway and the 72 modern rooms surrounding an alfresco restaurant and pool. The outdoor area is stunning, and often hosts nightlife events with performers including the likes of Sweet Micky, the famous *compas* singer and former president.

On Sundays, the hotel restaurant hosts a very popular boozy brunch buffet (US$30).

Hotel Kinam   HOTEL **$$$**
(Map p232; ☑ 2944-6000, 2955-6000; www.ho telkinam.com; Pl St-Pierre, Pétionville; r old/new incl breakfast US$80/169; ⓟ❋@🛜☒) This large, historic gingerbread hotel right in the center of Pétionville recently underwent a $26-million expansion, adding a shiny new wing. Rooms in the new section are well sized and modern, while vintage rooms are more basic and budget-friendly. The effect is charming, particularly on evenings when the pool is lit up and guests congregate for renowned rum punches.

Royal Oasis Hotel   HOTEL **$$$**
(Map p232; ☑ 2229-2030; www.royaloasishotel. com; 115 Ave Pan Américaine, Pétionville; s/d US$132/138; ⓟ❋🛜) The best part about this Occidental chain hotel is the sky-high rooftop, which is open to anybody and includes sweeping views of the city and mountains. The second best part is the ground-floor restaurant Haiku, which serves up fresh, high-quality sushi in a lovely setting. Rooms here don't stand out, and hot water is sometimes lacking. Breakfast is US$22.

✖ Eating

In Port-au-Prince the default menu is Creole, with a smattering of French and American dishes. If you're downtown, you should also consider the hotel restaurants – many restaurants close on Sundays and lots of places only open in daytime hours during the week (lunch is the big meal of the day). For a wider range of options, head up the hill to Pétionville.

Port-au-Prince

Les Jardins du Mupanah CARIBBEAN $$
(Map p228; ☑ 2811-6764; lesjardinsdumupanah@gmail.com; Rue Oswald Durand, Champs de Mars; sandwiches US$8, mains US$13; ⊙ 11am-4pm Mon-Sat) With floor-to-ceiling windows looking out over leafy gardens, Mupanah's cafe and restaurant offers one of the most elegant lunching experiences in the city. Artsy white imitation trees adorn the dining area, and well-dressed waitstaff provide top-notch service. The Caribbean-themed menu includes such items as Creole shrimp and a tropical chopped salad with grilled lobster and green papaya.

Café Terrasse INTERNATIONAL $$
(Map p228; ☑ 2944-1033, 3736-3132; 11 Rue Capois, Port-au-Prince; sandwiches US$5, mains US$12-24; ⊙ 10am-8pm Mon-Sat; 🛜) In downtown Port-au-Prince, Café Terrasse is a long-standing haunt for embassy and NGO types, serving up large, fresh salads, custom omelettes and hearty French fare. The eccentric owner has tastefully adorned the cafe with antique furnishings and old-timey art, and patio seating looks over Champs de Mars. Surprisingly cheap burgers and sandwiches are also available to go.

Pétionville

Caribbean Supermarket SUPERMARKET
(Map p232; ☑ 3113-3333; 51 Rue Métellus, Pétionville; ⊙ 8am-8pm Mon-Sat, to 2pm Sun; 🅿) This enormous supermarket in Pétionville is a one-stop shop for food. The glistening aisles includes imported and gourmet products and there's also an attached cafe serving some of the best coffee and sandwiches around. The caprese sandwich with prosciutto is particularly mind-blowing.

PORT-AU-PRINCE'S GINGERBREAD ARCHITECTURE

The vast majority of Haiti's unique gingerbread buildings are in Port-au-Prince, almost entirely the product of just three Parisian-trained Haitian architects: Georges Baussan, Léon Mathon and Joseph-Eugène Maximilien. There are a couple of hundred gingerbreads, and although many are now falling into disrepair, being expensive to maintain, they withstood the 2010 earthquake much better than many modern concrete buildings.

The key gingerbread characteristics are brick-filled timber frames adorned with lacy wooden latticework, high ceilings, and graceful balconies set over wide porches – all designed to take advantage of the prevailing winds. The old Palais National, built in 1881 (and blown up in 1912), was an early model, and its style was quickly appropriated as the height of bourgeois tropical living. The residential areas of Pacot and Bois Verna saw gingerbread houses reach their zenith during a 30-year spree that ended in 1925, when Port-au-Prince's mayor stifled the construction of wooden buildings due to their potential fire hazard.

Hôtel Oloffson (p227) is Port-au-Prince's most photographed example of gingerbread style. Built in 1887, it served as the family home to the son of President Sam, then as a military hospital during the American occupation, before being converted to a hotel in 1936. A walk along **Ave Lamartinière** in Bois Verna reveals a parade of great gingerbreads, while Lalue (Ave John Brown) has the famous **Le Manoir** at 126. Recently, the exquisite and refurbished gingerbread home **Maison Dufort** (Map p228; ☑ 2813-1694; studiofokal@fokal.org; Rue du Travail, Turgeau; ⊙ 9am-4pm) opened to the public.

There are few gingerbreads in Pétionville. The loveliest by far is the Hotel Kinam (p230), although this was built in the 1950s, long after the original gingerbread boom.

Preserving Haiti's Gingerbread Houses, a post-earthquake report by the World Monument Fund, is an excellent introduction to the challenges facing this unique aspect of Haitian heritage.

Pétionville

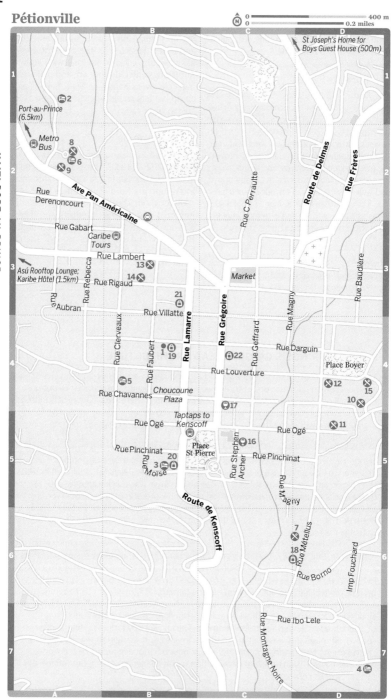

Pétionville

HAITI PORT-AU-PRINCE

Pâtisserie Marie Beliard BAKERY $
(Map p232; ☑ 2813-1516, 2813-1515; www.patisse-riemariebeliard.com; cnr Rues Faubert & Lambert, Pétionville; pastries US$1-5; ⊙ 6am-6:30pm Mon-Sat, to 1pm Sun) Hands down the best bakery in Pétionville, this bright French cafe is the perfect stop to fuel up before a city tour or a road trip. The *pain au chocolat* is divine, as are the cupcakes, croissants, sandwiches and pizzas. The quaint kitchen utensil wallpaper and inlaid brick give the place a homey vibe.

Harry's CREOLE $
(Map p232; ☑ 4404-9842; 97 Ave Pan Américaine, Pétionville; mains US$5-8; ⊙ 9am-late) A popular extended bar-resto, Harry's is always good value. Lunchtime offerings include Creole *plat du jour,* while pizzas seem more popular in the evening, when the place fills up with diners and drinkers. Live bands often perform, and hookah pipes are available.

★**Café 36** INTERNATIONAL $$
(Map p232; ☑ 2233-3636; www.cafe36haiti.com; La Lorraine Hotel, 36 Rue Clerveaux, Pétionville; tapas US$8-10, mains US$12-18; ⊙ 6am-10pm; P ⊗) Attached to the boutique hotel La Lorraine, this classy but chilled-out restaurant, event space and art gallery is the kind of place where you could eat for a week. And drink. And do trivia. And see some art. And eat more. Try Dominican dishes such as *kibbeh* and *acra,* or international salads and beef carpaccio.

★**L'Estaminet** BRASSERIE $$
(Map p232; ☑ 4824-1329, 4873-2163; 157 Rue Chavannes, Pétionville; mains $11-22; ⊙ 7:30am-11:30pm Mon-Sat, 4pm-11:30pm Sun) Recently opened by Jean Pierre, a whimsical, serial restaurateur who rarely ceases to delight, L'Estaminet is his best offering yet. The stylish brasserie boasts an extensive wine list along with cheese plates, homemade pastas and a tender beef filet drizzled with a decadent sauce of your choosing. Art and books abound, and jazz seems to emanate from the very walls.

Haiku ASIAN $$
(Map p232; ☑ 2813-0136, 2813-0151; Royal Oasis, 12 Rue Louverture, Pétionville; mains US$17, sashimi US$12, nigiri US$3; ⊙ 11am-10:30pm Mon-Sat, 2-10pm Sun; ⊗) Situated within the Royal Oasis hotel complex, this new Pan-Asian restaurant serves up the best sushi in Pétionville, along with an excellent Thai, Vietnamese, Chinese and Japanese dishes. The fresh fish is top quality, and the setting is lovely and modern, with indoor seating at a sleek white sushi bar and a covered outdoor terrace.

Magdoos MIDDLE EASTERN $$
(Map p232; ☑ 4823-2665, 3821-2121; www.facebook. com/magdoosresto; Rue Ogé, Pétionville; mains US$7-15) Wednesday nights this place gets packed with expats and NGO types looking to capitalize on special US$5 appetizers and drinks. But really, an evening at Magdoo's need not be justified by bargain offers. The popular Lebanese restaurant drips with style, and its menu includes incredible humus, tabbouleh and other Middle Eastern favorites.

Presse Café CAFE $$
(Map p232; ☑ 2816-9292; 28 Rue Rigaud, Pétionville; snacks US$3-7, mains US$10-13; ⊙ 7am-9pm Mon-Wed, to midnight Thu-Sat; ⊗) Presse Café is delightful for its casual bistro air. Decorated with old newspapers and photos of jazz heroes, it's a great place for a relaxed snack and drink, and even better for its lunchtime buffet (US$14). On Thursday and Friday evenings there's usually live music.

PÉTIONVILLE

The suburb of Pétionville was founded by President Boyer, although it never became the replacement capital he hoped for. Urban sprawl has long since incorporated Pétionville into greater Port-au-Prince, but the district has maintained its own identity as the center of gravity for Haiti's elite, and a hub for many businesses and banks.

Pl St-Pierre is the heart of Pétionville and the action flows downhill from here, with streets laid out in a grid (surprisingly well signed for Haiti). This is where you'll find the best restaurants, galleries and upmarket shops. At the bottom of the hill a chaotic street market spills along Rue Grégoire toward Rue de Delmas.

Quartier Latin　　　　INTERNATIONAL **$$**
(Map p232; ☑ 3445-3325; 10 Place Boyer, Pétionville; mains US$5-22; ⊙11am-midnight) An established mainstay, Quartier Latin throws French, Italian, Asian and Spanish dishes into the mix, and serves up generous and tasty dishes as a result. There are a few tables outside in the garden and a generally relaxed atmosphere. There's live jazz music on Friday and Saturday nights, too.

★**Papaye**　　　　　　FUSION **$$$**
(Map p232; ☑ 4656-2482; 48 Rue Métellus, Pétionville; mains US$18-28; ⊙noon-2:30pm & 7-11pm Tue-Fri, 1-11pm Sat) 'Caribbean fusion' aren't words you expect to see written in a Haitian restaurant review, but Papaye carries off the idea with considerable aplomb, taking Creole dishes and jamming them up against Asian, European and other culinary influences. Somehow it works, producing one of Haiti's classiest restaurants.

🍷 Drinking & Nightlife

This is a city that knows how to party. On any given night of the week, residents pour into their regular haunts to throw down, oftentimes until the wee hours. Mondays are trivia night at La Lorraine (p230), Tuesdays are karaoke night at Zest. Wednesdays are US$5 appetizers at Magdoos, Thursdays are rum sours at Yanvalou (p234), and so on.

Asú Rooftop Lounge　　　　LOUNGE
(☑ 2819-2222; Karibe Hôtel, Juvenat 7, Juvenat; ⊙5pm-1am Tue-Fri, 2pm-1am Sat) The place to see and be seen, Karibe Hôtel's rooftop lounge is unquestionably Pétionville's most fabulous venue to throw back a few cocktails – especially on Fridays. A fire pit, an elevated pool with colored lights, and crystal chandeliers all feed into the atmosphere of excess, and a permanently installed DJ booth starts pumping house music at around 10pm.

Tito's Tacos　　　　　　BAR
(Map p232; ☑ 4890-8226; www.facebook.com/titostacoht; Rue Stephen Archer, Pétionville; ⊙9am-10pm Mon-Thu, 24hr Fri & Sat) Yes, you can get decent Mexican food here, and whole chickens, and Prestige, of course. But the main reason to come is that after dinner, this relatively unremarkable outdoor taco joint occasionally hosts wild parties and raves, with Haiti's most talented DJs spinning. You might even need a password to get in.

Zest　　　　　　　　KARAOKE
(Map p232; ☑ 4429-4994; 81 Rue Gregoire, Pétionville; ⊙noon-late) A lounge in the center of Pétionville that attracts a young, rambunctious crowd. Tuesday night karaoke is very popular.

☆ Entertainment

Music is everywhere in Port-au-Prince, as many taptaps (minibuses) have their own mega sound-systems. For something more organized, look for billboards posted on major junctions advertising upcoming concerts.

Keep in mind that taxis can be extremely hard to find late at night.

Hôtel Oloffson　　　　LIVE MUSIC
(Map p228; ☑ 3810-4000; 60 Ave Christophe, Port-au-Prince) On Thursday nights, from about 11pm, crowds gather here to dance until the small hours to the Vodou rock and roots music of RAM – the hotel band. A potent blend of African rhythms, *rara* horns, guitar and keyboards, the shows have an irresistible atmosphere. At the center of everything is band leader (and Oloffson owner) Richard A Morse.

Yanvalou　　　　　　LIVE MUSIC
(Map p228; ☑ 4329-1347; yanvaloubar@gmail.com; Ave N, Pacot; ⊙11am-11pm) Thursday nights in Haiti's capital are synonymous with Yanvalou. At around 9pm, the artsy cafe and

bar begins to swell with the city's in-crowd, be they expats, UN workers, embassy types or local business owners. Some sip rum cocktails in the courtyard while others socialize by the bar. Eventually a Vodou folklore band shows up and everybody dances like crazy.

Sylvio Cator Stadium   SPECTATOR SPORT
(Map p228; cnr Rue Oswald Durand & Ave Mgr Guilloux, Port-au-Prince) Hosts Port-au-Prince's two biggest soccer clubs: Racing Club Haïtien and Violette Athletic.

🛍 Shopping

Port-au-Prince is Haiti's marketplace. For the most memorable of all souvenirs, head to the Grand Rue Artists (p225), a Vodou junkyard extraordinaire. Down the street at the Marché de Fer (Map p228; Grand Rue, Port-au-Prince; ⊙7am-5pm), you can also find everything from paintings and *artisanat* (handicrafts) to Vodou flags.

For the best metalwork, head straight to the source at the artisan's village at Croix des Bouquets (p239).

Papillon Enterprise   ARTS & CRAFTS
(Apparent Project; ☑3194-1267; www.papillon-enterprise.com; 14 Rue Cassagnol Prolongee, Delmas; ⊙9am-5pm, tours 9-11:30am & 1-3pm Mon-Fri) Formed in 2009, this top-notch organization has built a successful artisan's workshop staffed by Haitians who make art out of various recycled materials such as paper, glass bottles, aluminum and steel drums. A tour of the boutique features the jewelry and crafts, but also introduces visitors to hard-working Haitians with compelling stories of how they provide for their children.

The staff are incredibly warm and diligent, and the adorable open-air cafe across the street, which is also part of the project, serves up excellent smoothies and coffee.

Pascale Théard Creations   ARTS & CRAFTS
(www.pascaletheard.com; Rue Salomon 17, Delmas; ⊙9am-5pm) An upscale art boutique with everything from custom sandals to flatware to Vodou bracelets to chandeliers made out of recycled tires. The business owner, Pascale Théard, is a mover and shaker in the local art community.

Comité Artisanat Haïtien   ARTS & CRAFTS
(Map p228; ☑2946-5256; 29 Rue 3, Pacot; ⊙9am-4pm Mon-Fri, 10am-1pm Sat) Established in 1972, this craftmakers' cooperative has worked to promote Haitian crafts and provide fair wages for its artisans. The shop here is strong on well-priced metalwork, stone sculptures, lively painted boxes and miniature taptaps.

ℹ Information

DANGERS & ANNOYANCES
Police station (☑2257-2222, 2222-1117, emergency 114; Rue Légitime, Port-au-Prince; ⊙24hr)

INTERNET ACCESS
Most hotels have wi-fi, but internet cafes are plentiful and cost around HTG150 per hour.

MEDICAL SERVICES
Haiti Air Ambulanc (☑2812-8700, 2812-8701; www.haitiairambulance.org; Sonapi industrial Park)e Helicopter ambulances accessible to those who buy a membership (two weeks/one year US$25/36).
Hôpital Bernard Mevs (☑3771-8247; 2 Rue Solidarite; ⊙24hr) A reputable hospital with a

HAITI PORT-AU-PRINCE

ITINERARY: PORT-AU-PRINCE & AROUND

The gravitational pull of Port-au-Prince inevitably sucks in both Haitians and foreign visitors alike: this is the trip for art, culture and even a little bit of hiking.

The traditional place to start getting your bearings in Port-au-Prince is Champs de Mars, which was still under reconstruction at the time of research, but possible to tour. Next, visit the Vodou art cooperative of the Grand Rue Artists before strolling among the gingerbread houses of the Pacot and Bois Verna districts. The artists' village of Croix des Bouquets (p239) is a good half-day trip, but if you really want to get out of the city for some fresh air, head uphill to the Parc National la Visite (p238) for a day's hiking, which is best concluded with a stay in Furcy (p238), ideally in the tree house at O-zone the Village. Back in the city, eat in the restaurants in Pétionville, and swing by the many art galleries. Finally, be sure to time the close of your stay so you can call in at the Hôtel Oloffson on a Thursday night to see a RAM concert and to have one last rum punch.

ART GALLERIES

Impromptu open-air art galleries can be found throughout Port-au-Prince, with canvases hung on fences and walls, all quickly executed copies of the Haitian masters. Large congregations are found along the wall of the **Hotel Kinam** (p230) in Pétionville and along Delmas 33. Prices should never really top US$20.

If you're after something more specific, try the following galleries, where staff are knowledgeable and will be able to give more information about specific artists and schools of painting. Prices range from reasonable to astronomical, depending on the artist.

Galerie Marassa (Map p232; ☑4834-2328; galeriemarassakinam@gmail.com; Hotel Kinam, Pl St-Pierre, Pétionville; ⊗9am-6pm) Recently relocated to the Hotel Kinam, this specialized and exclusive gallery exhibits a good base of contemporary and naive Haitian artists, as well as metalwork, crafts and Vodou flags.

Galerie Monnin (Map p232; ☑3446-8464; www.galeriemonnin.com; 17 Rue Lamarre, Pétionville; ⊗10:30am-6pm Tue-Fri, to 4pm Sat) In a lovely building, this is Port-au-Prince's oldest private art gallery. Lots of landscapes, but with a wide selection of different Haitian schools.

Galerie Nader (Map p232; ☑3709-0222; 50 Rue Grégoire, Pétionville; ⊗10am-6pm Mon-Sat) A huge gallery over two floors, with a large collection of mostly moderns and some naives. The owner also has an extensive private collection housed as a museum at a separate address.

Galerie Flamboyant (Map p232; ☑3909-9231; 9 Rue Darguin, Pétionville; ⊗10am-6pm Mon-Sat) A small gallery with a nice mix of naives and moderns.

Expressions (Map p232; ☑3713-0522; 55 Rue Métellus, Pétionville; ⊗10am-6pm Mon-Sat) A well-regarded Pétionville gallery, with one of the largest and most wide-ranging selections of Haitian artists.

---

trauma center, run in partnership with Project Medishare.

Hôpital du Canapé Vert (☑2245-0984, 3767-8191; 83 Rte de Canapé Vert, Canapé Vert; ⊗24hr) Excellent doctors and emergency service, recommended by expats.

Hôpital François de Sales (☑2223-2110, 2222-0232; 53 Rue Charéron, Port-au-Prince; ⊗24hr) Decent hospital for visitors and expats.

St Luke Family Hôpital (www.stlukehaiti.org; Next to Petit Freres, Tabarre; ⊗8am-5pm) A leader in internal medicine; down the street from the US Embassy.

MONEY

ATMs are widespread. To beat bank queues and maximize safety, head to supermarkets to change money; most have dedicated counters and security guards.

Sogebank (Rte de Delmas 30, Delmas; ⊗8:30am-3:30pm Mon-Fri)

Scotiabank (cnr Rues Geffrard & Louverture, Pétionville; ⊗9am-4:30pm Mon-Fri)

Unibank (118 Rue Capois, downtown Port-au-Prince; ⊗8am-4:30pm Mon-Fri)

POST

Post Office in Pétionville (Pl St-Pierre; ⊗8am-4pm Mon-Sat)

Post Office in Port-au-Prince (Rue Bonne Foi, Port-au-Prince; ⊗8am-4pm Mon-Sat)

TOURIST INFORMATION

Ministry of Tourism (☑3816-3208; www.haititourisme.gouv.ht; 8 Rue Légitime, Port-au-Prince)

ℹ Getting There & Away

AIR

International flights depart from Aéroport International Toussaint Louverture (p265) and domestic flights from Aérogare Guy Malary (p265); the two are adjacent on the northern outskirts of Port-au-Prince.

Numerous international carriers offer services to and from Aéroport International Toussaint Louverture, including JetBlue Airways, American Airlines, Spirit Airlines, Air France, Air Antilles Express, Insel Air, InterCaribbean Airways, Delta, Cubana, Copa, Aeromexico and Avianca. Airlines running domestic flights to and from Aérogare Guy Malary include Sunrise Airways (p265) and Mission Aviation Fellowship (p265).

It takes around 30 to 45 minutes to reach the city center from the airports, depending on the time of day. Airport taxis are run by the Association des Chauffeurs Guides d'Haïti. Fares should be between US$25 and US$40. You can take a taptap to or from the airports (HTG10); they wait outside the terminals and drop passengers off at the corner of Blvd Toussaint Louverture and Rte de Delmas.

BUS

Port-au-Prince has no central bus station; instead, there is a series of mildly anarchic departure points according to the destination. Most buses and taptaps leave when full – exceptions are for Cap-Haïtien, Les Cayes and Jérémie, which you can buy seats for in advance.

For destinations in the south and southwest, go to **Estasyon Portail Léogâne** (Map p228; Grand Rue, Port-au-Prince). Taptaps go from here to Jacmel (US$4, three hours), Les Cayes (US$10, four hours) and all points in between. Large air-conditioned **Transport Chic** (Map p228; ☑ 3107-5423; Rue Oswald Durand, Port-au-Prince) buses leave for Les Cayes (US$10, five hours) from just north of Sylvio Cator Stadium.

For Jérémie (US$12, nine hours), **Grand'anse Tours** (Map p228; ☑ 3746-6777, 2811-8064; 81 Rue Geffard, Port-au-Prince) buses leave from north of the Champs de Mars, on the southwest corner of Rue Geffard and Rue Pavée.

For taptaps to Cap-Haïtien (US$12, seven hours) go to **Estasyon O'Cap** (Grand Rue, Port-au-Prince). Taptaps to Gonaïves (US$6, three hours) and the Côte des Arcadins also leave from here. Note that this area is considered unsafe, and that several companies run large, air-conditioned buses to Cap-Haïtien from near the airport, including **Sans Souci Tours** (☑ 2810-8000, 4861-5656; Blvd Toussaint Louverture).

Buses to Croix des Bouquets (US$1, 30 minutes) depart from the **junction of Rue des Fronts Forts and Rue du Centre** (Map p228). Taptaps to Kenscoff (HTG20, 30 minutes) leave from **Pl St-Pierre** (Map p232) in Pétionville.

For Santo Domingo in the DR, **Caribe Tours** (Map p232; ☑ 3785-1946; cnr Rues Clerveaux & Gabart, Pétionville), **Metro Bus** (Map p232; ☑ 2949-4545; www.metroserviciosturisticos. com; 69 Ave Panaméricaine, Pétionville) and **Capital Coach Line** (☑ 2942-1800, 2813-1880; www.capitalcoachline.com; Blvd 15 Octobre, Tabarre) all have daily departures at around 8am, arriving in Santo Domingo nine hours later, with tickets costing around US$40, plus border taxes.

CAR

Many of the car-rental companies are near the airport.

🛈 Getting Around

MOTO-TAXI

Useful for weaving through traffic jams, but certainly not the safest form of transport. They cost around HTG50 for short trips; haggle for longer distances.

TAPTAP

Port-au-Prince's taptaps run along set routes and are a very cheap and convenient way of getting around. The usual fare is HTG10 per trip. Routes are painted on the side of the cab doors. All stop on request. Shouting 'Merci chauffeur!' or banging on the side of the vehicle will stop the driver. Particularly useful routes include Lalue to Pétionville, Rte de Delmas to Pétionville and Canapé Vert to Pétionville. Routes running north–south include Aéroport to Nazon (crossing Delmas and Lalue), and Saline to Martissant (along Grand Rue).

TAXI

Collective taxis running set routes are called *publiques*, recognizable from the red ribbon hanging from the front mirror. Hail as you would a taptap. Fares are set at HTG25. If you get into an empty *publique* and the driver removes the red ribbon, he's treating you as a private fare and will charge accordingly – up to US$20 if you're going a long way. State clearly if you want to ride *collectif* and share the ride with others. *Publiques* don't tend to travel between Port-au-Prince and Pétionville, so hiring is often the best option. There is one radio-taxi firm, especially useful if you're out late: **Nick's Taxis** (Map p232; ☑ 3401-1021; 31 Ave Pan Américaine, Pétionville). It costs around HTG800 between downtown and Pétionville.

AROUND PORT-AU-PRINCE

Route de Kenscoff

The main road from Pétionville's Pl Saint-Pierre winds steeply uphill toward the cool of the mountains. After just a few kilometers you're in a rich agricultural area, with steep terraced fields clinging to the sides of the mountains, and the congestion of the city replaced by sweet cool breezes.

The crisp air of Kenscoff makes it a popular weekend destination for city dwellers – at 1980m above sea level, it's often referred to as the Switzerland of the Caribbean (there are even a few weird Caribbean–Alpine architectural hybrids). With sweeping views

HIKING IN PARC NATIONAL LA VISITE

The Massif de la Selle, a series of spectacular ridges still dotted with pine forest, divides Haiti's southeast. You can do one of Haiti's best hikes here – a day of trekking that takes you through the western section of the mountains, known as Park National la Visite, and toward the Caribbean. The route traverses four mountains and takes in some truly beautiful terrain, from wooded slopes to almost-rolling green hills, as well as offering lovely views out to sea. Once you reach Seguin you'll find the weird *kraze dan* (broken teeth) rock formations – great slabs of karst jutting up from the ground like so many discarded giant's dentures. A decent degree of fitness is required to do the trek, which usually takes six to eight hours. Take plenty of water and some food, as well as suitable clothing: the altitude ascends above 2000m in places, so there can be strong sun and wind, as well as unexpected rain and chill.

To reach the trailhead, take a taptap from Pétionville to Kenscoff, and change for Furcy. From there, you can walk to Carrefour Badyo, then bear left to follow the track to Seguin. By 4WD, it's a 15-minute drive to Badyo, and then you have to start hiking. Once at Seguin, you descend to Marigot (another couple of hours), and from here it is a taptap ride to Jacmel (US$1, one hour). At Furcy it's possible to hire horses with guides, but you'll have to pay for the return trip from Seguin.

In Seguin, about half-way between Furcy and Marigot, the **Auberge de la Visite** (✆ 2246-0166, 3851-0159; www.facebook.com/auberge.lavisite; Seguin; r per person incl full board US$80) is a delightful place to rest.

everywhere you look and the brooding cloud-capped backdrop of Massif de la Selle behind you, it's tailor-made for day walks. Coffee and vegetables are grown in great quantities here, giving Kenscoff an interesting local market.

◎ Sights

Fort Jacques　　　　　　　　FORT
(US$3; ☉ dawn-dusk) Fort Jacques was erected during the burst of fort-building following independence in 1804. It was built by Alexandre Pétion and named after Jean-Jacques Dessalines, and though it is well preserved, the structure was slightly damaged in the 2010 earthquake. The ruined **Fort Alexandre** is a short walk away. Overlooking Port-au-Prince, they both offer grand views. The forts are a 3km walk or moto ride from the main road – take the sharp uphill road opposite Fermathe's covered market.

🛏 Sleeping & Eating

Le Florville　　　　　　　HOTEL **$$**
(✆ 3289-9911; 19 Rte de Kenscoff, Kenscoff; r incl breakfast US$65-100; 🅿) A lovely hotel on the Route de Kenscoff, with just five tidy rooms and a winning restaurant. Eating here is a large part of the appeal, with the restaurant's high wooden ceiling, and a mix of French and Creole dishes (mains US$12 to US$30). The outside terrace offers spectacular views,

and Sunday brunch features a troubadour band. Don't miss the ribs.

L'Observatoire de Boutilliers　CREOLE **$$**
(✆ 3454-0118; Boutilliers; mains HTG800-1500; ☉ 10am-10pm) Just off the Route de Kenscoff, this romantic mountain-top restaurant offers the best possible view of Port-au-Prince and beyond. The food is pricey (but decent, with all the typical Haitian favorites, including goat, port and conch, as well as burgers and wings) and service can be slow, but just remember: the point is the glorious view.

🛈 Getting There & Away

Taptaps leave Pétionville throughout the day from the corner of Rue Gregoire and Villate, departing when full (HTG20, 30 minutes) and passing through Fermathe. Change at Kenscoff for Furcy.

Furcy

In the tiny, picturesque village of Furcy, pine trees abound and the whiff of fresh cilantro is in the air. There are stellar views of the Massif de la Selle, and locals rent out horses (around US$5 per hour) to take visitors to a waterfall above the village (it's 1½ hours on foot). Whatever your plans, don't forget some warm clothes – temperatures drop once the sun starts to dip.

🛏 Sleeping & Eating

★ O-zone the Village
HOSTEL $

(📞 4806-6929, 2811-5170; www.facebook.com/pg/
ozonethevillage; Pl Furcy; dm incl breakfast from
US$30, s/d incl breakfast US$40/60; 🅿 🛜) 🖊
Unique in Haiti, this inspired mountain
stay is encircled by pine trees and constructed with recycled materials – discarded
wire-holders as walkways, old tires as art,
reclaimed wood and liquor bottles as walls.
There's a rugged, artsy feel to the place, and
it features one of the only dorms around,
along with a rustic tree house guests enter
via a hanging bridge.

On windy nights there's a lot of creaking
up in the tree house, but on the bright side,
that is sometimes drowned out by raucous
events and late-night parties. A new kid-
zone aimed at attracting families includes a
trampoline and a playground, and there are
also some fantastic dirt bike trails and hikes
in the area.

Lodge
LODGE $$

(📞 3458-5968; s/d/tr incl breakfast
US$100/120/140; 🅿 ❄ @) Owned by the same
people responsible for Barbancourt rum,
this Canadian-style stone-and-wood cottage
sits high in the mountains, surrounded by
pine trees. Decorated with a keen eye for
detail, the cozy rooms meet every need, and
one even features a private sauna. The res-
taurant menu (mains US$15 to US$27) in-
cludes baby back ribs, lamb, and a powerful
rum sour.

★ Sesanet
GUESTHOUSE $$$

(Madame Helene's; 📞 3443-0443; s/d incl half
board US$125/150; 🅿) With just three rooms,
this charming, secluded guesthouse is usually full – and for good reason. The owner,
Madame Helene, has filled the place with
exquisite art and homey touches, and her
fusion meals (French and Middle Eastern;
dinner US$35) are something truly special.
Specialties here include tabbouleh, guinea
fowl and rabbit, all prepared with whatever
is fresh at the market.

The property features excellent mountain views and a children's play area, complete with a ping pong table. To get there,
head for Furcy and soon after the paved
road ends, look for the barber shop on the
right, and a road to the right shortly after.
Turn there and follow to a gate with a sign
for Sesanet.

ℹ Getting There & Away

To arrive in Furcy, rent a car or hop a moto-taxi
from Kenscoff (HTG150, 45 minutes) up the
mountain. Make a left at Kenscoff Commissariat,
then right after the fast-food places and continue
uphill. Those continuing on to Parc National la
Visite will eventually reach the entrance, from
where you can hike over the mountains to Seguin.

Plaine du Cul-de-Sac

The fertile Plaine du Cul-de-Sac runs east
from Port-au-Prince toward the Dominican
Republic. Once the heart of the colonial
plantation system, it's of interest to visitors
for its metalworking community in Croix des
Bouquets, and for its bird-watching sites at
Trou Caïman and Lac Azueï, which straddles
the border. To the northwest, the road leads
into Haiti's central district, where every year
the village of Ville-Bonheur becomes the focus of a major Vodou pilgrimage.

On your way out of Port-au-Prince, check
out **Parc Historique de la Canne à Sucre**,
a 19th–century sugar mill that now stands as
a museum, and hit **Le Daily Gourmet Cafe**
(📞 4868-9890; www.facebook.com/ledailycafe;
Rue Roumain, Tabarre; mains US$8-15; ⊙ 8am-
4pm Mon-Fri; 🖊) for a delicious buffet-style
lunch. From there on out it'll be standard
street food and bar-restos.

Croix des Bouquets

Almost sucked in by Port-au-Prince's inex-
orable urban sprawl, Croix des Bouquets is
the setting for one of Haiti's most vibrant art
scenes. Its Noialles district is home to the *boss
fè* (ironworkers), who hammer out incredible
decorative art from flattened oil drums and
vehicle bodies.

Croix des Bouquets' metal-art tradition
was begun by the blacksmith George Liautaud, who made decorative crosses for his
local cemetery. In the early 1950s, he was encouraged by the American De Witt Peters to
make freestanding figures and incorporate
Vodou iconography into his work. The result
was an explosion of creativity, with Liautaud
and his apprentices creating a uniquely Haitian form of art: carved iron. Although Liautaud died in 1991, his legacy is the thriving
community of artists in Croix des Bouquets.

Steel drums are the most common ma-
terial for the art. They're cut in half and
flattened, the designs chalked and then cut

out with chisels. Once free, the edges are smoothed and relief work beaten out. The smallest pieces are the size of a book; the most gloriously elaborate can stand over 2m. Popular designs include the Tree of Life, the Vodou *lwa* La Siren (the mermaid), birds, fish, musicians and angels.

Those interested in Vodou should consider a stop at the **Isidor Gallery** (☑ 3724-5617; jbjjgalleryisidor@yahoo.fr; Rte Noailles, Entree Remy 89; ☺ hours vary), where artist and Vodou priest Jean Baptiste Jean Joseph (JBJJ) performs ceremonies and sells tapestries, beaded pillow cases, flags and other spiritual works.

Buses from Port-au-Prince (US$1, 30 minutes) depart from the junction of Rue des Fronts Forts and Rue du Centre. Taptaps from Port-au-Prince (HTG20, 30 minutes) leave from Carrefour Fleuriot in Tabarre, on Boulevard du 15 Octobre. For Croix des Bouquets, get out at the police post, where the road splits left to Hinche and right to the DR. Take the right-hand road, then turn right at Notre Dame Depot. For Noailles, turn right at the Seventh Day Adventist Church, and follow the sound of hammered metal: the artist village is signed.

Ville-Bonheur & Saut d'Eau

An otherwise unprepossessing town, Ville-Bonheur and the nearby waterfall Saut d'Eau become the focus of Haiti's largest Vodou pilgrimage every July 16. True to form, elements of Catholicism and Vodou have been blended to produce something uniquely Haitian.

It all began in 1847 after someone's vision of the Virgin Mary in Ville-Bonheur drew pilgrims, who were convinced of the town's healing abilities. A church was built on the site of the vision, but local devotees soon spiritually associated it with Saut d'Eau, which was sacred to Erzuli Dantor – an lwa often represented as the Virgin. As a result, both Catholic and Vodou adherents now make the pilgrimage in huge numbers. A Catholic mass is said in the church and a statue of the Virgin Mary is carried around town. Vodou pilgrims then trek 4km to the Saut d'Eau waterfalls, a series of shallow pools overhung by greenery, where they bathe in the sacred waters, light candles and whisper requests to those lucky enough to become possessed by Erzuli herself.

During the pilgrimage, the area around the Church of Our Lady of Mt Carmel is turned into a huge campground for pilgrims. The few guesthouses are inundated. One great accommodations option is the bright and clean **Auberge du Mont Carmel** (☑ 4844-8935; r incl breakfast US$50; P ❄ ☎ ⛵), just before the waterfall. Alternatively, there are accommodations in nearby Mirebalais, including the **Mirage Hotel** (☑ 2210-0631; 11 Rte Départmentale; s/d incl breakfast US$85/105; P ❄ ☎ ⛵).

Buses and taptaps leave from Estasyon Mirebalais in Port-au-Prince (US$2.50, 2½ hours) between Grand Rue and the cathedral, at the junction of Rues des Fronts Forts and du Centre.

Côte des Arcadins

From Port-au-Prince, Rte National 1 stretches north along the coast before turning inland toward Gonaïves and Cap-Haïtien. The area is named for the Arcadins, a trio of sand cays surrounded by coral reefs in the channel between the mainland and Île de la Gonâve.

The first main town after leaving the capital is **Cabaret**, 'Papa Doc' Duvalier's modernist construction, built as a symbol of his regime and ruthlessly satirized for its pretensions in Graham Greene's novel, *The Comedians*. Just beyond is **Arcahaie**, where Dessalines created the Haitian flag from the rags of the Tricolor in 1804.

Past Arcahaie are the beach resorts, which offer safe, shallow swimming and snorkeling in clear water. On weekends they come alive with visitors from the capital; it's worthwhile booking accommodations in advance.

◉ Sights & Activities

The coast is good for diving, which can be arranged by **Pegasus** (☑ 3411-4775; nicole marcelinroy@yahoo.com; Kaliko Beach Club, Km 61, Rte National 1; ☺ 8am-5pm) or **Marina Blue Dive & Excursion Center** (☑ 2811-4043; www.marinabluehaiti.com; Moulin sur Mer, Km 77, Rte National 1; open water certification US$275, dives US$100; ☺ 8am-5pm).

Plage Publique   BEACH
(Km 62, Rte National 1) This beach is tucked in between the Kaliko Beach Club and Wahoo Bay, and offers basic facilities, food sellers, sound systems and booze – it's a great place to see regular Haitians at play.

Musée Colonial Ogier-Fombrun MUSEUM

(☑ 3701-1918; Km 77, Rte National 1; US$5; ☉ 10am-6pm) On the grounds of hotel Moulin sur Mer, Musée Colonial Ogier-Fombrun and its old sugar mill are housed in a restored colonial plantation. It's definitely worth a look: there's an eclectic collection of exhibits, from a reconstruction of a colonist's room to slave shackles. At the entrance is a framed letter from Toussaint Louverture to the present owner's ancestors. Official opening hours are optimistic – if you visit during the week, you'll probably have to ask for it to be opened.

🛏 Sleeping & Eating

Along this coast are the country's two all-inclusive resorts and a few other high-end stays. All of these hotels have their own restaurants, and guests stay put for all meals.

★ Royal Decameron
Indigo Beach Resort & Spa HOTEL $$

(☑ 2815-0111, in USA 855-308-0375; www.decameron.com; Km 78, Rte National 1; all-incl r from US$79; P ✳ @ ☎) On the site that once housed Club Med, this bright and breezy hotel was recently purchased by the international chain Decameron All-Inclusive Hotels & Resorts. The newly expanded hotel (400 rooms!) sits on a gorgeous white sand beach with dazzling turquoise water, and cocktails flow freely from four bars and three tasty restaurants.

Swimming pools, sports fields and water toys abound, and guests can expect encounters with tourists from abroad, local UN staff, NGO types and well-heeled Haitians escaping the grit of Port-au-Prince for a laid-back weekend on the beach.

Moulin sur Mer HOTEL $$

(☑ 3701-1918, 2813-1042; www.moulinsurmer.com; Km 77, Rte National 1; r incl breakfast from US$115; P ✳ @ ☎) Recently renovated, this large and charming complex has a nice selection of rooms, including 'gingerbreadized' rooms near the beach and more Spanish-hacienda style ones further back. There's the beachside Boucanier seafood restaurant, a new on-site scuba shop, and gardens full of sculptures. The Musée Colonial Ogier-Fombrun is a short (complimentary) golf-buggy ride away.

A day pass including use of the resort amenities and unlimited food costs US$40 per person.

Ouanga Bay HOTEL $$

(☑ 3407-2020; ouanga@hotmail.com; Km 63, Rte National 1; r incl breakfast from US$115; P ✳ ☎) This hotel is relatively small, but offers a cute and immaculate beach and breezy rooms. The palm-thatched restaurant extends over the water, making it an ideal place to graze on fresh seafood (mains US$12 to US$16) and watch the boats go by.

Kaliko Beach Club HOTEL $$$

(☑ 2940-4609; www.kalikobeachclub.com; Km 61, Rte National 1; all-incl r US$159-175; P ✳ @ ☎) This modern resort recently became the country's second all-inclusive property, and features a series of linked pools and cute octagonal bungalows set amid shady grounds. There are various water-sports options along the pebbly beach, and also Pegasus, a dive shop that can arrange certification and charters. Day passes to the resort include food and cost US$45.

HAITI CÔTE DES ARCADINS

ITINERARY: IN THE NORTH

This itinerary encapsulates the best of Haiti's historical and cultural heritage, with stops for beach time and plenty of adventure.

From Port-au-Prince (p224), catch an internal flight up to **Cap-Haïtien** (p242). Take a full day to make a tour out to the **Citadelle** (p245) and the ruined palace of Sans Souci – and call ahead to book a dance performance and feast at Lakou Lakay in **Milot**. Back in Cap-Haïtien, explore the architecture of the old city and grab a few Prestiges at one of the popular waterfront resto-bars. The following day, take a vehicle and boat-taxi to the uninhabited **Île-à-Rat** (p247), where you can snorkel and dine on fresh crab purchased from a local fisherman, then spend a restful night in Labadie or Cormier Plage. If you're after some real adventure, rent a 4WD vehicle and drive out to Boukan Guinguette in Môle Saint-Nicolas (p247) for beach camping and kitesurfing. On the way back to Port-au-Prince, pause in **Cabaret** to stock up on *tablet pistach* (local peanut brittle) before an indulgent stay at Haiti's premier all-inclusive hotel, the Royal Decameron.

ⓘ Getting There & Away

Hotels offer private transport to and from the area, and intrepid travelers can catch a bus or taptap to Gonaïves or Saint-Marc (US$3.50, 2½ hours) from Estacyon O'Cap beside the Shell petrol station, at the corner of Blvds Jean-Jacques Dessalines (Grand Rue) and La Saline in Port-au-Prince; advise the driver where you want to be dropped. Return transportation is a lot more hit and miss; you're reliant on flagging down passing buses.

NORTHERN HAITI

If you're interested in how Haiti came to be as it is today, head north. From Columbus' first landfall on Hispaniola to the key events of the slave revolution, it all happened here.

Base yourself at Cap-Haïtien, Haiti's second city. Once one of the richest colonial ports in the world, it's the ideal jumping-off point to visit the magnificent Citadelle Laferrière, a true castle perched high on a mountain, with the ruined palace of Sans Souci sitting below, looking like something from a tropical Hollywood adventure movie. There are plenty of smaller forts along the coast, while Île de la Tortue evokes memories of the golden age of piracy.

The crashing Atlantic waves give the north some spectacular coastline and great beaches. Cormier Plage and Plage Labadie are a stone's throw from Cap-Haïtien and are ideal places to unwind.

Cap-Haïtien

POP 171,000

Haiti's second city feels a world away from the throng and hustle of Port-au-Prince. During the French colonial era it was the richest city in the Caribbean, and even if that grandeur has long since faded, the city still maintains a relaxed atmosphere, and the old port architecture of high shop fronts and balconies makes it a pleasant place to wander. Most people refer to the city simply as 'Cap,' or 'O'Kap' in the high-lilting local Creole accent of its residents.

There isn't too much to do in Cap-Haïtien beyond enjoy the atmosphere, but it's an ideal place to base yourself to enjoy the nearby attractions, including the Citadelle Laferrière and the beaches around Plage Labadie.

Despite its rich history, there is still a lot of poverty in Cap-Haïtien. On the way to the city center from the airport, travelers pass

one of the country's most dilapidated and trash-covered slums.

History

Razed five times (by both humans and nature), Cap-Haïtien has a turbulent history, inextricably linked to Haiti's colonial past and independence struggle.

Cap-François was founded in 1670 by Bertrand d'Ogeron, who recognized the superb natural harbor of its location. As St-Domingue grew as a colony, the port was renamed Cap Français, and sat at the hub of the booming plantation economy. Sugar, coffee, cotton and indigo – and the slave trade – swelled its coffers. By the middle of the century, Cap Français was so rich it was dubbed the 'Paris of the Antilles.'

This Paris was destined to burn in revolutionary fire. Early rebellions had been squashed here, the inhabitants witnessing the executions of Mackandal in 1758; Vincent Ogé, who had agitated for mulattoes' rights, in 1790; and the Vodou rebellion of Boukman a year later. The city was sacked when revolution erupted, and completely torched in 1803 on the orders of Toussaint Louverture, lest it fall into the hands of Napoleon's invading army. At Vertières on its outskirts, Dessalines won the final victory that brought independence, and renamed the city Cap-Haïtien as a symbol of freedom. When Christophe became king he renamed it Cap Henri, but the name reverted on his death in 1820.

Leveled by an earthquake in 1842, Cap-Haïtien has arguably never fully recovered. Its central political and economic role has been long-ceded to Port-au-Prince, and even today the road to the capital is very poorly maintained.

Cap-Haïtien

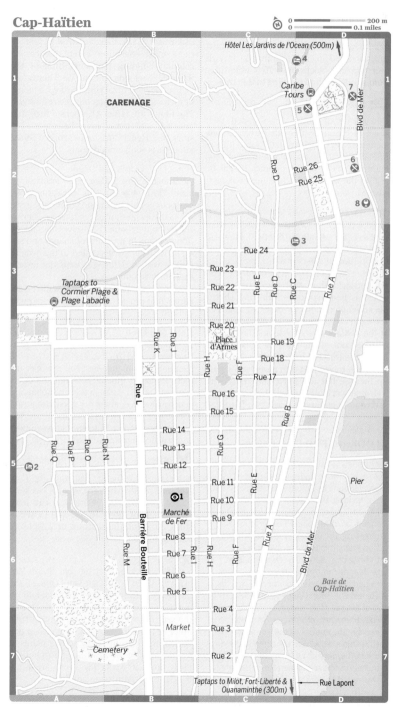

0 — 200 m
0 — 0.1 miles

Hôtel Les Jardins de l'Ocean (500m)

4

Caribe Tours

7

5

Blvd de Mer

6

8

CARENAGE

Rue D

Rue 26

Rue 25

Rue 24

3

Rue 23

Rue 22

Rue E

Rue D

Rue C

Rue A

Rue 21

Taptaps to Cormier Plage & Plage Labadie

Rue 20

Place d'Armes

Rue 19

Rue K

Rue J

Rue H

Rue F

Rue 18

Rue 17

Rue 16

Rue L

Rue 15

Rue B

Rue 14

Rue 13

Rue G

Rue 12

Rue 11

Rue E

Pier

Rue Q

Rue P

Rue O

Rue N

Rue 10

2

Marché de Fer

Rue 9

1

Rue 8

Rue A

Rue 7

Rue I

Rue H

Rue F

Rue 6

Blvd de Mer

Rue 5

Baie de Cap-Haïtien

Rue M

Barriére Bouteille

Rue 4

Market

Rue 3

Cemetery

Rue 2

Taptaps to Milot, Fort-Liberté & Ouanaminthe (300m)

Rue Lapont

⊙ Sights

Marché de Fer MARKET

(Iron Market; Rues 9 & 11, btwn Rues I & K; ⊙ dawn-dusk Mon-Sat) The city's iron market sprawls over four city blocks and offers everything from vegetables and clothing to toiletries.

🛏 Sleeping

Hotels in Cap-Haïtien have upped their game in recent years, with budget accommodations becoming available for as little as US$50 a night, alongside a number of good midrange and high-end options. Rooms fill fast on the weekend, so advance booking is advised.

★ **Habitation des Lauriers** HOTEL $$

(☑ 3836-0885; www.habitationdeslauriers.com; cnr Rues 13 & Q; s/d with fan US$50/60, with air-con US$90/120; [P][@][🛜][🏊]) The best value option in Cap-Haïtien offers striking views of the city from its mountaintop perch on the western outskirts, along with top-notch service, delicious home-cooked meals, and charming accommodations for every budget. A diverse mix of guests socialize on the veranda of the historic main house and around the dipping pool, surrounded by lush gardens, hummingbirds and butterflies.

Budget travelers stay in more basic rooms up the hill, but the warm owners provide welcome cocktails, affordable excursions and complimentary airport pick-up to all.

LOOKING FOR COLUMBUS

Although La Isabela and Santo Domingo in the DR are celebrated for their connections to Columbus, the site of La Navidad, the first attempted Spanish settlement in the Americas, remains unknown and a holy grail for archaeologists. It's believed to be close to Cap-Haïtien in Haiti, probably built on the site of a Taíno village around Bord de Mer de Limonade. If you don't want to dedicate yourself to archaeology, the easiest way to get close to La Navidad is at **Musée du Panthéon National** (p225) in Port-au-Prince, where you can see the anchor of the *Santa María* (the ship's wood was salvaged to build the settlement of La Navidad in 1492, but burnt to ashes when the settlement was razed in 1493)..

★ **Hostellerie du Roi Christophe** HOTEL $$

(☑ 3687-8915; hotroi24b@hotmail.com; cnr Rues 24 & B; s/d US$105/126; [P][✳][🛜][🏊]) Cap-Haïtien's most charming hotel, this French colonial building has something of the Spanish hacienda about it. There's an elegant, leafy central courtyard with plenty of rocking chairs, and a terrace restaurant. The rooms are large, with period furniture and art, and many have balconies. The story that Henri Christophe worked in the kitchens is sadly apocryphal.

Hôtel Les Jardins de l'Ocean HOTEL $$

(☑ 2260-1655; Rue 9, Carenage; r incl breakfast from US$90; [P][✳][🛜]) This expat-run hotel seems to ramble up the side of the hill it sits on, so there's no shortage of terraces offering sea views (the rooms themselves have none). Rooms come in a variety of shapes and sizes, all individually decorated to the owner's taste – we loved the one with the mosaic wall of broken mirror.

The owners have recently installed solar panels that provide 24-7 electricity – a rarity in Haiti.

Hôtel Mont Joli HOTEL $$$

(☑ 4802-7181; www.hotelmontjoli.com; Rue B, Carenage; s/d US$120/150; [P][✳][🛜][🏊]) On a hill overlooking Cap, the Mont Joli was once the place to go. It's quieter now, but still offers some of the best views in the city. Rooms are generously sized, there's a good restaurant with bar, and a terrace to chill out on. The pool is the deepest in town, but was under construction during our visit.

🍴 Eating

NGO workers living just outside Cap-Haïtien salivate when speaking of weekend forays into the city, where they can feast on a variety of international and local cuisines, either on the seafront or within upscale hotels.

★ **Lakay** CREOLE $$

(☑ 3188-6881; info@lakayhaiti.com; Blvd de Mer; mains US$8-19; ⊙ 11:30am-3am) One of the busiest restaurants in Cap-Haïtien, and it's not hard to see why. There are tables facing the seafront where you can enjoy a drink, otherwise step inside to eat under bamboo thatch and load up on generous plates of Creole food or pizza. The atmosphere is lively, and at weekends there are often bands (US$4 admission applies).

Cap Deli
DELI $$

(☑ 2817-2807; www.facebook.com/pg/capdelihaiti; cnr Rues 29 & A; mains US$6-15; ☺ 10am-10pm Mon-Sat, 1-10pm Sun; 🐟) Step off Cap-Haitien's sun-baked streets into this cool, tidy new eatery, the closest thing you'll get to new American food in Haiti. The menu, posted in bubbly handwriting on a giant chalkboard, includes gourmet burgers, cheese steak sandwiches and even teriyaki wings. Service is excellent, and the decor, with its inlaid brick and glossy wood-paneling, is definitely up to snuff.

Kokiyaj
INTERNATIONAL $$

(☑ 3227-4821; Blvd de Mer; mains US$8-15; ☺ 8am-midnight) A self-styled sports bar above a supermarket sounds unimpressive, but this restaurant is actually a cut above. As well as Creole classics there are some good continental and American mains, pleasant service and a well-stocked bar.

Drinking & Nightlife

Cap-Haitien offers a lively nightlife scene, with most of the bar-restos concentrated along the Blvd de Mer and emanating *compas* music late into the night. For a more local scene, head to the Place d'Armes, where Haitians gather to watch football matches over Prestige and popcorn.

Boukanye
BAR

(☑ 4453-6344, 3354-6344; www.facebook.com/Boukanye; Blvd de Mer, btwn Rues 24 & 25; ☺ 7am-late Mon-Sat, 6pm-late Sun) This new, waterfront bar and restaurant is pirate-themed, with a spectacular view of Cap-Haitien's bay. It's an ideal spot for a Haitian spaghetti breakfast or a burger (mains US$10 to US$25), but even better for the late-night parties fueled by *compas* music and the potent Buccaneer punch.

ⓘ Information

There's a useful cluster of banks and ATMs along Rue 10-11A.

Banque de L'Union Haïtienne (BUH; cnr Rues 11 & D; ☺ 8:30am-5pm Mon-Fri, to noon Sat)

Hôpital Justinien (☑ 2262-0512, 3356-2004; cnr Rues 17 & Q; ☺ 24hr) Cap-Haitien's main hospital.

Post office (cnr Rues 17 & A)

Rien Que Pour Vos Yeux (82 Rue 17) Well-stocked pharmacy.

Sogebank (cnr Rues 11 & A) Has an ATM open during banking hours.

Unibank (cnr Rues 11 & A)

ⓘ Getting There & Away

AIR

Hugo Chavez International Airport (p265) is 3.5km east of the city (US$7/1.50 by taxi/moto-taxi). Sunrise Airways (p265) has four daily flights to Port-au-Prince (from US$55, 30 minutes).

International airlines servicing this airport include American Airlines, InterCaribbean Airways and IBC Airways. International flights are currently limited, but are scheduled for expansion.

BUS

Bus company **San-Souci Tours** (☑ 4855-7071; Rte National 1) has routes between Cap-Haïtien and Port-au-Prince (HTG900, seven hours), departing at 6am, 7am, 9am, 11am and 2pm and dropping off in Port-au-Prince near the airport. Buses travel via Gonaïves (three hours), with a stop for the bathroom or a quick bite.

Caribe Tours (cnr Rues 29 & A) runs a direct coach service to Santiago (US$20, four hours) and Santo Domingo (US$30, nine hours) in the DR.

For Cormier Plage and Plage Labadie, taptaps leave from the corner of Rues 21 and Q in Cap-Haïtien (HTG25, 30 and 40 minutes respectively). For the Citadelle, taptaps to Milot (HTG20, one hour) leave from Stasyon Pon near the main bridge. Transportation to Fort-Liberté (HTG30, two hours) and Ouanaminthe (HTG60, three hours) also leaves from here.

ⓘ Getting Around

Publiques (collective taxis) have a set rate of HTG15 anywhere in town – a few are signed as taxis, otherwise look for the red ribbon hanging from the front windshield mirror. Taptaps (HTG5) run two main routes along Rue L (also called Rue Espanole) from the corner of Rue 15 to the Barrière Bouteille, and along Rue A from the corner of Rue 10 to the airport.

Moto-taxis here should never cost more than HTG50.

The Citadelle & Sans Souci

The awe-inspiring mountain fortress of Citadelle Laferrière is a short distance from Cap-Haïtien on the edge of the small town of Milot. Built to repel the French, it's a monument to the vision of Henri Christophe, who oversaw its construction. A visit here is an essential part of any trip to Haiti, and actually takes in two sites – the Unesco World Heritage–listed fortress itself and the palace of Sans Souci.

The site entrance is at the far end of Milot, next to the huge dome of Église Immaculée Conception de Milot, facing the ruins of Sans Souci. Opposite this is the ticket office. There are many guides and horse wranglers here. One that comes recommended is Maurice Etienne, who also runs the Lakou Lakay cultural center. A reasonable fee for a good guide is US$20 to US$30, plus the hire of a horse.

◎ Sights

★ Citadelle Laferrière — FORTRESS

(Citadelle Henry; Sans Souci & Citadelle US$25; ⊙7am-4pm) Haitians call the Citadelle the eighth wonder of the world and, having slogged to the 900m summit of Pic Laferrière (or ridden horseback for US$15), you'll likely agree. This battleship-like fortress gives commanding views in every direction. Completed in 1820, it employed 20,000 people and held supplies to sustain the royal family and a garrison of 5000 troops for a year. With 4m-thick walls up to 40m high, the fortress was impenetrable, although its cannons were never fired in combat.

Inside the ramparts the fort has a series of drawbridges and blind corners to fox attackers. These lead through a gallery containing the first of several cannon batteries. The Citadelle contains over 160 cannons, mostly captured in battle from the English, the Spanish and the French. Throughout the fort are huge piles of cannonballs – once 50,000 in total – though many have been stolen.

At the heart of the fort is the central courtyard, with its officers' quarters. Christophe himself was buried here after his suicide – his grave is under a huge boulder that forms part of the mountain. On the level above is the whitewashed tomb of his son Prince Noel.

It's possible to spend a couple of hours exploring the site, which constantly reveals hidden passages, halls and new views from its ramparts. Sheer drops protect the Citadelle from every angle except its rear, where you can look south to Site des Ramiers, a huddle of four small forts protecting its exposed flank.

In the main courtyard there's a small shop that sells postcards and drinks, and the finest public bathroom in all the land was recently installed inside the fort. A new museum and gallery are also set to open in the fort's interior in 2017.

Sans Souci — HISTORIC SITE

(US$15; ⊙7am-4pm) Built as a rival to Versailles in France, Henri Christophe's palace of Sans Souci has lain abandoned since it was ruined in the 1842 earthquake. The years of neglect have left an elegantly crumbling edifice, slightly alien against its tropical backdrop. Finished in 1813, Sans Souci was more than just a palace, designed to be the administrative capital of Christophe's kingdom, housing a hospital, a school and a printing press, as well as an army barracks.

The palace is approached by a grand staircase once flanked by bronze lions. You enter a series of rooms – the throne room, banqueting halls and private apartments. Although the walls are now bare brick they would have been hung with rich tapestries and paintings, all designed to show that although Haitians had once been slaves, they were now a cultured nation. The palace originally had three stories and huge French picture windows. From his apartments, Christophe maintained correspondences with the Czar of Russia and the English abolitionist William Wilberforce.

Behind the palace are the remains of the King's and Queen's ornamental gardens. To one side are the remains of the hospital and, opposite, the old barracks, home to the Royal Corps of freed slaves from Dahomey.

Just above the palace site, a roughly paved road winds up the mountain to the Citadelle.

🛏 Sleeping & Eating

Lakou Lakay — CREOLE $$

(☑3614-2485; Milot; meals US$10-20) This cultural community center is a longstanding institution that has seen better economic times but remains delightful. Run by guide Maurice Etienne and his family, the center welcomes visitors with traditional dancing, folk songs and drumming, along with a huge Creole feast (reservations required). Rooms for visitors (US$50 per person) are very simple.

❶ Getting There & Away

Taptaps from Cap-Haïtien (HTG20, one hour) drop you a short walk from Sans Souci. Don't plan to return too late, as transport dries up by late afternoon.

MÔLE SAINT-NICOLAS

The prosperous town of Môle Saint-Nicolas is well worth a visit, not only because it is the site where Christopher Columbus first made landfall on Hispaniola in 1492, but also because it is the first town in Haiti to offer its residents 24-hour electricity, mostly generated by solar power. The grid was set up in 2016 by Sigora, a San Francisco–based technology company, and as you stroll through the town you'll see solar panels atop street lights, homes and businesses.

The surrounding areas are also brimming with historical sites, including caves with Taíno paintings, forts, a powder warehouse and a watchtower. The biggest attraction, though, is the kitesurfing camp.

The incredibly far-flung (closer to Cuba than Cap-Haitien) **Boukan Guinguette** (☑ 3845-2874; www.boukanguinguette.com; Plage de Raisinier, Môle Saint-Nicolas; beach camping HTG850, s/d incl breakfast US$65/80; P 🛜) is more than worth the drive; this is the first and only kitesurfing school in Haiti. The well-constructed bungalows and restaurant-bar are top-notch and will be attractive even to travelers who prefer to remain spectators. Tents for beach camping are also available and highly recommended.

The camp is perched seaside, on a cerulean bay that receives year-long downwind gusts of up to 25 knots, allowing kitesurfers to gear up fairly often, particularly in December through April and July through September. Lessons are available (US$50/250 per one hour/six hours), as is equipment rental (US$50/70 per two hours/half-day).

Other activities available include hiking to nearby historical sites, kayaking, snorkeling, sailing and motor boating, with plans to introduce scuba diving in the near future.

Reaching the area is a lengthy and difficult process. The cheapest way is to take a taptap from Port-au-Prince (HTG600, 10 hours) which leave four times a week from the roundabout in front of the industrial park Sonapi, about 1km west of the airport. Taptaps leave at 6am on Tuesday, Wednesday, Friday and Saturday and return from Môle Saint-Nicolas on Sunday, Monday, Wednesday and Thursday between 8pm and 10pm, arriving the following day. Travelers can also rent a 4WD vehicle to drive from Port-au-Prince or Cap-Haïtien, passing through Gonaïves and Anse Rouge. (Another more arduous but stunningly beautiful coastal route goes from Cap through Port Marigot, Anse à Foleur and Port-de-Paix.) A final option is to charter a flight through **Mission Aviation Fellowship** (p265).

❶ Getting Around

Horses are the normal method of reaching the Citadelle. Each generally comes with two handlers (both of whom expect a tip of around US$5 on top of the US$15 rental price). From Sans Souci to the Citadelle takes a couple of hours by horse, although a 4WD can make it to a parking area 30 minutes' walk short of the top.

Beaches West of Cap-Haïtien

A rough road leads west from Cap-Haïtien, winding along the northwest coast of the cape toward some of the loveliest coastal scenery in the country, where green hills tumble straight into the Atlantic, the two divided by sheer cliffs or stretches of delicious golden sand.

The road hits the north coast of the cape near **Cormier Plage**, the picture of a Caribbean beach and resort, where white breakers roll in to shore and rum punches are the order of the day. Further around the point is **Plage Labadie** (also called Coco Plage), a walled-off peninsula rented by Royal Caribbean Lines for its cruise-ship guests, who arrive three or four times a week.

From Plage Labadie, *bateaux-taxis* (water taxis) ferry passengers to the beaches further west and to the uninhabited island of Île-à-Rat, one of the country's most beautiful places to spend a day sunning, snorkeling, and feasting on freshly caught seafood.

❂ Sights

Île-à-Rat   ISLAND
(Amiga Island) Your basic paradise, this tiny island offers fine white sand, a lush core of trees, and cool turquoise water where snorkelers encounter sunken, centuries-old cannons and anchors. Christopher Columbus is said to have stopped by, and indigenous artifacts have also been unearthed

here. Boat taxi captains in Labadee charge around US$40 for a round-trip excursion and US$15 for cooking up a lunch of lobster, fish, octopus or enormous crabs purchased from local fishermen. Load a cooler of rum and Prestige.

🛏 Sleeping & Eating

Norm's Place
GUESTHOUSE $$

(📞 3917-3155, in USA 954-822-7548; normsplacelabadee@yahoo.com; Labadie; s/d incl breakfast US$60/80; 🅿 ❄ @ 🌐 🐕) For HTG100, a *bateau-taxi* hop between Plage Belli and Labadie village (ask for 'Kay Norm') drops guests at this charming guesthouse built from a restored French fort. Large rooms have four-poster beds with mosquito nets, there's a garden for lounging, and a warm welcome throughout. Meals are home-cooked on request.

Cormier Plage Resort
HOTEL $$$

(📞 3702-0210; www.cormierhaiti.com; Rte de Labadie; s/d incl half board US$120/198; 🅿 ❄ @ 🌐) Dotted amid palm trees, this pleasant resort has 34 big and airy rooms looking out to sea, and is meters from the gently shelving golden beach. The property also features an aviary, a spa and a tennis court, and the restaurant is great for seafood (though service can be slow).

❶ Getting There & Away

Taptaps going to Cormier Plage and Plage Labadie (both HTG25, 30 and 40 minutes respectively) leave from the corner of Rues 21 and Q in Cap-Haïtien. Taptaps terminate (and leave from) the western side of Plage Labadie by the boundary fence of the Royal Caribbean Lines compound, from where brightly painted *bateaux-taxis* (HTG50) ferry passengers to Plage Belli and Labadie village.

Gonaïves

POP 105,000

Gonaïves may not be much to look at, but travelers keen on understanding Haiti's history will definitely appreciate a stop in this large, political city. On January 1, 1804, it was here that Dessalines signed the act of Haitian independence, creating the world's first black republic. Just outside Gonaïves, the town of Dessalines is surrounded by historic, mountain-top forts that defended the city throughout the 1800s. In more recent years, Gonaïves has

also played a revolutionary role – riots here in 1985 showed the writing was on the wall for 'Baby Doc' Duvalier, while the rebel capture of Gonaïves in 2004 marked the beginning of the end for Aristide.

Souvenance and Soukri – the two biggest Vodou festivals in the country – are two more reasons travelers might opt to base themselves in the area. People from all over Haiti congregate near Gonaïves to take part in these marathon ceremonies.

✨ Festivals & Events

Souvenance
RELIGIOUS

Souvenance begins on Good Friday, and continues for a week, to the constant sound of *rara* music. Prayers are offered to sacred tamarind trees, initiates bathe in a sacred pond and bulls are sacrificed for the Vodou spirits.

Singing and dancing go on every night, along with rituals said to have originated in the maroon camps, the secret communities of runaway slaves. Ogou, the warrior *lwa* who helped inspire slaves during the revolution, is particularly revered.

Souvenance is held off the road between Gonaïves and Cap-Haïtien, about 20km north of Gonaïves. The festival has become well enough known that the place where it is held is also now known as Souvenance. As you leave Gonaïves on the road to Cap-Haïtien, you cross a bridge over the Rivière Laquinte and take the first right after the bridge to Souvenance. There are small houses for rent around the temple, but many of the participants just sleep on straw mats in the shade.

Soukri
RELIGIOUS

Soukri is a ritual dedicated to the Kongo *lwa*. The service is divided into two branches: 'the father of all Kongo' takes place on January 6, and the second, larger ceremony, 'the mother of all Kongo,' occurs on August 14. The rituals last two weeks each, a true test of endurance. Many of the celebrations are similar to those in Souvenance.

To visit these ceremonies, introduce yourself to the head of the Vodou society when you arrive.

Soukri takes place off the road from Gonaïves to Cap-Haïtien. Continue northward past the turnoff for Souvenance until you reach a small market town, Les Poteaux. A turn opposite the Saint-Marc

Catholic Church leads to the *lakou* (a collection of dwellings) known as Soukri.

🛏 Sleeping

Hotel Admiral Killick   HOTEL $$

(☑ 3498-2605; 90 Av des Dattes; r incl breakfast from US$80; 🅿 ❄ 🛜 🏊) The best hotel option in Gonaïves has decent rooms and a swim-up bar. It's also named for an admiral in the Haitian navy who blew up his own ship, killing himself and several of his men, rather than surrendering the ship to the Germans during the 1902 Fermin rebellion.

❶ Getting There & Away

Gonaïves is roughly halfway between Port-au-Prince and Cap-Haïtien, with a bus station east of the main square next to the National gas station on the main highway. There are buses to Port-au-Prince (HTG350, 3½ hours) and Cap-Haïtien (HTG250, three hours).

SOUTHERN HAITI

Haiti's south is about taking it easy. Pulling out of Port-au-Prince, the urban hustle is soon replaced by a relaxed air as you head toward the Caribbean.

Of the southern coast, Jacmel is the gem: an old port full of pretty buildings, handicrafts shops and a fabulous new beach boardwalk. East of there, Kabic Beach offers a more bohemian, back-to-nature vibe.

Further west, things are sleepier and still recovering from Hurricane Matthew. The gritty town of Les Cayes is an embarkation point for the gorgeous beaches of Île-à-Vache, a bit sandier after the storm but otherwise intact, while the formerly idyllic Port Salut still looks rough and lacks electricity.

The southern 'claw' is bisected by the Massif de la Hotte, and after a spectacular mountain crossing the road terminates at Jérémie, the sometime City of Poets, which has recovered steadily from the storm with the help of countless NGOs.

Jacmel
POP 48,000

Sheltered by a beautiful 3km-wide bay, the old port of Jacmel is one of the most friendly and tranquil towns in Haiti, and host to one of its best Carnivals.

Part of Jacmel's charm lies in its old town center, full of mansions and merchants' warehouses with a late-Victorian grace poking out from behind the wrought-iron balconies and peeling facades. Although some of Jacmel's historic buildings were damaged in the earthquake, the town has received a facelift in recent years, including the installation of innumerable urban mosaics, the most impressive of which are displayed along the new, kilometer-long beachfront boardwalk, Promenade du Bord de Mer, which buzzes with activity day and night.

The town is also the undisputed handicrafts capital of Haiti, with dozens of workshops producing hand-painted souvenirs, from wall decorations to elaborate papier-mâché masks produced for the Carnival festivities.

History

Founded by the French in 1698 near the old Arawak settlement of Yaquimel, Jacmel was a prosperous port by the close of the 18th century, when the town's large mulatto population began demanding equality with the whites. Soon after, under André Rigaud's leadership, Jacmel became an important battleground in the Haitian independence struggle, and remained a center of mulatto power when Haiti split into two following Dessaline's death in 1806.

Jacmel also played a small role in the South American independence movement. Pétion hosted Simón Bolívar here in 1816 when the Venezuelan revolutionary leader was assembling his army, hospitality that Bolívar returned by abolishing slavery after liberating his country.

By the middle of the 19th century, Jacmel was serving as a major Caribbean loading point for steamships bound for Europe. It was the first town in the Caribbean to have telephones and potable water, and (in 1895) the first to have electric light. The town center was destroyed by a huge fire in 1896 and then rebuilt in the unique Creole architectural style that remains to this day. Port trade, however, began to dry up following WWII and the Duvalier era, leaving the annual Carnival the one time of year when Jacmel truly recreates its glory days.

⊙ Sights

★ Bassin Bleu   WATERFALL

(HTG100; ⊙ dawn-dusk) Bassin Bleu is tucked into the mountains 12km northwest of Jacmel, a series of three cobalt-blue pools linked

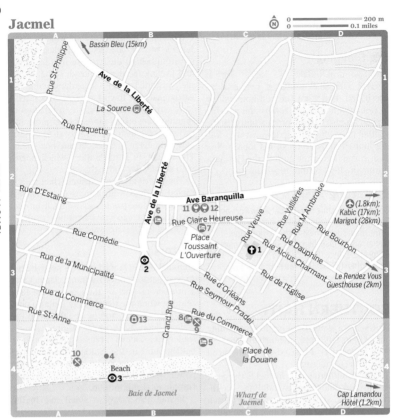

by waterfalls that make up one of the prettiest swimming holes in Haiti. Experience Jacmel will take you to a hamlet close to the pools via moto-taxi, then a local guide will escort you down an uneven path (at one point you'll rappel down a rock face) to the gorgeous pools, where kids often jump from high rocks.

The three pools are Bassin Clair, Bassin Bleu and Bassin Palmiste. Bassin Clair is the most beautiful of the three, deep into the mountain at the bottom of the waterfall, sheltered and surrounded by smooth rocks draped with maidenhair and creeper ferns. You're sadly less likely to see the nymphs that, according to legend, live in the grottoes, although be warned that they've been known to grab divers attempting to discover the true depth of the pool.

While the mineral-rich waters of Bassin Bleu are a delight at most times of the year, they turn a muddy brown after heavy rainfall.

Promenade du Bord de Mer WATERFRONT

(Jacmel waterfront) Installed by ex-President Michel Martelly, this new, kilometer-long boardwalk along Jacmel's waterfront has become popular with locals as a spot to socialize and relax. It's magical to go for a stroll over the boardwalks elaborate mosaic tile designs, checking out local jewelry and paintings, trying street food or interacting with passers-by. Time your visit to coincide with illuminated street lights.

Cayes Jacmel VILLAGE

From the small fishing village of Cayes Jacmel, about 14km east of Jacmel, the beach spreads a further 3km to Plage Ti Mouillage, a gorgeous white-sand beach fringed with coconut palms, plus a bar for drinks and seafood. Cayes Jacmel is known for making the rocking chairs seen throughout Haiti.

Cyvadier Plage BEACH

This beach is about 10km east of Jacmel, down a small track leading from the Cayes Jacmel road. The beach is part of the Cyvadier Plage Hôtel. The small half-moon-shaped cove flanked by rocky cliffs has no undertow.

Plage Raymond-les-Bains BEACH

About 13km from Jacmel this popular beach is a long stretch of sand with palm trees and mountains as a backdrop.

Maison Cadet NOTABLE BUILDING

(cnr Ave de la Liberté & Grand Rue) A key building to look out for is the grand Maison Cadet, with its red-iron 'witch's hat.'

Cathédrale de St Phillippe et St Jacques CATHEDRAL

(Rue de l'Eglise) This pretty white cathedral built in the mid-1800s is close to the old iron market.

☞ Tours

Experience Jacmel ADVENTURE

(☎ 3322-7557, 3722-5757; www.experiencejacmel. com; Promenade du Bord de Mer; ⊙8am-1pm) The most reputable tour company in the south, Experience Jacmel offers city tours, Carnival-focused art excursions, journeys to Bassin Bleu, and even a Vodou night tour involving an encounter with a Vodou priest. Local owner Markensy is as nice and helpful as they come, and incredibly knowledgeable about the town.

🛏 Sleeping

Despite its obvious tourist attractions, Jacmel isn't over-endowed with hotel beds. Many of the midrange and top-end hotels are actually outside Jacmel, heading east from Ave Baranquilla. If you plan on visiting during Carnival, advance booking is absolutely essential.

Guy's Guesthouse HOTEL $

(☎ 3708-8418; Ave de la Liberté; s/d/tr US$35/50/70; ❄ 🢅) There are invariably a few NGO workers staying at Guy's and it's easy to see why it remains popular. Although some bathrooms are shared, everything is kept very clean, the rooms are comfy, and the staff friendly and helpful. Breakfasts are huge, and the restaurant out the front is a good place for lunch or dinner.

Le Rendez Vous Guesthouse GUESTHOUSE $

(☎ 3800-9090, 2274-1079; lerendez_vousresto bar@yahoo.fr; Rte de Cyvadier; r with fan/air-con incl breakfast US$40/45; P ❄ @) Outside Jacmel opposite the airstrip, you'll find this simple, friendly place. There are nine uncluttered rooms, an open-sided bar-restaurant, and lots of greenery with chickens and ducks pecking about.

★ Cyvadier Plage Hôtel HOTEL $$

(☎ 3844-8264; www.hotelcyvadier.com; Rte de Cyvadier; s/d with fan US$60/73, with air-con US$80/95; P ❄ @ ❄) Off the main highway, this is the furthest of the beach hotels from the center of Jacmel, but also one of the best. Good rooms in a cluster of buildings face the terrace restaurant and out to the private cove of Cyvadier Plage (nonresidents welcome).

Colin's Hotel HOTEL $$

(☎ 3704-4877, 2818-8686; www.colinshotel. com; 13 Rue St-Anne; r incl breakfast from US$80; P ❄ 🢅 ❄) Just off the new beach boardwalk, the oversized rooms at this colorful hotel surround a large courtyard and pool area. The downstairs restaurant is very good and stands out for its friendly, efficient service, and the sea views from just about anywhere in the hotel are fantastic.

Cap Lamandou Hôtel HOTEL $$

(☎ 3720-1892, 3920-9135; www.cap-lamandou. com; Rte de Lamandou; r US$118; P ❄ @ 🢅 ❄) On the edge of Jacmel, but a bit of a hike off the main road, the Cap Lamandou is one of Jacmel's glitziest hotels. Rooms are

DON'T MISS

JACMEL'S CARNIVAL

Jacmel's **Carnival** (☉Feb) celebrations are famous across Haiti, and every year thousands of partygoers descend on the city to take part in this fantastic spectacle. Jacmel turns into one giant street theater for the event: it's a world away from the sequins and sparkle of Carnival in Rio de Janeiro.

The Carnival season starts buildup in late January, with events every Sunday leading up to the giant celebrations and procession on the Sunday of the week before Shrove Tuesday (it's held a week earlier than other Carnivals so it doesn't clash with Port-au-Prince's party).

The streets suddenly swell and everywhere you look are strange figures in fantastical papier-mâché masks – the signature image of Jacmel Carnival. You can see the masks being made and on display in the ateliers year-round. Jungle animals jostle with mythical birds, giant fruit and *lwa* (Vodou spirits). Mixed in with the procession are celebrants dressed as Arawaks and colonists, and horned figures covered in molasses and soot, who tease revelers with their sticky grab. St Michael and his angels ritually fight the devil, while gangs of monsters – caricaturing military misrule – growl scarily at the crowds. There's even a donkey dressed up in peasant clothes and sneakers (an old Carnival favorite).

Music is everywhere, from bands on organized floats to *rara* (one of the most popular forms of Haitian music) outfits on foot. It's an enormous party. The procession kicks off roughly around noon, with celebrations continuing late into the night.

immaculate, with wi-fi throughout and lovely views over the bay. The bar leads onto the central terrace and pool, which has more steps descending to the sea if you're in need of a dip.

Hôtel Florita HOTEL $$

(☑3785-5154; www.hotelflorita.com; 29 Rue du Commerce; s/d US$80/100; ❄@) Damaged in the earthquake but rebuilt, this converted mansion from 1888 oozes charm. There are polished floorboards and period furniture, while rooms are whitewashed and airy, with mosquito nets and balconies. Despite service at a snail's pace, the bar and restaurant are great, and chock-full of art.

Hôtel de la Place GUESTHOUSE $$

(☑3706-3913; 3 Rue de l'Eglise; s/d US$50/75; P❄) A pleasant old building overlooking Place Toussaint L'Ouverture, and a popular place to enjoy Carnival. Rooms are modern, although some are a little on the small side; most manage a view. The ground-floor terrace bar seems designed for hours of people-watching.

Jaclef Plaza Hôtel HOTEL $$

(☑3757-6818; Rte de Cyvadier; s/d US$65/75; P❄@☎) A hotel just outside town with a good range of facilities, a bar and conference rooms. The 150 guest rooms are very well sized but a shade characterless, something that's overcompensated for with a reckless love of chintz.

✖ Eating

The best restaurants in the city are housed in hotels, including Hôtel Florita (p252), Colin's Hotel (p251) and Cyvadier Plage Hôtel (p251). A local specialty are tiny sweet *ti malice* (bananas), and there's plenty of street food around. Between July and January, look out for women selling *pisquettes,* tiny fish sautéed in huge numbers.

Cafe Koze CAFE $

(☑4147-5000; www.facebook.com/pg/cafekoze; Rue du Commerce; mains HTG200, lobster roll HTG300; ☉noon-9pm Tue-Sun; ☎) When the wait at Hotel Florita becomes unbearable, head next door to the newer and more efficient Cafe Koze, an espresso bar and lounge with great pizza, tapas and occasionally a lobster roll special. On weekends there is live music.

Manje Lokal CREOLE $

(Jacmel beach; mains US$4-6; ☉noon-midnight) Right off the boardwalk behind a concrete wall with an opening at the center, this is a collection of half-a-dozen shacks (with accompanying sound systems), each serving up plenty of beer and cheap food. Fish, chicken and plantains are all filling staples, and the party here sometimes goes late into the night.

☻ Drinking & Nightlife

Nightlife in Jacmel is lively on the Promenade du Bord de Mer and Ave Baranquilla, where the music and partying go as late as the patrons feel like staying.

La Taverne BAR
(☑ 3486-9218; Ave Baranquilla; ⊙ noon-late)
Constructed of brick and stone, this low-lit
drinking establishment offers the best rum
sours around, along with regular salsa-dancing performances.

Belle Epoque Barak BAR
(☑ 3890-2180, 3666-5723; Ave Baranquilla;
⊙ 2pm-late) A favorite with expats, this bar
is known for its late-night parties fueled
by house and hip hop music. The chicken
wings and burgers are also pretty tasty.

🛍 Shopping

Jacmel is a souvenir-buyer's paradise. Its
most famous output is the papier-mâché
Carnival masks, but other handicrafts include hand-painted boxes, wooden flowers,
and models of taptaps, jungle animals and
boats. Prices are cheap, and there's no hard
sell. Most of the shops and a number of galleries can be found on Rue St-Anne near the
Hôtel la Jacmelienne sur Plage.

Moro ART
(☑ 3467-4518, 3166-6363; 21 Rue du Commerce;
⊙ hours vary Mon-Sat) One of Jacmel's better
artisanat (handicrafts) galleries, Moro
features Carnival masks and costumes and
the all-popular 'sitters' – colorful plywood
characters that perch on ledges.

ℹ️ Information

Banque Nationale de Crédit (Grand Rue;
⊙ 8:30am-4pm Mon-Fri)

Dola Dola (cnr Aves Baranquilla & de la Liberté;
⊙ 8am-4pm Mon-Sat) Moneychanger.

Hôpital St Michel (☑ 2288-2151; Rue St-Philippe; ⊙ 24hr) For emergencies, but not
great.

Pharmacie St-Cyr (48 Ave Baranquilla;
⊙ 8am-8pm)

Philippe Agent de Change (Ave Baranquilla;
⊙ 8am-7pm Mon-Sat) Changes euros and
Canadian dollars.

Post office (☑ 4890-0000; Place Touissaint
L'Ouverture; ⊙ 8am-4pm Mon-Sat)

Unibank (Ave de la Liberté; ⊙ 8:30am-4pm
Mon-Fri) Gives Visa advances.

ℹ️ Getting There & Away

La Source (☑ 4300-9525; 16 Av de la Liberté,
near Maré Geffard) buses (HTG200, three
hours) and taptaps (HTG100, 2½ hours) to
Port-au-Prince leave from the Bassin Caïman
station 2km out of town. Transport runs from
before dawn until about 5pm, departing when

full. The ride along Rte National 4 (Rte de l'Amité) is particularly scenic. At Carrefour Dufort
the road joins Rte National 2 to the capital.
If you want to travel west, get off here by the
Sodigaz gas station and flag down passing
buses before noon, as there are no direct buses
from Jacmel in this direction.

The **airport** (☑ 3701-4005; Rte de Cyvadier) is
about 6km east of town, but there are currently
no scheduled flights.

ℹ️ Getting Around

A moto-taxi around town costs around HTG25.
Even trips as far as Cyvadier Plage should give
change from HTG40. Taptaps run all day along
Ave Baranquilla.

Kabic

About 30 minutes east of Jacmel, just down
the street from Cayes Jacmel, this small fishing village turned lush Bohemian beach getaway graced the map just a few years ago,
attracting artist types with a desire to feel
closer to nature and further from the gritty
capital. The town is tiny, with just a few hotels and restaurants and a picturesque azure
beach that offers decent waves for surfers.
The friendly locals, referred to as Kabiquois,
make guests feel welcome and are one of
the main reasons so many return time and
again.

🏃 Activities

During the day people relax on the beach
or go surfing; the reef and rock breaks off
Kabic are suitable for all levels. The area is
home to Haiti's first and only surf school,
Surf Haiti (☑ 4906-2119, 3159-9414; www.
surfhaiti.org; Kabic Beach; lessons US$15, board
rental half-day/full day US$10/20; ⊙ dawn-dusk),
which also runs its own guesthouse up the
mountain. Kabic has increasingly attracted
surfers and hosted its first international
surf competition in 2016.

🛏 Sleeping & Eating

From an eccentric guesthouse to a beachfront resort to a bungalow-style stay, Kabic
has a good mix of overnight options for all
budgets.

Just off the main drag, a small but impressive collection of open-air, beachfront
restaurants serve up seafood dishes and
Creole cuisine. At Villa Nicole (p254) and **La
Reference** (Kabic Beach; mains US$5; ⊙ 9am-
9pm), expect just-caught lobster, conch, fish

ITINERARY: IN THE SOUTH

Haiti's laid-back south will have you relaxed in no time, with opportunities for nature hikes, cultural immersion and plenty of seafood feasts.

Take a short flight (or a long day's drive) from Port-au-Prince to Jérémie (p256), in the far southwest. Explore the town and beaches west, such as **Anse d'Azur** (p257), and sample *komparet*, a regional ginger-bun treat. Head south over the **Massif de la Hotte** mountains, and break for the night in Les Cayes (p256). You've done the hard traveling now, so enjoy your pick of Haiti's best beaches. It's a short boat trip out to the gorgeous Île-à-Vache (p255), or an equally short drive to Port Salut (p255). Either way, all your Caribbean clichés of white sand, palm trees and grilled fish on the beach will be easily fulfilled. When you're done, turn east. The Port-au-Prince highway splits near Léogâne, so let it take you to Jacmel (p249). Check out the town's historic quarter, and fill up on souvenirs with the handicrafts the town is famed for, and try a surf lesson in the Bohemian enclave of Kabic (p253). With that, you're ready to return to the capital.

and octopus, served with coconut rice and fried plantains. Wash it all down with fresh coconut water. **Sur Le Toit** (☑ 2209-4038; Kabic Beach; barbecue HTG175) has an ambitious menu but often only serves BBQ.

★ **Chic Chateau**   GUESTHOUSE **$**
(☑ 4751-6703; www.facebook.com/ChicChateau-Haiti; Kabic Beach; s/d incl breakfast US$50/60; P 🛜 🖳) 🍴 Up a bumpy side road from Kabic beach, Chic Chateau is challenging to find and harder to leave. Two unimposing structures make up this elegant, solar-powered stay: an open-air main house with sheer, flowing curtains, a sun deck and a dipping pool, and a two-story guesthouse next door that borrows its cylindrical shape from Taíno architecture.

Both spaces are beautifully arranged with antiques from the expat owner's travels in Haiti and Africa, and the whole place has incredible sea views. Don't miss the Creole eggs, or the sunset champagne boat ride the owner arranges with a local fisherman.

La Colline Enchantée   HOTEL **$$**
(☑ 3703-0448; www.facebook.com/collineenchantee; Marigot; s/d incl breakfast from US$77/99; P 🛜 🖳) This tidy collection of apricot, thatched-roof cottages is the talk of the south. Just down the road from Kabic in Marigot, the hotel is set back from the sea on a grassy hill, with nice views and an away-from-it-all vibe that city dwellers will adore. The restaurant is excellent, and the rooms feature broad porches with rocking chairs. Nice pool, too.

Kabic Beach Club   RESORT **$$**
(☑ 2274-1220, 3780-6850; www.kabicbeachclub.com; Kabic Beach; s/d with air-con US$120/130,

r without air-con US$115, all incl breakfast; P ❄ 🛜 🖳) Behind a stone wall just opposite the beach, this clean, modern resort looks like it could have been transplanted from Miami Beach, with a couple of sleek white buildings and pools and some whimsical art scattered about. Nice ocean views and a decent restaurant, too.

Villa Nicole   BOUTIQUE HOTEL **$$$**
(☑ 3389-4500, 3387-4500; www.villanicolejacmel.com; Kabic Beach; s/d incl breakfast $121/154; ❄ 🛜) This seaside hotel feels a bit sterile for Kabic Beach, but is nonetheless a very comfortable and pleasant place to stay. The rooms are plush and the poolside restaurant serves up incredibly time-consuming but tasty meals (go with the lobster). Although the beach is a bit rocky in parts, it makes for great swimming.

❶ Getting There & Away

Moto taxis from Jacmel to Kabic run around HTG75 in the daytime and HTG125 at night, and taptaps (HTG25) travel up and down the beachfront road from sunrise until 8pm. Jacmel's taptap station is on the corner of Ave Baranquilla and Rue des Beaux Enfants, and the ride from Jacmel to Kabic takes around 30 minutes.

The Southwest

From Port-au-Prince, Rte National 2 runs the length of Haiti's southern 'claw' to Les Cayes. After crawling through Carrefour, the road winds through a succession of medium-sized towns along the coast: Léogâne, known for its distilleries and stone sculptors; Grand-Goâve, a jumping off point for dolphin- and whale-watching trips and visits to secluded and outrageously beautiful beaches, which can be done with boating tour company **Toupamer** (☑ 3685-7505; richardboyer1@hotmail.com); and Petit-Goâve, famous for its sweet *dous makos* (a type of Haitian fudge).

The coastal road used to be popular for weekend beach visits from the capital before Hurricane Matthew tore into the south, and snarling traffic made the resorts of Côte des Arcadins a more attractive prospect. From Miragoâne the road cuts inland and heads across the mountains southwestward to Les Cayes, a somewhat seedy jumping-off point for the recovering Jérémie, still-pristine Île-à-Vache and decimated Port Salut.

Île-à-Vache

POP 15,400

The so-called 'Island of Cows,' Île-à-Vache lies about 15km south of Les Cayes. In the 16th century it was a base for the Welsh pirate Henry Morgan as he terrorized Santo Domingo and Colombia. Three centuries later Abraham Lincoln tried to relocate emancipated black American slaves here, but it was a short-lived and ill-provisioned experiment.

The island today is scattered with rural houses, plantations, mangroves, the odd Arawak burial ground and some great beaches, but the government seemingly has big plans for the eastern side of the island. A proposed $260-million project over 17.3 sq miles would include resorts and hotels with as many as 2500 rooms, along with a golf course and an airport. Due to conflicts with local residents, though, the project has been in a holding pattern since 2015.

🛏 Sleeping & Eating

Accommodations options include two contrasting upmarket resorts and one collection of budget-friendly bungalows, although some islanders in the village of Madame Bernard have been known to rent rooms to foreigners for around US$10.

Village Vacances   BUNGALOW $$
(Vacation Village; ☑ 3170-8385, 3637-4391; www.thevacationvillage.com; r incl full board US$70) This rustic option on the northern coast of Île-à-Vache has opened up the island to travelers on a budget. Just a small collection of bungalows, hammocks, and a restaurant, Village Vacances excels in customer service and particularly in the kitchen, which lovingly prepares elaborate meals with whatever is fresh from the on-site farm or the sea.

★ **Abaka Bay Resort**   RESORT $$$
(☑ 3721-3691; www.abakabay.com; Anse Dufour; s/d incl full board US$135/220; ❄ @) This hotel has one of the most fabulous beaches in the Caribbean, a smooth white curve of a bay, met by lush foliage and a series of pleasant bungalows and villas. The atmosphere is laid-back, but the service is still exacting. Private transport to and from the island costs an additional US$50 per boat.

Port Morgan   RESORT $$$
(☑ 3923-0000; www.port-morgan.com; Cayes Coq; s/d incl full board from US$115/205; ℗ ❄ @ ≋) Served by a yacht harbor, Port Morgan is all bright-and-breezy gingerbread chalets with lovely views out to sea. There's a small beach, an excellent restaurant serving French-influenced cuisine, and various kayaks and other water-sports equipment for rent.

❶ Getting There & Away

All three hotels on Île-à-Vache offer transfers from the Les Cayes wharf from US$50 to US$60 per trip (which can be split among groups). Otherwise, *bateaux-taxis* (water taxis) leave from the wharf several times daily (US$2, 30 minutes) for Madame Bernard.

❶ Getting Around

Getting around on foot is easy; you can do a pleasant day walk in a loop between the two resorts via Madame Bernard, taking in the viewpoints of Pointe Ouest and Pointe Latanier.

Port Salut

POP 2330

A once-picturesque road leads west from Les Cayes to the spectacular beaches of Port Salut, but these days the view is diminished by broken trees, trashed buildings and other hurricane damage. At the time of writing, electricity had not yet been restored, and all area businesses were running on generators and lacked wi-fi.

The one-street town is strung for several kilometers along the coast, and still offers wide swaths of palm-fringed white sand with barely a person on it, and the gorgeously warm Caribbean to splash around in. The largest cave in Haiti, Grotte Marie Jeanne, is about 45 minutes up the coast in Port-à-Piment, and definitely worth a visit.

HAITI THE SOUTHWEST

LES CAYES

You'd be hard-pressed to find a sense of urgency in Haiti's fourth-largest city. More popularly known as Aux Cayes, Les Cayes is an old rum port sheltered by a series of reefs that has sent many ships to their graves (its first recorded victim was one of Columbus' ships on his final voyage to Hispaniola). Pirates were another threat, notably from nearby Île-à-Vache. Today Les Cayes has little to offer the visitor, although it's a good stopping-off point for other destinations in the south. The best place to stay is **Cayenne Hôtel** (☑ 3105-3959; lacayenneht@yahoo.fr; Rue Capitale; s/d incl breakfast from US$60/80; [P][✸][@][🌊]) and the best place to eat is **Bistro Gourmand** (☑ 2270-5718; Rue Geffrard; mains HTG400; ⊘ 9am-10pm).

Voyageur (☑ 3633-2361; voyageurbus@gmail.com; Meridien Hotel, Rte National 2) and **Transport Chic** (p237) have luxury air-conditioned minibuses running daily between Les Cayes and Port-au-Prince (US$10, four hours). Buy tickets the day before, and take photo ID.

◉ Sights

Grotte Marie Jeanne   CAVE

(☑ 3638-2292, 3702-3941; Port-à-Piment; HTG100; ⊘ 8am-4pm) About 45 minutes north of Port Salut, this massive cave is the largest and most impressive in Haiti. Visitors today can tour three areas of the cave, one of which is completely dark, and the whole thing takes about three hours. None of the guides here speak English, so bring a translator and call ahead for a tour.

Since 1999, the cave's 36 known chambers on three different levels have been the subject of scientific studies and mapping projects. Indigenous Taínos used the cave to perform sacred ceremonies, and escaped slaves were known to hide in them.

🛏 Sleeping & Eating

In addition to the town's two main hotels, there are a few other options along the coastal road going north.

Auberge du Rayon Vert   GUESTHOUSE $$

(☑ 3713-9035, 3779-1728; www.aubergedurayonvert.com; Rue Point-Sable; s/d US$77/88; [P][✸][@]) Stylish and immaculate rooms are the order of the day here, with locally made furniture and modern bathrooms, and the beach seconds away. The restaurant-bar is the best in Port Salut, serving up heaping portions of fresh seafood accompanied by fine wine (mains US$11 to US$22).

Hôtel du Village   CHALET $$

(☑ 3634-0689; portsaluthotelduvillage@yahoo.fr; Rue Pointe-Sable; s/d incl breakfast US$65/85; [P][✸]) A government-owned hotel comprising a series of chalets. The rooms are decent, although you're not likely to spend much time in them since the front doors open straight onto the sand. Much of the hotel's outdoor restaurant and bar area was destroyed by Hurricane Matthew, but the hotel owner is rebuilding a sturdy (if tacky) concrete gazebo on the beach.

Sunset Cove Restaurant   INTERNATIONAL $

(☑ 3664-0404, 3797-0978; Rte Départmentale 205; mains HTG200; ⊘ hours vary) This restaurant opened recently amid the wreckage of an old hotel called Dan's Creek, once a seafront gem with a hint of gingerbread and lots of promise. The scenery is still pretty bent, but the grilled conch and pizzas are decent.

Chez Kaliko   SEAFOOD $$

(☑ 3878-9601; Port Salut beach; mains US$12; ⊘ hours vary) Joe, the owner of this beachfront shack in Port Salut, doesn't know his business' opening hours, and doesn't seem aware of time in general. But if you've got several hours to spare and are a fan of fresh octopus, conch and grilled fish, this is the best place to get it.

❶ Getting There & Around

Taptaps to Les Cayes (HTG200, 45 minutes) leave throughout the day

Moto-taxis zip up and down the length of the town; expect to pay HTG50 for a 10-minute ride.

Jérémie

POP 42,390

Jérémie, the capital of Grand'Anse Département, was hit hard by Hurricane Matthew, which took out many of the city's trees and blew the tin roofs off innumerable homes. Hard work on the part of locals and visiting

NGO employees has gotten the city back up and running, though, making this one of the most pleasant and surprisingly tidy places to visit in all of Haiti.

The town is centered on Place Alexandre Dumas, with its red-and-white cathedral. Rue Stenio Vincent runs parallel to the sea, with numerous interesting old buildings and coffee warehouses, many of which are neglected. Continuing past the grubby beach takes you to **Fort Télémargue**, a crumbling fort that makes an excellent spot to watch the sunset.

History

Jérémie has a rich history. In 1793 it was the landing point for Britain's short-lived invasion of Haiti. After independence it was a major center for mulatto power, and its inhabitants grew rich on the coffee trade, sent their children to be educated in Paris and wore the latest French fashions. Jérémie was known as the 'City of Poets' for its writers. Its most famous sons were Thomas-Alexandre Dumas, whose son wrote *The Three Musketeers,* and the poet Émile Roumer. In 1964 the town was the focus of an attempt to overthrow 'Papa Doc' Duvalier, who responded in murderous fashion by ordering the massacre of virtually all of Jérémie's mulatto population of around 400 men, women and children, leaving the city politically and economically isolated.

🏖 Beaches

Anse d'Azur BEACH

About 5km northwest of Jérémie is this gorgeous sandy bay with a sunken German U-boat and several caves that any Caribbean country would envy. A return moto-taxi will cost around US$3 to US$4.

🛏 Sleeping

⭐ **Place Charmant** GUESTHOUSE **$$**

(✆ 3882-0965, 3701-5874; www.placecharmant.com; 2 Calasse; r incl half board from $US77; P@☎) Slightly out of town and with great views out to sea, this is a wonderful home-away-from-home. There are a variety of rooms, from bungalows to new guest apartments, but the biggest draws are the great food and genial owner Bette, a knowledgeable expat nurse. Since the hurricane, this has been the hotel of choice for aid workers and missionaries.

Auberge Inn GUESTHOUSE **$$**

(✆ 3727-9678; info@aubergeinnhaiti.com; 6 Ave Emile Roumer; s/d/tr without bathroom US$75/120/150; P@) The decor makes the Auberge Inn feel as much a home as a guesthouse. Dinner on request is excellent, and there's a selection of books, maps and handicrafts for sale, but the fact that most rooms share a single bathroom is a drawback.

Hôtel La Cabane HOTEL **$$**

(✆ 2278-1378, 4011-4178; Ave Emile Roumer; s/d with fan US$55/88, with air-con $77/112; P✷@) Some rooms in this bright pink hotel are a little small, or maybe they just feel that way because of the ostentatious dark-wood furniture squeezed in. The airy restaurant is decorated with paintings of Jérémie's famous literary and political sons.

Hôtel le Bon Temps HOTEL **$$**

(✆ 2278-2936; hotelbontemps@yahoo.fr; 8 Ave Emile Roumer; s/d from US$70/90; P✷@) Next to Jeremie's Auberge Inn, this old hotel runs on solar power but lacks hot water. The helpful owner speaks English, and some of the rooms have skylights rather than windows.

🍴 Eating

Konparet Madam Senec BAKERY **$**

(✆ 2714-4489; Rue Stenio Vincent; konparet US$1) The *konparet* (ginger buns) at this hole-in-the-wall store are luscious and unrivaled, made with Olivia Senec's decades-old recipe of sugar, coconut, cinnamon, ginger, flour, sweet banana and butter. She's been at it for 55 years, and also sells other regional confections such as *bonbon siwo.*

Ilan-Ilan HEALTH FOOD **$**

(✆ 3724-6662, 4865-7564; 85 Rue Source Dommage; mains HTG300; ☺8am-11pm) Whatever's fresh ends up on your plate at this cute little restaurant along the way to Plage Anse and Jérémie's airport, with favorites including fish, beef and herby tasting goat. Natural fruit juices with energy boosts are also a draw, and word on the street is that Sean Penn dined here recently.

Chez Patou CREOLE **$**

(✆ 4203-1977; Rue Monseigneur Boge; snacks US$2-5, mains US$4-9; ☺8am-10pm) A great place to fill up, this airy red-and-white building has a decent range of sandwiches and burgers, along with hearty servings of Creole standards, spaghetti and ice cream. The hurricane blew off the roof and trashed the place, but the affable owner has cleaned it all up.

HAITI THE SOUTHWEST

WORTH A TRIP

CAMP PERRIN

At the foot of the Massif de la Hotte range, Camp Perrin is a good base for exploring Parc National Macaya. The town is little more than two streets with a few shops and bar-restos; the hotel **Le Recul** (✆3785-0027, 3454-0027; lereculhotel@gmail.com; Camp Perrin; s/d US$88/98; P❋🕾🗺) is the best sleeping option. The town was founded in 1759 by the French, who left behind a network of irrigation canals. A different watery attraction not to be missed is the beautiful **Saut Mathurine** waterfall with its deep green pool, a 15-minute moto-taxi ride away. **La Mathurine Hotel & Restaurant** (✆3672-4334, 3644-1131; lamathurine@yahoo.com; r incl breakfast from US$20; P) is a great spot to spend the night near the waterfall.

Taptaps to Les Cayes (US$2, 1½ hours) leave several times daily, picking up passengers along the main street. Buses to Jérémie usually pass through in the middle of the day.

Le Boucanier
CREOLE $

(Rue Stenio Vincent; mains US$5-12; ⏱6-11pm) This typical bar-resto has a wide-ranging Creole menu, but there are usually only one or two dishes available, typically barbecued chicken or *griyo* (pork) served with plantain and salad.

★ Entertainment

Alliance Française
ARTS CENTER

(✆3617-2307; 110 Ave Emile Roumer; ⏱9am-5pm; 🕾) Hosts concerts, films and an annual cultural festival every April. Also offers an excellent internet connection.

ℹ Information

Unibank (Place Alexandre Dumas)

ℹ Getting There & Away

The quickest way in and out is the Mission Aviation Fellowship (p265) flight from Port-au-Prince (US$135, 30 minutes), with scheduled flights every Tuesday and Thursday. Demand is high, so book as far in advance as possible. The grassy airstrip is 5km northwest of Jérémie.

Grand'Anse Tours (p237) runs buses every morning for Port-au-Prince (HTG500, eight hours) from a lot on the southern outskirts. Buses stop at all main towns en route, but you'll be asked to pay the full Port-au-Prince fare irrespective of your destination.

ℹ Getting Around

Moto-taxis ply the streets, charging around HTG50 for most rides.

UNDERSTAND

Haiti Today

Haiti is now the poorest country in the Western hemisphere, and has long been a major recipient of international aid. The 2010 earthquake and 2016 hurricane not only created new challenges, but also laid bare the fault lines in Haitian society and the body politic.

In 2016, violent protests and dubious accusations of voter fraud repeatedly delayed the presidential election, forcing an interim government and an extra round of voting in which only 21% of the country took part. The winner, a banana exporter with no previous political experience, was finally declared in 2017. But President Jovenel Moïse faces some pretty enormous obstacles: Haiti's economic growth continues to slow, inflation and unemployment are spinning out of control, and on top of it all, Hurricane Matthew caused an estimated US$2.7 billion in damage.

Even if Moïse comes up with a viable plan, he'll likely end up thwarted by Haiti's parliament, which seems configured to create political gridlock. Meanwhile, the mainly mixed-race oligarchies who speak only French and own half the country's wealth continue dominating manufacturing and import/export, and remain the powers standing behind the president's throne. Within the high walls of Pétionville are the best French restaurants and boutiques and riches unimaginable by the vast majority of Haitians.

History

Haiti's earliest inhabitants called their island Quisqueya – 'cradle of life.' Despite its size, it has often played a key role in world history: Christopher Columbus founded the first European settlement in the Americas here, and under French slavery it became the richest colony – an iniquity that led to two firsts: the only successful slave revolution in history and the founding of the world's first black republic. Unfortunately, modern Haiti has suffered from self-serving leaders, foreign interventions and natural disasters, preventing it from living up to the promise of its revolutionary heroes.

The Taínos, the Spanish & the French

Hispaniola's earliest inhabitants arrived around 2600 BC in huge dugout canoes, coming from what is now eastern Venezuela. They were called the Taínos, and by the time Christopher Columbus landed on the island in 1492, they numbered some 400,000. However, within 30 years of Columbus' landing, the Taínos were gone, wiped out by disease and abuse.

The Spanish neglected their colony of Santo Domingo, and through the 17th century it became a haven for pirates and, later, ambitious French colonists. In 1697 the island was formally divided, and the French colony of St-Domingue followed soon after.

The French turned St-Domingue over to sugar production on a huge scale. By the end of the 18th century it was the richest colony in the world, with 40,000 colonists lording it over half a million black slaves. Following the French Revolution in 1789, free offspring of colonists and female slaves demanded equal rights, while the slaves themselves launched a huge rebellion. Led by the inspiring slave leader Toussaint Louverture, the slaves freed themselves by arms and forced France to abolish slavery.

The World's First Black Republic

French treachery dispatched Toussaint to a prison death, but in May 1803 his general, Jean-Jacques Dessalines, took the French tricolor flag and, ripping the white out of it, declared he was ripping the white man out of the country. The red and blue were stitched together with the motto Liberté ou la Mort (Liberty or Death), creating Haiti's flag.

Dessalines won a decisive victory against the French at the Battle Vertières, near Cap-Haïtien, and on January 1, 1804, at Gonaïves, Dessalines proclaimed independence for St-Domingue and restored its Taíno name, Haiti, meaning 'Mountainous Land.'

Dessalines crowned himself Emperor of Haiti and ratified a new constitution that granted him absolute power. However, his tyrannical approach to the throne inflamed large sections of society to revolt – his death in an ambush at Pont Rouge in 1806 marked

HAITI'S EARTHQUAKE

At 4:53pm on January 12, 2010, Haiti was shaken to its core when shock waves from a fault line 13km below the earth's surface caused a 7.0-magnitude earthquake. Haitians quickly dubbed the earthquake Godou-Godou, named for the sound it made as the buildings collapsed. It's thought that 230,000 people were killed, 300,000 injured and 2.3 million people displaced, while over 180,000 buildings were either damaged or destroyed. Striking at the heart of what was already the poorest country in the Americas, Godou-Godou is one of the largest natural disasters on record.

The earthquake prompted an enormous humanitarian response, with billions of dollars in international assistance flooding into Haiti, and tens of thousands of volunteers and soldiers arriving to assist. But much of that 'help' was misguided and even counterproductive, undermining Haiti's potential to help itself. The Interim Haiti Recovery Commission (IHRC) set up to coordinate billions of dollars in reconstruction aid and led by Bill Clinton delivered only disorganized development experiments and unfinished projects. The Red Cross raised half a billion dollars and claimed to have built 130,000 homes, but investigative reports revealed it had only built six permanent homes. Even today, not all of the rubble has been cleared, and tens of thousands of people remain in tent cities.

the first of many violent overthrows that would plague Haiti for the next 200 years.

Dessalines' death sparked a civil war between the black north, led by Henri Christophe, and the south, led by Alexandre Pétion. Christophe crowned himself king, while Pétion became president of the southern republic. It took both their deaths (Christophe by suicide) to reunite the country, which happened in 1820 under new southern leader Jean-Pierre Boyer, who established a tenuous peace.

During his reign Boyer paid a crippling indemnity to France in return for diplomatic recognition. The debt took the rest of the century to pay off and turned Haiti into the first third-world debtor nation. Boyer also sought to unify Hispaniola by invading Santo Domingo. The whole of the island remained under Haitian control until 1849, when the eastern part proclaimed independence as the Dominican Republic.

The next half-century was characterized by continued rivalry between the ruling classes of wealthy mixed race families and blacks. Of the 22 heads of state between 1843 and 1915, only one served his full term in office; the others were assassinated or forced into exile.

US Intervention

By the beginning of the 20th century, Haiti's strategic proximity to the new Panama Canal and increased German interests in the country reignited American interest. When Haitian President Vilbrun Guillaume Sam was killed by a mob in 1915, the US sent in the marines, with the stated aim of stabilizing the country.

During its nearly 20-year occupation of the country, the US replaced the Haitian constitution and built up the country's infrastructure by instituting the hated corvée, labor gangs of conscripted peasants.

The occupation brought predictable resistance, with the Caco peasant rebellion led by Charlemagne Péraulte from 1918 to 1920, in which thousands of Haitians were killed before the assassination of Péraulte effectively put an end to the uprising – an episode of Haitian history still bitterly remembered in the country today. The occupation proved costly and the US pulled out in 1934.

The Duvaliers & Aristide

Haiti's string of tyrannical rulers reached its zenith in 1956 with the election of François 'Papa Doc' Duvalier, whose support came from the burgeoning black middle class and the politically isolated rural poor.

Duvalier consolidated his power by creating the notorious Tontons Macoutes. The name refers to a character in a Haitian folk story who carries off small children in his bag at night. The Tontons Macoutes were a private militia who used force with impuni-

HURRICANE MATTHEW

In the early hours of October 4, 2016, Hurricane Matthew became the first Category 4 storm to come ashore in Haiti in 52 years. Winds of up to 230km/h battered the southern coast for hours, blowing off tin roofs, leveling poorly constructed homes and snapping trees like matchsticks. It was the worst humanitarian crisis since the 2010 earthquake, and hundreds died – news outlets reported up to 1000 deaths, although official sources in Haiti claim it was 546.

Ill-equipped to respond to the crisis, the Haitian government requested assistance from other countries, and aid groups, missionaries and UN peacekeepers descended on Haiti's south, concentrating their efforts in the coastal city of Jérémie and surrounding villages, all of which were hit directly. A total of 200,000 homes were destroyed, and agricultural and commercial activity and fishing came to a halt in most of the region, zapping the livelihood of much of the population. In the Grand'Anse and Sud departments, between 70% and 100% of the crops were destroyed.

In early 2017, the UN partnered with aid organizations and the Haitian government to launch a US$291-million response plan that would ostensibly assist 2.4 million victims of both the earthquake and Hurricane Matthew over the next two years. Supposedly the plan hinges on lessons learned from the failed response to the 2010 earthquake. Rather than focusing on relief, the idea is to implement longer-term solutions that allow Haitians to play a more active role.

ty in order to extort cash and crops from a cowed population.

'Papa Doc' died on April 21, 1971, and was succeeded by his son Jean-Claude 'Baby Doc' Duvalier. Periodic bouts of repression continued until major civil unrest forced Baby Doc to flee to France in February 1986.

Control changed hands between junta leaders until finally the Supreme Court ordered elections for December 1990. A young priest named Father Jean-Bertrand Aristide, standing as a surprise last-minute candidate with the slogan 'Lavalas' (Flood), won a landslide victory.

Aristide promised radical reforms to aid the poor, but after just seven months he was pushed out of office. An alliance of rich, mixed-race families and army generals staged a bloody coup. Despite international condemnation, an embargo against the junta was barely enforced, and thousands of Haitians fled political repression in boats to the USA.

Many had seen Aristide as a radical socialist, so when a joint US-UN plan was finally brokered for his return, it was on the condition that he sign up to an economic restructuring plan that eviscerated his original ideas for reform.

Culture

Vodou

It's hard to think of a more maligned and misunderstood religion than Vodou. Even its name sparks an instantly negative word-association game of voodoo dolls, zombies and black magic – less a religion than a mass of superstitions. The truth is somewhat distant from the hype. Vodou is a sophisticated belief system with roots in Haiti's African past and the slave rebellion that brought the country to independence in 1804. Central to Haiti's national identity, these roots have also led to the demonization of Vodou in the West. For three centuries, slaves were shipped to Haiti from the Dahomey and Kongo kingdoms in West and Central Africa. As well as their labor, the slaves brought with them their traditional religions; Vodou is a synthesis of these, mixed with residual Taíno rituals and colonial Catholic iconography.

Vodou played a large part in both the inspiration and organization of the struggle for independence. The Vodou ceremony at Bois Cayman in 1791, presided over by the slave and priest Boukman, is considered central to sparking the first fires of the Haitian slave revolution. However, Vodou's relationship to power has always been a rocky one. Both Toussaint Louverture and Jean-Jacques Dessalines outlawed Vodou during their reigns, fearing its political potential. Overseas, the 'bad example' of slaves emancipating themselves led to Vodou being castigated in the US and Europe throughout the 19th century. The bad press went into overdrive during the 1915–34 US occupation. Coinciding with the advent of Hollywood and the dime-store pulp novel, concocted stories of darkest Africa in the Caribbean – all witch doctors and child sacrifice – were eagerly eaten up by the Western public.

Haitian governments have played their part, too, with several ruthless anti superstition campaigns in the 20th century egged on by the Catholic Church. In the 1930s and early 1940s Vodou altars were burned and *mapou* trees (sacred trees where spiritual offerings are made) cut down. 'Papa Doc' Duvalier chose to co-opt the Vodou priests, which led to a violent backlash after his son's fall from power in 1986. By this time, however, progressive Catholics in the Haitian church had begun to reach an accommodation with Vodou. In 1987 a new constitution guaranteeing freedom of religion was put in place, and in 1991 Vodou was finally recognized as a national religion alongside Christianity.

Music

Haitian music has been used for many things: an accompaniment to Vodou ceremonies, a form of resistance in politics, and also just to dance the night away.

One of the most popular forms is *rara*. During Carnival, Port-au-Prince and Jacmel fill with rivers of people who come to hear *rara* bands moving through the streets on floats. Most bands compete for the song prize with a special composition, which has been recorded and played constantly on the radio during the lead up to Carnival. In the country, *rara* bands march for miles, with percussionists and musicians playing *vaskins* and *kònets* (bamboo and zinc trumpets). Each instrument plays just one note but, together with the drummers, they combine to create mesmerizing riffs.

Dance music has always taken in foreign sounds. Cuban *son* has influenced the troubadour bands that entertain in restaurants and hotels, singing and gently strumming guitars. Merengue, the Dominican big-band sound, has always been played enthusiastically on dance floors, and in the 1950s evolved into *compas direct* (or just *compas* for short), with its slightly more African beat. A joy to dance to, its greatest exponents are Nemours Jean-Baptiste and the late Coupé Cloué.

Racines (roots) music grew out of the Vodou-jazz movement of the late 1970s. Vodou jazz was a combination of American jazz with Vodou rhythms and melodies. For many, this new music reflected the struggle for change in Haiti. The lyrics were a clarion call for the revival of long-ignored peasant culture. *Racines* was propelled by Vodou rhythms overlaid with electric guitars, keyboards and vocals. The most notable *racines* bands are Boukman Eksperyans, Boukan Ginen and RAM. During the military dictatorships of the late 1980s and the coup years of the 1990s, many of these bands endured extreme harassment and threats from the military.

Haitian popular music and politics seem destined to be intertwined: in the 2010 presidential election, musician Wyclef Jean was only disqualified from running for office on a technicality, while *compas* singer Michel 'Sweet Micky' Martelly went on to win the vote for high office. The influence of Wyclef (and fellow ex-Fugees member Pras Michel) has also helped refresh Haitian music – given the proximity to the USA, it's no surprise that *rap kreyòl* (Haitian hip-hop) is a growing genre, with early exponents such as Torch blazing a musical trail.

Painting

Haiti's streets can seem like one continuous gallery, from the painted advertisements on buildings, and the myriad canvases hung on fences, to the brightly decorated taptaps (buses). The roots of Haitian painting are deep indeed.

While early elite Haitian art of the 19th century followed the European portrait tradition, the Haitian peasantry were forging their own path: painting murals to decorate the walls of Vodou temples and making elaborate sequined flags to use in ceremonies. This link to the *lwa* (Vodou spirits), with their visual language of *vévé* (sacred symbol) signs, is central to Haiti's artistic vision.

This tradition was brought front and center in the 1920s by parallel literary and visual-art movements. Modern Haitian literature was born through Noiriste, while visual artists founded the Indigéniste movement. Both sought to reclaim Haiti's African roots from the Francophilia of the elite. Subject matter switched from literal representation to idealized subjects, such as peasant life and landscapes. This style of art is often dubbed 'naive' or 'primitive,' partly due to its simple style and avoidance of classical perspective.

The Indigénistes paved the way for the arrival of the American, De Witt Peters, in Port-au-Prince. Trained in the arts, Peters recognized the extraordinary flavor of the primitivist work, and helped artists to develop their skills by setting up the Centre d'Art in Port-au-Prince in 1944. Here he discovered Hector Hyppolite, a Vodou priest now considered Haiti's greatest painter. A flood of brilliant artists soon arrived at the Centre d'Art, untutored but producing incredible work that stunned the international art world. At the same time, Peters also discovered Georges Liautaud, the carved-iron sculptor of Croix des Bouquets. Through its work, the Centre d'Art helped give painters such as Hyppolite, Philomé Obin and Wilson Bigaud the recognition they deserved, and was of such importance in the development of Haitian art that its opening is often referred to as 'the miracle of 1944.'

Throughout the 1950s, naive art became standard, pressed into easily recognizable images to serve the booming tourist market (the same paintings are still offered today). The Foyer des Arts Plastiques movement, led by Lucien Price, reacted against this by injecting a social ethic into Indigéniste: artists moved away from magic realism to portray the harsh realities of Haitian life.

The next great theme arose with the Saint-Soleil group of the 1970s. Spontaneity was key for artists such as Louisianne St Fleurant and Jean-Claude 'Tiga' Garoute, who often painted *lwa* as abstract forms or bursts of energy.

Modern Haitian art continues to go from strength to strength, including painters such as Frantz Zéphirin, Magda Magloire and Pascale Monnin, and the inspired junkyard Vodou sculptures of the Grand Rue artists.

SURVIVAL GUIDE

ℹ Directory A–Z

ATMS

Automated teller machines are increasingly common in Port-au-Prince, Pétionville and Cap-Haïtien, but have yet to catch on in much of the rest of the country. They're the simplest way to manage your money on the road, although obviously you'll need to make sure you're liquid when heading out of the capital. Most ATMs are directly on the street, with some in secure booths. Always be aware of your surroundings when using an ATM and pocketing a wad of cash – use machines in large grocery stores that staff security guards when possible.

CREDIT CARDS

Most midrange and all top-end hotels (and many Port-au-Prince restaurants) will happily let you flash the plastic. Visa, MasterCard and (to a slightly lesser extent) American Express will all do nicely. With an accompanying passport, cash advances on credit cards can be made in the larger banks.

DANGERS & ANNOYANCES

Many governments advise against nonessential travel to Haiti, and certainly caution is advised.
➡ UN troops have helped the country deal with large-scale gang and kidnapping problems, but keep your ear to the ground for protests around election time, which can get violent and should be avoided.
➡ To avoid street crime, use hotel safes for anything you're not willing to lose. Hide your money in pockets, and avoid taking out smart phones on the street.
➡ Common annoyances include a poor electricity supply, snarling traffic, begging, and getting stared at or called *blanc*, which is a generic word for a foreigner.

EMBASSIES & CONSULATES

All of the embassies and consulates are in Port-au-Prince or Pétionville. Australia, New Zealand and Ireland do not have diplomatic representation in Haiti; British citizens can seek assistance at the UK Embassy in Santo Domingo.

Brazilian Embassy (☑ 2256-0900; ppinto@ mr.gov.br; 168 Rue Darguin, Pétionville)
Canadian Embassy (☑ 2812-9000; www.port-au-prince.gc.ca; Rte de Delmas btwn Delmas 71 & 75, Port-au-Prince; ⊙7am-3:30pm Mon-Thu, to 12:30pm Fri)
Cuban Embassy (☑ 2256-3504; www.cuba diplomatica.cu/haiti; 3 Rue Marion, Pétionville; ⊙8am-12:30pm Mon-Fri)

Dominican Embassy (☑ 2813-0887; emba domhaiti@gmail.com; 121 Ave Pan Américaine, Pétionville)
French Embassy (☑ 2999-9000; www.amba france-ht.org; 51 Rue Capois, Port-au-Prince)
Mexican Embassy (☑ 2229-1040; embmxhai@ yahoo.com; 2 Musseau cnr Delmas 60, Port-au-Prince)
US Embassy (☑ 2229-8000; http://haiti. usembassy.gov; 41 Rte de Tabarre, Tabarre; ⊙7am-3:30pm Mon-Fri)
Venezuelan Embassy (☑ 3443-4127; embav enezhaiti@hainet.net; 2 Blvd Harry Truman, Port-au-Prince)

HEALTH

Travel in Haiti is generally safe as long as you're reasonably careful about what you eat and drink. The most common travel-related illnesses, such as dysentery and hepatitis, are acquired by consumption of contaminated food and water. There is a small but significant malaria risk in certain parts of the country, and you should check before travel as to required prophylaxis. Following the 2010 earthquake, Haiti suffered a widespread cholera outbreak.

HEALTH INSURANCE

Travel insurance that includes health coverage is highly recommended. Policies vary widely, but it's essential to have as much medical coverage as possible (including emergency evacuation cover). Medical services insist on payment on the spot, so collect all the paperwork you can when being treated so you can claim later. Some policies ask you to call them (they'll usually call you back) so that an assessment of your problem can be made.

INTERNET ACCESS

Online access isn't a problem in any decently sized Haitian town, and internet cafes open and close frequently. Broadband connections are increasingly standard, along with webcams, CD burning and USB connections for uploading digital photos. Prices cost around HTG50 (US$0.75) per hour. The more expensive the joint, the better the electricity supply is likely to be. If you're bringing a laptop, wi-fi access is increasingly widespread.

EATING PRICE RANGES

Prices are based on the average cost of a main dish and include tax.

$ less than US$10
$$ US$10–20
$$$ more than US$20

OPENING HOURS

Many restaurants and most businesses close on Sunday.

Banks 8:30am to 1pm Monday to Friday; some major branches also open 2pm to 5pm.

Bars & Clubs 5pm to late.

Offices 7am to 4pm Monday to Friday; many close earlier Friday; government offices close for an hour at noon.

Restaurants 7am to 9pm.

Shops 7am tp 4pm Monday to Saturday; some close earlier Friday and Saturday.

PHOTOGRAPHY

Taking photos of airports and police buildings is forbidden, and it's a good idea to obtain permission first before snapping a policeman or a UN soldier.

Haitians are well aware of their country's poverty, and often dislike being photographed in work or dirty clothes. Always ask permission – whether you're in a market or the countryside, producing a camera out of the blue can occasionally provoke a reaction. This goes double at Vodou ceremonies, where you should always check with the *houngan* or *mambo* (respectively male or female Vodou priest) before you start clicking away.

PUBLIC HOLIDAYS

Government offices and most businesses will be closed on the following days:

Independence Day January 1

Ancestors' Day January 2

Carnival February (three days before Ash Wednesday)

Good Friday March/April

Agriculture and Labor Day May 1

Flag and University Day May 18

Ascencion Day 39 days after Easter

Corpus Christi May/June

Anniversary of the death of Jean-Jacques Dessaline October 17

Anniversary of the death of Toussaint Louverture November 1

All Soul's Day November 2

Anniversary of the Battle of Vertières November 18

Christmas Day December 25

TELEPHONE

Cell/Mobile Phones Haiti uses the GSM system. The main operators are Digicel and Natcom. Coverage is generally good. The providers have international roaming agreements with many foreign networks, but it can be cheaper to buy a local handset on arrival in Haiti for about US$20, or a SIM card for about US$5. Take a copy of your passport to the dealer for identification.

Landlines Connections can sometimes be patchy. Most businesses list several numbers on their cards and many people carry two cell phones on different networks.

Calling The quickest option is to find a phone 'stand' – usually a youth on the street with a cell phone that looks like a regular desk phone, who will time your call and charge accordingly.

Costs Within Haiti calls cost around US$0.10 per minute, and to call overseas around US$0.90 per minute. Top-up scratch cards are available from shops and ubiquitous street vendors.

Codes Haiti's country code is ☏509. There are no area codes. To make an international call, first dial ☏00.

TIPPING

Most Haitians don't tip, but in tourist areas it is usual to tip and certainly all gratuities are happily accepted. Restaurant bills generally include a 10% tax and a 5% service charge, and if you'd like to add a little extra for great service, nobody will be upset. It's also considerate to give bellhops and drivers a little something extra for a job well done.

VOLUNTEERING

The country attracts many volunteers, but whether they are actually helpful to Haiti is another matter. Many organizations can offer life-changing experiences for volunteers, but the prime objective must be to provide sustainable benefits for the local population. The website Good Intentions Are Not Enough (www.goodintents.org) is a good place to start to dissect this thorny issue.

Fondam Haiti (www.fondam-haiti.org) Working on reforestation in the southwest, particularly Port Salut.

Gheskio (☏in USA 646-962-8140; www.gheskio.org) A Haitian HIV/AIDS NGO, working since 1982 and providing free health care for HIV patients.

SLEEPING PRICE RANGES

The following price ranges refer to a double room with bathroom; breakfast is usually included, along with a ceiling fan. Air-conditioning is often included in midrange and top-end properties.

$ less than US$70

$$ US$70–US$130

$$$ more than US$130

Lambi Fund (☑ in USA 202-772-2372; www. lambifund.org) A grassroots civil society NGO, working on sustainable development, environment and civic-empowerment programs in rural areas.

Partners in Health (☑ in USA 857-880-5100; www.pih.org) Set up by Dr Paul Farmer, providing health care across rural Haiti.

WORK

Paid work is in short supply in Haiti. Official unemployment estimates mask far higher figures, and wages are desperately inadequate. Competition for jobs is enormous, so to find work you need to be able to demonstrate you have skills that no one in the domestic market possesses. Fluency in French and/or Creole is virtually essential. After you've been in the country for 90 days you must register as a resident with the Department of Immigration, for which you'll need a letter from your embassy and your employer, a health check and a Haitian bank account proving solvency. You must also apply for a Haitian work permit at the **Ministère des Affaires Sociales** (Ministry of Social Affairs; Map p228; ☑ 2940-0928; www.mast.gouv.ht; Rue de l'Entrrement, Port-au-Prince).

Many foreigners working in Haiti and not in business are involved in aid and development. ReliefWeb (www.reliefweb.int) and DevNet (www.devnetjobs.org) are good places to look for jobs in the development sector in Haiti.

ⓘ Getting There & Away

Most travelers enter Haiti by air through Port-au-Prince, with the most common flight routes all being from the US – Miami, Fort Lauderdale and New York. The international airport at Cap-Haïtien also handles a small number of incoming flights.

By land, there are several border crossings with the Dominican Republic, and direct bus services link Port-au-Prince with Santo Domingo, and Cap-Haïtien with Santiago. There are no international boat services to Haiti.

Flights and tours can be booked online at www.lonelyplanet.com/bookings.

AIRPORTS & AIRLINES

Haiti has two international airports: **Aéroport International Toussaint Louverture** (☑ 4865-6436) in Port-au-Prince and **Hugo Chávez International Airport** (☑ 4478-5057, 2262-8539) in Cap-Haïtien. Numerous international carriers offer services to Haiti, including Sunrise Airways, JetBlue Airways, American Airlines, Spirit Airlines, Air France, Air Antilles Express, Insel Air, InterCaribbean Airways, Delta, Cubana, Copa, Aeromexico and Avianca.

LAND

The Haitian-Dominican border has three official crossing points. Most useful to travelers is the Malpasse-Jimaní crossing between Port-au-Prince and Santo Domingo, followed by the northern Ouanaminthe-Dajabón crossing on the road between Cap-Haïtien and Santiago. A third, and little-used, crossing is from Belladère to Comendador (aka Elías Piña).

There are direct coach services linking the two capitals, and also Cap-Haïtien to Santiago. Included in the cost of the tickets are border fees that all travelers have to pay. Entering the DR you must pay US$10 for a tourist card. The situation with fees entering and leaving Haiti by land is fluid – officials regularly ask for US$10 to stamp you in or out, and ostensibly the money goes toward promoting the destination, strengthening the tourist police (Politour) and training for careers in tourism.

The Haitian border can be slightly chaotic if you're traveling independently, particularly at Ouanaminthe with its sprawling local market. Onward transport is plentiful, however, along with the occasional hustle – any tourist is going to stand out in this scenario.

ⓘ Getting Around

AIR

Domestic flights operate from **Aérogare Guy Malary** (☑ 2250-1127), near the international terminal. The two airlines that operate there are **Sunrise Airways** (☑ 2811-2222, 2816-0616; www.sunriseairways.net; Aérogare Guy Malary) and **Mission Aviation Fellowship** (MAF; ☑ 3791-9209, 2941-9209; www.maf.org; Aérogare Guy Malary; ⊙7am-4pm Mon-Sat).

Haiti's small size means that flights are short (no flight is longer than 40 minutes), saving hours on bad roads. The planes are small, typically carrying 16 passengers or fewer. One-way tickets usually cost around US$100.

BOAT

Public boat taxis are common and relatively affordable in the north and south of Haiti for transport between locations not connected by roads. Hiring private boats is less economical.

BUS

Getting around Haiti by bus and minibus isn't always comfortable, but it's the cheapest way to travel within the country, and services run to most places you'll want to get to. Sturdy beasts, buses have the advantage of taking you to places that you'd usually need a 4WD to reach.

CAR & MOTORCYCLE

Although having your own wheels is a convenient way of seeing Haiti, be aware that you need both nerves of steel and a sense of humor. Terrible roads, a lack of road signs, and the perils of wayward pedestrians and oncoming traffic are all part of the mix.

MOTO-TAXI

The quickest and easiest way to get around any town is to hop on the back of a moto-taxi (motorcycle taxi), often just referred to as a 'moto'. A trip will rarely cost more than about US$0.75, although rates can climb steeply if you want to travel any serious distance. Motos in Port-au-Prince are more expensive than elsewhere.

If you want to wear a helmet, you'll need to have one with you. This is a very good idea, considering how people drive in Haiti. Moto drivers and passengers are regularly injured and even killed in accidents.

TAPTAP & CAMIONETTE

Smaller vehicles than buses ply the roads carrying passengers. A taptap is a converted pick-up, often brightly decorated, with bench seats in the back. Fares are slightly cheaper than a bus. The same rules for buses apply to taptaps, which leave from the same *estasyon:* they go when full, the comfy seats next to the driver are more pricey, and you can hail one and get off where you like.

Taptaps are better suited for short trips, and in many areas are likely to be the only feasible way of getting around. Halfway between a taptap and a bus is the *camionette*. There are no seats, just a few ropes dangling from the ceiling for people to hold on to.

TAXI

Port-au-Prince and Cap-Haïtien operate collective taxis called *publiques* for getting around town. You might find them hard to spot initially, as they look like any other battered car, but look for the red ribbon hanging from the front mirror and license plates starting with 'T' for transport.

Major towns sometimes have radio-taxi firms with meters.

Understand Dominican Republic

Dominican Republic Today

The Dominican Republic has enjoyed an economic heyday of late, with tourism booming and free-trade zones flourishing, but stubborn problems have lingered, namely corrupt politicians and trouble with Haiti. Add to that some pretty bad weather and you can bet that average Dominicans, who are no strangers to hardship, approach the present with a healthy dose of skepticism. Regardless, they certainly know how to celebrate and appreciate the good stuff: music, dancing, baseball, and, above all, family.

Best on Film

La Hija Natural (Love Child; 2011) A teenager's anguished attempt to find and get to know her estranged father. Dominican entry for Best Foreign Film at 2011 Academy Awards.

Sugar (2009) Story of a Dominican baseball prospect's journey to minor leagues in middle America.

Ladrones a Domicilio (Robbers of the House; 2008) A political satire and slapstick comedy involving a robbery and kidnapping, and corruption in everyday life.

Best in Print

Dead Man in Paradise (JB Mackinnon; 2009) Canadian journalist JB Mackinnon, the nephew of a priest murdered during the Trujillo regime, tries to piece together the unsolved crime.

Fiesta del Chivo (Feast of the Goat; Mario Vargas Llosa; 2000) Peruvian novelist Mario Vargas Llosa's imaginative telling of dictator Rafael Trujillo's final days.

The Brief Wondrous Life of Oscar Wao (Junot Díaz; 2007) Inventive story of a self-professed Dominican nerd in New Jersey and the tragic history of his family in the DR.

The Farming of Bones (Edwidge Danticat; 1998) Danticat's novel movingly recreates the events around the 1937 massacre of Haitians in the DR.

Politics & Economy

In true Dominican fashion, let's start with what's working. In 2015, a constitutional reform allowed presidents to run for a second consecutive term, and the sitting president Danilo Medina unsurprisingly seized the opportunity. He was reelected in 2016 in a landslide, which probably had a lot to do with the fact that during his first term, social services were expanded and the economy grew rapidly.

In 2015, GDP was growing at 7 percent, the fastest rate of any country in Latin America, thanks to healthy tourism, construction and mining industries. Inflation was relatively low, and around $1 billion was coming in via remittances from more than a million Dominicans living abroad. Although sugar, coffee and tobacco had for decades been the country's largest employers, the service sector overtook agriculture both in the number of jobs it provided and the revenue it brought in. In 2016, more than 6 million tourists are predicted to have visited the DR, which will generate more than $6.5 billion in revenue.

Corruption & Drugs

Corruption has long been a problem in the Dominican Republic, at all levels of government and within the private sector. The most recent example is the Odebrecht scandal, in which a Brazilian construction company paid US$92 million in bribes to DR government officials to secure public contracts, which in turn allowed the company to collect US$163 million in profit, according to US Justice Department documents. The DR wasn't the only place Odebrecht bribed, but it was one of the big ones.

In 2015, the alleged dirty dealings of DR Senator Felix Bautista were voted the worst corruption in the world by Transparency International's Unmask the Corrupt campaign. Bautista has been accused of money laundering, abuse of power, and elicit enrichment, though judges from within Bautista's political party have dismissed the cases. Widespread corruption has contributed to the DR becoming a transshipment hub for narcotics, with hundreds of flights and boats arriving yearly on its shores with cocaine from South America en route to the US and Europe.

Weather Challenges
Global warming and extreme weather events have wreaked havoc on the Caribbean in recent years, causing flooding, ocean acidification and beach erosion. DR's capital Santo Domingo is predicted to be among the five cities in the world most affected by rising sea levels, and lately the north has been hard hit with heavy rains and flooding.

In late 2016, just after Hurricane Matthew swung through and decimated southern Haiti, heavy rains fell for more than two weeks on the DR's north coast, causing widespread damage to the country's agriculture and infrastructure and forcing the president to declare a national emergency. Thankfully, the Dominican Republic is taking climate change seriously. Its fishermen have organized grassroots projects to protect mangrove nurseries and the government has made it clear that adapting to a warmer world is a priority.

The Other Half
Many Dominicans are still angry about the Haitian occupation of their country that ended in 1844, among other issues. And in a country where darker skin is often associated with lower social standing, the government has instituted a series of laws/regulations that have effectively marginalized even Dominican citizens of Haitian descent.

In September 2013, the Dominican Constitutional Court ruled that 'people born in the Dominican Republic to undocumented parents' weren't automatically afforded citizenship themselves. The decision, which applied to anyone born after 1929, was widely and strongly condemned by human rights activists, foreign governments and influential Dominican writers, artists and intellectuals as a racist ruling that targets Dominicans of Haitian descent. In response to this, the government created a 'regularization process' in 2015 that allowed people to apply for residency. The government claims that 364,965 people have 'regularized' their documentation, although activists claim the number is much lower.

Trade disputes are also commonplace, including unverified accusations that the DR ships lesser and unsafe goods to Haiti and that Haitian products are glaringly absent from Dominican stores. Nationalists from both sides have talked of building a wall that lines the entire 300km (190 miles) border.

POPULATION: **10,606,870**

AREA: **48,670 SQ KM**

GDP PER CAPITA:
US$15,900 (2016 EST)

UNEMPLOYMENT: **13.8% (2016 EST)**

POP BELOW POVERTY LINE :
41.1% (2015 EST)

if the Dominican Republic were 100 people

73 would be mixed race
16 would be white
11 would be black

belief systems
(% of population)

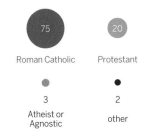

75 — Roman Catholic
20 — Protestant
3 — Atheist or Agnostic
2 — other

population per sq km

DOMINICAN REPUBLIC — HAITI — USA

👤 ≈ 35 people

History

Since 1492, when Columbus landed on Hispaniola, the Dominican Republic has seen wave after wave of foreign interlopers. The destruction of the native population led to periods of neglect and conflicts between the French and Spanish colonial systems. Shaping the DR as much as anything is its relationship with Haiti, its onetime invader and island neighbor. Though decades of dictatorial misrule left scars, physical and psychological, Dominicans are proud of their heritage, and in recent years nationalist pride has surged.

The Taínos

Christopher Columbus, Hernán Cortés, Francisco Pizarro, Juan Ponce de León and Vasco Nuñez de Balboa all spent time in what is now the DR.

Hispaniola had been inhabited for three millennia before Christopher Columbus sailed into view, colonized by a successive wave of island-hopping incomers from South America. Most notable were the Arawaks, and then the Taínos ('the friendly people'), who prospered on the island for around 700 years until the clash of civilizations with Europe brought their ultimate downfall.

The Taínos were both farmers and seafarers, living in chiefdoms called *caciques*, with a total population of around 500,000 at the time of Columbus' arrival. Each chiefdom comprised several districts with villages of 1000 to 2000 people.

Comparatively little of Taíno culture has survived to the modern age. Pottery and stone tools form the most common artifacts, along with jewelry of bone, shell and gold that was panned from rivers. Clothing was made of cotton or pounded bark fibers. While Taíno artifacts are relatively few, the crops they bequeathed to the world were revolutionary, from tobacco to yams, cassava and pineapples. Hispaniola's inhabitants, however, were barely to survive their first encounter with Europe.

The Columbus Brothers

In 1492 Christopher Columbus sailed from Spain with 90 men in the *Pinta,* the *Niña* and the *Santa María,* bound for Asia. He sailed west rather than east, expecting to circumnavigate the globe, instead discovering the New World for the Old. After stops at the small Bahamian island of Guanahaní and present-day Cuba (which Columbus initially mistook

TIMELINE	4000 BC	1200 BC	AD 500–1000
	Earliest evidence of human colonization of Hispaniola. Stone-flaked tools found at archaeological digs are thought to have been brought by hunter-gatherers migrating from the Yucatan peninsula in Mexico.	Ancestral Arawaks arrive in Hispaniola, via the Lesser Antilles. Dubbed 'the Saladoid culture,' they live in settled agricultural communities, and are best known for their sophisticated pottery.	A third wave of migration arrives in Hispaniola, with the rich seafaring culture of the Taínos. The population expands rapidly, and is divided into a series of interdependent but competing chiefdoms.

for Japan), a mountainous landscape appeared before the explorers. Columbus named it 'La Isla Española' or 'the Spanish Island,' which was later corrupted to 'Hispaniola.' He made landfall at Môle St-Nicholas in modern Haiti on December 7, and days later ran the *Santa María* onto a reef. Here on Christmas Day he established Villa La Navidad, the first settlement of any kind made by Europeans in the New World.

Columbus was greeted with great warmth by the Taínos, who impressed him further with their gifts of gold jewelry. Capturing a handful of Taínos to impress his royal patrons, he sailed back to Spain to be showered with glory. He returned within a year, leading 17 ships of soldiers and colonists.

La Navidad had been razed by the Taínos in reprisal for the kidnappings by the settlers, so Columbus sailed east and established La Isabela, named for Spain's queen, on the north coast of the DR; the first church in the Americas was erected here. However, La Isabela was plagued with disease, and within five years the capital of the new colony was moved to Santo Domingo, where it has remained.

Columbus' early administration was a disaster and appointing his brother Bartholomé proved no better. Their haphazard rule soon had the colonists up in arms, and a replacement sent from Spain returned the brothers home in chains. The colony would now be run with military harshness.

The Taínos were the ones to bear the brunt of this. They were already stricken by European illnesses that sent their numbers crashing, but on top of this Spain introduced *encomienda,* forced labor requiring the natives to dig up quotas of gold. The Spanish broke up Taíno villages, killed their chiefs and put the entire population to work. Within three decades of their first meeting with Europeans, the Taínos were reduced to a shadow of their previous numbers.

European Competition & Colonization

As Taíno civilization collapsed, so did the gold mines, and no amount of imported African slaves could make up the shortfall. Spain dropped Hispaniola as quickly as it had found it, turning its attention instead to the immense riches coming from its new possessions in Mexico and Peru. Santo Domingo was reduced to a trading post for gold and silver convoys, but couldn't even hold onto that position with the opening of new trade routes via Cuba. After the English admiral Sir Francis Drake sacked Santo Domingo in 1586, it was effectively abandoned for the next 50 years, further signaling the decline of Spanish Hispaniola.

For the next three centuries, Europe was riven by war. Imperial Spain slipped into a slow decline, and the English and French took advantage, competing not just in the Old World but in North America

'I cannot believe that any man has ever met a people so good-hearted and generous, so gentle that they did their utmost to give us everything they had' – Christopher Columbus on meeting the Taínos.

1492	1503	1496	1500
Christopher Columbus makes landfall on Hispaniola on Christmas Day and founds the settlement of La Navidad (Nativity) near modern-day Cap-Haïtien in Haiti, before returning to Spain with Taíno captives.	Queen Anacaona of the Taíno kingdom of Xaragua in central Hispaniola is arrested by the Spanish governor and publicly executed, effectively marking the end of Taíno independence on the island.	Nueva Isabela founded by the Spanish. Rebuilt as Santo Domingo after a 1502 hurricane, it quickly receives a royal charter, making it the oldest European city in the New World.	A Santo Domingo governor captures Christopher Columbus and returns him to Spain in shackles; Queen Isabella orders him released soon after.

and the Caribbean. Hispaniola was considered a great prize. The colony was stagnating under Spanish rule. Both the English and French encouraged piracy against the Spanish, even licensing the pirates as 'privateers,' and the rugged coast and mountainous interior of Hispaniola made it an ideal base for operations. Although a few captains became notorious raiders, most divided their time between hunting the wild cattle and pigs that thrived on the island and plundering for booty. The lack of any governmental control also made the island a haven for runaway slaves.

For security, the Spanish convoys sailed en masse once a year, a system that effectively cut Hispaniola off from trade with the mother country – not only were visiting ships few and far between, but the colonists were banned from trading with non-Spaniards. The colony shrank to the area around Santo Domingo, leaving the rest of the island open for the taking.

The English attempted to come in through the front door in 1655, but their army of 13,000 soldiers was repelled at the gates of Santo Domingo. Years of neglect meant the 125,000-person Spanish colony missed out on the sugar rush for now (Spanish investors had preferred to put their money into booming Cuba), relying primarily on cattle ranching for its lifeblood. Slave imports had never been high, as they simply couldn't be afforded, and slaves made up less than 1% of the population.

French tobacco farmers grabbed more and more territory until France had formed a de facto colony (which would become Haiti). The Spanish could do nothing, especially as France was beating them on the battlefields of Europe. At the close of the 17th century, France had managed to grab the western two-thirds of Hispaniola, christening them the colony of Saint-Domingue. It was the richest colony in the world due to sugar and slavery (around half the world's sugar and coffee came from the colony and the produce of 8000 plantations was providing 40% of France's foreign trade).

Pre-Colonial Sites

Cueva de las Maravillas, La Romana
....
Reserva Antropológica del Pomier, San Cristóbal
....
Parque Nacional Cotubanamá, near Bayahibe
....
Piedra Letrada, Constanza
....
El Corral de los Indios, near San Juan de la Maguana

PIRATES OF THE CARIBBEAN

The purported remains – mostly pieces of cannons, anchors and wood – of the *Quedagh Merchant,* which belonged to the Scottish privateer Captain William Kidd, were found in the waters off Isla Catalina near the shores of the Casa de Campo resort. The ship was scuttled and set on fire after Kidd returned to England to face charges of piracy. Despite the fact that he was often acting under the authority of the English navy, he was convicted of piracy and hanged in London in 1701.

1510	1519–1533	1586	1605
King Ferdinand of Spain issues first royal charter to import slaves to Hispaniola. Demand booms, to supplement rapidly crashing Taíno workforce.	A Taíno *cacique* (chief) named Enriquillo leads a rebellion against the Spanish in the Bahoruco mountains near the present-day DR–Haiti border.	Following the outbreak of war between England and Spain, Sir Francis Drake leads a devastating naval raid against Santo Domingo, leaving the city virtually razed.	Spain sends the army to relocate most of its colonists to Santo Domingo city by force, to prevent contraband trade with foreign merchants, effectively abandoning claims to western Hispaniola.

Separation Anxiety

While France and Spain's power in Europe waxed and waned, so, too, did their imperialist ambitions. And conflict within the colonies became an avenue for waging proxy wars against their rivals. So when the enslaved African population of western Hispaniola's Saint-Domingue rose up in bloody revolt, Spain supported the revolution. However, once the French agreed to abolish slavery, the former slaves turned their attention to liberating the entire island – the Spanish colony had about 60,000 slaves of its own. Lacking the appetite, will and ability to forcefully oppose the uprising, Spain and France haggled over the details, one of which involved the injunction that Spanish colonists abdicate their lands in exchange for ones in Cuba.

In 1801, frustrated by the slow pace of negotiations, François Dominique Toussaint Louverture, a former slave and leader of the rebel forces, marched into Santo Domingo and, without French authority, declared that the abolition of slavery would be enforced throughout the island. At odds with French leaders, especially Napoleon Bonaparte who now viewed him as a loose cannon, he was betrayed to the invading forces, who sent him in chains to France, where he died of neglect in a dungeon in April 1803.

Jean-Jacques Dessalines, who had been one of Toussaint's chief lieutenants, crowned himself emperor of the Republic of Haiti (an old Taíno name for the island) with the clearly stated ambition of uniting Hispaniola under one flag. Free, educated mulattoes were spurned, laborers were forced back onto the plantations to rebuild the economy, the remaining whites were massacred and the Spanish colony was invaded by General Henri Christophe whose forces participated in mass killings of civilians in Santiago and Moca. Dessalines' rule was brutal and the reaction inevitable – in 1806, he was killed in an ambush outside Port-au-Prince.

For the Spanish colonists in Santo Domingo, this new imperialist threat compelled them to ask Spain to reincorporate them into the empire. But through neglect and mismanagement Spain completely bungled its administration of Santo Domingo and on November 30, 1821, the colony declared its independence once again. Colonial leaders intended to join the Republic of Gran Colombia (a country that included present-day Ecuador, Colombia, Panama and Venezuela) but never got the chance – Haiti invaded and finally achieved its goal of a united Hispaniola.

Dominicans chafed under Haitian rule for the next 22 years, and to this day both countries regard the other with disdain and suspicion. Resistance grew until February 27, 1844 – a day celebrated as Domini-

The *trinitaria*, a bougainvillea that blooms purple, red and magenta, also refers to Juan Pablo Duarte, Francisco del Rosario Sánchez and Ramón Mella, the three fathers of the republic, and to the secret cells of three that were organized in 1838 to struggle for independence from Haiti.

HISTORY SEPARATION ANXIETY

Between 1844 and 1916, the Dominican Republic had 40 different governments.

1655	1697	1821–22	1844
An English military expedition is dispatched by Oliver Cromwell to conquer Santo Domingo. Although beaten back, the navy saves face by managing to grab Jamaica as a permanent Caribbean foothold.	The Treaty of Ryswick settles the nine-year pan-European War of the Grand Alliance. As a result, Hispaniola's borders are settled, dividing the island into Spanish Santa Domingo and French St-Domingue.	Colonists of Santo Domingo, known as Spanish Haiti, declare independence from Spain in November 1821, only to be invaded by Haiti nine weeks later and incorporated into a united Hispaniola.	Coalition of Santo Domingo intellectuals and rebel Haitian soldiers sparks a largely bloodless coup and the Dominican Republic declares its independence from Haiti, after 22 years of occupation.

can Independence Day – when a separatist movement headed by Juan Pablo Duarte captured Santo Domingo in a bloodless coup. The Puerto del Conde in Santo Domingo marks the spot where Duarte entered the city. Despite the reversal of fortunes of the two countries in the 20th century, many Dominicans still view Haiti as an aggressive nation with territorial ambitions.

Fearing another invasion and still feeling threatened by Haiti in 1861, the Dominican Republic once again submitted to Spanish rule. But ordinary Dominicans did not support the move and, after four years of armed resistance, succeeded in expelling Spanish troops in what is known as the War of Restoration. (Restauración is a common street name throughout the DR, and there are a number of monuments to the war, including a prominent one in Santiago.) On March 3, 1865, the Queen of Spain signed a decree annulling the annexation and withdrew her soldiers from the island.

Power from the North

With no strong central government, the newly independent Dominican Republic was a fractured nation, divided up among several dozen *caudillos* (military leaders) and their militias. From 1865 until 1879 there were more than 50 military uprisings or coups and 21 changes in government. In 1869, after Buenaventura Báez, the leader of a coalition of plantation owners, mahogany exporters and a significant portion of residents of Santo Domingo, was installed as president, he attempted to sell the country to the US for US$150,000. Even though the treaty was signed by Báez and US president Ulysses S Grant, the agreement was defeated in the US Senate.

The US was to involve itself once again in Dominican affairs, this time at the invitation of General Ulises Heureaux, who stabilized the musical chairs of political and military leadership from 1882 until his assassination in 1899. The general, known as Lilí, borrowed heavily from American and European banks to finance the army, infrastructure and sugar industry. But after a sharp drop-off in world sugar prices, Lilí essentially mortgaged the country to the US-owned and -operated San Domingo Improvement Company just before his death. Because the Dominican government was bankrupt, the US government intervened in 1905 by taking control of the customs houses and guaranteeing repayment of all loans, stopping just short of ratifying President Theodore Roosevelt's plan to establish a protectorate over the DR.

Despite some economic growth, after the assassination of another president in 1911, Dominican politics mostly remained chaotic, corrupt and bloody. In 1916, under the dual pretext of quelling yet another coup as well as guarding the waters from German aggression during WWI,

---

Colonial Sites

Zona Colonial, Santo Domingo

Fuerte de San Felipe, Puerto Plata

La Vega Vieja, La Vega

Parque Nacional La Isabela, north coast

Casa Ponce de León, near San Rafael del Yuma

Why the Cocks Fight, by Michele Wucker, examines Dominican-Haitian relations through the metaphor of cockfighting.

1849	1865	1870s	1880–1884
Buenaventura Báez begins the first of five terms – between 1849 and 1878 – as president of the DR. One of his first acts is an attempt to have his country annexed by the USA.	Two years after the initial uprising in Santiago, triggered by the Spanish authority's continual erosion of Dominican rights, the DR gains independence by defeating Spanish troops in the War of Restoration.	Baseball is first introduced to the Dominican Republic by Cubans fleeing their own country during the Ten Years War.	A handful of modern sugar mills begin operating in San Pedro de Macorís, the start of the Dominican sugar industry.

President Woodrow Wilson sent US marines to the DR – they remained for the next eight years. (Similarly, Wilson sent the marines into Haiti in 1915, claiming, ironically, that unrest there made it vulnerable to a German invasion – the occupation lasted 20 years.) Though deeply imperialistic, the US occupation did succeed in stabilizing Dominican politics and the economy. Once the DR's strategic value to the US had dropped, and a new strain of isolationism had entered American discourse, the occupation ended and the troops were sent home.

The Rise of Caudillo

Like the calm before the storm, the years from 1924 to 1930 were in many ways positive, led by a progressive president, Horacio Vásquez, whose administration built major roads and schools and initiated irrigation and sanitation programs. Vásquez extended his four-year term to six, a constitutionally questionable move that was nevertheless approved by the Congress. When a revolution was proclaimed in Santiago, Rafael Leónidas Trujillo, chief of the former Dominican National Police (renamed the National Army in 1928), ordered his troops to remain in their barracks, effectively forcing Vásquez and his vice president from office. After a sham election in which he was the sole candidate, Trujillo assumed the presidency. Within weeks he organized a terrorist band, La 42, which roamed the country, killing everyone who posed any threat to him. An egomaniac of the first degree, he changed the names of various cities – Santo Domingo became Ciudad Trujillo, for example – and lavished support on San Cristóbal, the small city west of the capital where he was born; a never-used palace Trujillo had built there can still be visited.

Trujillo ruled the Dominican Republic with an iron fist from 1930 to 1961, lavishing over 21% of the national budget on the ever-expanding Guardia Nacional and creating a handful of intelligence agencies dedicated to suppressing any dissent. The torture and murder of political prisoners was a daily event in Trujillo's DR. Two of the more infamous incidents were the kidnapping and murder of a Spanish professor teaching in New York City, who had criticized his regime, and plotting to assassinate the Venezuelan president Rómulo Betancourt. Trujillo, in spite of being part black, was deeply racist and xenophobic; he sought to 'whiten' the Dominican population by increasing European immigration and placing quotas on the number of Haitians allowed in the country.

During these years, Trujillo used his government to amass a personal fortune by establishing monopolies that he and his wife controlled. By 1934 he was the richest man on the island. Today there are many Dominicans who remember Trujillo's rule with a certain amount of fondness and nostalgia, in part because Trujillo did develop the economy. Factories were opened, a number of grandiose infrastructure and public works

Alan Cambeira's *Azucar! The Story of Sugar* is a fascinating novel that portrays the human toll of sugar production in the DR, with much of the information, descriptions and events based on real events.

In honor of the Mirabal sisters, Minerva, Paria and Maria Teresa, activists who were murdered by Trujillo's agents, the UN declared November 25, the day of their death, Inter national Day for the Elimination of Violence Against Women.

1904–1905	1916–24	1930	1937
US Marines are sent to Santo Domingo to assist the Dominican government fighting rebels; customs collections are turned over to the US.	After years of civil wars, the US occupies the Dominican Republic under the pretense of securing debt payments owed by the defaulting Dominican government.	After six years of relatively stable government, Rafael Trujillo, the chief of the Dominican National Police, declares himself president after an election in which he was the sole candidate.	In the culmination of his xenophobia, paranoia, racism and tyranny, dictator Rafael Trujillo orders the extermination of Haitians along the border; tens of thousands are killed in a matter of days.

projects were carried out, bridges and highways were built, and peasants were given state land to cultivate.

Border Bloodbath

The zenith of the Haiti xenophobia was Trujillo's massacre of tens of thousands of Haitians in 1937. After hearing reports that Haitian peasants were crossing into the Dominican Republic, perhaps to steal cattle, Trujillo ordered all Haitians along the border to be tracked down and executed. Dominican soldiers used a simple test to separate Haitians from Dominicans – they would hold up a string of parsley (*perejil* in Spanish) and ask everyone they encountered to name it. French- and Creole-speaking Haitians could not properly trill the 'r' and were summarily murdered. Beginning on October 3 and lasting for several days, at least 15,000 – and some researchers claim as many as 35,000 – Haitians were hacked to death with machetes, their bodies dumped into the ocean.

Trujillo never openly admitted a massacre had taken place, but in 1938, under international pressure, he and Haitian president Sténio Vincent agreed the Dominican Republic would pay a total of US$750,000 as reparation for Haitians who had been killed (US$50 per person). The Dominican Republic made an initial payment of US$250,000 but it's unclear if it ever paid the rest.

Trujillo's nicknames included Hot Balls, the Goat, the Chief and the Butcher.

False Starts

When Trujillo was assassinated by a group of Dominican dissidents on May 30, 1961, some hoped that the country would turn a corner. The promise of change, however, was short-lived. President Joaquín Balaguer officially assumed the office. He renamed the capital Santo Domingo. After a groundswell of unrest and at the insistence of the USA, a seven-member Council of State, which included two of the men who'd taken part in Trujillo's deadly ambush, was established to guide the country until elections were held in December 1962. The first free elections in many years in the DR was won by the scholar-poet Juan Bosch Gaviño.

Nine months later, after introducing liberal policies including the redistribution of land, the creation of a new constitution and guaranteeing civil and individual rights, Bosch was deposed by yet another military coup in September 1963. Wealthy landowners, to whom democracy was a threat, and a group of military leaders led by Generals Elías Wessin y Wessin and Antonio Imbert Barreras installed Donald Reid Cabral, a prominent businessman, as president. Bosch fled into exile but his supporters, calling themselves the Constitutionalists, took to the streets and seized the National Palace. Santo Domingo saw the stirrings of a civil war; the military launched tank assaults and bombing runs against civilian protesters.

Trujillo's titles include Benefactor of the Fatherland, Founder and Supreme Chief of the Partido Dominicana, Restorer of Financial Independence, First Journalist of the Republic and Doctor Honoris Causa in the Economic Political Sciences.

1956	1956–59	1961	1962–63
Ozzie Virgil (Osvaldo Virgil) becomes the first Dominican to play in the baseball major leagues as an infielder for the New York Giants.	More than 1000 Japanese refugees fleeing WWII are welcomed to the Dominican Republic by dictator Rafael Trujillo, and hundreds jumpstart Constanza's agricultural pursuits.	Despite the support he has received over the years from the US as a staunch anticommunist ally, Rafael Trujillo is assassinated by a group of CIA-trained Dominican dissidents.	In the first democratic election in nearly 40 years, Juan Bosch, leader of the left-leaning Dominican Revolutionary Party, is elected president and later removed in a coup orchestrated by a three-person junta.

The fighting continued until the USA intervened yet again. This time the Johnson administration, after losing Cuba, feared a left-wing or communist takeover of the Dominican Republic despite the fact that Bosch wasn't a communist and papers later revealed US intelligence had identified only 54 individuals who were part of the movement fighting the military junta. The official reason was that the US could no longer guarantee the safety of its nationals and so over 500 marines landed in Santo Domingo on April 27, 1965. A week later and only 40 years since the previous occupation, 14,000 American military personnel were stationed in the Dominican Republic.

Caudillo Redux

Elections were held in July 1966. Balaguer defeated Bosch. Many voters had feared a Bosch victory would lead to civil war. Bosch would go on to contest elections in 1978, 1982, 1986, 1990 and 1994, always losing. Balaguer, meanwhile, would outlast every Latin American ruler except Fidel Castro. Not the typical authoritarian dictator, Balaguer was a poet and a writer – in one book he argues against interracial marriage – who lived in the servant's quarters of his female-dominated home.

Taking a page from Trujillo's playbook, Balaguer curtailed opposition through bribes and intimidation and went on to win reelection in 1970 and 1974. Despite economic growth, in part fueled by investment and aid from the USA, which saw Balaguer as a staunch anticommunist ally, Balaguer lost the 1978 election to a wealthy cattle rancher named Silvestre Antonio Guzmán. The transfer of power wouldn't come easily, however: Balaguer ordered troops to destroy ballot boxes and declared himself the victor, standing down only after US president Jimmy Carter refused to recognize his victory.

As a result of plunging sugar prices and rising oil costs, the Dominican economy came to a standstill under Guzmán's administration; he committed suicide shortly before leaving office in 1982. His successor, Salvador Jorge Blanco, adhered to a fiscal austerity plan under pressure from the International Monetary Fund, measures that were far from popular with many ordinary Dominicans. (Blanco, who passed away in 2011, is the only president in the DR to have been prosecuted for corruption.) But old dictators don't go easily and Balaguer, 80 years old and blind with glaucoma, returned to power in the 1986 election.

For the next eight years Balaguer set about reversing every economic reform of the Blanco program; the result was five-fold devaluing of the Dominican peso and soaring annual inflation rates. With little chance of prospering at home, almost 900,000 Dominicans, or 12% of the country's population, had moved to New York by 1990. After Balaguer won the 1990 and 1994 elections (amid accusations of electoral fraud),

Life in Santo Domingo during the Trujillo regime was regimented: begging was allowed only on Saturdays, laborers were awakened with a siren at 7am, while office workers were given an extra hour to sleep in; their siren was at 8am.

1965	1966	1973	1974
Lyndon Johnson ultimately sends 42,000 US Army personnel and Marines to invade the DR, ostensibly to prevent a civil war. The troops remain until October 1966.	Trujillo's former vice-president, Dr Joaquín Balaguer, is elected president.	A state of emergency is declared by Balaguer after a small guerilla invasion fails; Bosch goes into hiding after Balaguer implicates him in insurgency.	The rare blue mineral Larimar is discovered on a beach in the province of Barahona and named after Larissa Méndez (daughter of one discoverer Miguel Méndez) and the sea (mar).

the military grew weary of his rule and he agreed to cut his last term short, hold elections and, most importantly, not be a candidate. But it wouldn't be his last campaign – he would run once more at the age of 92, winning 23% of the vote in the 2000 presidential election. Thousands would mourn his death two years later, despite the fact that he prolonged the Trujillo-style dictatorship for decades. His most lasting legacy may be the Faro a Colón, an enormously expensive monument to the discovery of the Americas that drained Santo Domingo of electricity whenever the lighthouse was turned on.

Moving away from the Past

The Dominican people signaled their desire for change in electing Leonel Fernández, a 42-year-old lawyer who grew up in New York City, as president in 1996; he edged out three-time candidate José Francisco Peña Gómez in a runoff. Still, the speed of his initial moves shocked the nation. Fernández forcibly retired two dozen generals, encouraged his defense minister to submit to questioning by the civilian attorney general and fired the defense minister for insubordination – all in a single week. In the four years of his first presidential term, he presided over strong economic growth and privatization, and lowered inflation and high rates of unemployment and illiteracy – accusations of endemic corruption, however, remained pervasive.

A Brief History of the Caribbean: From the Arawak and Carib to the Present by Jan Rogoziński does an excellent job of placing Hispaniola into the larger currents of Caribbean history.

Hipólito Mejía, a former tobacco farmer, succeeded Fernández in 2000 and immediately cut spending and increased fuel prices, not exactly the platform he ran on. The faltering US economy and September 11 attacks ate into Dominican exports, as well as cash remittances and foreign tourism. Corruption scandals involving the civil service, unchecked spending, electricity shortages and several bank failures, which cost the government in the form of huge bailouts for depositors, all spelled doom for Mejía's reelection chances.

More of the Same

Familiar faces reappear again and again in Dominican politics and Fernández returned to the national stage by handily defeating Mejía in the 2004 presidential elections. In 2005, to the consternation of many, the Dominican Supreme Court ruled that the children of visitors 'in transit' were not afforded citizenship. This ruling defined illegal immigrants, which virtually all Haitian workers are, as 'in transit', meaning that even those Haitians who were born in the DR and lived their entire lives there were denied citizenship. And on the border, by the end of 2007 there were 200 UN soldiers, mostly from other Caribbean countries, helping to buttress the DR army's attempts to stop the flow of drugs and arms across the Haitian border. In early 2008 tensions flared again along the

1979	1982	1986	1996
Hurricane David becomes the only Category 5 storm to make landfall in the Dominican Republic this century. It kills more than 2000 Dominicans and left 200,000 homeless.	Distraught over revelations of financial corruption and improprieties, incumbent President Silvestre Antonio Guzmán commits suicide, with just over a month left in term.	After an eight-year hiatus, Joaquín Balaguer, 80 years old and blind, is elected to his fifth term as president despite his previous administration's corruption and dismal human rights record.	After massive election fraud and widespread national and international pressure, Balaguer agrees to step down after two years and Leonel Fernández is elected president.

border over accusations of cattle rustling and reprisals, and Dominican chickens being turned away because of fears over avian flu.

In May 2008, with the US and world economies faltering and continued conflict with Haiti, Fernández was reelected to another presidential term. He avoided a runoff despite mounting questions about

BIG SUGAR

After the island's gold reserves were quickly exhausted and the native population decimated, Spanish colonists harvested the first sugar crop in 1506. While the tropical climate and topography rendered it an ideal physical environment, labor was in short supply. Slaves imported from Africa rebelled and fled to the western part of the island – soon after, Spain discovered sugar was being sold to France and Holland and so decided to burn all they could.

It wasn't for another several hundred years, when in the mid-19th century prosperous Cuban plantation owners began to seek out new territory, that sugar took root once again in the DR. Cuba's failed 10-year war of independence only accelerated the migration, and only when slavery was abolished in other Spanish colonies like Cuba and Puerto Rico in the 1870s could the DR begin to compete in terms of production costs.

The first steam-powered sugar mill (*ingenio*) was opened in 1879 near San Pedro de Macorís on the southeast coast. This commercial port town was soon booming, with more than a half-dozen modern plants in operation by 1920. San Pedro, which would later become synonymous with baseball, became a relatively elegant and cosmopolitan town known for its poets as well as sugar wealth. When the European sugar industry was destroyed by WWI, Caribbean suppliers stepped into the void. Sugar became the DR's leading export and the US its leading buyer.

But Dominicans, able to survive with their own small plots of land, were largely uninterested in the backbreaking, low-paying work. Companies started turning to workers from the British-speaking Caribbean islands, who were more eager for seasonal labor and disinclined to push for better pay or improved working conditions. These migrant workers from the eastern Caribbean came to be called *cocolos* and the close quarters where they lived *bateyes*. A backlash was inevitable – in 1919 a law was passed banning non-Caucasians from immigrating to the DR. Though thousands of *cocolos* and their families remained around San Pedro working for the mills, Haitians began to replace them during the harvest, in part because it was easier for the companies to 'repatriate' them when the work was over.

When the bottom dropped out of the price of sugar on the world market in the 1930s, around the same time Trujillo came to power, the financial well-being of the industry in the DR was inextricably tied to quotas obtained through negotiations with the US. Just as he did in other sectors of the economy, Trujillo consolidated control and ownership in his family and coterie and was able to influence many members of the US Congress into supporting his regime through continued trade in sugar.

2003–04	2008	2010	2010
A growing financial crisis sparks widespread public unrest and protests, including a general strike in which several people are killed and scores injured by police.	In May Leonel Fernández convincingly wins reelection to his third presidential term; a 2002 constitutional amendment allows him to again run for office.	Haiti's cholera epidemic, following the devastating earthquake, spreads into the DR, reigniting border conflicts.	President Leonel Fernández orders the drafting of a new constitution that bans all forms of same-sex unions and abortion. It also revokes the right of a president to run for two consecutive terms.

the logic of spending US$700 million on Santo Domingo's subway system, rising gas prices, the fact that the DR still had one of the highest rates of income inequality in Latin America and the government's less-than-stellar response to the devastation wrought by Tropical Storm Noel in late October 2007. Over 66,000 people were displaced from their homes by the storm and around 100 communities were completely isolated, some for over two weeks, because of damaged roads and bridges. There were massive layoffs in the agricultural industry after crop production took a major hit.

Though considered competent and by some even forward-thinking, Fernández was also a typical politician beholden to special interests. The more cynical observers long claimed that the Fernández administration was allied with corrupt business and government officials, and they were proven correct long after Fernández left office, when the Odebrecht scandal unraveled in 2016. During Fernandez's term, the construction giant caught bribing DR officials with $92 million had nine projects going on in the country.

Aftershocks

The Last Playboy: The High Life of Porfirio Rubirosa, by Shawn Levy, tells the life story of the DR's most famous womanizer and Trujillo intimate.

In the aftermath of the devastating earthquake that struck Haiti in January 2010, the Dominican government provided medical and humanitarian assistance, and much of the aid from other countries was shipped overland through the DR. However, the thaw in relations only lasted so long. Haiti's cholera epidemic that erupted the following year led to the temporary closure of some border crossings, which ignited more conflict: several Haitians were killed and scores injured in protests. A rising number of incidents at the end of 2010 and beginning of 2011 left dozens of Haitians dead and hundreds injured in clashes in poor barrios around the country. Some Dominicans, claiming they were trying to evict illegal Haitians, say they were justified by the threat of cholera and crime. In the beginning of February 2011, the Dominican government initiated a widespread crackdown, deporting 'illegal' Haitians back over the border.

2012	2013	2016	2016
Danilo Medina wins the presidential elections (after Fernández decided not to pursue constitutional changes that would have allowed him to run for a fourth term).	A Constitutional Court ruling strips citizenship from hundreds of thousands of Dominicans with Haitian ancestry.	DR government officials are implicated in the Odebrecht scandal, one of the biggest corruption cases in history, for accepting $92 million in bribes.	Danilo Medina wins reelection a year after the constitution is changed (again) to allow a president to run for a second consecutive term.

Music & Dance

Life in the Dominican Republic seems to move to a constant, infectious rhythm, and music has always been an important part of the country's heritage. Despite, or perhaps in part because of, the country's tumultuous history of bitter divisions, revolutions and dictatorial rule, the DR has made significant contributions to the musical world, giving rise to some of Latin music's most popular and influential styles.

Merengue

Merengue is the national dance music of the Dominican Republic. From the minute you arrive until the minute you leave, merengue will be coming at you full volume: in restaurants, public buses, taxis, at the beach or simply walking down the street. Rhythmically driven and heavy on the downbeat, merengue follows a common 2-4 or 4-4 beat pattern and Domnicans dance to it with passion and flair. But what sets merengue apart from other musical forms is the presence of traditional signature instruments and how they work within the two- or four-beat structure. Merengue is typically played with a two-headed drum called a tambora, a guitar, an accordion-like instrument known as a melodeon, and a *güira* – a metal instrument that looks a little like a cheese grater and is scraped using a metal or plastic rod.

If you hit a dance club and take a shine to the music, you may want to pick up some CDs before leaving the country. A few of the most popular musicians include Johnny Ventura, Coco Band, Wilfrido Vargas, Milly y Los Vecinos, Fernando Villalona, Joseito Mateo, Rubby Perez, Miriam Cruz, Milly Quezada and, perhaps the biggest name of all, Santo Domingo–born Juan Luis Guerra. Rita Indiana y los Misterios, led by the eponymous vocalist and an accomplished writer, have created an 'experimental' merengue sound, blending alternative rock and pop with traditional forms.

Even if you don't dance – something Dominicans will find peculiar – you'll be impressed by the skill and artfulness of the way even amateurs move their feet and hips in perfect time to the music. The *merengue típico*, or traditional folk genre, is a fast two-step dance characterized by the close proximity of the dancers. The most prevalent of the folk styles, called *perico ripiao*, originated in the northern valley region of Cibao and is still commonly played today.

From its humble rural beginnings, merengue evolved into a more modernized orchestral 'big band' style, largely due to its elevated status as a national symbol embraced by Trujillo in the 1930s. In typical Trujillo fashion, he ordered many merengues to be composed in his honor. While the earlier traditional forms established the complexities of the rhythm and the development of the dance, it was the orchestral style, called *orquesta merengue* or *merengue de salon*, that drove merengue's rise to prominence by the 1980s, becoming a worthy competitor of salsa. By the 1990s, contemporary merengue had incorporated electronic drum beats and synthesizers, and this new sound was heard blaring out of cars, stereos and nightclubs from Puerto Rico to New York City.

Hit Songs

El Super Nuevo – 'Superman Sin Capa' (reggaeton)

Joseito Mateo – 'El Negrito del Batey' (merengue)

Luis Vargas – 'Volvio el Dolor' (merengue)

Antony Santos – 'Voy pa'lla' (bachata)

Don Miguelo – 'Que tu Quieres' (reggaeton)

For most Dominicans, talk of merengue's origins – and Dominican merengue didn't emerge as its own distinct genre until the mid-19th century – are wrapped up in notions of national and racial identity. Earlier versions existed in Cuba and Haiti, but Dominicans are often disinclined to admit African and Haitian influences on their culture. Many theories point to European-derived ballroom-dance styles. According to one popular myth, merengue originated in 1844, the year that the Dominican Republic was founded, to poke fun at a Dominican soldier who had abandoned his post during the Battle of Talanquera in the War of Independence. The Dominicans won the battle and, while celebrating the victory at night, soldiers mocked the cowardly deserter in song and dance. Eurocentric critics emphasize merengue's European elements; Afrocentric scholars may emphasize its African and Haitian elements; and those who celebrate racial amalgamation point to its synergistic nature.

Bachata: A Social History of Dominican Popular Music, by Deborah Pacini Hernandez, and *Merengue: Dominican Music and Dominican Identity,* by Paul Austerlitz, are academic examinations of the DR's two most important musical contributions and obsessions.

Bachata

Whereas merengue might be viewed as an urban sound, *bachata* is definitely the nation's 'country' music, of love and broken hearts in the hinterlands. Born in the poorest of Dominican neighborhoods, *bachata* emerged in the mid-20th century, after Trujillo's death, as a slow, romantic style played on the Spanish guitar. The term initially referred to informal, sometimes rowdy backyard parties in rural areas, finally emerging in Santo Domingo shanties.

The term *'bachata'* was meant as a slight by the urban elite, a reference to the music's supposed lack of sophistication. Often called 'songs of bitterness,' *bachata* tunes were no different to most romantic ballad forms, such as the Cuban bolero, but were perceived as low class, and didn't have the same political or social support as merengue. In fact, *bachata* was not even regarded as a style per se until the 1960s – and even then it was not widely known outside the Dominican Republic.

Since 1986 merengue and *bachata* superstar Juan Luis Guerra has won almost every major music award possible, including two Grammys, 18 Latin Grammys and three Premios Soberanos, the DR's highest musical award.

But widespread interest and acceptance grew largely because of the efforts of musician and composer Juan Luis Guerra, who introduced international audiences to this rich and sentimental form. Already credited with developing a more modern and socially conscious merengue, Guerra nearly single-handedly brought *bachata* out of obscurity, paving the way for many Dominican artists to come.

While merengue continues to be the more popular style, *bachata* has risen in popularity, particularly in New York City's Dominican community. Among the big names are Raulín Rodríguez, Antony Santos, Joe Veras, Luis Vargas, Quico Rodríguez, Frank Reyes and Leo Valdez. *Bachata Roja* is a compilation of classic *bachata* from the early 1960s to late 1980s, the pre-electric era when the music was entirely guitar based and drew on a variety of musical traditions, including Mexican *ranchera,* Puerto Rican *jíbaro,* Cuban bolero, guaracha and *son.* The record includes legendary musicians such as Edilio Paredes and Augusto Santos.

THE GÜIRA

The *güira* is a popular musical instrument used to infuse a song with a rhythmical rasping sound. It was originally adopted by Hispaniola's indigenous people – the Taínos – who employed dried, hollowed-out-gourds and a forked stick to produce music for their *areítos* (ceremonial songs). Today the *güira* has been modernized – but not by much. Instead of using vegetables, the modern *güira* is made of latten brass; it typically looks like a cylindrical cheese grater that is scraped with a long metal pick. The rasping sound is essentially the same – the modern-day instrument just lasts a little longer. The next time you hear a merengue or a *bachata* song, listen for this centuries-old sound.

COCOLOS

....

Cocolos (English-speaking immigrants from the eastern Caribbean who primarily settled in the region around San Pedro de Macorís) have their own distinctive musical and dance culture. A good time to experience this hybrid of African and Caribbean rhythms is February 27, the national holiday celebrating Dominican independence from Haiti.

Salsa

Salsa, like *bachata*, is heard throughout the Caribbean, and is very popular in the DR. Before they called it salsa, many musicians in New York City had already explored the possibilities of blending Cuban rhythms with jazz. In the 1950s, the Latin big-band era found favor with dancers and listeners alike, and in the mid-1960s, Dominican flutist, composer and producer Johnny Pacheco founded the Fania label, which was exclusively dedicated to recording 'tropical Latin' music.

In 1818 the Spanish colonial governor ordered nighttime dancing in the street without a permit to be illegal.

With Cuba cut off from the United States politically as well as culturally, it was no longer appropriate to use the term 'Afro-Cuban'. The word 'salsa' (literally 'sauce') emerged as a clever marketing tool, reflecting not only the music but the entire atmosphere, and was the perfect appellation for a genre of music resulting from a mixture of styles: Cuban-based rhythms played by Puerto Ricans, Dominicans, Africans and African Americans.

By the 1970s salsa was hot, not only in the US, but also in South America and Central America. Even European, Japanese and African audiences were treated to this new sound. In the 1980s, salsa evolved into a bland version of itself – the so-called '*salsa romántica*' genre – and during this time Dominican merengue served up some worthy competition. Since the 1990s, however, salsa rebounded and spread throughout the globe, living on in new generations of musicians and dancers alike.

Top Music Festivals

Carnival – end of February, all over the country

....

Dominican Republic Jazz Festival – end of October and beginning of November in Puerto Plata, Santiago and Cabarete

....

The following individuals and groups enjoy particularly favorable reputations in the DR: Tito Puente, Tito Rojas, Jerry Rivera, Tito Gómez, Grupo Niche, Gilberto Santa Rosa, Mimi Ibarra, Marc Anthony and Leonardo Paniagua.

Reggaeton & Rap

Reggaeton, a mix of American-style hip-hop and Latin rhythms, has exploded onto the Dominican scene. Reggaeton has a distinctly urban flavor, and its fast-paced danceable beats, street-life narratives and catchy choruses make it the party music of choice for many young Dominicans. In terms of origins, Panama claims it was the first country to bring Spanish-influenced reggae to the underground scene in the late 1970s. But it was Puerto Rico that gave the music a whole new beat and name in the 1980s and '90s.

Santo Domingo Merengue Festival – last week in July/first week in August

....

Puerto Plata Merengue Festival – November

Since that time, reggaeton has become increasingly popular throughout the DR, and Dominican artists have made their own stamp on the genre. Like hip-hop in the US, reggaeton has evolved from a musical genre to an entire culture, with its own brand of fashion and commerce. Artists to look out for include the well-known reggaeton duo Wisin & Yandel, Pavel Núñez, an established star whose music is a mix between folk and Latin, and Kat DeLuna, a pop singer whose music is a hodgepodge of styles and rhythms.

Rap Dominicano, a relatively new musical sub-genre, is pounded out of the Dominican barrios, and has taken its place alongside reggaeton as one of the most popular forms of music among Dominican youth. Although rap is an imported genre and the sounds blasting from the speakers don't resemble the typical sounds of the DR, Dominican rap artists have managed to weave the sounds of *bachata* and merengue into their tracks, rapping about an urban upbringing that is uniquely their own. A few artists to look out for are El Lapiz Conciente, Vakero, Joa, Toxic Crow, Punto Rojo and R1.

Baseball: A Dominican Passion

Not just the USA's game, *beísbol* is an integral part of the Dominican social and cultural landscape. Dominican ballplayers who have made the major league are the most revered figures in the country, and over 400 have done so, including stars like David Ortiz, Albert Pujols, Robinson Canó and Sammy Sosa. In 2015, 83 players on the opening day rosters came from the DR, and pitchers Juan Marichal and Pedro Martinez have both been inducted into the Hall of Fame.

Drafting Dilemmas

The Eastern Stars: How Baseball Changed the Dominican Town of San Pedro de Macorís, by Mark Kurlansky, is a comprehensive history of baseball in the DR, with a focus on San Pedro de Macorís, known as the 'city of shortstops'.

For a young prospect in the Dominican Republic the financial incentives of just being drafted, let alone actually playing a single game, in the major leagues are considerable. The average bonus (US$100,000) alone can provide a down payment on a home and provide for family members. However, the odds are overwhelmingly against success – only 3% of those signed make it to the majors – and when a young teenager pins their hopes on baseball (players are eligible for recruitment at 16), education usually falls by the wayside.

A series of high-profile issues have arisen, complicating the often incestuous relationship between Dominican baseball and the major leagues. Nearly every team has an academy – a mix of university dormitory, work camp and health club. Problems include steroid use, which isn't technically illegal in the DR, fake birth certificates intentionally misstating a player's age (younger to overstate potential and older to allow recruitment) and the increasingly questionable role that unregulated *buscones* play in the whole system. Taken from the Spanish verb *buscar*, to look for, *buscones* are more than merely scouts. They train, feed, house and educate promising players, grooming them to be signed by the majors in the hopes of one day gaining a large percentage of whatever signing bonus their prospects earn. An estimated 2% of those kids will go on to make a living in baseball.

According to critics, the legacy of this homegrown corruption helps explains why a disporportionate number of players caught violating the major league's drug policy are Dominicans (the most high-profile case of course involves the Yankees' Alex Rodriguez who is of Dominican descent).

BASEBALL TEAMS

Tigres del Licey (Santo Domingo)

Leones del Escogido (Santo Domingo)

Águilas Cibaeñas (Santiago)

Estrellas Orientales (San Pedro de Macorís)

Los Toros del Este (La Romana)

Gigantes del Cibao (San Francisco de Macorís)

Getting to First Base

The origin of baseball in the DR is intertwined with the beginnings of the sugar industry, first in Cuba and later in the DR. Around the same time that American business ambitions were directed toward the Caribbean, particularly Cuba, baseball was being established in the States. When Cuban plantation owners fled their country during a failed war of independence in 1868, they brought with them their passion for the game, which they learned from the Americans (where and when the game was originally established is open for dispute).

Workers from the English-speaking Caribbean who were brought to the DR to work in the cane fields were already skilled cricket players, bringing a familiarity with the general concepts of batting, pitching and fielding. With few leisure activities available, plant owners encouraged baseball rather than cricket and organized competitive teams into a 'sugar league.' Cubans, Americans and Dominicans in Santo Domingo, La Vega and near Santiago also formed their own teams.

But it was the US embargo of Cuba that began in 1962 (as well as free agency that began in the 1970s) that really accelerated the recruitment of Dominican players, since fewer Cubans were willing to defect – a requirement imposed by the government. Major-league scouts turned to other Caribbean countries, including the DR, to pick up the slack and Dominicans, unlike Puerto Ricans who are American citizens, were not subject to draft rules at the time.

Take Me out to 'El Partido de Beísbol'

The Dominican professional baseball league's season runs from October to January, and is known as the Liga de Invierno (Winter League). The winner of the DR league competes in the Caribbean World Series against other Latin-American countries. The country has six professional teams. Because the US and Dominican seasons don't overlap, many Dominican players in the US major leagues and quite a few non-Dominicans play in the winter league in the DR as well.

Needless to say, the quality of play is high (the DR went undefeated in winning the World Baseball Classic in 2013), but even if you're not a fan of the sport, it's worth checking out a game or two. It's always a fun afternoon or evening. Fans are decked out in their respective team's colors waving pennants and flags, as rabidly partisan as the Yankees–Red Sox rivalry, and dancers in hot pants perform to loud merengue beats on top of the dugouts between innings. Games usually don't start on time and the stands aren't filled until several innings have passed. The best place to take in a game is Estadio Quisqueya (p84) in Santo Domingo. For tickets, head to the stadium with time to spare before the start of play (as early as possible for big games).

From June to August there is also a Liga del Verano (Summer League) if you're in the DR outside of regular season. Various major-league franchises – the San Francisco Giants, the Toronto Blue Jays, the Arizona Diamondbacks and the New York Yankees, to name a few – maintain farm teams in the DR, and summer-league play is a semiformal tournament between these teams. Games are held at smaller stadiums around town.

Santiago's baseball team was originally named 'Sandino' in honor of Augusto César Sandino, the Nicaraguan guerrilla leader who resisted the US invasion forces. After Trujillo came to power he forced the team to change its name to Águilas Cibaeñas.

Rob Ruck, a history professor at the University of Pittsburgh, wrote about baseball fanaticism in the DR in his book, *The Tropic of Baseball: Baseball in the Dominican Republic*.

The movie *Sugar* (2008) tells the story of a young Dominican baseball prospect drafted to play in the US minor leagues, and the loneliness and dislocation he and other players experience.

Arts & Architecture

The legacy of Hispaniola's diverse peoples, from the Taíno inhabitants to European settlers and Haitian emigres, has translated into a mix of artistic voices and styles. Walking city streets lined with some of the finest examples of Spanish colonial architecture in the New World, you'll hear a soundtrack of merengue beats. Many writers are preoccupied with politics, history and questions of national identity and a through line in the visual arts has been a romanticization of the Dominican rural life.

Painting

The Dominican art scene today is quite healthy, thanks in no small part to dictator Rafael Trujillo. Although his 31 years of authoritarian rule in many ways negated the essence of creative freedom, Trujillo had a warm place in his heart for painting, and in 1942 he established the Escuela Nacional de Bellas Artes (National School of Fine Arts). Fine Dominican artwork predates the school, but it really wasn't until the institution's doors opened that Dominican art underwent definitive development.

The Eduardo León Jimenes Art Contest in Santiago began in 1964 and is the longest-running privately sponsored art competition in Latin America.

If the artwork looks distinctly Spanish, it's because the influence is undeniable. During the Spanish Civil War (1936–39), many artists fled Franco's fascist regime to start new lives in the Dominican Republic. Influential artists include Manolo Pascual, José Gausachs, José Vela-Zanetti, Eugenio Fernández Granell and Juan Fernández Corredor.

In the late 1960s in Santiago, Grupo Friordano, as well as other small groups of socially engaged artists, began politically conscious and ideological aesthetic movements. Painters such as Daniel Henríquez, Orlando Menicucci and Yoryi Morel considered their work as engaged critiques of society; Morel painted traditional rural scenes and helped develop a distinctly Dominican vernacular style.

Those colorful and bright canvases of simple rural scenes lined up on virtually every street corner and piece of pavement where tourists are expected are actually reproductions of iconic Haitian paintings; these are often churned out with house paint.

If you visit any of the art galleries in Santo Domingo or Santiago, keep an eye out for Cándido Bidó's bright, colorful paintings of scenes from his native Cibao valley (Bidó passed away in 2011); Adriana Billini Gautreau, who is famous for portraits that are rich in expressionist touches; the cubist forms of Jaime Colson, emphasizing the social crises of his day; Luis Desangles, considered the forerunner of folklore in Dominican painting; Mariano Eckert, representing the realism of everyday life; Juan Bautista Gómez, whose paintings depict the sensuality of the landscape; Guillo Pérez, whose works of oxen, carts and canefields convey a poetic vision of life at the sugar mill; Ivan Tovar's surrealist Dali-esque works; the traditional realist paintings of Ada Balcácer; Marian Balcácer, a photographer who lives in Italy; the steel sculptures of Johnny Bonnelly; and, finally, the enigmatic and dreamlike paintings of Dionisio Blanco.

Also well represented is what's known as 'primitive art' – Dominican and Haitian paintings that convey rural Caribbean life with simple and colorful figures and landscapes. These paintings are created by amateur painters – some would say skilled craftspeople – who reproduce the same painting hundreds of times. They are sold everywhere there are tourists; you're sure to get an eyeful regardless of the length of your trip.

A good resource on Dominican art is the authoritative *Enciclopedia de las Artes Plásticas Dominicanas* (Encyclopedia of Dominican Visual Arts) by Cándido Gerón. Illustrations and Spanish text are followed by English translations; look for copies at used bookstores in the Santo Domingo's Zona Colonial.

Architecture

The quality and variety of architecture found in the Dominican Republic has no equal in the Caribbean. Santo Domingo's Zona Colonial, a well-preserved grid of Spanish colonial buildings, is a showcase of landmarks. An imposing fortress – the oldest still intact in the Americas – stands adjacent to mansions and Dominican and Franciscan convents. The Americas' oldest functioning cathedral, the Catedral Primada de América, whose construction began in 1514, stands in the center. You'll see plenty of the baroque, Romanesque, Gothic and renaissance styles which were popular in Europe during the colonial times.

Elsewhere in Santo Domingo and Santiago you can see examples of Cuban Victorian, Caribbean gingerbread and art deco. The buildings in Puerto Plata vary between the vernacular Antillean and the pure Victorian; sometimes English, sometimes North American. Sugar magnates in San Pedro de Macorís built late-Victorian style homes with concrete (it was the first city in the DR to use reinforced concrete in construction). And rural clapboard homes – Monte Cristi in the far northwest has these in spades – have a charm all their own: small, square, single-story and more colorful than a handful of jelly beans, you'll find yourself slowing down to take a longer look.

More contemporary and postmodern architecture is best seen in homes commissioned by wealthy Dominicans, in upscale neighborhoods in Santo Domingo and Santiago. Elsewhere, including Jarabacoa in the central highlands, along the southeastern coastline around Punta Cana, and around Puerto Plata on the north coast, are enclaves of vacation homes; these communities are worth a look for creative and high-concept design.

Easily the best book on architecture in the country is *Arquitectura Dominicana: 1492–2008*, edited by Gustavo Luis More (available at bookstores in Santo Domingo and the Museo Centro León in Santiago). Another excellent resource is *Interiors*, a book of photographs by Polibio Diaz, which shows glimpses into the homes of ordinary Dominicans with respect and care.

Literature

The Dominican Republic's literary history dates to the Spanish colonial period (1492–1795). It was then that Bartolomé de Las Casas, a Spanish friar, recorded the early history of the Caribbean and pleaded for fair treatment of the Taínos in his famous *Historia de las Indias* (History of the Indies). In the same era, Gabriel Téllez, a priest who helped to reorganize the convent of Our Lady of Mercy in Santo Domingo, wrote his impressive *Historia general de la Orden de la Merced* (General History of the Order of Mercy).

During the Haitian occupation of Santo Domingo (1822–44), a French literary style became prominent, and many Dominican writers who emigrated to other Spanish-speaking countries made names for themselves there. With the first proclamation of independence in 1844, Félix María del Monte created the country's principal poetic form – a short, patriotic poem based on local events of the day.

Dominican poetry flourished in the late 19th century, primarily through the three figures of Salome Ureña, Joaquín Pérez and Gastón Fernando Deligne. Pérez's collection, *Fantasías Indíginas* (Indian Fantasies), imagines

Buildings Not to Miss

Museo Alcázar de Colón, Santo Domingo

Catedral Primada de América, Santo Domingo

Basilica de Nuestra Señora de la Altagracia, Higüey

Catedral de la Concepción, La Vega

Best Art Museums

Centro León, Santiago

Museo de Arte Moderno, Santo Domingo

Museo Bellapart, Santo Domingo

encounters between Spanish conquistadores and the native Taíno. In the 20th century, Pedro Mir established himself while living in exile in Cuba during the Trujillo regime and was later named Poet Laureate in 1984.

During the late 19th and early 20th centuries, three literary movements occurred in the DR: *indigenismo, criollismo* and *postumismo. Indigenismo* exposed the brutalities the Taínos experienced at the hands of the Spaniards. *Criollismo* focused on the local people and their customs. And *postumismo* dealt with the repression that Rafael Trujillo's iron-fisted leadership brought. Some writers, such as Manuel and Lupo Hernández Rueda, used clever metaphors to protest against the regime. Juan Bosch Gaviño, writing from exile, penned numerous stories that openly attacked Trujillo. Bosch, who held the presidency for only seven months in 1963, is one of the more influential literary figures in the DR, both as an essayist tackling social problems and as a novelist and short-story writer.

San Pedro de Macorís is known for its poets: Gastón Fernando Deligne, Pedro Mir and René del Risco Bermúdez, among others, were either born here or drew their inspiration living in this city.

Only a few Dominican novels have been translated into English. Viriato Sención's *They Forged the Signature of God,* winner of the DR's 1993 National Fiction award (after realizing that the book was critical of both Trujillo and himself, Balaguer rescinded the prize) and the country's all-time best seller, follows three seminary students suffering oppression at the hands of both the state and the church. Though slightly preachy, it provides another perspective on the Trujillo regime besides the exceptional *Fiesta del Chivo* (Feast of the Goat) by the Peruvian novelist Mario Vargas Llosa.

Ten years after publishing the short-story collection *Drown,* Junot Díaz received critical acclaim for his 2007 novel *The Brief Wondrous Life of Oscar Wao,* a stylistically inventive story of a self-professed Dominican nerd in New Jersey and the tragic history of his family in the DR. Less well known, but perhaps a more devastating picture of the Dominican diaspora's rejection of the conventional American Dream, is Loida Maritza Pérez's *Geographies of Home.* For Spanish readers, other recommended young Dominican authors are Pedro Antonio Valdez *(Bachata del angel caído, Carnaval de Sodoma),* Aurora Arias *(Inyi's Paradise, Fin del mundo, Emoticons)* and Rita Indiana Hernández *(La estrategia de Chochueca, Papi).*

In the Time of the Butterflies is an award-winning novel by Julia Álvarez, about three sisters slain for their part in a plot to overthrow Trujillo. Also by Álvarez is *How the García Girls Lost Their Accents,* describing an emigrant Dominican family in New York. Other well-known contemporary Dominican writers include José Goudy Pratt, Jeannette Miller and Ivan García Guerra.

Dominican Landscapes

If wealth was measured by landscape, the DR would be among the richest countries in the Americas. Sharing the island of Hispaniola, the second-largest island in the Caribbean (after Cuba), it's a dynamic country of high mountains, fertile valleys and watered plains, and an amazing diversity of ecosystems. The rich landscape is matched by an equally rich biodiversity with over 5600 species of plants and close to 500 vertebrate species on the island, many of these endemic.

The Land

The island's geography owes more to the Central American mainland than its mostly flat neighboring islands. The one thing that Hispaniola has in spades is an abundance of mountains. Primary among mountain ranges is the Cordillera Central that runs from Santo Domingo into Haiti, where it becomes the Massif du Nord, fully encompassing a third of the island's landmass. The Cordillera Central is home to Pico Duarte, the Caribbean's highest mountain (at 3087m), which is so big it causes a rain shadow that makes much of southwest DR very arid. Other ranges include the Cordillera Septentrional, rising dramatically from the coast near Cabarete, and the Cordillera Orientale, along the southern shoreline of Bahía de Samaná.

Between the ranges lie a series of lush and fertile valleys. Coffee, rice, bananas and tobacco all thrive here, as well as in the plains around Santo Domingo. In comparison, sections of southwest DR are semi-desert and studded with cacti.

The unique landscape of Hispaniola is due to the 90-million-year-old movements of the earth's crust. As it slowly ground past North America, the Caribbean Plate cracked and crumpled to form the islands stretching from Cuba to Puerto Rico. Further collisions formed the Lesser Antilles, the coastal mountains of Venezuela and much of Central America. The plate is still moving at 1cm to 2cm per year, and continues to elevate Hispaniola.

The Dominican Republic has the highest mountain in the Caribbean – Pico Duarte (3087m) – and the lowest point in the Caribbean – Lago Enriquillo, a lake 40m below sea level.

Wildlife

The problems of colonizing an island are clear, with plants heavily reliant on seeds and roots arriving on floating rafts of vegetation, often with animal hitchhikers. Reptiles make the best long-distance voyagers and over 140 species are found on the island, compared to around 60 amphibians and 20 land mammals (only two of which survived the arrival of Europeans). The rest of the country's fauna is made up of a rich variety of birds, marine mammals and bats.

The Birds of the West Indies, by Herbert Raffaele et al, covers birds across the West Indies, including migratory species you may see in the DR.

Birds

More than 300 species of bird have been recorded in the DR, including more than two dozen found nowhere else in the world. Abundant, colorful species include the white-tailed tropicbird, magnificent frigatebird, roseate spoonbill and greater flamingo, plus unique endemic species such as the Hispaniolan lizard-cuckoo, ashy-faced owl and Hispaniolan emerald hummingbird.

Travelers are most likely to encounter birds on beaches and coastal waterways – specifically herons, egrets, ibis, rails, pelicans and gulls. Some of the best spots for twitchers in the DR are Parque Nacional Jaragua (p211), Parque Nacional Los Haitises (p121), Parque Nacional Monte Cristi (p177) and Laguna Limón (p119). More determined travelers taking the time to wander into some of the rich wildlife areas in the DR's interior can expect to encounter a tremendous variety of forest birds.

Favorites among birdwatchers include the odd palmchat, DR's national bird, which builds large apartment-like nests where each pair sleeps in its own chamber.

Land Mammals

The arrival of Europeans, who introduced many disruptive species of their own, proved disastrous for Hispaniola's land mammals. Rats, cats, pigs and mongooses all tore through the local wildlife with severe consequences.

Just two native mammal species remain, clinging to survival in scattered pockets throughout Haiti and the DR. These are the hutia, a tree-climbing rodent, and the solenodon, an insectivore resembling a giant shrew. The solenodon is particularly threatened, and both species are nocturnal, making sightings extremely difficult.

Most of the humpbacks visiting the DR spend the winter gorging on krill in the feeding grounds of the Gulf of Maine, off the US coast. They don't eat during their entire Caribbean stay.

Marine Mammals

The DR is world famous for its marine mammals, with manatees and humpback whales the star attractions. Travelers, however, are more likely to see dolphins unless they arrive in the right season or make a special trip to the right habitat.

Several thousand humpback whales migrate south from frigid arctic waters to breed and calve in the tropical waters of the DR each winter (with their numbers peaking in January and February). The Bahía de Samaná is one of the foremost places in the world for boat-based whale-watching,

Manatees feed on the seagrass meadows surrounding Hispaniola, hence their alternative name of 'sea cow' (their closest relative is, in fact, the elephant). Weighing up to 590kg and reaching 3.7m in length, manatees are shy, docile creatures; Santuario de Mamíferos Marinos Estero Hondo (near Punta Rucia) and Parque Nacional Monte Cristi (p177) are two of the better places to try to spot them.

Want to put a name to that frog or gecko? Consult *Amphibians and Reptiles of the West Indies*, by Robert Henderson and Albert Schwartz.

Fish & Marine Life

The shallow coastal waters and coral reefs that surround the DR are home to a tremendous variety of sea life. So many species of tropical fish, crustaceans, sponges and corals can be found here that it takes a specialized field guide to begin to sort them out. Where they remain relatively intact and unfished – such as at Sosúa and Monte Cristi – they are stupendously beautiful. Some of the more colorful Caribbean reef fish include fluorescent fairy basslet, queen angelfish, rock beauty and blue tang, but each visitor will quickly find their own favorite.

The warm waters are also home to four species of sea turtle: green, leatherback, hawksbill and loggerhead. You may have occasional encounters with these turtles while snorkeling, but from May to October they can be viewed in places such as Parque Nacional Jaragua (p211), coming ashore at night to lay their eggs on sandy beaches.

Reptiles & Amphibians

Reptiles were Hispaniola's most successful vertebrate colonists. You can expect to see lots of lizards (geckos in particular), but also keep your eye out for snakes, turtles and even the American crocodile (or caiman), found in sizable numbers in the brackish cross-border Lago Enriquillo – on the Haiti side it's Lac Azueï.

There is also a Hispaniolan boa, its numbers reduced by mongoose predation. At opposite ends of the spectrum are the Jaragua lizard, which is the world's smallest terrestrial vertebrate (adults measure only 2.8cm), and the massive 10kg rhinoceros iguana. Frogs are the most numerous amphibians.

NATIONAL PARKS OF THE DOMINICAN REPUBLIC

The DR, home to some of the largest and most diverse parks in all the Caribbean, has set aside over 10% of its land as *parques nacionales* (national parks) and *reservas científicas* (scientific reserves) and is doing a reasonably good job of protecting these important local resources in the face of external pressures. This is especially important in coastal areas, where resorts are devouring open spaces and destroying fragile coral reefs with huge numbers of tourists. Enforcement has been less effective in the DR's central mountains, where logging and encroachment by farmers continues in many areas. Together, Parque Nacional Jaragua, Lago Enriquillo and Parque Nacional Sierra de Bahoruco form the Jaragua-Bahoruco-Enriquillo Biosphere Reserve, the first Unesco biosphere reserve in the country.

Parque Nacional Armando Bermúdez This 766-sq-km park in the humid Cordillera Central is blanketed in pine trees, tree ferns and palm trees, and is home to the hawk-like Hispaniolan trogon.

Parque Nacional Cotubanamá Located in the southeastern part of the country, this park (formerly known as Parque Nacional del Este) consists of dry and subtropical humid forest, with caves featuring Taíno petroglyphs, as well as the sandy beaches of Isla Saona. Look out for manatees and dolphins off the coast.

Parque Nacional Isla Cabritos In the southwest, this park is a 24-sq-km island surrounded by the saltwater Lago Enriquillo. It is a refuge for crocodiles, iguanas, scorpions, flamingos, crows and cacti. Sadly, it is closed indefinitely to visitors.

Parque Nacional Jaragua At 1400 sq km, this is the largest park in the DR. It is made up of an arid thorn forest, an extensive marine area and the islands of Beata and Alto Velo. The park is rich in birdlife, particularly sea and shore birds, and its beaches are nesting grounds for hawksbill turtles.

Parque Nacional José del Carmen Ramírez This 764-sq-km park is home to the Caribbean's tallest peak – Pico Duarte – and the headwaters of three of the DR's most important rivers: Yaque del Sur, San Juan and Mijo. Although there is occasional frost, the park is considered a subtropical humid mountain forest.

Parque Nacional La Isabela Located on the north coast, this park was established in the 1990s to protect the ruins of the second European settlement in the New World. An on-site museum contains many objects that were used by the earliest European settlers.

Parque Nacional Los Haitises Situated on the Bahía de Samaná, this park's lush hills jut out of the ocean and are fringed with mangroves, tawny beaches and several Taíno caves. Bamboo, ferns and bromeliads thrive, along with the Hispaniolan parakeet.

Parque Nacional Monte Cristi This 530-sq-km park in the extreme northwest contains a subtropical dry forest, coastal lagoons and seven islets. It is home to many seabirds, including great egrets, brown pelicans and yellow-crowned night herons. American crocodiles also inhabit the park's lagoons.

Parque Nacional Sierra de Bahoruco Located in the southwest, this 800-sq-km park stretches from desert lowlands to 2000m-high tracts of pine. Along with the broad range of plant life (orchids abound), it's rich in birds, including the endemic white-necked crow and the Hispaniolan parrot.

Parque Nacional Submarino La Caleta Only 22km from Santo Domingo, this 10-sq-km park is one of the country's most visited. Containing several healthy coral reefs and two shipwrecks, it is one of the top diving spots in the country.

Plants

Hispaniola presents a bewildering assortment of plants. In every season there is something flowering, fruiting or filling the air with exotic fragrances, and it makes the place truly magical. Nearly a third of the 5600-odd species are endemic, spread across more than 20 discrete vegetation zones, ranging from desert to subtropical forest to mangrove swamp.

Of these vegetation zones, by far the most prevalent is the subtropical forest, which blankets the slopes of many of the DR's valleys and is found throughout the Península de Samaná. This is a majestic landscape, dominated by royal palms with large curving fronds, and native mahogany trees.

True tropical rainforest is rare, both because areas receiving enough rainfall are scarce and because the grand trees of this forest type have been extensively logged. Green-leaved throughout the year, these dense humid forests support a wealth of tree ferns, orchids, bromeliads and epiphytes. Examples can still be found in the Vega Real, which is located in the eastern end of the Valle de Cibao, adjacent to the Samaná region.

Above 1830m, the habitat gives way to mountain forests characterized by pines and palms, as well as ferns, bromeliads, heliconias and orchids. Although threatened by coffee plantations and ranching, large tracts still exist in Parques Nacionales Armando Bermúdez and José del Carmen Ramírez.

Thorn and cacti forests abound in the southwest corner of the DR. Parque Nacional Jaragua, the country's largest protected area, consists largely of thorn forest, cacti and agaves, and receives less than 700mm of rain a year.

Mangrove swamps are a characteristic feature along the coast around the DR's Bahía de Samaná and pockets along the northern coastline. They're hugely important wildlife habitats, serving as nurseries for many marine species and nesting grounds for water birds, as well as buffering the coast against the erosive power of storms and tides.

One of the coldest parts of the country is Reserva Científica de Valle Nuevo, southeast of Constanza on the way to San Jose de Ocoa, with temperatures as low as -8°C and vegetation similar to the European Alps.

Environmental Issues

The DR has a rapidly growing population and millions of tourists a year, all of whom put severe pressure on the land. Water use, damage to marine ecosystems and, most of all, deforestation, present acute environmental challenges. Despite the government's continual efforts in setting aside pristine land, and at times banning commercial logging, parks and reserves remain chronically underfunded, and illegal logging and agricultural encroachment remain a problem, especially in the central highlands. It's estimated that the DR has lost 60% of its forests in the last 80 years.

One of the more puzzling issues concerns the rising and receding waters of Lago Enriquillo. In 2004 the waters began rising, and by 2014, tens of thousands of acres previously occupied by yuca, banana and cattle farms had become eerily submerged, with the government attempting to move an entire town threatened by flooding. The Ministry of the Environment, to the outrage of many residents and environmentalists, began clearing the Loma Charco Azul Biological Reserve (part of the Jaragua-Bahoruco-Enriquillo Biosphere) in 2013 in order to replace lost agricultural acreage. But later that year, the lake began to recede, and it has continued to do so, apparently due to drought. Scientists don't fully understand what's happening with the lake, but Isla Cabritos, an island and national park surrounded by the lake, has closed indefinitely to visitors.

Coastal resorts and villages continue to have a tremendous impact on the very seas that provide their livelihood. Pollution, runoff and other consequences of massive developments have destroyed many of the island's foremost reefs. Overfishing and the inadvertent destruction caused by careless humans transform reefs into gray shadows of their former selves.

Vertebrate species particularly endangered on Hispaniola include the West Indian manatee, American crocodile, rhinoceros iguana, Hispaniolan ground iguana and dozens of frog, turtle and bird species.

Survival Guide

Directory A–Z

Accommodations

Compared to other destinations in the Caribbean, lodging in the Dominican Republic is relatively affordable. That said, there is a limited number of options for independent travelers wishing to make decisions on the fly and for whom cost is a concern.

In some places, such as Santo Domingo, you can stay in restored colonial-era buildings with loads of character with comfortable accommodations (Santo Domingo's Nicolas de Ovando is the choicest example) for less money than you would spend for a night at a bland international-chain-style hotel (Holiday Inn, Marriott and Sheraton, among others have a presence). And a good number of all-inclusives, especially outside the holidays and the high season, can be remarkably good deals considering what you get.

From US$200 and up (the ceiling is high for the most exclusive resorts), there's a big jump in terms of the quality of furnishings, food and service, and in the Dominican Republic, maybe more than elsewhere, you truly get what you pay for.

Pay budget room rates and you won't necessarily feel like you're on vacation, especially in the cities, but there are some exceptions. The DR only has a few hostels, and little backpacker culture of the sort found in the rest of Latin America, Europe and elsewhere. The walled compounds generically called *cabañas turisticas*, with names suggestive of intercourse or romantic love, on the outskirts of most large towns are short-time hotels for couples seeking privacy. Following are some guidelines to keep in mind:

➡ Assume that low-season rates are 20% to 50% less than high-season rates.

➡ Rooms booked a minimum of three days in advance on the internet are far cheaper (especially so at the all-inclusive resorts) than if you book via phone or, worst-case scenario, simply show up without a reservation.

➡ Be sure the rate you are quoted already includes the 23% room tax. We've been shocked when paying the bill after making reservations and booking online.

➡ The Dominican government doles out stars, from one to six (very few have received a six), though the qualifications for the rankings probably wouldn't match North American or European standards.

➡ Hotels geared towards business travelers, especially in Santo Domingo and Santiago, offer weekend discounts.

➡ Reservations are recommended for independent hotels in the high season.

All-Inclusive Resorts

Easily the most popular form of lodging in the DR is the all-inclusive resort. Much of the prime beachfront property throughout the country is occupied by all-inclusives. By far the largest concentrations are in the Bávaro/ Punta Cana area in the east, followed by Playa Dorada in the north; Boca Chica and Juan Dolio, both within easy driving distance of Santo Domingo, have small concentrations as well.

If you're looking for a hassle-free vacation, it's easy to understand the appeal of the all-inclusive. The majority offer at least one all-you-can-eat buffet and

---

BOOK YOUR STAY ONLINE

For more accommodations reviews by Lonely Planet authors, check out http://lonelyplanet.com/dominican-republic/hotels. You'll find independent reviews, as well as recommendations on the best places to stay. Best of all, you can book online.

several stand-alone restaurants (these sometimes require reservations once you've arrived and sometimes cost extra) and food is usually available virtually around the clock. Drinks (coffee, juice, soda, beer, wine, mixed drinks) are also unlimited and served up almost 24/7 from restaurants, beach and pool bars, cafes, discos etc. Most are located on the beach and have lounge chairs and towels, as well as several pools. A variety of tours are on offer daily, including snorkeling, diving, trips to parks and sights in the surrounding area, city tours and horseback riding. If there isn't a golf course on the property, no doubt the concierge can arrange a tee time.

Several companies dominate the resort landscape in the Dominican Republic. Names like Melia, Barcelo and Wyndham are plastered on signs everywhere from Puerto Plata to Bávaro. Often there will be several Melias, Barcelos or Wyndhams in the same area, ranging widely in terms of quality and costs – it can get confusing. While choosing the best resort for you or your family requires some homework, it's well worth the effort. Too often people's vacations are ruined by unrealistic expectations fostered by out-of-focus photos and inaccurate information found online; mediocre food is the most common complaint.

And if it's your first time visiting the Dominican Republic, it's difficult to have a sense of the geography of the area you're considering. For example, the Bávaro/Punta Cana region is quite large, and while some resorts are within walking distance of one another and local restaurants and shops, others are isolated and without a rental vehicle you might end up feeling stranded.

In reviews, all-inclusive options will state 'all-incl' in the practicalities list.

Camping

Other than the basic free cabins en route to Pico Duarte, there are only a handful of formal campgrounds. You might have some luck in rural mountain areas or along deserted beaches – inland, you should ask the owner of the plot of land you are on before pitching a tent, and on the beach always – this can't be stressed enough – ask the Cestur (tourist police) or local police if it is allowed and safe.

Hostels

A few hostels have popped up in recent years, complete with dorm beds and international camaraderie.

Rental Accommodations

If you'll be in the Dominican Republic for long – even a couple of weeks – renting an apartment, condo or villa can be a convenient and cost-effective way to enjoy the country. Many homes and condos are in private, secure developments, have reduced week- and month-long rates and often many bedrooms, making them ideal for large groups (personal chefs are sometimes an option); alternatively, look for 'apartahotels,' which have studio, one-bedroom and two-bedroom apartments, usually with fully equipped kitchens. Some hotels have a small number of units with kitchens – such cases are indicated in the listings.

Children

All-inclusive resorts can be a convenient and affordable way for families to travel, as they provide easy answers to the most vexing of travel questions: when is dinner? Where are we going to eat? What are we going to do? Can I have another Coke? For independent-minded families the DR is no better or worse than most countries – its small size means no long bus or plane rides, and the beaches and outdoor activities are fun for everyone. At the same time, navigating the cities can be challenging for parents and exhausting for children. For excellent general advice on traveling with children, check out Lonely Planet's *Travel with Children*.

Practicalities

All-inclusive resorts have the best child-specific facilities and services, from high chairs in the restaurants to child care and children's programming. That said, not all resorts cater to families with young children (some even have adults-only policies). Independent travelers will have a harder time finding facilities designed for children.

Child safety seats are not common, even in private

cars, and are almost unheard of in taxis or buses. If you bring your own car seat – and it's one that can adapt to a number of different cars – you may be able to use it at least some of the time.

Breastfeeding babies in public is not totally taboo, but nor is it common. It is definitely not done in restaurants, as in the US and some other countries. Nursing mothers are recommended to find a private park bench and use a shawl or other covering. Major grocery stores sell many of the same brands of baby food and diapers (nappies) as in the US.

Customs Regulations

Other than the obvious, like weapons, drugs and live animals, there are only a few specific import restrictions for foreigners arriving in the Dominican Republic. Visitors can bring up to 200 cigarettes, 2L of alcohol and 1 box of cigars. It's best to carry a prescription for any medication, especially psychotropic drugs.

It is illegal to take anything out of the DR that is over 100 years old – paintings, household items, prehistoric artifacts etc – without special export certificates. Mahogany trees are endangered and products made from mahogany wood may be confiscated upon departure. Black coral is widely available but although Dominican law does not forbid its sale, international environment agreements do – avoid purchasing it. The same goes for products made from turtle shells and butterfly wings – these animals are facing extinction. It is illegal to export raw unpolished amber from the DR, though amber jewelry is common and highly prized.

Most travelers run into problems with the export of cigars, and it's not with Dominican customs as much as their own. Canada, European countries and the US allow its citizens to bring in up to 50 cigars duty-free.

Electricity

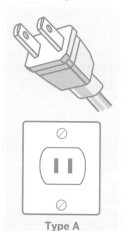

**Type A
110V/60Hz**

Food & Drink

Some visitors to the Dominican Republic never experience a meal outside of their all-inclusive resort, which can seem like a bargain. For travelers hoping to eat out on their own, food can be surprisingly expensive. Of course, prices tend to be much higher in heavily touristed areas, such as the Zona Colonial in Santo Domingo (comparable to US and European prices), and cheaper in small towns and isolated areas. However, outside of informal food stands and cafeteria-style eateries, a meal without drinks at most restaurants will cost a minimum of RD$325 or US$7 (after the 16% ITBIS tax and 10% service charge have been added on). Many restaurants have a range of options, from inexpensive pizza and pasta dishes to pricey lobster meals.

GLBTI Travelers

As a whole, the Dominican Republic is quite open about heterosexual sex and sexuality, but still fairly closed-minded about gays and lesbians. Gay and lesbian travelers will find the most open community in Santo Domingo, though even its gay clubs are relatively discreet. Santiago, Puerto Plata, Bávaro and Punta Cana also have gay venues, catering as much to foreigners as to locals. Everywhere else, open displays of affection between men are fairly taboo, between women less so. Same-sex couples shouldn't have trouble getting a hotel room.

Health

From a medical standpoint, the DR is generally safe as long as you're reasonably careful about what you eat and drink.

Centers for Disease Control (www.cdc.gov/travel) Detailed health overview curated with tips and updated notices.

MD Travel Health (www. mdtravelhealth.com) Complete travel health recommendations for every country, updated daily, at no cost.

Sitata (www.sitata.com) Customized medical reports, pre-trip vaccination recommendations, alerts on disease outbreaks and other breaking health news.

World Health Organization (www.who.int/ith) Available online at no cost as well as in book form – *International Travel and Health* – which is revised annually.

Availability & Cost of Health Care

Medical care is variable in Santo Domingo and limited elsewhere, although good privately run clinics and hospitals can be found in and around the more heavily touristy areas. Many doctors and hospitals expect payment in cash, regardless of whether you have travel-health insurance. Modern pharmacies are easy to find in cities and mid-sized towns.

Infectious Diseases

The most common travel-related diseases, such as dysentery and hepatitis, are acquired by consumption of contaminated food and water, so limit your risk by following safe food and water habits.

Zika outbreaks have been reported in the Dominican Republic. The Center for Disease Control (CDC) warns that because of the risk of birth defects in babies born to women infected with Zika while pregnant, pregnant women should avoid the DR.

Also, it's worth noting there's a small risk of malaria (in the western provinces and in La Altagracia, including Punta Cana) and dengue fever (in Santiago, inland and north coast). In these areas, long pants and long sleeves, mosquito repellent and bed nets are recommended (dengue bites are during the daytime).

Tap Water

Only purified water should be used for drinking, brushing your teeth as well as hand washing.

Vaccinations

Typhoid and hepatitis A and B vaccinations should be considered, along with a prescription for a malaria prophylaxis like Atovaquone-proguanil, chloroquine, doxycycline, or mefloquine.

Insurance

As always, you should purchase travel or health insurance that covers you abroad.

Internet Access

The Dominican Republic has a surprisingly limited number of internet cafes; most charge RD$35 to RD$70 per hour. Many of these cafes also operate as call centers.

Wi-fi access is widespread in cafes and restaurants, as well as at midrange and top-end hotels and resorts throughout the country. Travelers with laptops won't have far to go before finding some place with a signal. However, the majority of the all-inclusives, as opposed to most midrange and even budget hotels, charge daily fees (around US$15 and up) for access. Many hotels that advertise the service free for guests only have a signal in public spaces like the lobby and limited or poor access in guest rooms.

Most internet cafes have Spanish language keyboards – the '@' key is usually accessed by pressing 'alt', '6' and '4'.

Legal Matters

The Dominican Republic has two police forces – the Policía Nacional (national police) and Cuerpo Especializado de Seguridad Turística (tourist police, commonly referred to by its abbreviation, Cestur).

Cestur officers are generally friendly men and women whose job is specifically to help tourists. Many speak a little bit of a language other than Spanish. They wear white shirts with blue insignia and can usually be found near major tourist sights and

centers. You should contact Cestur first in the event of theft, assault or if you are the victim of a scam, but you can equally ask them for directions to sights, which bus to take etc.

It's best to have as little interaction with the Policía Nacional as possible. If a police officer stops you, be polite and cooperate; heavily armed roadway checkpoints aren't uncommon, particularly in regions bordering Haiti – they're looking for drugs and weapons. They may ask to see your passport – you're not required to have it on you, but it's a good idea to carry a photocopy. You might also be asked for a 'tip' in cash or merchandise; feign misunderstanding or simply politely decline. More often than not, you'll simply be waved through.

Money

ATMs

ATMs can be found throughout the DR.

Credit Cards

Credit and debit cards are more and more common among Dominicans (and more widely accepted for use by foreigners). Visa and MasterCard are more common than Amex but most cards are accepted in areas frequented by tourists. Some but not all businesses add a surcharge for credit-card purchases (typically 16%) – the federal policy of withdrawing sales tax directly from credit-card transactions means merchants will simply add the cost directly to the bill. We've had reports of travelers being excessively overcharged when paying by credit card, so always check the bill before signing.

Currency

The Dominican monetary unit is the peso, indicated by the symbol RD$ (or sometimes just R$). Though the peso is technically divided into 100 centavos (cents), prices are usually rounded to the nearest peso. There are one- and five-peso coins, while paper money comes in denominations of 10, 20, 50, 100, 500, 1000 and 2000 pesos. Both US$ and RD$ are accepted in tourist areas. Many tourist-related businesses, including most midrange and top-end hotels, list prices in US dollars, but accept pesos at the going exchange rate.

Money Changers

Moneychangers will approach you in a number of tourist centers. They are unlikely to be aggressive. You will get equally favorable rates, however, and a much securer transaction, at an ATM, a bank or an exchange office (*cambio*).

Taxes & Refunds

An ITBIS (Industrialized Goods and Services Transfer Tax) of 18% sales tax is levied on most goods and services, and in restaurants, a 10% service charge may also be included in the bill. Be sure to ask when booking hotels if the quoted price includes the tax.

There is no refund mechanism for VAT-exempt goods for the average traveler.

Tipping

A shock to many first-timers, most restaurants add a whopping 28% (ITBIS of 18% and an automatic 10% service charge) to every bill. Menus don't always indicate whether prices include the tax and tip.

Hotels A 10% service charge is often automatically included; however, a US$1 to US$2 per night gratuity left for cleaning staff is worth considering.

Taxis Typically, you can round up or give a little extra change.

Tours You should also tip tour guides, some of whom earn no other salary.

Restaurants Tipping generally not expected since 10% automatically added to total. If especially impressed, you can

add whatever else you feel is deserved.

Opening Hours

Opening hours vary throughout the year. We've provided high-season opening hours; hours generally decrease in the shoulder and low seasons.

Banks 9am to 4:30pm Monday to Friday, to 1pm Saturday.

Bars 8pm to late, to 2am in Santo Domingo.

Government Offices 7:30am to 4pm Monday to Friday, officially; in practice more like 9am to 2:30pm.

Restaurants 8am to 10pm Monday to Saturday (some closed between lunch and dinner); to 11pm or later in large cities and tourist areas.

Supermarkets 8am to 10pm Monday to Saturday.

Shops 9am to 7:30pm Monday to Saturday; some open half-day Sunday.

Post

Mail service in the DR can't be relied upon, no doubt in part because mailing addresses are non-existent in much of the country. It can take as long as a month for a letter to arrive from the US. Your best bet is FedEx or UPS; within the country, use either Caribe Pack or Metro PAC; each bus company's own package delivery entity is located in their respective terminals.

Public Holidays

New Years Day January 1

Epiphany January 6

Lady of Altagracia January 21

Juan Pablo Duarte Day January 26

Independence Day February 27

Good Friday Friday before Easter

Easter Sunday March/April

Labor Day May 1

PRACTICALITIES

➡ **Newspapers** *El Listin Diario* (www.listin.com.do), *Hoy* (www.hoy.com.do), *Diario Libre* (www.diariolibre.com), *El Caribe* (www.elcaribe.com.do), *El Día* (www.eldia.com.do) and *El Nacional* (www.elnacional.com.do), plus *International Herald Tribune*, the *New York Times* and the *Miami Herald* can be found in many tourist areas. Local papers cost RD$25.

➡ **Radio & TV** There are about 150 radio stations, most playing merengue and *bachata* (popular guitar music based on bolero rhythms), and seven local TV networks, though cable and satellite programming is very popular for baseball, movies and American soap operas.

➡ **Weights & measures** The DR uses the metric system for everything except gasoline, which is measured in gallons, and at laundromats, where laundry is measured in pounds.

Corpus Christi June 15

Restoration Day August 16

Our Lady of Mercedes Day
September 24

Constitution Day November 6

Christmas Day December 25

Safe Travel

The Dominican Republic is not a particularly dangerous place to visit, but tourists should be aware of the following:

➡ Street crime is rare, but locals advise tourists to avoid talking on or looking at cellphones in public (thieves are known to snatch them).

➡ Don't walk on beaches at night, and consider taking a cab when returning home late from bars.

➡ Car theft is not unheard of, so don't leave valuables inside your car.

➡ Tensions along the Haitian border flare up occasionally: check the situation before crossing.

➡ To prevent cholera, use purified water for drinking, brushing teeth and hand washing.

Telephone

Remember that you must dial ☑1 + 809, 829 or ☑849 for all calls within the DR, even local ones. Toll-free numbers have ☑200 or ☑809 for their prefix (not the area code).

The easiest way to make a phone call in the DR is to pay per minute (average rates per minute: to the US US$0.20; to Europe US$0.50; to Haiti US$0.50) at a Codetel Centro de Comunicaciones (Codetel) call center or an internet cafe that operates as a dual call center.

Calling from a hotel is always the most expensive option.

Mobile Phones

Cell (mobile) phones are ubiquitous and iPhone and Galaxy are both popular smart phone brands. Travelers with global-roaming-enabled phones can receive and make cell phone calls. It's worth checking with your cell-phone carrier for details on rates and accessibility – be aware that per-minute fees can be exorbitant. If you have a GSM phone, and you can unlock it, you can use a SIM card bought from Orange or Claro (prepaid start-up kit US$30). Or you can buy a new cell phone (the cheapest is around RD$800; DR cell phones work at 1900 MHZ, the North American standard) and pay as you go (around RD$4 per minute for a call and a recharge costs RD$200). In terms of customer service, Orange has a better reputation than Claro.

Phonecards

These can be used at public phones and are available in denominations of RD$50, RD$100, RD$150, RD$200 and RD$250.

Time

The DR is four hours behind Greenwich Mean Time. In autumn and winter it is one hour ahead of New York, Miami and Toronto as well as Haiti – extremely important to keep in mind if heading to or from the border. However, because the country does not adjust for daylight saving time as do the USA and Canada, it's in the same time zone as New York, Miami and Toronto from the first Sunday in April to the last Sunday in October.

Toilets

There are public restrooms in most public buildings and restaurants. It's rare that somebody will try to charge you for use, but nearly every bathroom will instruct you

to dispose of the toilet paper in a waste basket instead of the toilet. Septic systems are sensitive here, so try to avoid contributing to a blockage.

Tourist Information

Almost every city in the DR that's frequented by tourists has a tourist office, and a number of less-visited towns do as well. In general, the information you get at tourist offices will feel a bit canned, but it can certainly still be helpful. Some tourist offices offer maps, bus schedules or a calendar of upcoming events, which are handy. The official DR tourism website, www.godominicanrepublic.com, is a useful resource.

Travelers with Disabilities

Few Latin American countries are well suited for travelers with disabilities, and the Dominican Republic is no different. On the other hand, all-inclusive resorts can be ideal for travelers with mobility impairments, as rooms, meals and daytime and nighttime activities are all within close proximity, and there are plenty of staff members to help you navigate around the property. Some resorts have a few wheelchair-friendly rooms, with larger doors and handles in the bathroom. Dominicans tend to be extremely helpful and accommodating people. Travelers with disabilities should expect some curious stares, but also quick and friendly help from perfect strangers and passersby.

Two associations in Santo Domingo that provide information and assistance to travelers with disabilities are the **Asociación Dominicana de Rehabilitación** (☑809-689-7151; San Francisco de Macoris; ☺8am-4pm Mon-Fri), and the **Fundación Dominicana de Ciegos** (☑809-538-4161; cnr Av Expreso V Centenario &

Tunti Cáceres; ☺7am-3:30pm Mon-Fri).

Download Lonely Planet's free Accessible Travel guide from http://lptravel.to/Access ibleTravel.

Visas

The majority of would-be foreign travelers in the Dominican Republic do not need to obtain visas prior to arrival.

Tourist cards (you don't need to retain this for your return flight) are issued for US$10 upon arrival to visitors from Argentina, Australia, Austria, Belgium, Brazil, Canada, Chile, Denmark, France, Germany, Greece, Ireland, Israel, Italy, Japan, Mexico, the Netherlands, Portugal, Russia, South Africa, Spain, Sweden, Switzerland, the UK and the US, among many others. Whatever your country of origin, a valid passport is necessary.

Tourist Card Extensions

A tourist card is good for up to 30 days from the date of issue. If you wish to stay longer, it's unnecessary to formally extend – instead you'll be charged RD$1000 when you depart the country for any stay up to 90 days. Another way to extend your time is to leave the DR briefly – most likely to Haiti – and then return, at which point you'll be issued a brand-new tourist card. (You may have to pay entrance and departure fees in both countries, of course.)

To extend your tourist card longer than three months, you must apply in Santo Domingo at the **Dirección General de Migración** (Map p78; ☎809-508-2555; www.migracion.gob.do; cnr Av 30 de Mayo & Héroes de Luperón; ☺8am-2:30pm Mon-Fri) at least two weeks before your original card expires (up to nine months will cost RD$1000).

Volunteering

Many NGOs operating in the DR are primarily community networks attempting to develop sustainable ecotourism. Formal volunteering programs may be hard to come by, but if you speak good Spanish and don't mind some elbow grease (or office work), you may be of some use to them. A few more established organizations that accept volunteers:

CEDAF (Centro para el Desarrollo Agropecuario y Forestal; ☎809-565-5603; www.cedaf.org.do; José Amado Soler 50, Ensanche Paraíso, Santo Domingo) This nationwide NGO helps local farmers develop sustainable ways to use the land.

Fundación Taigüey (☎809-537-8977; www.taiguey.org) This is a network of small NGOs, several of which focus on ecotourism.

Grupo Jaragua (☎809-472-1036; www.grupojaragua.org.do; Santo Domingo) The largest and oldest NGO in the southwest. Based in Santo Domingo, it concentrates on biodiversity and conservation through microfinancing to assist locals with bee farming etc.

Mariposa Foundation (☎809-571-0610; www.mariposadrfoundation.org; Calle Principal, La Cienega, Cabarete) Dedicated to empowering and educating girls living in and around Cabarete through a 'holistic' program that involves English-language classes, health and wellness seminars, athletics and family involvement. Minimum three month commitment, generally teaching in varying

EMBASSIES & CONSULATES

All of the following are located in Santo Domingo.

EMBASSY/CONSULATE	TELEPHONE	ADDRESS
Canadian Embassy	☎809-262-3100	Av Winston Churchill 1099
Cuban Embassy	☎809-537-2113	Calle Francisco Prats Ramírez 808
French Consulate	☎809-695-4300	Calle Las Damas 42
German Embassy	☎809-542-8950	Av Gustavo Mejia Ricart 1986
Haitian Embassy	☎809-686-7115	Calle Juan Sánchez Ramírez 33
Israeli Embassy	☎809-920-1500	Calle Pedro Henriquez Ureña 80
Italian Consulate	☎809-732-6971	Av Lope de Vega
Japanese Embassy	☎809-567-3365	Torre Citigroup Bldg, 21st fl, Av Winston Churchill 1099
Netherlands	☎809-262-0320	Nuñez de Cáceres 11
Spanish Embassy	☎809-535-6500	Av Independencia 1205
UK Embassy	☎809-472-7111	Av 27 de Febrero 233
US Embassy	☎809-567-7775	Av República de Colombia 57

capacities. Located near Kite Beach.

Punta Cana Ecological Foundation (Map p112; ☑809-959-9221; www.puntacana.com/ecological-foundation.html) One of the pioneers of sustainable development in the DR; projects targeted at coral reef restoration and preserving the natural environment in the Punta Cana area.

REDOTUR (Red Dominicana de Turismo Rural; ☑809-487-1057; www.redotur.org) Promotes alternative and sustainable tourism projects.

SOEPA (☑809-863-8833; www.facebook.com/Sociedad-Ecologica-de-Paraiso-SOEPA-395909647173421/) Sociedad Ecologica de Paraíso, founded in 1995, is dedicated to the preservation and protection of the environment and natural resources in the area around Paraíso; its biggest project is maintenance and development at Cachóte.

Women Travelers

Women traveling without men in the Dominican Republic should expect to receive some attention, usually in the form of hissing (to get your attention), stares and comments like '*Hola, preciosa*' (Hello, beautiful). Although it may be unwanted, it's more of a nuisance than anything else. If you don't like it, dressing conservatively and ignoring the comments are probably your best lines of defense.

That is not to say that women travelers shouldn't take the same precautions they would in other countries, or ignore their instincts about certain men or situations they encounter. Robbery and assaults, though rare against tourists, do occur and women are often seen as easier targets than men. Young, athletic Dominican men who 'target' foreign women, especially in beach resort areas like Punta Cana, are referred to as 'sanky-pankys'. Their MO is subtly transactional, usually involving 'promises' of affection in exchange for meals, drinks, gifts and cash from generally older North American and European women.

Work

It can be difficult for a foreigner to find work in the Dominican Republic, as opportunities are limited unless you have special skills and speak Spanish. Otherwise, your only options will likely be teaching English, doing something in the tourism industry or working at a call center. Salaries are very low, so don't expect to have much extra spending money.

Transportation

GETTING THERE & AWAY

There are a variety of ways to get to and from the Dominican Republic, including flights into international airports, overland crossings, international cruiseships and ferries. Flights, cars and tours can be booked online at lonelyplanet.com/bookings.

Entering the Country

The vast majority of tourists entering the Dominican Republic arrive by air. Independent travelers typically arrive at the main international airport outside of Santo Domingo, Aeropuerto Internacional Las Américas. Passing through immigration is a relatively simple process. Once disembarked, you are guided to the immigration area where you must buy a tourist card (US$10). You're expected to pay in US dollars (Euros and GBP are accepted, but you lose out substantially on the rate); then join the queue in front of one of the immigration officers. You're allowed up to 30 days on a tourist card. The procedure is the same if you arrive at one of the other airports such as Puerto Plata or Punta Cana; the latter is easily the busiest airport in the country in terms of tourist arrivals.

Air

Regardless of where you plan to travel in the DR, there is an international airport close by. You may even want to consider flying into one place, such as Santo Domingo, and out of say, Puerto Plata, to maximize the time you spend experiencing different areas of the country.

Airports

There are nine so-called international airports, though at least three are used only for domestic flights. For information on most, check out www.aerodom.com. Perhaps the cheapest route between North America and the DR is Spirit Airlines' Fort Lauderdale to Santiago (around US$195 round-trip).

Aeropuerto Internacional Arroyo Barril (DAB; ☑809-248-2718) West of Samaná, a small airstrip used mostly during whale-watching season (January to March).

Aeropuerto Internacional del Cibao (☑809-233-8000; www.aeropuertocibao.com.do) Santiago's airport is the third-largest in the country, and offers frequent international air service to major destinations. There's a good selection of rent-a-car agencies at the airport, too.

Aeropuerto Internacional de Puerto Plata (Gregorio Luperón) (POP; ☑809-291-0000; www.puerto-plata-airport.com) Most convenient airport for north-coast destinations like the beach resorts around Puerto Plata, Sosúa and Cabarete.

Aeropuerto Internacional La Isabela Dr Joaquín Balaguer (JBQ, Higüero; ☑809-826-4003) This airport is just north of Santo Domingo proper. It handles mostly domestic flights.

Aeropuerto Internacional La Romana (☑809-813-9000; www.romanaairport.com; Casa de Campo) Near La Romana and Casa de Campo; handles primarily charter flights from the US, Canada, Italy and Germany; some flights from Miami, NYC and San Juan, Puerto Rico.

Aeropuerto Internacional Las Américas (SDQ; José Francisco Peña Gómez; ☑809-947-2220) The country's main international airport is located 20km east of Santo Domingo.

Aeropuerto Internacional María Montez (BRX; ☑809-524-4144) Located 5km from Barahona in the southwest; charters only.

Aeropuerto Internacional Punta Cana (Map p112; ☑809-959-2473; www.puntacanainternationalairport.com; Carretera Higüey-Punta Cana Km 45) Serves Bávaro and Punta Cana, and is the busiest airport in the country.

Aeropuerto Internacional Samaná El Catey (AZS; Presidente Juan Bosch; ☑809-338-0150) Located around 40km west of Samaná; Península de Samaná's main air gateway.

Land

These are the four points where you can cross between Haiti and the DR. Note that in recent years, tensions at the borders have sometimes been high due to new policies in the DR that have led to an increase in deportations of Haitians and even Dominicans of Haitian descent.

Jimaní–Malpasse This, the busiest and most organized crossing, is in the south on the road that links Santo Domingo and Port-au-Prince. Disputes here have created strong tension according to a local news source.

Dajabón–Ouanaminthe Busy northern crossing on the road between Santiago and Cap-Haïtien (a six-hour drive); try to avoid crossing on market days (Monday and Friday) because of the enormous crush of people and the risk of theft.

Pedernales–Ainse-a-Pietres In the far south; there's a small bridge for foot and motorcycle traffic; cars have to drive over a paved road through a generally shallow river. Migrant camps are set up on the Haitian side of this border for those who have been deported and have nowhere else to go.

Comendador (aka Elías Piña)–Belladère Certainly the dodgiest crossing, but also the least busy. On the Haiti side, the immigration building is several hundred meters from the actual border. Transportation further into Haiti is difficult to access.

Practicalities

Immigration offices on the Dominican side are usually open 8am to 6pm, and 9am to 6pm on the Haitian side. Arrive as early as possible, so you are sure to get through both countries' border offices and onto a bus well before dark. When deciding between either crossing in the late afternoon or staying an extra night and crossing in the morning, choose the latter – safety concerns aside, onward transportation is less frequent or non-existent after dark.

Leaving the DR You need your passport and are likely to be asked more questions than if leaving via an airport, usually only out of curiosity that a tourist would travel this way. Officially, you are supposed to pay US$20 to leave the DR, which gives you the right to re-enter at the same point for no extra charge. However, border officials have been known to ask for an extra US$5 to US$10 to leave and the full US$20 to re-enter for no other reason than they can. It's worth politely pointing out that you have already paid the full fee. If you're only interested in leaving without returning the fee should be US$10.

Entering Haiti Pay a US$10 fee (US dollars only).

Public Transportation Caribe Tours and Capital Coach Lines service the Santo Domingo–Port-au-Prince route daily; Caribe Tours also has daily departures from Santiago for Cap-Haïtien. From the north coast it's easy enough to reach Dajabón, but then you have to transfer to a Haitian vehicle on the other side.

Private Transportation Rental vehicles are not allowed to cross from one country into the other, and you need special authorization to cross the border with a private vehicle.

Sea

International cruise ships on Caribbean tours commonly stop in Santo Domingo, Cayo Levantado in the Península de Samaná and at the new Amber Cove port near Puerto Plata.

Caribbean Fantasy, run by **America Cruise Ferries** (Map p58; ☑San Juan, Puerto Rico 787-622-4800, Santiago 809-583-4440, Santo Domingo 809-688-4400; www.acferries. com), offers a passenger and car ferry service between Santo Domingo and Puerto Rico (San Juan). The trip takes about 12 hours and departs three times weekly.

DEPARTURE TAX

The departure tax of US$20 is almost always automatically included in the price of the ticket.

GETTING AROUND

The DR is a fairly small country, so in theory at least it's easy to drive or take public transportation from one side of the country to the other. In practice, however, the inadequate road network will behoove some with limited time and a sufficient budget to consider flying.

Air Useful if short on time, though the most expensive option and sometimes unreliable depending on time of year.

Bus Two major companies, Caribe Tours and Metro, provide comfortable; frequent service along a network of major cities and towns.

Car Most convenient option if seeking freedom of movement, especially if interested in exploring rural and mountain regions.

Guaguas Basically small buses or minivans, ubiquitous, least expensive and least comfortable, but often the only available public transport.

Air

If making flight connections in Santo Domingo, keep in mind that it's an hour drive between Aeropuerto Internacional Las Américas and La Isabela. The main domestic carriers and air-taxi companies include Aerolíneas MAS (www.aerolineasmas. com), Dominican Shuttles (www.dominicanshuttles. com), Air Century (www. aircentury.com), Servicios Aéreos Profesionales (www. sapair.com) and M&N Aviation (www.mnaviation.com).

CLIMATE CHANGE & TRAVEL

Every form of transport that relies on carbon-based fuel generates CO_2, the main cause of human-induced climate change. Modern travel is dependent on airplanes, which might use less fuel per mile per person than most cars but travel much greater distances. The altitude at which aircraft emit gases (including CO_2) and particles also contributes to their climate change impact. Many websites offer 'carbon calculators' that allow people to estimate the carbon emissions generated by their journey and, for those who wish to do so, to offset the impact of the greenhouse gases emitted with contributions to portfolios of climate-friendly initiatives throughout the world. Lonely Planet offsets the carbon footprint of all staff and author travel.

Bicycle

The DR's highways are not well suited for cycling, and Dominican drivers are not exactly accommodating to people on bikes; the situation is hectic to say the least. However, mountain biking on the DR's back roads and lesser-used highways can be rewarding, and a number of recommended tour companies operate in Jarabacoa and Cabarete. If you're planning a multiday ride, definitely consider bringing your own bike. If you're joining a bike tour, most tour operators will provide you with one.

Boat

The only regularly scheduled domestic passenger boat route in the DR is the ferry service between Samaná and Sabana de la Mar, on opposite sides of the Bahía de Samaná in the northeastern part of the country. The journey is subject to weather and departures are frequently canceled. There is no car ferry service here, so unfortunately, if you arrive in Sabana de la Mar with a rental vehicle, you'll have to leave it behind and return by the same route you arrived.

Bus

The DR has a great bus system, utilizing buses similar to Greyhound in the US, with frequent service throughout the country. Virtually all 1st

class buses have toilets in the back and TVs in the aisles showing movies (loudly) en route. Air-conditioning is sometimes turned up to uncomfortable levels. Fares are low – the most expensive 1st class ticket is less than US$10 – and you must buy your ticket before boarding. Unfortunately, there are no central bus terminals in the majority of cities and each company has its own station location. They almost never stop along the road to pick up passengers but drivers are often willing to drop passengers off at various points along the way; they will not, however, open the luggage compartment at any point other than the actual terminal.

Reservations aren't usually necessary and rarely even taken. The exceptions are the international buses to Port-au-Prince, Haiti, operated by Caribe Tours and Capital Coach Lines. During Dominican holidays you can sometimes buy your ticket a day or two in advance, which assures you a spot and saves you the time and hassle of waiting in line at a busy terminal with all your bags.

First-class carriers include:

Capital Coach Lines (☑809-530-8266; www.capitalcoach-line.com; Av 27 de Febrero 455) Offers daily bus services to and from Port-au-Prince on comfortable, air-con buses.

Caribe Tours (Map p64; ☑809-221-4422; www.caribetours.com.do; cnr Avs 27 de Febrero

& Leopoldo Navarro) One of the country's two main bus companies; has most departures and covers more destinations.

Metro (Map p78; ☑809-544-4580; www.metroserviciosturisticos.com; Francisco Prats Ramírez) Metro serves nine cities, mostly along the Santo Domingo–Puerto Plata corridor. Fares tend to be slightly more expensive than Caribe Tours.

Car & Motorcycle

Though the DR's bus and *guagua* system is excellent, having your own car is invariably faster and more convenient. Even if renting a car isn't in your budget for the entire trip, consider renting one for a select couple of days, to reach sights that are isolated or not well served by public transportation; pretty much a necessity for the southwest.

Driving Licences

For travelers from most countries, your home country driver's license allows you to drive in the DR. Be sure it's valid.

Fuel & Spare Parts

Most towns have at least one gas station, typically right along the highway on the outskirts of town. There are a couple of different companies, but prices are essentially the same for all. At the time of research, gas prices were around RD$212 per gallon. Many gas stations accept credit cards and many also have ATMs – all are full service.

With the cost of gas so high, a growing percentage of vehicles have been jerry-rigged to run on much cheaper propane gas (RD$100 per gallon) – you'll usually see a station (Unigas, Propagas or Tropigas) at the exit and entrance of any good-sized town.

Play it safe and always keep your gas tank at least half full. Many *bombas* (gas stations) in the DR close by 7pm, and even when they are open they don't always have gas. If you're traveling on back roads or in a remote part of the country, your best bet is to buy gas from people selling it from their front porch. Look for the large pink jugs sitting on tables on the side of the road.

The most common car trouble is to end up with a punctured or damaged tire caused by potholes, speed bumps and rocks or other debris in the road. The word for tire is *goma* (literally 'rubber') and a tire shop is called a *gomero*. If you can make it to one on your busted tire, the guys there can patch a flat, replace a damaged tire, or just put the spare on.

Insurance

The multinational car-rental agencies typically offer comprehensive, nondeductible collision and liability insurance for fairly small daily fees. Smaller agencies usually offer partial coverage, with a deductible ranging from US$100 to US$2000. Several credit-card companies, including Amex, offer comprehensive coverage for rentals, but you should check your own insurance policy before declining the rental company's.

Maps

If you rent a car, it's worth buying a good map to the area you'll be driving in. In Santo Domingo, **Mapas GAAR** (Map p58; ☏809-688-8004; 3rd fl, cnr El Conde &

Espaillat; ⊙8am-5:30pm Mon-Fri, 9am-1pm Sat) publishes and sells the most comprehensive maps of cities and towns in the DR. Both the *National Geographic Adventure Map* and Boch maps of the Dominican Republic can be recommended.

Rental

Familiar multinational agencies like Hertz, Avis, Europcar, Alamo and Dollar have offices at the major international airports (or pickup service like at Punta Cana), as well as in Santo Domingo and other cities. Not only are their online rates sometimes much less than those of local or national agencies, but their vehicles are of better quality and they provide reliable and mostly comprehensive service and insurance (it should be noted that an additional 'airport terminal charge', around 8%, is tacked on to the bill). If you plan to do any driving on secondary roads along the coast or in the mountains, a 4WD is recommended. Rates typically cost US$30 (for a standard car) to US$120 (for a 4WD) per day. Motorcycles can also be rented, but only experienced riders should do so because of poor road conditions.

Road Conditions

Roads in the DR range from excellent to awful, sometimes along the same highway over a very short distance. The *autopista* (freeway) between Santo Domingo and Santiago has as many as eight lanes, is fast moving and is generally in good condition. However, even here, always be alert for potholes, speed bumps and people walking along the roadside, especially near populated areas. On all roads, large or small, watch for slow-moving cars and especially motorcycles. Be particularly careful when driving at night. Better yet, *never drive at night*. Even the most skilled person with the reflexes of a superhero will

probably end up in a ditch by the side of the road.

Some of the highways, including Hwy 3 heading out of Santo Domingo to the east and Hwy 2 leaving the city to the west, have toll fees of fairly nominal amounts (RD$35), while the Santo Domingo–Samaná highway (DR-7) is a relatively whopping RD$412. For the former it's best to have exact change that you can simply toss into the basket and quickly move on.

Road Rules

The first rule is there are none. In theory, road rules in the DR are the same as for most countries in the Americas, and the lights and signs are the same shape and color you find in the US or Canada (speed limit signs are in kilometers per hour). Driving is on the right and seat belts are required. That said, driving is pretty much a free-for-all. In fact, in 2013, the World Health Organization (WHO) ranked the DR as the world's most dangerous country for drivers, just ahead of Thailand. Pedestrians, equally indifferent to common sense safety precautions, are also frequently victims. The combination of powerful public transport unions and the general public's opposition to education and licensing regulations are continuing obstacles to improving safety standards.

In small towns, nay in all towns, traffic lights – when working – are frequently ignored, though you should plan to stop at them. Watch what other drivers are doing – if everyone is going through, you probably should, too, as it can be even more dangerous to stop if the cars behind you aren't expecting it. Many city streets are one way and often poorly marked, creating yet another hazard. Often, in lieu of stop signs, culverts (basically, the opposite of speed bumps), deep enough to damage the undersides of low clearance vehicles unless taken at the slowest of speeds, signal stops. Prohibitions against drinking and driving are widely flouted and it's not uncommon to spot a speeding motorcyclist sipping rum.

Guaguas

Wherever long-distance buses don't go, you can be sure a *guagua* (pronounced 'gwa-gwa') does. *Guaguas* are typically midsize buses holding around 25 to 30 passengers. They rarely have signs, but the driver's assistant (known as the *cobrador*, or 'charger', since one of his jobs is to collect fares from passengers) will yell out the destination to potential fares on the side of the road. Don't hesitate to ask a local if you're unsure which one to take. *Guaguas* pick up and drop off passengers anywhere along the route – to flag one down simply hold out your hand – the common gesture is to point at the curb in front of you but just about any gesture will do. Most *guaguas* pass every 15 to 30 minutes and cost RD$35 to RD$70, but unless you have the exact amount some *cobradors* may pocket the change of unwary foreigners. It's a good idea to carry change or small bills and to find out the exact cost in advance. When you want to get off, tap the roof or bang on the side of the van.

Guaguas are divided into two types – the majority are *caliente* (literally 'hot'), which don't have air-conditioning, naturally. For every four or five *caliente* buses there is usually an *expreso*, which typically has air-conditioning, makes fewer stops and costs slightly more. Within these two categories there's a virtual rainbow of diversity in terms of vehicle quality and reliability.

Hitchhiking & Ride-Sharing

Hitching is never entirely safe, and we don't recommend it. Travellers who hitch should understand that they are taking a small but potentially serious risk. That said, Dominicans, both men and women, do it all the time, especially in rural areas where fewer people have cars and *guagua* service is sparse. It's also common in resort areas like Bávaro, where a large number of workers commute to Higüey or other towns nearby every morning and evening. It is, however, rare to see foreigners hitchhiking, and doing so (especially if you have bags) carries a greater risk than for locals.

Local Transportation

Bus

Large cities like Santo Domingo and Santiago have public bus systems that operate as they do in most places around the world. Many of the larger city buses are imported from Brazil, and are the kind which you board in the back and pay the person sitting beside the turnstile. Other city buses are more or less like *guaguas*, where you board quickly and pay the *cobrador* when he comes around. In general, you will probably take relatively few city buses, simply because *públicos* follow pretty much the same routes and pass more frequently.

Metro

Santo Domingo has a good metro system that is continuing to expand.

Motoconcho

Cheaper and easier to find than taxis, *motoconchos* (motorcycle taxis) are the best, and sometimes only, way to get around in many towns. An average ride

should set you back no more than RD$30. That being said, you might have to negotiate to get a fair price and we've heard of travelers unknowingly dropped off far short of their intended location. Accidents resulting in injuries and even deaths are not uncommon; ask the driver to slow down (*¡Más despacio por favor!*) if you think he's driving dangerously. Avoid two passengers on a bike since not only is the price the same as taking separate bikes but the extra weight makes scooters harder to control. For longer trips, or if you have any sort of bag or luggage, *motoconchos* are usually impractical and certainly less comfortable than alternatives. By law, drivers are required to wear helmets though it's generally ignored, as are any tickets issued.

Públicos

These are banged-up cars, minivans or small pickup trucks that pick up passengers along set routes, usually main boulevards. *Públicos* (also called *conchos* or *carros*) don't have signs but the drivers hold their hands out the window to solicit potential fares. They are also identifiable by the crush of people inside them – up to seven in a midsize car! To flag one down simply hold out your hand – the fare is around RD$12. If there is no one else in the car, be sure to tell the driver you want *servicio público* (public service) to avoid paying private taxi rates.

Taxi

Dominican taxis rarely cruise for passengers – instead they wait at designated *sitios* (stops), which are located at hotels, bus terminals, tourist areas and main public parks. You can also phone a taxi service (or ask your hotel receptionist to call for you). Taxis do not have meters – agree on a price beforehand.

Language

The official language of the Dominican Republic is Spanish. Some English and German is also spoken by individuals in the tourist business. Dominican Spanish is very much like Central America's other varieties of Spanish. Note though that Dominicans tend to swallow the ends of words, especially those ending in 's' – *tres* will sound like 'tre' and *buenos días* like 'bueno día.'

Spanish pronunciation is relatively straightforward as the relationship between what's written and how you pronounce it is clear and consistent – each written letter is always pronounced the same way. Also, most Spanish sounds are similar to their English counterparts. Note that the kh in our pronunciation guides is a throaty sound (like the 'ch' in the Scottish *loch*), v and b are similar to the English 'b' (but softer, between a 'v' and a 'b'), and r is strongly rolled. If you read our pronunciation guides as if they were English, you will be understood. In our guides, we've also indicated the stressed syllables in italics.

The Dominican Academy of Language published its first Dominican-language-based dictionary in 2013.

BASICS

Hello.	*Hola.*	o·la
Goodbye.	*Adiós.*	a·dyos
How are you?	*¿Qué tal?*	ke tal
Fine, thanks.	*Bien, gracias.*	byen gra·syas
Excuse me.	*Perdón.*	per·don

WANT MORE?

For in-depth language information and handy phrases, check out Lonely Planet's *Latin American Spanish Phrasebook*. You'll find it at **shop.lonelyplanet.com**, or you can buy Lonely Planet's iPhone phrasebooks at the Apple App Store.

Sorry.	*Lo siento.*	lo syen·to
Please.	*Por favor.*	por fa·vor
Thank you.	*Gracias.*	gra·syas
You're welcome.	*De nada.*	de na·da
Yes./No.	*Sí./No.*	see/no

What's your name?
¿Cómo se llama Usted?	ko·mo se ya·ma oo·ste (pol)
¿Cómo te llamas?	ko·mo te ya·mas (inf)

My name is ...
Me llamo ...	me ya·mo ...

Do you speak English?
¿Habla inglés?	a·bla een·gles (pol)
¿Hablas inglés?	a·blas een·gles (inf)

I don't understand.
Yo no entiendo.	yo no en·tyen·do

ACCOMMODATIONS

I'd like a ... room.	*Quisiera una habitación ...*	kee·sye·ra oo·na a·bee·ta·syon ...
single	*individual*	een·dee·vee·dwal
double	*doble*	do·ble

How much is it per night/person?
¿Cuánto cuesta por noche/persona?	kwan·to kwes·ta por no·che/per·so·na

Does it include breakfast?
¿Incluye el desayuno?	een·kloo·ye el de·sa·yoo·no

air-con	*aire acondicionado*	ai·re a·kon·dee·syo·na·do
bathroom	*baño*	ba·nyo
bed	*cama*	ka·ma
campsite	*terreno de cámping*	te·re·no de kam·peeng
guesthouse	*pensión*	pen·syon
hotel	*hotel*	o·tel
youth hostel	*albergue juvenil*	al·ber·ge khoo·ve·neel

KEY PATTERNS

To get by in Spanish, mix and match these simple patterns with words of your choice:

When's (the next flight)?
¿Cuándo sale   kwan·do sa·le
(el próximo vuelo)? (el prok·see·mo vwe·lo)

Where's (the station)?
¿Dónde está   don·de es·ta
(la estación)?   (la es·ta·syon)

Where can I (buy a ticket)?
¿Dónde puedo   don·de pwe·do
(comprar un billete)? (kom·prar oon bee·ye·te)

Do you have (a map)?
¿Tiene (un mapa)?   tye·ne (oon ma·pa)

Is there (a toilet)?
¿Hay (servicios)?   ai (ser·vee·syos)

I'd like (a coffee).
Quisiera (un café). kee·sye·ra (oon ka·fe)

I'd like (to hire a car).
Quisiera (alquilar kee·sye·ra (al·kee·lar
un coche).   oon ko·che)

Can I (enter)?
¿Se puede (entrar)? se pwe·de (en·trar)

Could you please (help me)?
¿Puede (ayudarme), pwe·de (a·yoo·dar·me)
por favor?   por fa·vor

DIRECTIONS

Where's ...?
¿Dónde está ...?   don·de es·ta ...

What's the address?
¿Cuál es la dirección? kwal es la dee·rek·syon

Could you please write it down?
¿Puede escribirlo, pwe·de es·kree·beer·lo
por favor?   por fa·vor

Can you show me (on the map)?
¿Me lo puede indicar me lo pwe·de een·dee·kar
(en el mapa)?   (en el ma·pa)

at the corner	en la esquina	en la es·kee·na
at the traffic lights	en el semáforo	en el se·ma·fo·ro
behind ...	detrás de ...	de·tras de ...
in front of ...	enfrente de ...	en·fren·te de ...
left	izquierda	ees·kyer·da
next to ...	al lado de ...	al la·do de ...
opposite ...	frente a ...	fren·te a ...
right	derecha	de·re·cha
straight ahead	todo recto	to·do rek·to

EATING & DRINKING

What would you recommend?
¿Qué recomienda?   ke re·ko·myen·da

What's in that dish?
¿Que lleva ese plato? ke ye·va e·se pla·to

I don't eat ...
No como ...   no ko·mo ...

That was delicious!
¡Estaba buenísimo! es·ta·ba bwe·nee·see·mo

Please bring the check/bill.
Por favor nos trae por fa·vor nos tra·e
la cuenta.   la kwen·ta

Cheers!
¡Salud!   sa·loo

I'd like to book a table for ...	Quisiera reservar una mesa para ...	kee·sye·ra re·ser·var oo·na me·sa pa·ra ...
(eight) o'clock	las (ocho)	las (o·cho)
(two) people	(dos) personas	(dos) per·so·nas

Key Words

appetizers	aperitivos	a·pe·ree·tee·vos
bar	bar	bar
bottle	botella	bo·te·ya
bowl	bol	bol
breakfast	desayuno	de·sa·yoo·no
cafe	café	ka·fe
children's menu	menú infantil	me·noo een·fan·teel
(too) cold	(muy) frío	(mooy) free·o
dinner	cena	se·na
food	comida	ko·mee·da
fork	tenedor	te·ne·dor
glass	vaso	va·so
highchair	trona	tro·na
hot (warm)	caliente	kal·yen·te
knife	cuchillo	koo·chee·yo
lunch	comida	ko·mee·da
main course	segundo plato	se·goon·do pla·to
market	mercado	mer·ka·do
menu (in English)	menú (en inglés)	oon me·noo (en een·gles)
plate	plato	pla·to
restaurant	restaurante	res·tow·ran·te
spoon	cuchara	koo·cha·ra
supermarket	supermercado	soo·per·mer·ka·do
vegetarian food	comida vegetariana	ko·mee·da ve·khe·ta·rya·na
with	con	kon
without	sin	seen

Meat & Fish

beef	*carne de vaca*	*kar*·ne de *va*·ka
chicken	*pollo*	*po*·yo
duck	*pato*	*pa*·to
fish	*pescado*	pes·*ka*·do
lamb	*cordero*	kor·*de*·ro
pork	*cerdo*	*ser*·do
turkey	*pavo*	*pa*·vo
veal	*ternera*	ter·*ne*·ra

Fruit & Vegetables

apple	*manzana*	man·*sa*·na
apricot	*albaricoque*	al·ba·ree·*ko*·ke
artichoke	*alcachofa*	al·ka·*cho*·fa
asparagus	*espárragos*	es·*pa*·ra·gos
banana	*plátano*	*pla*·ta·no
beans	*judías*	khoo·*dee*·as
beetroot	*remolacha*	re·mo·*la*·cha
cabbage	*col*	kol
carrot	*zanahoria*	sa·na·o·rya
celery	*apio*	*a*·pyo
cherry	*cereza*	se·*re*·sa
corn	*maíz*	ma·*ees*
cucumber	*pepino*	pe·*pee*·no
fruit	*fruta*	*froo*·ta
grape	*uvas*	*oo*·vas
lemon	*limón*	lee·*mon*
lentils	*lentejas*	len·*te*·khas
lettuce	*lechuga*	le·*choo*·ga
mushroom	*champiñón*	cham·pee·*nyon*
nuts	*nueces*	*nwe*·ses
onion	*cebolla*	se·*bo*·ya
orange	*naranja*	na·*ran*·kha
peach	*melocotón*	me·lo·ko·*ton*
peas	*guisantes*	gee·*san*·tes
(red/green) pepper	*pimiento (rojo/verde)*	pee·*myen*·to (ro·kho/ver·de)
pineapple	*piña*	*pee*·nya
plum	*ciruela*	seer·*we*·la
potato	*patata*	pa·*ta*·ta
pumpkin	*calabaza*	ka·la·*ba*·sa
spinach	*espinacas*	es·pee·*na*·kas
strawberry	*fresa*	*fre*·sa
tomato	*tomate*	to·*ma*·te
vegetable	*verdura*	ver·*doo*·ra
watermelon	*sandía*	san·*dee*·a

Other

bread	*pan*	pan
butter	*mantequilla*	man·te·*kee*·ya
cheese	*queso*	*ke*·so
egg	*huevo*	*we*·vo
honey	*miel*	myel
jam	*mermelada*	mer·me·*la*·da
oil	*aceite*	a·*sey*·te
pepper	*pimienta*	pee·*myen*·ta
rice	*arroz*	a·*ros*
salt	*sal*	sal
sugar	*azúcar*	a·*soo*·kar
vinegar	*vinagre*	vee·*na*·gre

Drinks

beer	*cerveza*	ser·*ve*·sa
coffee	*café*	ka·*fe*
(orange) juice	*zumo (de naranja)*	*soo*·mo (de na·*ran*·kha)

TALKING LIKE A LOCAL

Here are a few typical regionalisms you might come across in the Dominican Republic:

apagón	power failure
apodo	nickname
bandera dominicana	rice and beans (lit: Dominican flag)
bohío	thatch hut
bulto	luggage
carros de concho	routed, shared taxi
chichi	baby
colmado	small grocery store
fucú	a thing bringing bad luck
guapo	bad-tempered
guarapo	sugarcane juice
gumo	(a) drunk
hablador	person who talks a lot
papaúpa	important person
pariguayo	foolish
pín-pún	exactly equal
una rumba	a lot
Siempre a su orden.	You're welcome.
tiguere	rascal
timacle	brave

milk	*leche*	*le·che*
tea	*té*	*te*
(mineral) water	*agua (mineral)*	*a·gwa (mee·ne·ral)*
(red/white) wine	*vino (tinto/ blanco)*	*vee·no (teen·to/ blan·ko)*

EMERGENCIES

Help!	*¡Socorro!*	*so·ko·ro*
Go away!	*¡Vete!*	*ve·te*

Call a doctor!
¡Llame a un médico! ya·me a oon me·dee·ko

Call the police!
¡Llame a la policía! ya·me a la po·lee·see·a

I'm lost.
Estoy perdido/a. es·toy per·dee·do/a (m/f)

I'm ill.
Estoy enfermo/a. es·toy en·fer·mo/a (m/f)

It hurts here.
Me duele aquí. me dwe·le a·kee

I'm allergic to (antibiotics).
Soy alérgico/a a soy a·ler·khee·ko/a a
(los antibióticos). (los an·tee·byo·tee·kos) (m/f)

SHOPPING & SERVICES

I'd like to buy ...
Quisiera comprar ... kee·sye·ra kom·prar ...

I'm just looking.
Sólo estoy mirando. so·lo es·toy mee·ran·do

May I look at it?
¿Puedo verlo? pwe·do ver·lo

I don't like it.
No me gusta. no me goos·ta

How much is it?
¿Cuánto cuesta? kwan·to kwes·ta

That's too expensive.
Es muy caro. es mooy ka·ro

Can you lower the price?
¿Podría bajar un po·dree·a ba·khar oon
poco el precio? po·ko el pre·syo

There's a mistake in the check/bill.
Hay un error ai oon e·ror
en la cuenta. en la kwen·ta

Question Words		
How?	*¿Cómo?*	*ko·mo*
What?	*¿Qué?*	*ke*
When?	*¿Cuándo?*	*kwan·do*
Where?	*¿Dónde?*	*don·de*
Who?	*¿Quién?*	*kyen*
Why?	*¿Por qué?*	*por ke*

Signs	
Abierto	Open
Cerrado	Closed
Entrada	Entrance
Hombres/Varones	Men
Mujeres/Damas	Women
Prohibido	Prohibited
Salida	Exit
Servicios/Baños	Toilets

ATM	*cajero automático*	*ka·khe·ro ow·to·ma·tee·ko*
internet cafe	*cibercafé*	*see·ber·ka·fe*
post office	*correos*	*ko·re·os*
tourist office	*oficina de turismo*	*o·fee·see·na de too·rees·mo*

TIME & DATES

What time is it?	*¿Qué hora es?*	ke o·ra es
It's (10) o'clock.	*Son (las diez).*	son (las dyes)
It's half past (one).	*Es (la una) y media.*	es (la oo·na) ee me·dya

morning	*mañana*	*ma·nya·na*
afternoon	*tarde*	*tar·de*
evening	*noche*	*no·che*
yesterday	*ayer*	*a·yer*
today	*hoy*	*oy*
tomorrow	*mañana*	*ma·nya·na*

Monday	*lunes*	*loo·nes*
Tuesday	*martes*	*mar·tes*
Wednesday	*miércoles*	*myer·ko·les*
Thursday	*jueves*	*khwe·ves*
Friday	*viernes*	*vyer·nes*
Saturday	*sábado*	*sa·ba·do*
Sunday	*domingo*	*do·meen·go*

January	*enero*	*e·ne·ro*
February	*febrero*	*fe·bre·ro*
March	*marzo*	*mar·so*
April	*abril*	*a·breel*
May	*mayo*	*ma·yo*
June	*junio*	*khoon·yo*
July	*julio*	*khool·yo*
August	*agosto*	*a·gos·to*
September	*septiembre*	*sep·tyem·bre*
October	*octubre*	*ok·too·bre*
November	*noviembre*	*no·vyem·bre*
December	*diciembre*	*dee·syem·bre*

TRANSPORTATION

Public Transportation

boat	barco	bar·ko
bus	autobús	ow·to·boos
plane	avión	a·vyon
train	tren	tren

first	primero	pree·me·ro
last	último	ool·tee·mo
next	próximo	prok·see·mo

I want to go to ...
Quisiera ir a ...   kee·sye·ra eer a ...

What time does it arrive/leave?
¿A qué hora llega/sale?   a ke o·ra ye·ga/sa·le

Please tell me when we get to ...
¿Puede avisarme   pwe·de a·vee·sar·me
cuando lleguemos a ...?   kwan·do ye·ge·mos a ...

I want to get off here.
Quiero bajarme aquí.   kye·ro ba·khar·me a·kee

a ... ticket	un billete de ...	oon bee·ye·te de ...
1st-class	primera clase	pree·me·ra kla·se
2nd-class	segunda clase	se·goon·da kla·se
one-way	ida	ee·da
return	ida y vuelta	ee·da ee vwel·ta

airport	aeropuerto	a·e·ro·pwer·to
bus stop	parada de autobuses	pa·ra·da de ow·to·boo·ses
platform	plataforma	pla·ta·for·ma
ticket office	taquilla	ta·kee·ya
timetable	horario	o·ra·ryo
train station	estación de trenes	es·ta·syon de tre·nes

Driving & Cycling

I'd like to rent a ...	Quisiera alquilar ...	kee·sye·ra al·kee·lar ...
4WD	un todo-terreno	oon to·do·te·re·no
bicycle	una bicicleta	oo·na bee·see·kle·ta
car	un coche	oon ko·che
motorcycle	una moto	oo·na mo·to

Numbers

1	uno	oo·no
2	dos	dos
3	tres	tres
4	cuatro	kwa·tro
5	cinco	seen·ko
6	seis	seys
7	siete	sye·te
8	ocho	o·cho
9	nueve	nwe·ve
10	diez	dyes
20	veinte	veyn·te
30	treinta	treyn·ta
40	cuarenta	kwa·ren·ta
50	cincuenta	seen·kwen·ta
60	sesenta	se·sen·ta
70	setenta	se·ten·ta
80	ochenta	o·chen·ta
90	noventa	no·ven·ta
100	cien	syen
1000	mil	meel

child seat	asiento de seguridad para niños	a·syen·to de se·goo·ree·da pa·ra nee·nyos
diesel	petróleo	pet·ro·le·o
helmet	casco	kas·ko
hitchhike	hacer botella	a·ser bo·te·ya
mechanic	mecánico	me·ka·nee·ko
gas/petrol	gasolina	ga·so·lee·na
service station	gasolinera	ga·so·lee·ne·ra
truck	camion	ka·myon

Is this the road to ...?
¿Se va a ... por   se va a ... por
esta carretera?   es·ta ka·re·te·ra

(How long) Can I park here?
¿(Por cuánto tiempo)   (por kwan·to tyem·po)
Puedo aparcar aquí?   pwe·do a·par·kar a·kee

The car has broken down (at ...).
El coche se ha averiado   el ko·che se a a·ve·rya·do
(en ...).   (en ...)

I have a flat tyre.
Tengo un pinchazo.   ten·go oon peen·cha·so

I've run out of gas/petrol.
Me he quedado sin   me e ke·da·do seen
gasolina.   ga·so·lee·na

I need a mechanic.
Necesito un/una   ne·se·see·to oon/oo·na
mecánico/a.   me·ka·nee·ko/a (m/f)

Behind the Scenes

SEND US YOUR FEEDBACK

We love to hear from travelers – your comments keep us on our toes and help make our books better. Our well-traveled team reads every word on what you loved or loathed about this book. Although we cannot reply individually to your submissions, we always guarantee that your feedback goes straight to the appropriate authors, in time for the next edition. Each person who sends us information is thanked in the next edition – the most useful submissions are rewarded with a selection of digital PDF chapters.

Visit **lonelyplanet.com/contact** to submit your updates and suggestions or to ask for help. Our award-winning website also features inspirational travel stories, news and discussions.

Note: We may edit, reproduce and incorporate your comments in Lonely Planet products such as guidebooks, websites and digital products, so let us know if you don't want your comments reproduced or your name acknowledged. For a copy of our privacy policy visit lonelyplanet.com/privacy.

OUR READERS

Many thanks to the travelers who used the last edition and wrote to us with helpful hints, useful advice and interesting anecdotes:

Aided Ceballo, Alison Estabrook, Anders Nielsen, Dara Rose, Hanna & Martin Alexandersson, Harvey Schwartz, Maartje Folbert, Richard Weil, Robert Walker, Robert Merriam

WRITER THANKS
Ashley Harrell

Thanks to: David Roth for hiking Pico Duarte with me. Vince DeGennaro and Grace Tilly for the hospitality. Kevin Raub, Bailey Freeman and Paul Clammer for their help and expertise. Soulouque for the wild ride. Caroline and Kaitlyn for the girl-time. Diane Pellerin for the dancing. Paul Guggenheim for the ideas and company. Sam Luok for existing. Tania Simonet for loving food like I do. Amy Benziger

for the truest friendship I've ever known. And JC Taillandier, for just everything.

Kevin Raub

Thanks to my wife, Adriana Schmidt Raub, who has to put up with me being gone more than being home (she might like it!). Bailey Freeman, Ashley Harrell and all my partners-in-crime at LP. On the road, Kim Beddall, Pierre and Monick Rouleau, Terry Baldi, Flora Tours, Paul and Audrey and all at the Dive Academy, Catherine DeLaura, Gill Thomas, Kate Wallace, Mael Moisan, Simon Suarez, Andria Mitsakos and Christina Little.

ACKNOWLEDGEMENTS

Climate map data adapted from Peel MC, Finlayson BL & McMahon TA (2007) 'Updated World Map of the Köppen-Geiger Climate Classification', Hydrology and Earth System Sciences, 11, 163344.

Cover photograph: Isla Saona, Bertrand Gardel/Getty ©

THIS BOOK

This 7th edition of Lonely Planet's Dominican Republic guidebook was researched and written by Ashley Harrell and Kevin Raub. The previous edition was written by Michael Grosberg and Kevin Raub.

This guidebook was produced by the following:

Destination Editor Bailey Freeman

Product Editor Jessica Ryan

Senior Cartographer Corey Hutchison

Book Designers Gwen Cotter, Ania Bartoszek

Assisting Editors Sarah Bailey, Nigel Chin, Bruce Evans, Rosie Nicholson, Monique Perrin, Saralinda Turner

Cartographer Rachel Imeson

Cover Researcher Naomi Parker

Thanks to Ronan Abayawickrema, Lauren O'Connell, Ellie Simpson, Angela Tinson, Tony Wheeler

Index

Map Legend

Sights

- Beach
- Bird Sanctuary
- Buddhist
- Castle/Palace
- Christian
- Confucian
- Hindu
- Islamic
- Jain
- Jewish
- Monument
- Museum/Gallery/Historic Building
- Ruin
- Shinto
- Sikh
- Taoist
- Winery/Vineyard
- Zoo/Wildlife Sanctuary
- Other Sight

Activities, Courses & Tours

- Bodysurfing
- Diving
- Canoeing/Kayaking
- Course/Tour
- Sento Hot Baths/Onsen
- Skiing
- Snorkeling
- Surfing
- Swimming/Pool
- Walking
- Windsurfing
- Other Activity

Sleeping

- Sleeping
- Camping

Eating

- Eating

Drinking & Nightlife

- Drinking & Nightlife
- Cafe

Entertainment

- Entertainment

Shopping

- Shopping

Information

- Bank
- Embassy/Consulate
- Hospital/Medical
- Internet
- Police
- Post Office
- Telephone
- Toilet
- Tourist Information
- Other Information

Geographic

- Beach
- Gate
- Hut/Shelter
- Lighthouse
- Lookout
- Mountain/Volcano
- Oasis
- Park
- Pass
- Picnic Area
- Waterfall

Population

- Capital (National)
- Capital (State/Province)
- City/Large Town
- Town/Village

Transport

- Airport
- Border crossing
- Bus
- Cable car/Funicular
- Cycling
- Ferry
- Metro station
- Monorail
- Parking
- Petrol station
- Subway/Subte station
- Taxi
- Train station/Railway
- Tram
- Underground station
- Other Transport

Note: Not all symbols displayed above appear on the maps in this book

Routes

- Tollway
- Freeway
- Primary
- Secondary
- Tertiary
- Lane
- Unsealed road
- Road under construction
- Plaza/Mall
- Steps
- Tunnel
- Pedestrian overpass
- Walking Tour
- Walking Tour detour
- Path/Walking Trail

Boundaries

- International
- State/Province
- Disputed
- Regional/Suburb
- Marine Park
- Cliff
- Wall

Hydrography

- River, Creek
- Intermittent River
- Canal
- Water
- Dry/Salt/Intermittent Lake
- Reef

Areas

- Airport/Runway
- Beach/Desert
- Cemetery (Christian)
- Cemetery (Other)
- Glacier
- Mudflat
- Park/Forest
- Sight (Building)
- Sportsground
- Swamp/Mangrove

OUR STORY

A beat-up old car, a few dollars in the pocket and a sense of adventure. In 1972 that's all Tony and Maureen Wheeler needed for the trip of a lifetime – across Europe and Asia overland to Australia. It took several months, and at the end – broke but inspired – they sat at their kitchen table writing and stapling together their first travel guide, *Across Asia on the Cheap*. Within a week they'd sold 1500 copies. Lonely Planet was born.

Today, Lonely Planet has offices in Franklin, London, Melbourne, Oakland, Dublin, Beijing and Delhi, with more than 600 staff and writers. We share Tony's belief that 'a great guidebook should do three things: inform, educate and amuse'.

OUR WRITERS

Ashley Harrell

Curator, Santo Domingo, North Coast, Central Highlands, Haiti. After a brief stint selling day-spa coupons door-to-door in South Florida, Ashley decided she'd rather be a writer. She went to journalism grad school, convinced a newspaper to hire her, and starting covering wildlife, crime and tourism, sometimes all in the same story. Fueling her zest for storytelling and the unknown, she traveled widely and moved often, from a tiny NYC apartment to a vast California ranch to a jungle cabin in Costa Rica, where she started writing for Lonely Planet. From there her travels became more exotic and farther flung, and she still laughs when paychecks arrive.

Kevin Raub

Writer, Punta Cana & the Southeast, Península de Samaná, The Southwest & Península de Pedernales. Kevin Raub grew up in Atlanta and started his career as a music journalist in New York, working for *Men's Journal* and *Rolling Stone* magazines. He almost didn't accept this assignment, his third through the region, until he found out the road to Sabana de la Mar was finished – he just couldn't bear another go on the formerly tortuous, pothole-ridden road. This is Kevin's 46th Lonely Planet guide. Follow him on Twitter and Instagram (@RaubOnTheRoad).

Read more about Kevin at:
lonelyplanet.com/profiles/Kraub

Published by Lonely Planet Global Limited
CRN 554153
7th edition – Oct 2017
ISBN 978 1 78657 140 3
© Lonely Planet 2017   Photographs © as indicated 2017
10 9 8 7 6 5 4 3 2 1
Printed in China